Desert Visions and the Making of Phoenix, 1860–2009

Desert Visions and the Making of Phoenix, 1860–2009

Philip VanderMeer

University of New Mexico Press | Albuquerque

First paperbound printing, 2012
Paperbound ISBN: 978-0-8263-4892-0

18 17 16 15 14 13 12   1 2 3 4 5 6 7

Library of Congress Cataloging-in Publication Data

VanderMeer, Philip R., 1947–
  Desert visions and the making of Phoenix, 1860–2009 / Philip VanderMeer.
      p. cm.
  Includes bibliographical references and index.
ISBN 978-0-8263-4891-3 (cloth : alk. paper)
  1. Phoenix (Ariz.)—History. 2. Phoenix (Ariz.)—Economic conditions. 3. Phoenix
(Ariz.)—Social conditions. 4. Phoenix (Ariz.)—Politics and government. 5. City and
town life—Arizona—Phoenix—History. 6. City planning—Arizona—Phoenix—
History. 7. Social change—Arizona—Phoenix—History. 8. Cities and towns—United
States—Growth—Case studies. I. Title.
  F819.P57V358 2010
  979.1'73—dc22

                            2010033059

For Mary, with love and gratitude

Contents

TABLES   xi

FIGURES   xii

ACKNOWLEDGMENTS   xv

Introduction   1

Part I The First Desert Vision: An American Eden   9

1 Civilizing the Desert: The Initial Phase   11

Physical Realities and Early Settlement   11

The Town That Agriculture Built   16

Building a Town   20

Establishing the Public City   27

Building a Hydraulic System: Controlling and Using Water   29

Climate and Health   33

2 Building the Modern City: Physical Form and Function   37

Phoenix in an Urban Context, 1890–1920   38

The Changing Urban Form   42

The Changing Urban Form I: Downtown   42

The Changing Urban Form II: From Streetcar Suburbs to Automobile Suburbs   48

Remaking or Saving the Desert   52

3 Shaping the Modern American City: Social Construction   57

Making a Moral City   57

Making a Cultured City   61

A Lively City   65

Social Structures and Diverse Peoples   68

Governing the City   71

Selling the City   76

Crisis and Completion: The 1930s   79

Controlling the Climate   83

The Phoenix Economic Elite   85

Phoenix in 1940   88

Part II Creating and Pursuing a New Vision, 1940–60   93

4 Creating a New Vision: The War and After 95
How the Military Reshaped Phoenix   95
   Building an Aviation Industry   97
   The Expansion of Military Aviation   99
   The Military and Phoenix Politics   103

Postwar Trials and Shaping a New Vision   105
   The Growth of Tourism   106
   Migration and Health   109
   Overcoming Climate and Distance   112
   Planning the Future   115
   Phoenix Leaders and a New Vision   118

Conclusion   121

5 Building a New Politics   125
Political Conflict   126
From Charter Reform to Charter Government   129
The Nature and Success of Charter Government   134
Political Debates and City Services   138
Managing and Planning for a Growing City   141
The Top Job: Water   143
Getting Around the City   146
Growth and Other Services   149

6 Growing the City: Economic, Cultural, and Spatial Expansion   153
Growth of the Postwar Economy   154
Planning for Manufacturing   156
High-Tech Firms and a Changing Economy   160
Shaping Identities: Western and Outdoor Cultures   164
"High Culture" and the Arts   167
Growth and Annexation   171
A Dramatically Different Place   180

Part III Elaborating and Modifying the High-Tech Suburban Vision   183

7 From Houses to Communities: Suburban Growth in
   the Postwar Metropolis, 1945–1980   187

Building Homes   190
   Houses for a Growing Population   190
   Phoenix Builders and the Home Building Industry   192
   Building Homes in Phoenix   196
   The Structure and Size of Phoenix Homes   201
   Building Affordable Housing   203

Building Communities   206
   The Shift to Community Building   207
   New Approaches to Residence: Retirement Communities   210
   "New Towns"   215
   Planned Communities   217
   From Agricultural Satellites to Supersuburbs   221
   Shopping for Community   225

   Conclusion   227

8 Political Change and Changing Policies in
   the 1960s and 1970s   231
   Charter Government and Politics of the Center   232
   Charter Government as a Liberal Movement   235
   A Conservative Turn and Charter Government's Demise   240
   Taxes and Revenues   243
   The Politics of City Services   248
   Civil Rights, Poverty, and City Politics   253
   Mexican American Political Activism   259

9 Changing the Urban Form: The Politics of
Place and Space   265

The Politics of Housing   266
The Politics of Place and Space: Downtown   269
The Politics of Place and Space: Older Neighborhoods   273
Planning, Land Use, and Sprawl   276
Planning to Live in the Desert   279
Planning and the Urban Village   287
The Growth Crisis   289

10 An Uncertain Future: Looking for a New Vision   295

Creating a New Economic Vision   298
    Prelude: A Maturing Economy, 1960–1980   298
    Continuing Economic Strengths after 1980   300
    Rising Economic Problems   302
    The Collapse of High Tech   305
    A Building and Financial Crisis   308
    Planning and Responses to Economic Challenge   311

Creating a New Political Vision   314
    Leadership and a New Politics   314
    Representing Citizens and Governing the City   320

A New Urban Vision   324
    Building the City: The Downtown Era   324
    The Reemerging Role for Culture and the Arts   328
    Sports, Politics, and Identity   331
    Envisioning "Neighborhoods That Work"   335

Population and Communities: Growth in the Desert   337
    A Hispanic City?   337
    A Growing City   339
    Communities and Community   344
    Living Together in a Desert: Metropolitan Issues   350
    Fighting over Growth   357

Conclusion Desert Vision, Desert City   361

NOTES   367

INDEX   445

Tables

Table 2.1 Western inland cities, 1870–1930.   39

Table 2.2 Population in the largest Arizona towns and cities.   40

Table 3.1 Western cities in 1940.   89

Table 4.1 Defense spending in western metropolitan areas, 1940–45: regional median averages (in $ millions).   96

Table 5.1 City elections, 1949–59.   137

Table 5.2 Condition of Phoenix streets, 1950 and 1960.   148

Table 5.3 Traffic and safety improvements in Phoenix, 1950–60.   149

Table 6.1 Annual per capita manufacturing wages in Arizona, 1958.   156

Table 6.2 New manufacturers in the Phoenix area, 1948–60.   159

Table 6.3 Population of metropolitan Phoenix and Maricopa County, 1940–60.   172

Table 7.1 Population of metropolitan Phoenix, 1960–80.   191

Table 7.2 Number of moves per Phoenix area household, 1960–67.   207

Table 7.3 Valley malls, 1957–81.   226

Table 8.1 Charter Government collapses: 1975 City Council votes by group (averaged).   242

Table 8.2 Federal spending in Phoenix.   246

Table 9.1 Per capita water use in southwestern cities, 1981.   284

Table 9.2 Condition of Salt River Project canals and laterals, 1956–73.   286

Table 10.1 Population of metropolitan Phoenix, 1980–2008.   340

Figures

Figure 1.1 Signs of the Hohokam irrigation.   15

Figure 1.2 Hohokam and modern canals in the Salt River Valley.   17

Figure 1.3 Heyman Furniture Building, 1895, at Washington Street and 1st Avenue.   26

Figure 1.4 Beyond Main Street.   26

Figure 2.1 Central Phoenix, 1924.   43

Figure 2.2 Downtown Phoenix in 1929, taken from the courthouse.   47

Figure 2.3 A shady residential street, 1917 (Culver and 12th Street).   53

Figure 2.4 Lush canal vegetation, 1924.   54

Figure 3.1 The Palace Saloon—one of many on Washington Street.   59

Figure 3.2 One of the large movie "palaces," the Fox was the first to provide air-conditioning.   67

Figure 3.3 "Parlor Car Apache" of Arizona Tours, Inc., in front of the Santa Fe Depot in Phoenix, around 1930.   77

Figure 3.4 Lobby of the Arizona Club, where city leaders met.   88

Figure 4.1 Wartime employment changed opportunities and ideas in Phoenix.   99

Figure 4.2 The ease of trailer life in Phoenix.   108

Figure 5.1 The Charter Government Committee's campaign against corruption was an important reason for its initial success.   132

Figure 5.2 Phoenix area water systems in 1960, showing the city's expanding service region and facilities.   144

Figure 6.1 Baggage carriers loading Motorola products, 1960.   163

Figure 6.2 Phoenix annexations, 1950–60.   176

Figure 6.3 Undeveloped land in the Phoenix urban area, 1958.   179

Figure 7.1 Housing construction in Maricopa County, 1960–80.   194

Figure 7.2 Selling Maryvale.   199

Figure 7.3 Making the outdoors into the "good life" in suburbia.   202

Figure 7.4 Planned communities in the Phoenix area, 1980.   211

Figure 7.5 Sun City new floor plan, 1967.   213

Figure 8.1 Phoenix revenue sources, 1960–80.   244

Figure 8.2 One view of "progress" in building the Papago Freeway.   251

Figure 8.3 Phoenix Inner City, 1963.   257

Figure 8.4 Joe Eddie Lopez and Daniel Ortega at Chicanos Por La Causa meeting.   262

Figure 9.1 Older Neighborhoods immediately north of downtown.   274

Figure 9.2 Annexation and city size, 1958–78.   279

Figure 9.3 Floodwaters hit Sky Harbor Airport, 1979.   282

Figure 9.4 Urban village boundaries, 1985.   290

Figure 10.1 Aviation in Phoenix.   303

Figure 10.2 The collapse of Motorola.   307

Figure 10.3 Building activity in Maricopa County, 1980–2006.   309

Figure 10.4 Mayor Hance's reaction to Goddard's 1983 victory.   317

Figure 10.5 City of Phoenix annexation, 1984.   343

Figure 10.6 Annexation conflict in north Phoenix, 1985.   343

Figure 10.7 Stucco-tacky housing.   346

Figure 10.8 Housing in Verado.   349

Acknowledgments

One of the pleasures of completing a long-term project like this is the opportunity to reflect on and thank the many people who helped along the way. I benefited greatly from the help of various librarians and archivists. I have been especially fortunate in being able to work primarily in the Phoenix area, which permitted me to avail myself of the abilities and support of these people. The substantial holdings of the Arizona State University Library were made more accessible by the assistance of the library's able staff. In the Archives and Special Collections, Chris Marin was especially helpful, as were Rob Spindler and Mike Lotstein. Becky Burke located obscure and missing items in the Government Documents section, while Deborah Koshinsky and Jim Allen aided me in working through collections in the Architecture Library. Dawn Nave and Dave Tackenberg assisted my efforts to examine the many useful collections of the Central Division of the Arizona Historical Society, especially the Phoenix History Project. Catherine May facilitated my access to the archives of the Salt River Project and helped me identify important materials. I am also grateful to the staffs of the Arizona Library and State Archives (Melanie Spurgeon), the Phoenix Public Library (Linda Risseeuw), the Arizona Historical Foundation, and the Auraria Library of the University of Colorado, Denver.

Over the years I have been researching and writing on Phoenix, I have been aided by the work of two able graduate research assistants, Victoria Jackson and Karla Alonso, and by Kevin Norton's voluntary research on city directories. My work with Arizona State University graduate students has strengthened this project, and I particularly wish to acknowledge the contributions of Fred Amis, Trace Baker, Jerry Briscoe, Mike Casavantes, David Dean, Robin LaVoie, Jane Lawrence, Nicolas Locher, Matt Lord, Vince Murray, Mark Pry, Mark Scott, and Mark Simpson. Several undergraduate students—notably Jeff Dean, Linda Miller, and Ian Storrer—also contributed to my understanding of the city's history. Jim Hanley, from the home owner association management firm of Rossmar and Graham, helped clarify some important aspects of contemporary HOA policy. Finally, I want to thank former Mayor Terry Goddard, who spoke to me with great insight and frankness about his experiences.

Several colleagues generously gave of their time to read and comment on the manuscript. Heidi Osselaer "returned the favor" of my work on her dissertation and then excellent book with her extensive and helpful notes on this manuscript. Peter Iverson, my longtime and good friend, encouraged me through general counsel and specific observations on the text. Karen Smith, who has written insightfully on the city's early years, offered good suggestions on my chapters relating to that era. All of them improved the manuscript in important ways.

Other colleagues shared research materials with me. Arturo Rosales loaned his extensive collection of newspaper articles on Mexican Americans in Phoenix; Jan Warren Findley offered material produced by one of her classes on a 1950s subdivision; and Carol Heim provided photocopies of changes in the Arizona's annexation law. With the encouragement of department chair Noel Stowe, ASU gave me release time from teaching, which advanced my progress in completing this study.

My greatest debt is to my wife, Mary. She shared directly in some of this work when she was the photo editor on my earlier history of the city's postwar period, *Phoenix Rising* (2002), from which some of the material for this book is drawn. For that project she chose and secured the permissions for numerous photographs, wrote captions, and essentially laid out the book. For this volume, although she is an excellent editor and writer, she had none of the direct responsibilities, for she had her own projects on which to work. However, she heard more detail about the researching and writing of this book than anyone except the author or a therapist should have to endure. Her kind attention, gentle questioning, and unfailing encouragement were essential to my completing this study. For that and for so many reasons, this book belongs to her.

Introduction

The history of Phoenix over the last fifty years has prompted very different perspectives. The city's tremendous growth has been its most prominent characteristic, touted by city leaders and many observers as reflecting popular choice. A massive in-migration has fed a burgeoning economy, as new residents have found jobs, affordable housing, and a pleasant living style. Some analysts have considered it within the context of other Sunbelt and postmodern cities. Rather than faulting its differences from traditional cities, they have praised its decentralized form as reflecting new urban patterns in an era of global and technological change.

Critics have objected on various grounds. Observers from older midwestern or eastern cities have often found it unfamiliar and unattractive. They, like a number of urban theorists, have stressed that it has lacked vertical growth, a dense population, and a vibrant downtown. It seems, then, less like a city than a sprawling suburb. A related social criticism alleges a lack of an urban "culture," stretching from the culinary to the fine arts, and portrays the area as bland, sun drenched, and superficial. Others have faulted it on ecological grounds, seeing its growth as unsustainable and harboring suspicions that placing a city in a desert violates a basic principle about cities, population, and natural resources.

Form, location, and culture have been central issues for Phoenix from its beginning, as early migrants sought to create something that people further east, the cultural standard bearers, would view favorably. Throughout its history, residents have pursued growth with this in mind. For the last half century they have reveled in the city's rise relative to other urban places, and they have taken this quantitative measure as indicating larger achievements. This dynamic has made both pride and insecurity consistent elements of the city's past. Equally central is a persisting mixture of perspectives about the central character of this place, as migrants have continued to bring expectations rooted in places from which they came.

I, too, am a migrant to Phoenix, coming with expectations and a cultural perspective. I moved to the area in 1985, a midwesterner by birth, by residence, and through my historical research. Studies and work had taken me to the various states of the Old Northwest, and from observation and study I knew the lay of that land. Central Arizona confounded my knowledge and perspective. Its topography of mountains and valleys contrasted with rolling, forested hills and grassy prairies; the burden of its ovenlike summers was the seasonal reverse of frigid Michigan winters; and its regularized canals and irrigation ditches bore little resemblance to Indiana's itinerant creeks and streams. Illinois's checkerboard of sections and townships, the regular location of its county seats, and the wide distribution of its towns and cities represented very different natural and constructed landscapes than the clusters of cities and towns in Arizona.

Living in Mesa, working in Tempe, and visiting Phoenix and Scottsdale, I found that the built environment of these cities was more familiar. Detached, single-family homes were built in various architectural styles, especially different types of ranch homes, which were common throughout the country. The landscaping of yards varied more substantially. Some had lawns and deciduous trees; others sprouted citrus trees or tropical plants; while the most divergent, to my midwestern eyes, contained cacti and rocks or stones. The cities had grassy playgrounds and shade trees, while parks on the urban periphery and some places within the cities were mountains or buttes, rocky with low-lying vegetation, unlandscaped, and open to the sun. The juxtaposition of arid desert with landscaped lawns and swimming pools suggested a contrast that was both historical and contemporary, built and natural, visual and cultural.

These differences, these tensions, pushed my interest past a standard curiosity about the place in which I lived and beyond my midwestern sense of this as a truly different, even "exotic" locale. The reasons for my own migration I understood, but why had so many others come? What had they been expecting, and what did they find? How did they change this place, and how did it change them? My efforts to understand how and why this area had grown began with my observations and moved to reading. At that time very little had been written about the history of the area, but the pioneering work of my colleague Bradford Luckingham and my own efforts in directing substantial research on it by graduate and undergraduate students helped me see this region in more complex terms.

My perspective was also reshaped because the last twentysome years have been an extraordinary period in the city's history. Reflecting national urban changes and especially new ideas about both western and global cities, public officials and people from many professions within Phoenix and its major satellite suburbs have thought, talked, and worked to redefine this city and the metropolitan area. And some have explicitly described this as a crucial era. In 2001 the insightful *Arizona Republic* columnist Jon Talton argued that Phoenix was at a "tipping point" in its development. Arizona State University urbanist Nan Ellin framed it historically, likening the era to other moments of significant change in key cities—Paris in the 1860s, New York in the 1910s, and Los Angeles in the 1950s.

Prodigious amounts of construction either completed or in process have been creating a vastly different built environment in downtown Phoenix and in several surrounding cities. The building of a highway system and the opening of a light rail system have produced multiple, sometimes conflicting changes in urban form. Concerns about resources, the environment, and sheer size have stimulated greater skepticism, or even resistance, to growth on the Valley's periphery and new approaches to development within the central areas of the city. The new built environment has provided venues for public audiences and has affected the nature of the city's development. The arrival of major league sports teams both roused the enthusiasm of fans and became an important part of urban development. The proliferation of museums and cultural facilities resulted from the significant growth of many cultural organizations and their audiences. Together with an increasing diversity of population, these changes reflected a more mature, even cosmopolitan character, and the rippling effects could be seen in multiple areas, even in the significantly more diverse cuisine of the city's restaurants.

My observation of these changes and my study of the area compelled me to look beyond the perspective I had brought with me to Phoenix. Instead of seeing the city in traditional terms, I began viewing it through a different lens—if not a "postmodern" perspective, then at least one not simply dependent on forms and standards established many decades before. After writing *Phoenix Rising*, a relatively brief history of postwar Phoenix, I began a more comprehensive study of how and why Phoenix grew. Starting from its origins in the 1860s and tracking its development to the present state as the nation's fifth largest city, I sought to understand how such unusual growth occurred in what many now consider—and even more did earlier—an unlikely place.

The complexity and size of this subject has forced me to make many choices about what topics to cover and to what extent. Some issues that are interesting but peripheral to my purpose I have had to ignore; other topics of importance I could only cover briefly. While I have attempted to balance my coverage of basic themes across the different periods of city history, my attention to specific topics has varied to reflect their changing importance. Perhaps the most obvious issue in terms of coverage is the definition of *Phoenix*. The narrow meaning of this name is the incorporated municipality, but it has been commonly used to refer to the larger metropolitan area. This is not a concern before 1960, when other communities were so small, but for the years in which they grew, the question of coverage became more complex. In general, I consider most topics across the region except for politics. This was partly a question of sources and structure, but it also reflects the reality that the city of Phoenix has been the dominant political voice in the area.

My study develops five major thematic areas across the years from 1860 to the present. The natural environment has set the basic context for the development of this city and others in the Salt River Valley. Set within the Sonoran Desert, its climate, topography, and vegetation defined the early expectations of settlers, but the Salt River's waters and the Valley's alluvial soils provided opportunities for change. Residents have promoted different views of this environment during the course of the city's history, but the fact of it has always been the first element in shaping the type of city that grew.

The second, urban form, also reflected the broader cultural values that residents held and created, as well as the economic systems they built. Their initial goal was to make Phoenix a "modern American city," and their efforts to shape their built environment continued to follow this objective into the late twentieth century. However, the speed of the city's growth and its proximity to California affected the forms of housing, neighborhoods, and the larger development of the city in important respects.

The economy of Phoenix, a third theme, shows important continuities but even more significant shifts. Initially based on agriculture, with tourism and health seeking as added revenue sources, the city expanded as a government center and as a retail and wholesale center. Aviation and air-conditioning not only changed the postwar economic context, they also made up part of the new economy. Aerospace and electronics provided the main substance for the city's new manufacturing sector, but tourism grew increasingly important, as did the construction generated by the continued population influx. By the 1990s, however, this economic model was showing considerable signs of wear, and city leaders began, slowly, pursuing new ventures.

The social and cultural values of Phoenix were brought by immigrants but also shaped by the area's environmental, urban, and economic character. Some of these values—like ideas about urban landscaping—have changed over time, but others—like an interest in the outdoors, recreation, and an active lifestyle—have remained constant. The overarching goal of creating a modern city that would impress a national audience prompted periodic changes in the Valley's popular culture, but the emphasis on the fine arts and culture remained constant. In the 1950s city leaders talked quite explicitly about their value in attracting and retaining employees in the new electronic and aerospace businesses, but in every era boosters, builders, developers, and city advocates supported these institutions as a key element in the city's development.

The final theme of this work is public leadership, both from the political officials who held elective or appointive office and from community leaders, those men and women who served in community organizations or ad hoc groups, or whose stature gave them importance and influence without their holding any specific position. While any city's fortunes reflect its location and population, the quality of its leadership can also materially affect its position, as the history of Phoenix clearly demonstrates. Before World War II, Phoenix was a relatively undistinguished city whose leadership was congenial and open to newcomers, but in the postwar era it achieved enormous success. This was not because it followed some unique economic plan; its strategy was largely what many western cities followed. Instead, Phoenix grew because of the leadership's holistic approach, connecting economic, political, and social factors, and their ability to carry out their common strategy effectively. Leaders also adapted to changing circumstances and values, particularly in accepting the political mobilization of minority groups, the rise of social politics, and the expanding definition of city services.

Examining the broad history of Phoenix, I see several sets of expectations, several notions of what the city was about and what its future would hold, and these form several different eras. This desert area prompted specific visions of the Phoenix which its residents sought, successively, to implement—a transplanted vision, then an adapted vision, and then, currently and incompletely, a vision reflecting both place and time. The initial vision, "An American Eden," was a familiar, imported plan for an agricultural settlement. While the process of transforming a desert into profitable farms had unique elements, it more generally represented a fully familiar attempt at environmental transformation that Americans had pursued for hundreds of years. Only the particulars varied. Settlers believed in the efficacy of human efforts and the bounty of nature; they envisioned Phoenix as the service center for its agricultural hinterlands. They constructed an environment of buildings and landscapes that resembled what they knew and that would impress national observers. Furthermore, they intentionally and thoughtfully created social, cultural, and political institutions and values to mark Phoenix as a modern, progressive American city.

In the 1940s war called forth massive energies that led to the creation of new structures, relationships, values, and expectations. The Valley had traditionally relied on the federal government for crucial resources, and the New Deal had increased the distribution of federal funds, but World War II taught Phoenix leaders how to pursue development, while Cold War spending offered significant opportunities for economic growth. In addition, technological innovations, notably in aviation and air-conditioning, let Phoenix take advantage of these new options, and the city's tourist trade greatly profited from national prosperity. But the primary factor enabling Phoenix to boom as it did was its rapid adoption of a "High-Tech Suburban" vision. More than reliance on electronics and aerospace manufacturing, it was the holistic approach to development, including citywide governance, an emphasis on administrative autonomy and inexpensive city services, aggressive annexation, community development and affordable housing, and the development of cultural institutions. The combination of public and private actions enabled this plan to work.

The city's implementation of this vision spurred rapid growth by attracting new businesses, adding population, constructing new neighborhoods, and expanding city boundaries. But the original vision was not flawless, and during the 1960s and 1970s city leaders addressed problems inherent in that vision, as well as structural problems shared by cities across the nation. The civil rights movement and the mobilization of minority groups changed city politics and expanded the city's policy interests. Simultaneous suburban sprawl and the decay of downtown raised serious questions about urban form and the role of city government. Even more significant than policy debates over specific issues like in fill, taxes, or transportation was that many Phoenicians began worrying about the environmental, social, and political costs of growth, and they started to explore what sorts of controls the city might adopt.

By the 1990s the rising concerns had begun to foster major changes in how the city grew. Debates over how and where the city was being built, changes in the structure of the economy, and the increased vibrancy of the cultural sector suggested that the postwar vision was no longer the primary force shaping ideas or actions. While many individuals offered their own plans for the future, only the successful actions of political leaders could mold these disparate views into a single perspective, a new vision that would reshape this city. The task of building a twenty-first century desert city involves issues of form and culture, but most of all it means confronting the importance of location. The story of the city's future, like the narrative of its past, must start with the impact of human habitation on the land and with the particular character of that place.

Part I △△△

The First Desert Vision: AN AMERICAN EDEN

From the city's founding in the 1860s until the onset of World War II, the leaders and residents of Phoenix followed a vision of its future that reflected the physical realities of central Arizona and the American culture of the time. This vision was rooted in agriculture, for the area's beginnings and its growth during this period depended primarily on the development of farming in the Salt River Valley. Irrigation made these efforts successful, and it fostered an awareness that human labor and ingenuity had transformed this area—Phoenicians felt a sense of pride in civilizing the desert. Their sense of place also led them to create the supporting elements of this vision, seeking residents and tourists by emphasizing the "healthfulness" of the climate and the beauty of the scenery. Living in this area involved a struggle not only against physical elements but also to fulfill cultural expectations. Phoenicians sought to create a "modern" and "American" city, for their own sakes and to gain the esteem of others. Thus, the initial Phoenix vision grew from the culture that settlers brought and the place in which they lived. Like most Americans, they dreamed and worked for growth and economic prosperity. They imagined making Phoenix the largest city in Arizona and it having an importance beyond that, but they also saw the city's prospects in an agricultural and regional context. And by 1940 the city had achieved its expected place: it had become the largest city in Arizona and New Mexico, but distinctly smaller and less significant than El Paso or cities to the north like Denver and Salt Lake City.

To realize this vision, Phoenicians worked to change the natural environment, to create a complementary built environment, and to develop the accouterments of modern American culture. They employed exaggerated rhetoric, but their accomplishments were impressive, for while every community grapples with its natural environment, the Arizona desert was more daunting than most other places. Boosters deprecated concerns about the summer climate by comparing it with the weather elsewhere and touting the benefits of a "dry heat"; later, and with considerable effect, they redefined "harsh" as "healthy." More substantively, they sought to reshape the climate—and more importantly the land—by damming the rivers, channeling water into canals, and creating new ecosystems. By irrigating fields and watering the town site, they created greenery, shade, flowers, and saleable produce. These changes allowed boosters to describe the Valley "as a veritable paradise," to compare the climate with that of Italy or Egypt, and to liken its irrigated agriculture to that of ancient regions, biblical Canaan, the Nile, or southern California.[1] The application of capital, engineering, and labor transformed the physical appearance of the Salt River Valley and created a prosperous agricultural economy. But it also fostered a somewhat dangerous belief in the malleability of nature and the near-limitless power of human ingenuity.

Building the city was an integral part of transforming the desert, for residents considered the city's physical characteristics an important demonstration of its essential success. This effort started with the initial town plat, which designated public space, and continued as the town erected significant public buildings. The types of buildings, both public and private, commercial and residential, held considerable importance, for their size, design, and construction demonstrated the affluence and confidence of the community. The emergence of a distinct downtown by the 1920s represented both similarities to and differences from other American cities, while the structure of the city's suburbs reflected a variety of transportation influences. The extent and quality of city services and urban amenities also represented significant accomplishments. The various reports of buildings and services produced during this time read like ritualized booster rhetoric, but these descriptions were not fundamentally inaccurate. The larger perspective that shaped the language of these writers also formed the vision that guided the city's planners and builders.[2]

Phoenicians also touted their community as "modern" and "American." They did not emphasize their southwestern location, except in struggling to overcome the problems of isolation from the East. Instead, their standards for modernity were drawn from their communities of origin. Like other communities organized before this, Phoenicians stressed the presence of businesses, professionals, tradespeople, and prosperous farmers to demonstrate both what was available and to show that the community could support a complex and growing economy. Similarly, the impulse to create schools, churches, and societies reflected the real needs of the people and demonstrated that they were "cultured, liberal, and progressive." Being "American" also meant being white and Anglo. While some persons of color resided in the city and had developed separate institutions, town leaders during this period attempted to ignore them as much as possible.[3]

Thus, the history of Phoenix from its founding to the beginning of World War II was the story of developing and implementing a plan for civilizing the desert. It grew steadily, not dramatically, as a prosperous agricultural community, the territorial and then state capitol, a marketing center, and a tourist destination. But how did Phoenix develop and realize this vision? Why did it become the dominant city in the Salt River Valley, and how did it surpass the initial leads of Prescott and Tucson to become the largest city in the state? If one expands the context, how did the urban form that Phoenix developed compare with other American cities, and what type of society did Phoenicians attempt to create? And how did Phoenicians balance the use of private and public actions? To answer these questions one must begin by examining the area in which the city sits.

1

Civilizing the Desert: *The Initial Phase*

PHYSICAL REALITIES AND EARLY SETTLEMENT

The defining geological and geographic features of the Salt River Valley are as obvious and significant today as they were a hundred or ten thousand years ago. The Sierra Estrella Mountains define the southwest limit of this central Arizona region, which is also bordered by mountain ranges on the northwest, north, and east, stretching roughly 80 miles from the White Tank Mountains to the Superstition Mountains. Various buttes and mountains protrude from the Valley floor, most notably the ten-mile range of the South Mountains, a southern boundary roughly 40 miles from the northern Phoenix Mountains. The Valley is open to the west, following the Salt River as it joins the Gila River flowing in from the southeast. To the southeast, stretching around the South Mountains, the Valley also flows into the larger Sonoran desert, extending down to Tucson and ultimately to Mexico. The large Valley area bounded by these mountains totals roughly 17,700 square miles.[1] More malleable but no less fundamental, the Salt River provides water that sustains abundant life in this Valley. Human decisions have produced many types of landscapes within the Valley—such as grassy lawns, desert oases, and tropical gardens—but beyond the outskirts of settlement is a sparser and harsher natural landscape that prevailed before irrigation. Although dams, canals, and air-conditioning made life in this desert comfortable, climate remains a real and persistent force shaping life in the area.

Confrontation with this environment gives the history of Phoenix, especially the early decades, a particular direction. The course of American expansion and settlement is the story of settlers facing major issues and problems— scarcity, danger, and the absence of facilities and institutions. They responded, to varying degrees, by creating and building. "Boosterism"—a community's self-promotion based on optimism, bravado, and fraud—provided a crucial aspect of this process, as settlers struggled to attract additional residents and capital. But while every community shared some experiences of settlement and growth, they often differed in critical ways. For Phoenix, location was a vital and defining characteristic. In the nineteenth century, without a navigable river or direct railroad connection, in a desert largely surrounded by mountains, and a thousand miles from the nearest sizable cities like Omaha or Kansas City, Phoenicians felt a strong and understandable sense of isolation, a reality that continued well into the twentieth century despite improved transportation and communication. Like many westerners, they often felt unfairly ignored or mistreated by economic or political powers in "the East." Producing crops and raw materials for those distant markets, dependent on their capital for needed loans, and with seemingly marginal political power compared to established political machines and urban bosses, they struggled to shape their own destiny.

Climate and topography posed major challenges for these settlers. Heat, minimal rainfall, and desert terrain forged an environment that compelled settlers to make hard choices between their imported culture and their new physical environment. Here, as in most other places, settlers attempted to combine elements of both. The physical realities required concessions as well as innovations in the built environments they created, the ways they lived, and how they farmed. Irrigation was the most obvious and significant element in this process, involving considerable effort and ingenuity for Phoenicians to create prosperity from this new situation. Yet they also decided how to build the physical and social structure of their community that represented inherited and imported values, partly to suit their own desires and sensibilities, but also to appeal to potential settlers. Both the personal desires to recreate familiar settings as much as possible and the goals of boosterism led Phoenicians to live and speak as they did.

The term *desert* has a significantly varied and contested meaning in American history. In the early nineteenth century Americans accepted the geographers' label for the Trans-Mississippi West as the "Great American Desert." Exploration and settlement shrank the scope of this perceived area by the 1870s, eliminating the Great Plains and Rocky Mountains but still including the intermountain region. This change reflected not only familiarity, but also the belief that civilization and settlement could alter climate, that human habitation and agriculture had increased rainfall in the area. While the drought that began in numerous places in the late 1880s caused many residents of the Great Plains to question that view, a more general conviction that human intervention could substantively transform nature and living conditions remained an article of faith throughout the West.[2]

Perceptions of Central Arizona as a "desert" were not false, but the implications most often drawn were wrong. Phoenix is situated in the Sonoran Desert, one of four North American deserts.[3] The traditional American expectations of the term *desert*—emptiness, deadness, and sand dunes—are strikingly inaccurate for this region. In reality, it contains abundant life; the density and diversity of its wildlife make it "one of the richest deserts of the world," with more than thirty-five hundred species of plants and hundreds of animal species.[4] Besides the familiar types of cactus—particularly the area's signature cactus, the saguaro, but also many others such as cholla, ocotillo, and prickly pear types—the area hosts native palo verde, ironwood, mesquite, and cottonwood trees; it is home to lower vegetation like creosote bushes and yucca plants; and the numerous types of wildflowers bloom expeditiously or riotously, depending on the amount of spring rains. The wildlife has included javelinas, coyotes and wolves, bobcats, jackrabbits, otters (in riparian areas), and birds as diverse as cactus wrens, hawks, hummingbirds, quails, and woodpeckers.

But if settlers were surprised by the abundant life in this valley, they had a more accurate understanding of its climate, which many found alien, even hostile. The area is very arid, with humidity levels below ten percent during the early summer. It averages only about seven inches of rain annually, which generally falls within two seasons: the months of January to March sometimes see heavy downpours, while the summer "monsoons" during late June to August bring moisture from the south and east as part of intense weather patterns. More importantly, the summers are very hot, with daily high temperatures over 100 degrees for most of four months and periodically exceeding 110 degrees. Boosters downplayed the discomfort this caused, but even southern migrants from central Texas to the Atlantic coast found the height and duration of these temperatures unfamiliar and unpleasant. Those who stayed developed coping strategies for this season, and many felt compensated by the region's balmy winters and the nearly year-round growing season. Still, the heat established effective limits on population growth in the area until technology and air-conditioning intruded.[5]

In the 1860s the Salt River Valley was an unusual place in several respects, but most strikingly because it contained no human inhabitants. Neither the Spanish nor the Mexicans had settled there, restricting their movements to the southeastern area of modern Arizona, with Tucson as the major town.[6] Nor did Indians live there at this time, perhaps because conflict between tribes north and south of the valley had made residence too precarious. Yet the area was potentially attractive because of the Salt River. Although not generally navigable, the Salt had a substantial and year-round flow, for it draws on a large watershed of roughly 13,000 square miles covering east-central Arizona and through its tributary, the Verde River, drains much of the north-central part of the state. Over the eons its flooding had laid a thick layer of fertile alluvial soil on the Valley floor, and the land nearer the river sustained substantial plant and animal wildlife.[7] It supported diverse ecosystems, including an area along the southern bank that W. H. Ingalls described in the 1860s as "low and inclined to be swampy; with timber cottonwood along banks, and mesquite and willow brush."[8]

The first Anglo settlers to central Arizona came, not for water, but for minerals, and in 1863 they established mining camps at Wickenburg and Prescott in the foothills and mountains north of the Salt River Valley. Their intrusion aroused the antagonism of local Indian tribes, and the U.S. Army established Camp McDowell in September 1865 to provide protection.[9] To acquire foodstuffs locally, the army contracted with John Y. T. Smith, who began harvesting wild hay growing in the Valley near the Salt River, and in 1867 Smith hired Jack Swilling to help him. An adventurer and entrepreneur, Swilling had lived in the territory since 1862 and had seen various tribes practicing irrigated farming. As he looked at the Salt River Valley, he saw a major opportunity.[10]

Swilling realized that despite its current lack of habitation, the Valley contained abundant evidence of previous settlement. As many as fifty large mounds marked the ruins of former multistoried dwellings, while more numerous smaller ruins with pots and other material were scattered across the Valley. More importantly, he saw signs of a canal system that could have supported extensive agriculture for a sizeable population. What Swilling recognized were the remnants of prehistoric Hohokam settlements. Some fifteen hundred years previously, these people had begun building an extensive system of up to a thousand miles of canals, some of which extended twenty or thirty miles, with the largest canals measuring fifty feet wide and twenty feet deep. At its peak the population reached somewhere between twenty-five and fifty thousand people.[11] Then, because of floods and drought, the increasing salinity of soil, and civil strife, the population began to dwindle, and by 1450 the area had been abandoned. Over four centuries the structures disintegrated, but although the canals had partly filled in, their forms were easy to recognize and invited activity (figure 1.1).[12] Swilling hired miners from Wickenburg to begin redigging the canals and to reestablish farming in the Valley. These efforts drew the interest of others, and in 1870 roughly two hundred settlers chose a town site, which was quickly platted in the standard Anglo grid pattern with a courthouse square. The place they selected was over a mile north of the river, on higher ground relatively free of ruins and with limited desert growth.

Figure 1.1 Signs of the Hohokam irrigation. This canal was one of many that visitors to the Salt River Valley observed. The form of the canals and the network they comprised made it obvious that the Valley had been the site of extensive farming. *Source:* South Canal, Pueblo Grande Park of Four Waters, Phoenix. Photograph by Todd Bostwick.

Almost accidentally it was near the center of the Valley, a decision that would come to have great significance in shaping the hierarchy of Valley communities. They named the site Phoenix, after the mythical bird rising from its ashes and as a passing acknowledgment of the area's past.[13]

THE TOWN THAT AGRICULTURE BUILT

Phoenix was never a "western" town, certainly not a stereotypical western town. It had no Mexican heritage and only an ancient Indian connection, and except for its initial decades its minority population remained relatively small. Although the surrounding area contained cattle and ranches, it was never a "cow town," like Abilene or Dodge City, and although the Arizona Packing Company would become important starting in the 1920s, the slaughterhouse industry never achieved the defining role it held in cities like Fort Worth or Kansas City. Nor was Phoenix linked closely to mining, with its boom-bust patterns and its industrial labor force. Some Phoenix investors had mining interests, and the town supported some mining-related businesses, but mining companies operated from the mine sites at Prescott, Jerome, Morenci, and Bisbee, and the significant investment funds needed to develop such industrial enterprises came from centers of capital like San Francisco and New York.

Instead, Phoenix grew primarily because of agriculture. Like innumerable towns across the nation during the nineteenth century, its growth and prosperity depended on its agricultural hinterland. Its businesses, the focus of its economy, the importance of transportation, and the pace of its growth all reflected this fundamental reality. As area farmers prospered, so too did Phoenix residents. Agricultural prosperity fueled investment and speculation in land by both farmers and city residents. Finally, while an agricultural economy fluctuated, depending on weather and crop prices, it did not experience the kind of boom-bust pattern common to other types of towns. This agricultural, land-based economy fundamentally shaped the perceptions of Phoenicians about their future and their opportunities. They believed in growth and the need to "boost" their town and area, and they believed that some secondary economic activities could add to their prosperity. But they understood Phoenix to be primarily reliant upon agriculture, which established some basic limits to how fast it would grow and defined how big it would become.[14]

The Swilling Canal (later called the Salt River Valley Canal, as well as the Town Ditch) began two decades of active canal building in the Valley, and this prompted the emergence of agricultural towns dispersed throughout the area.[15] Within ten years, another five canals had been dug: one north of the river and four on the south side. These canals linked directly to the establishment of additional agricultural communities. The Tempe Canal (1870), dug seven miles upriver (east) from Phoenix, served a community first named after its founder, Charles Hayden, and then changed to Tempe. In 1877 and 1878 two groups of Mormon immigrants dug canals some eight miles further upstream that supported the town of Mesa.

Development of canals and the Valley advanced significantly with the construction of the Arizona Canal (1883–85). Starting much further upstream, running far to the north of the other canals through territory unserved by prehistoric canals, it was much larger (fifty-eight feet wide at the top and seven feet deep) and extended significantly further to the west. In addition, it was built, not by landowning farmers to service their farms, but by the Arizona Improvement Company, owned by speculative capitalists who sought profits from selling water and land along the canal. The Arizona Canal made possible the settlement of the northwestern communities of Peoria (1888) and Glendale (1892), as well as Scottsdale (1895) in the northeast. Finally, two canals dug later in the southeast eventually led to the establishment of

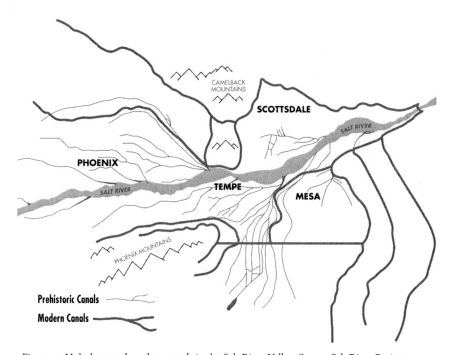

Figure 1.2 Hohokam and modern canals in the Salt River Valley. *Source:* Salt River Project.

Chandler (1912), roughly nine miles south of Mesa, and Gilbert (1910), some seven miles southeast of Mesa (figure 1.2).[16]

The size of the Valley and the ability to transport water across it encouraged the development of multiple settlements, but they did not predetermine the distribution of population or the relative importance of the settlements. Phoenix always remained the largest and then the dominant community in the valley because it began first, because it was located in the center of the Valley, and because of the decisions of the settlers themselves. (But while these other communities had little importance during this period, a century and more later they would develop a significant role as part of a "multi-nucleated" metropolis.[17])

Canals changed the appearance and reality of life in the Valley, enabling the creation of new ecosystems. Settlers immediately planted trees along the canals, aiding a natural process, and the combination of sun and water transformed the landscape. Cottonwood, ash, poplar, and willow trees added shade, color, and definition to the rural areas, supplementing native mesquite and palo verde trees. Canals and ditches distributed water throughout the towns, where trees were even more important, providing windbreaks and shade. Phoenicians considered this botanical transformation an integral part of civilizing the desert, as vital as the construction of buildings and an economy. The change was almost immediate and remarkable to both residents and visitors. An 1881 publication described Phoenix as having "groves of cottonwoods and lines of the graceful Lombardy popular diversify the landscape in every direction," a panoramic map of 1885 displayed an image of the town that it described as being "embowered in shade trees and shrubbery," while a pamphlet from 1894 claimed that "so dense is this forest of verdure that the traveler approaching it from any direction will not see the house until he is fairly within the town."[18]

Boosters, working independently and through organizations like the Phoenix Board of Trade, touted the reliability of irrigated agriculture, claimed that Valley soil equaled the best "garden spots of the world," including "the 'Polders' of Holland or the 'Black Lands' of Russia," and asserted that virtually any crop could be grown profitably there.[19] In fact, the long growing season and the relative predictability of water from irrigation created many options, but heat and the particular soil types meant that Valley agriculture was better suited to some crops than to others. Thus, basic elements of agriculture in the Valley persisted throughout this era, but through continuing experimentation Valley farmers diversified what they raised. Their earliest crops were alfalfa (which remained the dominant crop until the 1920s) and grains (mainly wheat and barley), and by the late 1870s many farmers had introduced livestock. Vegetables were also important, particularly root crops such as turnips, beets, onions, and potatoes, but also traditional Indian crops like squash and beans, and later on lettuce was added to this mix.

By the 1880s farmers were growing increasing varieties and amounts of fruits, particularly strawberries, apricots, peaches, and grapes. Citrus cultivation began in 1889, promoted by the Arizona Improvement Company and Rev. Winfield Scott. An army chaplain who had seen citrus growing in California, Scott purchased land near what he would later found as Scottsdale and began raising citrus and other fruits. The citrus effort quickly became successful, and by 1895 roughly 150,000 trees had been planted, most densely in the "Orange Belt," near the Arizona Canal. By this time the Valley had become a significant agricultural area within the Southwest, with more than 125,000 acres being irrigated and farmed. Climate and expanding irrigation had provided the basic means for this rapid expansion and had shaped the choice of crops, but improved transportation played a key part in this process.[20]

Wagon roads provided the initial transportation options for Phoenix and the Valley, linking the area directly to Prescott, Florence, and Tucson; more distantly to Yuma; and then to California. This changed in 1879, when the Southern Pacific Railroad reached the town of Maricopa, a twenty-three-mile journey from Phoenix taking six hours by stagecoach and sixteen by freight wagon. This enhanced opportunities for trade and travel, but the main Southern line ran through Tucson. Founded in 1775, territorial capital from 1867 to 1877, and the territory's largest town (its population was 3,224 in 1870 and 7,007 in 1880), Tucson's acquisition of a direct rail connection promised to bolster its existing advantages and transform it into the dominant community in the territory and perhaps in the Southwest.

Recognizing the need to improve their situation and respond to Tucson's gain, Phoenix leaders raised the money to construct a spur line to their community. In June 1887 the rails reached Tempe, and a month later they entered Phoenix; eight years later, a spur connected Mesa to the Southern line. Equally important, the Atchison, Topeka, & Santa Fe tracks reached Phoenix from the north in 1895. This changed the city from being on a dead end to being on a through route, served by two competing lines, and firmly linked to the national transportation system. These rail connections greatly enhanced the opportunities for Valley farmers, letting them change from wagon shipments for central Arizona towns to transporting goods to markets across the nation, and expanding the nascent competition with California. The easier and more direct passenger service increased the prospects for migration and tourism. Thus, land prices, population, and agricultural production all boomed with the arrival of the railroad.[21]

BUILDING A TOWN

The development of farming and transportation fostered the growth of many economic services, new social institutions, and a significant built environment. Economic forces stimulated these developments, but the desires of Phoenicians to create a "modern American" town gave them drive and direction. Roughly a decade after its founding, the Phoenix population reached 1,708. More impressive than this respectable rate of growth, the village featured key institutions and a surprisingly well-developed occupational structure. A branch of the Bank of Arizona opened in 1878. Another vital public institution began service in the same year, when C. E. McClintock started the *Salt River Herald* (which became the *Phoenix Herald* in 1880), followed after several years by the *Arizona Gazette*. By 1881 two hotels had opened: the Phoenix Hotel and the more substantial Bank Exchange Hotel, started by Emil Ganz, who later served as mayor. Phoenix also offered a wide range of shops: general stores and butcher shops, dry goods stores and laundries, liveries, a floor mill, an ice factory, and lumberyards. Certain professionals—lawyers, doctors, and ministers—as well as various tradesmen—carpenters, painters, blacksmiths, tailors, barbers, and photographers, among them—found employment in the young community.[22]

Phoenicians developed social structures and amenities almost as quickly as they built an economy, reflecting the cultures they brought as well as their aspirations. Two churches were established by the first wave of settlers, and within a decade three denominations—the Methodist Episcopal, Presbyterian, and Roman Catholic—had erected houses of worship. A second crucial institution begun as soon as settlers arrived was a school, demonstrating the community's legitimacy and providing a crucial meeting place. Legitimacy through the pursuit of knowledge also inspired the organization of both a library association in 1877 to bring books to the community and the Maricopa Literary Society a year later. While women actively built these associations, men engaged in organizing various fraternal lodges, starting with the ubiquitous Masons. In Phoenix, as elsewhere, such groups provided key social networks and a means of quickly integrating new arrivals into the community.[23] The desire for social interaction found some expression in groups like the Phoenix Brass Band, but other connections were more common. In most western communities the first settler brought liquor, and the second opened a saloon, and Phoenix was no different: by 1881 it hosted fifteen saloons, more than any other type of business. In addition to dispensing alcohol, the saloons offered musical and theatrical entertainment, and besides the school, they provided the only secular, semipublic space for people to congregate.[24]

Over the next two decades, the town's economic and social development advanced at a healthy pace. The population reached relatively modest levels of 3,152 in 1890 and 5,544 in 1900, but the economic institutions and the range of occupations continued to resemble those of a larger community.[25] By the end of the century, four daily and six weekly newspapers fed the community's political and other interests. Financial services expanded considerably: by 1892 the city boasted six banks plus two building and loan associations, while real estate and business services firms also flourished.

Predictably, bankers were prominent community leaders and involved in multiple economic enterprises. Given the size of the city, these men were often partners in various ventures. Emil Ganz, who built a hotel in 1879 and owned a liquor business, was president of Arizona National Bank and served as mayor in 1885 and 1889. William Christy, politically prominent in Iowa, came to Phoenix and first engaged in farming, but he soon joined William Murphy in founding Valley Bank and later in creating the Arizona Improvement Company. Christy and Murphy also partnered with Moses Sherman, who owned the water and streetcar companies, which he used to help develop his real estate interests. Hotels also attracted investment from important business leaders. Chicago emigre John Adams arrived in 1896 and immediately began building the Adams Hotel, which offered finer accommodations than the other establishments and served as a meeting place for local, county, and state politicians—and those seeking to influence them. Fittingly, Adams served as mayor in 1897 and 1905.

The town also housed a wide variety of stores and shops offering foods and furnishings; artisans and skilled workers like tinsmiths, upholsterers, black-smiths, and tailors tendered their services; contractors and men in building trades allied with numerous persons working in the area of real estate; while the number of professionals—especially lawyers and doctors, but also archi-tects and civil engineers—showed the town's prosperity and growth. A sense of shared enterprise and an interest in growth, common to many new communi-ties, strongly characterized this town and was reflected in various informal ways.

The Chamber of Commerce, organized in 1888, represents the most important formal effort at fostering this sense and pursuing common goals.[26]

The town's vibrant social life also demonstrated the interest in community development. The "joining" impulse fueled the growth of organizations, most notably fraternal societies, but also some social groups, like the Arizona Club. Various other types of organizations also appeared, like the Grand Army of the Republic and the Illinois Association, but the one having the greatest social impact was the Ladies Benevolent Society, organized in 1890, which provided relief to the poor and sick, and occasionally investigated their treatment in hospitals and the poor house. Organized religion expanded to include seventeen churches, mostly mainline Protestant churches, but also one Catholic and various unique congregations, while several church societies attracted growing memberships. The dominance of evangelical churches had important implications for this community, because these groups emphasized moral behavior rather than fine points of doctrine. The community's growing efforts to develop a middle-class Victorian culture reflected the moral and cultural standards of these groups.[27]

The city continued to emphasize the vital role of schools in the community's social and cultural development. Phoenicians loudly and regularly touted the quality of their schools, which included four grammar schools and one high school by the century's end. They valued these institutions because they represented learning and opportunity, they served as important community meeting places, and they offered a way to demonstrate the community's worthiness. Living in a new frontier western town, Phoenicians felt a strong need to develop their culture and to report, as one author did in 1894, that

> the society of Phoenix can lay just claim to being cultured, liberal, and progressive. Reading rooms, libraries, social and benevolent organizations are fully established here, and the amenities of social life are observed as fully as in lands of an older civilization.

New intellectual organizations emerged, like various women's reading groups and a history club, while new cultural organizations included the Chautauqua Society and the Orpheus Society. A Signor Fernari started a (short-lived) Conservatory of Music, but by 1899 the town supported five music teachers and five companies selling musical instruments, as well as two art supply firms.[28]

Besides reflecting boosterism and traditional efforts to promote a new community, these claims and activities represent a societal divide that grew during the late nineteenth century. Boosters and town leaders combined their interest in a separate "high" culture with a religious/cultural emphasis on moral reform to create a culture of refinement and edification. On the other side of the societal divide, "popular" culture included amusements and entertainments, and in Phoenix this was flourishing.[29] Traveling stock companies presented variety shows, and theatrical troupes offered a range of shows or plays on successive nights. Outdoor theaters using temporary walls provided inexpensive venues for such performances, but the Phoenix Opera House opened in 1886 and allegedly contained 800 seats. Besides housing entertainment, it filled a vital need for public space and was "used for literary and social club meetings, Catholic bazaars, high school exams and commencements," school programs, and various public meetings such as those on water storage issues. This structure was superseded in 1898 by the Dorris Opera House, a larger four-story building, which served a similar array of entertainment and civic events. Public amusements also developed, especially by the 1890s, with outdoor roller rinks, a merry-go-round, and Phoenix Park, which offered a community swimming pool.[30]

The most popular but also the most disruptive amusements were the various activities—musical and theater shows, billiards, gambling, and prostitution—connected with the town's saloons. Many of the establishments in this growing industry were centrally placed: from nineteen in 1892 the number grew to thirty-three in 1899, of which half clustered in the five main blocks on Washington Street, the town's main street. Most of the saloons explicitly listed gambling facilities and implicitly provided prostitutes. The town's growth provided citizens with alternative public meeting places, but the saloons continued to draw many customers, in part because competition between saloons encouraged them to offer food and substantial amusements. City ordinances in the 1880s made some attempts at regulation by forbidding public drunkenness and Sunday liquor sales, as well as instituting minimal regulation of prostitution, and an 1894 ordinance restricted houses of prostitution to a city block away from the center of town. Churches sought more restrictions, as did the chapters of several national groups, including the Salvation Army, the Good Templars (a temperance fraternal order), and especially the local chapter of the Women's Christian Temperance Union (WCTU), which started in 1884 and established an office with a public reading room a block from the Washington Street saloons.[31]

Anglo Phoenicians' concern with community morality and behavior, and more generally with developing Phoenix as a modern American city, also fueled their attitudes toward the four minority groups in the area, each of which had a different presence and raised somewhat different worries. Except for students at the Indian School, Indians did not live in Phoenix, but Anglos complained about their loitering in town. They did live nearby, however, for Pima and Maricopa tribes resided on the Gila River Reservation, established in 1859 some eighteen miles south of the town site, and the Salt River Reservation, established in 1879 ten miles east. Chinese began arriving during the 1870s, and most worked for laundries, groceries, or restaurants or as laborers. Like many Anglo Californians, Anglo Phoenicians viewed this population with distaste, associating it with opium, gambling, and squalor. In 1895 the desire to oust them from the community inspired several Anglo businessmen to buy and close up several buildings in Chinatown, and partly as a result the total Chinese population (nearly all male) declined between 1880 and 1900. However, not all Phoenicians felt this way, as some demonstrated by creating a Chinese Mission by 1899. African Americans constituted a slightly larger group, and they created a significantly stronger institutional base, with an African Methodist Episcopal (South) church and separate associations for Masons, Odd Fellows, and Knights of Pythias. Their treatment in Phoenix during this period roughly resembles the move towards separation and segregation they experienced elsewhere in the nation.[32]

Mexican Americans comprised easily the largest non-Anglo group in Phoenix and the Valley. Making up roughly half the population in 1870 and 1880, their numbers rose only slightly thereafter, lagging much behind the general population increase.[33] Despite this reduced percentage, the population was large enough to include a small middle class of shopkeepers and merchants. It also supported numerous institutions. Unlike other Valley groups, Mexicans created a social/national association, and instead of fraternal orders they organized mutual benefit organizations—Alianza Hispano-Americano (1898) and the Society Beneficentes Mutual Co-Operative (as of 1899). Mexicans associated closely with the Catholic church, but a Mexican Methodist Episcopal church represented a successful missionary approach to this population. Several Spanish-language newspapers operated during this era, but the use of Spanish was a divisive issue, raising fears among Anglo Phoenicians about Mexican resistance to assimilation or a cultural challenge from any "foreign" element.

While Anglo Phoenicians viewed each group somewhat differently, they felt that all minorities posed cultural and economic problems, as well as endangering how outsiders viewed the community. The proportion of minorities in Phoenix declined during this era partly because more Anglos found the town attractive, but the limited change in minority population numbers hints that other factors, particularly public attitudes, were involved. Booster rhetoric of this era reflects deliberate efforts to define a preferred culture and people. As one such author wrote in 1892, Phoenix was "thoroughly American and its citizens are live and go-ahead people full of push and enterprise."[34]

Changes in the city's built environment were as striking and important as its social and economic growth. Phoenicians believed that the physical structures and architecture of their community revealed not only their prosperity, but also their character—their ambitions, their modernity, and their status as living in a fully American town. Location and isolation were crucial factors in shaping these views. Since importing building materials was very difficult and expensive before the railroad arrived, most buildings constructed in the first dozen years of Anglo settlement were made of adobe, the sun-dried clay that the Hohokams had also used. Although abundant, inexpensive, and appropriate for the climate, it was not durable, it did not have a finished or uniform appearance, and it had severe load-bearing restrictions. Consequently, in its first decade Phoenix "had a decidedly rough, frontier-town appearance."[35]

Conditions changed rapidly after 1879. Construction of a factory making fired brick and the greater ease of importing lumber and glass via the railroad led to a building boom and a dramatic shift in building patterns, which was also influenced by the presence of four architects. Brick quickly became the preferred material for homes, businesses, and the new school building. Over the next several decades numerous homes were built in Victorian styles common across the nation, including Queen Anne, French Second Empire, and Victorian Eclectic. Such homes involved features like multiplaned roofs, exotic finials, cupolas, spires, and ornate trim, and their larger lots featured lawns, flowers and "luxuriant growth of semi-tropical plants," picket fences, and increasing numbers of shade trees.[36]

Wood was also used for homes and initially for businesses, but fires in 1885 and 1886 led to a ban on using wood in the center city. This prohibition coincided with the prosperity induced by the arrival of the railroad, and by the mid-1890s a number of new brick structures with plate glass windows had been built downtown, where multistory buildings were now common.[37] These buildings often made accommodations to the weather, providing arcades, colonnades, porches, substantial awnings, and shades to protect pedestrians from the sun as they walked on the newly built sidewalks. But apart from such features, the physical structures of downtown Phoenix did not appear

Figure 1.3 Heyman Furniture Building, 1895, at Washington Street and 1st Avenue. Phoenicians viewed this substantial structure as important evidence of the city's maturation, as was the newly electrified streetcar system. *Source:* Luhrs Family Photographs, Arizona Collection, Arizona State University Libraries.

Figure 1.4 Beyond Main Street. Washington Street and 2nd Avenue in 1900, showing a forested city behind. *Source:* McCulloch Brothers Photographs, Herb and Dorothy McLaughlin Collection, Arizona State University Libraries.

recognizably "western." Resembling neither the rustic wooden style nor the Hispanic architecture of places like Tucson or Santa Fe, the downtown buildings instead looked like Anglo American, neoclassical, or new European architectural styles. With its Opera House topped by its turrets and mansard roof, for example, downtown Phoenix looked, intentionally, like eastern American cities of the time (figures 1.3 and 1.4).[38]

Although the use of adobe declined greatly after 1880, several earlier-made structures remained, to the growing dissatisfaction of some Valley residents. Then a flood swept through the Valley in February 1891, and besides devastating the dams, canals, and bridge, its main urban destruction was described as the "melting down" of as many as fifty adobe houses. The *Arizona Republican* approved. "Phoenix, as a city, was benefitted" since these "miserable adobes . . . have rendered the city unsightly for a number of years." The writer hoped that this would "relieve the valley forever of the dreadful mud house." The *Arizona Daily Gazette* was slightly less euphoric, suggesting that "while it will work a hardship on some families, it will in the end prove a blessing to this valley." Left unsaid in these reports but noted by a later historian was the personal and differential impact, "making homeless hundreds of Mexicans."[39] The connection between architecture and culture was made clearly in an 1893 description of Phoenix: "On every side are to be noted the evidences of thrift and enterprise. Here are none of the sleepy, semi-Mexican features of the more ancient towns of the Southwest, but in the midst of a valley of wonderful fertility, has risen a city of stately structures, beautiful homes, progressive and vigorous."[40]

ESTABLISHING THE PUBLIC CITY

Decisions about the role and nature of their government were another way for Valley settlers to develop their community and demonstrate their modern and progressive values. Through the first decade the community's only public features were canals, which irrigated the urban landscape; its one public institution, small but important, was the school, begun in 1872. After a decade of growth, town residents began developing public services and creating political opportunities: they formally incorporated the town of Phoenix in 1881 and landscaped as public parks the two blocks in the town site originally reserved for public use. In the next several years the city took a few additional steps, passing several ordinances, mainly concerning sanitation; collecting some fines and license fees; and hiring a marshal.[41]

In 1885 a slightly revised charter provided for four council members chosen from wards, with a mayor, marshal, and treasurer elected at-large. Then, as in numerous other communities, public crises stimulated public actions. After two smallpox epidemics, the city created a public health department and hired a permanent health officer. Serious fires in 1885 and 1886 prompted the establishment of an equipped volunteer fire department, and it fueled a growing demand for a water system. Begun in 1887, within two years the system had eleven miles of pipe, mainly serving businesses. During the next decade workers laid another sixteen miles of pipe, enabling residents to shift from using wells or buying water by the bucket. The companion system to this, the Phoenix Sewer and Drainage Department, started in 1892.[42]

The town also acquired other key urban amenities after 1885, initially serving businesses and then expanding to residents. The city council granted a franchise in 1886 to a gas lighting company; two years later an electric power company started providing power for businesses and streetlights. A rudimentary telephone system began in 1886, and by 1897 it had 280 customers and connections to other Valley towns. More important, Moses Sherman and M. E. Collins began developing a streetcar system in 1887. By 1890 these mule-drawn cars traveled 5.5 miles of track, and in 1893 the system was converted to electricity, which increased the speed, range, and convenience. Besides providing another visible sign of the city's modern status, the lines also influenced the development and placement of new subdivisions, in this period to the west and northwest.[43] Noting these features, *Appleton's Annual Cyclopedia* claimed in 1889 that the city "has all the improvements required in a modern town."[44] These services attracted residents and enabled more people to live outside the original town site boundaries. An 1893 territorial law allowed the city to annex surrounding territory, with agreement from residents, which it did, growing from the 0.5 square miles of the original town site to 2.13 square miles in 1900.[45]

Governmental institutions, structures, and functions also enabled Phoenicians to expand their town's status and importance, and that created conflict with other communities throughout the territory. The competition began early, in 1871, when the County of Maricopa was established and Phoenix became the new county seat. After a dozen years of housing county government in rented office space, in 1884 a two-story brick county courthouse building was completed on Washington Street, on one of the two blocks reserved for public use. Three years later the other block was filled by a new city hall, whose tower made it the tallest structure in the city.

In 1885 the territorial legislature began creating basic public institutions for the territory. The decision about where to place them generated an intense struggle between communities, one in which Phoenix came out surprisingly well. Tucson, the older and still much larger town, secured what most considered a lesser prize—the university and an allocation of $25,000. The city's outraged citizens, perceiving a slight and seeing little economic value in the institution (and perhaps anticipating only trouble ahead), jeered their representatives and considered rejecting the award.[46] The Valley's second town, Tempe, did unexpectedly well in the institutional sweepstakes, winning the normal school, but Phoenix won the main prize—the state asylum— valued for providing more employment and a more substantial structure than the other institutions.

The federal government increased the city's gains in 1891 by choosing it as the location for a major school for Indians. Thirty buildings were constructed within a decade. With more than seven hundred students and numerous staff, the Phoenix Indian School was the second largest such institution in the nation. Anglo Phoenicians valued this for providing visibility, revenue, and employment, but its mission of "civilizing the savage" also fit their larger goals.[47] Easily the most significant boost to the city's status and institutional base, though, occurred when Phoenix was named the territorial capital in 1889. This honor had previously belonged to Tucson and then Prescott after 1875, but the changing patterns of territorial development prompted a continuing debate over the issue. Finally, recognizing Phoenix's claims of centrality and size, and responding to the city's offer of ten acres of land, landscaping, plus street and streetcar connections, the legislature decided to move the capitol "irrevocably" to the growing city. These new government offices provided employment for Phoenicians and, together with attracting clients and petitioners, represented a distinct influence on the city's economy. They also presented some increased opportunity to influence territorial, and later state, governmental decisions. But they were more important for confirming the emerging role for Phoenix as the dominant city in central Arizona and strengthening its ability to compete with Tucson and other cities for influence within the larger southwestern region.

BUILDING A HYDRAULIC SYSTEM: CONTROLLING AND USING WATER

Water was the lifeblood of this agricultural area, and thus of Phoenix, but its irregular flow threatened the community's vitality. If flowing water in a desert is surprising, then desert floods must appear even more unusual, yet this has featured significantly in the history of the Valley's inhabitation. Irrigation systems have certainly played the largest part in shaping the contours of the Valley, but the persistent, periodic need for flood control has had a complementary and conflicting role. In 1868, within a year of the initial settlement, the Salt River flooded, and in 1874 and 1875 more significant floods destroyed most of the dam and canal structures.[48] These were quickly rebuilt, however, and the area continued to grow; more canals were constructed, and the population grew to 3,152 in 1890. But on February 18, 1891, the heavy rains came again. By February 19 the confluence of the Verde and Salt rivers spread over eight miles, and near Phoenix the Salt widened to more than three miles.

This torrent of water wreaked havoc on the irrigation system. It washed out the diversion dams and poured into the canals, destroying several miles of the Tempe Canal, flooding three miles of the Mesa Canal border, and overflowing miles of the Highland Canal. The Arizona Canal, the largest water channel, suffered even greater damage. Canals that had been built to move water around the Valley and to Phoenix now overserved that function, as they enabled flood waters to pour down the Salt River Valley Canal and laterals into the center of the city. The greatest destruction affected adobe buildings, but several other structures in the city were seriously damaged. Even greater devastation occurred on the river, as flood waters washed out the prized railroad bridge near Tempe, also eliminating telegraph service.[49] The bridge, dams, and canals were repaired relatively quickly, and, as noted above, some Phoenicians felt that the destruction of the adobe structures was beneficial. A more significant consequence was that Phoenicians decided hereafter to build to the north, away from the river.

Fears of floods soon receded, especially because conditions soon turned to drought. Below-average rainfall from 1898 to 1904 reduced the river from a flow in January 1895 of 83,000 cubic feet per second (cfs), down to 35,000 cfs in 1897, and to 20,000 cfs in 1903. As a result, from 1895 to 1905 the amount of land under cultivation declined by a fifth, and the economy of Phoenix stagnated.[50] Certainly these drought conditions reinforced the perception that this area was a desert that needed to be reclaimed. In 1889 the Irrigation and Reclamation Committee of the U.S. Senate had held hearings in Phoenix about irrigation, and in 1896 the city hosted the 5th National Irrigation Congress. Thus, as participants in a national movement seeking increased federal support for irrigation, as residents of an area benefiting from irrigation, and spurred by the post-1891 drought, Phoenicians and other Valley residents began exploring options and places for building a storage dam on the Salt River.

Following the proposal of an earlier investigative group, a committee of the Phoenix Board of Trade in April of 1900 recommended a dam site, which a public meeting in August confirmed. A committee representing various parties chose Benjamin A. Fowler to lobby Congress for help. A recent migrant to the Valley who had political connections, Fowler worked with congressmen and members of the new Roosevelt administration to promote passage of the Newlands Reclamation Act (1902), which provided federal funding for irrigation projects and the selection of a Salt River dam as the first project under this legislation. The project's final obstacles—the clarification of claims to the water and the improvement of the canal distribution system—were overcome when Valley farmers created the Salt River Valley Water Users' Association in 1903 and in subsequent years when the federal government consolidated canal ownership and constructed several connecting canals. Work began immediately, although delayed by flooding in 1905 and 1908, resulting in completion of the Granite Reef Diversion Dam in 1908 and the Roosevelt Dam in 1911.[51]

This project marked a crucial transition in the history of the Valley and of Phoenix. Most importantly, it provided a fairly reliable and regular supply of water. While annual rainfall was steady during the 1910s, the Valley experienced great variation during the next decade, with four years of severe drought and another three of below-average rainfall. Roosevelt Dam alleviated this problem by storing water available in the wetter years of 1923 and 1926.[52] It also provided some flood control (although this was not perfect), and it offered relatively inexpensive hydroelectric power, which soon became a major benefit. Federal government financing made this project possible, but local boosterism and cooperative community efforts provided the essential drive.

The amount of land in production had fallen by a fifth from 1895 to 1905, during the drought, but the return of rain brought those numbers back to their former level by 1908. After the completion of Roosevelt Dam, the quantity of cultivated land increased dramatically, rising by a third from 1910 to 1920, gaining another third during the 1920s, and from the late 1920s to 1940 averaging 360,000 acres. Expanding acreage created more opportunities, and the number of farmers more than doubled, from 2,130 in 1910 to 4,359 in 1921. This growth was encouraged by publicity campaigns operated by the Board of Trade, the Santa Fe Railroad, and the U.S. Reclamation Service.

The availability of water let farmers bring new land into cultivation, as well as affecting land ownership and stimulating the creation of new towns. The Reclamation Act restricted the distribution of its water to farms of no more than 160 acres, which led to land sales in the southeast Valley and the towns of Gilbert and Chandler.[53]

A second reason for the expansion and profitability of agriculture was World War I. Besides causing general price hikes, it greatly boosted prices for long-staple cotton because this was needed for military items, including airplane wings, balloons, and uniforms, and it was essential for the Goodyear Tire and Rubber Company's new pneumatic truck tires. Because Valley farmers were reluctant to grow this new crop, in 1916 Goodyear vice president Paul Litchfield purchased 8,000 acres south of land in the Salt River Project area, which were watered by wells. Goodyear's subsidiary, the Southwest Cotton Company, managed the operation from a company "town," or village, of Goodyear (later renamed Ocotillo). The company also purchased 14,000 acres in the west Valley, where its town of Litchfield Park (1916) relied on water from wells and the Gila River.[54] Escalating prices and financial incentives from Goodyear soon eliminated farmers' initial hesitation, and acreage in long-staple cotton skyrocketed from 7,300 acres in 1916 to 180,000 in 1920. Unfortunately, the last increase came as the price of cotton plummeted, and the market crash bankrupted many farmers as well as related businesses. These farm foreclosures caused more consolidation in land ownership, and by 1924 the number of farms had declined by 20 percent.

After the crash, farmers quickly reverted to dairy farming and a diversity of crops, including alfalfa and grains, fruits, and vegetables; they also expanded citrus, olive, and date farming, and by the late 1920s they were marketing more poultry and lettuce. By the end of the 1920s, some Valley farmers resumed the cultivation of long-staple cotton, but more chose to grow the short-staple variety, creating a permanent shift in Valley farming. Despite the short-term changes of fortune, Valley agriculture remained quite profitable. The significant income directly related to farming, plus expansion of the associated economic activities involving warehouses, processing plants, marketing, agricultural implement dealers, and growers' associations, as well as banks and land investment, continued to fuel the growth of Phoenix. The "principal business" of Phoenix, a Chamber of Commerce pamphlet confirmed in 1922, "is that which relates directly or indirectly to agriculture."[55]

Roosevelt Dam created significant water storage, but it was only the first step in creating the Valley's hydraulic system. Three additional dams were built on the Salt River in the 1920s, primarily for hydroelectric power and secondarily for water storage. But flooding continued elsewhere. After Cave Creek flooded in 1916, 1919, 1921, and 1922, the construction of a dam in that northern Phoenix area reduced but did not entirely eliminate that threat. Flooding on the Verde River in 1916, 1923, and 1932 led to construction of Bartlett Dam in 1938, but serious flooding in that year washed away some of the construction and some equipment. Additional floods—on the Gila River in 1915, on the Agua Fria and New rivers in 1931, and on Queen Creek in 1933—stimulated demands for action by the Maricopa County Board of Supervisors. Far from being unusual, flooding somewhere in the Salt River Valley was a typical occurrence.[56] Contrary to whatever Phoenicians' increasing sense of mastery might have led them to believe, Nature was not so easily tamed.

CLIMATE AND HEALTH

From the beginning of settlement, boosters praised the availability of water, the growing season, and the greenery of the Valley, and comments by visitors verified those claims. Boosters' descriptions of the climate, however, were less accurate, and they sometimes stretched the truth beyond the melting point. Writing in 1877, Hiram Hodge accurately noted the pleasant winters, but he also claimed that the summer climate, "although quite warm, is not oppressive, or debilitating." Patrick Hamilton asserted in 1881 that "while the heat in summer is high, its peculiar dryness prevents any injurious effects, and sunstrokes are rarely heard of in Arizona." While many residents might dispute these sanguine reports of summer heat, their general views of the climate related to ideas about health. Both authors used the same language to assert that "no country in the world [had] a purer, healthier climate," with Hamilton noting the therapeutic effects for persons "suffering from pulmonary complaints or rheumatic affections."[57] These opinions were mirrored by "climatologists," doctors who championed the effect of climate on human health. Their presence in Colorado and southern California had boosted settlement in those regions, beginning in the 1870s, and by the 1890s Arizona had attracted numerous adherents to these views. Writing in the *New York Medical Journal* in 1900, for example, Dr. E. Payne Palmer asserted that Phoenix offered the healthiest climate in the nation.[58]

Aided by increased accessibility from the new rail connections, Valley boosters in the 1890s began touting its attractiveness for nonagricultural reasons. Railroads, the Board of Trade, and investment companies advertised the healthful nature of the climate as a way to change national perceptions of the Arizona desert. A publication in 1908 advised that the climate was a natural "healing sanitarium" for tuberculosis, asthma, hay fever, bronchitis, and catarrhs, as well as preventing typhoid or malaria. A climate analysis written in 1910 by a section director of the U.S. Weather Bureau added the claim that persons suffering from "the irritated and exhausted nervous system and overwrought brain" could find sleep and thus overcome "all forms of nervous debility and nervous prostration." But most of the appeal, starting in the 1890s, was to persons suffering pulmonary problems—"lungers" as they came to be called—and by 1910 the Valley was "one of the most popular destinations in the western U.S. for migrant consumptives."[59]

The presence of these ailing immigrants impacted the Valley most notably by encouraging medical care. St. Joseph's (1895), St. Luke's (1907), and Deaconess (1911) hospitals were all started to treat consumptives, and after that they broadened their services. A second consequence was that concern about these ailing immigrants led to the creation of certain philanthropic organizations. But negative reactions to this influx also grew. Phoenix banned tents within the city in 1903, some businesses and landlords refused service to these sufferers, and a promotional pamphlet warned the ill not to expect free medical care. The more affluent could afford care in small cottages or sanatoriums, but the poor clustered in tents or shacks on the northern outskirts of town, in Cave Creek or Sunnyslope.

The recognition that tuberculosis posed a public health threat, the concern about providing for a flood of indigents with TB, and a fear that the Valley's national image would be as a TB haven prompted a shift in attitudes and actions during the 1910s. The simplistic claims that residence in the Valley alone would have tonic affects, as well as general invitations to immigrate, disappeared. The Valley still attracted persons with pulmonary problems, but by the 1920s they received medical treatment instead of simply relying on open air. Valley boosters continued to champion the attractive climate, but during the 1910s their focus shifted to drawing in other groups. Pursuit of the ailing was a settlement strategy; appealing the healthy would be the new focus.[60]

The early history of Phoenix was much like that of many other communities established in the nineteenth century. Entrepreneurs first ventured forth, buying land and platting a town site. They were quickly followed by others, and after the first public facilities were built—a saloon and a school—others followed soon after. Economic growth led to increased occupational diversity, various types of business, and a range of social and cultural organizations. Formal government was also established in fairly rapid order. The town's boosterism was typical of new communities; so, too, was its reliance on agriculture. What distinguished it was the town's geographic setting and its interest in how others viewed it.

Phoenicians took great pains to boast about the agriculture conditions of the area, for they knew that the notion of farming in the desert would seem incomprehensible to most people. They also recognized that most Americans would consider the desert climate harsh not only for agriculture but for culture in general. If agricultural towns were generally viewed as cultural backwaters, a southwestern desert town would seem an even less likely place for civilization to prosper. So Phoenicians loudly and relentlessly emphasized the "modern" and "American" character of their community: they built in familiar forms, quickly adopted new urban amenities, and established institutions that championed community, education, and morality. They believed they could reshape parts of nature through dams and canals, and parts that were less amendable to change, like climate, they managed by touting its healthful benefits.

By 1900, Phoenix had developed a social, cultural, and political framework; by the 1910s, it was the heart of a prosperous agricultural region, a community bound to its hinterland like agricultural service towns in Nebraska or Georgia or Ohio. But in structure, culture, and public life, Phoenix would experience considerable change from 1900 to 1940. Chapter 2 focuses on post-1900 changes in the form and function of the city—its position in the regional urban hierarchy, its development of more complex internal forms, and the consolidation of social structures. Chapter 3 then covers public activities, like the struggle to create an efficient and "progressive" city government, as well as campaigns for moral reform and cultural development. The city's popular culture provided another face, as did the campaign to promote tourism. Finally, despite the trials of the Great Depression, the city drew some important lessons and was better positioned to deal with the challenges of the war years.

2
Building The Modern City:
Physical Form and Function

In 1912 Arizona became the last of the forty-eight contiguous states to enter the Union, last partly because its population was relatively small, and over the next thirty years it remained one of the least populous states. Roughly a third of its residents lived in cities, but unlike more urbanized states, this population was not distributed in a spatially regular hierarchy of towns, villages, hamlets, and farms. And by contrast with the relatively predictable urban development in many other states, where populations either boomed or simply grew, and might perhaps plateau after a period of growth, some Arizona communities displayed highly erratic patterns of boom and bust, or simply a boom and gradual fade. These conditions complicated the relationship of Phoenix to communities in central Arizona, the state, and the region.

Phoenicians built their city in imitation of urban forms elsewhere, but they necessarily responded to the unique conditions of their location. They created a downtown reflecting the city's economic role within the area but with functions and structures like those of larger cities. The expansion and development of the city's residential neighborhoods also followed national transportation and architectural patterns. But their ways of dealing with the environment continued to set the city apart. They developed a unique role for canals as part of a continuing effort to structure a society by taming nature. But even at this early point, while Phoenix produced the form and function of a modern city, dissenting voices challenged this vision of the desert.

PHOENIX IN AN URBAN CONTEXT, 1890–1920

Central place theorists envision a base community surrounded by an agricultural hinterland, connected to similar communities spaced at roughly equal intervals and related to a larger central town that offers additional and more specialized services. The larger town, and others of similar size and functions, connect to a still larger and central city, and so forth, completing the hierarchy. In its simplest form, the theory posited equal distances between places, but in any application topography, natural resources, and transportation alter town location and the urban hierarchy. Moreover, different functions—like port facilities, manufacturing, or government—could also affect the outcome. Such complexities demonstrate the limits of a simple, deterministic version of central place or urban hierarchy. However, the simple model does clarify different urban functions, and in seeking to explain the competition between different urban places, it highlights the importance of particular services, market areas, and the role of community leaders.[1]

Examining the urban hierarchy that developed in the inland West during the later nineteenth century puts the growth and position of Phoenix into perspective (table 2.1). Except for Salt Lake City (1847) and Spokane (1881), these cities were founded only about a decade earlier than Phoenix; four were also state capitals, and none were ports or had major manufacturing industries. However, each grew much more rapidly and had become much larger than Phoenix. While these difference reflect various factors, the main point is that an agriculturally based city like Phoenix, even with rail transportation and some government functions, did not become a major western city. Even in the Southwest, its position remained limited and subordinate to El Paso. In fact, its growth before 1920 more closely resembles that of Emporia, Kansas, or Walla Walla, Washington, than that of Denver or Topeka. The *Salt River Herald*'s observation in 1878 that the town's growth during that decade "has not been feverish nor of the mushroom order" remained appropriate for subsequent decades as well.[2]

The position of Phoenix within Arizona was more complex. As noted earlier, Phoenix started with the advantages of being first and having a central location. Into the 1890s it kept its position as the largest community in central Arizona because its aggressive and imaginative leaders saw the need for rail

Table 2.1 Western inland cities, 1870–1930.

City	1870	1880	1890	1900	1910	1920	1930
Phoenix	200	1,708	3,152	5,544	11,134	29,053	48,118
Salt Lake City	12,854	20,708	44,843	53,531	92,777	118,110	140,267
Denver	4,759	35,629	106,713	133,859	213,381	256,491	287,861
Omaha	16,083	30,518	140,452	102,555	124,096	191,601	214,006
Spokane			19,922	36,848	104,402	104,437	115,514
Lincoln	2,441	13,003	58,154	40,169	43,973	54,948	75,933
Topeka	5,790	15,452	31,007	33,608	43,684	69,159	85,200

Source: U.S. Bureau of the Census, 1870–1930.

connections and obtained them, persuaded the legislature to move the capital, and created various urban amenities. But Phoenix was not dominant within Arizona at this time; its future position was not certain, and during the early twentieth century it vied with other Arizona communities for growth, power, and influence. Since all of these communities were relatively small, fortunes and preeminence could change considerably in a decade.

After the initial years of settlement and harmony, competition with Tucson had grown, especially after Phoenix established direct rail connections and became the territorial capital. The two communities differed in various ways—Tucson was older, larger, more Mexican in population and more pueblo in architecture, and its economy included more commerce and was more linked to mining. From 1890 to 1910 Tucson maintained roughly the same edge in absolute population numbers, but in percentage terms Phoenix got much closer (table 2.2). As competition increased, attitudes had hardened. In 1911, for example, the *Arizona Republican* commented sarcastically that it was "exceedingly hard to harmonize the wonderful greatness of Tucson as heralded by its newspapers, in comparison with the unimportance and insignificance of Phoenix" when a recent report showed that Phoenix banks had double the assets of their southern rivals. But these two communities were not the only urban competitors. While both Phoenix and Tucson grew steadily, the population of several mining communities skyrocketed: in 1910 the neighboring southeastern towns of Bisbee and Douglas combined had more people than Phoenix and roughly the same as Phoenix plus all other Valley communities. Not only did this growth complicate Tucson's ambitions, but it was increasingly overshadowed within the region by El Paso.[3]

Table 2.2 Population in the largest Arizona towns and cities.

Towns and cities	1890	1910	1920
Bisbee-Douglas	1,535	15,456	19,121
Globe, Miami, Superior	803	8,473	16,197
Clifton-Morenci	1,358	9,874	9,163
Prescott, Jerome	2,009	8,185	9,040
Tucson	5,150	13,193	20,292
Phoenix	3,152	11,134	29,053
All Salt River Valley towns	4,537	15,859	40,207

Source: "Decennial Censuses: Arizona, Counties, Cities, Places, 1860–1990," http://www.ci.tucson.az.us/planning/data/demographic/decennials.pdf (accessed 7 January 2008); Charles Sargent, ed., *Metro Arizona* (Scottsdale: Biffington Books, 1988), 44, 50–51.

Phoenix had some obvious strengths in Arizona's interurban competition. Most importantly, the Roosevelt Dam provided a secure source of water, expanded the supply of irrigable land, and created hydroelectric power. Boosters continued to believe in the key importance of agriculture, arguing in 1911 that "in a stretch of a thousand miles the Salt River valley is the only big agricultural oasis, the one real natural base for the big city which is to be built between Los Angeles and El Paso." Statehood expanded the functions and resources of state government, creating jobs, attracting talented people, and making Phoenix the center of political and economic connections. Phoenix could also capitalize on its dominant position within the Valley, for it boasted a substantial range of businesses, professions, and skilled trades. While the other Valley communities featured some basic economic functions and some services related to agriculture, as of the early part of the century they relied on Phoenix for most nonessential needs.[4] Finally, Phoenix had key economic groups and institutions, like the Chamber of Commerce, promoting its future, and it had established a culture of civic cooperation.

The challenges facing Phoenix largely involved its transportation system and the question of how to expand its connections to neighboring communities. Without a bridge over the Salt River or enough adequate roads, residents of other communities, especially on the southern side of the river, had limited ability to shop in the capital city. In a larger sense, the city's future was restricted by its physical location and its resulting dependence on railroads, even though the connections improved during the 1920s. Distance was a serious constraint. A second long-term challenge was economic: the role of agriculture as the primary economic basis of the Valley, and the state's resource-based economy. The eventual exhaustion of copper mines and the uncertainty regarding prices, plus the limits inherent in an agricultural economy, imposed another constraint on any long-term growth ambitions. But in the short term, the area's transportation improved considerably with completion of the Central Avenue Bridge (1911) and the Ash Avenue Bridge in Tempe (1913) and with the paving of roads throughout Maricopa County. On top of the gains from completing the Roosevelt Dam, this propelled Phoenix through the 1920s to a dominant economic position within the state.

The city's growth reflected its natural advantages, but success also depended significantly on the vision and abilities of Phoenix leaders. As G. Wesley Johnson observed, men who arrived in the 1880s—William Murphy, Moses Sherman, William Christy, and Emil Ganz—had vision, knowledge, and connections.[5] They recognized the inherent potential of the area and understood what was necessary to achieve it. Their connections with banks and financiers in other states enabled them to pursue financing for key projects, and their drive helped them sell the Valley to other investors. Railroad competition made it easier to acquire these essential connections, but local leadership provided the necessary capital. They also demonstrated their mettle in vying successfully to win new government institutions. The Valley's attraction for health seekers was significant in this era, as it would be later, for it drew wealthy individuals like Dwight Heard, who, if healthy, would have stayed in Chicago or at least gone to a larger city. In partnership with his father-in-law, Heard purchased seventy-five hundred acres that he used for farming, ranching, and eventually real estate development, and he was a major force behind the Roosevelt Dam. A friend of national figures like President Theodore Roosevelt, he belonged to numerous civic groups, owned the newspaper, and was active in politics.

The city's growth during the early twentieth century enabled Phoenix to retain the sons of many leaders and to attract new men of ability, like grocer-turned-developer George Mickle, department store owners Baron Goldwater and the Korrick brothers, Abe and Charles, newspaperman Charles Stauffer, architect Les Mahoney, and the O'Malley brothers, who had many business interests. A defining characteristic of this group is that it was a commercial elite linked to an agricultural economy, not an industrial elite whose sudden prosperity fostered greater class and wealth divisions. Some held substantial real estate, and a number were well off, but, as Orme Lewis later observed, "there wasn't a rich person in Phoenix in the real sense of the word." Moreover, while they were certainly seeking their own advancement, their economic interest fostered a boosterism that promoted projects benefiting Phoenix and a focus on land development that linked the city with others in the Valley.[6]

THE CHANGING URBAN FORM

In the early twentieth century Phoenix made the transition from town to city as it grew in size, form, and complexity. The increase in size put Phoenix atop the state's urban hierarchy, but a far more significant impact of that shift was its effect on the spatial distribution of people and functions within the city. The economic context for this growth was the expansion of agriculture and the increased use of the railroad, but changes in intraurban transportation— first streetcars and then cars—most directly affected the city's form. Phoenix resembled the burgeoning cities of the Midwest and East in being affected by transportation innovations, but the spatial outcomes differed because the town held only about three thousand people when the transportation-induced process of change began. Instead of a built-out walking city being changed by the introduction of streetcars and the resulting streetcar city being reshaped by automobiles, the process was compressed, and many changes ran simultaneously, rather than sequentially. Still, both its downtown and its residential areas were shaped by these transportation innovations. Downtown was affected by rail, air, and autos, which changed the city's relationship to its surroundings; residential areas responded to the shift from streetcar to auto. During this era of transition, then, Phoenix looked far more like older American cities than it would later on.

THE CHANGING URBAN FORM I:

Downtown

Downtown presented the most visible part of the shift from town to city. This began with the development of city services and the construction of more substantial buildings, and, also, symbolically, by replacing the original Indian street names with numbered street and avenue names. By the early 1890s a clearer separation had appeared between businesses and residences, and that nonresidential part of Phoenix took the form that Richard Francaviglia has termed "Main Street," with businesses primarily along a single street—in this case along Washington Street, with secondary groupings along Center, Adams, and 1st Streets.[7] That spatial arrangement included some elementary

Figure 2.1 Central Phoenix, 1924. As tall buildings rose in the downtown area, streetcars connected different parts of the city, and a new central railroad depot brought in visitors and freight. *Source:* Based on *City Map of Phoenix, Lightning-Delivery-Company, 1926.* Arizona Collection, Arizona State University Libraries.

clustering by types of businesses, but in 1892 the city was still too small, with too few businesses, to need or support such specialized land use. A quadrupling in the number of businesses during the next two decades stimulated clusters of similar businesses and a pattern of specialized land use referred to as a "central business district" (CBD), with an elaboration of this development occurring in the 1920s (figure 2.1).[8]

During the first stage, financial, insurance, real estate, and nonfood retail businesses concentrated in the CBD; less attractive businesses, like blacksmiths and stables, left it entirely; and food and building-related firms spread throughout the city. By 1910 financial and insurance companies, which had increased steadily in numbers, had moved and formed a cluster around Central Avenue and Adams Street. Clothing stores concentrated along Washington, Central, and 1st Street, with the most visible cluster being the three department stores—Diamond's Boston Store and Korrick's were across the street from each other, with Goldwater's a block away. The physical positions of these stores symbolized their economic centrality within Phoenix and, over time, within the Valley and Central Arizona. Patrick Downey described his family's biweekly shopping trips from a small mining town east of the valley to Phoenix, "mostly for women's clothes."[9]

During the 1920s the downtown achieved a mature form that it held until the 1950s.[10] Finance, insurance, and real estate businesses grew more numerous and more highly clustered. The increased numbers of professionals also concentrated in downtown areas and buildings, especially the two largest groups. The abundance of attorneys (the Phoenix per capita figure was high by national standards) tended toward the southern downtown buildings, partly for easy access to the courts. In the 1920s, half of the doctors had offices at city center, but that changed by 1940: only a tenth had downtown offices, while 60 percent had offices in the Professional Building (1931), a few blocks north on Monroe.[11] Further marking the area's increased economic importance, by 1925 a total of eleven mining companies (most with operations in central Arizona) had downtown offices, as did the cattle, cotton, and wool growers' associations and seventeen labor unions. A decade later, another four growers' associations were represented there, but the collapse of the copper industry reduced the downtown presence of mining companies.

Changes in transportation greatly affected the number and location of other types of businesses. The 1920s saw a major improvement in the city's external lifeline, its rail connections. Phoenix Union Station opened in 1923, a new, consolidated depot, and three years later the rerouted Southern Pacific main line arrived in town, considerably enhancing the city's economic prospects and firmly establishing its rail parity with Tucson and El Paso.[12] Improved rail connections also stimulated the development of warehouses and wholesale shipping, as the number of wholesale distributors jumped from seven in 1919 to fifty-two in 1930.[13] These facilities, plus the expanding sectors of agricultural processing and the manufacturing of building supplies, concentrated to the south of the CBD, as they spread east and west near the railroad.[14]

Aviation opened a new area of interurban competition, one in which Phoenix initially struggled. A municipal airport opened in 1925, but it was too far from town and gradually faded before nearer, better funded, private fields. The first of these opened in 1927 on South Central Avenue, offering triweekly flights to Los Angles and Tucson, but Sky Harbor Airport, an even larger and better-equipped airport several miles east of downtown, opened in 1928. It quickly established successful service and attracted airlines from the other fields, forcing them to close. The early Depression years were difficult for Phoenix aviation, for only American Airways offered regular flights, and a handful of other aviation businesses survived. Conditions improved after 1935, however, when the city purchased Sky Harbor as a municipal airport. The improving economy supported expanded flight activity, and TWA established regular service to Phoenix.[15]

Improved rail and air transportation brought more visitors, which affected the number and quality of hotels. In the years after 1900, five major hotels—those having over fifty rooms, being more comfortably appointed, and located in the city center—served visiting businesspeople, vacationers, and seasonal visitors, while a number of lesser "hotels" and boardinghouses (increasing from five in 1909 to thirty by 1925) were scattered across the CBD but also nearer the warehouse district, and served both temporary and long-term residents. The San Carlos (1927) and the Westward Ho (1928) hotels were built to cater to wealthier vacationers.[16]

Automobiles, a third transportation development, held manifold implications for the economy of Phoenix as well as the structure of downtown. Although still largely a curiosity in 1910, this new vehicle worsened a long-standing problem of dusty streets, which the city workers had traditionally managed by sprinkling them with water. Paving offered a better solution, and in 1912–13 the city paved the streets and alleys of the original town site, as well as building sidewalks.[17] Cars gained rapidly in popularity after 1915, in both Phoenix and the nation, and in the 1920s they became a phenomenon, symbolized by the separate section of the Sunday newspaper that published articles on cars and car-related topics. Auto registrations in Maricopa County hit 14,707 in 1922, jumped to 25,397 in 1925, rose to 41,164 in 1930, and swelled to 45,866 in 1940, of which probably two-thirds were from Phoenix.[18]

Cars directly impacted the economy and urban structure. The economic effect is most obvious in the number of auto dealers, which rose from only three in 1909 to thirty-seven in 1925, and then declining in the 1930s. Cars involved more businesses than just dealers, of course. Auto-related services, which took up three pages in the 1909 city directory, filled five pages in the 1925 city directory, on top of the lengthy dealer listings. By 1929 the sales from the 140 garage, repair, and gas stations totaled 50 percent more than all clothing sales. The distribution of auto-related businesses within the city reinforced the larger structural pattern that had developed in Phoenix: merchants (dealers of cars and basic parts) clustered in downtown, in a new section along West Adams Street (from 2nd to 6th avenues) and North Central Avenue, while the less attractive services of auto painting, repair, and towing were scattered and often outside the CBD.[19] Cars also had other economic effects. They produced public revenue through the gasoline tax, the vehicle tax, and the drivers' license fee, which provided funds for substantial amounts of road construction throughout the county, further encouraging travel.[20]

The availability of cars and the improvement of roads markedly affected Phoenix retailers, and by 1930 they dominated the region—attracting customers not only from nearby towns like Tempe and Mesa, but also from more distant farming towns like Florence and mining towns like Globe. As evidence of this, retail sales exceeded those of regional rival El Paso and were the highest per capita of any U.S. city of comparable size.[21] This expansion was fueled by and further boosted an increased number of independent merchants, but more significantly, by an influx of national chains. J. C. Penney (1920), Sears and Roebuck (1928), and Montgomery Ward (1929) added competition to the local department stores and vitality to the downtown market, as did the arrival of three national variety stores: F. W. Woolworth (1914), S. H. Kress (1917), and J. J. Newberry (1927).[22]

The construction of numerous buildings during the 1920s and early 1930s boosted the economy, but this activity was at least as important for transforming the look and feel of downtown. While not big-city skyscrapers, the seven-story Dwight B. Heard Building (1920) and the ten-story Luhrs Building (1924) did initiate the construction of modern multistory office buildings that brought new urban realities to the area and symbolized the achievement of city status. The fifteen-story Luhrs Tower (1930) and the sixteen-story Westward Ho Hotel heightened the nascent skyline. These buildings also enabled Phoenix architects to present different styles. Public architecture up to the 1910s (the state capitol and Phoenix schools) followed fairly a predictable, neoclassical revival style, but after 1920 both private and public buildings showcased new forms. Spanish Colonial Revival was quite popular (for example, the Westward Ho Hotel, the City-County Building in 1928, and the Orpheum Theater in 1929), as was the Moderne style (evident in the Luhrs Tower, the Professional Building and the Fox Theater in 1931, and the Kress Building in 1933). Other major structures built in Mission Revival, Pueblo Revival, and Italian Renaissance Revival added to the interesting visual display and to the sense that Phoenix was connected to ideas and developments elsewhere.[23]

The Phoenix downtown that developed by the 1920s represented a different type of place and a configuration with different economic and social features than had existed previously. While it emerged later than downtowns in older, larger, and (generally) more eastern cities, it represented basically the same pattern as in those other American cities. Phoenicians shared the common American view that, in the words of historian Robert Fogelson, "every American city, large and small, had to have a downtown" and that "a prosperous downtown was as vital to the well-being of a city as a strong heart was to the well-being of a person."[24] While the particular historical conditions that produced this downtown structure would not persist past the 1960s, its nature shaped the expectations and goals of Phoenicians for decades after its demise.

During this era the downtown area functioned as a vibrant and accessible public place—a space occupied by many people of various social and economic types who engaged in different commercial and noncommercial activities. The substantial structures constructed in Phoenix during the 1920s were not skyscrapers, but they created a cityscape that Phoenicians perceived as new, different, and a virtual connection to a larger, grander public world (figure 2.2). Public buildings, particularly those built in the familiar neoclassical

Figure 2.2 Downtown Phoenix in 1929, taken from the courthouse. Downtown Phoenix boasted increasing numbers of substantial buildings (to the north) and bustling streets. *Source:* McCulloch Brothers Photographs, Herb and Dorothy McLaughlin Collection, Arizona State University Libraries.

revival style, were intended not simply to fill functional needs but to foster the sense of a public presence. The streets and sidewalks were teeming with people walking, looking, meeting, and talking. These streets were the common place for public events, like celebrations and parades on public holidays, as well as amusements like the races down Central Avenue in the Bell Hop and Chambermaid Games.

Such democratic mixing comprised a crucial part of the perception of downtown. Another aspect was access to the new consumer commercial culture, which people could attain by automobile, streetcar, or walking. The proliferation of stores and the dramatic increase in consumer goods made the downtown a cornucopia. Department, clothing, and shoe stores offered consumers a wide range of styles and prices; furniture and appliance stores presented an expanding array of more expensive options; while even greater choices spread from jewelry stores to less expensive items in variety stores. Of course, incomes limited people's abilities to purchase goods, but that was partly mitigated by the growing availability of credit. Besides purchasing goods, downtown visitors could eat at one of many restaurants, cafés, or lunch counters; consumers could avail themselves of repair services or personal services like a haircut or shoe shine; or they could attend a movie theater, all of which were available downtown. This consumer society was by no means egalitarian: income restricted access to consumer goods, and race limited access to some public accommodations (as discussed below).[25] Still, the combination of public places with an expanding consumer economy seeking customers meant that downtown was the place for people to be, where they went expecting to see others and to be seen.

THE CHANGING URBAN FORM II:

From Streetcar Suburbs to Automobile Suburbs

Besides the development of downtown, the early twentieth century shift from town to city involved significant changes in residential forms and structures, and these were greatly affected by shifts in transportation systems.[26] Because Phoenix was relatively small and its streetcar lines did not comprise a fully integrated system, streetcars did not have the kind of determinative effect as elsewhere. Nevertheless, they did influence the shape of the city in important ways. The earliest residential subdivisions were within walking distance, built adjacent to the original town site between 1880 and 1886. Creation of the streetcar system in 1887 "had a direct and profound impact on the growth and development of Phoenix neighborhoods" since "its reason for being [was] the development of Phoenix suburbs." Lines were built either to serve the developments of streetcar owner Moses Sherman or because of subsidies from property owners along the route. Of course, the primary influence on residence was still distance, and since the city population before 1910 was still small, most new subdivisions built in this period were within the 1.5 miles and part of a traditional "walking city." But streetcars could direct development within that area, and they did serve some subdivisions built beyond it. Finally, all streetcar lines and nearly all of the development went north from the railroad tracks.

Before 1900 one line ran northwest along Grand Avenue, through two new subdivisions, while adjacent areas not directly touched by the line did not develop for another two decades. Two other early lines ran north along 3rd and 10th streets, servicing the subdivisions started from 1887 to 1898, including two at 2.5 miles from city center, which was a mile beyond the next most northerly subdivision. That gap was filled after 1910 by development of the elite Las Palmas (1910) and Central (1910) districts on the east side of Central Avenue, served by the 3rd Street line. The extension of this line enabled the opening of more distant subdivisions, such as Longview Place (1912), which was 3.5 miles from city center. Construction of the Kenilworth line (1911), which ran north, mostly on 3rd Avenue, connected with similarly posh subdivisions west of Central—Kenilworth (1911) and Los Olivos (1911), developed by Dwight Heard. Thus, streetcars did not eliminate the pedestrian basis for development in Phoenix, but they reshaped the order in which subdivisions developed and, like elsewhere, supported the interests of the "growth machine."[27]

Streetcars influenced various aspects of subdivisions built from the 1890s to the 1920s: subdivisions were contiguous to the city (soon, if not immediately), streets followed a grid system, and lots were relatively narrow and small (e.g., 50 by 140 feet). But changes in residential architecture also shaped these neighborhoods. The Victorian homes that wealthier Phoenicians had begun building in the late nineteenth century significantly enhanced the aesthetic and architectural character of the city, but they were too large and expensive to satisfy the housing needs of many people, and the styles were not really appropriate for the area—as one observer claimed, they were "almost uninhabitable in the summer." Dr. John W. Foss, president of the Board of Trade, explained to the Phoenix Women's Club that "what we need are houses such as are to be found in semitropical climates and which are specially designed for coolness." Several versions of the bungalow style—the classical and the California Craftsman—met these needs, and the California style became very popular in the early twentieth century, especially after 1910. Typically four to six rooms, with a deep shaded porch supported by large pillars, these simple homes were small and affordable, and building plans were readily available from published "pattern books." The landscaping associated with this style of home included lawns and trees next to the street, often ash and California fan palm trees. This greenery added to its attraction in Phoenix, where boosters gushed, "Here is the ideal place for a real home. Flowers, gardens, lawns, palms, roses, and quiet restful places are in all parts of the city."[28]

But during the 1920s an automobile-driven dynamic replaced streetcars and streetcar suburbs in popularity. Cars were increasingly affordable, offering independence and flexibility, and their popularity after 1920 changed the calculus of urban residence throughout the nation. In Phoenix, however, the shift from streetcar to auto suburbs occurred somewhat differently and for slightly different reasons than in some other places. During this transition era of 1915 to 1925, the city was still small, and many residents in the north central corridor lived close to one of the three north-south streetcar lines (they were only 1 mile apart). Moreover, since much of the land between 1.5 and 4 miles from city center was still undeveloped, additional subdivisions could have been efficiently serviced by new or extended streetcar lines. This did not occur, in part, because cars became so popular, even among residents of northern suburbs with easy access to streetcars. That system, already underfunded and lacking any east-west connections between the three lines, was crippled by the sudden competition from cars, as ridership fell by half from 1920 to 1924.[29]

To revive the system, the city purchased it in 1926, relaid the tracks, and bought new cars. Usage increased until 1930, when the Depression, a hike in fares, and reduced service decreased patronage by half. The restoration of the nickel fare, economic recovery, and gradually expanding service brought the ridership to new highs by 1939.[30] But although streetcars remained a useful mass transit system in the urban core until the 1940s, they had faded by the 1920s as a practical alternative for developing new neighborhoods.

Streets constituted a defining element of auto suburbs. Unlike the regular grid pattern of walking and streetcar suburbs, the streets in auto suburbs within the 1-mile grid often curved and sometimes ended in cul-de-sacs, while blocks varied in length. Uniform setback distances for houses created a different feel to the neighborhoods, and the absence of sidewalks and tree lawns at the curb indicated that these areas were intended for cars, not pedestrians. Street paving, which had begun in the precar era with the downtown area, partly because of dust, expanded because with the popularity of cars: 7 miles were paved by 1915, then 25 by 1920, and 77 by 1930. But while paved mileage tripled in the 1920s, by 1930 it still represented less than half of the 161 miles of city streets. Like the paving of county roads, street paving was incomplete and not always expected. Unpaved streets were common and intentional in new subdivisions. Even developers of upper middle class subdivisions, in describing their projects, would mention routinely that their streets had been graveled, not paved.[31]

Clearly, a major motive for having gravel streets was that paving increased the cost of homes. But if pavement seemed inessential for neighborhood streets, it was considered a vital part of connecting with the "distant" city; subdivisions often specifically advertised their connections to paved streets. Such linkages were especially important because cars made it easier to build "leapfrog," or noncontiguous, developments. Streetcars had previously facilitated a bit of this type of growth, but by 1937 numerous unconnected subdivisions had sprouted in the swath of land running from the southeast to the northwest between the Grand and Arizona canals. In particular, developers of more expensive subdivisions found this access useful, enabling them to build near attractive environmental features, such as orchards or Camelback Mountain, or to place them near luxury resorts or golf courses. A final difference engendered by auto suburbs was an increase in lot size, partly because density was unimportant for transportation in this type of residential arrangement, and because land further from the city center was cheaper. Although lot sizes varied by subdivision, smaller lots in auto suburbs were often 50 by 175 feet, 25 percent larger than streetcar-area lots, while lots in wealthier subdivisions ranged from two to four times larger, increasing in size the further they were from the city center.

Simultaneous with the shift to auto suburbs came new housing styles. Builders began producing homes in various period revival styles—especially Spanish and Mediterranean, but also different types of English, French, and American Colonial—and by the 1930s bungalow homes were seldom built. The first period homes—Spanish and Tudor Revival—were built on lots in bungalow suburbs using the grid street system, but by the 1930s these and other period houses were built in auto suburbs. Houses in those suburbs also had garages or sometimes carports, a feature often added to bungalows. After 1935 some houses advertised cooling systems, but that was not a feature of the home design until still later (as discussed below). The more common amenity, even in wealthier homes, was the sleeping porch.[32]

The rapid suburban expansion of Phoenix during the 1920s meant a major construction boom involving roughly seventy-five hundred single-family houses, and boosters, realtors, and developers greatly increased their efforts to persuade people about the attractiveness of Phoenix and the blessings of home ownership.[33] Community boosters continued a tradition of promoting Phoenix as "a sophisticated city with attractive, modern housing," and they described the prospects of home ownership there in glowing terms: "Phoenix is a city to delight the home-seeker. Here is the ideal place for a real home."[34] Builders used familiar reasons to encourage purchasing a home—it promoted good citizenship, developed pride in one's possessions, and was a sound investment.[35] Despite their continued effort and the sense of prosperity and community building, these campaigns were generally ineffective. Less than a third of all dwellings in Phoenix were owner occupied, a modest to low level of home ownership, especially for a city of its size, age, and location. Whether this pattern reflects population mobility, or disbelief that homes were a good investment, or inability to afford them, the reality of living in Phoenix clearly fell short of the image and goal of blissful home ownership.[36] Still, the shift in the city's transportation system produced important changes in its residential forms and structures.

REMAKING OR SAVING THE DESERT

Like many cities, Phoenix benefited from the efforts of women's groups to beautify the city and improve its appearance.[37] In 1902 the Phoenix Women's Club began its improvement efforts with the railroad station, several years later it agitated for cleaning up vacant lots and the Five Points neighborhood, and from 1909 to 1913 it marshaled efforts to rid the city of billboards. But despite similarities with other cities in particular campaigns and in efforts to improve the built urban environment, the Phoenix perspective differed in key respects. Here, the notion of people remaking or controlling the natural environment was not simply a means of urban improvement or related to a particular project; it represented a necessary and fundamental part of the city's identity. More than simply encouraging people to plant roses, the Women's Club promoted these activities as part of a larger 1920s campaign whose slogan was "Do Away with the Desert."[38]

While this slogan sounds oddly naive to contemporary ears, Phoenicians in the 1920s considered it neither bombast nor foolishness, but a realistic goal that had been successfully pursued for the previous half century. A 1921 photo spread in the *New York World* reported this perspective, with its caption "Picturing a Man-Made State"; a 1924 pamphlet proclaimed (albeit prematurely) that "the dry inhospitable desert has been conquered." The latter publication noted that while strangers often associated Phoenix with "great silent desert lands" and "limitless wastes," in reality it was "a beautiful, well-cared for garden. True, she can give you the weird, wild desert, the rugged mountain peaks and the cactus strewed canyon if you wish, but she uses them only as a background, in striking contrast to the abundant foliage and the brilliant coloring with which she surrounds herself."[39]

This perception stemmed partly from the deliberate and successful efforts at landscaping streets and homes. Claims that Phoenix was "the Rose City" and that one saw "everywhere flowers, everywhere sunshine" had some basis in fact. Moreover, because of sustained efforts at tree planting, which began with the town's founding, by the 1920s the city had an estimated one hundred thousand trees within its borders. But perhaps even more important in shaping a perception of victory over the desert were the ecological and social systems created by canals (figures 2.3 and 2.4).[40] While the main canals necessarily followed the topography, the laterals and ditches were organized in a grid system, conveying a sense of order and mastery over this natural environment. Trees along the canals—cottonwoods, ash, eucalyptus, and mesquite—made

Figure 2.3 A shady residential street, 1917 (Culver and 12th Street). Phoenicians landscaped for shade, transforming their environment. *Source:* Courtesy Ron Heberlee.

Figure 2.4 Lush canal vegetation, 1924. Canals supported verdant growth and provided recreation. *Source:* McCulloch Brothers Photographs, Herb and Dorothy McLaughlin Collection, Arizona State University Libraries.

a vivid impression on observers, for in many areas they were "so thick that they provided a continuous canopy." Equally impressive were the rows of trees along streets with laterals beside them. For example, Alfred Simon reports that "North Central Avenue was lined with ash trees, on both sides, and the branches would meet above, and it was almost like driving through a tunnel."[41]

The canals effectively mimicked and multiplied the natural desert riparian environments, with the types of vegetation and animal life originally seen on the Salt River before Anglo settlement; the canals even produced some marsh areas with cattails and a profusion of birds. In addition, this landscaping affected the local climate. While assessing any climate shift is notoriously a complicated task, this creation of substantial shade and standing water correlate with climate data for this era that show slightly lower temperatures and humidity levels 10 to 20 percent higher than those prior to the building of the waterways.[42]

Canals also created a social environment. During the hot summer months, the shady canal areas attracted numerous visitors for activities as simple as sitting and picnicking, as mundane as laundering, and as solemn as baptism. Children and adults commonly canoed and fished, but canals were most popular, of course, for swimming. Children hung ropes from trees along the banks and even constructed makeshift diving boards. And as they got older and braver, they often water-skied, holding a rope attached to the bumper of a car driving down the road. Canals could be dangerous, of course, even fatal; they had variable currents and an uncertain bottom, and there was no formal supervision. Pools constituted one possible alternative, but the private pools charged admission and discriminated against minorities.[43] For the period before 1940, then, canals provided daily socialization opportunities.

Most Phoenicians were eager to "conquer" the desert, but many also wanted to explore and enjoy it. This desire stemmed from what originally attracted many people to the Valley: a healthy climate and opportunities for outdoor activities and living. Many connected health with the desert climate; they found it invigorating to be "living with air, day and night, dry, pure, and stimulating like champagne." And promoters advertised numerous outdoor activities. Foremost among them was golf, in part because it so clearly represented a manufactured environment and a conquering of the desert. Other recommended activities included tennis, riflery, archery, riding, and hiking. Less active persons might still wish to enjoy the desert occasionally, through picnics and excursions. To support these activities city leaders exercised considerable foresight and in 1925 managed to purchase from the federal government, as a city park, a mountain area of 16,500 acres some seven miles south of town.[44]

A few Phoenicians, visible as noted individuals or members of an organization, valued the desert as a unique environment. Frank Lloyd Wright, America's most brilliant architect, first came to Arizona in 1928 to help a former student, Albert McArthur, build the Arizona Biltmore Hotel. Within a few months Dr. Alexander J. Chandler had commissioned him to design San Marcos in the Desert, a luxury resort for Chandler's town. The work camp of Ocatilla, which Wright designed in preparation for building the resort, reflected Wright's growing love for the materials and openness of the desert. The camp burned down that summer, and the Great Crash of 1929 killed the San Marcos project, but Wright remained fascinated with the desert's light, topography, and vegetation, describing the saguaro cactus as a "perfect example of reinforced construction." He returned to the Valley in the winter of 1934, camping with some of his architecture students in what would much later become north Scottsdale. In 1937 he bought substantial acreage there and with associates and students began building Taliesin West, which would become his winter school and retreat. Wright's "organic architecture," incorporating natural materials and using light and air, represented a deep appreciation of the desert's natural beauty.[45]

Another form of this appreciation showed in the activities of Gustaf Starck, an engineer for the Salt River Water Users' Association, whose love and concern for desert horticulture led him to organize the Arizona Cactus and Native Flora Society in 1934. The society aimed to create a botanical garden that would both preserve and explain some of the desert vegetation. Starck's efforts gained some public support, but his greatest success was in winning the commitment of Gertrude Divine Webster. A wealthy migrant from Vermont, Webster used her connections to raise funds and in 1938 to obtain the state's permission to use land in the former Papago Saguaro National Monument. The following year the society dedicated the Desert Botanical Garden and began its program of restoring the desert. During this period the voices of Webster and the 121 members of her association amounted to only a whisper, compared to the clamor for doing away with the desert. Yet many who championed roses also saw beauty in desert flowers, and some, over time, came to see beauty in the desert itself. The changing balance and tension between these perspectives would later become a significant force in the city's development.[46]

In the early twentieth century Phoenicians labored to build their city in a form that would satisfy their needs and bring appropriate recognition from others. The city's rise in the urban hierarchy of the state and the Southwest certified its growing significance, while the evolution within the city of a downtown and attractive residential neighborhoods met what they considered to be the national standards for urban development. Phoenicians were very determined to shape both their built and their natural environment to reflect their values and to demonstrate their sense of effectiveness. Their efforts to construct a social, cultural, and political environment that would mirror their notions of a modern American city were part of their larger vision for Phoenix's place in the nation.

3
Shaping the Modern American City:
Social Construction

The creation of social or cultural organizations, like the construction of build-ings, often reflects the choices and efforts of one or several individuals. George Luhrs determined to build impressive buildings downtown; Blanche Korrick hosted musical events in support of the Musicians Club; and Maie Heard cre-ated the Heard Museum. But just as constructing buildings fit within a larger purpose, so too did developing social organizations. Phoenicians were not unique in seeking to shape their city's future, but they were firmly intentional in promoting the kind of development that occurred. Their vision of a pros-perous and modern city required the establishment of moral standards and effective governance; it meant creating and fostering "high culture," while also encouraging wholesome entertainment and recreation. And their promotion of tourism represented the most explicit effort to show these features and link them with a proper appreciation of place.

MAKING A MORAL CITY

As Phoenix struggled at the turn of the century to make the transition from town to city, it confronted problems of image and reality. While Phoenix could not realistically be considered part of the Wild West, boosters understood the need to dispel that image.

There was a time when Arizona was known only for its . . . cowboys, Indians, cactus, and lawlessness, [but] today it is best known for its health-giving climate, for its wondrous scenery, for its mines of wealth, and for its great agricultural valley of the Salt River. It is no longer the frontier—the sweeping wave of civilization has covered it. The cactus has been thrust back, and the plain has been made a garden. . . . Life and property are as safe as in any other part of the Union.[1]

Similarly, after lauding the physical, cultural, and educational facilities of Phoenix, an ad in a local paper asked whether the reader knew "that we do not carry pistols?" And Valley boosters often invoked an earlier report by *New York Tribune* editor Whitelaw Reid stating that the Valley was quite civilized and not violent.[2] Such efforts were not entirely successful, since this lawless image had been projected countless times in forms like dime novels or traveling Wild West shows, and since publicity for tourism even made some use of the image.

The more serious and immediate issues for Phoenicians were the same ones confronting many cities across the nation. A flourishing combination of saloons, gambling, and prostitution challenged the law and affronted the standards of community leaders. Some reformers opposed these vices on moral and religious grounds, condemning the behavior of participants. Others placed more emphasis on the societal consequences, regarding such conduct as socially regressive, as wasteful, perhaps, and certainly as retarding the progress of civilization. Still others feared this might create a bad image of the city, dissuading people from moving there and possibly obstructing statehood.[3] Thus, Phoenicians viewed these issues partly in terms of current local conditions: the expansion of vice activities in Phoenix and concerns about external perceptions of their town. National developments, like the appearance of large brewing corporations and their links with local saloons, contributed to the fears. But Phoenicians also shared in the rising national tide of moral qualms about the nature of American society. This encompassed many issues involving the family, children, and minority groups, it highlighted sexual misconduct, and it concentrated on the evils of liquor and the saloon. The moral reform activities of Phoenicians in the Progressive Era were both consciously and unconsciously influenced by those larger national patterns, as their largely successful efforts paralleled what was occurring in many different places across the nation.[4]

The organization of antiliquor and antivice forces in Phoenix began with the Woman's Christian Temperance Union (WCTU) in 1884 and was extended by the Good Templars and Salvation Army during the next decade. Other groups bolstered this movement. The Fortnightly Club organized in 1900, becoming the Phoenix Women's Club in 1901, and over the next several decades was active in numerous reform campaigns, including those combating vice. The Anti-Saloon League, which first organized in Arizona in Scottsdale but did not become active until 1909, lobbied local and territorial governments and coordinated the activities of the various antisaloon forces, particularly churches. These antivice campaigners worked at the territorial and especially the local level, and they adopted multiple approaches, attempting to secure legislation, have laws enforced, and persuade voters to act.[5]

Antivice efforts effectively began in 1900, when the Phoenix Common Council raised the annual saloon license fee from $100 to $200. Pursuing a second track, the following year it banned women from operating, working in, or patronizing saloons, and in subsequent years city ordinances attempted to exclude minors by setting a curfew and by criminalizing the sale of liquor to a minor. In 1906 the council boosted the license fee to a hefty $1,000, and a few years later required that license renewal petitions be supported by a majority of nearby property owners. Earlier territorial legislation had done little, partly because it was unenforced. A weak Sunday closing ordinance was replaced by a clear statute in 1907, which was enforced. Even more significant, in 1909 both the territorial legislature and the city council passed strict measures banning gambling and excluding women from saloons. This action effectively ended

Figure 3.1 The Palace Saloon—one of many on Washington Street. *Source:* Herb and Dorothy McLaughlin Collection, Arizona State University Libraries.

gambling in Phoenix, but while it removed prostitution from saloons, it did not entirely eliminate that practice from the city. A final measure redefining saloons was the 1909 ordinance that prohibited separate rooms in saloons, as well as tables and chairs, and required that any passerby have an uninhibited view inside a saloon (figure 3.1).[6]

The effectiveness of these measures is suggested by the fact that saloons, which had been rapidly rising in numbers, declined from thirty-two in 1906 to twenty-four in 1909 and to eighteen in 1910. But reformers wanted to eliminate, not merely reduce, the saloon. They had attempted this from 1902 to 1908 by seeking voter support in county option elections, but with insufficient success. In 1910–11 dry forces ingeniously invoked a law banning liquor sales within six miles of a labor camp, citing several workforces on nearby city construction projects. This device prevented some license renewals until saloon owners persuaded the workers to move their camps. The drys then returned to the voters, now using a 1909 local option law. Elections in 1911 and 1913 managed to dry up the county, but Phoenicians tenaciously voted wet, even after women received the vote in 1912. Having failed in county and local jurisdiction, the antiliquor forces changed jurisdictions in 1914 and through the initiative placed a state prohibition measure on the ballot. The success of the measure was in some doubt, but a three-fourths majority in Maricopa County secured its passage. Two years later a clearer law passed that definitively eliminated saloons from the city. As a fitting symbol of civic virtue triumphant, on December 29, 1916, the sheriff disposed of impounded liquor by sprinkling it on the city's unpaved streets.[7]

At first glance, men seem to have dominated the antivice campaigns in Phoenix, but that perception comes from examining only the actions of public officeholders, candidates for public office, lawyers, and church leaders, all of whom were men. A look at all active participants shows that women played crucial roles within both their own organizations and the larger groups. For example, the Woman's Enforcement League, organized to monitor prohibition enforcement, included thirty-five hundred members in Maricopa County. But women's activities and influence went far beyond antivice campaigns. Rather than having a narrow set of moralistic concerns, Phoenix women worked on a wide range of social causes that seemed appropriate areas for a woman's perspective. The WCTU had the dominant role in managing the Florence Crittenden Home for young women, and it led in organizing the Associated Charities in Phoenix in 1907, which assisted indigent health seekers, developed a training program for nurses, and opened day nurseries. The Phoenix Women's Club displayed even greater efforts. This organization of middle-class, educated women began as a study group but quickly expanded into municipal housekeeping activities, working on schools and for a public library, and lobbying for city beautification projects. They not only extended their activism to close the saloons and end prostitution, they also pushed for a juvenile court and a probation system, as well as for prison reform, and they maintained a program for studying contemporary social issues. But through these years they continued organizing cultural and intellectual activities for themselves and the community, demonstrating their larger motivation to build a more cultured and moral society.[8]

MAKING A CULTURED CITY

Community leaders believed that if Phoenix was to become and be accepted as a modern American city, they had to create institutions and to foster practices and values that people across the nation would respect. Meeting moral standards was essential, but they also needed to have a culture that would demonstrate their worthiness. During the early twentieth century a vibrant popular culture offered residents a range of acceptable activities and numerous facilities, but while popular culture could address the desires of many residents, it did not meet all tastes or satisfy concerns about the city's image. For this, the activities, institutions, and refinement of high culture were more important. As of 1900 these had advanced relatively little, and changing that would take considerable work. The growing cultural divide and the association between high culture and wealth or class appeared in various ways. For example, after the Phoenix Philharmonic Course, an organized set of musical performances, brought in a German contralto to perform, the *Arizona Republican* headline read: "Big Night Event for Society Folk."[9]

In the early twentieth century Phoenicians could connect with culture by attending events as audience members or by performing as artists themselves, although these options changed considerably over time. The Phoenix Opera House and then the Dorris Opera House (later the Elks Opera House) offered a facility primarily for variety shows and popular theater; upon occasion they brought in other performances, but these were mostly partial or popularized versions of high culture music or theater. By the 1920s the Musicians Club began booking various performers, including some major orchestras, and they began using larger facilities, including the Elks Theater and the Shriner Auditorium. The growing availability of cultural performances was threatened in the mid-1930s when the organizers encountered financial difficulties.

Jessie E. Linde, a classically trained vocalist, then took over the Musical Events Series, assuming the debt and booking concerts and other artistic performances. To reduce expenses she scheduled performances at the Phoenix Union High School Auditorium and used the school's field house for larger events. Despite such activities, Newton Rosenzweig accurately reflected the unhappy sense of most Phoenicians in claiming that Phoenix during this era was "very much off the beaten path—very little came here in the way of entertainment, things that had to do with what was going on in the outside world."[10]

Partly because visiting performances occurred relatively infrequently, but also because Phoenicians sought venues for their own expression, local artists provided the primary basis for establishing cultural opportunities and appreciation. Of the various cultural forms, music attracted the most activity. The city boasted ten music teachers by 1910 and sixty-eight by 1940. The Arizona School of Music provided music lessons and recitals on Saturday afternoons. During this period various musical organizations sprang up, but those without institutional support generally did not last. By the 1930s a volunteer Phoenix Symphony Orchestra was giving two concerts a year, and a community vocal group had been organized, but the high schools and junior college provided most of the Valley's musical groups. The main exception to this, the Musicians Club, continued to promote musical performance in the Valley, by themselves and by others. Organized in 1906, initially for young women, the club was transformed into an influential organization largely because of the dedication of Blanche Korrick, wife of department store owner Charles Korrick. A singer trained in Chicago and New York, she had performed on the Chautauqua circuit before her marriage. Arriving in Phoenix in 1920, she perceived an appalling lack of culture: "Nothing but cards and drinking. No music, no culture of any kind." Although she continued to train musically, her main focus was developing the Musicians Club. Over the years she held many of its recitals in her home, and for several years she hosted radio broadcasts of the performances. Her son later observed, "During the seasons from October to May, they would put on something two or three times a month."[11]

In 1921 another local group of performers, interested in theater and reflective of a national little theater movement, began offering theatrical productions, including some classical fare. Unlike earlier amateur productions, which involved only one-time performances, this group created a regular season of offerings, although they had no regular venue. In 1924, after Maie Bartlett Heard had hosted several musical reviews on the lawn of her estate, she let the group renovate an old stable on her property to use for rehearsals and performances. After creating a Board of Directors, they formally established the Phoenix Little Theater in 1928 with a membership of 424, including 100 active participants. They scheduled six to eight productions a year and began offering theater classes for children and adults. By the later 1930s they were printing their programs, and in 1938 they remodeled the theater with new seats and a heating system.[12]

Fine art in the Valley had a different history, for evaluating quality was more difficult and institutional support went to related fields. Beginning in the 1890s Dwight and Maie Heard collected Indian art and artifacts, which were publicly displayed in the Heard Museum after Dwight's death in 1929, but during this era such materials were considered culture in an anthropological sense, rather than art. Some type of art studio existed in the early 1900s, and the Miller-Sterling Gallery later exhibited works, mainly by Taos artists, but in 1917 it showed works by the local Sketch Club. From 1913 to 1929 the Phoenix Women's Club promoted the Arizona Art Exhibit at the state fair and bought the winning artworks after 1914. It donated these to the city, hoping they would be displayed in the Arizona Museum, which opened in 1927, but the small museum preferred to display archeological, Indian, and Territorial artifacts. These same interests were evident in the city's opening of the Pueblo Grande Museum in 1933. By the 1930s, however, the city included two groups of persons who considered themselves practicing artists. The first significant public support for art appeared in the 1930s, when the federal Works Progress Administration (WPA) funded the state's first art center in Phoenix. Directed from 1936 to 1938 by Philip Curtis (later an artist of considerable note who lived in Scottsdale), the Federal Arts Center hosted traveling exhibitions and organized art classes, a task that the Phoenix Fine Arts Association later assumed.[13]

Support for culture and learning took various forms, with groups like the Phoenix Fine Arts Association or the transitory Phoenix Music School. Several women's organizations proffered significant aid. The Harmony Club organized in 1898 to study and promote music and history. The Phoenix Women's Club started, according to its first President W. F. Nichols in 1904, "not only for study and self-improvement" but also to provide opportunities for women who "crave and need the mental stimulus . . . of other women who are thoughtful and earnest." Besides its reform activities, the club developed a broad cultural agenda to benefit members and nonmembers. Periodically it organized specific classes—in drama, for example, as well as in art and literature. The club also offered impressive self-education courses for members in art, music, literature, and history. At a more basic level, a desire of city women to support learning and knowledge led to joint private-public efforts to develop a public library. Another women's group, the Friday Club (1898), organized to push for a free public library, and the following year it transferred the tasks of gathering books and operating the library, now moved to City Hall, to the new Phoenix Library Association. After the association donated its fifteen hundred books to the city, the city council in 1902 passed a tax to support the library's operations. This propitious act enabled the city to be one of more than fifteen hundred cities to receive a library construction grant from Andrew Carnegie. With that $25,000 the library was completed in 1908, and branch libraries were erected in 1917 and 1935.[14]

Schools and education comprised the essential starting point for establishing the legitimacy of Phoenix. The number of public grade schools kept pace with the population, rising from six in 1909 to twenty in 1929, leavened by several parochial and private schools. The first high school, Phoenix Union High School, opened in 1895. The second, North High School, was not built until 1937, and accommodating population growth made it one of the largest high schools in the West. Responding to various educational concerns, it offered both advanced science courses and vocational education. The Phoenix public education system expanded to a third level in 1920, when Phoenix High transferred two buildings to the new Phoenix Junior College; and in 1928 it opened its own campus. At the same time, in neighboring Tempe, the two-year Normal School became the four-year Arizona State Teachers College.

Boosters always mentioned the importance of schools and touted their quality, reflecting their own sense of education's importance and recognizing that Americans elsewhere considered schools a key indicator of a progressive community. However, the booster discussions dealt almost exclusively with the facilities and size of the high school enrollment, not curriculum or standards. Orme Lewis reported that he and most other Phoenix boys enrolling at Stanford University in the early 1920s flunked out because they were ill prepared, and he claimed this nearly cost the high school its accreditation. An even more serious flaw—but what many persons at the time considered essential—was the racial segregation of African American school children. A 1909 school board policy, upheld by a 1912 state supreme court ruling that cited the national "separate but equal" standard, led to a separate school for grade children; high school students first met in a separate room, and in 1926 in a separate George Washington Carver school building.[15]

A LIVELY CITY

The culture of everyday life in pre–World War II Phoenix—the use of recreation and leisure time, the popular culture—represents a particular phase of cultural development. Although some elements of mass culture began appearing during this era, they did not form a critical mass of events, institutions, or materials, and it seems more appropriate to consider them as part of popular culture. Forms of mass media did begin developing, but they still contained a considerable diversity of material and appealed to multiple audiences. More generally, as Michael Kammen convincingly argues, popular culture can be distinguished from mass culture by its substantially smaller scale, by the personal access and decision making it affords, and by active participation.[16] Nor, during this period, did Phoenix present publicly competing folk cultures. While ethnic and racial groups defined for themselves patterns of primary association, key values, and ideas about leisure time, art, or music, they did not offer sizable, visible systems of cultural institutions or celebrations that competed for attention in the public arena. This reflects the very low proportion of European immigrants, the small Asian population, and the limited formal organization of the Mexican population, partly because it was so highly mobile. Thus, Anglo Phoenicians developed habits, behaviors, and memories that helped people shape a sense of who they were as residents of Phoenix.

Much of the popular culture in Phoenix related to the outdoors and physical activity, reflecting the advantages of the climate and the accepted value of outdoor living. As noted earlier, canals provided a popular site for swimming, boating, and picnics, and the shade made them especially attractive in the summer heat. Hiking and picnicking in the desert or a dozen city parks bestirred many people, while parks and playgrounds consistently hosted baseball and softball games. Other outdoor activities that attracted participation included tennis, riflery, archery, riding, and golf.

Many public events and much entertainment were staged outdoors. Open-air band concerts were common, for example under the band shell at Encanto Park, while numerous dancers—and watchers—were drawn to the three outdoor dancing pavilions. Cheap outdoor movie theaters—simple walls and no roofs, with benches on dirt floors—were erected after 1900 and attracted viewers until they started closing in the late 1920s, while traveling tent shows, including the Chautauqua, arrived in the 1920s and presented popular theater. Riverside Park regularly drew large crowds to dance in the pavilion, to see movies, to stroll through an animal zoo, or to use its water slide and swimming pool. Several other parks also offered swimming, while one had a roller rink.[17]

Outdoor spectator events drew sizable audiences. For a week in November the annual state fair combined activities related to agriculture with various amusements; in February a Wild West Rodeo offered entertainment; and the Phoenix Open Golf Tournament, begun in 1932 and revived after 1938 by the Thunderbirds, drew good crowds.[18] Baseball, in various forms, proved highly popular. In 1915 and from 1928 to 1932, Phoenix fielded minor league teams that played in a stadium at Riverside Park. Although the teams and leagues were short-lived, killed largely by having to play in the summer heat, their presence highlighted two important community goals: entertainment and promotion. A fan in 1915 explained that baseball "is a good clean sport for the business man," but that the "main reason why Phoenix should have baseball is that it gives the town lots of publicity." This perspective was reinforced by support for the team from a Baseball Committee of the Chamber of Commerce.[19]

Efforts to promote baseball in the Valley also included staging exhibition games with or between major league teams, which occurred periodically after 1915. These popular events drew thousands of fans and occasioned parades through the city, and in 1933 the governor declared the day of the event a holiday. One of the promotional goals—attracting a team for spring training—was achieved when the Detroit Tigers spent the 1929 season in Phoenix.[20] But the spectator events most consistently and widely popular were football games involving local high schools, the Phoenix Indian School, and Phoenix Junior College. The revenues from filling their 10,500-seat stadium for these games enabled the Phoenix Union High School to install lights in 1930 for night games. Thus, while Phoenicians grew more interested in national teams and commercialized sports entertainment, their primary experiences remained local events and people they knew.[21]

Theater and the movies comprised another important part of popular culture. Movies became available in the Valley around the turn of the century and sparked the construction of numerous theaters: thirteen went up in Phoenix, Mesa, and Tempe between 1905 and 1910 alone, and by 1920 six blocks of Washington Street contained thirteen theaters. This might suggest a burgeoning mass culture, but the underlying reality was more complex. The theaters ranged considerably in size: the larger averaged a thousand seats, while smaller ones held about two hundred and fifty. Most alternated between movies and live entertainment—some stock theater or road shows, but especially vaudeville. Large theaters showed the major new feature films, but smaller theaters typically showed briefer, less sophisticated fare, and admission prices reflected this difference. In 1918 the Rialto was constructed, a new "palace" theater with seating for eighteen hundred, which could accommodate the larger vaudeville crowds. Two similar theaters were also constructed—the Orpheum (1929) and the Fox (1931)—but by that time movies had become the widely preferred type of entertainment (figure 3.2). With such luxurious settings, refrigerated air (initially in the Fox Theater), and reliable sound systems, moviegoers flocked to attend these large theaters. As a consequence, twelve older theaters closed by the mid-1930s, mostly the smaller ones and all of those not on Washington Street. With this consolidation of theaters and the development of a single "movie experience" by the later 1930s, movies brought large audiences to downtown and started to present Phoenicians with a mass culture. The one major limitation to this mass culture was that by tradition in these audiences, like those for live artistic performances, African Americans were segregated.[22]

The development of radio in Phoenix followed a somewhat different pattern. Two stations started operating in 1922, broadcasting to a local area and with local programming. In 1930 KTAR affiliated with the NBC network and began receiving network programs. By 1940 the station was broadcasting network programs slightly more than half of its broadcasting hours. The second station received the KOY call sign in 1929 and made its mark by

Figure 3.2 One of the large movie "palaces," the Fox was the first to provide air-conditioning. *Source:* Luhrs Family Photographs, Arizona Collection, Arizona State University Libraries.

broadcasting live music. It did not affiliate with a national network until 1937, when it joined CBS, and by 1940 a third of its programming was national. By contrast with movies, then, radio in Phoenix provided a weaker connection with the emerging national mass culture, and one that would not develop until after the war.[23]

SOCIAL STRUCTURES AND DIVERSE PEOPLES

Phoenicians used social organizations to forge connections and groups within the community, but also to advance specific goals. During the early twentieth century they built upon some of their previous efforts. Fraternal organizations continued to flourish, as did women's social clubs. African Americans preserved their separate fraternal organizations, while Mexicans, Japanese, and Chinese sustained their protective associations. But in this new century, as the city grew and times changed, the joining tendency of Phoenicians broadened considerably to new types of voluntary associations. Some of these had economic goals, like professional or semiprofessional groups, associations of organizations such as agricultural producers or different types of retailers, or labor organizations or labor unions. Other focused on special interests, like the Red Cross and the Good Roads Association.[24]

The most important new groups, and quickly the most influential organizations in the city, were business service clubs. The first of these national organizations, the Rotary Club, had started in Chicago in 1905, followed by the Kiwanis and Lions clubs. They spread rapidly across the nation, and Phoenicians were among the earlier joiners, with a Rotary Club in 1914 (the 100th nationally), a Kiwanis Club in 1917 (the 55th), and a Lions Club in the 1920s. These organizations attracted membership from businessmen and professionals less interested in the secret, ritualized sociability of fraternal orders, which were restricted by gender but not by occupation. Their purpose included social interaction, but they also required some type of social service. Their combination of social, ameliorative, and civic purposes proved compelling; these organizations, especially the Rotary and Kiwanis clubs, attracted the most important men in Phoenix and exerted considerable influential over urban affairs. Although not formally excluded from these groups, women formed their own organization during these years, the Business and Professional Women's Club, which included women interested in public life and a number of whom would hold public office.[25]

Churches also provided a sense of community and advanced specific goals, and they flourished during the early twentieth century. The roster of organizations grew impressively from 22 to 110 in 1940, and it included mainline Protestant and Catholic churches, a number of evangelical, holiness, or pentecostal congregations, and other religious groups outside the Anglo American Christian mainstream, such as Greek Orthodox, Jewish, Buddhist, or Spiritualist. This division highlights the continuation of a earlier trend, namely, the popularity of churches that stressed strict moral behavior of their members rather than doctrinal orthodoxy. Churches further influenced the city through their buildings, which added a key element to the city's spatial organization. Initially, many major denominations built sanctuaries downtown, especially on Monroe Street. St. Mary's Catholic church stayed in its original structure, and the First Baptist (1929) and First Presbyterian (1927) congregations built new structures in the area, but Trinity Episcopal (1915) and Grace Lutheran (1928) churches moved north to the suburbs with their congregants.[26]

While the number and names of these organizations demonstrate the range of groups, membership more accurately indicates the relative importance of shared beliefs. This data is available only for Maricopa County, not Phoenix, but read a little cautiously, these federal census figures tell an important story. From 1906 to 1936 nearly half of the county's adults were church members, a relatively high level. Catholics were easily the largest group, consistently comprising 40 percent of the population; the mainline Protestant denominations constituted a third; while the remainder were divided into numerous small groups. Predictably, the religious affiliation of city leaders did not mirror this distribution, since their prominence reflected economic power, status, and connections: besides Jewish merchants and some non-Mexican Catholics, most belonged to mainline Protestant churches.[27]

Anglo Phoenicians viewed the city's population and its social organizations very positively and believed they would win respect from visitors and across the nation. As James McClintock phrased it, "Its people particularly are proud that it is an American city in all that the word *American* means. The percentage of foreign population is relatively small, though the picturesque Mexican is much in evidence on all public occasions."[28] Anglo Phoenicians' efforts to forge a modern American city caused them to expand the customs of discrimination that had begun with the founding of the town and fostered their support for more overt segregation in this era. Of course, these arrangements were not uniquely local, somehow grown exclusively in warm desert soil, although local circumstances and conditions confirmed those attitudes. Nor were they simply imported by the small group of migrants from southern states. Instead, they reflected common attitudes about races, cultures, civilization, and behavior that evolved in Phoenix much as they did elsewhere in the nation.

Some Anglo Phoenicians perceived these groups as less intelligent, following a tradition of seeing intelligence as a reflection of physical features. More commonly, they focused on character. The most serious complaints, which blurred individual behavior, cultural preferences, and class attitudes, concerned actions like gambling, drinking, prostitution, and the use of drugs. Anglo Phoenicians often criticized minorities as being dishonest or "sly," but their fundamental criticism and belief was that most minorities were lazy, that they lacked the type of drive that Anglo Phoenicians valued and considered necessary for building the town.

The pattern that increasingly emerged during these decades was "separate but unequal." This had started earlier with the creation of some separate organizations, but during these years pressure from Anglo Phoenicians extended the division across most social and economic categories. Ironically, while objecting to minority members' use of a foreign language or other efforts at maintaining a distinct cultural or national identity, Anglo Phoenicians defended separation and segregation as reflecting group preferences. School segregation of African Americans was justified by the claim that they would naturally prefer their children be educated "with their own." This perspective generated the proud claim in 1941 that "Phoenix is practically free from racial conflicts" and that Americanism "unites all racial and national groups into a cooperative group of citizens."[29]

The number of Indians who resided in Phoenix in the several decades after 1900 rose slowly to several hundred. Living near the Indian School to find work or selling goods near the railroad, their presence created little impression. The common image of Indians was as picturesque tourist attractions, living separately on nearby reservations. The very small population of Chinese grew little, and, like the few Japanese living in Phoenix, they built some separate religious and social institutions. African Americans increased in numbers a bit faster than the city's population, rising to 6.5 percent by 1940. Their numbers and the historical pattern of treatment made them the visible targets of de jure segregation in schools, of de facto segregation in public accommodations and in public facilities like swimming pools, and of discrimination in housing (because of restrictive covenants) and employment. In response, they developed a full range of associations for adults and children, creating a substantial institutional base for their community.[30]

Mexicans built the greatest number of institutions and comprised the largest group, but their numbers are harder to tally. By Keith Blakeman's careful analysis, they comprised 21 percent of the 1910 population, twice the previous estimates. Blakeman also shows that at least before 1920, Mexicans did not reside in rigidly segregated neighborhoods. While certain areas contained only Anglos, reinforced in the 1920s by racially restrictive housing covenants, in the previous decades most Mexicans and other minorities lived in racially mixed areas, often including Anglos, generally but not only in the southern and southeastern part of Phoenix.[31] But separationist and segregationist pressures were building during these years and were reflected in many behaviors and organizations. In 1915, in a decision with symbolic and real importance, the priest at St. Mary's Catholic Church began segregating worshipers, sending Mexican parishioners to the basement. In response, they began building Immaculate Heart Church, completed in 1928.[32]

GOVERNING THE CITY

During the early twentieth century changes in social and economic conditions prompted far-reaching debates about the nature of government. Many involved federalism or the scope of state government; some touched on the expanding range of government responsibilities; and others dealt directly with the form and activities of cities. Phoenix joined these debates, not because it faced the complex urban problems confronting large eastern and midwestern cities, nor because it suffered a crisis produced by a natural disaster, as did Galveston and San Francisco. But like nearly all cities it did encounter growing demands for services, it needed to decide how or whether to plan for growth, and it grappled with changing ideas about efficient management and the nature of democracy. Basic elements of urban life—water, sewers, streets—required decisions about quality and finance, while the city leaders' attempt to achieve some vision of the future meant deciding about urban planning issues. Phoenicians differed over using public authority to enforce moral policies, but they generally agreed that problems related to economic need should be left to private solutions. Finally, a growing respect for corporate and "scientific" approaches to organization and decision making, a desire by businessmen for access to government decisions, combined with increasing concerns about the character of the electorate, prompted conflicts over the structure and responsiveness of city government.[33]

By the early twentieth century Phoenix faced serious choices about public services and utilities. Water service had not expanded to match city growth, even after the Phoenix Water Company installed more water mains and fire hydrants in 1905. As a result, in 1907 the city bought the water company, making water hereafter a municipal service. The city also confronted a seriously inadequate private sewer system. Framing this as a public health issue, the city overcame private property concerns when voters in 1910 approved creating a municipal system and buying out the privately held Phoenix Sewer and Drainage Company. Cars required decisions about traffic issues and streets. Sprinkling alone consumed over 25 percent of the budget for streets, and the extent and type of paving raised various choices. The city's most obvious failing concerned the fire department. In 1911 it had only 5 full-time and 2 part-time employees, to go with some 120 volunteers; it had only one regular engine, plus a chemical engine; and the hydrants covered only a three-by-eight-block area of downtown. And the failure was visible: in 1910 fire destroyed the streetcar shops and Hotel Adams; in 1911 the Holmes Building and connected stores burned down, as did the insane asylum and the Arizona Alfalfa Milling Company.[34]

While city services loomed as a growing concern, many Phoenicians increasingly sought to use government to regulate morals, considering urban vice inherently wrong and a blot on the city's reputation. However (as discussed previously), their initial successes against saloons, gambling, and prostitution were short-lived. Laws were often ignored, inadequate, or overturned.[35] Moral reformers found this experience disturbing and suspicious, and it reinforced their emerging views about society and politics. They blamed the failure to enforce the law and manipulation of the law on those who ran government. In fact, the background and status of Phoenix city officials had been changing: while city councilors of the late nineteenth century had been bankers, business owners, and lawyers, the 1910 council included two contractors, a blacksmith, and a sheep rancher. Reformers considered such persons inadequately suited for public service. More importantly, they believed the weakness of the electorate had caused this problem. This view was explicitly voiced in warnings before the 1911 election that opponents were planning to use "400 illiterate Mexicans" to swing the election. More generally, reformers saw the weakness of the electorate as symbolized by the "loiterers" hanging around "Whiskey Row" on Washington Street.[36]

These concerns prompted discussions about city charter revision, beginning in 1906 and continuing over the next seven years, complicated by differences with the territorial legislature, by delays imposed by statehood, and by conflicts with the new state constitution. These efforts occurred within a national debate over competing ideas and models of urban reform, divisions evident in Phoenix's decade-long struggle over framing its government. Galveston, Texas, introduced the city commission form of government, with citywide elections of commissioners who individually administered certain city departments. This combination of legislative and executive functions, plus the addition of at-large, nonpartisan elections, was adopted by cities across the country. Still others adopted a variant created in Des Moines, Iowa, in 1909, which included direct democracy features of initiative, referendum, and recall.[37] Drafting a new charter for Phoenix in 1911 and 1912, the City Charter Commission and then an appointed board of freeholders adopted essentially the Des Moines model. Voters approved this commission-style government on November 8, 1912, but the state attorney general found that it conflicted with direct democracy provisions in the state constitution. He also objected to the proposed restriction of suffrage to "tax-paying electors." When the governor vetoed the measure, the city was forced to start again.

Acting quickly, Mayor Lloyd Christy appointed a five-person committee that selected a Charter Commission Committee (CCC) of one hundred men. When newly enfranchised women protested their exclusion, the mayor added twenty-five women to the committee. Despite its large number and its inclusion of both sexes and all parties, committee membership was effectively restricted to only the middle and upper middle classes. And party affiliation provided the only diversity on the fourteen-member board of freeholders committee that the CCC selected to draft a charter. The document that this committee presented in August 1913 differed significantly from the previous proposal by including a city manager. The first use in the nation of such a position had come in 1908, as an alternative to the commission form of management, but by 1913 many cities had adopted and were proposing various combined forms. The version approved by Phoenix voters in 1913 and implemented in March 1914 included a mayor and four commissioners, chosen at-large and in a nonpartisan election, with a city manager who appointed all other city officials, but with each commissioner having supervisory responsibility for particular government departments. With the appointment of William Farish as city manager, the new government began to operate, fulfilling the hopes of reformers.

A year later Farish had been fired and the charter amended, placing the manager under the control of the commission. Various accounts of this situation allege that Farish was fired because of his efforts to enforce efficient, honest government and that the amendment seriously undermined the reform nature of the original charter. These do reflect contemporary editorials, which charged that "political workers and the men who would get at the city treasury" were responsible, and the claim became part of the attack mounted by advocates of charter revision in the late 1940s.[38] But this version too conveniently adopts the Progressive Era tendency to see all conflicts as moral struggles and to denounce any opponents as "corrupt." Furthermore, it ignores the history of early twentieth-century political conflict and charter revision in Phoenix.

An early and important goal of that effort had been to change the influences on city government, reducing the role of the working class and minorities while increasing the power of businessmen and professionals. In general, this effort had succeeded, but by 1915 city growth had produced some diverse perspectives and interests within this latter group. Complaints about the 1915 revisions had more to do, first, with who had access to government rather than a simple contest for democracy and, second, with competing notions of management and authority. Farish may well have been an efficient manager, but the mixed commission-manager form in the 1913 charter had institutionalized conflicting lines of responsibility. This division was especially volatile because it related to a divergence that burgeoned within American society during the Progressive Era between the value ascribed to "experts" and a belief in representative government.

One clear result of the charter amendments was that the city manager became an integral part of Phoenix city politics, and over the next several decades the frequent shifts in political balances on the council yielded frequent changes in city managers. Such turnover was unusual for city managers, and critics cited this as showing a fundamental weakness in city government, corruption, or both. Yet this administrative system might be better understood as being like a mayor-council system with an additional layer of administration. Phoenix government during this period was relatively efficient, expanding government services fairly effectively and, with several exceptions discussed below, free from scandal. Although the commission reclaimed the power to appoint the heads of half the city departments, a civil service system was begun in 1924, extended by charter amendment in 1933, and as of 1940 covered all but 12 of the 646 city employees.[39]

The new charter government steadily improved city services. The fire department was professionalized, additional stations and substations were built, and new equipment was purchased. More streets and sidewalks were paved. The city water and sewage systems were crucial for the city's development and for convincing outlying areas to be annexed. In particular, the inadequate supply and poor quality of the city's water, from local wells, demanded a solution. After three reports, the city finally built a redwood pipeline for water from the Verde River in 1920, but it was poorly designed and had to replaced in 1930–32 with a much larger concrete pipe. With this measure and the additional water obtained in the 1930s from wells along the Verde and Salt rivers, Phoenix had a secure and sufficient water supply.[40]

City government also considered how to improve the built environment. Encouraged by the Chamber of Commerce, the city hired Edward Bennett, a nationally known planner, to draft an urban plan. In 1921 the city created a Planning Commission, and the following year it adopted a scaled-down version of Bennett's design. Focused more on functional improvements than on beautification, the city followed his plan in building new government buildings and the railroad station; by acquiring the airport and various parks, including South Mountain Park; and by creating a Parks and Recreation Commission. The Planning Commission persuaded the city to cover the central city canal known as the "Town Ditch," and in 1930 the commission recommended the city's first zoning ordinance, which "prohibited commercial uses in residential districts, and encouraged its development along major streets."[41]

But during the 1920s and 1930s complaints about city services were fewer and less vigorous than were allegations of rampant vice in the city. With Arizona's adoption of state prohibition in 1914, the saloons disappeared, but illegal use of liquor remained a nagging issue for the next two decades. The repeal of federal Prohibition in 1933 brought back the saloon—324 licenses were issued from mid-March to early May—but many of these did not survive. Moreover, high license fees and other regulatory legislation prevented a return of the old style saloon and its problems. Gambling did not reappear as a major concern, although Nevada's legalization of gambling in 1931 prompted some resort and guest ranch owners to suggest the same policy for Arizona.[42]

While liquor and gambling did not pose serious policing problems in this era, the continuation of prostitution generated periodic public outcries and crackdowns. The primary issue was not prostitution in general, but the existence of a specific red light district. While large American cities had eliminated their red light districts during World War I, usually because of demands from the military, Phoenix and many smaller communities continued to tolerate the public existence of brothels and districts. Arguing that active attempts at suppression would only disperse the trade throughout the city, Phoenix authorities essentially practiced a system of semiofficial regulation: madams of the nine houses and the two or three prostitutes per house were arrested monthly on vagrancy charges, fined, and released. Thus, prostitution generated income, but as fines that were officially recorded and part of city revenues, rather than as private payments to police or political operators. Although this system did not produce the corruption that some critics alleged, it tolerated behavior that social purity reformers considered immoral. Most importantly, by not requiring medical inspection, this system failed to deal with concerns about venereal disease, an issue that national social hygiene reformers had been pressing since the turn of the century and that had driven the military to exercise pressure on other cities during World War I.[43]

SELLING THE CITY

From the beginning Phoenicians worked hard at selling their city, championing its assets and boosting its image to achieve their vision of its future, and these efforts expanded and changed direction during the 1920s and 1930s. Their initial and continuing focus was to attract more residents by proclaiming that Phoenix was an agricultural "paradise," the "Eden of America," or the "American Nile."[44] Climate served as a secondary theme, and by the 1890s boosters were advertising its health-giving benefits. Several groups began producing promotional pamphlets by 1887 with intriguing titles like *Salt River Valley: Its Attractions for the Immigrant, the Capitalist, the Invalid* (1894), but promotional efforts increased substantially when the Board of Trade started a $12,000 advertising campaign in 1907, and the Santa Fe railroad began a concerted effort the following year. Besides being intended to attract permanent settlers, this literature included a new strategy of encouraging seasonal migrants. Although contemporary estimates of winter visitors around 1910 ranged from three thousand to five thousand (with no clear factual basis), these claims showed an awareness that tourism could benefit the area economically.[45]

The growth of tourism depended on the development of transportation, accommodations, attractions, and publicity. Expanded rail connections in the 1890s had been a first step, and development of the Ingleside Inn (1909) and the San Marcos resort in Chandler (1913) provided an additional boost. By 1916 the promotional literature no longer referred at all to possible health benefits, emphasizing instead the city's amenities and the different things to see, assorted tourist sites, and auto trips to nearby features. Promotional efforts blossomed during the 1920s. In 1924, the Phoenix-Arizona Club, a booster group organized in 1919, raised $40,000 from various Valley business interests to fund a promotional campaign that included printed pamphlets and advertising in magazines like *Time* and *Better Homes and Gardens*. The railroads ran complementary campaigns, with the Santa Fe running ads and the Southern Pacific using its *Sunset* magazine. Expanding on prior themes, these materials emphasized the area's scenery and stressed the rugged beauty of the Apache Trail, the former construction road to the Roosevelt Dam.[46]

Recommendations for car trips in the Valley increased over this period, and by the late 1920s the promotional literature also proposed bus tours from the state's two bus companies (figure 3.3). By then the dominant theme was "Where Winter Never Comes," and any mention of climate came in promoting the numerous activities available to visitors as part of the "outdoor life." One reason for the increased recommendations for car or bus trips was that more state highways were paved. In addition, the area offered new attractions, as dam construction created new structures and lakes for visitors to see. The growing tourist trade stimulated the building of cabins and motor courts, as well as of several new hotels and resorts. Besides the San Carlos and Westward Ho hotels in downtown, the Jokake Inn (1927), the Wigwam (1929), the Hermosa Inn (1935), and Camelback Inn (1936) catered to wealthier visitors, with a

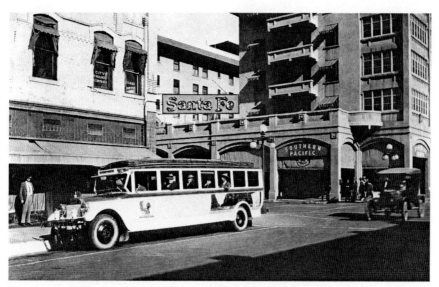

Figure 3.3 "Parlor Car Apache" of Arizona Tours, Inc., in front of the Santa Fe Depot in Phoenix, around 1930. *Source:* Herb and Dorothy McLaughlin Collection, Arizona State University Libraries.

range of indoor and outdoor attractions. The best known and most luxurious hostelry was the Arizona Biltmore (1929). Designed by a student of Frank Lloyd Wright, with only minimal help from the master, it was purchased by William Wrigley, of Chicago Cubs and chewing gum fame, after the builders lost money in the Depression.[47]

Efforts to attract the well-to-do followed tradition and yielded important results. Health problems were one reason that the wealthy came to visit. Delos Willard Cooke, a rich New York industrialist and financier, began wintering in Arizona because of his wife's ill health. He hired the local architectural firm of Lescher & Mahoney in 1926 to design El Vermadero, a 3,500-square-foot villa on sixty-five acres near the base of Camelback Mountain. Cleveland businessman John C. Lincoln, who spent increasing amounts of time in the Valley after 1931 because of the health difficulties of his wife, Helen, built the Camelback Inn. An even more significant addition to that area was La Colina Solana, the mansion built by William K. Wrigley. Overlooking the Biltmore Hotel, this elaborate "winter cottage" contained 16,850 square feet and twenty-four rooms. Other wealthy industrialists and old moneyed families also built winter homes in the area during the interwar period, while movie stars and other celebrities vacationed at the luxurious resorts and brought a sense of glamour to the Valley.[48]

Economic crisis pushed city leaders to pursue tourism more aggressively, and in 1930 and 1931 the Chamber of Commerce began a substantially increased national advertising campaign. After several years, and buoyed by the new label of the "Valley of the Sun," the campaign began showing results. State efforts also expanded, most obviously in the state government's *Arizona Highways* magazine, which would soon become nationally known. In 1937 its focus became promotion and tourism, and in 1938 the budget more than doubled, partly to pay for publishing color photographs.

Because of these efforts, economic recovery, and unsettled conditions abroad, Arizona tourism flourished. The number of winter visitors doubled over two years to 35,000 in the 1939–40 season and exceeded that growth in the following year, adding between $30 and $50 million to the Valley's economy. Air travel rose at a similar pace during this era, but American Airlines' thirteen daily flights still brought in only 4,023 passengers a year. Many more visitors arrived by train, roughly 25,000 annually, but the growing majority came by car, with many renting the 3,000 rooms at the increasingly popular "auto courts." By 1940 the promotion of tourism had achieved a comprehensive approach befitting such an economically valuable enterprise, as the literature touted natural sites and parks; man-made dams, lakes, and canals; Indian ruins and reservations; pageants and festivals; resorts and dude ranches; and outdoor living.[49]

CRISIS AND COMPLETION: THE 1930S

The 1930s were both the occasion of and the cause for Phoenix fulfilling its transition from town to city. The combination of developments related to the city's stage of growth and specific aspects of the Depression crisis brought to completion the city's economic dominance within the Valley, its primacy within the lower Southwest, a more complex version of its original economy, and the filling out of the structure and amenities of the city. Taken together they represent the culmination of the original vision that had guided the community forward.

In Phoenix and the rest of Arizona, the Depression brought misery to many people. In relative terms Arizona suffered less (and received more help) than some other states, and Phoenix, with its diverse economy, fared better than many other areas within the state. From the beginning, the mining communities were hurt worst, for the utter collapse of copper prices devastated the industry, driving employment down from 17,566 in 1929 to 3,300 in 1933. While conditions improved by decade's end, mining did not regain its former importance. In general, the economies of Arizona and Phoenix followed the national pattern of decline and recovery, except their troughs were less deep and their recoveries somewhat more robust, a condition reflecting the nature of the state's economy and the role of the federal government. According to one estimate, from 1933 to 1939 the federal government spent $342 million in Arizona, while the state paid a mere $16 million in taxes.[50]

The activities of the federal government had significantly affected Arizona during its six decades as a territory, and statehood in 1912 did little to change the basic relationship. The federal government maintained responsibility for reservation Indians, it owned vast amounts of land—in national forests, national parks and monuments, and as saleable land—and the Bureau of Reclamation had authority over dams and irrigation. Some of these activities directly influenced Phoenix, and the federal offices were located there. The federal government also fulfilled governmental tasks that gave it additional presence in Phoenix—the post office, federal courts, weather bureau—which were augmented during the 1930s by new, permanent programs like Social Security.[51]

But starting in 1933, the proliferation of special New Deal programs such as the Public Works Administration, the Civilian Conservation Corps, and the WPA, as well as new agricultural programs, vastly increased the visibility and importance of the federal government in the state and in Phoenix. By 1935 more than fifty federal agencies had offices in the city. This changed the city's relationship with the federal government, although it did not alter as much the status of Phoenix within the southwest. As one observer complained in 1941, "in far too many cases the Phoenix office of a Federal agency is merely a sub-office," while the regional offices were located in Albuquerque, Denver, or San Francisco. But more than just establishing offices, the federal government became directly involved as the county's largest employer by the mid-1930s, hiring nearly six thousand persons and spending roughly $10 million on salaries, materials, and equipment. The ripple effect of this income was significant; Barry Goldwater admitted in 1940 that this "huge expenditure of public moneys . . . has been of extreme importance to retailing."[52]

It had been equally vital for construction, the largest sector of the city's economy in the late 1930s, accounting for nearly a quarter of the employment, directly or indirectly. The benefits of New Deal construction programs went beyond the substantial employment they provided; these programs made permanent improvements in Phoenix by providing for the erection of buildings at the state fair grounds, North High School, Phoenix Junior College, and Arizona State Teachers College. Reclamation projects improved dams along the Salt River and made possible the building of Bartlett Dam on the Verde River; while a costly modernization project transformed the airport with new runways, buildings, and lighting. Road and road-related construction, core parts of both the PWA and the WPA, added 40 miles of paved streets (bringing the total to 117 miles), 95 miles of sidewalks, and 73 miles of curbs; widened key traffic arteries; built bridges; and extended sewers and waterlines.[53] The most significant project in expense and impact was the construction of public housing. Spurred to action by Father Emmett McLoughlin, the state legislature in 1939 passed enabling legislation for public housing, and as head of the new Phoenix Housing Commission Father Emmett supervised the construction of three complexes of public housing units. Although racially segregated and built in separate neighborhoods, the three complexes represented substantially improved housing for 558 families.[54]

When Del Webb observed in 1940 that the New Deal had "changed the whole method of construction as we know it," he referred to public building projects, his area of experience to that point, but he also recognized that federal programs had drastically altered the construction and improvement of private homes. Such efforts had virtually stopped by 1932, with only forty building permits processed in the next two years. Several New Deal programs secured and transformed home mortgages, restarted home construction, and proferred plans to reconfigure the designing and building of private homes. Creation of the Home Owners' Loan Corporation (HOLC) in early 1933 provided money for refinancing home mortgages, an opportunity that many Phoenicians embraced. HOLC also facilitated home ownership by establishing standardized house-appraising guidelines and long-term, self-amortizing mortgages.[55]

The Federal Housing Authority (FHA), created in 1934, brought even greater results. Title I of this program provided small installment loans for home repair or "modernization." First offered in August 1934, these "character" loans proved popular among Phoenix home owners, particularly as some bankers like Carl Bimson of Valley National Bank promoted their value, and spending on construction materials and home appliances rose substantially. The main FHA program simply insured long-term mortgages made by private lenders, but that enabled the FHA to set new mortgage standards, reducing the required down payment to 10 percent or less and lengthening the repayment period. First implemented in Arizona in early 1935, this program immediately boosted home construction. By 1939 building permits had reached the level of the late 1920s. Between 1935 and 1940 a total of 2,160 new homes were built, and the FHA had insured two-thirds of them. Those homes represented over 10 percent of the total housing stock in the city, and, strikingly, 61 percent of them were owner occupied, roughly twice the level for previous-built homes and the level of home ownership in the city in 1930.[56] Clearly, New Deal policies helped move Phoenix from the hope to the reality of home ownership.

Besides boosting construction and ownership, the FHA established guidelines for construction and design that significantly affected the construction industry and the nature of suburban America.[57] And just as FHA standards affected mortgage lenders, so also their standards encouraged Phoenix to adopt a building code in 1935. In 1936 the FHA financed three model homes as a way to advertise home buying and to encourage standardized construction.[58] The impact of FHA financing and standards is apparent in two Phoenix neighborhoods begun before the Depression. In Fairview Place, located in the near northwest, construction "jumped from just two homes in 1937 to seventy-four completed in the next two years," and "FHA design standards encouraged efficiency in both form and materials," which led to a shift in architectural styles. In Cheery Lynn, a near-northeast neighborhood that had seen various design changes and very slow progress since 1928, FHA standards "once again changed the look of construction. . . . Diversity was replaced by uniformity and consistency. Floor plans were simplified, materials were standardized, and ornamentation [was] reduced to a minimum. Period styles gradually evolved into the Transitional and Early Ranch Styles." These and other subdivisions responded to an importation of FHA standards after they had begun, but the logical extension of the FHA principles for reduced costs, standardization, and larger-scale construction was the design of an entire subdivision using FHA standards. The first of these, Womack Heights, consisted of thirty-two houses, which were built between July 1939 and July 1941. While the construction of most homes still involved the labor of only a few individuals, FHA guidelines set the stage for dramatic postwar changes.[59]

New Deal programs and developments of the 1930s also affected other economic sectors. Banking began the decade in crisis, and conditions worsened by the winter of 1932–33. Only quick action by Walter Bimson, the new president of Valley National Bank, got the governor to avoid bank failure by declaring a bank holiday, and subsequent New Deal banking measures stabilized the system. During the decade various New Deal policies, including the FHA's, provided opportunities for banks like Valley National Bank that welcomed new programs and ways of doing business. By 1940 the different reactions of financial institutions to these policies had reconfigured this industry: the number of savings and loan institutions had declined from eight to two, the number of banks had shrunk from six to three, and Valley National was the big winner, gaining significantly in profits and size.[60] Agriculture, the primary basis of the Valley's economy, suffered from falling prices after 1929, and various New Deal agricultural programs, especially the Agricultural Adjustment Acts, attempted to bolster prices, partly by reducing production. These worked fairly well in Arizona, as farm income rose during the 1930s. Limitations in the crop reduction program initially failed to lower the overproduction of cotton, but the new program implemented after the 1938 law did effect a significant reduction in that crop. Unlike much of the West, the Valley did not suffer from drought. Average temperatures were close to those of the 1920s, while rainfall was above average in most years of this decade.[61]

Phoenix's commercial position remained very strong throughout the decade. Retail figures show its continuing dominance of the county: it had 50 percent of the stores but 71 percent of the sales, and its per capita sales figures were double those of other Valley cities. While those communities served the basic needs of their residents, residents of Maricopa County as well as surrounding mining towns shopped in Phoenix for nonessential items. In 1932–33 Phoenix ranked 2nd among the nation's top 200 cities in per capita sales. The city later lost its lofty national ranking but maintained its regional role: in 1939, while only 198th in population, it ranked 109th in total sales.[62] The figures for Phoenix's wholesale trade show its increasing importance in the lower Southwest. In contrast with its relatively low population rank in 1940, Phoenix ranked among the top 75 U.S. cities in wholesaling. The number of both food and nonfood distributors increased substantially; the number of trucking and storage companies grew by 43 percent, and the number of firms wholesaling local agricultural products rose from six to thirty.[63]

While commerce showed overall signs of growth, manufacturing in Phoenix declined during the decade, dropping from 139 firms to 80 and from 2,181 employees to 1,250, roughly one-fourth the number who worked in retail. Yet even these figures exaggerate the importance of "manufacturing" in the Phoenix economy, for in both 1930 and 1940 the majority of firms and employees engaged in processing agricultural or food items—like the Arizona Flour Mill, the Holsum Bakery, the Crystal Ice Company, and the Tovrea Packing Company.[64] But while Phoenix lacked a substantial industrial base, significant changes occurred during the 1930s that had implications for later manufacturing and for living in Phoenix.

CONTROLLING THE CLIMATE

To live in a desert, Phoenicians had successfully altered their physical environment, building dams and canals to maximize the use of water and planting trees, shrubs, flowers, and lawns to create a landscape more like the tropics or the Midwest than the Sonoran Desert. The climate, however, was not so malleable. From the city's beginnings, Phoenix boosters had contended that summers were not really uncomfortable, using various anecdotal and statistical arguments, but residents knew that Phoenix summers were to be avoided or endured. Those who could leave went to mountain retreats in Iron Springs (near Prescott) or Flagstaff or vacationed at the Pacific Ocean. For those who stayed, work was more leisurely. Bob Goldwater later reminisced that summer afternoons in the department store were so slow that he and the staff played board games; Nicholas Udall remembered "putting rubber bands or something around your arms to keep the perspiration off the papers you were working on." Outside, people sought relief in shade, for the city's landscape design and the proliferation of trees were intended for comfort as much as beauty. In their homes, people used electric fans, if possible over ice; at night they often slept on porches or sometimes, as reporter Ben Avery remembered it, even on lawns.[65]

Refrigerated air systems—"air-conditioning," in modern parlance—were developed around 1900 by Willis Carrier, but for the first part of the century such systems were too cumbersome and expensive to gain much acceptance. Before 1940 a growing number of Phoenix businesses installed air-conditioning, starting with the Westward Ho Hotel in 1929 and followed by the Fox Theater in 1931, the Luhrs buildings in 1932, and the three department stores in the mid-1930s. Other theaters, larger stores, and some office buildings also made the change, but the expense kept many smaller businesses from purchasing this equipment.[66]

While air-conditioning cooled by removing moisture from the air, an effective alternative for the desert involved adding moisture and letting evaporation produce a cooling effect. With the availability of affordable electric fans some Valley residents had employed simple, home-style versions of this technique for temporary relief, but these typically cooled only limited areas and required refilling, and those using ice were relatively expensive. During the 1920s various companies and individuals began developing and producing individual models of self-sustaining units for "air cooling"—evaporative coolers, or "swamp coolers"—but the public manufacture and sale of a working window unit was only begun in 1931, by the Taylor Metal Works in Tucson.

Within the next few years numerous individuals and companies such as Southwest Manufacturing began making some type of cooler, ranging considerably in quality, and the popularity of these units grew rapidly. In 1935 a manufacturer with sixty-five employees wrote Carl Bimson that people were taking out FHA loans to buy his coolers. Phoenix reportedly had fifteen hundred units in that year, and in 1936 the Central Arizona Power and Light Company counted some five thousand coolers in the city. By 1937 manufacturers were producing quieter and more durable units, with copper tubing, metal grills, and blowers. These popular window units were widely advertised and sold, but they cooled only part of the house. By then, some companies were making a roof-mounted unit that used the house's heating ducts to cool the entire house. Builders quickly accommodated this innovation with a link to the duct work, a niche on the roof, or an opening on the outside walls. Additional improvements came in 1938, with a float valve, removable pads, remote controls inside the house, and a more finished casing, and these units were available in different sizes and capacities. Coolers were readily available in Phoenix by 1939, and while more elaborate styles were available at over $100, materials for a homemade version cost only $10.[67]

By 1940 the use of coolers was also expanding in New Mexico, Nevada, and California, but Phoenix legitimately claimed to be the "air-conditioned capital of the world" (meaning "air-cooled") in terms of both use and manufacturing. Virtually all new homes included coolers or were at least built to make their addition very easy, and most older homes had either central or window units. This simple innovation greatly affected the lives of Phoenicians, enabling them to overcome the summer heat that Del Webb called "the bane of the southwesterners' existence." The system had limitations, working less effectively at very high temperatures or when humidity levels rose, but it was a crucial first step in transforming basic living conditions in the area. It represented yet another instance of human ingenuity overcoming the area's obstacles, reinforcing the notion that nature was malleable. It also gave rise to a new industry, for by 1940 more than thirty manufacturers employed roughly two hundred persons, with additional jobs in related areas. More crucial than the employment it provided, this industry encouraged entrepreneurial talent, such as Oscar Palmer, who came to the business after repairing cars and radiators; or Gust and Adam Goettl, who worked for Southwestern Manufacturing, making sheet metal for coolers, before starting Goettl Brothers Metal Products in 1939 to make their own units. Most importantly, this industry financed the development of machine shops, metalworking, and other skills vital to the future development of manufacturing in Phoenix.[68]

THE PHOENIX ECONOMIC ELITE

Just as the city's economy during the 1930s presented substantial continuity mixed with change, so too did its economic and social leadership. The Depression seriously shifted the fortunes of some, like Albert, Charles, and Warren McArthur, whose financial difficulties forced them to sell their newly built Biltmore resort to William Wrigley. More typical were men who surmounted the challenge of declining office rents and a difficult real estate market. George Luhrs managed his family's office buildings and hotel; Roy Wayland's Professional Building opened in 1931 and successful attracted tenants from among Phoenix professionals; while George Mickle's Phoenix Title and Trust Building opened in 1931, and his title company weathered the difficult real estate market of the early 1930s. They, along with others like the O'Malley brothers and the Korricks, represented important continuity in the city's economic elite.[69]

Time affected this group, of course, especially through mortality. The death in 1929 of Dwight Heard, since the 1890s a major figure with manifold interests, left a gap in leadership, capital, and outside connections. Charles Stauffer took Heard's role as publisher of the *Arizona Republican*, and with his brother-in-law, Wes Knorpp, built a local media conglomerate by purchasing the *Phoenix Gazette* and several radio stations. Stauffer had been an active civic leader in the 1910s and 1920s, while Knorpp increased his community involvement in the 1930s. A second death in 1929 marked a generational transition, as Baron Goldwater's demise pushed his sons Barry and Bob to manage the family department store and advance the city's interests.[70]

The city's expansion also created opportunities for newcomers, and the Phoenix elite was open to accepting them. A few were actually recruited, like Walter Bimson, president of Valley National Bank. Born in Colorado in 1892, he briefly attended the University of Colorado, worked as a bank janitor, graduated from the University of Chicago, and after serving in the navy during World War I took a position with the Harris Trust and Savings Bank in Chicago. His work with commodity credits involved contacts with the Arizona Cotton Growers Association and Valley Bank and Trust, which occasioned his first trip to Phoenix in 1926; his connections expanded through a Harris Trust vice president, Frank Elliott, who spent winter vacations in the Valley. In January 1933 he became president of Valley Bank, the state's largest financial institution, whose assets had fallen by two-thirds and whose administrators had laid off half its work force. While maintaining the bank's traditional agricultural business, Bimson moved immediately and aggressively to get money to consumers, especially in small installment loans. He hired his brother, Carl, to expand the bank's involvement in FHA programs for home remodeling and purchase, gaining national recognition. His methods won friends and profits: bank assets rose immediately, reaching $45 million by 1939, an increase of 600 percent and half of all the state's bank assets.[71]

An equally important figure, Frank Snell, migrated to Phoenix and worked his way into city leadership during the 1930s. Born in Kansas City, Missouri, in 1899, Snell graduated from law school and came to Arizona at the urging of an uncle. After practicing law for several years in Miami, he moved to Phoenix in 1927. Although one of nearly 150 lawyers in the community, during the next decade Snell built a flourishing practice with connections that involved him across the range of Phoenix's economic activities—working for the Arizona Cotton Growers Association, the Arizona Edison Company, and the Central Arizona Power and Light Company; writing the incorporation papers for numerous businesses, such as Camelback Inn; and handling real estate such as John C. Lincoln's development of the posh Encanto subdivision and aspects of Henry Coerver's Arcadia neighborhood. In 1938 Snell moved his career to a new level, forging a partnership that enabled him to operate in boardrooms while partner Mark Wilmer worked the courtroom. Snell's power of persuasion and his sensitivity to the situations of others were keys to his success. He also knew a great many people through his considerable involvement and leadership in various community organizations, particularly the Kiwanis Club, the Chamber of Commerce, and the Arizona Club.[72]

The role of this elite was shaped by the nature of Phoenix and the social groups they created. During the 1930s, when the city was still relatively compact in size and modest in population, this group of wealthy, influential men met often and informally. With a total downtown area of no more than twenty blocks, and with shopping and movie theaters heavily concentrated along a few blocks of Washington Street, people routinely saw each other on the streets: "You couldn't go two blocks without meeting ten people that you knew well," said Snell. Business service clubs helped forge connections by recruiting members, offering regular club luncheons, and engaging in service projects. Snell later observed of this era that "men had a little more time. We knew each other better." After four or five years in the Kiwanis Club, he became president, and "I could call everybody by name, you know, and know their business." A common saying reflected the considerable importance of these groups: "The Rotary Club owned the town, the Kiwanians ran it, and the Lions enjoyed it."[73]

The Phoenix Chamber of Commerce provided an additional, broader gathering of business, professional, and community leadership, as well as valuable opportunities for making profitable contacts. The elite dominated the leadership of this group, notably presidents Les Mahoney (1933–35), Orme Lewis (1937–38), and Frank Snell (1939–40). Another, informal group met in the Arizona Club, on the ninth floor of the Luhrs Hotel, often for dinner (figure 3.4). While air-conditioning clearly enhanced its attraction during the summer months of the 1930s, men also came for the discussions. Among the regular attendees were Snell, Howard Conway (who did much of the paving in Phoenix), Charlie Korrick, Harold Diamond, Orme Lewis, Bob Goldwater, and occasionally Barry Goldwater. Snell joked that the participants "solved all the problems of all the city and the nation," but then added more seriously that "we really did talk about important things, and many were carried out." These men discussed serious topics, but city government and local politics were not among them. In a later reflection, Newton Rosenzweig explained

Figure 3.4 Lobby of the Arizona Club, where city leaders met. *Source:* Luhrs Family Photographs, Arizona Collection, Arizona State University Libraries.

that "we were all aware of the fact that we didn't have as stable a government as we might have. On the other hand, we, with one exception [the water pipeline fiasco] never had anything in the way of a serious problem." Some wealthier men from older Phoenix families served on the city council, but increasingly since the 1920s that activity had been left to others. Instead, this group focused on economic opportunities, building social relationships, and engaging in community service for hospitals or the community chest fund drives.[74]

PHOENIX IN 1940

In 1940 Phoenix reached a population of 65,411, ranking only 198th in the nation and 16th among Western cities (table 3.1). It had grown steadily, however, and during the previous two decades had advanced a bit more rapidly than before. It remained smaller than major Western cities, but it was larger than Tucson and Albuquerque, the other southwestern urban centers between El Paso and Los Angeles. Its retail and wholesale sectors reflected its dominance in this region and its traditional reliance on the prosperity of agriculture in the Salt River Valley.

Most Phoenicians felt comfortable with the status and condition of their community, with its interesting blend of downtown and suburbs, its social institutions, and its culture. The founding vision had been of a modern American community resting on a prosperous agricultural hinterland, and with only some modifications, that remained the community's expectation in 1940. As one writer joked, visitors were important because they could return home to tell that "we live in houses, can read and write English, and are not violent." Phoenicians praised their city's parks and schools and claimed that "homes are built to last for a long time, for the people who live here are content with their homes and their city."[75]

A sense that manufacturing needed to expand prompted the suggestion that "in the Egyptian Nile Valley of America, the farmer may provide the raw

Table 3.1 Western cities in 1940.

Region/city	Population	National rank
PACIFIC COAST		
Los Angeles	1,504,277	5
San Francisco	634,536	12
Seattle	368,302	22
Portland	305,394	27
San Diego	203,341	43
Tacoma	109,408	82
TEXAS-OKLAHOMA		
Dallas	294,734	31
Fort Worth	177,662	46
San Antonio	253,854	36
Oklahoma City	204,424	42
Tulsa	142,157	62
INLAND WEST		
Denver	322,412	24
Salt Lake City	149,934	57
Spokane	122,001	68
El Paso	96,810	98
Phoenix	65,414	198
Tucson	35,752	NA
Albuquerque	35,449	NA

Source: U.S. Bureau of the Census, *Sixteenth Census of the United States: 1940*, 1 (Washington, DC: Government Printing Office, 1942): 32–36.

materials of industry." But the larger argument focused on consumption, as a community leader contended that "national prosperity hinges on the prosperity of the farmer, for it is he who provides for the market for the manufacturer."[76] The continuing strength of this vision shows in an article projecting the city's future. The basis for growth would be obtaining water from the Colorado River, which, the author anticipated, would be used on "millions of acres of rich farm lands" and would add to the development of cheap power, mineral wealth, and forests. But, the author hastened to add, "This does not mean that the Phoenix of 1993 will be a large industrial city, nor would that be desirable."[77]

Yet this vision overlooked some important realities. Although agriculture was reasonably prosperous in 1940, it did not provide a broad basis for long-term economic growth and substantial employment in the region. Apart from questions about the profitability of agriculture, its reliance on cotton made it increasingly dependent on cheap agricultural labor. The weakness of the manufacturing sector meant that more employment was concentrated in lower-paying clerical and service jobs, and the wages Phoenix employers paid for those positions were below the national average.[78] A further problem for the community was housing, for while it seemed relatively affordable, this was partly because much of it was small, too much of it lacked proper ventilation and plumbing, and some of it was in poor shape. A survey in 1934 reported that less than a third was "satisfactory," while a 1939 study of 4,065 houses in the "slum" area (roughly one-fifth of all city housing) found that only 289 of those structures were "standard." Finally, an element linking these weaknesses was the mainstream community's views and treatment of minority populations. By maintaining minorities' inferior position, Anglo Phoenicians would fail to address basic elements of economic development.[79]

But if Phoenicians in 1940 still embraced their traditional vision, important changes had been occurring, especially in the 1930s, which opened the possibility of alternative futures. The increased role of the federal government, beyond the traditional resources management familiar to western states, now involving economic development and military spending, presented new and interesting possibilities. The new availability of "coolers" meant that Phoenix could become a place for year-round economic activity outside of agriculture. Tourism, which had begun as an adjunct to efforts promoting settlement, had blossomed into a separate economic strategy by the 1930s. By 1940, as the number of visitors soared, other spillover benefits started becoming apparent. With the possibility of indoor climate control and improved transportation, climate became a common interest linking different migration considerations. Outdoor living took on various meanings; people seeking relief from respiratory or arthritic complaints came to Phoenix, as health facilities replaced tent cities. Drawn by noneconomic motives, these new migrants represented a new blend of interests and talents. But the most important factor creating change and possible alternatives to this vision was the outbreak of war in Europe and America's nearing involvement. As Americans readied for and then were plunged into war, Phoenix confronted very different conditions and opportunities.

Part II   △△△
Creating and Pursuing a New Vision, 1940–60

In celebrating and pursuing growth, Phoenix was Everytown, following the American dream. From its beginnings into the early twentieth century, its expectations reflected a common frontier expansionism in which boosters described accomplishments in exaggerated language and painted fanciful notions about future expansion and prosperity. While resting on some real possibilities, such optimism was inflated by the ambitions and self-interest of boosters. Equally important, it reflected the absence of a fixed and determinative urban hierarchy and the lack of competing notions about why cities grew. Chicago's meteoric rise during the nineteenth century inspired boosters across the nation with the hope of imitating its success, although most who hoped to develop their cities identified more realistic exemplars. The model for ambitious Phoenix leaders was Denver, a western city whose economy rested on extractive industries and agriculture, a state capitol and trading center, and a community appreciated for the area's scenery and climate.

By the twentieth century, the widespread and widely exaggerated hopes of America's frontier boosterism had shrunk, replaced by a recognition of the emerging urban hierarchy. Western communities still grew more rapidly than national norms, and some cities changed in relative rank, but the passing decades showed increased stability in America's overall urban hierarchy and a more regular and predictable distribution of urban places. As population in the nation's cities rose, the bar for becoming a major city grew higher and more distant. The emergence of a different urban form, the industrial city, also created new limitations. These changes had a specific impact on Phoenix. By 1920 it had become the dominant city in Arizona and had increased its role within the Southwest, but it lagged far behind other western cities.

In reality, Phoenix had developed into a city like Topeka, another state capitol, similar in population and also dependent on agriculture. After 1920 Phoenicians' vision of their city's future comprised only a larger version of its past. Still referring to their Valley as "America's Egypt," Phoenicians expected it to remain a primary sector economy, reliant on agriculture, with some marketing of raw materials from nearby mines and forests, and with little increase in manufacturing.[1] Hoping for more tourism, they boasted about the dry desert air, warm winters, and the dramatic scenery. Phoenicians valued nature, but primarily for how it could be transformed into a saleable commodity to tourists, productive fields for farmers, or residential areas replete with trees, flowers, and greenery. Touting their city for its "civilizing" social institutions, they saw it as ideal for raising families, as a place of affordable homes, pleasant parks, and good schools. Finally, most Phoenicians spent little time on city politics or government beyond their concern with basic services.

World War II divides the history of Phoenix and demarcates its Edenic, prewar vision from the postwar, high-tech suburban vision. Of course, some continuity linked these eras. The city's early development had stemmed from cooperative community planning plus effective lobbying to obtain federal funds. This continued during and after the war, as increased spending provided new development opportunities and taught Phoenix leaders more about planning and working with the federal government. Postwar Phoenix also emphasized some characteristics it had previously touted: an area attractive for tourists and health seekers; an economy that included agriculture, wholesale distribution and retail sales; and a place with amenities suitable for families. And views about the natural environment and how to create a pleasing built environment changed very little.

But despite similarities, the two eras show striking differences, most obviously in the city's dramatic increase in size and in its economy. These changes reflected intentional efforts by city leaders to implement a different vision of the city's future, one begun during the war and expanded immediately afterward. For this, Phoenix followed a new model, shifting its orientation away from interior Western cities towards California, drawn by the wartime successes and strategies of its key cities. A blend of electronic and aerospace manufacturing, military spending, and increased tourism were to provide the economic growth to support a burgeoning population.

In broad outline, this strategy was not at all unique, of course. Many communities throughout the West and South pursued the same objectives, competing for military bases and defense contracts, advertising for tourists, and living between air-conditioning and swimming pools. Phoenix differed, not in basic economic goals, but in its striking success, a record especially unusual for a city in the interior West. Why, then, was it so successful? An important part of the answer is the nature of the city's postwar vision, especially its breadth and the connection of its different elements. Economic development was the objective, but Phoenicians saw this linked to a public-private partnership. Building affordable housing and attractive neighborhoods depended on efficient city services, which required creating an effective political and governmental system. For the city to attract and keep an educated workforce and to enrich the quality of community life, it needed to improve its culture and living styles. Besides having resources and vision, Phoenix benefited from the abilities of its leaders. Cooperative decision making and an openness to talented newcomers had characterized city leadership in previous decades, and those attitude proved even more important to the creation of a new Phoenix.

4
Creating a New Vision:
The War and After

HOW THE MILITARY RESHAPED PHOENIX

In its first era, Phoenix had some military connections. This relationship began in the 1860s, to meet Fort McDowell's need for local provisions, and for several decades military supply remained a source of local income. By the 1890s, with the frontier era ending, the military's influence in Arizona and Phoenix receded. The Valley's economy responded again to military influences, briefly, when World War I created a market for long-staple cotton, but when wartime demand evaporated, the agricultural economy returned to its earlier balance.

World War II produced more significant and longer lasting effects in Phoenix, as it did through much of the West. Historians investigating the war's impact within this region differ somewhat about the nature of that change. Gerald Nash's initial claim that the war produced economic shifts that "would have taken more than forty years in peacetime" prompted other studies noting that the economies within the region varied, that federal spending differed by place, and that some of the impacts were temporary. Still, as Nash later argued, the war did serve as a general watershed for the region in terms of military activities, encouraging a technologically oriented economy and inspiring a major population shift.[1] The war years show a higher level of military and defense-related spending in Pacific Coast states, as well as in Texas and Oklahoma, than in interior western states, a pattern also true for western cities (table 4.1). Thus, Phoenix felt the war's impact directly, but its economic experience resembled (while slightly exceeding) that of other cities in the interior West.

Table 4.1 Defense spending in western metropolitan areas, 1940–45: regional median averages (in $ millions).

Region/city	Contracts	Facilities	Total expenses
Pacific Coast	1,737	97	1,834
Texas-Oklahoma	339	83	434
Interior	68	44	150
Phoenix	90	73	163

Source: *County Data Book: 1947,* reported in Carl Abbott, *The Metropolitan Frontier: Cities in the Modern American West* (Tucson: University of Arizona Press, 1993), 10.

Military decisions about facilities reflected different factors. Situating military functions in Pacific Coast cities, most obviously naval facilities, made practical sense because of existing resources and proximity to the ocean. Placing facilities in the interior West to protect them from enemy attacks was also reasonable strategy, but nonmilitary considerations and prior policy also influenced these decisions. New Deal programs had promoted economic development in the West and South, partly by encouraging small businesses. Wartime planners, working through the Defense Plant Corporation (run by the Reconstruction Finance Corporation) and the National Resources Planning Board, embraced the same goals and encouraged the geographic dispersal of defense plants.[2] And by early 1940 the military had decided that geography and climate made it wise to locate air training bases in the southern third of the nation.

The decision to locate military and defense facilities away from the coast made the Valley a potential site, as did its proximity to the burgeoning manufacturing activity in southern California. The area's geography, topography, and climate enhanced its value as a site, but it was still only one of numerous possible locations. The actual placement of facilities resulted from conscious efforts by city leaders. These efforts began in the late 1930s and reflected a web of personal connections, individual actions, and political influence. The war became a watershed in the history of Phoenix partly because it created specific facilities, but it achieved far greater importance because it led city leaders to rethink their understanding of the community's prospects, to create and pursue a new vision for the city. While parts of this vision were apparent in the 1930s, it took the war crisis and the war-induced opportunities to make the new possibilities comprehensible.

Building an Aviation Industry

The impetus for the Valley's wartime expansion of the 1940s had its origins in World War I. The Goodyear Tire and Rubber Company needed long-staple cotton, so it created a subsidiary, the Southwest Cotton Company, which bought land in the Valley and raised cotton. Goodyear Vice President Paul Lichtfield organized this effort, initiating a long-term connection with significant consequences for the Valley.[3] Like many visitors, Litchfield was fascinated with the desert. It confounded his expectations of Sahara-like dunes, for it was "blanketed everywhere with sagebrush and greasewood, the twisted rope that is mesquite, the glistening paloverde." And the effect of adding water, he noted, was almost magical, as "the desert, in the Biblical phrase, blossomed like the rose." Enamored by the area, he bought 160 acres in the west Valley on which he built a home in the 1920s. Although Litchfield assigned daily management of the Arizona enterprise to others, he supervised and maintained his company's connection with the state. In 1918 he helped design the company town of Litchfield Park in the west Valley, which included a company hotel for visiting company executives. In 1929 that facility was converted into a fashionable public resort, the Wigwam, replete with a nine-hole golf course, and in 1931 the company expanded its operations in the area by establishing a tire testing ground.[4]

An early advocate of flying, in 1910 Litchfield started Goodyear's aeronautics department, which produced a rubberized fabric useful for airplanes and for lighter-than-air craft—zeppelins, blimps, and observation balloons. Becoming president in 1926 allowed him to advance the company's aircraft-related manufacturing and experimentation with blimps, and in the 1930s the company produced two aerial aircraft carriers for the military. By the late 1930s Goodyear was filling major government contracts for aircraft components and its K series blimps.[5]

As the demands of military production increased, Lichtfield's familiarity with the Valley and Goodyear's investment there raised new options.

According to Lichtfield:

> With increasing orders coming in from Consolidated and other west coast manufacturers, I talked to Washington about putting up an auxiliary factory in Arizona. Washington did not think much of the idea. Where would I get the labor? But I pressed my point. Much of the work could be done out-of-doors. Planes could be flown and tested every day of the year. Arizona was far enough inland to be safe from enemy air raids, such as might threaten plants on the Pacific coast.[6]

The argument—and Arizona's close proximity to southern California, the site of massive aircraft production—were ultimately convincing. In 1941 the Southwest Cotton Company leased land near Litchfield Park to the government, and the Defense Plant Corporation erected a factory in which the Goodyear Aircraft Corporation built airplane parts, blimps, and balloons. Beginning operations in November 1941, the plant eventually had a workforce of seventy-five hundred employees (figure 4.1). This operation expanded significantly in 1943, when the plant began to modify navy bombers, and to test-fly these aircraft the Litchfield Naval Air Facility was built on adjacent land, with a huge hangar and long runway.[7]

Lichtfield's support for the Valley and its proximity to southern California encouraged the Defense Plant Corporation to fund the construction of two other facilities in the Valley for manufacturing airplane components. In a plant that opened in November 1942 near Sky Harbor Airport, the AiResearch company, headquartered in Los Angeles, made various types of equipment for high-altitude flying. To the west of Phoenix, starting in 1943, Alcoa operated the world's largest aluminum factory, which made aluminum into extruded forms for airplanes. At their peak these plants and the Goodyear facility employed nearly fifteen thousand workers, which had significant, multiple effects on the area. First, the Phoenix population could not meet this labor demand, even after reallocating local workers, so that three-fourths of the manufacturing workers were recent migrants to the Valley from out of state. This large and sudden population influx created a serious housing shortage. Many Phoenicians took in boarders, and the Federal Housing Authority funded the construction of temporary housing projects near the AiResearch and Alcoa plants. Second, this represented a twelvefold increase in the Valley's manufacturing workforce, as skilled workers were attracted and additional workers were trained in useful skills. Many people found these jobs attractive, for manufacturing wages were much higher than what most

Figure 4.1 Wartime employment changed opportunities and ideas in Phoenix. *Source: Arizona Republic*, 6 October 1944, 10.

workers had previously earned, and deposits in Valley banks rose 415 percent from 1939 to 1945.[8]

The Expansion of Military Aviation

The Valley's physical and perceived contours were also reshaped by creation of multiple military facilities to train pilots. Central Arizona was ideal for such activities, for it offered substantial areas of level ground and vast expanses without populations that might be bothered by frequent flights. As the area's history of flying had shown, its sunny skies and mild winds were perfect for aviation. An eight-year USDA survey reported that Phoenix had the best flying conditions of seven southwestern cities, for on roughly 95 percent of the days it offered excellent visibility of more than thirteen miles and a high ceiling of more than 9,750 feet.[9]

The Valley's main aviation facility, Sky Harbor Airport, was increasingly affected by federal government involvement, starting with WPA funding for airport improvement in 1937. After passage of the Civil Aeronautics Act of 1938, President Franklin Roosevelt authorized a Civilian Pilot Training Program (CPTP) to expand the nation's inadequate supply of pilots. The outbreak of war in September 1939 led to a major expansion of the program, which included Sky Harbor. After the airport manager, Carl Knier, complained that it could not handle the desired increase, on top of serving the army's Ferry Command, federal funds paid for a major facility expansion. This enabled the training program to grow significantly. In October 1940 Southwest Airlines took over the program from Knier, and by 1942 it ran the second largest CPTP in the nation.

Southwest also won army contracts to provide basic training for military pilots on an expanding number of Valley military airfields. In the spring of 1941 flights began at Thunderbird Field, north of Glendale, which offered primary training to American, Chinese, and British pilots; in September 1941 Falcon Field in northeast Mesa began instructing British cadets; and a second basic training program for American pilots opened in June 1942 at Thunderbird II Field, north of Scottsdale. By the fall of 1942 Southwest Airways employed over sixteen hundred persons in these four programs, and its flight instructors included locals like hotelier John Rockwell (the son-in-law of local notable John C. Adams), as well as in-migrants, like Bob Kersting, a lawyer who would remain in the Valley after the war.[10]

Even more substantial federal investments came in the form of two large army air bases created to provide military pilots with more advanced training. On January 15, 1941, the *Arizona Republic* reported plans to build a large advanced training base in the area. The site chosen for Luke Field, which would become the nation's largest fighter training center, was two miles north of Litchfield Park, in the west Valley. Construction started in March and proceeded rapidly: the first training flights took place in July, and when the first pilots graduated in August, many of what would eventually number 126 buildings were complete. A second major army facility, south of Mesa, was begun on July 16, 1941. Nearly as large as Luke Field and also built during

1941, Williams Field provided basic and intermediate training for bomber and fighter pilots.[11]

The placement of these facilities owed something to the Valley's excellent flying conditions, but two additional factors were also crucial in bringing this about: active public-private cooperation and intense political efforts by Phoenix leaders. Responding to rumors well in advance of the government's decision on the air bases, the city's Aeronautics Commission and the Phoenix Chamber of Commerce had been pressuring Arizona's federal representatives and had traveled to Washington to advance the city's cause. When these efforts bore fruit, and the army decided to locate an air base in the Valley, the Chamber of Commerce quickly arranged land options and financing for 1,440 acres that the city purchased for $40,000 and leased to the army for $1 a year. The city also convinced the utility company to extend service to the base and arranged for a railroad spur line. In similar fashion, Mesa acquired four square miles of land for Williams Field and leased it to the army at the $1-a-year rate. The experience in creating proposals for the federal government was invaluable, and the economic benefits from these projects far exceeded these expenses: construction costs alone totaled $6.2 million, with twenty-five hundred men employed in building Williams, and Luke's annual payroll was $3.5 million.[12]

Anticipating this type of return, many communities and states sought to obtain military facilities, and political factors played some role in the decisions about where to locate these facilities. In this struggle Arizona benefited considerably from the skills and position of Senator Carl Hayden. First elected in 1912 as the new state's only congressman, Hayden advanced to the Senate in 1926, where he would remain for forty-two years (the record for longest senatorial service until it was surpassed in 1998). Hayden described himself, modestly but accurately, as "a work horse, not a show horse"; he was known for diligent committee service and for rarely speaking on the Senate floor. Like many western politicians of the era, Hayden focused, not on ideology, but on resources. For any Arizona politician, water was the important resource, and this topic dominated Hayden's career: from his lobbying as a citizen in 1903 for the Salt River Project, to congressional negotiations over the division of Colorado River water in the 1920s—and Arizona's subsequent dispute of that compact—to his last senatorial accomplishment, the authorization of the Central Arizona Project in 1968. But Hayden's focus on water was in service to his larger goal of developing Arizona. Like other western politicians, he saw many ways the federal government could assist this goal, and he pursued those opportunities in Plunkitt-like fashion.

But while Hayden was no ideologue, he did hold to broader political ideals, consistently voting for FDR's policies and supporting him in key disputes. In the struggle over FDR's Supreme Court plan in 1937, Hayden publically criticized the court's "ultra-conservative majority" and lauded Justice Charles Evans Hughes' retreat from the confrontation. Such loyalty and his status as one of the most senior Democrats in the Senate won him an attentive hearing whenever he asked administration officials to place facilities in the Grand Canyon state. Correctly noting that "Carl carried a lot of clout in Washington," Frank Snell later reported that Hayden had "played a very important part" in the placement of these bases and that his involvement had also been crucial in getting the Alcoa factory located in the Valley.[13]

Hayden's success in winning federal support and contracts created major opportunities for developing a construction industry, and Del Webb was especially skillful in responding to these possibilities.[14] Growing up in California, Webb was a carpenter and baseball player until an accident ended his sports career and typhoid fever nearly ended his life. After a year's recuperation, Webb moved to Arizona for his health. Arriving in 1928, he worked as a carpenter until the contractor for an A. J. Bayless grocery store ran into difficulties, and Webb completed the job. During the initial years of the Depression Webb maintained his new business by building more grocery stores and other small buildings; later, he built larger stores for Sears, Montgomery Wards, and J. J. Newberry. Driven and highly organized, Webb succeeded by "following the money," and this meant government contracts. His state contracts included a pyramid tomb for Governor George W. P. Hunt in Papago Park and an addition to the State Capitol in 1938, but the federal government offered far greater opportunities. Concluding that "construction is no longer a private enterprise but rather a subsidiary of the federal government," Webb acted accordingly. He successfully pursued many federally funded construction projects, including the Phoenix Post Office (1935) and the construction camp for the Bartlett Dam.[15]

Military spending on building projects beginning in the late 1930s created even more opportunities, which Webb fully exploited. Rather than simply bidding on jobs, Webb put together a planning staff and, as Ted O'Malley later recalled, "he was sitting on the doorstep in Washington, D.C., and taking advantage of everything they could possibly pass out."[16] Starting in 1941 with a major renovation and expansion project at the army's Fort Huachuca, near the Mexican border, Webb worked simultaneously on building Luke and

Williams airfields. He went on to build nearly every military installation in Arizona, plus other facilities like the Japanese internment camps and POW camps. By 1941 his construction firm was the largest in the Southwest, and with other work throughout the area during the war, by 1945 he was positioned to work across the nation on the largest types of projects.

The Military and Phoenix Politics

Beyond training city leaders in project-building skills and creating military facilities, the war impacted Phoenix through the presence of men in uniform. The Army Desert Training Center, established by General George S. Patton, covered an area of 350 by 250 miles in western Arizona and southeastern California and included two bases (Camps Horn and Hyder) roughly 100 miles west of Phoenix. With troop trains constantly crossing the Valley and caravans of vehicles coming from the camps and airfields, Phoenix was flooded by young men looking to spend money and find entertainment. Rowdiness became a problem in Phoenix, as it did in all towns in this area. One night soldiers took over Yuma; on another occasion 300 troops rioted in Las Vegas. Racial tensions complicated these conditions, and armed confrontations involving black troops occurred in Phoenix and Indio, California.[17]

The presence of soldiers significantly increased the city's problems with gambling and prostitution. During the interwar years Phoenix, like many communities, had used unofficial regulation to control these vices. This policy had proved relatively effective, but the huge influx of military personnel created demands and opportunities that overwhelmed that system. Alarmed by a rising number of cases of venereal disease and dissatisfied with the city's response, on November 30, 1942, Colonel Ross Hoyt, the military control officer for all area airfields, employed a familiar tactic used successfully by military officials in Las Vegas, Fort Worth, and Savannah: he declared Phoenix temporarily off limits to all airfield personnel and threatened to make the order permanent unless the city cracked down effectively on vice.[18]

Because city leaders acknowledged that military "pay rolls constitute one of the community's largest sources of revenue," Hoyt's action transformed what many had considered a troublesome but essentially inevitable condition into a major political crisis.[19] By connecting political decisions with the city's economic health, it reengaged leading businessmen with management of the city. Phoenix officials sought to resolve the crisis by closing brothels, arresting prostitutes, controlling hotels, prosecuting taxi drivers who procured prostitutes, and establishing venereal clinics. While offering to "follow implicitly" whatever the military suggested, the comments of city officials showed their belief that the problem could not be easily controlled and perhaps not entirely eliminated. Military leaders labeled the city's efforts as half hearted, yet they knew the problem was complex and went beyond the brothels, for they admitted that "most of the disease cases we now encounter are nonprofessional." Their proposed solutions to this problem ventured onto treacherous political and legal grounds of broad restrictions on minors and controls of "suspect" women.[20]

A stalemate continued over the next several weeks, as city leaders touted arrests and increased restrictions, while the military judged their actions "ineffectual." Indicating the level of frustration with this crisis, the proposed violations of civil liberties became more draconian. State Adjutant General A. M. Tuthill claimed that the guilty women could easily be run out of the state. Phoenix City Manager Richard Smith recommended stopping incoming trains to check for prostitutes. And Governor Sidney Osborn threatened to declare martial law.[21]

Seeking an alternative to this escalating rhetoric and what he considered an uncooperative city leadership, on December 12 Colonel Hoyt contacted Frank Snell, now chairman of the local USO and a major leader of the Chamber of Commerce, and warned that he might make the off-limits order permanent. Snell immediately conferred with the chamber's board of directors, who forced city commissioners to meet them at the Adams Hotel. They talked into the early morning hours of December 15, with Snell, Wes Knorpp, and other chamber leaders demanding the appointment of a new city clerk, manager, and police chief. Snell defined this as a political management problem and explained that "we don't know that they're bad or inefficient or that there's anything else wrong with them, but we just don't have confidence in them." Faced with such nonnegotiable demands, the commissioners acquiesced in what Snell later called the "Card Room Putsch." The replacement of these officials satisfied Colonel Hoyt, who also reported a significant decline of new venereal cases, and on December 19 he lifted the off-limits order.[22]

Three weeks later, no longer facing the military's threat, the commission reversed itself and rehired the original officials. The newly politicized chamber leaders were furious, viewing this as duplicity and a weakness on moral issues, and they determined to pursue larger political changes. Organizing the Phoenix Citizens Good Government Council, they supported two candidates for city commission in the March 1943 election. Their victory, and subsequent election victories in 1944 and 1945, brought control of the city commission and even greater changes to city politics, which now reverberated with charges of inefficiency, cronyism, vice, and corruption.[23]

The war affected Phoenix, but not primarily, as in many cities, because of extensive investment (table 4.1). Rather, it provided lessons in development. It demonstrated the vital importance of personal contacts, both in making decisions and in getting things done. It also showed Phoenicians various methods of public-private cooperation. Both political leaders and private citizens noted how valuable federal government spending could be for the community. Work in the wartime defense plants contrasted dramatically with employment previously available in Phoenix, paying far better and attracting a more skilled and educated workforce. Finally, the war demonstrated the crucial importance and many uses of planning. All of these lessons would help reshape the future of this area.

POSTWAR TRIALS AND SHAPING A NEW VISION

While the defense spending and military activities introduced considerable change to the Valley, victory in September 1945 brought their near cessation, leaving mostly memories and empty buildings as signs of the war experience. The process began even before the guns were silent, when the army camps closed in May 1944. Pilot training also began to conclude in 1944, finishing at Sky Harbor, Thunderbird II, and then Thunderbird by June 1945. The program at Falcon Field just outlasted the war, closing in November. The Naval Air Station at Litchfield Park was turned into a storage facility, while demobilization and a reassessment of America's military needs shut down Luke Field in October 1946.[24] The last action did not surprise or especially disappoint Phoenicians, for they still expected to claim and use the facility for some aviation purpose. In April 1947, however, they were shocked to learn that the military planned to strip the base of virtually every piece of equipment and usable hardware, rendering the structures worthless. An angry city leadership appealed to their senators, and Mayor Ray Busey threatened to use city police to block further removal of equipment. While military authorities quickly halted further action, debate over the status of the base continued for more than a year, before its status was changed from surplus to future reactivation.[25]

While the loss of bases and airfields was disappointing, the disappearance of war manufacturing was potentially devastating. The rapid cancellation of war contracts stopped production and effectively ended the use of the three manufacturing facilities. AiResearch reduced its operations back to its Los

Angeles base, while Goodyear ended its activities by mid-1946. The federal government then declared these to be surplus properties, and Phoenicians hoped some firm would buy and use them. During the summer of 1945 the Alcoa plant seemed the best prospect for continued use, since Alcoa expressed interest, despite some concern over temporary excess productive capacity. This possibility foundered, however, because the federal government objected to Alcoa's virtual monopoly in this industry, and it decided to sell the Phoenix and other western aluminum plants to encourage competition.[26]

These developments seemed to presage a future of economic retrenchment, at least temporarily. Manufacturing, which had been such a minor part of the Phoenix economy before the war, had boomed dramatically during 1942–43, even more strongly than in the nation overall. After declining somewhat in 1944, it plummeted in 1945, dipping below national levels. It seemed headed toward prewar status, bearing out a common prediction "that Phoenix would go back to being pretty much what it had been before the war." Wartime expansion and changes, it appeared, might have been only a deviation, not a basic shift in course.[27]

Instead, this postwar slump proved both temporary and brief, yet it highlights the complexity of the city's transition into a new phase of development. Facilities built during the war would prove useful, but not immediately, and the lessons and perspectives encouraged by the war would only bear fruit in the right circumstances. The city's economic recovery and expansion in the immediate postwar period began with characteristics that had previously fueled the Valley's progress. Tourism and health-related migration, which had started in the nineteenth century, helped revived the economy, bringing new revenue and new people into the Valley. Aviation and "climate control," which had developed in the 1930s, were necessary conditions for growth, making it possible for the city to adopt a new orientation. But it was the decisions by the Phoenix leadership, their interest in new directions and planning, which would make a new vision realizable. Their belief that growth was vital and would be generally beneficial shaped their actions and the future of the city.[28]

The Growth of Tourism

Valley boosters began promoting scenic and lifestyle tourism in the 1920s and did so with increased energy in the following decade. Although tourism ebbed during the war, in 1945 boosters moved quickly to take advantage of increasingly favorable conditions. Wartime savings, increased productive capacity, and pent-up desires fueled a huge boom in automobile production; an extensive program of road construction increased significantly after 1956 with the inauguration of the interstate highway system. Americans took to the roads because larger salaries and higher wages meant they could afford to travel; they had time for trips because paid vacations became increasingly common and because Social Security and private pensions enabled retirees to travel.[29]

The Phoenix Chamber of Commerce, as one of its major functions, actively promoted tourism though national advertising campaigns. Earlier efforts had won occasional financial support from local government, but this connection became regularized in the postwar era. By the mid-1950s both Maricopa County and the City of Phoenix were paying $50,000 annually to fund advertising campaigns, and this support rose to $85,000 by 1962. Together with the chamber's own expenditures, and reinforced by the increasingly popular *Arizona Highways* magazine, this yielded an attractive national campaign. It also demonstrated an effective use of public-private cooperation to promote economic development.[30]

Tourism most obviously affected the Valley in terms of lodging. During the prewar era seven major downtown hotels catered to business visitors and vacationers; so, too, did the area's smaller, less expensive hotels, which included some newer facilities in or just beyond the northern section of the Central Business District (CBD). In and just below the southern part of that district a group of second-class hotels catered to working class residents, while a third cluster in the southeastern CBD sector were seedy and rented rooms "by the hour." After the war, downtown hotels catered mostly to business visitors, with roughly 80 percent occupancy, while the increased business trade went mostly to newer hotels built three to five miles further north and to five "highway hotels" constructed on East Van Buren Street, which was U.S. Highway 80 and just north of the airport. These changes in hotel location and occupancy reflected both city growth and a specialization in lodging facilities that emerged from larger cultural and economic shifts begun before the war.[31]

While the San Carlos and the Westward Ho hotels were built in the late 1920s to cater, in part, to wealthier vacationers, their success with that clientele diminished because they provided comfort but not amenities, and downtown Phoenix had relatively few diversions. By contrast, the Arizona Biltmore and the Camelback Inn, built a few years later and some eight miles north of downtown, offered wealthy visitors greater luxury and outdoor activities like swimming or golf. By 1960 the city boasted fourteen resorts, with various services, and eleven of them clustered near Camelback Mountain. But this lodging density was overshadowed by that of north Scottsdale, touting eighteen resorts and twice the number of rooms as in Phoenix resorts. "Guest ranches" also catered to more well-to-do visitors, offering accommodations that were more western in style, although not necessarily rustic. Of the fourteen ranches in the immediate Phoenix area, six were a mile or so south of the resorts, while the others were scattered to the north and west of town.[32] Visitors who stayed at hotels, resorts, and ranches were mostly older, were often retired, arrived by train or plane, and came for health and climate reasons.[33]

The majority of visitors were a bit younger, drove there by car, and stayed at one of the area's many, more affordable motels. By 1961 the Valley boasted 380 motels, 236 of which were in Phoenix, with most along a few major highway routes, primarily Van Buren Street. Bright neon signs advertising availability lit up the roads, with televisions and swimming pools to lure customers. National motel chains, which offered predictable quality and service, were represented by the Bel-Air Motel, Ramada Inn, and Holiday Inn. Trailer courts also offered an option for travelers, providing parking, utility hookups, and sometimes other amenities (figure 4.2). Spaces were relatively inexpensive

Figure 4.2 The ease of trailer life in Phoenix. *Source:* Phoenix History Project, Arizona Historical Society Museum.

and could be rented by the month (rates were as low as eighteen dollars a month), making them attractive for persons with more time to vacation. By 1960 a majority of trailer courts were used for permanent housing, but some offered places for temporary lodging, they were located primarily along the major travel routes, and they were often near motels.[34]

Tourism, and specifically tourist lodgings, grew very rapidly. In 1951 the Valley had rooms for fewer than ten thousand visitors; a decade later that figure had escalated to forty-three thousand. Half of these rooms were in Phoenix and mostly in motels, which were the cheapest accommodations, running five to ten dollars a night for a double. (First-class hotels cost ten to fifteen dollars; and resorts and dude ranches, twenty-five dollars.) Motels were a visible presence and economically significant, comprising 16 percent of the city's entire commercial land area, but they constituted only part of what tourism brought to the city, since lodging made up less than a fourth of all tourism revenues, which included food, recreation, and transportation, among other expenses.

Tourism produced major economic benefits: the total income from tourism increased from $60 million in 1946 to $100 million in 1950 and $290 million in 1960. That exceeded the value of the state's agricultural produce and verged on matching the income from mining. But some businesspersons and economic leaders attempted to downplay the impact of tourism, even claiming (falsely) that "tourists are no longer the vital part of our economy that they once were. You might say they're the frosting on the cake." The reason for this attitude was that tourism provided a limited base for economic development, because it was seasonal. Motels filled with winter tourists, but summer occupancy rates could fall below 50 percent, while restaurant revenues declined by a third. As a result, some facilities, including resorts, closed during the summer. While tourism encouraged growth, it could not provide the basis for the kind of vibrant and powerful economy that some leaders were now seeking.[35]

Migration and Health

The same mild winter temperatures, dry desert air, and dramatic scenery that attracted tourists to visit the Valley also enticed people to move there. Being physically present in the area was often crucial in changing people's preconceptions about Phoenix, and this made tourism additionally important. Part of learning about the area involved culture, demonstrating to visitors that not "every male over twelve wears six guns and spurs" and that "we live in houses, can read and write English, and are not violent." Understanding the physical environment also required firsthand experience. As hotelier Sylvia Byrnes phrased it, "Easterners on their first trips to the Arizona desert were truly visitors in a foreign land." Foreign, yes, but like Paul Litchfield, many succumbed to its charms. Even before postwar tourism, military service had brought involuntary visitors to the Valley and stimulated an interest in the area. Some returned later and settled, men like John Rhodes, a lawyer and later a congressman, or Evan Mecham, who became a successful car dealer and eventually governor. This migration of the ex-military was aided by the G. I. Bill, because the benefits that enabled veterans to buy homes, start businesses, or return to school were portable.[36]

The war had also prompted the migration of civilians, as production needs and job opportunities drew people to Phoenix, and even when war production and those jobs ended, some workers stayed. For others, the mobility induced by war opportunities encouraged them to seek new places and possibilities, following a basic American tradition of mobility. An appreciation of the climate and a growing sense that the Valley was a place of opportunities led people to move or seek the possibility of moving. In the mid-1950s an industrialist reported that in studying Phoenix as a possible plant site his company's survey team "found that the chamber of commerce had on file letters from thousands of skilled and semi-skilled craftsmen from all over the United States who were seeking employment in Arizona. An analysis of this labor market showed that hundreds of precision tool makers, jewelers, specialists in the electrical fields, and supervisory type personnel would move to Arizona provided they could be assured of employment." Mayors, too, received numerous letters of inquiry from persons interested in moving to Phoenix because of the climate and seeking information about economic opportunities.[37]

Motorola found the climate a major advantage in hiring. Plant manager Robert Barton claimed that "we can run an ad in the trade magazines mentioning three places to work—Phoenix, Chicago, and Riverside, in California. We'll draw twenty-five-to-one replies for Phoenix compared with the other cities." Moreover, "We don't have to pay a premium to get them to come here, either. The premium is free—sunshine." Daniel Noble went further and claimed, only half facetiously, that "if the engineers and the scientists of the country knew about the perfection of Phoenix' winter weather and understood the joys of Western living without snow, or ice, or smog, there would be such a rush of applicants for positions that corporations of the country would have to set up shop in Phoenix to stay in business."[38]

Climate influenced the location decisions not only of job seekers but also of those who hired. The decisions by company owners, CEOs, or managers to expand or relocate their companies were frequently made because of their firsthand experiences in the Valley. Many had initially come as winter visitors, and some had purchased homes to use during the season. Thus, Paul Litchfield expanded and renewed Goodyear's facilities in the Valley based on his personal knowledge of the area; Phil Wrigley later brought his Chicago Cubs baseball team for spring training; and John Ross, who bought the home of Delos and Florence Cooke, moved his Aviola Radio Corporation to the Valley. Some part-time residents relocated themselves, like Lewis J. Ruskin, founder of a Chicago drug and pharmaceutical chain, who came to Scottsdale as a winter resident in 1951 and moved there permanently in 1955; while others came more directly for retirement, like *Time* magazine publisher Henry Luce and his wife Clair Booth Luce, congresswoman and ambassador. Still others established another base of operations, like winter visitor Merle Cheney, who, after selling his Cleveland chemical company, moved permanently to the Valley and became a land developer in Scottsdale. Boosters, like Carl Bimson of Valley National Bank, talked explicitly about demonstrating the Valley's natural and business climates to people with wealth and connections in hopes of attracting important new residents and investors.[39]

Some wealthy migrants came for their health. Although the primary Valley promotional theme changed in the 1920s from health to vacation, and despite improved health care throughout the nation, moving to the Arizona desert continued to be a sensible, pain-easing, and sometimes lifesaving prescription for people suffering from respiratory ailments or arthritis. But for every wealthy migrant like John C. Lincoln, many others of minor means came to the Valley seeking health and found an especially opportune environment:[40] like Del Webb, who came in 1928 after suffering from typhoid fever; and John Goettl, the metalworker-turned-manufacturer who arrived in 1934 because of lung problems; and John C. Hall, rejected by the military for health problems, who moved to the Valley in 1943 to work in the AiResearch plant and later became a major home builder.

Of course, most who came did not reach that level of success. Some migrants had few skills, but ill health cuts across lines of wealth and ability, altering the normal dispositions to move and increasing the mobility of persons with skills. Studies throughout the 1950s demonstrated the continuing connection of health and migration to the Valley. One survey in 1952 found that three-fourths of the workers who moved came because of health. An assessment of the area's growth in 1957 claimed that "much of the skilled labor now employed in Arizona's new industries has been on tap for several years, brought to the State by reasons of their own health or that of some members of their family." A careful study done in 1959 found lower levels, but still concluded that health considerations had inspired more than a quarter of the recent migrants.[41]

Overcoming Climate and Distance

Both tourism and health-related migration had greatly aided the Phoenix economy since the nineteenth century, although they gained in importance after the war. By contrast, the traditional problems of climate and distance, which had begun diminishing before the war, were effectively vanquished in the postwar era. Efforts at indoor climate control became quickly and widely successful. By the early 1940s most Phoenix homes had some type of evaporative cooler, and during the war these were even standard in military barracks and other facilities. Production of these units surged after the war, aided by new home construction, and by 1951 nearly every Phoenix home was at least equipped with window units, with central cooling becoming most common. This development greatly improved life in the Valley, easing the oppression of summer heat, reducing the summer exodus, and shifting the economy from seasonal to year-round. The Valley's prewar dominance in manufacturing these units continued into this era; in 1951 five local companies produced over half of the coolers made in the nation, led by the Goettl brothers' International Metal Products and Oscar Palmer's Palmer Manufacturing.[42]

Coolers were a godsend, but given their limited effectiveness during the hottest and more humid weather of July and August, Phoenicians continued to hope for an affordable system of home air-conditioning. During the 1930s, when central air-conditioning units were too expensive for homes or small businesses, various refrigerator manufacturers began building window units. Prices fell in the late 1940s, with improved designs and mass production. Manufacturers and utility companies encouraged the sale of units as providing "year around living comfort," and Phoenix led the nation in the number of homes cooled by window air conditioners. Central air-conditioning became standard in businesses, but cost still restricted the use in homes: by 1955 only 3,782 units had been installed. The situation changed rapidly in the next six years, because of increasing affluence, because of the huge number of new homes built in the Phoenix area, and because the FHA agreed in 1957 to cover the cost of central air-conditioning in new homes. The Salt River Project noted the rapidly growing popularity of such units, rising from 1,199 units installed in 1957 to 2,875 in 1958 and to 3,345 in 1959. By 1960 a quarter of all Phoenix homes had central air, which was twice the number having only window units. Coolers were still twice as common in existing homes, and builders continued to install them, more often in less expensive homes, but central air was increasingly common and desirable.[43]

Even more than coolers, air-conditioning changed Valley living. Providing total climate control, it eliminated any seasonal inconveniences and conveyed a sense of mastery over the unpleasant realities of nature. Both systems took people off the streets and put them indoors, but unlike coolers, which operated with open windows or doors to exhaust moist air, homes with air-conditioning had to be sealed, cutting off street sounds and isolating the inhabitants. A further difference was that because air-conditioning consumed far more energy, it was more expensive to operate, and it increased the Valley's demand for power. Yet utility companies endorsed the change, touting the benefits of better sleep and reduced housework, because homes were less open to dust. A spokesman for Arizona Public Service Company explained that "all in all, air-conditioning is not just cool air. No sir! It's proving to be a new way of life for the family."[44]

Climate was one barrier overcome during these years; distance was the other. The Valley's growth had been shaped by the quality of its transportation links. Phoenix leaders had fought skillfully to connect the city with the transcontinental rail system, a project completed by the direct link finished in 1926. Rail passenger traffic had actually declined nationally in the 1930s but rose during the war, and some anticipated a rosy future for Phoenix. In February 1945 the Southern Pacific Railroad announced plans to operate "new, fast streamlined Southern Pacific trains" to connect Phoenicians "going to Chicago and New Orleans, or to Los Angeles and San Francisco as soon as the equipment can be made available." But instead of expanding, passenger rail traffic shrank, and while Phoenix benefited from rail freight facilities, El Paso and Los Angeles had established leads as distribution centers.[45]

Phoenix's interest in roads had grown with the popularity of automobiles and trucks. The state's Good Roads Association, the state highway department, and the availability of federal highway funds had facilitated the development of a fairly extensive system of federal and state highways within Arizona. The postwar surge of automobile sales and traffic strengthened the importance of maintaining and improving highways. Tourism made this even more vital, for in these decades it was primarily automobile based, shaping the location and nature of motels, as well as providing substantial income for service stations and other auto-related businesses. Trucking, which had developed during the 1930s, expanded significantly, enhancing the position of Phoenix as a distribution center within the state and providing connections to California that offered some alternative to railroad ties. While improved rail and highway connections could improve the Valley's position, they could not lessen the significant distances to important locations other than southern California or alter the linear nature of those connections. But air travel could and did.[46]

Unlike ground transportation, which passed through individual places with limited difference in time or expense, the speed and cost of air travel discouraged many stops and promoted the role of central locations.[47] Starting in the 1930s, Phoenix had provided a convenient stopping place for transcontinental flights, because of the distance limitations for planes of the era and good flying conditions in the Valley. Maintaining direct connections to distant cities—keeping Phoenix the primary flight destination in the Southwest—required the city to make timely investment, and that relied on public perception. Virtually all of the Valley's wartime changes had educated people about aviation and how crucial it was to the Valley's future. While the wartime expansion of Sky Harbor Airport and construction of two air bases and four feeder fields offered concrete forms for future activity, the views and presence of thousand of pilots, students, and trainers percolated through public opinion. All three war production plants manufactured aviation equipment and parts. Moreover, their executives publicly promoted an aviation perspective. Paul Litchfield proposed that "the word *Arizona* should be synonymous with *zone of the air*" and argued that "Arizona is now in a position to take part in this future development." In 1944 the manager of AiResearch Manufacturing Company told the Tempe Chamber of Commerce that "rapid growth in air commerce which can be expected to materialize in the near future promises to have a great influence on every type of business in the Salt River Valley and will affect the lives of nearly every Arizona resident."[48]

That growth challenged the hopes of Phoenix in 1946. Because the new, larger planes were unable to land safely at Sky Harbor, both American Airlines and TWA decided to drop Phoenix from their transcontinental routes. The city responded immediately, as voters passed bonds to expand the airport and extend the runways, and service quickly resumed. The continuing need for expansion and improvements led to additional bond approvals in 1948 and 1957, which funded improved runways, a control tower, surrounding roads and buildings, and new terminals in 1952 and 1962. This support showed public awareness that aviation was crucial for city growth, plus an eagerness to seek federal funds. Just as they had previously obtained WPA and other federal funding for Sky Harbor, so city leaders successfully pursued federal dollars available under the 1946 Federal Aid to Airports Program.

Airport expansion went hand in hand with expanded service. Before 1950 both American Airlines and TWA flew nonstop flights from Phoenix to larger cities in California, Texas, and Oklahoma, while two smaller carriers—Frontier and Bonanza—flew to communities within the state and to nearby cities like El Paso and Las Vegas. During the 1950s faster planes extended direct service as far as Seattle and Chicago; Western and Continental airlines added more western travel options; and additional small carriers provided more links to nearby cities. After 1960, jet service offered a further world of opportunities. Tourism flourished because of easy air access, as passenger traffic more than tripled in the next decade, twice as fast as the national increase. By the mid-1950s Sky Harbor was the country's tenth busiest airport in passenger service; in 1961 it ranked sixth. Aviation meant more than tourism and personal travel. Sky Harbor's location was a key element of its success (although this would be an increasing controversial position), for it gave visiting businesspeople quick access to downtown, only a few miles away. With land near or immediately adjacent to the airport available for business facilities, the airport took on even greater importance. The development strategy that unfolded during this era involved the manufacture of high-value, lightweight goods that could be shipped relatively cheaply by air, combined with easy trucking to and from California. Finally, the arrival of the Arizona Air National Guard in 1952 provided another user of the facility, but it also highlighted the airport's larger connection with national policy and federal spending.[49]

Planning the Future

The postwar expansion of aviation, air-conditioning, and migration created major new economic opportunities, but to take full advantage of them required going beyond traditional booster goals and methods to create a new vision for the city's future and more deliberate action to achieve it. When the war began, Arizonans did not anticipate that it would bring substantial, permanent change to the nation or the Valley. But the war stimulated new thinking about the future because it had concretely illustrated the impact of a dynamic economy that attracted professionals and skilled workers, emphasized the importance of training and technology, showed that government could play a key role in bringing this about, and provided experience in accomplishing these goals. Valley leaders also encountered advocates for change, new industrial leaders like Paul Litchfield and executives from AiResearch, or visiting speakers like Paul Hoffman, the president of the Studebaker auto company and head of the Committee for Economic Development, which focused on postwar economic conversion; Hoffman spoke to the Phoenix Chamber of Commerce on "Your Postwar Future."[50] Stimulated by these influences, some prominent Phoenix businessmen and professionals began thinking about the postwar era as offering more than a return to peace and the prewar status quo. Their vision of the city's future differed from its past, it was holistic—involving political, social, and cultural changes—and it required deliberate action. But how should they plan for that new future and how could they accomplish that plan?

California cities offered examples of how to proceed, particularly San Diego. In July 1942, with the war only seven months old, it began postwar planning, probably the earliest effort by any city. A committee with representatives of various economic interests as well as several public officials, and funded by $240,000 from the San Diego Chamber of Commerce, commissioned a study and a postwar plan. The major recommendations emphasized military bases, aircraft manufacturing—a relatively "clean" industry that would not bring serious pollution—and tourism and indicated the need to plan for a range of urban services.[51] After the committee completed its work, it organized a celebration for October 1944 and invited guests from Arizona, including Phoenix Mayor J. R. Fleming, Phoenix Chamber of Commerce President W. C. Quebedeaux, Paul Litchfield, and Frank Snell. Speaking at the event, Arizona Secretary of State Dan Garvey presented a response quite unaffected by this exemplar of postwar planning and suggested a partnership between San Diego and Arizona. "'You have the port, the industries, the skilled labor market, and the B-24s,' he said. 'We have the minerals, the foods, the timber, the cowboys, and the sunshine.'" Garvey saw nothing to emulate and envisioned a future for the state that would differ little from the past.[52]

Garvey's lack of perception was typical of the state's political leadership, which had been slow to think creatively about change or about planning for the future. During the 1930s the state had responded, narrowly, to various New Deal programs with ideas for specific actions, but it had avoided the larger questions. The main federal agency for planning, the National Resources Planning Board (NRPB), started in 1935 by emphasizing national planning, but from 1941 until its demise in 1943 it encouraged planning on regional and state levels. It organized a conference on postwar planning for western states in October 1943, but Arizona did not participate. In February 1944, a second meeting attracted representatives from five states, but not from Arizona.[53]

The first signs of change appeared in October 1944, when Governor Sidney Osborn and Senator Hayden decided to organize meetings with the heads of large industries in the state, "particularly the war plants, soon, to determine what can be done from a governmental standpoint to encourage expansion of industry in Arizona." This reflected only interest, not an actual plan, but it did show a new awareness, which Osborn continued when he hosted the western governors conference in December.[54]

The following year saw growing discussions of economic development and suggestions for enhancing the role of government. For example, on December 16, 1945, Arizona Corporation Commissioner William Eden declared that the state's future required industrialization, for its traditional "raw material economy" made the state a "colony of Eastern interests" and retarded income development. If the ultimate goal was clear to Eden, the means to accomplish it were not. Raising questions about freight rates, about subsidizing industry, and about distinguishing between "healthy and diseased industries," he proposed contracting for an economic study, for "at present no one seems to know what it is all about." Noting reports that some business leaders were organizing to push economic development, he argued that success required a joint effort by business, labor, and government.[55]

Phoenix did not follow Eden's suggestion for a broadly based group, or the NRPB model of government planning, or the San Diego model of government involvement in a business-led effort. It likewise ignored the element common to all three approaches—contracting for an economic study. Instead, the Chamber of Commerce established its own plan for economic development. But while the initial thrust was rather narrowly business directed and economically oriented, the type of economic development being sought had connections with political and cultural matters that would lead to a broader definition of the planning process and involvement by a greater range of participants.

In the early 1940s the chamber was a modest-sized community group of about five hundred members—businesspersons and some professionals— and included members of the different service clubs. Part of its attraction was purely social, but members also found the meetings valuable occasions for networking. Over the years the chamber had promoted various issues, such as Valley beautification and road building. In the 1920s it began running periodic advertising campaigns to promote tourism, but its economic perspective consistently placed agriculture as the top concern. In 1944 the organization began addressing the larger issues of economic change. Prompted by its president, F. W. Albury, the chamber appointed a Post-War Development Committee, with subcommittees on aviation and tourism.

In the spring of 1945, chamber President Herbert R. Askins, who would serve as the Assistant Secretary of the Navy (1951–53) in the Truman administration, moved the organization much further toward planning and a new economy. New bylaws defined the chamber's purpose as economic development, and, aiming to extend the type of activity that successfully placed Luke Air Field, they allowed the organization to purchase and hold property for that purpose. More than a dozen committees were created to advise the chamber about manufacturing, conventions, public relations, and state trade. To manage this much larger program, the chamber abandoned its strictly volunteer tradition, hiring a full-time staff, including a public relations director who had worked for Goodyear, and recruiting Lewis E. Haas from San Francisco as the new director. This clear focus and an energetic membership drive boosted total membership to nearly two thousand by the end of the decade and made the organization a driving force in the Valley's future.[56]

Phoenix Leaders and a New Vision

The chamber and its formal leadership were vital in planning and realizing a new economic vision for the city, but achieving this new economy depended on making numerous changes in urban governance, politics, education, and cultural life. For action in these areas, as well as in economic development, certain individuals played crucial leadership roles. This postwar leadership included many men who had been influential during the 1930s, but like that earlier group, they readily embraced new members and a younger generation. This openness was matched by diversity in occupation, religion, and political interests. All of them belonged to the same basic economic group, however, and they shared the same civic commitment. Most importantly, living in close proximity, they served and ran the same associations and service clubs, and they met socially in the Arizona Room in the Luhrs Hotel or at the Phoenix Country Club. Their personal connections, their face-to-face contacts, and their shared experiences greatly helped them achieve agreement and obtain support in implementing ideas about community development. [57]

Among the most visible leaders were downtown merchants, especially the owners of the three downtown department stores—Abe and Charles Korrick, Harold Diamond, and Bob and Barry Goldwater. Since 1900 they (and Baron Goldwater before 1929) had been crucial players in developing the city's economy. Operating out of both economic self-interest and civic regard, they had been closely attentive to developing downtown and various civic functions, and they had been part of the group at the Arizona Room. They remained important players during this period, although their influence would later diminish with the decline of downtown and the growth of the city. Barry Goldwater was the obvious exception to this shift, but his role was political, and he soon moved to the national stage.[58]

Builders became increasingly important and numerous within the Phoenix leadership. Del Webb was the most visible and played some role in Phoenix development, but Webb's interests and activities were more national than local. Both Sam Mardian and David Murdock moved to the Valley in the 1940s, and in the early 1950s each shifted profitably from residential to commercial construction. Ted O'Malley was a second-generation Phoenician whose family had founded O'Malley Lumber Company and expanded into various building supply companies, development businesses, and investment firms. Ted worked in these enterprises, participated in the chamber, belonged to many charitable and social groups, and worked especially with hospitals and health care. Newton and Harry Rosenzweig, also a second-generation family, continued the family jewelry stores, invested in development projects, and worked in politics. Other second-generation leaders as well as other young leaders formed the Junior Chamber of Commerce. Meeting socially at the Adams Hotel, they also arranged various projects, and their membership included Frank Murphy and Dr. Les Kober.[59]

Eugene Pulliam was a significance addition to the city's leadership. The owner of a string of midwestern newspapers, headed by the *Indianapolis Star*, Pulliam purchased the *Arizona Republic* and the *Phoenix Gazette* newspapers from Charles Stauffer and Wes Knorpp in 1946. Although Pulliam preferred to work with other community leaders behind the scenes rather than in the public eye, he believed strongly in community service, even more than the previous publishers, and contributed financially to various local causes. Pulliam's primary public interest was politics. He made his papers active participants in public debates, especially on local matters, and pursued a political and economic agenda with a style reminiscent of press barons of an earlier era. Both the *Republic* and the *Gazette* featured front-page editorials and banner headlines, blistering stories and sarcastic critiques, bombast and hyperbole that sometimes seemed nothing more than a vehicle for Pulliam's conservative views—of labor unions, the federal government, the Democratic party, and taxation as the road to socialism. People complained, often rightly, about preferential coverage or limited treatment of some issues, or about slanted stories (denounced as "Pulliamism"). But accusations of bias did not deter Pulliam, and beneath his somewhat combative support of local government, his views periodically reflected a tinge of the Bull Moose Progressivism of his youth, or even his intermittent support of the New Deal.[60]

The most important figures in the postwar era, as they had been in the 1930s, were Walter Bimson and Frank Snell. Walter's influence (and to a lesser extent his brother Carl's) grew along with Valley National Bank. Continuing the successful policies of the 1930s, which included consumer signature loans and small business loans, during the war years he added a simple $300 loan plan for persons serving in the military. In 1945 Valley National Bank made two-thirds of all loans in the Valley and was the largest bank in the Rocky Mountain states area. During the next fifteen years the bank built branch offices and acquired control of other Arizona banks (including Frank Brophy's Bank of Arizona by 1955), becoming the dominant financial force in the Valley and state. Bimson's strategy helped Valley National Bank prosper, which also stimulated the Valley's economic development. His belief in the reciprocal relationship—that promoting Arizona's growth would benefit the bank—also guided his actions and increased his influence. This philosophy of boosterism and interdependence led the bank in 1944 to begin publishing an annual summary of Arizona data, the *Arizona Statistical Review*, and a pamphlet describing Arizona's growth, *Arizona Progress* (1946), which it distributed to banks around the country for decades after.[61]

Bimson's philosophy and his position at Valley National Bank put him at the forefront of important economic and social institutions in the Valley and made him a key actor in efforts to recruit new businesses. His pragmatism and his willingness to use government to advance important goals were vital for the city's success. In addition, his personal interests in culture played a crucial role in the creation and growth of important cultural institutions. A youthful fondness for drawing continued throughout his life, developing into an adult's pleasure in fine art. He was a major benefactor of the Phoenix Art Museum, providing personal financial support, encouraging others to supply assistance, and advocating public funding for an art museum building.[62]

Frank Snell had the greatest influence of any Phoenix leader. "He was probably the most powerful man that ever existed in Arizona," claimed Tom Chauncey, another prominent city leader, at the time of Snell's death. "But I'll tell you, he was humble with it."[63] Equally notable, Snell generally operated behind the scenes or in cooperation with others, using his connections, reputation, and persuasive powers to achieve his goals. Snell's legal work connected him with a widening range of major economic interests; as his firm grew after 1938, so did his contacts. Working for major established interests like Goodyear, he also attracted business from newcomers, such as doing the incorporation work for Sam Mardian's construction company. His involvement in community affairs had further expanded his influence. To solve the 1942 vice crisis, it was Snell that Colonel Hoyt had contacted, and Snell had forced a resolution. In 1945 he helped push the chamber to its new role and served on the committee that hired Lew Haas as director. He obtained crucial refinancing for the chamber, but, marking his importance, the bank agreed to the loan only if Snell remained as vice president.[64]

Convinced that international trade would be important to Phoenix, immediately after the war he helped organize the American Graduate School of International Management, whose board he chaired for six years.[65] In 1945 Snell worked with Walter Bimson and Ted O'Malley to help local investors purchase Central Arizona Light and Power Company from a New York holding company. In 1952 he merged it with several other utility companies to create Arizona Public Service Company, for which he served as corporate counsel and board member. Throughout the decade, Snell worked actively to recruit businesses to Phoenix. Besides economic development, he helped reform city government and revise its politics, serving on the Charter Revision Committee and shaping government personnel through service on the Charter Government Committee. Finally, he contributed to cultural and educational affairs, serving on various boards. More than any other individual, Frank Snell connected the city leaders and manifold elements of life in Phoenix and successfully promoted a new vision for the city.

CONCLUSION

Wartime developments helped transform Phoenix by creating facilities, experiences, and new ideas. Air bases and manufacturing plants offered new economic opportunities, but for the city to attract professionals and skilled workers, it had to support training and technology. The role of government assumed a new importance. The potential impact of federal programs and spending heightened the traditional interest in Washington and reinforced the role of congressional representatives in seeking federal largesse. The Valley's success in obtaining war facilities demonstrated the benefits of planning and of cooperation between local government and private interests; it provided a clear template for how to accomplish this in the future. Finally, the war's effects extended beyond the traumatic lessons of war in general and prompted a new perspective for individuals. The military sent men all over the world, and, as Newton Rosenzweig explained, "it opened my eyes to the fact that the world wasn't just a few square miles out in the middle of the desert here in Arizona."[66] This newfound Phoenician awareness included heeding what other cities were doing, but it also meant an interest in the larger world. In Phoenix this took various forms, like creating an international business school, or the political decisions of Barry Goldwater to endorse internationalist Dwight D. Eisenhower rather than the isolationist Robert Taft in the 1952 presidential election. While postwar Phoenix leaders did not become "one worlders," their broader interest in and awareness of the nation and the world were an important part of their new vision for the city's future.

Aviation also played a key role in this transformation. The city's military experience came almost entirely through its air bases and airplane manufacturing facilities, and they remained central to the postwar economic gains. Federal funds built Sky Harbor Airport into a substantial facility, enabling the Valley to develop economic connections and passenger services that overcame the area's historic obstacles of distance and isolation. Modern Phoenix was a product of the air age—as well as of the age of air-conditioning. The possibility of a year-round economy and comfortable residence, partially realized by prewar evaporative cooling, reached fruition with postwar air-conditioning, made available by FHA support and relative inexpensive hydroelectric power. By contrast, tourism and Arizona's attraction for health seekers had a relatively long tradition, and their impact on migration to the state increased after the war. The demographic and economic changes they brought were matched by an increased interest in economic planning and national developments.

Most importantly, the city's leadership was open to newcomers, linked by friendship and social ties, and was optimistic about future opportunities for themselves and the city. In the immediate postwar period the economic and social leadership was relatively inclusive and connected through a network of organizations. Phoenicians' tradition of participating in voluntary and civic associations grew even stronger during these years, enhanced by a sense of efficacy. Edward "Bud" Jacobson illustrates the nature of these connections. The son of a Chicago lawyer, after a bout of rheumatic fever he followed his doctor's advice and went to Arizona. Upon graduating in 1946 from the University of Arizona law school, a now-healthy Jacobson decided not to return to Chicago and join his father's law firm. Instead, he stayed in Arizona and became the first law clerk for the state's Supreme Court. The reason, he later explained, was that Phoenix was "a very warm place that you could really feel was home. Chicago was pretty big and everything that basically needed doing had been done long ago. Here, it was a sort of 'you all come,' and if anything needed doing, that's the way it was done." He described his involvement in starting the Phoenix Symphony by explaining that "a group of people got together and thought we ought to have one." And he noted that "you can't do that in a big city." He illuminated the city's attraction by his matter-of-fact explanation that "I was simply out here and there were a bunch of eager people wanting to make the town better, and they sort of rang the dinner bell, and we all helped. It wasn't glamorous—it was great."[67]

—

5

Building a New Politics

City government held a central place in the new postwar vision. While economic planning would be largely done by the private sector, especially the Chamber of Commerce, civic leaders recognized that public-private partnership had landed the beneficial defense plants and air bases, and that it was a key part of the strategizing they observed in San Diego. Believing that growth was desirable, possible, and generally beneficial, Phoenix leaders sought a city government that could provide efficient and economical services.[1] But in the 1940s the city administration was already failing to cope, and changing it would require a transformation of local politics.

In struggling against entrenched political groups and escalating political factionalism, reformers benefited from larger forces affecting demographic and economic growth. Since other southwestern cities experienced similar political battles, these cities and their leaders shared information and developed similar strategies. Even more importantly, the National Municipal League heavily influenced Phoenix politics and governance through publications and direct advice. Its model city charter had inspired Phoenix's original reform charter of 1913. In the 1930s the league transferred its urban consulting activities to the Public Administration Service, and both organizations shared office space in a building on the University of Chicago campus with some twenty other national organizations that dealt with public administration and government officials. These organizations shaped the development of Phoenix government during this period, both directly, through contacts and programs like the All-America City Program, and indirectly, through their influence on other cities and urban leaders.[2]

The city's charter reform movement evolved in two stages. The first (1947–48) saw the writing and adoption of an amended charter; the second (in 1949) involved the creation of a political movement, the Charter Government Committee (CGC), to safeguard those changes and to promote an effective city administration. This committee, and the larger group it represented, proved a highly effective political force, winning virtually every mayor and council race for twenty-five years. This resulted partly from the electoral system the charter created, and partly because of the development and implementation of effective political strategies. However, the group's electoral success also reflected the effectiveness of city governance during this era. Beneath the gloss that the charter group and the city government applied to their management of city affairs, Phoenix city government created a record of considerable success in an era of enormous growth. Its decisions about city services and its highly effective management were essential for the city's expansion and prosperity.

POLITICAL CONFLICT

When the city commission reneged in 1943 on the "card room putsch" deal to fire city officials, it started a political dynamic that dominated city politics for the rest of the decade. Chamber leaders organized the Phoenix Citizens Good Government Council (PCGGC), which supported candidates who won the annual city elections from 1943 to 1945 and controlled city government. It attempted to curb vice and encourage city growth, and in its efforts to promote more general reform, the commission contracted for a study of city government. Seeking change was not novel: in 1941 former mayors Walter Thalheimer and Dr. Reed Shupe had proposed basic revisions of the city charter, and more charter amendments were on the ballot in the fall of 1945, but like most initiatives, these were rejected by voters.[3] In 1940 the commission had hired the Public Administration Service to study and make recommendations for city parks. But selecting that organization to examine the entire system of local government in 1945 was a much more significant step: it would produce a detailed document, and, knowing the organization's perspective, one could predict at least some of its recommendations.[4]

Completed in December 1945, the study consisted of ten reports, which were printed serially in the *Arizona Republic* and *Phoenix Gazette*. Some of the recommended changes had been proffered before, but as part of a comprehensive evaluation and governmental revamping and because the Public Administration Service had independent standing, they received more consideration. The central conclusion was that strengthening city administration required abandoning the existing "weak manager" system. In particular, the reports advocated transforming the city manager into an independent administrator, consolidating various boards and agencies into the main structure of city government, and strengthening the municipal civil service system. They proposed cooperating with the county on health and libraries, adding equipment for the fire department, and completing a "sorely needed" reorganization of the police department. It was, as intended, a thorough review of city administration, and it proposed comprehensive and cohesive changes, though the study did not address a possible economic role for the city, which some people were beginning to consider.[5]

With the ink on this study not yet dry, political dynamics and discussions in Phoenix shifted.[6] In the February 1946 election, the PCGGC lost control of city government to a new Greater Phoenix Ticket, created by Ray Busey. Elected mayor, and with two allies elected to the commission, Busey was a local Democratic leader who criticized the PCGGC as the tool of a small group of businessmen, and he proposed charter revisions that would include district representation. The 1947 contest brought a fourth slate representative to the commission, Nicholas Udall, the son of former mayor John Udall and a member of one the state's noted political families.[7] While this seemingly cemented the mayor's control of city government, the political kaleidoscope turned again in the spring of 1947.

In April the city auditor revealed that a serious financial crisis would require increased city revenues, and in May allegations rose anew about official toleration of prostitution. Some favored a policy of constraint rather than one of repression because, as Mrs. J. G. Thurman explained, prostitution was inevitable and would cease only "when the male gender grows a halo and sprouts little white wings."[8] What complicated the dispute was a continuing lack of clarity or consensus on whether individual commissioners should have administrative authority over specific city departments, in this case, the police. The dispute split the Greater Phoenix bloc and began a period of harsh political conflict and escalating factionalism. In October the majority bloc heightened the clash by appointing a new city manager, James Deppe, formerly PCGGC's executive secretary.

In May 1948 Nicholas Udall ran for mayor, teaming with two candidates for commissioner and campaigning on the slogan of "End the Discord at City Hall. We'll Bring Unity to Phoenix."[9] After their election this group immediately abandoned their slogan as they fractured over appointing a replacement commissioner for Udall. The compromise winner represented yet another political faction, the Biz Vets, a coalition of small businessmen and military veterans. Growing increasingly unhappy with Deppe's administration and politics, in August Mayor Udall sought to fire Deppe, charging him with incompetence and with following the direction of the alleged city boss, Ward "Doc" Scheumack, manager of the Valley Paint and Supply Store. Udall's effort failed, and the attempt moved the political conflict to a new level.

By raising the charges of bossism and corruption, Udall connected to political rhetoric with a long tradition in American politics, rhetoric which was filling the nation's newspapers and airwaves in the postwar era. Urban reformers throughout the Southwest borrowed the language and complaints that were standard fare in larger Eastern cities and that would gain great national visibility in the congressional hearings of 1950–51. In Phoenix, this charge would win increasing currency among reformers and especially in Phoenix newspapers. Doc Scheumack wielded far less political influence than his critics suggested, but the reports had currency because both he and his detractors, including Udall, found it useful to exaggerate his power.[10]

This clash was most important because of how it shaped the subsequent struggle. By publically denouncing Scheumack, Udall brought him into the open, and he became a visible and increasingly active political player. Deppe's response to Udall completed his own transformation and clarified a basic weakness in the political system. The most common criticism of Phoenix government—by contemporaries and later historians—was the brief tenure of city managers, but Deppe showed that stability could be worse.[11] Previous managers had been objects of political disputes; Deppe altered this pattern and became, himself, a political actor. By aligning himself with changing commission majorities, firing city employees for political reasons, and linking himself with outside political forces—increasingly to Scheumack—Deppe threatened to change the nature of city governance in fundamental ways. The combined effects of factionalism, the intrusion of outside forces, and a politically active manager became even more obvious during the following year.

FROM CHARTER REFORM TO CHARTER GOVERNMENT

At the same time that factionalism heated up after the summer of 1947, Ray Busey revived the issue of reforming the city charter by announcing on October 23, 1947, the formation of a forty-person Charter Revision Committee. As Busey accurately observed, "These people were carefully selected to represent practically every facet of our social structure. Both major political parties and most of the religious beliefs were evident among them. Capital, labor, education, national and racial backgrounds, as well as industrial men were there." It was a uniquely diverse and powerful group. Some members had political experience, including four former mayors and a number of judges; others had useful expertise; and many were prominent community leaders, like Frank Snell. Working under the chairmanship of Charles Bernstein, a lawyer and head of the Chamber of Commerce, the committee finished its work in August 1948.[12]

The committee had considered several options, including Udall's plan for a strong mayor who would be separate from the council and Busey's suggestion for choosing council members in partisan elections from districts. However, it rejected them in favor of proposals that more closely reflected the Public Administration Service recommendations and, as later mayor Jack Williams noted, were "the essential features of the model charter of the National Municipal League." Specifically, they proposed changing to a council form of government; eliminating the administrative duties of council members; increasing the city manager's authority and permitting the selection of a nonresident as manager; increasing the council membership to six; electing all members biennially at the same election; and choosing members at-large in a nonpartisan election. This structure closely resembled what a number of southwestern cities—including Dallas, San Antonio, Albuquerque, and San Diego—were adopting, reflecting both similar influences and shared information.[13]

Voters overwhelmingly endorsed these proposals in November 1948, as a vigorous campaign by the committee and Pulliam's newspapers defeated the public opposition of three commissioners, Deppe, and Scheumack. But instead of settling the issues and bringing the changes that supporters expected, a period of more intense political manipulation and conflict began. To fill the two new council positions created by the new charter, the three anticharter members chose like-minded candidates, ignoring public sentiment; this enlarged majority immediately reappointed Manager Deppe, effectively negating a major aim of charter revision and the public vote. Deppe grew bolder in January, firing the city clerk for political reasons, and when the council deadlocked over selecting a replacement for a council member who had resigned, the new clerk cast the deciding vote. A few months later, Deppe fired an additional five officials for political reasons. In March 1949 another audit revealed that lower revenues and higher expenses—some linked to poor administration—had created a deficit in the city budget, requiring a special election to approve a half-cent sales tax. June saw renewed allegations that city officials were tolerating increased prostitution and gambling. Councilman Jack Blaine was particularly incensed, accusing Manager Deppe of permitting gambling at the dog racing track and in the Arizona Club and of allowing brothels to remain open because "you are merely the tool of Doc Scheumack."[14]

In July 1949 anger at political manipulation, factionalism, fiscal malad-ministration, and allegations of corruption sparked the organization of a committee that would control the next quarter century of the city's political history. Several months earlier, Dix Price, president of Young Democrats, and Ronald Webster, head of Young Republicans, had decided to act cooperatively to oust the existing political administration. Learning that Alfred Knight had initiated similar efforts with an older group of businessmen, they developed a joint plan of action, and in July they formed the Charter Government Com-mittee (CGC) to select a slate of candidates for city office. Despite similar names, the CGC had different origins than the Charter Revision group, it was much larger (100 members), and—as discussed below—its membership dif-fered in important ways.[15]

But despite the differences, the two groups had similar methods and structure, and what connected them was the ethos of the National Municipal League (NML). Its principles had shaped the new form of government, and the NML's 1934 pamphlet *The Cincinnati Plan of Citizen Organization for Political Activity* described how to organize and operate a group exactly like the CGC. Reform leaders did not refer publicly to this publication, but the Charter Revision Committee relied on advice from the NML, and their investigation of urban government would certainly have uncovered this important pamphlet. Alfred Knight provided a specific personal connection, for this primary activator of the CGC had lived in Cincinnati and participated in that city's reform movement. And as Amy Bridges observes, "All accounts (including Price's) agree that it was Alfred Knight who had the ideas."[16]

The CGC's initial task was to select candidates for the November election. After some debate, it accepted the request for support from two incumbents: council member Charles Walters and Mayor Nicholas Udall. Of the other five CGC nominees, none had previously held political office, but each had been very active in community organizations, especially the Junior Chamber of Commerce. They held a similar social standing, but they represented both political parties and a range of religious affiliations. Hohen Foster was the managing partner of the Barq Bottling Company; Frank Murphy was a successful insurance man; Harry Rosenzweig was a prominent jeweler; and Margaret Kober, one of several women on the CGC, was the wife of a doctor active in civic affairs and was herself active in numerous health-related groups.[17]

The final slot was initially filled by Jim Vickers, a labor representative, but he withdrew, apparently after being pressured by other labor leaders. This enabled Rosenzweig to seek an acceptance from Barry Goldwater, the committee's consensus choice and the man who had convinced both Murphy and Kober to accept CGC nominations. Handsome, known for his photographs and movies of the state, and widely active in public affairs, he had rejected previous offers and had assured his brother that he would not leave the family store, which they jointly managed, to run for office. But after some discussion and a good deal of bourbon with his boyhood friend, Harry Rosenzweig, Goldwater agreed to run. Feeling guilty for changing his mind and leaving Bob to tend the store, Goldwater penned an explanation, saying, "I don't think a man can live with himself when he asks others to do his dirty work for him. I couldn't criticize the government of this city if I, myself, refused to help." He then reminded Bob of their family's tradition of political service and added, "Don't cuss me too much. It ain't for life, and it may be fun." It was, indeed.[18]

The 1949 contest represented the final step in the political dynamic that began in 1943. Factionalism peaked, with four mayoral candidates, including two "independent" Deppe critics: former mayor Ray Busey and Jack Blaine, councilman and Biz Vets leader. The six council seats drew twenty-three candidates, but the main contest (as it was for mayor) was between two competing slates. The Scheumack-Deppe forces, organized as the Civic Achievement Group, had considerable strengths. The slate included four incumbent councilmen, one of whom was running for mayor; the Phoenix Central Labor Council endorsed three of its council candidates; and it had substantial campaign funds. The thrust of its campaign was claiming credit for improving the airport, parks, and library. The well-financed, well-organized CGC forces mailed postcards to registered voters, ran newspaper ads, and addressed various public meetings throughout the community, with Udall and Goldwater as their leading spokesmen. Their campaign refuted the Civic Achievement Group's claims of responsibility for city improvements, and they discussed topics such as the need for major improvement of the city health department, but they focused on hiring a professional city manager

Figure 5.1 The Charter Government Committee's campaign against corruption was an important reason for its initial success. *Source: Arizona Republic,* 6 November 1949. The Reg Manning Collection, Arizona Collection, Arizona State University Libraries. Courtesy Col. David Manning.

and used a simple underlying theme: the CGC was the "efficient and decent government which will cost you less" alternative to "the political boss system, with its vicious machine (figure 5.1)."[19]

CGC candidates won in a landslide. Udall, who faced three credible opponents, received an impressive 60 percent of the vote. Five of the CGC council candidates averaged two-thirds of the vote, while Goldwater won support from every three of four voters. The results showed the electorate clearly endorsed the ticket as a whole, with only minor variations due to personal popularity. On these grounds the CGC could reasonably claim public endorsement for their platform. In addition, their victory reflected substantial public interest: turnout more than doubled from past elections, to 41 percent of the eligible electorate (and 76 percent of the registered voters).[20]

The election initiated a new era in Phoenix governance and politics. The new council hired a professional city manager, Ray Wilson, who avoided city politics and removed politics from administrative and personnel decisions. Over the next eleven years Wilson reorganized and reduced the number of city departments, reformed budgeting and purchasing procedures, and improved and expanded city services. This nonpolitical administrative efficiency, combined with the city's record of civic activism and involvement in public decisions, helped the city win numerous awards. The election and administrative successes ended the era of nonproductive factionalism and ushered in a period of relative political stability, as CGC slates handily won every election for the next decade.

As part of marking the new era, city leaders worked to create a usable history. Through official documents and in each election campaign, they sought to shape the civic perception of the past, claiming that "from the start political bosses took advantage of weak charter provisions, and the citizens endured years of unstable, inefficient, and oft-times corrupt city government for which Phoenix earned an unenviable national reputation." They cited the turnover of city managers as demonstrating the "instability of city government" and fundamental administrative failure, and they conflated decades of politics into an era of bossism and conflict. Exaggerating the extent and tolerance of vice by claiming the city had been "wide-open," they claimed that "*organized prostitution and gambling were wiped out*" and that the city had gained the "reputation as one of America's cleanest cities." Painting this new past in greater contrast and darker hues was an important step in creating and embracing a new vision of the city's future.[21]

THE NATURE AND SUCCESS OF CHARTER GOVERNMENT

The day following the 1949 election, the CGC chairman, Spencer Nitchie, announced that the group was disbanding, and as originally promised in July the various committees ceased to operate. However, instead of permanently dissolving, the group was actually going into periodic hibernation: over the next twenty-five years, roughly three months before each biennial election, the CGC reappeared to nominate, finance, and campaign for a slate of candidates. To ensure continuity and revival, after an election the CGC chairman retained formal authority; before the next election he revived the organization by appointing an executive committee, and together they selected finance, nominating, and campaign committees.[22]

The Charter Government group adapted this strategy from an approach that the Cincinnati reformers had first developed.[23] Recognizing that reform efforts often failed because they were too ephemeral—"morning glories," in the language of machine politician George Washington Plunkitt—the Ohioans created a permanent organization with a citizen board, a paid staff, and a corps of volunteers. They distinguished between a political machine, which motivated supporters by offering favors, and their organization, a "political party," whose adherents favored certain policies. Charter Government held similar views about machines and politics, preaching a model of "selfless" civic participation as opposed to self-interested, interest-group politics. The CGC went beyond the Cincinnati Plan seeking to avoid "the possibility of the development of a political machine," as Mayor Jack Williams explained, for by disbanding after an election, it could not pressure the government and "there is nothing for a machine to tie to." Government, they believed, should make broad policy decisions based on nonpartisan, citywide standards—what was "good" for "all citizens"—while "politics" was a four-letter word meaning the pursuit of self-interest or the benefit of a limited group. The public good, or common good, would be achieved by allowing able people of goodwill and without personal or political agendas to choose the city's course, leaving the details to administrators. To accomplish this, city government turned to volunteer groups and created citywide committees to decide city funding priorities.[24]

The selection of candidates followed the same approach. The nominating committees acted on recommendations, not applications, and screened them for reputation and possible conflict of interest. They chose people active in service clubs, volunteer organizations, or on city boards or commissions, but not those who were politically experienced or ambitious. The nominees had not previously held elective office and, with a few notable exceptions like Barry Goldwater and Jack Williams, did not hold office afterward. According to Rhes Cornelius, the committee looked for candidates "who don't seek the job—they have to be sort of high-pressured into taking it," people who could be "forced to do it as a matter of civic pride." Jack Williams explained that they would not choose anyone "who has expressed a desire to become a member of the City Council." Partly because of this perspective, the CGC financed and organized their campaigns, and they ran as part of a team. The one clear exception to this selection pattern occurred in 1953 with Adam Diaz. Desiring to have one of their own on the council, Mexican American leaders solicited the aid of then-Senator Barry Goldwater. Not coincidently, Diaz was subsequently nominated and elected.[25]

Both the Cincinnati and Phoenix models were influential throughout the Southwest in the postwar era, as groups in other cities in the region sought to imitate their methods. In 1959, for example, a committee chairman for the Dallas Citizens Charter Association wrote to Mayor Williams for information on how the CGC was organized and operated. The Charter Government group had certainly created a model worth imitating; despite its disclaimer, in nominating and financing candidates it most resembled a successful political machine. But it was not totally divorced from policy perspectives, as reflected in its strong connection with the National Municipal League and its notions of proper city policies. Barry Goldwater spoke at the league's 1950 conference, corresponded with the leadership, and served into the 1960s as one of the league's vice presidents. More important, the city competed successfully for the league's All-America City Award, which was inaugurated in 1949. Phoenix won in 1950 and 1958 (entering but being excluded in 1951 as a previous winner), and it supported the successful candidacy of Maricopa County in 1954.[26]

Significantly, the CGC was not a revival of the Charter Revision Committee of 1947–48, despite their similar names, their overlapping memberships, and their National Municipal League links. Some Charter Revision group members opposed organizing the CGC, in part because it reflected a different approach to government. CGC slates were diverse in certain ways: they had Democrats and Republicans, a range of religious affiliations, at least one woman per council, and, beginning with Adam Diaz in 1953, a Mexican American in one position. Yet neither the CGC nor its candidates represented the full spectrum of the city's population or political groups.[27] The clearest absence was organized labor.

Charter leaders did not discuss this explicitly, but several factors were probably involved. Debates over state labor and tax policies inevitably involved city leaders. Conflict over a 1947 right-to-work initiative undoubtedly created hard feelings, and labor organizations also opposed other legislation of that era, like repeal of the inventory tax in 1949. But it was not inevitable that these differences over economic and tax policies would carry over to the organization of city government and its policies. Indeed, the separation of city government from such other considerations was one of the main policies of charter leaders. But at least a majority of organized labor disagreed. The Phoenix Central Labor Council's endorsements in the 1949 contest put it at odds with the CGC, and it stayed there.[28]

Social factors also played a role. Charter Government leaders were active in civic groups, and they knew each other from business service clubs, the chamber of commerce, and social groups. By contrast, some labor leaders worked in civic associations, but their social contacts and socialization relied more heavily on fraternal organizations, the Democratic party, and, of course, unions. Finally, and most fundamentally, labor disagreed with Charter Government's basic premise that politics should be "selfless." Instead, labor held to an interest-group perspective and saw politics as the allocation of power and benefits. And with their exclusion from the CGC, they enjoyed little of those.

In 1949 the Charter Government slate won by a hefty margin, and their winning percentage rose still further during the 1950s (table 5.1), but these results included hints of future problems. First, opposition to the slate was concentrated in particular city neighborhoods. In 1949 Charter candidates won only a third of the vote in eight of the nine south-central precincts south of Van Buren Street—the poorest areas of town—and barely half in the next tier of precincts reaching to Roosevelt Street; but in the wealthy northwest precincts it averaged nearly 75 percent. Over time the gap diminished, and in 1959 only three precincts gave the Charter slate less than majority support, but the continuing disparity showed clear limits to Charter Government's new vision. Second, from a high of 41 percent of the electorate in 1949, voter turnout dropped in the 1950s. Charter Government aspired to increase citizen participation in government, but, ironically, its electoral dominance had the opposite effect.[29]

A major reason for Charter Government's electoral success was the system in which all council members were selected at-large in the same election. Charter candidates campaigned as a slate, and this showed in the voting results: each member won nearly the same number of votes, with the weakest

Table 5.1 City elections, 1949–59.

Year	Office	Charter Government	%	Votes	Main opposition	Votes	Total	voter turnout
1949	MAYOR	Nicholas Udall	60	13,270	Civic Action Thomas Imler	3,935	22,157	41
	COUNCIL	Average	67	14,103	Average	4,334	21,212	
1951	MAYOR	Nicholas Udall	80	17,381	E. H. Braatelien	4,381	21,762	39
	COUNCIL	Average	79	16,972	Average	4,399	21,371	
1953	MAYOR	Frank Murphy	67	12,086	Economy Jack Choisser	5,940	18,026	29
	COUNCIL	Average	67	11,665	Average	5,250	17,380	
1955	MAYOR	Jack Williams	83	12,858	Taxpayers Sam Levitin	2,544	15,402	27
	COUNCIL	Average	68	12,918	Average	3,246	18,992	
1957	MAYOR	Jack Williams	82	17,128	Democratic Charter Government Rogers Lee	3,845	20,973	23
	COUNCIL	Average	79	15,911	Average	4,305	20,216	
1959	MAYOR	Sam Mardian	71	28,929	Phoenix Russell Kapp	11,860	40,789	32
	COUNCIL	Average	72	27,731	Average	11,014	38,745	

Source: Registered Voters and Votes Cast for Mayor and Council, Primary and General Election, Phoenix, 1949–1979 (Phoenix: City of Phoenix, 1980).

candidate running only about 5.5 percent below the slate's mean vote.[30] While personal popularity or name recognition may have boosted the vote totals of a few persons, incumbency made little difference in the results.

Because a single candidate running alone had little chance of winning, and because citywide campaigns were expensive, critics found it essential to organize their own mayor-council slates. They imitated the CGC strategy of balancing their ticket, especially in religious affiliation, but they differed in several important respects. Instead of experience in citywide service clubs or on government boards, these candidates represented local fraternal organizations, veterans groups like the American Legion, or unions. They were also more explicitly political and partisan—in identification, in having worked for a party organization, or in having held a state or county government job. Most importantly, many were strikingly less elite in occupation, wealth, status, or education. As bus drivers, beauticians, housewives, clerks, or retired railroad workers, they lacked the citywide contacts, the name recognition, and the job-related skills necessary to win in citywide elections without political party help. Only the Phoenix Ticket in 1959 recognized that limitation. Besides a balance of party, religion, and gender, its members held roughly the same status as the Charter Government slate, and several had been active in community organizations. Their prominence and connections forced the CGC to run its most aggressive race since 1949, but its combination of structure, strategy, organization, and candidate selection continued to prove unbeatable.[31]

POLITICAL DEBATES AND CITY SERVICES

City election campaigns in the 1950s involved both style and substance, largely replaying the 1949 campaign debates, but with slightly different emphases.[32] Both sides issued grave warnings about the dangers of bosses and "patronage-hungry politicians," referring to their opponents, and Charter Government supporters frequently linked this rhetoric with denunciations of vice. A voter initiative in 1950 to legalize gambling kept that issue alive and allowed Charter Government to remind voters about prior allegations of open gambling at racetracks and in private clubs.[33] The stakes in this debate were raised in 1953, when Adam Diaz claimed that the Economy Ticket intended to relax controls on vice. This evoked heated rebuttals (and a lawsuit from Ray Busey), and other CGC candidates came to Diaz's defense. In an allegation combining problems of vice and traffic control, John Sullivan reported that "prostitutes ran wild when we were elected to office four years ago," and Margaret Kober touted Charter Government's accomplishment in eliminating prostitution and gambling in 1950 and preventing their return.[34]

In nearly every election, voters heard allegations that non-CGC candidates were seeking support from the Democratic party, but the fear of partisan action was mainly unfounded: some opponents were Democratic notables, but their campaigns were personal and did not reflect formal or organizational support.[35] Democratic affiliation and support might have been an advantage, since Maricopa County voted Democratic for most offices, but the Charter Government argument that there was no Democratic way to pick up garbage seemed persuasive. Furthermore, while many opposition candidates were Democrats, so too were two-thirds of the CGC slates. Most importantly, the meaning of party affiliation was complicated, particularly in connection with political issues. Loyalties formed in earlier times and perhaps other places often rang dissonantly in a postwar Arizona confronting new ideas about the federal government or issues like civil rights. In short, party labels alone were not a very reliable guide to the ideology of Charter Government or its opponents.[36]

Some Charter challengers took another, perhaps clearer, approach by labeling CGC nominees a "country-club council" and claiming that the committee actually ran the city through the city manager's office. In reality, the council members were more socially diverse than this suggests, but nearly all came from the same affluent north-central area of town. An obvious solution to this distribution would have been to elect council members from districts. This was a perennial opposition theme: several opposition tickets specifically proposed it, and CGC candidates denounced it at every opportunity. Mayor Jack Williams, who had gained widespread public recognition as a radio announcer since 1929, responded with the familiar chorus, "There should be no north, no south, no east, and no west," arguing that ward elections would divide and weaken the council.[37]

The persistent discussions of the city government's efficiency revolved primarily around the issue of the city manager. Critics alleged that Wilson, a nonelected administrator, had too much power and offered to replace him with a Phoenix native, while council members and mayors defended him as a professional with a record of great accomplishments. In 1959 mayoral candidate Russell Kapp broadened the complaints to attack the "monolithic bureaucracy long entrenched, controlled by a small group" that had become "contemptuous of the people it is supposed to serve." Financial management also stirred debate. In 1955 mayoral candidate Sam Levitin alleged that Phoenix spent more per capita than any other comparable city—an argument refuted by Councilman Wes Johnson, an accountant by occupation. In both 1955 and 1957 the opposition complained about unfair or inadequate treatment of firefighters and the police and also decried the inadequate city bus service.[38]

The most substantive discussions concerned taxes, which assumed increasing importance and related directly to the larger issues of government management and urban growth. Charter Government officeholders consistently trumpeted their success in reducing property taxes by 25 percent, from $2.28 per $100 of assessed value in 1949 to $1.75 by 1955.[39] Opposition mayoral candidates in both 1957 and 1959 claimed that water rates had increased by one-third during this period, and those revenues were supporting nonwater expenses, a charge that Charter supporters hotly denied.[40] Sam Levitin made a more serious allegation: that Charter Government had failed to repeal the "temporary" city sales tax passed in April 1949, and that without this revenue property taxes would have been $3.09. Levitin argued that the city's economic health and its ability to expand services owed more to sales tax revenues than to government efficiencies. Describing both property and sales taxes as "poor man's taxes," he contended that an income tax would have been more equitable.[41]

Levitin was factually wrong on several counts: voters had made the tax permanent in 1954, and the per capita sales and property taxes totaled less than pre-1949 property taxes.[42] But in raising the larger issues of taxing mechanism and equity, Levitin had identified an emerging Arizona tradition and one that would eventually pose a serious problem for Valley cities. Already in 1950 the state depended on sales taxes more than did other Rocky Mountain states and far more than the national average.[43] After Phoenix lowered property tax rates in 1949 and 1955, it received roughly 30 percent of its revenues from property taxes, about 20 percent from its sales tax, and another 10 percent from the state sales tax.[44] Yet sales taxes, especially on hotels and motels, offered an appropriate method for taxing nonresidents who paid neither income nor property taxes. This included both tourists and persons living outside the city who came for business or pleasure.[45] Thus, equity was important, but reaching it was a more complex challenge than critics admitted. It required including different types of taxation and providing the revenues that were crucial for the city's economic health during a period of vital expansion.

MANAGING AND PLANNING FOR A GROWING CITY

While critics focused on taxes and political structure, Charter Government leaders emphasized the effectiveness of city governance, and with good reason: their accomplishments in planning, management, and delivery of services during the 1950s were very impressive, especially considering the city's condition in 1950 and the challenges created by the city's tremendous growth. This record was largely responsible for Charter's electoral victories and for the city's successful efforts to annex the suburbs expanding around it. Economic conditions during the Depression and war years had hampered previous administrations, but the city officials had also failed in significant ways. During the late 1940s city governments had extended some services, selling bonds to expand the airport (as noted above), water system, and street paving, but these efforts failed to meet the population's growing needs and involved poor administrative decisions, like using long-term bond funds to pay current operating expenses.[46] Postwar inflation posed additional problems by increasing expenses more rapidly than revenues, leading to the budget crisis in 1949.[47] The city council eased the immediate financial difficulty by enacting a temporary sales tax, but that group lacked the vision and will to address the larger financial situation. The city's growth was only possible because Charter Government officials created an efficient city administration and guaranteed adequate city revenues.

Administrative reforms began abruptly in January 1950. Upon taking office, City Manager Ray Wilson instituted numerous significant changes in organization and personnel management, many of which followed the earlier Public Administration Service recommendations. Wilson immediately reorganized city government from twenty-seven reporting agencies to twelve departments, consolidating a dozen agencies into a Department of Public Works and five departments into a Department of Finance. In subsequent years he created departments of planning and of urban renewal. Wilson substantially improved personnel management by establishing a new classification of positions and a new pay plan, plus a personnel committee and employee training programs.[48] During the next decade he cut the employee work week from 48 to 40 hours, improved employee health and pension plans, encouraged the staff to attend professional conferences and write for publications, and purchased data processing machines that increased staff efficiency.[49]

Certain services, notably financial and legal, were made more professional. The finance director redesigned the budget as a "program of municipal services for the year and the means of financing" them, instead of merely stating the estimated revenues and expenditures.[50] To improve fiscal management, Wilson and the director installed an accounting system that followed the professional standards established by the Municipal Finance Officers Association, another organization housed with the NML and PAS. Further developing the connections with such national groups, the city joined the U.S. Conference of Mayors and the American Municipal Association.[51] The rationalization of city practices also involve the recodification of the Phoenix City Code, making current legal information readily available.[52]

The planning department was reactivated in 1951 and was very busy. By 1952 the administration identified twenty-two planning items, and from 1950 to 1960 it produced or contracted for twenty-eight planning reports. Compared with cities of roughly the same size in 1961, Phoenix had a larger planning staff and spent more on such efforts.[53] The city also worked diligently to involve citizens in community planning. In November 1956 Mayor Jack Williams appointed three persons to the Phoenix Growth Committee, and working with numerous civic groups they formed a citizens' committee of 464 people who recommended a $70 million bond issue to fund a broad community development program. Adopted by voters in May 1957, this program and process were the primary reason that Phoenix won the 1958 All-America City Award. In 1961 a similarly created Phoenix Growth Committee involved 742 citizens, and voters also endorsed their $103 million bond program.[54]

Finances complicated Wilson's efforts. Prior budget problems had caused an understaffing of certain departments, plus the more serious problem of the "extremely poor condition of the city's capital goods." The dilapidated state of its motor vehicles (the average age of city trucks, cars, and heavy equipment was over ten years) necessitated extensive spending on replacements.[55] The nature and scope of the city's growth created more general and longer-term complications. The city could by and large keep pace with the need to hire more personnel, but additional infrastructure took preparation time, and the expense often required further bonding authority. Most strikingly, in the late 1950s several annexations brought in large areas needing facilities that took time to build. But long-term strategy required the city to plan for expansion, and through the decade the city generated support for annexation in outlying areas by providing services for a fee. Finally, plans for the city's infrastructure and services needed to take into account the nonresident visitors drawn daily to Phoenix, the center of a growing metropolis.

The city's dynamic growth and its complex planning and administrative needs highlight its successful performance during the 1950s. The number of employees per capita—one measure of administrative efficiency—rose slightly after 1950 (to 124.9 per 10,000), declined by mid-decade, and then dropped significantly (to 65.1) by 1960. Amy Bridges' comparative urban analysis also showed Phoenix in a positive light. Using U.S. Census Bureau calculations on the number of urban employees providing core services, she shows Phoenix was the fifth lowest of seven southwestern cities and much below the levels in eastern, "machine" cities. Phoenix also ranked fifth lowest in taxes, and despite its major bond campaign it ranked a close fourth in lowest debt per capita.[56]

THE TOP JOB: WATER

The city's most important actions concerned water, the lifeblood of development in Phoenix and the Valley. In the previous era, leaders had focused on building dams and canals to distribute an adequate and affordable supply of water to farmers. The new postwar vision of urban development required a new infrastructure. Its dramatic population growth compelled Phoenix to achieve an equally dramatic increase in its sources of water and the construction of huge pipelines, pumping stations, and treatment plants to deliver it. In 1945 the city relied on groundwater from wells near the Verde River and near Scottsdale and on surface water from the Verde River, but these could not meet the city's long-term needs. That guarantee of a sufficient supply of water for the near future came in a 1952 agreement with the Salt River Water Users Association; by 1959 the Salt River Project provided 85 percent of the city's growing water needs. Yet the city continued to explore groundwater sources, such as new wells near Glendale. It acquired additional wells by purchasing private water companies in outlying areas in 1948, 1957, and 1960, but that was done primarily to centralize the water system, enabling the city to control the amount of pumping, and to encourage outlying suburbs to seek annexation.[57]

To deliver this water to a rapidly increasing number of customers, the city needed to construct a substantial and costly infrastructure. Adding to previous expenditures, in 1957 the city dedicated half of its $70 million bond funds to the water system and $33 million of the $103 million approved in 1961 (figure 5.2). Two systems of large pipelines distributed water within the city, each connected to pumping stations and reservoirs. Equally vital, the presedimentation and treatment plants in the city and on the Verde River made the water drinkable. Thus, between 1950 and 1960, the city solved the issues of supply, quality, and delivery, having more than tripled its water production capacity to 242 million gallons per day.[58]

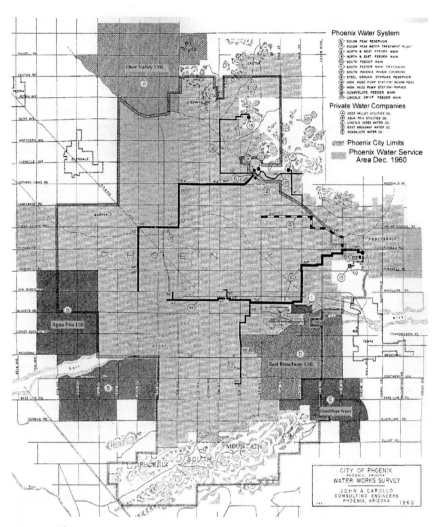

Figure 5.2 Phoenix area water systems in 1960, showing the city's expanding service region and facilities. *Source:* Based on a map in *Official Statement, Relating to the Issuance of $9,000,000 Water System Revenue Bonds, Series 1960: (Payable Solely from Water System Revenues): Interest Exempt from All Present Federal Income Taxes* (Phoenix: City of Phoenix, [1960]), 12.

Consumer usage and expense were also crucial measures of the city's success in managing water. Before 1951 most customers simply paid a flat rate, but by July 1952, the water system had installed meters for all customers. Not surprisingly, usage patterns seem to respond to this change: the average per capita consumption (a rough measure of usage), which had been about 246 gallons per day from 1945 to 1950, dropped to a new level of 212 gallons after 1951. A subsequent drop to a lower average of 189 gallons from 1954 to 1958 suggests an additional influence on usage patterns: the shifting preference of home owners from water-consuming evaporative coolers to air-conditioning. The city also attempted to shape usage for particular goals by modifying price: in 1953 the city council lowered the summer rate for water "to encourage the use of water for lawns, shrubs, and trees." Most important to the city's development was that Phoenix water was cheap, among the least expensive of all major western cities, and roughly 40 percent cheaper than prices charged by private water companies in the Valley.[59]

Water supply and distribution aided the city's economic and social policy goals, but they also forced Phoenicians to think outside of political boundaries. The larger context involved the long-running debates over Colorado River water with other western states, especially California. A second outside connection (which would become much more important later) was raised by the water claims of various central Arizona Indian nations. The interrelated nature of the Valley's hydrology had the most immediate and obvious impact on how postwar Phoenicians thought about water resources. While knowledge of this subject would grow exponentially over time, and most actions were years in the future, already in 1945 some Arizonans were complaining that unregulated pumping was lowering the water table in central Arizona and causing numerous problems.[60] By 1960 Phoenix was working with neighboring cities to plan for additional water supplies and to develop common water treatment plants.[61]

This interrelationship was also evident in the development of a sewage treatment system. Concerns about polluting the groundwater and the spread of contagious disease encouraged the efforts of Phoenix and other Valley governments to reduce the widespread use of privies, cesspools, and septic tanks. In 1956 Phoenix built a sewage treatment plant with Glendale, and in 1957 it connected to the sewage systems in the unincorporated suburbs of Maryvale and Sunnyslope. One-fifth of the 1957 bond funds went to expand this system, including an additional treatment facility. Describing the city's growing system in September 1958, Mayor Jack Williams explained that lines already existed for an area of thirty-five square miles lying north of the city and that lines were planned for territory to the city's south. Another 20 percent of the 1961 bonds were devoted to the sewer system, and additional funds paid for a system of storm sewers. Thus, while the Phoenix sewer system was built to cooperate with surrounding areas, it also aimed to bring them into the city.[62] In effort, money, and success the city focused most on water services.

GETTING AROUND THE CITY

Phoenix leaders faced the same types of issues and implemented the same strategy in dealing with transportation matters, creating an infrastructure to deal with the city's existing needs, but also planning for expansion and connections to the surrounding area. In many respects the story of transportation in postwar Phoenix followed national trends and values. In Phoenix, the American love affair with the automobile became passionate. The number of vehicles tripled from 1947 to 1957, and even factoring in the city's population growth, Phoenicians had more cars (one per 2.7 persons) than the average American (one per 3.0 persons). City traffic, up by half between 1941 and 1947, grew by half again in the next decade, boosted by more cars and because the numbers riding in each car declined by a third, to 2.3 persons.[63]

The city's public transportation system suffered badly during this era, because of the enthusiasm for cars, the city's sprawling and increasingly low density character, and a flawed understanding about the connection between transportation, population, and various economic and ecological issues. By the 1940s, the Phoenix streetcar system, like such systems across the nation, suffered from aging equipment and faulty service, and undercapitalization prevented any improvement or expansion. The Valley's pattern of leapfrog and scattered growth encouraged the greater use of buses, a more flexible mode of transportation. Finally, after a disastrous fire in 1947 destroyed one of the trolley barns, the system closed in 1948.[64]

City officials initially considered the bus system an important service. City publications touted it to residents as "Your Best Bargain," for by instituting various economies, the city held fares to a comparatively low rate of ten cents. Yet in 1952 it also warned about higher costs and the complication of competing with a private line. These problems grew rapidly, with the familiar circular pattern of increased costs and fares leading to declining routes and ridership. Conditions worsened because of competition within the city, legal restrictions that prohibited routes going outside city boundaries, and private companies refusing to sell. When the city finally sold the bus system to a private company in 1959, it was because it had seen no practical alternative and concluded that a system of public transportation was probably unnecessary.[65]

The city's postwar expansion and love of cars produced the sorts of physical changes in Phoenix that appeared across the nation, like dramatic increases in traffic and auto-dependent subdivisions. But they also reflected a new process. Previously, street improvements, such as the paving of existing streets, had represented the modernization of city transportation or the increase of an individual's status related to his or her home. In the more expansive and interconnected postwar city, street improvement in Phoenix became part of a growth dynamic, increasingly dominated by a new and seemingly endless cycle of need and fulfillment. Despite substantial expenditures and repeated efforts at planning during this era, the management of transportation spun increasingly out of the city's control.

Urban growth meant more streets: from 161 miles in 1930 to 346 in 1950 and 1,630 in 1960. This extensive system yielded two problems: road condition and maintenance, and traffic management. Mayors addressed the seriousness of these issues and sought to improve the city's performance. The streets suffered, first, from a lack of pavement: paved streets had increased by 131 miles between 1930 and 1950, but the mileage of unpaved streets had also risen, by 52 miles. The major and continuing problem was that Maricopa County did not require contractors to pave the streets in their subdivisions, and for various reasons—to create a more rural atmosphere, build less expensive houses, or make greater profits—many did not. But more cars and traffic brought greater difficulties with dust, safety, noise, and comfort, necessitating pavement. In addition, the county did not regulate the quality of paving until 1954, and some streets had been poorly paved and needed repair.[66]

Street conditions vitally concerned the city, since it handled street maintenance, which included pavement repair and street oiling. In 1952 a quarter of all paved streets needed repair "soon," and in 1960 the city spent $1 million (5 percent of the total budget) on maintenance. The city handled the far more expensive task of upgrading streets by shifting much of the financial burden to property owners. When half of the home owners on a particular street agreed to make improvements, they would form a neighborhood improvement district. The city paid almost nothing for improving "local" or "collector" streets, which described the vast majority of street mileage (table 5.2); it covered a third of improvement costs for most "arterial" streets; and it used federal aid to pay half the upgrade expenses for streets designated as part of the federal urban highway system.[67] This system offered the advantage of restricting costs to those who benefited directly, instead of spreading them to the entire city; its weaknesses stemmed from burdening individuals and making a citywide problem dependent on individual initiative. By 1960 some 880 miles of city streets were in good condition, but nearly as many, over 750 miles, needed

Table 5.2 Condition of Phoenix streets, 1950 and 1960.

Street condition	1950 All streets	1960 Local or collector	1960 Arterial streets
Paved, good	159	772	108
Needs improvement	188	598	152
Total	347	1370	260

Source: *Phoenix Reports: 2½ Years of Progress: January 1, 1950, to June 30, 1952* (Phoenix: City of Phoenix, 1952), 18; Advance Transportation Planning Team, *Epilogue '83: An Update of Transportation—1980, Then and Now* (Phoenix: City of Phoenix, 1983), 28–29.

work. Predictably, conditions varied by city area. They were worse in the south, with roughly 60 percent of the streets south of Van Buren needing repairs, but even north of that line a third of the streets needed repair.[68]

An overlapping problem was traffic, which grew rapidly in volume and by 1960 began to decline in speed. Phoenix leaders worked diligently on traffic control and safety issues during the decade (table 5.3), and the city won numerous awards for traffic safety. Serious efforts to deal with traffic volume had begun in the 1940s. A major plan in 1949 proposed a practical approach to the central issues of traffic management: building highways and widening arterial streets. Over the next dozen years four more studies monitored the increasing traffic conditions and essentially reiterated the same recommendations. The 1960 Wilbur Smith study reported that "long range street and highway needs in the Phoenix Urban Area and Maricopa County are tremendous by all measures," estimating the necessary expenditures at $228 million. Understandably balking at such an expensive commitment, the city adopted a more modest plan, which neighboring towns also endorsed, maintaining the larger community approach to transportation problems. Yet judging by past performance, even this scaled-back effort provided little assurance of future actions. By 1960 the city had completed some of the 1949 recommendations for widening arterial streets, but it had only built seven miles of the recommended north-south Black Canyon Highway.[69]

Several major problems had stymied highway construction and continued to do so after 1960. The first was inadequate funding. Although the city had fumbled several opportunities to obtain money for planning, state policies severely hampered its ability to get construction funding during this period

Table 5.3 Traffic and safety improvements in Phoenix, 1950–60.

Year	Traffic signals	Walk signals	Streetlights
1950	85	18	1,656
1960	290	314	13,042

Source: Annual Financial Report, 1960–61, vii; "The Phoenix Story of Municipal Government since 1950," 8, October 9, 1961, typescript in box 2, folder 11, City of Phoenix Government Records Collection, Arizona Historical Society, Tempe.

for the substantial miles of needed highways. The malapportioned Arizona legislature grossly underrepresented urban areas, and its priorities for federal highway money reflected a strong rural bias, as did the formula for distributing revenues from the state's (low) gasoline tax. A second obstacle was the opposition from certain businesses. This blocked the initial route consideration in the late 1940s, and it appeared as a major factor in a public hearing in February 1957 on a highway proposal. Businesses in any community worried that a new highway would bypass them; the situation in Phoenix was worse because prominent among the businesses being bypassed were roughly 90 percent of the city's motels. Given their numbers and the importance of tourism to the Phoenix economy, motel owners and their allies were able to prevent the city from making any meaningful progress.[70]

Thus, while Phoenix grew as an automobile-dependent sprawl of suburban housing, this pattern reflected the influence and availability of cars, not highways. In this respect Phoenix differed from most other expanding cities, for its growth occurred in the absence—although some saw a promise—of highway construction. More than certain economic factors and a specific built environment, it was cultural values, mental maps, and future possibilities that powerfully influenced the emerging shape of this city. Expectations drove many Phoenicians to ignore the ugly realities of its nonhighway traffic and the consequences for amenities such as clean air and access to desert open spaces.[71]

GROWTH AND OTHER SERVICES

The same goals that guided the development of the water and transportation infrastructure—managerial efficiency and maintaining connections with surrounding communities—also shaped the development of other services, including public safety. Here, too, city officials struggled to surmount the problems of growth, but in somewhat different ways. Management of the police department was highly politicized during the 1940s, with heated public debates over the enforcement of vice policies and frequent replacement of police chiefs. This, combined with the city's weak finances and a departmental culture that was more traditional and personal than professional, forged the department's relatively weak condition in 1950. Wilson moved quickly to modernize and reorganize operations. He also replaced the fleet of aging police cars, and the department installed an overdue three-way FM radio system. During the next decade the department grew from a force of 173 to 616 officers and 82 civilians, and from 20 cars in 1950 to 291 by 1961. Compared with police departments in cities of a comparable size, Phoenix had standard levels of compensation and equipment, but it ranked below average in numbers of officers per capita, partly because hiring had not caught up with the large increase in population brought by annexations in 1958–60.[72]

A second municipal service, the Phoenix Fire Department, shared similarities with the police, but it also differed in fundamental respects. Both oversaw public safety, but police regulated behavior, while the fire department dealt with economic losses and influenced the cost of insurance. The fire department also expanded during the 1950s, but its increase in personnel, from 171 to 357 firemen, represented only a third of the growth rate for the police force. The fire department also needed more costly equipment and facilities. The city built hydrants, it expanded the fire alarm system, and to its three fire stations as of 1950, it added another seventeen during the decade. Starting with seventeen pieces of relatively old firefighting equipment (averaging 16.5 years of age), the department acquired newer, better, and additional equipment by 1960. However, as reported in a 1961 study and shown in comparative urban data, this still fell short of what was needed.

Given the fire department's dependence on infrastructure, the city's dramatic spatial growth between 1958 and 1960, increasing from 36 to 187 square miles, seriously hampered the department's effectiveness. Although the newly annexed territory contained a few areas with facilities, large areas had none, and the patchwork, or leapfrog, development of subdivisions complicated the task of providing service. The demand for additional city firemen and equipment was also too difficult to meet. As a result, for some years after these annexations, the city retained the services of private fire companies in some areas. In 1960 one-third of the city lacked the recommended level of coverage from fire engines. Compared with twenty-six cities in the same population category, Phoenix had the fewest firemen per capita and less equipment—especially fewer big fire trucks. Tellingly, it was in the lower fire insurance class (with five other cities) and had next-to-the highest number of deficiency points, so that fire insurance was more expensive for home owners.[73]

Phoenix fared better in expanding and improving other services. In 1950 it began depositing garbage in a sanitary landfill instead of a dump; by mid-decade it collected both garbage and trash twice a week and without charge. The park system also grew, as planners forecast a shorter work week and more spare time, requiring "the community to provide facilities whereby this time can be used effectively." To the 1950 total of twenty-two parks, the city added twenty-three (seven of which it annexed from the county). This included the 1959 purchase from the state of Papago Park, a third large park (along with South Mountain and Encanto parks) that would provide various facilities. The city also increased the number of school playgrounds (which were also public recreation places) from twenty-six to ninety-seven. A new library, built in 1952, met the city's needs at the time, but rapid growth soon rendered that facility insufficient. One branch library was completed by 1960, and others were being planned, but it would be some years before library facilities caught up to the city's needs, and in the meantime the several bookmobiles were the main option for people on the city periphery.[74]

By the early 1960s the political and governmental parts of the city leaders' new vision for Phoenix had been substantially accomplished. The factional, personal, and parochial squabbling of the 1940s had been replaced by debates over city policies and larger discussions about city growth. While its opponents denounced Charter Government as rule by a small group, they were largely contesting the distribution of benefits from growth, not the notion that growth was the city's primary goal. Moreover, Charter's striking electoral success indicated both its effective political strategy and its broad community support. Transforming the city's political image was central in its strategies and success, but creating an effective administration was equally vital. Efficient delivery of inexpensive services was the key to the group's political victories, but it was also essential to realizing the larger goals of annexing the surrounding areas and building a vibrant economy. While the definition of necessary services would later be contested, for the period leading into the 1960s Phoenix city government was a striking success.

6
Growing the City:
Economic, Cultural, and Spatial Expansion

The economic and social leaders of Phoenix became politically active not only for the sake of effective and efficient government but also to serve their larger goal of building a bigger and more prosperous city. Several key factors marked their efforts and explain their accomplishment. Their wartime experiences taught them about connections between the military, government, and politics, and they successfully applied those lessons and skills in the postwar era. They recognized the importance of planning, and they understood the interactive relationships between political, economic, and cultural growth.

Leadership was crucial but not sufficient to produce such growth. While the city benefited substantially from national developments and historical trends, the confluence of spending on national defense, the rise of aviation and electronics, and the availability of air-conditioning made growth in the desert possible, but not inevitable. The vision of a new economy did not come to everyone at the same time, and during the first postwar years the city moved somewhat tentatively toward this change. The development of culture, which had been a goal of Phoenix boosters for decades, took on more focus and added significance in this era. Besides traditional expectations and personal preferences, key leaders pushed substantial improvement of the educational and cultural institutions in the Valley, because they recognized these were crucial for recruiting and retaining the skilled and educated workforce that economic development required. And this reflected their belief that growth was generally and broadly beneficial. The combination of these factors enabled the city to prosper, to grow in population, and to annex large amounts of adjacent territory, as well as fostering the transformation of several Valley towns into new suburbs. This metropolitan form differed from the area's previous configuration, as well as from urban patterns in areas further east.

GROWTH OF THE POSTWAR ECONOMY

In important respects the postwar economy of Phoenix continued to reflect the area's inherent character and resources. The fertile soil and plentiful water supply maintained agriculture's vital role in the area's employment and income, while climate encouraged the expansion of tourism and the continued in-migration of health seekers. The growth of air travel and the availability of air-conditioning bolstered both tourism and population growth. The new city leaders had greater aspirations for the city than this, however, drawing on their wartime experiences with defense spending and the income obtainable from electronics and aviation-related manufacturing. But Phoenix faced steep competition from many other cities that had drawn the same lessons, and its hopes for continuity were dashed when the end of World War II brought lower spending for military personnel, weapons, and war-related manufacturing.

California provided the greatest contrast with Phoenix and the best model. Various of its cities had focused on military-related activity for decades, and that had yielded both a substantial investment by the military and a critical mass influencing the economic development of the host cities. World War II significantly affected Phoenix, creating physical structures and new perspectives, but it was America's postwar foreign and military policies that actually changed the Valley's future. As President Harry Truman pressed Congress in the spring of 1947 to increase military assistance to Greece and Turkey, Phoenix was fighting its own battle, threatening to use police to prevent the federal government from removing any buildings from Luke Field. As the Cold War expanded, with the implementation of the Marshall Plan, the establishment of NATO, and continued development of airpower and missiles, America's military budget rose. Finally, the outbreak of the "hot" war in Korea in June 1950 returned America's role and military spending to levels like those of World War II, where they would remain, and this new commitment provided a significant, direct, and continuing impact on Phoenix.[1]

After faltering immediately after the war, Arizona's economy more than tripled from 1947 to 1960, with gains in all economic sectors.[2] Agriculture, the traditional basis of the Valley's economy, flourished during this era, led by increased production of cotton, lettuce, and livestock, and the acreage in production rose to 485,000 acres in 1955 and to 519,160 acres in 1959.[3] The county's retail sector grew nearly sixfold, expanding from 45 to 58 percent of the state's retail sales. Wholesaling also prospered, with more trucking firms, more warehouses of national companies such as Westinghouse, Pittsburgh Glass, and H. J. Heinz, and a nascent international export business.[4] Stimulated especially by the increase in tourism, service-sector employment increased slightly faster than the general rate of economic growth, while the flood of people moving to Phoenix kept construction employment strong at nearly 10 percent of the nonagricultural workforce.[5] Increased employment and economic expansion brought greater prosperity, as Arizona's average annual wages rose from $2,894 in 1949 to $4,697 in 1959.[6]

Manufacturing was the most important sector, because it was the dynamic force that expanded the economy and because manufacturing wages were higher than those in other fields and raised the community's standard of living. In 1949 average annual wages in manufacturing were $3,083, just below construction wages and above the other categories. By 1958 the average had jumped to $5,568, but that included considerable variation by industry (table 6.1).[7] Jobs in manufacturing airplane and aerospace components paid the best and were the most numerous, followed by jobs in manufacturing electrical machinery, other machinery, various types of metal fabrication, and jobs in manufacturing building materials. The least remunerative manufacturing jobs were in apparel and furniture manufacturing. This hierarchy helps to explain the Phoenix plan for economic development and the degree of its success.

The prewar manufacturing base of Phoenix was primarily meatpacking, some metalworks, and minor clothes making. The growing part of that sector was in the production of evaporative coolers, and in 1951 five manufacturing plants produced half of the nation's coolers. But competition and changing market conditions disrupted this pattern. Within a decade three of these firms closed. International Metal Products became the largest cooler manufacturer in the world and employed 850 workers, but after the firm was sold in 1960, its expansion occurred in places other than Phoenix. Other manufacturers adapted to new markets. In 1960 Chill-Vac Cooling (300 workers) produced

Table 6.1 Annual per capita manufacturing wages in Arizona, 1958.

Annual wages	Industry
$ 6,466	Aircraft
$ 5,797	Machinery
$ 5,301	Metal fabrication
$ 4,634	Food, lumber, printing
$ 4,210	Miscellaneous
$ 3,960	Furniture
$ 2,717	Apparel

Source: Calculated from data in *Arizona Statistical Review, 1961* (Phoenix: Valley National Bank, 1961), 21.

air conditioners, and Wright Manufacturing (475 workers) made air conditioners and heat pumps. Goettl Brothers Metal Products shifted in the 1950s to manufacturing window air conditioners and residential units, developing heat pumps by 1960, and then becoming the largest residential air-conditioning contractor in the nation.[8]

Besides manufacturing coolers and air conditioners, the initial postwar hopes for additional manufacturing in Phoenix focused on finding purchasers, or at least tenants, for the three wartime factories. These efforts bore partial success in 1946, when the Aviola Radio Corporation bought the former AiResearch plant to produce radio components, and the Reynolds Metals Company leased the aluminum extrusion plant. This represented some continued production in high-wage industries, but with competition from California and Texas cities in the years of low military budgets, it seemed unlikely that such plants could bring substantial employment.[9]

PLANNING FOR MANUFACTURING

Community leaders increasingly sensed that Phoenix needed an economic plan and a cooperative approach to attracting new businesses. The Chamber of Commerce provided the impetus and general context for this approach. Immediately after the war it reorganized, expanded its membership, and hired a new director, Lew Haas. Initially, through its monthly publication, *Whither Phoenix*, and national advertising campaigns, the chamber promoted the city generally, but focused on tourism and conventions. During the next several years, its interest in business and industrial development increased, providing additional impetus to reform Phoenix city government and change various fiscal and labor policies.[10]

An honest and efficient city government was essential for successful economic development, first, to allay the concerns of local businesses currently outside city boundaries and, second, to make the city attractive to new businesses. The city government also acted directly, contributing money to the chamber's ad campaigns, negotiating inducements for business resettlements, expanding Sky Harbor Airport, and even sending officials like the mayor to recruit specific businesses. In 1949 voters approved the city government's proposal to reduce taxes on manufacturing inventory and equipment; state laws eliminated an inventory tax and a sales tax on manufactured goods sold to the federal government.[11]

Some boosters credited these measures and a 1946 voter-approved Arizona right-to-work law with creating a probusiness climate that prompted subsequent business development, but the desert climate had far greater influence, providing dry air that aided manufacturing and weather that attracted skilled laborers and lowered rates of illness and absenteeism. Businesses gained from a modernized tax system, but cheap land and utilities were more important benefits. Finally, the right-to-work law and newspaper fulminations had a limited effect on the Phoenix labor movement. Unions organized and workers struck, with some success, but their relative failure stemmed more from the nature of the economy—with its large employment in service, retail, and wholesale sectors and the volatile construction business—than from the plans of owners.[12]

Efforts at planned expansion of manufacturing started in 1948 with the chamber's creation of an Industrial Development Committee. In the next two years it achieved some success, with fifty new businesses employing 1,750 people opening in the Phoenix area. The most notable addition was the return of the Goodyear Aircraft Company, which reacquired its wartime plant in 1949 to build plastic pilot enclosures, wings for training planes, and bags for blimps. A decade later it was building support equipment for missiles and employed 2,000 workers. The economy also benefited in 1949 when the Reynolds Metals Company bought and began expanding the aluminum extrusion plant it had been leasing; by 1952 it had become the largest such plant in the world.[13]

Business recruitment accelerated in 1950, boosted by production for the Korean War and the federal policy of disbursing war-related manufacturing. By 1952 an additional seventy new firms opened, providing jobs for 6,680 workers. This included AiResearch, which returned to the Valley in a plant located north of Sky Harbor Airport in 1951 to build gas turbine engines, starters, pneumatic control valves, and (later) precision controls for missiles. By 1960, the company employed 3,800 workers. Other, smaller firms—like the 300-employee Phoenix Parachute Company—opened for the first time. Nearly all the major firms initially focused on aviation and electronics for military use, encouraged by the proximity to the U.S. Army electronics proving ground, established at Fort Huachuca in 1954, and to California. But while this industrial expansion began with military contracts, the plants they financed and the skilled workers they attracted provided both initial prosperity and the basis for increased consumer production in the years to come.[14]

The expansion of manufacturing in Phoenix resulted from a coordinated effort involving the Chamber of Commerce, city government, the Arizona Development Board, and interested businesses. Everyone favored "smoke-less" industries and rejected options like a proposed refinery, because of the potential harm to the environment. They also sought electronics and aviation firms because they employed people with higher income, skills, and education. The recruitment team included a utility company representative (Adrian Babcock), a chamber employee (Floyd Rains), and representatives of the leading banks (James Patrick of Valley National Bank and Patrick Downey of First National Bank of Arizona). Some of the persuasion was personal. Downey, once the industrial relations director for AiResearch, suggested to his former employer, Cliff Garrett, that he could easily reopen in Phoenix simply by hiring back his former employees, many of whom had stayed in town.[15]

More typically, the recruiters "prepared quite extensive charts, maps, dwelling on the tax situation, dwelling on the weather, on the lack of rainfall," and they followed these presentations by inviting company representatives to town. Working with officials of city government, they offered financial incentives but required some payment, believing that "it was not good business to give things away" because companies would behave better "if they paid for it." Recruiters also provided assistance in relocation. Carl Bimson recounted that for one employer, Valley National Bank sent a crew to furnish their employees with information on the cost of homes, type of schools, tax rates, recreation, and the weather. "When they came out, [we] helped to locate them in homes, made special deals for loans."[16]

Their efforts were highly successful, and over the 1950s manufacturing grew much faster than other economic sectors, with its workforce more than doubling to nearly 20 percent of the area's total. The lion's share of this growth resulted from the 290 new manufacturers who had come to the Phoenix area

Table 6.2 New manufacturers in the Phoenix area, 1948–60.

Type	No. of firms	No. of employees	% of all	Notable companies	Products and sizes
Aerospace	13	7,484	31.7%	AiResearch, Goodyear, Sperry Phoenix, Rocket Power	3 firms over 1,000 employees; 3 had under 20.
Electronic	23	6,990	29.6%	GE, Motorola, U.S. Semiconductor	3 firms over 1,000 employees; 11 had under 20.
Manufacturing support	73	2,363	10.0%	Acme Steel, Western Rolling Mills, Garland Steel, National Malleable & Steel Castings Co.	Structural steel, steel rolling mill, products; also plastic. Median no. of employees = 17.
Housing/ building materials	70	2,040	8.7%	Union Gypsum, Jokco Mfg., Palmer Excelsior	Windows and doors; furniture; lights; draperies; air conditioners.
Clothing	18	1,874	8.0%	E. L. Gruber, Albert of Arizona, Grundwald-Marx, Raco Apparel, Penn-Mor Mfg.	All clothes, especially underwear. 6 firms over 100 employees; 8 had under 50.
Food	23	1,187	5.0%	Carnation and Shamrock dairies; Rosita Food Products	5 dairies and bakeries had over 100 employees; others were small.
Other	70	1,645	7.0%		Average = 11 employees.
Total	290	23,583	100.0%		

Source: Calculated from *290 New Manufacturers in the Phoenix Area since March 1, 1948* (Phoenix: Industrial Department, Phoenix Chamber of Commerce, 1960).

since 1948, creating 23,583 jobs and with a payroll of $122 million (table 6.2). Only one in five of those new jobs stemmed from traditional employment in food, clothing, or building materials, which grew partly because of the population increase. Three times as many jobs developed from aviation and electronics, many of them related to military contracts (as were jobs with older firms like Reynolds). These firms were attracted by and further stimulated the growth of subcontractors: tool and die companies, precision grinders, and other skilled machine and engineering firms. Firms like Phoenix Engineering and Manufacturing Company, which grew from 12 to 100 employees during the decade, prospered on work from many of the large companies.[17]

HIGH-TECH FIRMS AND A CHANGING ECONOMY

After the mid-1950s Phoenix attracted a number of significant national companies. One of those was Sperry Phoenix, a subdivision that developed aerospace navigation systems, automatic flight controls, and guidance systems for pilotless drones. Drawn by financial underwriting from the city and community, it started with a research center and hangar near Sky Harbor and completed its major facility in 1957 in Deer Valley, on the city's northwest fringe.[18] In the same year General Electric established its computer division in Phoenix, having won a contract to provide computer equipment for Bank of America. GE quickly established a major presence in the Valley with substantial manufacturing facilities in Deer Valley, main offices in Phoenix, and a computer service center at Arizona State College.[19] By 1960 GE had 2,000 employees, Sperry had 1,100, and they were joined by other aviation and electronic firms such as U.S. Semiconductor and the Aircraft and Electronics Division of the Kaiser Corporation. But easily the largest firm, and the one that significantly shaped the Valley's economic future, was Motorola.

Paul Galvin founded Motorola in 1928 and in 1940 hired a person who would prove crucial to the company's future—Daniel Noble, an engineering professor at Connecticut State College. During the 1930s Noble had developed an educational radio broadcasting station for the school and then converted it to the new FM system; he subsequently designed mobile FM communications systems for the state's forestry and police departments. Noble continued this work for Motorola, and during World War II he created the first FM-based walkie-talkie systems for the military. By the late 1940s Motorola had developed radio communications equipment and had become a leading manufacturer of televisions, but its future, and that of all electronics firms, changed in 1948 with the development of the transistor.[20]

Interested in the possibilities of solid-state electronics, Noble, now the head of research for Motorola, convinced Galvin to establish a research lab. Favoring a southwestern site because of the climate, Noble chose Phoenix for its machine shops and transportation facilities, its strategic location near the New Mexico atomic energy works and California defense contractors, its record of effective wartime production, and its dual character as both a growing urban area and a place with a "resort atmosphere." The lab opened in the winter of 1948–49, but a contract with New Mexico's Sandia Laboratory involving atomic weaponry, followed by the outbreak of the Korean War, changed Noble's plan. Motorola quickly built a military research and production facility in Scottsdale in 1950, and Noble successfully pursued government contracts, particularly with the Atomic Energy Commission. This enabled Motorola to expand its facility in 1956 and prompted the decision to move the headquarters of the Military Electronics Division from Chicago in 1957 to an additional plant in Scottsdale. In subsequent years the division won substantial military contracts working on navigation systems for bombers, instrument flight equipment, missile guidance, and radar-mapping devices.[21]

Although war and the success of military contracts delayed some of the solid-state research Noble had intended, he used that funding to subsidize his research in semiconductors. He also saw technical benefits from this plan. "The government, with contracts, will constantly be working on the leading edge of the art," he later explained, creating new "technical information and techniques, and the general flow of information is relevant to your total movement in the field of electronics." By the mid-1950s Motorola achieved a major advance in developing the first power transistor, which substantially improved the performance of industrial and consumer radios. In 1956 the company created its Semiconductor Products Division and built a Phoenix plant, which it expanded fivefold by 1960 (figure 6.1). In 1966 the division opened a plant to research and manufacture integrated circuits in Mesa, drawn by the city's willingness to pay for and provide roads and utility connections. Thus, by beginning with military contracts and expanding into consumer product production, by the late 1960s Motorola had built five large facilities in the Valley, with two subdivisions employing roughly twenty thousand workers, making it Arizona's largest employer.[22]

But Motorola's importance to the Valley's development went beyond buildings and employees. Noble argued forcefully that Motorola's well-being required a major improvement of higher education in the Valley. To retain its employees and improve itself, Motorola needed its employees to have easy access to good university and graduate-level training, especially in engineering and computer science. But Noble also made a broader argument, contending that the Valley's economic development generally depended on expanding and upgrading the system of higher education.

When Noble arrived in Phoenix in 1948 and examined Arizona's higher education system, Phoenix College was only a two-year institution, and

Arizona State College in neighboring Tempe was still a small teaching school. For several years he tentatively explored a relationship with the University of Arizona but concluded that the institution was too far from the Valley to be a practical partner. This left Arizona State College as the most likely option, and with its booming enrollments it seemed to offer improving prospects. And perhaps Noble saw its possibilities as a research institution because of his experiences years earlier at Connecticut State College.

Noble talked frequently with President Grady Gammage, encouraging his efforts to transform the institution into a university with significant training in science and engineering, and in 1955 Gammage persuaded the Arizona Board of Regents to accept his plan to reorganize the school into four colleges and hire an engineer, Lee Thompson, as one of the deans. The following year, joined by Walter Bimson, Noble and Gammage won permissions to create a separate school of engineering and offer an undergraduate engineering degree. For the next decade Noble was a leading campaigner for advancing the institution, invoking the models of Stanford University and MIT. Although he admitted in 1956 that the institution's existing standards "were wholly inadequate to meet the extraordinary needs of the complex technological industries," he touted its capacity to improve, and a few years later he praised the "tremendous strides" the engineering program had made.[23]

Executives at AiResearch and Goodyear voiced their support for Noble's ideas. A key issue in GE's decision about whether to locate in Phoenix was its concerns about ASC's programs in engineering and science. Encouraged by conversations with President Gammage and by the establishment of the new engineering degree, GE not only located in the Valley, it also donated a large computer to the school (its first) and leased office and laboratory space on campus, where GE researchers worked on various computing problems. By articulating his vision of a research institution and a partnership between the college and the larger community, Noble not only aided in developing the school's science and engineering programs, he also helped redefine the institution's role in the Valley.[24]

The importance of education in this emerging economy climaxed in the campaign to upgrade the institution. In 1958, following the combined efforts of the college students and faculty, various employers in the Valley, and Phoenix boosters, led by the Pulliam newspapers, the state's voters approved changing ASC to Arizona State University, with the right to offer graduate degrees (a change that the University of Arizona and a huge majority of Tucson voters opposed).[25] By 1962 the undergraduate

Figure 6.1 Baggage carriers loading Motorola products, 1960. Electronics manufacturers like Motorola could ship their products by air. *Source:* Herb and Dorothy McLaughlin Collection, Arizona State University Libraries.

engineering programs were accredited, in record time; were being praised by outside reviewers; and were attracting 10 percent of the university enrollment, including more than 300 Motorola employees, with 115 working on master's degrees and 5 pursuing PhDs. This educational connection was made possible, in part, by an ASU program initiated by Motorola, which enabled its employees to pursue graduate degrees while still working, an option chosen by more than 100 Motorola employees plus 200 employees of other Valley firms.[26]

But Noble had broader notions about the potential role of this new university and saw its future prospects as crucial for the well-being of Motorola but also of the Valley. Without enhanced engineering and scientific education, Motorola "could not expand and could not maintain leadership," he declared. "We could not hold our superior brain power here in the city." He also articulated a connection between ASU and economic development in the Valley: "Phoenix cannot hope to compete with other areas in attracting the technical product industries, and holding them, without the development of engineering and science education and research at Arizona State University to a high level of scholarship and maturity."[27] Prompted especially by Noble's reiteration of these views, by the early 1960s both university officials and community leaders commonly invoked the notion that "development of Arizona's industrial and business potential depends upon the university's future" and pointed to California and Boston as the academic and business examples the university and city should follow.[28]

SHAPING IDENTITIES: WESTERN AND OUTDOOR CULTURES

While endeavoring to build the city's economy, city leaders also considered its culture, continuing previous efforts to make the city respectable and adding a sense that its culture must be enhanced as part of the drive to achieve national significance. Prewar Phoenix had looked like an aspiring agricultural city: it had presented a deliberately "American" style, with growing awareness of mass culture, a substantial interest in outdoor activities, and a classic middle-class concern with fine arts and "culture." The first shift from this specific blend of values occurred in the 1930s with the appearance of activities and celebrations that were self-consciously western and that reflected an effort to bolster tourism.[29]

Of course, some of this did connect with the area's real life: Valley farmers and ranchers had always raised cattle, and mining had been important in central Arizona. The change involved bringing to town activities that had existed in rural outskirts or surrounding mountain areas but with very limited connection to Phoenix's history. Rodeos, for example, which had a long history in Prescott, were initiated in Phoenix and other Valley communities during the 1930s. This shift deliberately played on romantic stereotypes and an American awareness that the frontier times really had ended, a realization that fueled the popularity of western movies in the 1930s and 1940s and television programs in the 1950s—some of which were filmed in the state. A calendar of Valley activities in the 1950s mimicked those themes and included "the bi-weekly Desert Sun Ranchers Rodeos in Wickenburg; weekly travelcades by the Spanish-attired Dons club, topped by the annual search for the Lost Dutchman Gold Mine in the Superstition Mountains; the Wickenburg Gold Rush Days"; "the Phoenix Jaycees World Championship Rodeo in March";

and, finally, "dances like the Cattle Rustlers Ball and the Valley of the Sun Square Dance Festival and Fiddlers Jamboree."[30]

Although the area's natural environment was clearly western, the Valley's built environment was not. Phoenicians had intentionally selected architectural styles that avoided a frontier look, although the imitation of California housing styles grew after the 1910s. The one specific exception to this was Scottsdale's deliberate effort at self-marketing. In near total contrast with the agricultural reality of its past, the community adopted the Chamber of Commerce's label of the "West's Most Western Town" and remodeled its downtown to give it a wooden "cow town" facade. By the 1960s, however, this theme was rapidly lost among the upscale shopping areas, art galleries, and resorts that offered luxurious accommodations and activities like golf. The western theme persisted only in a few select areas, with specific commercial purposes. Starting in the 1960s, Legend City, an amusement park between Phoenix, Tempe, and Scottsdale, attempted with mixed success to mimic Disneyland's Frontierland. In the following decade, entrepreneurs built two imitation western towns on the northeastern urban periphery. Frontier Town was essentially a collection of stores and did not succeed, but the Wild West "town" of Rawhide offered a range of entertainment, spectacle, commerce, and food that continued to attract an audience.[31]

In several other respects Phoenix did reflect a western and smaller town character. Publications often advised visitors that "life in Phoenix, both for vacationists and residents, is friendly and informal." This advice referred generally to living style, manners, and modes of dress. Phoenicians attempted to build on this more casual style and the national interest in the West by wearing and manufacturing western-style clothing. Although jeans would retain their local and national acceptance, observers in the early 1960s noted "the sudden decline in popularity of 'Western' fashions for both women and men." Local clothing manufacturers persisted for a time by selling other western-style clothing items, but national trends would eventually swamp these local efforts.[32]

In other respects, such as cuisine, Phoenix clearly displayed its tradition, which was western but with limited ethnic variety. Like the chance of buying a Model T car in a color besides black, Phoenicians had restricted choices in the types of meals they could order. Nearly all restaurants during the 1950s were either "American," specializing in hamburger and steak, or local grills, offering chili, or national fast-food chains, plus various Mexican establishments. Even the select listings in *Point West* magazine, the champion of Valley cosmopolitanism, primarily featured steak houses, with just a smattering of other cuisines, mainly Italian.[33]

A continuing and deeply rooted facet of Phoenix culture was the attraction of active living and the outdoors. "Outdoor living is a cultivated way of life," claimed one author, and Phoenicians touted their involvement in activities and exercise like hiking, horseback riding, hunting, and fishing, as well as skiing and boating, as reflecting their appreciation of nature and physical activity. The growing popularity of athletic events and sports generally provided more chances for people to participate, entertainment for spectators, and evidence of the area's social and economic development. This was enhanced by the postwar expansion of facilities, as the parks department constructed swimming pools and tennis courts, and the burgeoning popularity of golf pushed the total number of courses to twenty-one by 1960.

While high school athletics, particularly football, still attracted enthusiastic audiences, they lost their role as the community's primary sporting events. Population growth and the proliferation of high schools fragmented the community's identification, but the main reason was the growth of the ASU athletic program. As the school's successful football teams achieved regional prominence and national ranking, their games became the Valley's prime athletic attraction. The creation by Harry Rosenzweig and other prominent city leaders of the athletic booster group the Sun Angel Foundation further showed that identification with ASU was spreading from Tempe to the Valley, and it paralleled and reinforced other forces encouraging a metropolitan identity.[34]

Various other sporting programs, events, and activities drew public interest and created economic opportunities. The Phoenix Open Golf Tournament and the Thunderbird Tennis Tournament gained popularity, while horse- and dog-racing facilities attracted increasing audiences and were profitable businesses.[35] But baseball remained the Valley's most valued sport, reflecting ideas about the nature and values inherent in the game, but also because it connected the city to other places. As minor leagues resumed and expanded after the war, a Class C Arizona-Texas League opened in 1947 featuring the Phoenix Senators, along with teams in Mesa, Tucson, Bisbee, Globe-Miami, El Paso, and Juarez. Surmounting league and team changes, the Phoenix team achieved some success, and playing as the Phoenix Stars in 1954 it drew 114,450 fans, but air-conditioning and television were killing the league. The shift of two major league teams to California in 1958 offered a new opportunity, as the displaced San Francisco Seals of the Pacific Coast

League migrated to Phoenix. But low attendance, partly because of an aging and inadequate stadium, sent the team fleeing to Tacoma in 1960.[36]

Phoenicians' disappointment over this was partly mollified by the Valley's developing role as a regular host for major league spring training. This began in 1947, with the arrival of the New York Giants in Phoenix and the Cleveland Indians in Tucson. The Chicago Cubs came to Mesa in 1952, and the Baltimore Orioles trained first in Yuma and then in Scottsdale, replaced in 1959 by the Boston Red Sox. This base made it possible, after the major leagues expanded in 1961, for the Valley to acquire additional teams, with the larger total morphing into the Cactus League and stimulating both sports tourism and greater local interest in the game.[37]

"HIGH CULTURE" AND THE ARTS

The growth of the fine arts in Phoenix—music, theater, and art—represented a deliberate effort by city leaders to transform the Valley's "culture," a term they applied only to those fine arts and high (as opposed to popular) culture. In part, this represented the continuation of earlier efforts, interests, and perspectives. Some of these leaders—husbands or wives—were themselves amateur artists, and some labored for love of the arts. But others acted to enhance the city's reputation and avoid the "hick town" label, for they recognized that culture and education, as much as tall buildings or a burgeoning economy, were signs of urban status. As Mayor Sam Mardian noted, "Any city, if it amounts to anything, has to develop culturally." But postwar leaders also perceived a direct connection between their specific economic plans and the development of high culture. They believed that cultural institutions helped recruit electronics and similar businesses and that "in order to attract [their employees] to Phoenix, you need facilities like the art museum and the symphony." Thus, postwar efforts at cultural refinement married traditional attempts to "civilize" the town with a new vision of economic development, which involved both private and public support.[38]

City leaders especially supported the art museum, partly because a collection was permanent, while performances were temporary, but more because of the influence of key individuals. Building and filling the art museum took significant labor, and, as later president Sam Applewhite noted, "Of course, the man who put the Phoenix Art Museum over was Walter Bimson." The city's leading banker, involved with much of the economic development in this era, Bimson had a longstanding interest in art. His brother Carl recalled that as a boy in Colorado Walter was "always crazy about art." He took a course in show-card lettering, and he did airbrushing, wood burning, and pen drawings. He started college in journalism, wanting to be a cartoonist, and applied for a job at the *Denver Post*. He then switched to architecture, but financial pressures forced him to leave college to work for a bank, and he took correspondence courses, which drew him to Chicago and a career in banking. Throughout his life Bimson collected art, and during the 1950s he organized city leaders behind the museum. Rhes Cornelius, of the Phoenix Title and Trust Company, served on the museum board and admitted, "I had no interest in art at that time—I just did it as a civic venture, of course, and because somebody asked me to be on the Board."[39]

The city's first art museum opened in 1949, in a small building near the Civic Center. While city leaders set aside public space for a proper museum, they decided not to spend public money on a building, and Bimson helped raise funds to construct a museum on the Civic Center site in 1959. But when that structure quickly proved too small, city leaders changed policy in 1961 and proposed funding an addition with city bonds, which voters endorsed, and they spent public funds to underwrite the museum's operating budget. Belief in the institution's economic importance is evident in the support from major economic leaders, particularly bankers, and from public officials. Mardian favored public funding for the museum even though he admitted, like Cornelius, to having no particular interest in art—"just the overall interest in knowing that a community needs cultural activities to attract to the city the type of people that Phoenix seemed to be attracting—in electronics."[40]

A crucial part of the museum's success was obtaining donations of artworks. Here, too, Bimson was highly important as an example, both in providing some of his own pieces and in persuading others to do likewise. The most notable early gifts came from Lewis Ruskin, the founder of a Chicago pharmaceutical chain who moved to the Valley in 1955 and thereafter donated thirty-one paintings worth over $3 million. Building on these examples, the museum's director, Forest M. Hinkhouse, successfully encouraged the donation of artworks from persons living in the Valley and others in the East, obtaining an Asian collection, for example, from Henry and Clare Booth Luce.[41]

Besides promoting the museum, Bimson and others sought to encourage local artists. For many years Bimson provided the $500 annual prize for a local art competition; he bought many of the prizewinning pieces and displayed them at the Valley National Bank. The most substantial effort to help a local artist involved Philip Curtis, who had directed the New Deal's federal Art Center in Phoenix. Returning after the war, Curtis began developing a national reputation, but as Ruskin discovered in 1961, Curtis was distracted from painting by the need to sell his art. Working with nine other investors (including Bimson and Kax Herberger), Ruskin created the Philip Curtis Trust, a $25,000 fund to support the artist for three years, with repayment from the sale of paintings. The investment paid off, as the artist's production and reputation increased, and the investors got their money back and artworks.[42]

By contrast, the city assisted the performing arts in three different ways. Providing an audience for visiting national performers was the easiest type of support to achieve, though no simple task. In this regard the efforts of Jessie Linde were central. A tireless booking agent and promoter, starting in the 1930s, Linde brought artists to the Valley, hosting some in her home, educated Phoenix audiences in concert etiquette, and desegregated them. Frustrated with having to use Phoenix Union High School Auditorium, she persistently argued that city should build a facility. A second stage of support for performing arts, local productions by amateurs, required developing an audience and improving the quality of local performers, and the latter proved a challenge during this period. The highest goal was supporting local professionals whose skills reached nationally recognized levels, and this was not attainable in this era.[43]

Theater in Phoenix during the immediate postwar era meant the Phoenix Little Theater (PLT) and the Sombrero Playhouse. The Sombrero was a private commercial venture that presented some popular stage and movie stars in off-Broadway comedies and dramas. Begun in 1948 by actress Ann Lee Harris and director Richard Charlton, the playhouse operated as a dinner theater from January through April and as a movie theater during the rest of the year. It survived by offering popular entertainment that was not especially challenging to audiences, but by 1968 its formula no longer worked, and the theater closed.[44]

The amateur PLT continued more through the actions of a group of volunteers than because of a few key individuals. Having presented plays since the 1920s in a renovated stable on Maie Heard's property, the group received a substantial boost in 1949 when the city funded a 394-seat facility as part of a new Phoenix Civic Center. PLT prospered in this new home, and in 1965 it joined with the Arizona Repertory Theatre, a new professional group, and the Phoenix Children's Theatre to form the Phoenix Theatre Center. This collaboration required expanding the facility, which the city partially underwrote, but the partnership quickly became a debacle. Complaining of financial and scheduling problems, the repertory group quit and thereafter folded. Construction disasters on the Phoenix Children's Theatre facility prompted their departure in 1967, leaving PLT with a crushing debt and difficult scheduling decisions.[45] The folding of the Arizona Repertory Theatre and the closing of the Sombrero Playhouse marked the end, for the time being, of live professional theater in Phoenix.

Compared with theater and art in Phoenix, classical music had deeper roots and more sources of participation and support. The availability of private musical training, especially on the piano, had spread some appreciation among the middle and upper classes, and schools offered general training and created instrumental and choral groups. But prewar Phoenix had created no professional musical groups, no community vocal groups presented classical music, and its limited volunteer symphony had ceased operating in 1943. The Musicians Club of Phoenix had constituted the core support for quality classical music, both as an audience and as performers, and its key personnel played significant roles in postwar developments. Various choral and ensemble groups were formed in this era, but a symphony orchestra was needed for the development of classical music and musical culture in the Valley.[46]

The most important leader of the Musicians Club and the person having the greatest role in developing the symphony was Blanche Korrick, a classically trained singer and wife of prominent department store owner Charlie Korrick. In May 1947, she and five other community leaders formed the Phoenix Symphony Association and began making plans. Drawing on her familiarity with musical fund raising in New York and Los Angeles, Korrick established the Symphony Guild to raise money and develop public support, and within several months she had collected the necessary $25,000 to start the symphony. The new association then hired as its first conductor, John Barnett, the assistant conductor of the Los Angeles Symphony. Limited local talent required Barnett to import and pay key players, mainly members of the Los Angeles Symphony. Finances also limited his role to part-time; he commuted from Los Angeles and while in Phoenix stayed with the Korricks.[47]

Barnett conducted the first concert in November 1947 and another three concerts over the next two years. In 1949 the board decided to upgrade the orchestra and hired a resident conductor, Robert Lawrence, whose position included a professorship at Arizona State College. In 1952 the board hired Dr. Leslie Hodge, who expanded the season to eight concerts and held the post until 1959. Although the orchestra was "professional," in that members were paid two dollars per rehearsal and ten dollars for each performance, the musical training and professional experience of local members varied greatly.

A number had limited musical education and held jobs unrelated to music; others had significant musical training; and some were employed in the field of music, particularly as music educators, like violinist Helen Swindall, who had graduated from New York's Juilliard School of Music. A few, like Louise Lincoln Kerr, were musicians by design and intent. A classically trained musician who had played with the Cleveland and Pasadena orchestras, after moving to Phoenix Kerr composed music, organized performances by musicians in her home, assisted in developing the symphony, and performed in it.[48] As the organization improved, its concert venue, the Phoenix Union High School Auditorium, became increasingly unacceptable. Efforts since 1948 to obtain public funding for a Phoenix auditorium had failed, but the completion in 1964 of Gammage Auditorium at ASU, designed by Frank Lloyd Wright, provided both an excellent concert hall and a challenge to Phoenix, whose symphony orchestra was now at home in Tempe.[49]

By the early 1960s the proponents of fine arts in Phoenix could claim considerable success, with the construction of some facilities, the emergence of professional groups, and a rising level of financial and audience support. The allocation of public funds was crucial in these efforts, and this reflected a conviction that strong cultural institutions and programs were vitally important in order for Phoenix to attract and retain educated, cultured individuals. But critics pointed out the limitations and indicated how far the city had yet to go before it could reasonably compare itself to cities of comparable size, which were older, more "cultured," and had numerous well-funded cultural institutions. One of these critics noted the absence of key groups, such as opera and ballet, and the fact that cultural performances disappeared in the long summer months. "For a city with cultural aspirations," he concluded, "this situation is frankly inexcusable," and added that "much of our state is a cultural Sahara."[50]

GROWTH AND ANNEXATION

The cultural and economic development of the city related also to its increased population and physical size. In 1940 Phoenix was a modest-sized city of 65,414. Ten years later it included 106,818 people, ranking ninety-ninth among U.S. cities; by 1960 the city's population had boomed to 439,170 people, and it ranked twenty-ninth in the nation. These numbers reflect the leadership's successful efforts to expand the economy, plus their challenging task of expanding city services. However, numbers cannot adequately convey the complexity of population expansion throughout the Valley or how Phoenix

Table 6.3 Population of metropolitan Phoenix and Maricopa County, 1940–60.

Population categories	1940	1950	1960	Growth 1940–50
Phoenix	65,414	106,818	439,170	63.3%
All urban places	87,506	161,315	557,473	84.3%
Unincorporated Phoenix	44,452	76,668	32,131	72.5%
U.S. Census: metro Phoenix	121,828	216,038	552,043	77.3%
Total urban	131,958	237,983	585,958	80.3%
MARICOPA	186,193	331,770	663,510	78.2%
Phoenix: % of urban	49.6	44.9	74.9	

Population categories	1940	1950	1960	Date of incorporation
Towns and villages				
Tolleson	1,731	3,042	3,886	1910
Gilbert	837	1,114	1,833	1914
Buckeye	1,305	1,932	2,286	1929
Avondale		2,505	6,151	1946
Goodyear		1,254	1,654	1946
El Mirage			1,723	1951
Peoria			2,593	1954
Cities and towns				
Glendale	4,855	8,179	15,696	1910
Tempe	2,906	7,684	24,894	1894
Mesa	7,224	16,790	33,772	1883
Chandler	1,239	3,799	9,531	1920
Scottsdale	[1000]	[2032]	10,026	1951
Nonmetropolitan towns				
Wickenburg	995	1,736	2,445	1909
Gila Bend			[1813]	1962

Source: Arizona Statistical Review, 1951, 18; *Arizona Statistical Review,* 1961, 9. Note: Population data are for incorporated areas, except estimates for Scottsdale and Gila Bend.

struggled to avoid being overcome by this huge growth. These two decades witnessed the basic decision about the role of Phoenix within the emerging metropolitan area. Like cities such as Dallas and San Jose, and unlike Denver, Phoenix emerged, not simply as the symbolic metropolitan center having certain features and attractions, but as the dominant city in population, size, and power. This occurred because of deliberate planning and concerted effort by the city's new leadership. They perceived expansion as being interrelated with economic, political, and cultural developments, all of which were essential for creating a new and prosperous future.

Before 1940 the Valley supported several types of urban places apart from Phoenix: agricultural villages, small towns, and fringe subdivisions (table 6.3). Furthest from Phoenix, to the west and southeast, various small towns, villages, and hamlets had emerged, a few of which were incorporated. They existed solely because of agriculture and depended on the availability of ground or dammed water (see chapter 1). They usually had a general store, sometimes a few other shops, and perhaps a school, and in most places a relatively high proportion of the population were poor minorities who worked the fields. Surrounded by cultivated fields and relatively distant from Phoenix, even by 1960, these communities grew only marginally in the two decades after 1940.[51]

A second cluster of towns—Glendale, Tempe, and Mesa—were older, were much closer to Phoenix, and had achieved more substantial forms by 1940, including commercial areas with grocery stores and additional businesses such as auto services and movie theaters. They also boasted other features, such as the Mormon Temple (1927) in Mesa, while Tempe was home to Arizona State College. After 1940 these towns, plus Scottsdale and Chandler, experienced much greater growth. All of them gained something from the increased tourism that was drawn to Phoenix but spread throughout the Valley. To a lesser extent they obtained economic benefits analogous to those of Phoenix. Mesa succeeded in converting Falcon Field, the wartime airport, into an economic asset and began seeking to attract aerospace businesses. The dramatic postwar increase of enrollment at ASU fueled the development of Tempe. And after incorporating in 1951, Scottsdale moved rapidly to develop resorts and upscale shopping.[52]

The effect of the Valley's population growth on these adjacent towns would come mainly after 1960. The agricultural hamlets, as well as new communities built outside of the immediate Phoenix area, would change mostly after 1980.

Virtually all of these towns would become incorporated, and given the state's annexation and incorporation laws, they would push the metropolitan area into a new political, and to a certain extent social, form. Because of their location, the four larger towns (and to a lesser extent, Chandler) followed a different pattern. After 1950 they began growing much more rapidly, they achieved a population size that began to support more independent economic and social features, and their areas of peripheral growth began reaching those of the other major towns and of Phoenix. This led to annexation campaigns that expanded the sizes of these cities but that also conflicted with some of Phoenix's plans.[53]

The third area, fringe subdivisions immediately around Phoenix, experienced by far the most substantial population growth. In 1940 and 1950 these unincorporated suburban neighborhoods included a population twice as large as that contained in all other communities outside of Phoenix and two-thirds the size of Phoenix itself. While Phoenix grew by almost two-thirds during the 1940s, the unincorporated population expanded even more rapidly, and in 1950 it constituted a third of Maricopa County's urban residents, while Phoenix had less than half.[54]

Reacting to growth by proposing annexation was, of course, a familiar response in Phoenix, as it was elsewhere. During the previous five decades the city had periodically expanded its boundaries, growing from 0.5 to 9.6 square miles. This traditional booster goal of enlarging the city was strengthened in the postwar era by a larger vision of the city's future. A new awareness of the actions of other cities, such as San Diego, stimulated greater ambitions for the city and a determination to accomplish them. As Mayor Ray Busey phrased it, "We wanted Phoenix to be the economic center of the Southwest."[55]

But conditions in the immediate postwar era involved a different balance of factors and would make annexation somewhat contested and difficult. Since the late 1930s, growth had spread into noncontiguous areas and had outdistanced annexation, so that surrounding areas had come to include more territory, population, and businesses. This accumulation meant that several sites of adjacent population had more than a few years of history and some nascent community identity. The changing nature of housing construction, building standards, and neighborhood development also posed problems. Finally, adjacent territories included not only residences but also industrial areas in the west and southeast of the city.

In the late 1940s, Mayors Busey and Udall strongly advocated annexation, but the territory actually added fell far short of their goals. Business resistance was central to this failure. Private water companies were hostile because they feared competition with the city. However, when city bond elections later provided the funds to purchase these companies, their opposition melted away. Other businesses disliked city bureaucracy and especially certain city taxes. The voters' repeal of the inventory tax in 1949 eliminated that objection. During the 1950s major industries, such as Reynolds Aluminum, fought against annexation, claiming that existing city maintenance codes were inappropriate for their sort of businesses and that city zoning would prohibit their expansion and restrict future sales. The city adjusted these requirements in 1958 and reassured businesses about taxes by guaranteeing that it would not revoke existing tax exemptions.[56]

The final problem, as the lawyer for these businesses phrased it, "was a genuine distrust of the city that had been built up in years long ago."[57] Suspicion and ill regard for the city had become strong by the late 1940s, and during the 1950s Charter Government forces worked diligently to assure both businesses and residents of the fringe areas that the city administration was honest and efficient. This effort included the Charter Government's reiteration of its "creation myth," in which it painted great contrasts with previous city governments. It was also another reason that the administration trumpeted its winning of the All-America City Award in 1951 and 1958.

Soon after being appointed city manager in 1950, Ray Wilson strengthened the Planning Department, which he ordered to study the surrounding fringe areas and to develop a comprehensive plan for annexation. In his first public report on the new city administration, Wilson lauded the successful management of different parts of city government, emphasized the importance of planning in all aspects, and vigorously argued for annexation, going beyond the traditional simple endorsement of "bigger." Wilson denounced "unplanned sprawl" because it "creates health and sanitation problems, traffic congestion, crime, substandard building, and many other problems." Left unmentioned, but a central cause of these problems, was that county zoning and building codes were recent and inadequate. Another study several years later expanded this critique, noting additional problems produced by the failure to plan: streets that did not connect, industry in inappropriate places, and the virtual absence of neighborhood recreation facilities. Part of the cause, the study noted, was that fringe areas had "an unusual amount and distribution of undeveloped land within urbanized areas. Leap-frogging of development has disrupted the continuity of urban growth" and created numerous difficulties.[58]

This type of development made services costly, and Wilson presented Phoenix as the logical and efficient provider. Private delivery was more expensive and, given the pace of growth in the Valley, only a short-term solution. The only real alternative was separate incorporation, and this, he argued, would bring many problems: it would be more costly, increase taxes, produce conflicting laws, and cause "deterioration of the central city and serious damage to the economy of the whole community." To illustrate the danger of suburban incorporation, he noted the conditions of other cities, such as St. Louis. After Phoenix won the 1958 All-America City Award, Wilson refined his argument for annexation. While still emphasizing the cost efficiencies that a larger city could produce, he added a revenue argument—saying that annexing shopping centers would add to the city's sale tax revenues. Finally, he defended annexation as a way of retaining the civic leaders who were migrating to suburbs.[59]

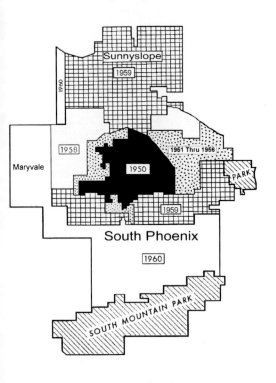

Figure 6.2 Phoenix annexations, 1950–60.
Source: Modified from *Annual Financial Report* (Phoenix: City of Phoenix), 1960–80 editions, and *Arizona Statistical Review, 1960.*

These strong beliefs in annexation were checked by city finances and public attitudes for the first five years, although the city developed campaign methods in 1951 and 1952 that it would soon use to acquire larger areas. In 1953 Wilson hired John Burke as director of annexation; Burke began devising plans, and a few years later the city began to act. One factor expediting the process was that Phoenix paid people to circulate annexation petitions. Equally important, the city began extending services to more surrounding areas—water to 60,000 nonresidents in 1957; sewers to Sunnyslope and Maryvale; and police and fire services to other neighborhoods.[60] This pseudo annexation demonstrated the benefits of city services but at a slightly higher cost than to city residents. City officials explained that annexation would bring more services, and that taxes would cost less than what residents already paid for services. The city's flexibility in eliminating "unnecessary restrictions, without reducing the building requirements" was also crucial and resulted in key annexations of industrial areas in 1958 and 1959 (figure 6.2).[61]

While planning, zoning, and the quality of construction were important considerations for the city, with implications for the integrity of the built environment, the quality of life, and the city budget, Phoenix's greatest risk was strangulation by suburban incorporation. Phoenix faced two threats of such action, in Sunnyslope to the north and in South Phoenix. Supporters of incorporation touted the benefits of self-reliance and a smaller community, but the combined opposition of residents favoring annexation and those preferring not to incorporate prevailed.

Begun as a tent community for respiratory victims in the 1910s, Sunnyslope grew slowly over the next decades. By the 1940s its proponents began efforts to improve its public image, advertising that it contained no slums or poverty and was "neither a sick colony nor a tubercular camp." Instead, they trumpeted, it was "THE PLACE TO LIVE IN SUBURBAN PHOENIX," combining "all the desert's attractiveness" with "the advantages of city life."[62] By the late 1940s, it boasted over 150 businesses, a variety of locally based social or economic organizations, and public services provided by the county, all of which encouraged some residents to seek a separate legal identity for the community. Five times—in 1949, 1953, 1955, and twice in 1958—they lost elections to incorporate, with areas of slightly different boundaries. By the end, however, hope was gone, and the final election was primarily a defensive maneuver intended simply to delay annexation. After it failed, Phoenix quickly introduced an annexation measure, which "prevent[ed] any further moves toward incorporation of any part of" Sunnyslope, and completed the annexation in April 1959.[63]

A second struggle sprouted in South Phoenix, an area mostly south of the Salt River. With a population in 1950 of over sixteen thousand, this area contained various types of neighborhoods, from slum to middle class to rural, and a diverse population of roughly one-third African Americans and Mexican Americans. The movement for incorporation, led by R. C. Moore and the South Phoenix Municipal Association, attracted various supporters, including many African Americans, who hoped a separate municipality might offer more opportunity for political influence and office. As the campaign developed, however, even some of the initial supporters moved into opposition, and the election on February 17, 1953, effectively ended the incorporation hope when it garnered only 10 percent of the votes. Annexation came in 1960, as the city moved to bolster its population numbers for the 1960 census count (figure 6.2). Linking South Phoenix with Maryvale (the westside community that overwhelmingly favored annexation) into a single annexation district made it easier and faster to obtain the necessary signatures. While African Americans and other persons hoping for improved services favored annexation, some residents who feared increased taxes and regulation filed a lawsuit, but the courts rejected their complaint and upheld the annexation.[64]

The incorporation of the small, entirely residential community of Paradise Valley in 1961 was the sole exception to this pattern, and it was soon surrounded by Phoenix and Scottsdale. When the legislature passed a law in 1961 prohibiting incorporation of an area within six miles of a city, it effectively ended the possibility that other adjacent urban areas might pursue this goal in the future.[65]

The final challenges to Phoenix's growth were efforts by several neighboring cities to annex areas lying between them and the rapidly growing urban hub. In the mid-1950s Phoenix worked out an amicable division of territory with Glendale, but it fought with cities to the east. When Tempe attempted to encircle an area of adjacent territory, Phoenix successfully protested in court. A more serious conflict involved Scottsdale, which annexed aggressively after it incorporated in 1951, seeking to expand to the west. In the battle between these cities, Phoenix cleverly used paid petition circulators, defined areas of annexation that overlapped Scottsdale's target areas, and relied on assistance from the courts. Thus, when the courts overturned a preemptive annexation by Scottsdale in 1961, Phoenix quickly annexed much of the same area. Although the struggle continued for a few more years, the two cities resolved the remaining issues in 1964, deciding on a partition line for future annexations that held for the next two decades.[66]

The simplest measure of Phoenix's success is that in 1940 and 1950 the city had comprised only a third of the county and half the urban population, while in 1960 it made up two-thirds of the county and three-fourths of the urban area. Annexation accounted for all of this change: three-fourths of the 1960 population lived in areas annexed since 1950 and half in areas annexed since 1958. The city's success reflected clever tactics, speed, the conflict of development and community ideals, and the importance of services. While the ideal of living in a small community may have drawn more fringe area residents than did the allure of being part of a greater urban area, the rapid pace of development visibly and undeniably undermined the possibility of maintaining a rural lifestyle, whatever incorporated or unincorporated entity one lived in. The key factor in tipping the balance toward annexation was the attraction of efficient government and affordable services. Thus, while annexation did not fully please everyone affected by the change, the process—particularly when compared with that elsewhere—was relatively harmonious.[67]

A related factor influencing the decisions of new residents and of the city was that the county was an ineffective planning agent. Although appreciating the freedom and lower housing prices, a majority of residents favored the benefits of community planning. City planners saw the disadvantages of annexing unconnected residential areas, but they perceived greater danger from inaction. They chose, then, to expand the city as far and as quickly as possible, considering this the only sure way to make certain that these surrounding areas would be built to reasonable standards, including features like connected and paved streets, sufficient parks, and rational zoning. Thus, by the late 1950s annexation decisions increasingly involved areas that were the product of leapfrog development (figure 6.3). Although annexing large

Figure 6.3 Undeveloped land in the Phoenix urban area, 1958. *Source:* Modified from plate 10 in *Land Use of the Phoenix Urban Area* (Phoenix: Advanced Planning Task Force, 1959).

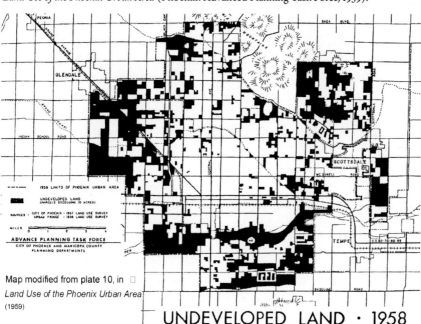

UNDEVELOPED LAND · 1958

portions of undeveloped land posed numerous problems and contributed to suburban sprawl, at this stage of development, it seemed the more prudent alternative.

A DRAMATICALLY DIFFERENT PLACE

By 1960 Phoenix had achieved national recognition.[68] It had become the leading city in the Southwest and the fastest growing city of its size in the nation. In merely two decades it had become a dramatically different place. The most obvious change involved a vast increase in size: the incorporated area ballooned from 9.6 to 187.4 square miles, while the population grew from 65,414 to 439,170. Although substantial growth was a common story for western cities during this era, the considerable change in Phoenix's position in regional and western hierarchy was the stuff of dramas. During the next two decades Phoenix not only kept pace with the fast growth in this region, it greatly exceeded it. Starting in 1940 as nearly the smallest of the major western cities, by 1960 it ranked ninth in population, surpassing every Rocky Mountain and Great Basin city except Denver, and it had even grown larger than some Pacific Coast cities. The city expanded even more dramatically in area, trailing only Los Angeles, Houston, and Dallas and closing in on the heels of San Diego.[69] During this era western cities grew more rapidly than those elsewhere in the nation and assumed greater prominence in the national urban hierarchy (increasing from two to seven of the top twenty urban communities). Ranking twenty-ninth in 1960, Phoenix was not yet part of that national elite, but growth had radically changed its status and suggested the promise of greater changes in the future.

Phoenix was also part of a larger story of western and Sunbelt economic growth and prosperity, one that involved the expansion of aviation and electronics linked to national defense spending, national migration, and suburbanization. Besides following this economy strategy, the city was also aided by the climate's attractiveness for health seekers and by the propitious development of affordable air-conditioning. While Phoenix differed from other cities of the region in some particulars, for the most part its new position came through determined effort and planning. It was simply more successful than its competitors.

The city's success reflected a new vision of its future that developed during the 1940s. Stimulated by wartime lessons and activities, encouraged by technological advances, and aided by postwar opportunities, key leaders assembled in stages a new strategy for development, one that recognized and emphasized the interrelationship between various aspects of community development. The role of an able and cohesive leadership group was central to this effort. Their understanding of these connections, their willingness to pursue the goals defined by other key leaders and provide benefits to a range of groups, and their ability to lead and accomplish tasks determined the city's success.

For the city to support and expand economic growth it had to attract the right industries, which required government assistance, and it had to attract and retain a sizable and skilled workforce. A key to sustaining this development was maintaining an effective government and providing services. These depended on the city's fiscal health, and to protect that the city had to avoid suburban strangulation. The creation of a dominant city within the metropolitan area was also essential for planning and orderly development. This did not mean, of course, creating high-density residential areas as in older eastern cities; the availability of affordable land made the suburban dream an attainable reality in the Phoenix area. Instead, planners worked to create a rational structure for neighborhoods, to provide needed services, and to ensure the construction of good, affordable homes. Economies of scale helped make it possible to provide many services, but because water resources existed independent of political boundaries, the emergence of a central city was crucial for this stage of the Valley's development.

By 1960 the key economic, political, social, and cultural elements of the new vision for Phoenix were in place. The concerted efforts of city leaders had been crucial to this accomplishment, but like any such enterprise, it succeeded because it rode a wave of historical changes, here involving westward migration and urbanization, the rise of aviation and electronics, and changing national and international realities. Yet the city's future included few certainties and no pause from difficult decisions. The achievement of this new order undermined the forces that brought it about. The city's growth would soon enlarge the group of leaders and lead to a loss of personal connections and close relationships. The larger population included a greater diversity of interests, values, experiences, and needs, which would prompt challenges to the original, unitary vision. And while the city benefited from some historical changes, it would suffer from others. In particular, dependence on the automobile would have enormous implications for the health of the city's downtown, the structure of its suburbs and metropolitan area, and a host of environmental and ecological issues.

Part III △△△
Elaborating and Modifying the High-Tech Suburban Vision

The high-tech suburban vision that Phoenix leaders developed and implemented after World War II reflected key elements of postwar American culture, especially a belief in the possibilities of growth, the transformative power of technology and science, and a prosperous future of suburban homes, malls, and cars. The rapid growth of high-tech manufacturing and tourism in Phoenix boosted construction and was tied to continuing economic strengths in agriculture, retail, and service. This prosperity confirmed Phoenicians' belief in progress and the new vision. The creation of an effective city government helped make this economic expansion possible, and by providing efficient and economical services Phoenix was able to envelop its rapidly sprawling suburban fringe. An appreciation of the area's climate and scenery fostered an interest among Phoenicians in nature and outdoor activity, while the continued ethic of boosterism, combined with a pragmatic drive to attract and retain a more educated workforce, pushed expansion of the city's cultural institutions.

By 1960 Phoenix had reached a size and institutional development roughly comparable to Denver, its prewar model, yet during the 1940s its aspirations and goals had shifted to those exemplified by California cities, especially San Diego. This began with its economic model, and it developed through economic, financial, and cultural connections that flourished through the 1960s and 1970s. Phoenicians also relied on California for housing and building styles, and by the 1970s they began drawing on that state for models of neighborhood development and community planning. But also by the 1970s some Phoenicians were recoiling from urban-related ills such as smog and traffic congestion, highways and sprawl, and rising cost of living, ills they associated with that California model of growth. A fear of their city becoming "like L.A." encouraged Phoenicians to consider the strategies of other booming cities throughout the West. Even more unique places like Las Vegas or Miami suggested patterns that might be worth emulating, particularly in terms of entertainment and tourism. Ultimately, Phoenix adopted no single city as a model, nor could it, given its continued growth. As the city pushed steadily up through the ranks of America's largest cities—to twentieth in 1970, ninth in 1980, and sixth in 2000—its status, achievements, and quality of life were increasingly judged by comparison with the nation's other large cities.

In chasing their high-tech suburban vision, Phoenix leaders pursued particular goals and responded to specific local issues, but their challenges were generally those confronting all the nation's cities. Postwar Phoenix lacked sufficient housing for its existing population, and this problem increased significantly because of the general impact of migration to the Sunbelt, the Baby Boom, and the success of the city's development program. Nationally, the demand for housing prompted fundamental changes in housing construction, and Phoenix builders were in the vanguard of the innovators. New approaches were essential to meeting the need for housing and especially the demand for affordable, detached, single-family homes. Since Phoenix leaders and community residents considered this central to their vision, they viewed the quantity and quality of new housing, its affordability, plus the substantial jump in home ownership as signal accomplishments.

Despite this success, by the late 1950s some Phoenicians began echoing the views of those who looked beyond individual homes and faulted the new suburbs in which they were built as being monotonously uniform, exclusively residential, and auto dependent. During the 1960s and 1970s builders and developers in Phoenix and elsewhere responded to these criticisms, partly because the increasing scale of subdivisions gave them more opportunities to design neighborhoods. More importantly, the criticism and the changing market pushed builders to change. To do so, they borrowed techniques and innovations from different types of developments, and in the Phoenix area this included the emerging market for retirement communities, a revived interest in building self-sufficient "new towns," and the construction of semi-independent, master-planned communities. But while these developments reflected more careful planning, they also provoked later debates over sprawl and the privatization of public functions. This shift from home building in the 1940s to community building in the 1970s (see chapter 7) bridges the initial development of the city's postwar vision and the efforts to elaborate and improve it.

Politics played a crucial role in allowing Phoenicians to realize the postwar vision, shaping what government did and did not do. In developing Charter Government through the 1950s, Phoenix leaders had taken a limited approach to governance, essentially implementing a politics of structure and service, which rested on a citywide political system, an ethos of public service, and a narrow definition of government's responsibilities. The emphasis in this type of politics on the efficient delivery of basic services initially produced substantial public satisfaction and enabled the city to annex surrounding suburban areas. Its effort to create consensus and occupy the political center was successful into the mid-1960s, but thereafter different political currents pulled it successively in different directions. By the 1970s CG had become relatively conservative, outdistanced by the city's greater size, by a changing political climate, and by new ideas about politics. In the last years of the decade, CG dissipated as a political force.

One basic weakness in Charter Government's approach to politics was its notions about representation and participation. These were challenged in the 1960s by forces that championed a different approach, a politics of people. As the city's tremendous growth pushed council members further and further from the people they were to represent, more and more citizens rejected Charter's central tenet that only citywide leaders could effectively pursue some general good for the entire city. Instead, they argued that a more democratic and effective politics required the representation of groups, areas, and interests. Some Charter critics during the 1950s had pushed neighborhood goals in preference to citywide goals, but opponents in the 1960s offered a different and more significant critique, arguing that the city's general good was reached when representation responded to the diversity of the population. First articulated by African Americans and connected to the civil rights movement, this perspective gained strength as the growing activism of Mexican Americans further demonstrated that an open, participatory system was necessary to resolve the real differences among legitimate and diverse interest groups. Finally, public recognition of racial and economic conflicts forced the acceptance of new public issues, as city government during the 1960s to the 1980s moved beyond its initial, limited definition of city services to include actions relevant to social issues and problems, especially those of the inner city.

A second challenge to Charter's approach to politics and growth arose out of increasing concerns about the structural development of the city, concerns reflected in a politics of place and space. The precipitous decline of downtown after the war had worried some people, but no significant action was taken until the late 1960s, and no clear strategy emerged. By the early 1970s, however, many Phoenicians began to see a connection with other urban problems. They worried about the environmental and social consequences of leapfrog development and suburban sprawl, and various studies suggested the need to plan and control growth. These fears connected with a concern for downtown development and decay in the inner city, and with a growing interest in renovating the older well-to-do neighborhoods near downtown. The city attempted to balance the concerns and problems of different areas by adopting an urban village model of development.

These developments of the 1960s and 1970s had substantially altered key elements of the high-tech suburban vision, but it remained the basic blueprint for development. Beginning in the 1980s even more significant changes occurred, ultimately blurring the vision. Following Charter Government's defeat in the late 1970s, Phoenix voters opted for a district system of representation that transformed city politics. Death or retirement of the major postwar leaders and the emergence of multiple private leadership groups left a vacuum that subsequent mayors worked to fill, attempting to define new public goals and to call forth new public-private partnerships. This leadership was most obviously needed to create a replacement for the dying economic plan. The original hope of building a broad-based high-tech sector had dwindled to the reality of a narrow set of businesses, mainly semiconductor manufacturing, which was increasingly vulnerable to the evolving global economy. Nor did the growth industries of tourism and construction offer a reliable basis for significant long-term prosperity. By 2000, however, a coalition of public, private, and university leaders had begun a major new effort to create a substantial biomedical sector that could serve as a fresh engine for the area's economy.

Along with changing ideas about politics and the economy, Phoenicians also moved after 1980 to alter the postwar vision's emphasis on growth, particularly on the relative importance assigned to different areas. The reversal of attitudes about downtown was a striking change, as major planning efforts, plus considerable public and private investment, produced waves of construction. These developments transformed the appearance of the built environment and created many new cultural and recreational opportunities, but even they did not fully create the type of vibrant, active downtown that other major cities had produced. Still, the increased construction of residences, a new university campus, and the ongoing completion of a light rail system held the possibility of accomplishing this. A complementary effort involved greater support for the city's older neighborhoods, which included major programs for historic preservation, home maintenance, and community development.

Although the city continued to expand geographically, the attitudes and policies toward growth altered considerably, with various efforts made to direct, control, and even prevent this spread. Impact fees shifted the cost of extending services to developers and new residents, while "village" planning committees attempted to structure and restrict the types of development in their areas. Growing complaints about the impact of development on the environment prompted efforts to reduce the use of water, especially groundwater, and to landscape in ways that reduced water use and increased shade. Traffic congestion and its effect on air quality fueled a major highway building effort starting in the 1980s and construction of a light rail system after 2000. Concerns about sprawl and development led the city to continue acquiring mountain and desert lands for recreation and a buffer between developed areas.

But while the attitudes in Phoenix towards development changed greatly from what they had been forty or a hundred years before, these views had a diminishing impact on the nature of development in the Valley. Although the expanding city boundaries still included vacant land, development spread well outside Phoenix and increasingly outside the inner ring of suburbs into further reaches of the Valley. Many residents of the Valley recognized that the major issues they faced were truly metropolitan in character, but leaders of the twenty-five incorporated municipalities did not always see development issues in the same light. The creation and implementation of a vision for the Valley's development became significantly more complex.

7

From Houses to Communities:
Suburban Growth in the Postwar
Metropolis, 1945–1980

The end of World War II propelled the nation into a new era of rising prosperity, growth, and social change. Peace and the return of soldiers unleashed Americans' desires for families, homes, and material possessions that the Depression and war had checked. Marriage and birthrates soared, while wartime savings, government loan guarantees, and financial grants to veterans fueled the demand for houses and cars, changing how and where Americans lived. Home construction boomed, and new homes meant new owners: home ownership rose by half, from 43.6 percent in 1940 to 61.9 percent in 1960, and inched even further to 64.4 percent in 1980.[1]

Some of this growing population went to cities, but mostly it flooded the suburbs, tripling their portion of the population between 1940 and 1980, from 15.3 to 44.8 percent.[2] That movement and the contours of suburbia owed much to federal government policies and spending. Creation and funding of the Interstate Highway System significantly encouraged sprawling suburbs, with their ubiquitous ranch houses and shopping malls. Along with mortgage loan guarantees from the Federal Housing Administration and Veterans Administration, the FHA's policies shaped the architecture of housing and the structure of subdivisions. They also helped to change the home building industry, as the prewar system in which individual builders made single homes for specific buyers crumbled before prefabrication, mass production techniques, and economies of scale. Thus, the tremendous initial postwar demand for affordable housing fostered the growth of suburban subdivisions with similar types of housing.[3]

Millions of Americans flocked enthusiastically to these new suburban dwellings and neighborhoods, which generated unabashedly positive views from these home owners, as well as government administrators, builders, and many observers. But criticism followed closely behind settlement. Some critics derided the postwar housing as "ticky-tacky," insubstantial, and uninteresting; and they noted that the exclusively residential subdivisions isolated the inhabitants and made them auto dependent. Social commentators faulted these suburbs as being homogeneous in race and income, describing the migration out of urban areas as "white flight." More generally, urban advocates argued that cosmopolitan and lively cities were being replaced by intellectually sterile environments devoid of a sense of community.[4]

The nature of suburban "sprawl" also generated increasing criticism by the 1960s. While disagreeing about the precise meaning of the term, analysts felt they knew it when they saw it. In general, they referred to an unregulated process of "leapfrog," or noncontiguous growth, wasteful land use from low-density neighborhoods of single-family homes, dependence on cars, and a weak connection with other built areas, especially center cities. The objections included various consequences, such as decentralization and the decline of downtown, the loss of wilderness or farmland, and the rising use of cars, which increased gasoline consumption and pollution while diminishing both public and pedestrian transportation.[5]

Suburban forms began changing by the 1960s, partly because the initial postwar demand for housing had been met and partly because rising affluence encouraged the construction of larger homes with more amenities. More importantly, the criticisms of isolation, unimaginative design, and auto dependence—issues relating to both individual housing and the structure of society—prompted new approaches to suburban planning. These efforts drew on strains of new town thinking and building, which had begun with Ebenezer Howard's Garden City movement of the 1890s and took form in new towns in the 1920s and New Deal town-building efforts in 1930s. The clearest, though most demanding, representation of this approach was building new communities. The essential elements of such constructions were mixed land use, citizen involvement in local-level governance, social interaction, significant employment, housing at various prices, and "commitment to aesthetic values, open space preservation, human scale, and personal identity."[6]

Despite hopeful beginnings and some successes, relatively few such towns were constructed, and over time most of them failed to sustain their initial promise. Too few of these developments effectively fostered community, and even fewer provided appreciable employment opportunities.[7] Yet other attempts at planning, influenced to varying degrees by new town thought, did affect suburban construction. They were modeled after earlier efforts, notably in California, and were reflected most fully in large master-planned communities or suburbs, which were rapidly proliferating.[8]

The construction of homes and suburban developments in Phoenix from 1945 until 1980 followed this basic outline of national patterns, but it also differed, reflecting important regional, metropolitan, and local influences. The most important factor is that Phoenix, like other Sunbelt cities, pursued an aggressive annexation policy that brought developing and undeveloped land within city boundaries. The housing and land use patterns within this newly built area are properly labeled as "suburban," even though they grew within what was or would become part of the city proper. Thus, discussions of suburbia and sprawl are appropriate to the city of Phoenix, as are examinations of the changing form of the city from single centered to multinodal.[9]

But sprawl and suburban development also characterized the small cities and towns surrounding Phoenix. The largest of them—the initially small cities of Mesa, Tempe, Scottsdale, and Glendale—were also the closest (roughly ten to fifteen miles from city center to city center). Having developed as agricultural satellite cities before the war, as separate communities but dependent on Phoenix, their tremendous postwar growth expanded their boundaries, changed their economies, and altered key aspects of their relationship with the center city. By the end of the 1970s, then, a new metropolitan system had emerged. The sprawling city of Phoenix had become largely suburban, characterized by relatively low density, noncontiguous growth, and a decentralized, multinodal structure. The nearest "suburbs" had changed dramatically, spilling up to one another's boundaries, over former farmland, and into the desert. And outside these areas, other communities, both old and new towns, began a new ripple of growth.

The postwar demand for housing hit Phoenix as hard as any place in the nation. Partly in response to this, but also reflecting a culture of innovation, the city's builders were particularly quick to adopt and create major changes in the methods of home construction. Also characteristic of building in Phoenix was the emphasis on affordability, which was an important part of the city's efforts to attract newcomers. Although the nature of housing and the structure of new subdivisions represented the same forms to which national critics objected, Phoenix moved more swiftly and substantially than many places into developing master-planned communities and new towns. And Phoenix builders also found synergies between different types of developments. Malls and cars significantly affected the developing structure of Phoenix and its suburbs, but in this area their interconnection was different than in most of the nation. Phoenix was relatively successful in its home building and community development efforts, but by the 1970s a variety of issues, including the scope of growth, began raising more fundamental challenges.

BUILDING HOMES

Houses for a Growing Population

The burgeoning population growth of Phoenix and its environs that had begun in the immediate postwar era continued unabated in the two decades after 1960 (table 7.1). With its population increasing by a third in each decade, the city's rank among the nation's most populous cities rose from twenty-ninth in 1960 to ninth in 1980. Its place among the cities of the rapidly growing West also rose, from ninth to fifth, trailing only Los Angeles, Houston, Dallas, and San Diego. In physical size it rated even higher, going from ninth in area to fourth, reflecting its continued annexation practices.[10] This rapid and substantial increase not only required ongoing economic growth and the extension of city services, it also created a demand for the quick production of very substantial amounts of housing. The character of this demand greatly influenced the emergence of the Phoenix housing industry and determined the shape that the metropolis would take. The city of Phoenix and its immediate surrounding area remained the primary focus of this demand, but after 1960 it increasingly spread to the four major satellite cities, which developed substantial populations and struggled to create separate identities.

This population growth could only occur, of course, because of a synergy of economic development, expanding city services, and home construction. Numerous employment opportunities and the expectation of even more created the main parameters for migration, with climate and health being additional factors, but housing production operated in advance of economic development or migration, and it existed somewhat independently of such factors, as evidenced by the periodic surplus of new homes. Thus, persons involved in the Phoenix home building industry were responding to and

Table 7.1 Population of metropolitan Phoenix, 1960–80.

	1960	**1970**	**1980**
Phoenix	439,170	584,303	789,704
Suburbs	119,862	300,457	597,207
Maricopa County	663,510	971,228	1,509,175
Phoenix: % of urban	78.6%	66.0%	56.9%
Other Cities			
Mesa	33,772	63,049	152,453
Tempe	24,894	63,550	106,919
Glendale	15,696	36,228	96,988
Scottsdale	10,026	67,823	88,364
TOTAL	84,388	230,650	444,724
Established towns			
Chandler	9,531	13,763	29,673
Gilbert	1,833	1,971	5,717
Avondale	6,151	6,626	8,134
Buckeye	2,286	2,599	3,434
Goodyear	1,654	2,140	2,747
Tolleson	3,886	3,881	4,433
El Mirage	1,723	3,258	4,307
Peoria	2,593	4,792	12,251
Youngtown	1,559	1,886	2,254
Recent towns			
Litchfield Park		1,664	3,657
Surprise		2,427	3,723
Sun City		13,670	40,664
Sun City West			3,741
Sun Lakes			1,944
Paradise Valley		6,637	10,832
Carefree			986
Cave Creek			1,589
Fountain Hills			2,771
Guadalupe			4,506
Nonmetropolitan towns			
Gila Bend	1,813	1,795	1,585
Wickenburg	2,445	2,698	3,535

Source: U.S. Bureau of the Census, 1960–80.

anticipating demand—but also seeking to stimulate it, and succeeding. What they built and sold represented national trends and the influence of market factors, but also the nature of local materials, the local workforce, and capital markets, as well as the geography and climate of the Valley. It also reflected the values and beliefs of those home builders, their sense about what Americans wanted in their homes.

Of course, the federal government provided the context for and a primary influence on home building. Del Webb had observed in 1940 that the enormous power of the federal purse had dramatically reshaped the nature of the large-building construction industry, and the same change occurred in housing construction. The FHA and the VA offered mortgage insurance that all parties found highly attractive, so that FHA standards—begun in the 1930s as guidelines on matters like house size, layout, building materials, and construction techniques, as well as features of subdivisions—became virtual requirements in the postwar era.[11]

The FHA's construction and financing standards aimed to promote what it considered good-quality, affordable housing that would hold its value. Unlike some builders elsewhere in the nation whose sales talk involved "making people dissatisfied with their present homes" or even "ashamed" of living in older homes, Phoenix builders took a positive approach and fully embraced FHA goals, believing that this would enable them to make a healthy profit.[12] This perspective was congruent with larger community goals, because the availability of affordable housing was central to how Phoenix advertised itself: unlike crowded eastern cities with multifamily properties for renters, this was a community of sizable single-family dwellings with yards, a place where average people could afford to purchase a quality home.[13] That focus remained constant, despite dramatic changes over the thirty-five years after the war's end. The builders, the nature of construction, the kinds of houses, the amenities, the financing, and the marketing of homes altered on a scale reminiscent of the late nineteenth century's commercialization of agriculture or the transformation of manufacturing. This focus on housing affordability, despite ongoing changes in the housing industry, produced major consequences for the shape of the metropolis, the economy of the area, and the nature of life in the Valley.

Phoenix Builders and the Home Building Industry
Prewar housing development in Phoenix generally involved multiple persons in the overall development process, but only a few individuals and intensive

labor in the actual construction. One person bought the land; that person or someone else would plat it, put in (unpaved) streets, dig a septic system, and connect to private water and power utilities. An individual builder, working with one or several helpers, would then construct the house—doing everything from mixing cement and framing and roofing the structure to installing plumbing and building cabinets. When housing construction resumed in Phoenix after the war, most builders initially followed this method, but the process changed quickly and significantly. By the mid-1950s many builders had shifted or were shifting into mass production, while others moved in the other direction, concentrating on high-end custom homes. Regardless of market niche or housing type, subdivisions were becoming larger (and some were much larger), construction tasks were more specialized, and builders took over all the stages of development, from land acquisition to home sales. The vertical integration of housing construction had arrived.[14]

While a few builders, like Porter Womack and Alfred Anderson, had begun adopting new construction techniques in the late 1930s and remained in business into the 1950s, most prewar builders did not survive the transition. The postwar builders who took their places came to the job from other backgrounds and experiences. Some claimed Arizona as home, but more had arrived from other states—many from Arkansas, Oklahoma, and Missouri. A number of these men entered the business because their fathers or brothers were contractors; while a few had obtained apprenticeships, like Ralph Staggs, who had worked before the war with Del Webb's construction firm. Still other men became builders by different routes, like Clarence Suggs and Herman Meredith, who moved from insurance to realty, or Maxwell Dorne of Paradise Builders, who had previously worked as a designer. A few postwar immigrants—like Kenneth Rosing—had substantial construction experience (and perhaps not coincidentally tended to build more expensive custom homes), but many had worked only briefly as builders. Many of them started by working on one or only a few houses; their assets often amounted to their wartime savings, and these or personal loans got them started. James G. Hart, for example, became a builder in 1945 with assets of $600, a car, and a trailer. He obtained one improved lot in a subdivision and managed to arrange financing. After completing and selling that single house, he got additional lots and eventually built thirty-one houses in that subdivision. Similarly, John F. Long built his first house with his wife and financed it with a VA loan. Accepting an unsolicited offer for the house, he used the profits from this sale to fund his subsequent construction projects.[15]

This initial postwar building system demanded little capital of builders, providing easy entry into the business and, given the demand for housing, substantial profit, but such opportunities did not last long. The rapid change in home building, reflecting the fluid nature of the Phoenix market, reduced that openness within a decade, with a range of results. Some individuals and firms either could not compete successfully or decided to shift their activities, like Sam Mardian's family company, which moved into commercial construction. Others had modest success, but those who best understood and adapted to mass production of housing reaped handsome rewards, measured in both absolute and relative terms. In a community where wealth had traditionally been derived from land and which had no large industrial fortunes, some builders quickly became part of the economic elite. By 1960 home builders John F. Long, Ralph Staggs, and John Hall, commercial builders Herman Chanen and David Murdock, and Del Webb, who was involved in both areas, represented the new apex of the Phoenix wealth hierarchy.[16]

Figure 7.1 Housing construction in Maricopa County, 1960–80. *Source: Arizona Statistical Review,* 1961–81.

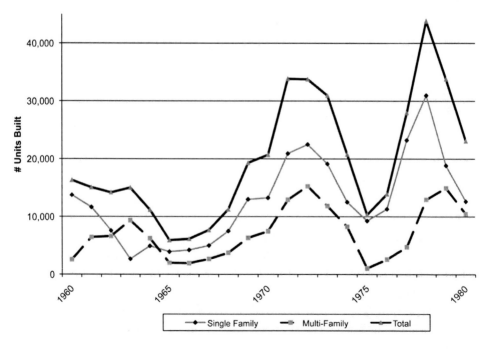

Construction not only created individual fortunes, it also comprised a significant economic sector. The value of building permits grew enormously from 1950 to 1980, rising from $66 million to $1.2 billion. Employment offered another measure of the importance of this section, as construction labor in the 1950s and in prosperous subsequent years constituted 8 to 10 percent of the nonagricultural workforce, while real estate brokers and salesmen made up another 3 percent.[17] However, the fortunes of this industry fluctuate, and the Valley experienced more gyrations than most places (figure 7.1).

The first collapse occurred in the early 1960s, when the national economy was booming and other sectors of the Phoenix economy were vibrant. In the initial stage of this collapse, from 1960 to 1963, the number of single-family homes constructed plummeted by 80 percent, and construction-related employment dropped by a third. Some builders, like Gene Hancock, blamed the collapse on higher interest rates, but most people acknowledged that the industry had simply overbuilt. In 1963 banker A. B. Robbs, Jr., claimed that "the customer for today's homes has been used up two years before."[18] While completed houses were eventually sold, land bought essentially on speculation posed a larger problem, even for major builders. Unable to afford payments on large parcels of land he had purchased, John Long sold them at a $1.2 million loss; Ralph Staggs had land for which he had already paid half of the $3,000-per-acre price and simply deeded it back to the original owners. The number of builders, which had risen from about forty in the mid-1950s to eighty by the early 1960s, plunged to twenty by 1965.[19]

In attempting to survive, builders devised various strategies.[20] Initially, many switched to building multiple-family dwellings, but by 1963 that market was also saturated. Some pursued contracts for commercial and office buildings, though competition was stiff for limited work. Glen Hancock was on the verge of folding his business when he discovered alternative work in remodeling homes. The largest builder, John F. Long, faced the largest problem, and he responded in various ways. First, he purchased, rehabbed, and resold homes that the FHA and VA had repossessed (Maryvale alone had more than thirteen hundred such homes). He also pursued office and commercial building. His riskiest venture was constructing mobile homes, which he began in the summer of 1964. Factory production methods for these structures closely resembled the mass production techniques he had implemented in building houses, and the construction costs were relatively low, but the early postwar notion that Americans would accept such structures proved ephemeral, and in 1969, when the regular housing market began improving, Long shut down this operation.[21]

The industry boomed during the next five years, followed by another serious slump in 1974–76. This crash saw a 50 percent drop in construction employment and a three-fourths decline in housing. In July 1974 unemployed construction workers totaled ninety-five hundred and comprised a third of all persons seeking unemployment compensation. By 1977, as the city's population growth began accelerating, the housing market recovered and soon reached new heights, but another collapse of the single-family housing market started in 1979, partly because of skyrocketing interest rates. In these crises, unlike that of the 1960s, builders generally avoided selling land at a loss, partly because some had acquired only options to buy land, rather than contracts. Equally importantly, major national companies—often based in other Sunbelt states, like California, and with much greater financial assets— had taken over the Phoenix building industry. Some companies, like Lenar, Kaiser Aetna, and Grant, opened offices in the Phoenix area, while other firms entered the market by buying out most of the major homegrown builders: Ralph Staggs sold to the Singer Corporation; Nu-West bought John Hall's business in 1978; Clarence Suggs sold out to U.S. Homes; while Frank Knoell and Gene Hancock also sold to large national public companies.[22]

The late 1970s marked the end of the transformational postwar building era. A system with numerous small or medium builders, requiring little capital and small-scale operations, had changed by the 1960s into a hierarchy topped by a few major builders. During the 1970s, control shifted from those individuals to national corporations, which operated in multiple states. Through this process, the construction industry became a vital part of the Phoenix economy, having a major impact on income and employment in the area and directly affecting the health of various economic institutions, most notably banking. Also significant, and not so encouraging, was the volatility of home building in Phoenix. While construction is highly sensitive to changing economic circumstances, the boom-bust cycle in Phoenix represented an exaggerated version—one in which speculative instincts and beliefs in a prosperous future overrode more sober estimates of economic realities.

Building Homes in Phoenix

In producing affordable and profitable housing, Phoenix builders were in the vanguard of builders across the nation and especially in the Sunbelt. Some of their success reflected local conditions, like the skill and availability of labor and the cost of land, but much of it resulted from their abilities and interests. During the first decade after the war, builders developed most of the basic techniques responsible for lower costs and increasing the speed of construction.[23] By the mid-1950s many were adopting at least some of the elements of mass production and preassembly that were also emerging elsewhere in the nation. They used premixed cement for slab concrete pads, and they installed prebuilt trusses and cabinets and prehung doors. John Dolan innovated by building walls on the ground and then raising them into place; Hugh Knoell built walls on a factory assembly line and transported them to the site.[24]

John F. Long generally was a step quicker and went further than his Phoenix competitors; by the late 1950s he was one of the ten largest builders in the country and arguably the top low-cost builder. By the mid-1950s he not only used but also made numerous house components off-site—including trusses, doors, and plumbing trees. By 1960 he had built a new fabrication shop with a hundred thousand square feet and was manufacturing counters and cabinets, as well as all interior wall sections, closets, gable ends, and overhangs. His shop devised and made equipment—such as a truck-mounted pump and storage tank for painting and a machine for forming sidewalks and rolled curbs—but it also copied the machinery and innovations of other builders, like the huge chain conveyor and saw machine that Long saw on a visit to the National Homes plant in Lafayette, Indiana. Other Phoenix area builders imitated Long's example, but only Hall and Staggs had the resources and skill to operate at the same preassembly level.[25]

The adoption of mass production techniques in home building— what Ralph Staggs called a "reverse assembly line"—occurred fairly rapidly in Phoenix, although some builders were more intuitive and quicker to innovate—again, mostly notably Long, but also Staggs and Hall. To achieve a specialized division of labor meant assigning workers to specific tasks and moving them from house to house. This imitated the method developed in manufacturing a century earlier, but the adoption of these techniques in Phoenix owed relatively little to direct factory experience: only John Hall, employed at AiResearch during the war, had worked on an assembly line. Instead, the builders' innovations followed their direct observations of building realities, their reading about builders like William Levitt, their hearing about developments in California housing construction, and stimulus from the FHA to reduce costs and increase production. What made the shift possible, though, were the opportunities for volume production and the local labor market.

The increased scope of Phoenix home building created an economy of scale that made these techniques profitable. In the immediate postwar era, subdivisions were relatively small, containing roughly 30 to 80 houses, which were constructed by various builders. By the mid-1950s subdivisions averaged closer to 180 houses, and in the larger ones a single builder produced all of the houses. At the high end of the scale, John Hall started a subdivision of 348 homes, while Ralph Staggs's Northeast Village included approximately 400. But it was John Long's Maryvale subdivision, eventually totaling 25,000 homes, that demonstrated the possibilities of mass production (figure 7.2). By 1959 the new scale of construction had become apparent: Long started 2,577 houses that year, followed by Staggs with 1,522 and Hall with 1,179. By 1967 Hall had built a career total of roughly 15,000 houses; Staggs had finished 14,000 homes in fifty-eight subdivisions by his retirement in 1972; and by the late 1970s Long had built more than 30,000 homes. But if all builders adopted the lessons of specialization, not all adopted the same management strategies. While one group, including Long, pushed to bring all aspects of building under their control, others, notably Staggs, subcontracted much of the work. Similarly, some builders, like Long, hired architects, while others, like Staggs, designed their own houses.[26]

Skilled labor provided the second key element in the initial Phoenix housing boom. The significant postwar immigration to Phoenix included numerous skilled laborers, which enabled builders to divide home construction into various skilled tasks. This was also union labor, and although periodic contract negotiations had contentious moments (as in 1962 and 1965), the relationship between builders and union laborers remained largely cooperative for the first several decades. In lauding the community's "great spirit of cooperation," Frank Snell specifically included labor, noting that Phoenix "did not have the unpleasant labor situations that many other communities have." Certainly one helpful factor was that most builders differed little from such laborers themselves, and some, like Ralph Staggs, had been union members. It was not coincidence, then, that John Long was the AFL-CIO's Man of the Year in 1958. By the mid-1960s, however, some builders were complaining about production bottlenecks caused by restrictive union work rules, and in the 1970s increasing wages led to changes in construction and greater use of nonunion labor.[27]

Materials also crucially affected the affordability and changing construction of Phoenix houses. Since the 1930s the federal government had encouraged builders to use cheaper materials, and plywood, concrete, and cinder block helped reduce costs. Private builders, like Kaiser Homes in California, also

Figure 7.2 Selling Maryvale. Because of his success in accelerating the pace of home construction and lowering the costs, particularly in his Maryvale community, John F. Long also innovated new methods of selling homes. These were subsequently imitated by other builders, notably Del Webb in selling Sun City. *Source:* John F. Long Properties.

tested different building materials, and in Arizona, John Long set up a building materials research facility in 1958 to focus on cost and durability.[28] The most important change in postwar building materials in Phoenix was the rapid shift to using locally manufactured cinder block. In 1945 Paul and Bill Thomas started the Superlite Builder's Supply Company, making block from volcanic scoria. Because the blocks were relatively inexpensive, as were the associated labor costs, builders quickly switched to using them instead of wood. Long estimated that using block saved him $500 per house (about 5 percent of the price). Roughly half of the homes built between 1945 and 1950 were made of block, and by the early 1960s they had been used in an estimated 85 percent of Phoenix area homes. By 1962 Superlite was the largest block manufacturing plant in the nation.[29]

The use of block also suited the decision of Valley builders to build ranch-style homes. Based on prewar California Bungalow styles and benefiting from the promotional efforts of architect Cliff May and *Sunset* magazine, ranch homes were popular throughout the nation, but especially in the Valley.[30] A few examples of this style of home had been constructed before the war, but the postwar housing demand, the relative ease of construction, and the emphasis on affordability made this the near-universal choice of Phoenix builders in the immediate postwar period. The early simple ranch style was a rectangular structure on a cement slab, having a low-pitched roof with asphalt shingles, a slightly overhanging eave with a small front porch, and a carport. Immediately after the war, builders constructed whole subdivisions of this basic model, but by the early 1950s they began shifting to modified versions, notably the California Ranch. This style had a more rambling or L-shaped form, a more varied gable or hip roof, larger eaves with no front porch, and often some type of ornamental trim. Builders also began dressing up the street-facing block wall with wood, brick, board and batten, or stucco. Additional diversity began in the late 1950s and spread into the 1960s, with the construction of modified ranch home styles—Spanish, American Colonial, French Provincial, Prairie, and "character"—as well as some trilevel homes. Other forms deviated in more than facade, such as the Contemporary Ranch style, with its nearly flat roof and extensive use of glass.[31]

By the late 1960s and 1970s, builders began offering a greater assortment of housing styles, such as the Los Ranchos type, which used stucco and a more rambling structure. Windows were often larger, and some builders included features that added light, such as skylights, inner atriums, or garden courtyards. Increased variety and structural complexity were made easier because builders revived the practice of framing houses out of wood. This occurred partly because it was the style of new builders from California, but also because rising wages for masons meant that building with block was no longer cheaper. Besides allowing more flexibility in exterior design, using wood also enabled builders to respond to rising energy costs and increasing ecological concerns during the 1970s by producing houses with much better insulation.

Diversity of design also reflected a growing unhappiness with the uniform housing styles in many subdivisions built before 1960. Ellis Suggs, president of the area Homebuilder's Association, noted that buyers "do not want their homes to look like the one across the street." More than simply improved taste was involved, of course. Several decades of economic growth and increasing affluence now enabled buyers to demand greater style and individuality in their housing. But while trends in the 1970s reflected improvements in housing, other developments would prove less beneficial. An influx of national builders, especially from California and Texas, began building acres of more expensive, two-story, Neo-Mediterranean-style houses, leading to growing problems that would become apparent in the 1980s.[32]

The Structure and Size of Phoenix Homes

The average size, internal structure, and setting of ranch homes in Phoenix and elsewhere changed significantly during this era, and Phoenicians had reason to believe that their community offered advantages over other places. Nationally, the average new house built in the 1940s was small, under 1,000 square feet, with two or three bedrooms and one and a half bathrooms. This increased to 1,230 square feet by 1957, roughly 1,400 square feet by the mid-1960s, and 1,645 square feet in 1975.[33] The average size of new houses in the metropolitan Phoenix area slightly exceeded the national figures for the early decade and matched it in the 1960s, although by the late 1970s that changed, as the average size rose to only 1,500 square feet. As one measure of the initial Phoenix edge, houses in Levittown, New York, averaged only 750 square feet, while most Long and Staggs houses in the early 1950s had 1,100 square feet, and the houses of other Phoenix builders ranged from 1,300 to 1,530 square feet.

Volume builders in the 1960s continued to offer small homes, but they responded to buyer demands by producing more larger models. Studies of housing patterns in Phoenix suburbs show appreciable variation. New houses in Mesa averaged 1,360 square feet from 1946 to 1955, increased to 1,450 square feet during the next decade, and reached 1,530 square feet between 1966 and 1973. Scottsdale houses built in this era were markedly larger. Those relatively few homes built before 1957 averaged 1,425 square feet; homes constructed in the boom of 1957–62 (when two-thirds of this era's housing was built) averaged 1,671 square feet; while the average new home in the subsequent decade topped 1,900 square feet.[34]

The increased house size related to the dimensions and number of rooms, but Valley builders and buyers also emphasized open floor plans and the internal arrangement of rooms. In the early 1950s some builders moved the living room to the rear of the house, opening onto a patio. By the early 1960s the typical home had two bathrooms and three or four bedrooms; living rooms were at the front of the house, while a family room with sliding glass doors was in the rear, next to the kitchen. Nearly as critical as house size and internal structure was the linkage to the backyard, which by the early 1950s was described as "an extension of the living area," so that builders "often are including a terrace, or patio, with the right kind of fence screening needed for privacy." Front yards were noted for their green lawns, trees, and bushes, but it was understood that "the back yard is the thing."[35]

This housing style fit Phoenix's culture of outdoor living and its championing of the Valley's climate, sunshine, and clean air. It also reflected the perspective developed in California and promoted by Cliff May and *Sunset* magazine, that "you do not just take the outdoors as it is. You manipulate it for your own purposes." The belief in human control of nature had been part of Valley culture since the beginning of settlement, but it especially matched the postwar belief in planning. This approach to nature fostered efforts to create "outdoor rooms" by expanding and roofing patio areas, adding barbecue grills, separating outside areas into "rooms" with partial walls and more elaborate landscaping, and, increasingly, building swimming pools (figure 7.3).[36]

Some private pools were constructed in the early 1950s, but a pool was

Figure 7.3 Making the outdoors into the "good life" in suburbia. *Source: This is Arizona: Fiftieth Anniversary* (special edition of *Arizona Days and Ways Magazine,* 11 February 1962), 73.

rather expensive, costing nearly $3,000, roughly a quarter to a third of the cost of a house. However, prices dropped considerably over the next decade: construction costs declined because of better equipment, experience, and volume production, and loan options became much more favorable, particularly when pool costs could be included in the home mortgage. By the early 1960s the advertised prices had fallen to between $1,700 and $2,000, and roughly thirteen thousand pools were built in the Phoenix area from 1960 to 1965. By 1977 the total number of pools in the Valley had reached sixty-seven thousand, found in roughly one of every seven homes. Further reflecting the view of backyards as "roofless rooms," pool designers had changed pool forms from rectangles to unique shapes that fit the house and backyard landscaping patterns.[37]

This outdoor room connected to a style of life, customs, and appearance proudly described as "informal" or "casual."[38] Phoenicians bragged that their "dress is far more casual than in other parts of the country," claiming that "sports shirts and slacks are perfectly acceptable business attire most of the year."[39] Observing their surroundings and neighbors, new residents also felt encouraged to pursue new notions about home furnishings. One recent migrant explained that living in Phoenix had led her to adopt a "contemporary and casual" decorating style, noting that "people are far more reserved in Wisconsin, and their homes reflect it." Housing designs replaced the dining room with a family room. The latter often included an eating area, but as one observer remarked, dinner guests might find themselves "eating from a TV tray in the living room" or "sitting on the floor" at a low table. Reflecting another common experience, a visitor to the 1962 Home Furnishings Exposition reported that her family often ate meals outside, where they had "comfortable furniture on our awning-covered patio and a swimming pool." As a result, she noted, "We're more inclined to stay home, because it's more comfortable there than anywhere else."[40] Both inside and outside, Phoenix housing offered a lifestyle that residents found attractive and that drew interested migrants.

Building Affordable Housing

Home buyers also appreciated the relatively low cost of Phoenix homes. Median values were $7,500 in 1950, and prices in 1953 for new homes ranged from roughly $9,000 for a smaller house (1,000 to 1,100 square feet) to $12,000 to $17,500 for a medium-sized home (1,300 to 1,500 square feet) and rising to $20,000 and above for larger and more luxurious homes. By the following year the increase in prefabrication, mass assembly, and volume production led to improved housing values. Hall and Staggs boosted the size of their base three-bedroom houses and maintained a price of $9,000, while Long lowered his price to $7,950, a cost below $7 per square foot, versus roughly $8 per square foot for his competition. In 1957 both Long and Hall were selling 1,400-square-foot homes for $10,950, with costs of $7.82 per square foot. (By way of comparison, in Levittown, New Jersey, in 1958 house prices ranged from $11,500 to $14,500.) From 1955 to 1960 single-family homes in metropolitan Phoenix increased in cost by only 9 percent, trailing the national increase of 23 percent. By several different measures Phoenix homes during the 1950s were a bargain compared with housing elsewhere in the nation, costing some 10 percent less.[41]

By the early 1960s, Long, Hall, and Staggs were selling houses to middle-income families at prices ranging from $9,000 to $16,000. However, by significantly expanding the prefabrication for his homes starting in 1959, Long retained his position as the lowest-cost builder. In 1962 he offered an exceptional value: a 1,879-square-foot home for $12,950, a cost of only $6.89 per square foot. Inflation made it impossible to maintain such prices, however, and a decade later the cost of middle-class housing ranged from $17,000 to $25,000. Besides inflation, the rising prices reflected some increase in house size but also, more importantly, additional equipment like central air-conditioning and electric heating, better appliances, increased amenities, plus higher-quality and more complex construction. Prices increased dramatically during the 1970s, topped by a 35 percent jump from 1978 to 1979, which exceeded the national average of 10 to 15 percent.

By the end of the 1970s, small homes and condominiums were selling for $30,000 to the low $40,000s. Such substantial inflation, plus the high interest rates for home mortgages, boosted the popularity of multifamily dwellings, which increased from a third to nearly half of all housing construction (figure 7.1). The major market for single-family homes stretched from the mid-$40,000s to the $70,000s, at roughly triple the costs of twenty years earlier. Finally, "one of the big changes" that observers noted in the area was "the increase in the buying of luxury homes," as a substantial number of subdivisions offered homes ranging from $90,000 to $220,000.[42]

Phoenix boosters and builders always considered the affordability of their housing very important, but by the 1970s changing market conditions and expectations had made this goal more difficult to achieve. The increased size of Phoenix houses most obviously and directly boosted their price, but consumer demands for changes in construction, such as increasing the insulation or adding features like interior tile, also played a role. In the short term, builders might maintain or even lower their prices by installing cheaper or lesser equipment, as some did in the mid-1960s by offering more homes with evaporative coolers instead of air-conditioning.[43] However, rising consumer expectations negated this as an effective long-term strategy. Builders also had little control over another element of price—the cost of land, which rose throughout these decades. For example, in 1946 Alfred Andersen paid $2,000 an acre for land for his Westwood Village subdivision, on the near-periphery of Phoenix; in 1952 adjacent land cost him $3,500 an acre.[44] Agricultural land in Deer Valley, further from the city, fetched $450 per acre in 1947, but ten years later it sold for $2,500 per acre and twice that by 1961. Builders like Ralph Staggs reported paying $2,500 to $3,000 an acre in the mid-1950s and $5,000 to $6,000 in the early 1960s.[45]

These escalating land costs, combined with the increasing costs of land improvements, substantially boosted the relative cost of home lots. During the late 1940s to 1950, lot prices accounted for roughly 10 percent of the cost of homes; that amount escalated to about 18 to 20 percent by the late 1950s to early 1960s; and by the late 1970s, in at least one family subdivision, lot costs had risen to 30 percent.[46] Not surprisingly, builders often sought to control their prices by reducing the sizes of their lots. The median-size lot in the Phoenix area in 1958 was 8,795 square feet, but changing times and circumstances had produced considerable variation. Lots in the old city core and immediately south of it averaged only 6,000 square feet, while areas south of the Salt River included a range of city and rural lot sizes, with the average being 11,934 square feet. Lots in the older, prestigious subdivisions like Kenilworth and Los Olivos typically measured 7,000 square feet (50 by 140 feet), while lots in the postwar subdivisions further north ran larger, measuring between 8,000 and 10,000 square feet. By contrast, mass builders Long, Hall, and Staggs built their homes on lots between 6,500 and 7,100 square feet in size, using smaller lots to reduce the overall prices of their homes. But beginning in the late 1960s many builders increased their lot sizes to meet market demand, and in areas like Mesa, where houses were less expensive, the lots averaged 9,100 square feet.[47]

Home loans were another key element affecting housing affordability, and builders worked to create the most attractive conditions for potential buyers. Down payments could be relatively low, sometimes only 8 percent, and John F. Long created a package requiring no down payment. Federal support through the FHA or VA proved crucial, insuring roughly half of all Phoenix loans in the mid-1950s (twice the national rate). Real estate funding came initially from local sources, but the booming market required more funds. New commercial banks attracted investments from eastern investors. The market also stimulated a major expansion of savings and loan companies, with Western Savings accounting for over half of the savings and loan mortgage business.[48]

BUILDING COMMUNITIES

The demand for Phoenix housing increased during these years partly because of the Baby Boom, a national trend, but migration to the Valley proved a far more important factor. Migrants to the Phoenix area came from virtually every state, but from the 1940s through the 1970s the bulk of them followed the historical patterns of migration to the Valley, reinforcing the existing cultural patterns and expectations. The Midwest contributed the most new residents, with persons from Illinois, Ohio, and Michigan consistently totaling one of every five migrants. A lesser share moved from the mid-Atlantic states, particularly New York; very few came from New England or the South; somewhat more came from the Pacific Northwest or the Southwest, particularly from Texas until the 1970s. The greatest number came from the neighboring state of California, but it also drew substantial migrants from other parts of Arizona.[49]

A shared regional culture was potentially an important source of stability for immigrants to Phoenix, for newness and population mobility overwhelmingly dominated city life. Besides the shifts caused by the area's tremendous overall growth, neighborhoods also altered because individuals changed residences. From 1960 to 1967 nearly two-thirds of the households moved, and of those, nearly half moved from one neighborhood to another. While roughly half of the households in the older city had moved during this period, the figure for neighborhoods to the north and south was roughly two-thirds, and over 70 percent of the residents of neighborhoods to the east and west had moved. Figures on multiple moves (table 7.2) suggest an even more complex pattern for the population and indicate some of the issues relating to community development.[50]

Traditionally, the city had been welcoming to newcomers. Stephen Shadegg attributed the "friendly open-handedness" of the area to the casual living style and a need for cooperation engendered by the harsh environment. Traditional booster culture had also fostered friendliness, for pursuing growth had meant accepting in-migrants as immediate contributors to community improvement. This openness also extended to leadership positions, for as noted earlier, able newcomers had not only been accepted, they had

become some of the city's top leaders. The city's physical structure, its
compactness and relatively small
size, had further encouraged this
pattern: the downtown fostered
face-to-face interaction, while well-
developed neighborhoods had supported various social organizations.

Initially, Phoenicians perceived
postwar growth as fitting this culture, and they saw the construction of houses and subdivisions as

Table 7.2 Number of moves per
Phoenix area household, 1960–67.

No. of moves	Percent
None	36
1	22
2 to 3	24
4 or more	18

Source: *Inside Phoenix, 1968* (Phoenix: Arizona
Republic, 1968), 30.

appropriate responses to housing demands. By the 1960s, however, growing
concerns about neighborhoods and city growth led to larger discussions
about the nature of society and community. Shadegg suggested that "under
the pressure of numbers in our growing mass civilization, this willingness
to be concerned with the problem of a neighbor appears to be rapidly dis-
appearing in certain areas."[51] Under the impact of continuing migration and
residential mobility, a perceived loss of social connections, and the recognition of the important changes brought by new techniques and the increased
scale of building, Phoenix builders began reevaluating the structure of the
neighborhoods they designed and constructed. To be sure, the changes they
made reflected national concern about suburbia and community, plus design
influences and ideas from outside the state, especially from California. But it
was the availability and relative affordability of land, as well as the interest in
imaginative projects, that produced the changes that appeared in many forms
in the next several decades: new subdivisions, retirement communities, new
towns, planned communities, and suburban cities.

The Shift to Community Building

Most home owners in the postwar era initially paid closest attention to the
costs, architecture, and sizes of their homes and lots, but over time both they
and society at large began examining more carefully the structures of the
areas where they lived. The transformation of home construction during the
immediate postwar period affected not only how builders worked and what
individuals could buy, but also the kind of society in which people resided.
Hugh Knoell, president of the Arizona Home Builders Association in 1953,
seemed to address this change. Noting that home construction was now part

of a larger process, he suggested that home owners were buying "an integrated unit of the community. The home builders in your city are really community builders."[52] But while Knoell was correct about changes in construction, to equate the increasing scale of production with the building of "community" meant ignoring the essential social dimensions of suburban life, exactly the concerns that drew growing attention from homes owners and social critics.

During the 1950s, subdivisions did grow larger, and individual builders increasingly produced all or most of the houses in a subdivision. Phoenix was a national leader in this trend, yet neither locally nor nationally did this shift have much effect on the shape or character of the subdivisions. By working within the standard one-mile grid of major streets in the metropolitan area, and given the few restrictions in city and county zoning and building standards, builders could still ignore the larger issues of constructing suburban society. Thus, the street layout of most subdivisions varied only marginally from a standard grid format, with some having slightly angled streets and an occasional cul-de-sac. Developers used land in these subdivisions almost exclusively for housing, with little provision for other features. In 1959 the urban fringe area of Phoenix included a minuscule 56 acres of playgrounds and parks (less than 1 percent of the area's 22,759 acres). Other public functions fared little better: no sites were designated for service structures like libraries or fire stations, and while some developers set aside land for schools, the city had to purchase the properties and build the schools. A final factor was the sprawling, leapfrog form of development. While Phoenix builders produced affordable homes, their designs were too often unimaginative, and the houses sat in isolated and auto-dependent subdivisions.[53]

Just as the rising criticism of identical housing styles during the 1950s yielded greater architectural variety, so too did objections to the nature of subdivisions encourage modifications in their structures. After 1960 subdivisions generally followed some design, with limited entrances, curvilinear streets, and cul-de-sacs; while planning for public land uses, especially parks and schools, increased. But instances of more substantial changes in constructing the city had begun in the early 1950s and included mixed-use development, specialty development, and planned communities.[54]

The first major innovation involved Park Central, a planned, mixed-use development. In 1950 three California developers—Ralph and A. J. Burgbacher, the sons of a Los Angeles general contractor and home builder, and Albert Behrstock—purchased more than 100 acres of the Central Avenue Dairy property, which was just three miles north of downtown. With

Ralph Burgbacher directing operations, the first construction phase of the project included 350 homes and 14 apartment buildings; phase two involved additional residences plus the construction of more expensive homes in a separate subdivision located a mile to the east.

Beyond the clusters of two-story apartment buildings, what distinguished this development was the inclusion of offices and commercial businesses as integral elements. In 1945 St. Joseph's Hospital had purchased ten acres of the dairy property on which to build a new facility; as this neared completion, Burgbacher constructed a major medical office building on adjacent land. As the key to this project, Burgbacher built Park Central shopping center, a collection of numerous stores including, most importantly, two department stores—Goldwater's and Diamond's. While other commercial properties were also developing outside of the central business district (CBD), this marked the first concentrated district and the first to include department stores. Being so close to downtown, the Park Central project represented an ominous trend.[55]

The expectations and context for building housing subdivisions in Phoenix changed in 1955 when John Long launched Maryvale, the first master-planned community in the Valley. Operating stealthily and through agents, he bought some sixty to seventy farms west of Phoenix, eventually totaling 15,680 acres. Careful reading of trade journals had previously helped him develop prefabrication and mass-assembly techniques; it also made him aware of architect Victor Gruen and his Los Angeles firm. Well-known since the late 1930s for store designs, in the later 1940s Gruen had expanded his planning interests to shopping centers and by the early 1950s was thinking about designs for the areas around such centers. Long wanted to build a community with various features, not just another residential subdivision, and he hired Gruen's firm to create the plan, even though it had not previously done such work. It was fortuitous timing for both parties. While Gruen's firm planned the noted Southdale Shopping Center and its surrounding environs near Minneapolis, its work on Maryvale advanced it to the next level of planning expertise. Long obtained a relatively complex community plan that featured various design features such as curvilinear streets plus many amenities that other new Phoenix neighborhoods did not have.

The initial impetus for Maryvale came from Long's understanding that building on a larger scale would help him increase efficiency and lower housing prices and that constructing related facilities would be profitable. But Long also valued community and maintained a sentimental attachment to the west Valley, where he had been born and continued to live. Thus, Long built the Maryvale homes and the state's largest shopping center to date, but he also donated land for libraries, schools, churches, medical facilities, and a YMCA. Long also gave land for the Maryvale golf course and 110 acres for seven parks, and he constructed public swimming pools and other park facilities. And when the young community had insufficient bonding capacity to pay for a school, Long built the school himself.

California connections comprised a final and vital element in this story. Gruen's Los Angeles location was crucial because it familiarized him with the area's multiplying examples of planned communities. Moreover, the financing for Maryvale came from California, and it was the planned-community aspects that convinced the lenders to make the investment.[56] And in marketing this community, Long went beyond Phoenix norms to hire a California actor, Ronald Reagan, as a pitchman.

New Approaches to Residence: Retirement Communities

While Long developed his larger community, other builders began pursuing a more specialized housing market, but one that also required a rethinking of suburban design. Rising affluence and higher Social Security payments, plus improved health and increased life expectancy, created new opportunities for retirees, and developers in various Sunbelt states began exploring the possibilities. Drawing on Phoenix's tradition of appealing to tourists and health seekers, some local builders were comfortable in designing for this targeted market. Starting with their experience in home building, they developed ideas and techniques to satisfy the interests and needs of retirees. Subsequently, they and other builders would use what they learned in this process and apply it to community building for nonretirement communities.

The Valley's first retirement venture, and allegedly the earliest in the nation, began in 1954, when realtor Ben Schleifer and builder Clarence Suggs bought a 320-acre farm some sixteen miles west of Phoenix. They planned a "retirement village" for persons aged fifty and over and began building inexpensive housing. Their residential community of Youngtown opened in 1955 and incorporated in 1960, when it contained roughly 900 homes (figure 7.4). Despite its growth, residents had mixed feelings about their community. Too distant from the city and from stores or other services, Youngtown suffered because the developers failed to realize what amenities might be needed, and they lacked the capital to build all of what they had promised.

Youngtown's main significance came from inspiring other projects that catered exclusively to seniors. The first and most explicit imitation came in 1958, when Mesa builder Ross Farnsworth began the retirement subdivision of Dreamland Villa, located just four miles from Mesa's then eastern boundary, in the "naturally soft mineral water belt." Starting with only 13 acres, Farnsworth expanded the subdivision over time, and by 1971 it included more than 600 acres, 2,100 homes, and more than 4,000 people. Dreamland Villa differed, then, by virtue of its expansion, but also because Farnsworth followed new development strategies. Most significantly, he built his subdivision next to a golf course, the first instance of what would become a crucial element of community building in Phoenix. Furthermore, rather than incorporating as a municipality or being annexed into Mesa, Dreamland Villa became a nonprofit organization and remained part of Maricopa County, becoming an island surrounded by the city of Mesa.[57]

In 1960 Ralph Staggs began another planned retirement village, Casa de

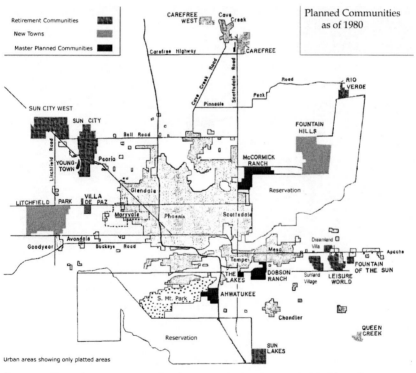

Figure 7.4 Planned communities in the Phoenix area, 1980. *Source:* Modified from figure 1 in Charles Sargent, *Planned Communities in Greater Phoenix: Origins, Functions and Control,* Papers in Public Administration no. 25 (Tempe, AZ: Institute of Public Administration, Arizona State University, 1973), 29. Courtesy Charles Sargent.

Sol, also east of downtown Mesa. Designed for 1,000 two- and three-bedroom homes, by 1963 it contained more than 200 homes. Other projects for seniors and retirees that emerged at this time were more modest in scope, with smaller and less expensive housing. The Desert Crest retirement home opened in Phoenix in 1958, as did the Shangri-La Apartments, which offered efficiency and one-bedroom apartments; they were followed quickly by several mobile home parks restricted to seniors. Builders of even these smaller retirement projects had learned from Youngtown's shortcomings and offered pools, a wide range of both sporting and craft activities, and some type of clubhouse. But easily the most important project inspired by Youngtown was Sun City.[58]

The success of this venture brought builder Del Webb national visibility, as his face graced the cover of *Time* magazine, but his company's importance predated this project, and Webb had little personal involvement in the first development stages of Sun City. During the 1950s Webb's company operated nationally, completing numerous military, industrial, and commercial projects in some twenty states, but it had built relatively little housing, and most of its Arizona projects were commercial. Seeking new business ventures in the late 1950s and aware of both Youngtown and projects in Florida, Webb directed company Vice President Thomas Breen to investigate constructing a retirement community, perhaps in Arizona. Breen and other company officials concluded, like other builders of Valley retirement housing, that success depended on designing an entire community with substantial amenities and completing these amenities before selling the homes. Thus, DEVCO, the company subsidiary that designed and built Sun City, began by creating a golf course, swimming pool, and other recreation sites; the "town hall" included an auditorium and meeting rooms; residents could use an arts and crafts center or the agricultural center; and the community design included lakes and stores. The modest homes were priced from $8,000 to $11,300, roughly within the lower half of the scale for Phoenix area housing at the time.[59]

The community opening on January 1, 1960, was a great success, attracting more than 100,000 people and with 272 homes being sold during that weekend. The office was so crowded that some salesmen had to sit on the floor to write contracts. The company was also pleased to discover that buyers had more money than anticipated, with half of them purchasing their homes in cash. In 1965, as sales of the original models had slowed, and in response to the better, larger, and more expensive housing in the Phoenix area, DEVCO began offering more substantial and more expensive models, sparking another sales boom (figure 7.5). When Sun City opened Phase II in

1968, it offered still better homes priced from $16,000 to $32,000; this trend continued through the 1970s and with the opening in 1978 of Sun City West, a sister community.[60]

See this fabulous new 1967
Experimental Model Home Today at the

GRAND OPENING IN Sun City

SEE THESE SPACE-AGE FEATURES:

① – Home designed around central garden and fountain
② – Water Purifying System
③ – Built-in Vacuum Cleaning System
④ – Kitchen Cabinets Grouped in unique storage wall
⑤ – Island Gas Bar-B-Q and Electric Range
⑥ – Built-in Food Center (mixer, blender, chopper, etc.)
⑦ – FM/AM Music – Intercom System Central Control
⑧ – Wet Bar with ice water on tap
⑨ – Swedish Steam Bath and Shower
⑩ – Whirlpool Bath and 6-foot tub

AND MANY MORE!

**See It Now
In Arizona's Most
Beautiful City**

DEL WEBB DOES IT AGAIN!

Once again, Del Webb demonstrates that the newest and most exciting concepts in home design become an up-to-the-minute reality at Sun City. No other builder in America encourages public participation in the design of new homes, but at Sun City, Del Webb and Sun Citizens work closely to bring this about. Now here's the proof . . . a home that brings the outdoors indoors . . . the all-new Experimental Model Home for 1967!

The Del Webb Development Company designed and built it specially to show you tomorrow's concepts in home design today. Many of its features will be incorporated in future Sun City homes. Because Sun City residents participate in choosing the features they want in their homes.

Yes, once you see it in person . . . once you discover the subtle blending of colors and coordination of materials . . . you will agree with us when we say it is indeed a home to remember.

Prove it to yourself. Drive to Sun City and see this remarkable new home . . . because seeing is believing! It may prove to be the wisest move you've ever made.

HOME LOCATION: 105TH DRIVE AND PEORIA AVE.

Sold by DEL E. WEBB DEVELOPMENT CO.

DEL E. WEBB CORPORATION
(COMMUNITY DEVELOPMENT DIVISION)

12 miles Northwest of Phoenix out Grand Ave.

Figure 7.5 Sun City new floor plan, 1967. By the mid-1960s Del Webb offered substantially upgraded homes in Sun City. *Source: Arizona Republic,* 13 November 1966.

Sun City achieved both national recognition and local success. The homes and other facilities were well built, and the properties sold quickly and appreciated in value. By 1980 the community's population topped forty thousand, and had it been incorporated, it would have been the Valley's fifth largest city (table 7.1). Despite this, public criticism of the project rose during the 1970s. Some opposed the basis of the community, arguing that such age segregation was socially deleterious, or they criticized the architecture as too bland. Others described the development as an isolated, sterile enclave because it was racially and politically homogeneous.

Sun City's decision to rely on county government and private services rather than to incorporate suggested a disinterest in the larger society, and the strongest criticisms on this issue arose because Sun Citians' opposition to raising taxes doomed every bond election in the neighboring Peoria school district to defeat for fifteen years. A partial settlement developed in 1975, when Sun City seceded from the Peoria district, removing the seniors' virtual veto of increases in school spending. Having chastised the retirees for obstruction, critics continued to fault them for avoiding a basic social responsibility. Community residents defended themselves by pointing out that they paid three-quarters of the school taxes, yet received no direct benefit, and that they had purchased homes expecting to pay no school taxes.[61] A key issue in the dispute was whether Sun City should be considered part of or separate from the larger community.

Most residents also dismissed the "enclave" criticism, seeing the demographics of the community as being more coincidental than intentional. They valued the community because it provided aging residents with vital support services, and by offering numerous physical and social activities, it encouraged residents to remain active. Already in 1962 residents had organized more than ninety clubs and organizations, and they arranged numerous social events. People participated in projects within Sun City, and many served as volunteers in neighboring communities and schools. While Sun City did not provide cheap housing for the elderly, neither was it an elite suburb. The sizes, prices, and features of housing in the community had increased over the years, but the rise had essentially paralleled housing trends in the metropolitan area.[62]

Sun City retirement communities created a large and highly visible presence in the West Valley, but sizeable retirement communities also appeared in the East Valley after 1970 (figure 7.4). This included the relatively small and isolated communities of Sun Lakes (1971) and Rio Verde (1972). More importantly, a growing concentration of adjacent or neighboring communities appeared in east Mesa. Leisure World (1971) was built just south of Dreamland Villa, with Fountain of the Sun (1970) to the east and Sunland Village (1979) to the west. Although operating on smaller scales than Sun City and perhaps with slight differences in their target market, these planned communities reflected the same type of suburban design, which often included lakes; they sought to create opportunities for social interaction; and they provided amenities, especially golf courses.

Despite the proliferation of these communities, the Valley's rapid growth meant that seniors did not comprise more of the population than elsewhere in the nation. Moreover, these communities were not especially exclusive, and they did encourage residents to remain active. But despite the broader perspectives of the developers and community leaders, the structure and age segregation of these communities tended to promote attitudes of suspicion, and separation from the society threatened the larger goal of community.[63]

"New Towns"

The proliferating critiques of postwar suburban design in Arizona and the nation provided a primary impetus for both these retirement communities and Maryvale. Long (and Gruen) focused on structural innovations, with a curvilinear street pattern, varied placement of houses on lots, and planning for commercial development, public facilities, and recreation. The retirement communities included some of these features but added an involved and involving system of social activities and recreation facilities to foster interaction and social relationships that addressed the specific needs of mobile retirees. During the 1960s and increasingly in the 1970s these models and strategies evolved further in other, nonretirement projects in the Valley.

Some nonretirement projects drew directly on the lessons of retirement communities, for builders of the latter, like Webb and Farnsworth, used those designs and some of the social planning in their nonretiree projects. The pattern of development also reflected the indirect influence of Arizona's past, for like most western states, Arizona had some older history of companies designing and building communities. Mining corporations had constructed company towns like Clarkdale and Ajo, and Goodyear had built the agricultural towns of Ocotillo and Goodyear, but these communities were relatively small and narrowly focused on employee housing plus some basic services.[64]

A more useful model came from the alternative to American (and European) cities that began with Ebenezer Howard's Garden City ideas in the 1890s and took form in new towns like Radburn in the 1920s and New Deal town-building efforts in 1930s. The burgeoning critique of postwar suburbia revived this approach by the late 1950s and led to the construction throughout the nation of communities of varying sizes, completeness, and independence that reflected New Town ideals. The design of various Arizona communities demonstrated the influence of this perspective, albeit an influence that often came directly from California sources. State law also affected these projects. A 1961 law prohibited incorporation of a town within six miles of an existing city, which strengthened the impulse to build New Towns at some remove from other municipalities. Beginning in 1966 the legislature also began discussing how to encourage planning and planned communities, which resulted in a 1970 law to encourage and regulate new urban developments.[65]

Three developments in Arizona sought with some success to be independent and self-contained New Towns. In 1963 Robert McCulloch bought twenty-six square miles of land along the Colorado River in western Arizona and started Lake Havasu City, which was planned by Charles Wood, Jr., one of the designers of Disneyland. McCulloch, who manufactured small engines, built the city as a test site for his outboard motors and as a real estate investment, and he imported the London Bridge to attract tourists.[66] Inspired by his success in this venture, McCulloch began a second project in 1968, also designed by Charles Wood. Fountain Hills began from twelve thousand acres in the far northeast Valley near the confluence of the Verde and Salt rivers and adjacent to the site where a planned dam would create a lake—and which would have flooded much of the Fort McDowell Indian Reservation. The town grew slowly, because the dam was delayed and ultimately not built and because it was quite distant from the developed urban area. It failed to become self-sufficient because it lacked significant employment opportunities and housing at varied prices. Instead, it offered a five-hundred-foot fountain to attract tourists and amenities like a golf course and pricey homes to attract retirees and upper middle class residents who commuted to Phoenix.[67]

The most ambitious New Town was Litchfield Park, some twenty miles west of downtown Phoenix. The Goodyear Company had built a village of that name in 1918 to provide housing for managers and employees at its fourteen-thousand-acre farm, had added the Wigwam resort in 1929, and in the 1950s had sold some homes to the public. With the water table dropping and the metropolitan region expanding, the company decided in the early 1960s to convert the farm into a city.[68] It hired Victor Gruen to create an ambitious master plan for a community of up to ninety thousand people. Besides the economic motive, the company's decision also reflected its longstanding interest in community. Goodyear believed that its town would compare favorably to the "very ordinary quality of present suburban development" in Phoenix. Speaking more pointedly, Litchfield Park's director of marketing observed that "our cities just happen, sprawling into ugly asphalt jungles with mishmash zoning, the monotony of row upon row of look-alike tract housing, streets congested with traffic, slums and ghettos. In short, America the ugly. Goodyear wanted Litchfield Park to be different."[69]

And it was. Gruen's plan followed his public writings and presented a hierarchical, organic city starting from the basic neighborhood unit, which clustered into communities, then into towns, and then into a city, with each level having higher-order services. The plan emphasized pedestrian traffic, a mix of housing types, restrictions and codes for property use, and a diverse economy supported by the allocation of areas for industry. It also included public facilities, schools, shopping, and a golf course. The elaboration and implementation of the plan involved the building of various commercial properties, construction of neighborhoods in different price ranges, and discussions regarding a hospital and some type of college—possible a junior college, but more hopefully a branch campus of Arizona State University.[70]

Litchfield Park had problems implementing the plan and struggled because of its location. A slump in the housing market and a predominance of more expensive homes reduced the community's intended size and diversity. New residents complained about the restrictions on the use of their properties. The delayed extension of Interstate Highway 10 to Los Angeles (expected in 1971 but not completed until 1990) meant lengthy travel times between Litchfield Park and Phoenix, hurting the prospects for local business and requiring long commutes for persons working in the city. The state legislature struck another blow when it killed a proposed branch campus of Arizona State University. Most importantly, with infrastructure costs running much higher than anticipated, Goodyear was slow in preparing industrial sites and lost potential buyers. As Hugh Kelly noted, "The development of our new town relies heavily on the impetus provided by new industry," and those potential buyers "will not settle for promises." Ultimately, Litchfield Park failed to attract significant employment for residents, largely eliminating its ability to develop as a self-sufficient town. With a population of 1,664 in 1970 and only 3,657 in 1980 (table 7.1), Litchfield Park emerged as only a small bedroom suburb. The community's municipal incorporation in 1987 represented a conservative step, to protect itself from being annexed by the population spreading west from Phoenix.[71]

Planned Communities

Although New Towns failed to achieve self-sufficiency, some of their broad designs and some elements of retirement communities were manifested in planned communities, a number of which developed in the late 1960s and 1970s. Some thirty subdivisions begun in this period in various areas of the Valley had a design population above one thousand, a size that permitted, and to some extent required, planning.[72] The importance of this was explained by Jerry Miller, the sales manager for John F. Long: "If you don't have a master plan, several square miles could be built up with houses without sites for schools, shopping areas, and parks."[73] Many subdivisions built during the 1950s had borne witness to this, and while city planning and zoning requirements helped prevent repetition, standards in the county and some suburbs were far more lax. Besides any altruistic interest in improving urban life or the pursuit of greater efficiencies, by 1970 builders engaged in planning in an effort to attract home buyers, and the quality of the planning depended on the builder, as well as on the size and location of the subdivision.

Of the "large" subdivisions started before 1980, the smallest eleven contained between 50 and 150 acres and were constructed by local builders. Half were in Phoenix and were ten to fifteen miles from downtown. They did not offer a neighborhood organization or facilities; most were located near a park and sometimes near a school, but had no other public facilities; and, given the grid layout of the Valley, all were relatively close to some types of commercial establishments. Two subdivisions in this size category had more features. Located in Mesa and Scottsdale, they were connected with larger subdivision developments and linked with home owner associations, a golf course, and other amenities.[74]

Another cluster included larger subdivisions, ranging from 500 to 1,200 acres, which were located outside Phoenix and between sixteen and twenty-six miles from downtown.[75] Golf courses were a central design feature for all but two of these communities, influencing the shapes of streets and the placement of houses. Subdivisions built in the western and southern parts of the Valley, which had previously been farmland, introduced water features; part of the Lakes subdivision in Tempe was built around a chain of man-made lakes. By contrast, communities in northern Scottsdale and Phoenix were set in desert foothills near mountains, and the lots, landscaping, and neighborhood design fit the characteristics of that area. Most of these communities included a mix of housing types and prices, schools, and access to nearby shopping and entertainment. But their most important contrast with the smaller and more centrally located subdivisions was their uniform use of home owner associations. Although there were some nineteenth-century antecedents, the use of such associations was essentially pioneered by J. C. Nichols in his Kansas City subdivision in 1910. Their popularity increased particularly after 1960 as an alternative to more cumbersome deed restrictions and less secure zoning, and they were used to protect home values and provide for common community resources and property. In these communities they aimed to complement the design features that encouraged community identity in the midst of a burgeoning suburban society, yet they also created a particular kind of community.[76]

The largest subdivisions built during this era were also the most institutionally complete—the three master-planned communities of Ahwatukee (2,100 acres), McCormick Ranch (3,116 acres), and Dobson Ranch (4,500 acres). Each was constructed on a single parcel of former ranch land, and unlike the more peripheral local of the aforementioned "larger" subdivisions, these communities were within fifteen miles of downtown Phoenix and close to existing subdivisions. When Ahwatukee began in 1971, it lay south of the Phoenix city boundaries, but its developers negotiated water and sewer hookups with the city in return for accepting future annexation, a process the city started in 1978. Like the other two communities, Ahwatukee used a curvilinear street pattern; it contained a mix of housing styles and types, including condos and retirement housing; it offered a golf course and tennis club, adjacent space for schools and churches, nearby shopping, and highway access to downtown Phoenix. The California-based development company, which had experience building master-planned communities in that state, also created a home owners' association, with various codes and restrictions on property usage.[77]

McCormick Ranch resembled Ahwatukee in many ways. It included many of the same features, but it aimed for a slightly wealthier clientele, reflecting its location in north Scottsdale, an area with relatively wealthy property owners. Kaiser Aetna, which purchased the property in 1969, cooperated with Scottsdale in producing a master plan for the entire area of the city, and Victor Gruen's firm produced a more detailed plan for the ranch area. It resembled both Ahwatukee and Litchfield Park in some design aspects—for example, in its inclusion of mixed housing, shopping, pedestrian walkways, golf courses, and lakes—but the housing was more expensive, and a resort sector was a central feature. Following the development strategy pioneered in Sun City, McCormick's developers made certain these amenities were in place when the first residences were sold in 1972. Although Gruen's original plan had included numerous school sites, revised plans eliminated many of them because new goals emphasized an older resident population. The community lacked highway access to Phoenix, although future improvements were anticipated, but it was near certain important sources of employment, particularly Scottsdale Healthcare. Finally, the home owners' association played an equally vital role in regulating the community.[78]

The third and largest master-planned community of this era, Dobson Ranch in southwestern Mesa, came the closest of any Valley development to being self-sufficient. Its housing ranged from apartments to sizeable single-family homes; the community included various types of business and professional offices, with a modest resort situated on the periphery; and along with fourteen shopping areas, the East Valley's largest shopping mall was built immediately north of Dobson Ranch on land purchased from the community's developer. Space within the community was allocated for churches and schools, both elementary and junior high, while a high school and community college were built on immediately adjacent land. Lakes were a central design feature, as was a golf course, but unlike those in most developments, this was a public course. Other public features also distinguished the community—a park, a library, as well as police and fire substations. Although the Dobson Ranch development itself did not offer substantial employment, the East Valley's largest hospital was built on twenty-four acres of adjacent land donated by the Dobson family, and one of the few Valley highways was extended to the community's northern border by 1977. The home owners' association managed common community areas, including various recreation facilities, and enforced the same types of codes and restrictions as other associations. With roughly forty-five hundred acres and a built-out population that reached fifteen thousand by the early 1990s, Dobson Ranch reflected the Valley's most significant effort to address the problems of urban sprawl and suburban design.[79]

The shift to larger and planned community development had numerous consequences. As the developers and planners intended, these were better designed and had more features than other subdivisions. While some of the smallest developments were strictly residential and offered only a limited range of housing, as had the initial postwar subdivisions, most of these communities included mixed housing and a range of commercial and recreational options. What this increase in size and features meant, of course, was a significant rise in the costs and financing needed to begin these projects. This prompted an influx of builders and developers from other states, especially from California, which also supplied project financing and designers.

In many ways these communities were more successful than the subdivisions built previously, but elements of their design differed significantly from those of traditional community structures, especially in establishing public features and responsibilities. While a few communities specifically included public functions—such as Dobson Ranch, which incorporated space for police and fire substations, as well as a public library—most did not. Communities in the two larger categories used golf courses as central features, but except for Dobson's municipal course, these were either country clubs or privately owned. Few of any planned communities except Dobson Ranch (and half of those in the smallest group) included a public park. Instead, most recreational facilities in the areas were owned and operated by their home owners' associations. While these organizations represented a major addition to urban/suburban life, by restricting participation to home owners they limited their ability to represent all residents, and their powers would become increasingly controversial in subsequent years.[80]

From Agricultural Satellites to Supersuburbs

The four municipalities adjacent to Phoenix were the Valley's next largest population centers. During the 1950s they began growing rapidly, with their populations doubling in each of the next two decades (table 7.1). In the 1970s two of them ranked among the fastest-growing U.S. cities of over 100,000: Mesa held second place, and Tempe ranked ninth. Aggressive annexation contributed substantially to suburban growth. In the late 1950s these four communities included less than 20 square miles; by 1970 they had spread to across more than 130 square miles, and to more than 230 in 1980.[81]

These communities were "suburbs," but as numerous authors have shown in recent years, that term harbors substantial variety. Each was clearly suburban in housing styles, land use, reliance on automobiles, and subordination to Phoenix, but their origins and the nature of growth in the Valley fostered a type of development outside the suburban "norm." Starting as agricultural satellites, separate from but dependent on Phoenix for important urban functions and services, they developed during these years into semidependent, unique communities, with independent features. Their size marks them as "supersuburbs," to use Carl Abbott's term, while their pattern of expansion through annexation puts them into David Rusk's category of "hyper-elastic cities." Both size and the metropolitan context are important for understanding these communities, but their internal features were also crucial. While sharing some common characteristics, they also followed distinct paths of maturation.[82]

The oldest and second largest of these communities, Tempe grew beyond its agricultural roots because it was home to what became Arizona State University. From a college in 1954 with roughly four thousand students, the institution morphed over the next twenty-five years into a university with an enrollment of thirty thousand. Besides attracting student residents and becoming a major community employer, ASU shaped the development of Tempe and made it a magnet for people throughout the Valley with its facilities and its athletic and cultural programs. Gammage Auditorium served as the Phoenix Symphony's home for nearly a decade, and ASU football games were easily the largest sporting event in the Valley.

The community's growth also followed the Phoenix strategy, with modest success in attracting manufacturing firms, especially electronics companies, which concentrated in industrial parks along the city's western boundary. Yet the city also showed some ambivalence about growth. Traditional businesses rapidly abandoned the Tempe downtown during the 1960s, creating vacancies filled by some counterculture businesses. An organization of these merchants initiated an arts and crafts fair, which grew steadily. They and other community members sought to direct the redevelopment of downtown to preserve historic buildings and independent stores, rather than creating an area of new buildings with upscale chain-store shopping. By 1980 this strategy had begun to demonstrate considerable success.

The city also evidenced ambivalence toward continued annexation. Although Tempe had expanded throughout the 1950s and 1960s, even vying with Phoenix for certain neighborhoods, this strategy came under attack by the 1970s. Critics felt that continued expansion to the south, with increasingly expensive housing, would generate greater conflict with the city's older northern section. In 1974 the smaller city of Chandler took advantage of this division and ended the argument: it annexed land to the south of Tempe, making that city landlocked.[83]

Scottsdale's initial postwar promotion used the historically inaccurate theme of "The West's Most Western Town," with wooden storefronts built for a section of downtown buildings, like a movie set. The reality of Scottsdale's development included a more prosaic aspect, with subdivisions in the southern and eastern parts of town containing relatively inexpensive homes and small lots, much like those in many areas of Phoenix. But the community's development also included another element. Motorola's construction of manufacturing plants starting in 1957 encouraged an influx of skilled workers and professionals. They helped make Scottsdale Arizona's wealthiest community in 1960, with "the highest household income, level of education, and percentage of persons employed in white-collar occupations."[84] This factor, plus the community's awareness of other development strategies in the Valley and an appreciation of Scottsdale's own historical and geographical character, prompted it to create a new development strategy by the mid-1960s.

After earlier efforts to annex developed territory to the west had been thwarted by Phoenix, Scottsdale began expanding rapidly to the north, growing from 3.8 to 68 square miles between 1960 and 1970 and to 88 square miles by 1980. A city plan in 1962 and a more important one in 1966 helped shape this drive. Seeking to capitalize on the proximity to mountains in the north and east and the attractiveness of those vistas, it prescribed expensive housing in this area. This produced the highest median housing values of any Valley community, a trend that increased with the construction of McCormick Ranch, followed soon after with similar planned developments to the north. Building on the community's tradition of attracting artists, the city encouraged the development of an art gallery district, and in 1975 it completed the Scottsdale Center for the Arts.[85]

The community's economic development plan followed one aspect of the Phoenix model, as Scottsdale took over the World War II Thunderbird II airfield in 1966 as a municipal airport and an area for business development. A second and more obvious similarity was city leaders' choice to build on Scottsdale's tradition of catering to tourism. The decision to develop the city "as a full service resort destination" produced not only numerous resorts but also "the maturing of specialty and high end retail areas." Thus, Scottsdale developed a second type of suburban community, which hosted upscale residential development and high-end commerce to attract shoppers from various communities in the Valley.[86]

Mesa created yet another pattern of development. For decades the largest of the small agricultural satellite towns, Mesa began the postwar era pursuing various growth strategies. But at the end of the 1950s it abandoned its faux western-themed tourist ventures and its marginally successful pursuit of convention business to focus on attracting manufacturing. Its initial efforts had included development around Falcon Field, the airfield acquired by the city after World War II, which had drawn businesses such as Rocket Power. Increased employment and residence in Mesa also came from the expansion of Williams Air Base and the establishment of the General Motors Proving Grounds. The city's efforts bore striking success during the 1960s with the addition of major industrial and manufacturing firms—Motorola's integrated circuit factory, a McDonnell-Douglas helicopter plant, and Talley Industries, a defense contractor and manufacturer of propellants. By the 1970s manufacturing accounted for one-sixth of Mesa's employment.[87]

Unlike Scottsdale and Tempe, Mesa did not produce a strategy for developing its downtown. While the city center deteriorated, the location of commercial areas and professional offices decentralized, as the sprawl of housing was accompanied by shopping centers, a modest-sized mall to the west, and in 1979 a large mall in the far southwest corner of the city. Mesa was unique in not levying a city property tax, relying instead on utility fees, retail sales tax, and construction-related sales taxes. This policy sometimes caused fiscal problems, but it also helped encourage the development of many retirement communities in central and east-central Mesa. It did not, however, undermine the highly ranked school system, which was funded by a separate tax. Mesa also differed by annexing mostly built-up areas rather than undeveloped land, a pattern evident in the 1970 population density figures (Mesa had 3,150 persons per square mile, Tempe had 1,658, and Scottsdale had only 985). Finally, Mesa differed in the nature of its housing, for developers chose to focus "on the middle and low income markets."[88]

The other traditional agricultural satellite was Glendale. Like Mesa it gained from the military's presence, for Luke Air Force Base had a substantial payroll. Higher education also had some impact, as Glendale received some economic benefit and status from the growth of the Thunderbird Graduate School of International Management. But unlike the other supersuburbs, Glendale did not experience an economic transformation. The city did not attract or develop much manufacturing, so that agricultural services remained important. Commercial patterns also differed: the city's first mall was not built until 1973, which partly explains why the traditional downtown did not collapse until the early 1980s. Thus, during this period Glendale did function mainly as a bedroom suburb, a residential home for persons who worked elsewhere.[89]

Of the other Valley communities, only Chandler and Peoria saw any appreciable population growth before 1980, and that occurred in the 1970s (table 7.1). The other towns remained small and agricultural in orientation, still too distant from the urban and urbanizing areas. But the four supersuburbs became integral parts of the metropolis by 1980. Their expansion and that of Phoenix ended the clear physical separation between them. The patterns of suburbanization created an increasingly common environment and metropolitan mindset and also threatened the distinctiveness of the smaller communities. To a large extent, however, they were successful in forging separate identities and roles. They followed different strategies in developing their signature downtowns and the character of their residential neighborhoods. While Phoenix businesses drew suburban commuters, suburban economies were sufficiently vibrant to employ many of their own residents as well as drawing persons from other suburbs and from Phoenix.[90] By maintaining their independence, they developed separate and unique political cultures and identities. Their success in creating independent cultural and commercial attractions paralleled the decentralized development of Phoenix and added to the emergence of a multinodal metropolis—what Joel Garreau termed "edge cities" and what other authors call "postsuburban."[91]

Shopping for Community

Postwar prosperity produced an explosion of consumer spending. Supplying this tremendous demand led to massive increases in stores and other places to shop, and this helped transform Phoenix and its major suburbs. Prewar shopping had concentrated heavily in Phoenix and its downtown, although each of the larger Valley towns contained a limited number of stores. In addition, some primary streets in Phoenix away from downtown featured miscellaneous stores, while a few shopping centers, focused on grocery stores, were built at some major street intersections.[92]

By the late 1950s the distribution of shopping had changed considerably to reflect population dispersal to the suburbs, the availability of cars, and more efficient designs. The initial commercial building activity had produced individual shops and service businesses "in strips along major traffic arteries, particularly those leading to the central core." With increased use of cars, this sort of linear development lost favor because single-use allocation of parking spaces was costly and inefficient. Instead, planners recommended and builders constructed shopping centers at major intersections, with businesses sharing parking. From 1950 to 1957, more than 6 million square feet of shopping area were built, with another 4 million under construction, and the pace increased thereafter. In 1957 the Valley featured twenty-six shopping centers with 288 stores, and it boasted of having the greatest number per capita of any city. A mere four years later it had fifty-eight centers and 845 stores. The scope of these projects increased: by 1968 each of thirteen large centers contained more than 100,000 square feet (averaging 162,000 square feet and twenty-six stores), anchored by grocery and drugstores, and typically including a bank, restaurant, and movie theater, along with other shops. A decade later the Valley had thirty-five of these "district" centers, with another eighteen located in surrounding cities.[93]

The spread of shopping centers represented a proliferation of commerce, revolving around food stores and some service. A second expansion of the 1950s, involving other types of commerce and greater spending, came in suburban downtowns. By 1961 they offered 629 stores with 830,000 square feet of shopping, equaling nearly 90 percent of the floor space in downtown Phoenix. Suburban downtowns were only a partial alternative, however, for their stores were smaller, their parking was limited, and they did not include the key attraction of major department stores. The development of malls more than countered these limitations (table 7.3).[94] The opening of the Park Central Mall in 1957 initiated an era of massive construction of malls: by 1963 seven malls had opened in north central Phoenix, offering four times the commercial space available in downtown Phoenix and all anchored by department stores. Two subsequent waves of construction further increased the shopping opportunities and distributed them to the east and west sides of the Valley. Nor did the initial construction mark an end to commercial development. All of the seven original malls expanded the number of their stores, and four increased their overall size by half.[95]

In Phoenix, as in other developing cities, malls represented not an anti-downtown movement but a substitute downtown. The range and arrangement of stores in malls mimicked and improved on the city's prewar pattern in which clothing, shoe, and other accessory stores were located near department stores, while specialty shops on secondary streets benefited from the traffic drawn by major stores. The second-stage Phoenix malls took the imitation a step further by adding elements like movie theaters, more restaurants, hotels, and even a library. These designs reflected the vision of important early mall architects, most famously Victor Gruen, of malls as a sort of "suburban downtown," an alternative to the auto-focused strip malls and shopping

Table 7.3 Valley malls, 1957–81.

Year opened	City	No. of malls	No. of tenants	Building area (sq. ft.)
1957–63	Phoenix	7	321	3,574,367
1961	Scottsdale	1	29	200,000
1972–73	Phoenix	3	288	2,506,098
1968–69	Mesa, Scottsdale	2	140	1,207,572
1979–81	Phoenix	2	234	1,555,400
1979	Mesa	1	166	1,177,500
TOTAL		16	1,361	11,372,400

Source: *Inside Phoenix* (Phoenix: Arizona Republic), 1968, 1978, 1989 editions.

centers, an updating of the small town. Gruen and others emphasized that besides shopping, malls should provide a social space for pedestrians, public art and beautiful interiors, and even public meeting rooms.

Throughout the nation, highway access and the lower cost of land encouraged the construction of many malls on the urban periphery. In Phoenix, by contrast, the slow construction of highways produced a different pattern, with only two of the first thirteen malls built close to highways. Furthermore, because Phoenix grew so rapidly, even those malls initially situated away from built-up areas were quickly engulfed by the expansion of commercial and residential developments. Thus, land cost influenced the placement of malls, but they also needed to be close enough to residential developments to attract sufficient patrons.

In some cases the relationship between mall and neighborhoods was even stronger, embracing Gruen's philosophy of making malls part of community development. The Paradise Valley Mall (1979) represented this sort of effort and served as the core for community-development efforts associated with the Paradise Village region of Phoenix. This 1,200-acre community included single- and multifamily housing, churches, schools, and parks. But while similar to other master-planned communities, Paradise Village never achieved the status of a new town or integrated community. Neither in Phoenix nor elsewhere in the nation did the public downtown aspects or the community center features of malls develop as the more optimistic proponents had wished. Indeed, by 1978 Victor Gruen had largely given up hope.[96]

CONCLUSION

Suburbanization was a central element of postwar American life, and this was especially true for Phoenix. Despite the limits on what any single place can reveal about such a common experience, when read carefully and in context, it can tell us important things. The experience of Phoenix illuminates what this was like in a very rapidly growing Sunbelt city, in terms of both individual experiences and the impact on the larger community.

Most Phoenicians liked the city's suburban expansion. The most important reason for this attitude was that houses were affordable and attractive, offering the increasing number of owners a lifestyle that they appreciated. Spacious ranch homes with a family room–backyard connection fit contemporary notions of progress, but also Phoenix's traditional stress on being modern and being oriented towards the outdoors. The tremendous demand for housing and the local value placed on affordability encouraged innovation in home building and determined what types of housing were produced. But the emphasis on mass production and the increasing sizes of subdivisions resulted in isolated neighborhoods with homogenous housing.

One response to this problem was for builders to modify the parameters of housing. By the 1970s, with rising levels of wealth and a different type of market in play, they appreciably diversified the types of housing in size, style, and cost. More importantly, they began designing communities. While it is useful to discuss those communities in their separate categories—retirement, or new town, or planned subdivision—in reality, such divisions were porous: some builders produced each of these types, and all builders observed and copied the innovations. Thus, curvilinear streets, mixed housing, access to shopping, various amenities, and some type of neighborhood organization became increasingly common in new subdivisions of various sizes.

But certain factors determined which of these features were implemented. The virtual absence of any public authority, either city or county, to plan effectively meant that builders made the decisions, and they were significantly influenced by available space and cost. Smaller communities had less variety and fewer amenities. Building on a larger scale required larger areas of land and cost more. Consequently, builders seeking to create more complex and more interesting communities moved increasingly to the urban periphery.

The near absence of governmental influence on this process is not unique; what is unusual is that the construction of highways played virtually no role in pulling population from city to suburb or in diverting it in a particular direction. Phoenix was remarkably slow to build highways: the area claimed only seventeen miles of highway in 1960 and only thirty-five by 1980. This reflected the opposition of certain businesses, but also a community fear of developing in the way Los Angeles had. As a result, population and subdivision expansion came first, followed by malls. Only in the 1970s were new malls being built in areas before residential construction, but even then they lay directly in the path of the rapidly expanding population.

More generally, the 1970s saw an accumulation of important changes that had implications for the future. The rising cost of land, added to rising construction costs, meant that housing was becoming less affordable than in the past. The retirement or other departure of longtime local builders and the takeover of home construction by other, mostly national firms meant different relationships with local financiers and the introduction of new expectations for home building and community development. Finally, the spatial expansion of the four oldest and closest suburbs physically connected them to Phoenix, while their expanding economic bases created positions of semi-independence and a postsuburban pattern.

While the creation of suburban housing and neighborhoods generally satisfied consumer demands and community interests, other parts of the city fared less well. The causal connection between suburbanization and the hollowing out of the center city is not simple or one-dimensional, but the popular fascination with growth at least distracted attention from troublesome problems. The expansion of poverty, the decay of residential areas, and the collapse of downtown's economic functions were not unique to this city, but in Phoenix they developed in a particular fashion, and they represented a serious challenge to the overall health of the community. By the end of the 1970s they began to appear less as problems of downtown and more as integral parts of the larger difficulty of building a sustainable city. But before dealing with these issues, Phoenicians had to confront questions about government and its composition.

8

Political Change and Changing Policies in the 1960s and 1970s

The success of the postwar vision required affordable houses and quality neighborhoods; but attracting buyers depended on able builders and a prosperous economy, as well as social and cultural amenities; and all of them relied, in one fashion or another, on an efficiently functioning city government. Building a livable and desirable city as outlined in the high-tech suburban vision was a balancing act. It was the interrelatedness of elements in the vision that made it both successful and difficult to maintain. And as Phoenix grew after 1960, keeping the balance among those elements became much more challenging.

During the 1960s and 1970s, cities across the nation faced serious problems, as suburbanization, malls, and urban highways drained city tax revenues and raised financial problems. While city managers struggled to sustain the existing infrastructure, people demanded more and better services. Cities grappled with growing areas of poverty and rising crime rates, which significantly increased the need for social programs. Politics became more volatile, transformed by the rising activism of minority populations, the struggles for civil rights and for effective antipoverty programs, and a contested role for the federal government.[1] Phoenix experienced much of this turmoil, but with a dynamic of its own. The timing and nature of the city's growth, its stage of development, created patterns a bit different than those of older and (initially) larger cities. In addition, the success of the Charter Government movement fostered another type of context for both politics and services.

The forces of Charter Government controlled city government nearly to the end of these two decades, seeking to maintain policies that would sustain their goals of effective leadership, responsible politics, efficient administration, and economical services. This approach fit its political strategy of controlling the political center—tacking right to counter conservatives who opposed taxes and favored the most limited type of government, and moving left to blunt liberal criticisms. Thus, it pursued a nonideological politics of growth and the efficient delivery of basic services, but this approach proved increasingly difficult to continue during these two decades.

One challenge came from those groups left out of the original vision, for during the 1960s racial minorities, the poor, and their allies disputed the narrow, service-oriented notion of city government and attempted to have it address larger social problems. Beyond the major differences over policy, this conflict involved a struggle over power as well as publicly recognizing groups whose presence in the city had been largely ignored for decades. The city's continuing growth posed further difficulties. Besides maintaining and improving services for the established neighborhoods, the city also had to provide them for new neighborhoods. Financing this expanding government required hard choices, particularly in terms of federal funds. Ultimately, Charter Government's approach to city governance and politics fell victim to the success of its growth policies and to changing political attitudes and mobilization. By the 1970s, Phoenix politics involved a different blend of actors and conflicting perspectives on who should serve in government, what government should do, and how best to develop the city. Emerging from an increasingly constrictive political structure and a narrow definition of city services, Phoenix politics broadened to become more open and inclusive, a politics of people, not just administrative policies.

CHARTER GOVERNMENT AND POLITICS OF THE CENTER

Politics remained central to the city's continued growth efforts after 1960. Leaders worked for consensus on the best policies to continue economic development, to address new social issues, and to sustain an open political style and an efficient city administration that residents supported. Their political efforts and postwar vision of growth were, thus, much broader than a narrow "growth machine" interest in land and property development, but over the next two decades the city's expansion created competition and conflict among existing groups, and the emergence of new interests brought further political complexity.[2] Into the 1970s, political control of Phoenix city government remained exclusively in the hands of Charter Government—with the sizable Charter Government Committee (CGC) and subcommittees appearing biennially, and with the direct control of the elected Charter Government slates of mayors and council members—but their uninterrupted electoral success suggests a degree of power and dominance that it did not possess. Charter Government retained office because of the committee's effective organization and hard work, but also because CGC and its nominees altered their strategies to meet different challenges and to defeat significantly different political opponents.

The CGC's core value was "selfless" civic participation; they touted the benefits generated by individuals allegedly seeking the general good. Council members were expected not only to reject the validity of interest-group politics, but, as Mayor Samuel Mardian explained to city council members, they would at times "be compelled by virtue of the public interest to render decisions which are not in accord with our personal viewpoints." As model forms of civic participation, they pointed to the activities of existing volunteer and business service organizations, but also to the special volunteer groups like the Valley Beautiful Committee created in 1963. Even more significant in terms of city governance were the sizeable groups appointed every five or seven years to evaluate city policy, programs, and spending priorities—and their recommendations were mostly followed. Three such groups were formed from 1957 to 1969, each time involving hundreds of citizens. During the 1970s a number of groups were organized to evaluate problems related to urban growth and recommend policies.[3]

In the 1960s and 1970s Charter Government resolutely championed the election of council members in citywide elections as the best way to promote its ideals of public service and an inclusive, growth-oriented urban vision. Critics of those goals continued to oppose at-large elections and argued that political activity reflected self-interest. Noting that most council members resided in a small part of the city, they challenged the claims of political selflessness, claiming that council members tended to serve the distinct interests of that section. They noted that the city's increased size not only expanded the distance between representatives and their constituents, but that it also made running for office significantly more difficult and expensive.

Critics gathered enough signatures to place a district system on the ballot in 1967 and 1975, but each time Charter Government's arguments for the value of a common purpose and the dangers of parochialism and division convinced voters to retain the at-large system.[4]

This same dynamic played out in CGC's biennial reconstitution, with its various subcommittees and its rules for selecting nominees for office. One of CGC's "iron-clad rules" was to avoid office seekers, so it solicited names from many sources, drafted its candidates, and imposed term limits. This strategy continued to draw strong supporters. In 1976, a member of the first Charter Government–elected council, Margaret Kober, explained that "I've been a loyal charterite and worked on every election ever since I was there [in 1949] and will continue to because I think that our principle is sound."[5] But despite such strong loyalties, Phoenicians eventually rejected this system. They did so partly because the city's growth changed the nature of officeholding and expanded its demands. Thus, while mayors in the 1950s viewed their office as part-time and heavily ceremonial, Samuel Mardian (1960–64) acted extensively in policy making and administration, and his successor, Milton Graham (1964–1970), became virtually a full-time mayor. By the late 1960s council members typically spent twenty to thirty hours per week on city business.[6]

CGC's political strategy matched its values and the political structure it built. During the 1950s the opposition slates often included relatively prominent liberals and drew more support in more heavily Democratic areas of the city, creating an impression that Charter Government was intentionally conservative. Although CGC did contain some conservative elements, the group itself was a coalition based in the political center, where it tried very hard to remain, and this was reflected in its balanced slates. In a nonpartisan system, without the standard binary partisan divisions, a centrist strategy could prove highly successful. However, it could also prompt political challenges that required great tactical agility. This was especially true in 1961 and 1963. Charter Government's liberal tilt brought success through 1967, but its sharp conservative shift in 1969—though subsequently modified—and the city's continued growth presaged the unraveling of this flexible strategy by the end the next decade.[7]

By the mid-1970s the changed responsibilities of office and the altered character of city politics reduced the appeal of officeholding for CGC's traditional types of nominees and increased it for a group of more politically oriented citizens. Phoenicians had also come to see governance not as simply implementing the logical option, but as the choice between different policies. Clear and important policy differences emerged in Phoenix during the 1960s, and conflicts over political leadership expanded throughout this period. Given how rapidly Phoenix was growing and the complexity of urban life, it is not the collapse of CGC in the mid-1970s that is surprising, but how it managed to stay in control of Phoenix for nearly a quarter of a century.

CHARTER GOVERNMENT AS A LIBERAL MOVEMENT

CGC's success and relative complacency were challenged in 1961 by a conservative slate whose members moved aggressively to define the contest on their terms. The struggle began in January, when Rev. Aubrey Moore, a local Baptist minister, initiated a struggle against the city's housing code. The council quickly repealed this measure, but several months later it revived the bill in amended form. This tactic galvanized conservatives and led to a vigorous campaign in the fall of 1961.[8] Rev. Moore led this fight, helping to organize an election slate called the Stay American Committee (SAC), running as one of its council candidates, and articulating some of its major themes in his weekly radio addresses.

Like prior Charter Government opponents, SAC wanted to elect council members from wards, reduce the city manager's power, and hire a local person for that job. SAC differed dramatically in its ideology: it claimed that Charter Government was the (mostly) unwitting dupe of a "communist conspiracy" and that its policies endangered representative city government. Denouncing zoning, housing codes, and land-use planning as steps toward eventual confiscation of all private property, SAC leaders lambasted urban renewal and the purchase of private water companies as elements of the Red menace.[9] No aspect of city life escaped their blasts. They excoriated the collection of money by city children for UNICEF, and they claimed that "the inexcusably snarled traffic conditions in Phoenix, the ill-timed and repeated tearing up of streets are part of the announced plan of those who would rule the world by planning confusion for the people."[10]

SAC's general anticommunist critique of Phoenix city government was invigorated by a special animus toward the National Municipal League (NML). Since 1940 Phoenix had developed a strong relationship with the NML, hiring it to study local problems, basing its charter on the NML's Model Charter, and regularly seeking managerial advice and assistance from its urban experts. The city had also hosted the organization's national meeting in 1960, and numerous Phoenix civic leaders served on the NML Steering Committee. SAC described this organization in code style as "1313," the building number of the league's Chicago headquarters, and alleged that the "World Government planners of 1313" intended, ultimately, to eliminate individual rights and private property. SAC also referred to the city government as a "UNESCO-METRO" government, claiming that it intended to annex all other Valley cities, which would become part of a "dictatorship under a socialistic U.N. one world system."[11]

SAC attempted to run a stealth campaign. Its "Letter to Patriotic Leaders" explained that "your campaign can only be won on a quiet basis—by telephone calls, doorbell ringing, and personal contact. Only with hard work and with as little noise as possible can this battle be won." Accordingly, SAC campaigned primarily in homes and to small groups. Its antipathy to city leaders and the print media showed in its refusal to debate publicly with CGC candidates and its reliance on issuing press releases, delivering radio addresses, and, at the end of the campaign, buying TV ads.[12]

SAC's strategy and allegations greatly frustrated members of the Charter Government. Normally, CGC campaigns boasted about their candidates' abilities, touted the accomplishments in city government, and promised to continue those policies. In this race, too, Charter Government candidates repeated those efforts in print, at numerous public meetings, and in an expanded television campaign. Numerous community and former Charter Government leaders defended it, and a two-page list of citizens endorsed it. But Charter Government supporters were mostly on the defensive, forced to respond to SAC's charges with lengthy rebuttals—describing SAC's misrepresentations of taxes, zoning, and the powers of the city manager, arguing that the housing code and urban renewal program no longer existed, and denying that Charter Government leaders, past or present, were "dupes" of a communist conspiracy.[13] For the most part Charter Government leaders and supporters did not retreat from their existing policies, and they vigorously defended their association with the National Municipal League. Their strongest defense against SAC's demonizing was to note that conservative icon Senator Barry Goldwater was one of the league's regional vice presidents. SAC blithely accused Goldwater of ignorance about the group's purpose and offered to educate him. This strategy failed not only for its presumptuous suggestion, but also because Mayor Mardian revealed that SAC's claims to have scheduled a meeting with Goldwater were false.[14]

While SAC claimed local issues as its inspiration, it was actually, along with many similarly named organizations in other cities, part of a semisecret national movement begun three years earlier during a fight against proposed changes in the governments of Miami and Dade County, Florida. Its mimeographed "fact sheets" and pamphlets on the dangers of "Metro government" and urban renewal were copies of those national materials, and its conspiracy theories reflected the beliefs of the John Birch Society, to which at least several of its members belonged. Confirming his group's larger goals, mayoral candidate Buck Hanner announced that upon winning in Phoenix, SAC intended to export its campaign to other Arizona communities and then to the nation. SAC's charges and tactics appalled and frustrated Mayor Mardian, and he wrote to warn other western mayors, many of whom had already encountered similar groups.[15]

While SAC garnered some support, its greatest success was in galvanizing the opposition, for Charter Government won support even from its liberal critics. CGC candidates were easily victorious in the fall of 1961, winning nearly three-fourths of the vote. This success was comforting, but victory accentuated existing problems. CGC's Nominating Committee had selected Republicans for all but one position and had included no Mexican Americans. Election results also revealed disturbing signs. Voter turnout actually fell, to 19 percent, the lowest level since before 1949. More ominous than apathy was the source of SAC's votes: four of the six precincts it won were in southern Phoenix, and it garnered 49.6 percent of the vote in the newly annexed South Phoenix area—a sign of continuing resentment.[16] Charter Government leaders also struggled to refute a national perception, encouraged by stories in the national media, that conservatives were creating a "Valley of Fear."[17]

A second transforming election came in 1963, when Charter Government fought a more substantive and complex struggle that went beyond its limited growth-promotion policies. A vigorous liberal slate, combined with a lesser threat from conservatives, created a serious debate over public issues, boosted voter turnout to one-third, and forced Charter Government into its first run-off election. The Action Citizens Ticket (ACT) included several prominent Phoenicians, including three-term Democratic Congressman Richard Harless for mayor and Ed Korrick, scion of the department store family and active in downtown renewal efforts, for council. The slate also revived the abandoned Charter Government tradition of including a Mexican American: Manuel Pena had begun his public activism on voter registration drives in Tolleson in

1947 and 1948 to integrate those schools, and he had since worked in various community groups, including the Phoenix Urban League. And by selecting Lincoln Ragsdale, an African American who had been continuously involved in protests and civil rights organizations since the late 1940s, ACT broke the color barrier.[18]

Fully as important as ACT's diverse slate was its platform: it substantively critiqued Charter Government's vision of growth by combining previous criticisms of Charter Government with a hard look at the problems produced by the city's dramatic expansion over the previous five years. Originating from the organizing efforts of Democratic, labor, and minority activists, ACT accepted the public endorsements of the Phoenix Central Labor Council and minority leaders, but the group rejected any suggestion that theirs was a partisan ticket. ACT's main theme was its pledge to "destroy the invisible government control exerted too long by a few individuals," referring to the influence of CGC and other power brokers, and it accused Charter Government of favoritism in its spending and taxation policies.[19] The ACT slate differed from previous opposition tickets by not criticizing district elections or the city manager system; it resembled them in criticizing the conditions of various city services, noting the inadequacies of the fire department and measuring the police department's ineffectiveness by the city's high crime rate, and they proposed to reform taxation. They tied these issues to a broader critique of Charter Government's approach to growth, charging it with failure to pursue land-use planning or construct freeways and with rushing to annex. Most significantly, ACT raised city problems that Charter Government had largely ignored—the dilemmas of unemployment, poverty, slums, and downtown decay—and as partial solutions they proposed recruitment of industry and the construction of youth centers.[20]

Charter Government leaders started by running a traditional campaign, touting their fourteen years in office, reiterating their basic platform, and relying on citizen endorsements. But the seriousness and credibility of ACT's charges and candidates forced the Charter Government campaign to respond with more detailed defenses of city government, and for this the leaders used position papers—which they had the city manager's office provide. As the campaign wore on, Charter Government shifted to the negative approach favored by the Pulliam newspapers, claiming that ACT was "dictated to by the liberal-labor element," that it intended to establish a Democratic political machine, and that it would raise taxes.[21]

Late in the campaign, a third, conservative Republican slate appeared. These candidates, too, complained about Charter Government's "favoritism," they denounced the "dictatorial attitudes" of the city's Planning and Zoning Commission, and they faulted city government for rising crime and low funding for police, poor street planning, inadequate services in newly annexed areas, and high taxes. This group received few funds, little attention, and few votes, but it influenced the outcome by helping to hold Charter Government council candidates below 50 percent of the votes, thus forcing a runoff election.[22]

In the end, Charter Government was again victorious. Its mayoral candidate, Milton Graham, obtained 53 percent of the vote in the primary election, and its council candidates won 57 percent of the general election council vote. But the results also revealed serious unrest. Turnout had jumped to 33 percent, and Ed Korrick, running ahead of other ACT candidates, came close to breaking Charter Government's monopoly. Most ominously, the candidates on the conservative slate had endorsed ACT candidates in the runoff election, raising the specter of a future left-right coalition.[23] Charter Government moved quickly to prevent this by accepting key ACT ideas and co-opting its supporters. First, as soon as they were in office, Mayor Graham and the council shifted to the left to address ACT's concerns, and by 1965 their support of civil rights and efforts to obtain federal urban funds (see below) had won liberal endorsement and wide public approval. As the second part of an agreement to win support, the CGC nominated two minority candidates for council—Dr. Morrison Warren, an African American educator, and Frank Benites, a Mexican American labor leader from South Phoenix. As a result, Charter Government's only opposition in 1965 was two conservatives—one for council and a write-in mayoral candidate.[24]

Two years later another conservative slate opposed Charter Government, largely on growth-related issues. Linked to conservatives who had run in the three previous elections and to supporters of the failed initiative of June 1967 that called for election of council members by district (as noted above), these candidates challenged "ineffective" police and inadequate fire services, high water rates, and spending on "frills" like city beautification and the purchase of Camelback Mountain, and they accused Charter Government of planning to institute a housing code. They complained that Charter Government represented only the "silk stocking district" and claimed, anew, that it was self-serving and secretive.[25] Their greatest criticism focused on plans to build a downtown convention center, but their inaccurate claims about the origins, planning, and financing undermined an already weakened position, and Charter Government won by a two-to-one margin.[26]

While most of the contest was predictable, one element was not. Before the campaign began, Mayor Graham challenged Charter Government's two-term rule by revealing his interest in a third term. After considerable debate, the Charter Government Nominating Committee finally endorsed Graham, thus breaking one of its "iron-clad rules" of operation.[27] Graham's easy victory and the ability of council incumbents John Long and Morrison Warren to run well ahead of their colleagues emphasized a larger concern of the CGC: the personal popularity of individual candidates exceeding the public support for the general slate. These concerns, plus policy differences, combined to produce a political eruption in 1969.

A CONSERVATIVE TURN AND CHARTER GOVERNMENT'S DEMISE

Graham's pursuit of a fourth term initiated the conflict, but the increasingly liberal policies of Graham and the city council conflicted with CGC's agreement with a conservative national shift from social reform to law and order, and CGC decided to make a dramatic change. The committee rejected, not only Graham, but also the incumbent council members, as they, in turn, rejected the CGC. In their place the CGC Nominating Committee put forth an entirely new slate: all Republican men, active in business service groups like Kiwanis and Rotary clubs and without political experience. Their campaign emphasized crime control, freeways, and Charter Government's traditional notions of limited officeholding.[28]

In response, Graham organized an impressive citizens' slate. It included the two minority councilmen, Warren and Benites, while the third two-term incumbent, John F. Long, endorsed Graham's slate. One of the single-term council members dumped by Charter Government also endorsed Graham, while a second, Dorothy Theilkas, ran for reelection as an independent. The social turmoil of the time also drew other council candidates. Charter Government's emphasis on crime and fiscal conservatism was shared by four "independent" council candidates, each of whom belonged to George Wallace's American Independent Party, opposed freeways, and favored a ward system.[29]

Charter Government's mayoral candidate, John Driggs, had extensive volunteer experience and additional public visibility because his family owned Western Savings and Loan. Benefiting from a hefty campaign fund and fervent newspaper support, Driggs won a slim victory in the primary. Since none of the twenty council candidates managed a majority, the top finishers—all from the two major slates—faced off in the general election. Although the Charter Government slate captured a majority, a relatively large number of voters split their ballots, many supporting Ed Korrick, which enabled him to beat the weakest Charter Government candidate and become the first outsider to win since Charter Government began in 1949.[30] A final complicating development in this election was that many Phoenix women were "seething" that neither major slate had included a women. A number of Phoenix women's clubs encouraged voters to support only the two independent women candidates. Their strong showing (close to the votes won by most of Graham's slate) and the 1,344 blank mayoral ballots demonstrated the political danger of sexism.[31]

During the next four years that Driggs was mayor, Charter Government largely controlled political developments, although it showed some political flexibilty. In 1971 it added Ed Korrick to its slate, and it rectified its previous mistakes by nominating an African American accountant, Calvin Goode, and a woman, Margaret Hance. Two years later Timothy Barrow won an easy victory to replace Driggs as mayor, and only two independent candidates ran for council, but one of them, Gary Peter Klahr, a maverick conservative who had being running for city council since 1967, won.[32] Howard Kraft, the CGC chair in 1973, announced that his goal was "to broaden the base of charter government," but this satisfied few critics. Many doubted this was possible if Charter Government used its traditional method of selecting candidates; others challenged the entire system, like a prominent Mexican American leader who criticized the "criteria used in selecting charter candidates." Mayor Driggs worried greatly about Charter Government's image and even suggested the possibility of eliminating endorsements, but to no avail.[33]

The end for this power group came suddenly in 1975, as a political tidal wave swept its members from the mayor's office and from control of city council. Councilwoman Margaret Hance, with multiple ties to the Charter Government group and now in the position of vice mayor, grew dissatisfied with its refusal to nominate interested and experienced officeholders, and when the CGC chose political novice Lyman Davidson as its mayoral candidate, Hance rebelled and ran against him. Having six other candidates for this office helped limit Davidson's vote to only 23 percent, but Hance won handily with 57 percent, becoming only the second woman in the country to be elected mayor of a major city.[34]

The race for city council seats in 1975 was even more contested, with a Charter Government slate, an American Party slate, and a shockingly large

Table 8.1 Charter Government collapses: 1975 City Council votes by group (averaged).

Candidate group	Primary election	General election
Charter Government slate	28,832	36,025
American Party slate	11,950	
Major independents	35,723	41,507
Minor independents	12,199	

Source: *Arizona Republic,* 5 November 1975, A1; *Registered Voters and Votes Cast for Mayor and Council, Primary and General Election, Phoenix, 1949–1979* (Phoenix: City of Phoenix, 1980).

number of independent candidates—fourteen. Phoenix voters made clear choices in the primary election, rejecting the American Party slate while picking six independents and the Charter Government slate (table 8.1). Independent candidates ran even more strongly in the general election, winning four seats. The first- and third-place finishers were the incumbent minority candidates, Rosendo Gutierrez and Calvin Goode, whom the CGC had refused to renominate, while Charter Government's only victorious candidates lagged in fourth and fifth place. In 1977 CGC met to endorse several candidates, but for the first time in twenty-five years it did not nominate a slate.[35]

The Charter Government system died primarily because the city in which it began no longer existed. Over the previous twenty-five years, Phoenix's population had grown to eight times its 1950 size. The passage of time and the influx of new residents created a population with little memory of the 1940s crisis that had inspired the movement. As the initial, relatively cohesive group of Phoenix's postwar leaders retired from public life, they were followed by various and competing groups of leaders, reflecting the city's growing diversity and size. The socioeconomic group that had identified with Charter Government remained an influential voting bloc and an important source of campaign funding, but other groups began achieving some influence. In particular, the increased size, political interest, and activism of minority populations changed electoral dynamics and transformed the political agenda (see below). Charter Government's ideals of a part-time, disinterested leadership had decreasing relevance, and the substantial boosts in mayoral and council salaries reflected an awareness of the greatly increased burden of holding city office. Increasingly, Phoenicians favored the open selection of leaders, endorsed the importance of experience, and perceived urban politics as a debate among perspectives rather than a search for consensus.

TAXES AND REVENUES

Charter Government's philosophy of governance involved promoting growth by creating an honest, efficient, and economical government that provided affordable services. Ray Wilson had demonstrated the benefits of increased managerial efficiencies during the 1950s, and over the next several decades the city continued to be well managed. But planning and operating city government involved the dual burden of continuing (and improving) services to the existing city while also coping with the city's tremendous expansion. In addition, national forces like inflation disrupted the city's best plans, and a changing social context transformed what people expected of cities. While providing services required decisions on many detailed matters, determining the types and levels of taxation to fund those services raised larger questions of preference and philosophy. Charter Goverment policies played a major role in shaping these decisions, but the final outcomes also reflected the actions of state and national governments over which the Phoenix leadership had much less influence than it would have liked.[36]

Charter Government's bedrock political and fiscal strategy was to hold the line on property taxes, and its candidates repeated that pledge religiously at every election. This proved politically popular, especially with businesses and retirees, but also with the general public, which increasing viewed this as the least desirable tax. The growing value of all property in Phoenix, from appreciation and city expansion, nearly tripled these revenues from 1960 to 1974, but the demands upon the city grew much faster, forcing it to find other revenue sources. As a result, property tax revenues fell from a third to one-eighth of the city's total revenues from 1960 to 1980 (figure 8.1). This downward trend reflected the national urban average, but other cities depended more on this source—from over half of their revenue in the beginning of this period to roughly a third at the end.[37]

Various user fees provided a second source of city revenues from direct, visible taxation of individuals. This remained a rather limited revenue category until the later 1970s, because many city services—including sewerage, plus garbage and trash pickup—were provided for free. This was not true for the city's most vital service, the water system. Those rates produced substantial revenue, but determining how to set them was frequently a prime election issue. The basic need for major facilities like filtration, pumping, and sewage treatment plants provoked little dispute. The conflicts were over expanding the water system by buying private water companies and providing water to newly annexed areas (more cheaply than before annexation). By the 1970s

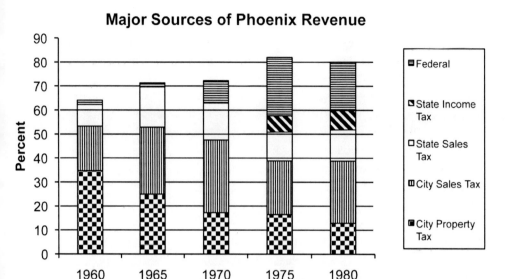

Major Sources of Phoenix Revenue

Figure 8.1 Phoenix revenue sources, 1960–80. *Source: Annual Financial Report* (Phoenix: City of Phoenix), 1960–80 editions.

water rates had tripled, but city officials consistently argued that these were fees for necessary services and were not being used for unnecessary expansion or to subsidize other services.[38]

Especially through the 1960s, Phoenix compensated for the declining importance of property taxes by its increasing reliance on various sales taxes. The city's own sales tax continued to rise as a revenue source, since it was the easiest to increase (this happened several times), it grew with prosperity, and it enabled the city to tax both nonresidents and winter visitors, whose purchases accounted for an estimated 10 to 20 percent of city sales. In 1969 the city added an unpopular "sin" tax on tobacco and liquor sales. Phoenix also relied on several types of state revenues during the 1960s: an increased state sales tax (those revenues rose over 500 percent) and an increased percentage of state gas tax revenues (which quadrupled to $4 million by 1970) that provided vital funding for streets and roads. In 1972 Arizona voters directed the state government to give cities 15 percent of the revenues from the new state income tax, which enabled the city to repeal the "sin" taxes and reduce the property tax from 1.75 to 1.43 percent.[39]

The 1970s were difficult for American cities, which suffered from high inflation, an aging infrastructure, and growing expectations for public services.

New York City's near bankruptcy most visibly signaled the urban crisis, but contemporary analysts talked about "crisis" conditions in other cities, like Detroit, Atlanta, and St. Louis. Conditions in Phoenix were less severe, for it benefited from continued economic growth and a relatively low level of public employment. Nevertheless, rising expenses demanded unusual policy changes. In 1975 the city was forced to cut positions and raise the property tax to 1.89 percent; in 1976 it doubled the sales tax to two cents, although it exempted food. (Public reaction changed the city's strategy, however, for a 1977 voter initiative repealed the sales tax increase.) The city was also obliged to institute user fees for sewer usage and trash pickup.[40]

Phoenix would have needed to raise taxes much more had it not received money from the federal government. City leaders' reluctance to accept federal funds flourished in the early 1960s but soon dwindled, as they confronted changes in the city's goals and problems. In addition, federal government spending grew dramatically and changed in character during this era, creating opportunities that Phoenix could not afford to ignore. From 1950 to 1960 federal grants to all cities—mainly for capital projects like building programs for airports or city services like sewers, roads, public housing, and hospitals—grew from $2 billion to $7 billion and increased to 44 grant-in-aid programs. By 1964 the number of programs had jumped to 115, while spending rose to $24 billion in 1970 and $43 billion in 1974. The new programs contained money for capital improvements but also substantial funds for job training, educational assistance, urban renewal, model cities, neighborhood development, and law enforcement.[41]

Nearly as important as the increased federal spending during the 1970s was the impact of distribution through two programs in President Richard Nixon's New Federalism policy: revenue sharing and block grants. The revenue-sharing program began in 1972 and granted money to cities and states largely on the basis of population. With no real federal oversight or restrictions, most cities used the money to pay for existing rather than new services. This permitted them to avoid raising taxes or even to lower them. The Community Development Block Grant Program of 1974 made federal money easier to obtain and more palatable by combining seven urban-related grant programs (such as Model Cities, urban renewal, or water and sewer systems) into one program. It required an annual application, but the process was undemanding, and 80 percent of the funds went to larger cities and used a formula involving population, poverty, and housing. The removal of many restrictions and the emphasis on population greatly assisted Phoenix and other Sunbelt cities, and it helped changed attitudes in Phoenix about seeking federal funds.[42]

In the immediate postwar era Phoenix had continued its prewar policy of seeking federal funds to improve the city's infrastructure, viewing this as a crucial aid in building the city's prosperity. In 1958 Mayor Jack Williams wrote to the chair of the appropriate Congressional subcommittee in strong support of these programs: "We feel that certain Federal grant-in-aid programs in which the City of Phoenix is participating are very vital to the future of the community. These include urban renewal, public housing, airport construction, and urban highway construction. Without Federal participation in these programs, the City of Phoenix alone would not have sufficient financial resources to undertake the programs."[43]

Williams' comments reflect the city's interest in obtaining funds for infrastructure, but also a growing willingness to seek funds for social purposes. These efforts halted abruptly near the end of 1960. Rev. Moore's successful campaign to repeal the housing code precluded the city from seeking federal funds for urban renewal, and Mayor Mardian responded by renouncing federal urban funds. His successor, Milton Graham, did the same when he came into office. These tactical moves fostered a persistent perception that the city had declared independence from federal funds, but its federal infrastructure funding actually doubled from 1961 to 1965. Increased federal spending redoubled these expenditures from 1966 to 1970, but the greatest and most significant shift involved the city's gaining federal antipoverty program funds (table 8.2). Despite the complaints of some critics, including the Pulliam newspapers, the city committed itself to both the programs and the funds.[44]

Table 8.2 Federal spending in Phoenix.

Era	Federal grants	Infrastructure		Social programs	
		Grants	%	Grants	%
1960–65	$ 7,454,188	$ 7,432,797	99.7%	$ 0	0
1966–70	$ 33,059,989	$ 13,981,025	42.3%	$ 15,931,314	48.2%
1971–75	$ 120,382,162	$ 27,161,943	22.6%	$ 53,224,037	44.2%

Source: Annual lists of federal grants and revenue-sharing funds in *(Comprehensive) Annual Financial Report* and summarized in *AFR*, 1975/76, 156–57, and *AFR*, 1980/81, 165–66.

Economic conditions in the 1970s made federal funds even more important. The city's expanding needs, the eroding values of its revenues because of inflation, and continuing public resistance to raising local taxes forced Phoenix politicians to revise their perspectives and policies even further. Federal funds jumped from roughly a tenth of the city budget in 1970 to more than a fifth during that decade (figure 8.1). Mayor Driggs, a banker and a Republican, followed a realistic but cautious policy and actively pursued federal moneys for certain programs, including public housing, job training, and the city's bus service. He used revenue-sharing funds for one-time expenses—a municipal building, land for a downtown park, and capital facilities like fire and police stations. His successor, Timothy Barrow, holding office in 1974 and 1975, an era of recession and continuing inflation, changed that policy to use substantial revenue sharing funds for operational expenses.

Mayor Hance entered office preaching a conservative fiscal message. She cut the limited local spending on antipoverty programs, instituted hiring freezes, and refused to contemplate raising city taxes. She warned against accepting federal funds and especially against using them to subsidize the operational budget, but economic realities and political pressures forced changes. She claimed to be pursuing federal funds as a "practical necessity," but she did so aggressively: from a $15 million total in 1974–75, before she took office, the city's federal grant funds averaged more than $40 million per year during the next six years. Furthermore, she continued to seek some federal funding for programs like public housing, as well as community and neighborhood development grants. Hance's approach to federal funding and city priorities mainly differed from that of her predecessors in that she used half of all revenue-sharing funds to increase police funding and another one-sixth for the fire department.[45]

Besides providing crucial funding for basic city services and implementing needed social programs, federal funds in this era also remained important for doing what Mayor Williams had described as allowing Phoenicians to do what they otherwise could not. A prime example is the preservation of mountain land within the city. Returning to Phoenix as a private citizen after his defeat in the 1964 presidential election, Barry Goldwater headed an effort to prevent development of Camelback Mountain. He solicited private donations and cajoled property owners to sell or donate their land, but when private sources had been exhausted, he swallowed his objections and successfully solicited federal funds, and in 1968 the private group he headed assumed ownership of the summit of this landmark. During the next five years another citizens' campaign worked to preserve additional mountain land further north of this. The final plan included private efforts and donations, money from the city's operating funds as well as bond revenue, but nearly a third of the resources needed to acquire the necessary areas and create the Phoenix Mountain Preserve came from federal funds, especially revenue-sharing funds.[46]

Despite its reputation and the conservative preferences of its mayors, Phoenix sought and obtained a significant increase in federal support during the 1970s, and opposition to this strategy dwindled markedly. The city's efforts benefited from changing national policies that offered fewer restrictions and less oversight than before. These policies also offered easier access to funds, as Phoenix enjoyed a sevenfold increase in block funds by 1978, the third highest increase among the nation's major cities. This success, plus the needs of both traditional infrastructure and newer social programs, shifted public debate away from the possible dangers of federal interference to questions of reasonable city policy.[47]

THE POLITICS OF CITY SERVICES

The city's ability to provide services efficiently and at reasonable cost had been vital for its initial postwar expansion. That remained true for the years after 1960, but the pace of growth, the demand for more services and higher revenues, and the problems of inflation greatly complicated this task. By the mid-1970s Phoenix had begun increasing fees and restricting certain services; by 1980 city leaders began talking more about the possible privatization of certain services.[48] Throughout this period, city government remained highly efficient and had a good national reputation. It was a finalist for All-America City honors in 1966 and won that award for the third time in 1979–80. Although the per capita number of city employees rose from 1967 to 1975, reflecting the city's increasing spending and program activities, this figure continued to be among the lowest for cities of comparable size.[49]

The water system remained highly successful during this era. Water production tripled, as the city continued to purchase private water companies (typically in newly annexed areas to the north) and to expand its water-treatment plants and other facilities. Although rates increased significantly over these two decades, by 1980 they were still below those of most other southwestern cities and half of what Tucson charged.[50] Perhaps the city's greatest weakness in the 1950s had been its sewer system, with some one hundred thousand people relying on cesspools. Between 1959 and 1964, the city invested significantly in building the system, and connections to the sewer system doubled; by 1970 virtually all structures within the city were connected. After the economic crunch of the mid-1970s, city leaders felt compelled to institute usage fees, but these were modest and common to most cities.[51]

The city's aviation services also represented continued success. While most major American cities expanded service by building new airports on the urban periphery, Phoenix improved and expanded Sky Harbor Airport, its in-town facility, by acquiring more land, updating its equipment, lengthening its runways, and attracting many additional airlines. To accommodate the tremendous increase in the number of passengers—from 859,744 in 1960 to 2.9 million a decade later and 6.6 million in 1980—the city built new terminals in 1962 and 1979. At the same time, Sky Harbor continued freight service and remained the local home for the National Guard. But while this expansion benefited the city as a whole, it was accomplished by eradicating the Golden Gate barrio to the west and south of Sky Harbor. To meet the demand for private planes and general aviation services, the city acquired airports at Deer Valley (1971) and Goodyear (1968). Although managed and promoted by the city, all three airports financed themselves through user fees and federal grants, not from general city revenue.[52]

Improving ground transportation proved more difficult, because rapid growth challenged both the city's fiscal resources and policy choices about development. Despite significant efforts during the 1950s, roughly seven hundred fifty miles of city streets in 1960 needed work. Fixing local and collector streets required action by the affected property owners, while the city was responsible for the major arterial streets. In 1960 Mayor Mardian declared that "the most important single item of [city] business" was improving streets, and the next twenty years saw important gains. By 1969 the mileage of deficient local or collector streets dropped by a third; by 1980 total street mileage had doubled, and the proportion that were judged to be "improved" (paved and often widened) rose from only half to nearly all.

The city fell short, however, in terms of major arterial streets, which handled 80 percent of the traffic: although the mileage of such streets nearly doubled to 212 miles in 1980, it was less than half of the estimated necessary mileage. The city's very rapid growth partly explains this problem, and traffic had increased twice as quickly as expected. Predictably, the accident rate increased by 39 percent, and the average speed on streets declined from twenty-eight to twenty-four miles per hour, which meant that trips took longer and were more expensive, and air pollution increased greatly. Inadequate revenues also hampered the city: the state increased the gas tax only slightly in 1963 and 1965, it gave no revenues to the city from 1971 to 1974, and it did not reapportion the gas tax revenues to help urban transportation needs until 1975. The provision of federal grants and revenue sharing were crucial for the improvements that did occur.[53]

The larger problem of increased traffic resulted from the city's low-density development and the ensuing dependence on cars. In this respect, of course, Phoenix resembled many American cities, but it was relatively unique in failing for decades to create a transportation system. The first, more understandable lapse was the city's neglecting to build some type of mass transit system. After divesting itself of the municipal bus system in 1959, city leaders had seen the plunge in average daily ridership from 58,000 in 1957 to 31,000 in 1960 but had imagined this as part of a "natural" shift from streetcars to buses to cars. But worsening traffic conditions, the discovery that many poor Phoenicians could not afford cars and depended on public transportation, and the near collapse of the system (with ridership down to 14,000 in 1970) forced a new policy. The city began subsidizing the bus system in 1969 and took it over in 1971. In 1973, admitting that "a balanced transportation system is badly needed," it began supporting the system with federal mass transit funds. By 1983 ridership had tripled to 43,000, but this did little to reduce the growing snarl of traffic.[54]

Phoenix city officials were hardly unique, especially among Sunbelt cities, in failing to challenge residents' preference for cars or to seek significant funding for mass transit. What was unusual, however, was their failure to deliver a sizable freeway system. The city's highway plan, created in 1949 and updated in 1960 to accommodate the U.S. Interstate Highway Act of 1956, envisioned a modest grid of freeways involving I-10 (connecting Tucson and Los Angeles), the existing north-south Black Canyon Highway of seven miles, and an east-west road slightly north of downtown. Despite city endorsement and the availability of federal highway money for the interstate portions, the project stalled for years because of cost and resistance from merchants and motel owners who feared, rightly, that rerouting traffic would cost them customers.[55]

In January 1969, the city council finally decided to build the crosstown Papago Freeway route as the extension of I-10 and chose a route through the Roosevelt neighborhood, just north of downtown. To deflect objections that the highway would physically split the neighborhood, the design called for the roadway to be elevated from 25 to 100 feet (figure 8.2). The proponents believed this would create a unique landmark; critics considered it a horrible eyesore.

Besides objecting to the expense, a growing number of Phoenicians worried that building freeways would simply encourage still greater urban sprawl. Finally, others criticized the specific route location as being too destructive of historic buildings and archaeological sites. This complex political battle, involving Pulliam's impassioned editorial opposition, three city votes, and a federal lawsuit, ultimately produced the worst solution: the basic location was unchanged; construction was delayed for over a decade, resulting in greater costs; and all highways were put on hold, so that in 1980 the Valley had still contained only thirty-five miles of freeway.[56]

Crime was a second problem facing Phoenicians. This began receiving significant public attention in 1963, after the FBI's annual *Uniform Crime Reports* indicated that Phoenix had a very high crime rate. The city increased the police budget and hired more officers, and in May public officials appointed a Valley-wide Citizens' Task Force. In the fall election campaign the ACT slate emphasized the issue and called for additional spending and attention to

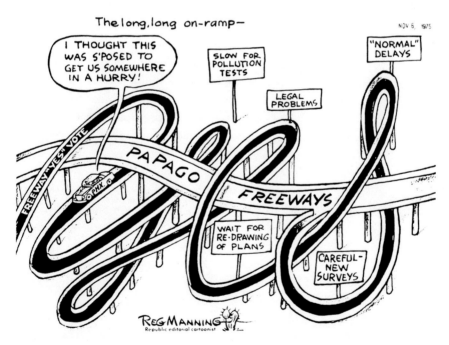

Figure 8.2 One view of "progress" in building the Papago Freeway. While many Phoenicians questioned aspects of the highway proposal, others became frustrated at the growing traffic congestion and the lack of progress in building roads. *Source: Arizona Republic,* 7 November 1975. The Reg Manning Collection, Arizona Collection, Arizona State University Libraries.

juveniles, while Charter Government contended that crime had many causes and that crime rates were higher in other western states. In January 1964 newly elected Mayor Graham labeled crime as the city's top problem and endorsed most of the crime task force's recommendations, including hiring more police, providing better equipment, reorganizing the department, and collecting more and better data.[57]

Reports over the next decade showed that crime continued to rise faster in Phoenix than elsewhere in the nation and that its major-crime rate was at or near the highest of any U.S. city. The city responded by beefing up the police force, hiring an additional 125 officers each year until 1975, a pace faster than the city's growth rate. From a level of 15 police per 10,000 population between 1960 and 1966, the force level increased to 21 per 10,000 in 1970 and to 27 per 10,000 in the years 1973 to 1980. This elevated the city from the bottom to the middle of the national city rankings, and in terms of southwestern cities this differentiated Phoenix's practices from the status quo policies of San Antonio and San Diego. The city also responded by modernizing equipment and procedures. Its commitment showed in the significantly increased spending levels, as law enforcement's share of the budget climbed from 20 percent in 1960 to 27 percent by the late 1970s, a change made possible by federal dollars.[58]

Increased crime levels were not unique to Phoenix, of course; this was a national phenomenon and a top domestic political issue.[59] FBI reports explained that, among other factors, rising affluence and more households vacant during the day provided greater opportunities for theft. Crime also grew more rapidly throughout the West, partly because it had a higher proportion of youths. Discussions of juvenile behavior and delinquency were rife during this era, but among cities with more than half a million people in 1970, Phoenix was alone in lacking a juvenile division in its police department. Criminal behavior certainly rose during this era, but some of the growth reflected major improvements in reporting, and many increases concerned relatively minor crimes. As Police Chief Lawrence Wetzel noted in 1974, "Twenty-four percent of the larceny crimes are under $10, yet they count the same as a murder in the FBI statistics; 65 percent of burglary crimes are under $50, yet they count the same as a grand theft in the FBI totals."[60]

But other serious factors also added to the problem. Nationally, social analysts argued that poverty and racial discrimination contributed to the increased crime rate and that any solution required more than just hiring additional police. Mayor Graham accepted this perspective and (as noted below) adopted programs to address the problems. Certain types of crime also appeared more commonly and scandalously in the Valley. Like many booming areas, it attracted swindlers, con men, and organized crime. Land fraud in the 1960s inspired wags to label Arizona "the Tainted Desert." Increasing instances of fraud and corruption, highlighted by a series of newspaper articles in 1974, forced police to pay more attention to such activities. The trial and conviction of land swindler Ned Warren revealed misuse of political influence and corruption of public officials, but the murder of *Arizona Republic* investigative reporter Don Bolles invigorated local and state efforts to prevent and prosecute fraud (the Phoenix police department created an Organized Crime Bureau), and it forced the state legislature to pass some important anticrime bills.[61]

Growth affected all city departments, but requirements for facilities and equipment continued to create unique problems for the fire department, as they had in the 1950s. It was not like the water and sanitation departments, which had extended services outside the city before those areas were annexed. Nor did it resemble the police department, which could cover new territory by making the relatively inexpensive purchase of a patrol car. The increased physical size of the city raised costs, and it took time to acquire equipment and build substations. As a result, starting from the city's major annexations from 1958 to 1960 and continuing throughout the 1960s, the Phoenix Fire Department was persistently understaffed and ill equipped. Not surprisingly, this became a common election issue. Compared to other cities of its size, Phoenix had proportionately fewer firefighters, fewer stations, and less powerful equipment. The city kept hiring additional firemen, but the number per 10,000 population only rose from 9.0 to 11.4 by 1980. However, the city did make greater progress in acquiring equipment and building substations in that period. Thus, in national rankings the department was near the bottom of the lowest major category until the mid-1970s, when it achieved a middle ranking.[62] Not coincidentally, public complaints diminished.

CIVIL RIGHTS, POVERTY, AND CITY POLITICS

Growth challenged the city's ability to extend services, but the inclusion within the city of certain geographic areas heightened that challenge. The annexation of South Phoenix added an area in great need of infrastructure and services; it also included a minority population who had begun to challenge traditional social arrangements and public policies regarding race. Since the late nineteenth century, the majority of Phoenicians had little discussed the presence of racial minorities, and since the 1920s they had largely ignored the conditions in which they lived. While the proportion of African Americans and Mexican Americans in the Phoenix population was somewhat lower than in other large cities and did not change from 1950 to 1980—remaining roughly five and fifteen percent, respectively—the national struggle over civil rights and a renewed awareness of poverty during this period also transformed politics in Phoenix.

The 1950s opened hopefully, with the election of two African Americans—Hayzel Daniels and Carl Sims—to the state legislature, and they were followed into public office by others. During the 1950s the city moved fairly quickly and without much dissent to address some key civil rights issues and prohibit overt discrimination by government in various forums: it banned discrimination at the municipal Sky Harbor Airport restaurant in 1952, desegregated public schools in 1953–54 and theaters in 1954, and in 1955 desegregated public housing and forbade discrimination in public employment. Minorities' achievement of these legal rights represented progress, but more basic problems of discrimination and inequality remained unaffected. As analyzed by Rev. George Brooks, one of the city's major civil rights leaders, Phoenix did not have "an attitude connected with resistance to integration," rather, its discrimination was "a very polite and subtle type of thing." By 1960 the continued residential segregation and the discrimination in employment and access to public accommodations, particularly restaurants, prompted civil rights groups, including the NAACP, the Congress of Racial Equality, and the Urban League, with leaders like Rev. Brooks and Lincoln Ragsdale, to organize picketing, boycotts, and sit-ins.[63]

Hearings held in Phoenix on February 3, 1962, by the U.S. Civil Rights Commission, as part of its nationwide investigations, provided a prominent public discussion that revealed differing views about the conditions facing racial minorities in Phoenix. Many witnesses documented the dire impact of residential segregation and discrimination in employment, but some employers and city officials presented a much rosier picture. The *Arizona Republic* editor saw no discrimination and opposed any federal or state legislation as unnecessary. Prominent business executive and community leader William Reilly saw progress being made and counseled patience and hard work. Vice Mayor Thomas Tang talked about balancing rights and responsibilities.[64]

Mayor Mardian offered the same perspective in his remarks to the commission and his written statement evaluating conditions in the city. He argued that substantial progress had been made recently; that Indians,

Mexican Americans, and Asians faced no discrimination or problems; and that African Americans encountered difficulties in only certain areas of private employment and housing. Although he acknowledged that federal laws had provided some benefits, he claimed that voluntary action was preferable and recommended that "minority groups should take advantage of this situation and obtain these gains gratefully." Mardian properly noted important areas of progress, but his description minimized conditions in Phoenix and ignored the larger problems that minorities faced. Having already testified to the problems, Ragsdale responded optimistically that "I think one of our great problems in Phoenix—this is a good town, the climate is right—but we want to get our political leaders, our so-called people in authority, to recognize that a problem exists." Brooks added that getting the tolerant majority to support greater action required leadership.[65]

Persons more sanguine about conditions in Phoenix emphasized the successful ending of legalized sanctioned segregation or discrimination, but they typically failed to see how discrimination worked. Mardian (and others) claimed that minorities faced no discrimination in voting, and it was true that Phoenix had no transparently discriminatory measures of the sort that many southern states used to prevent voting. However, the state's registration and English literacy requirements, plus the provision that private individuals could challenge voters, created the possibility of serious intimidation and harassment. These came fully into play shortly after the commission's hearings, in the 1962 election.

Worried about rising numbers of minority voters and the specter of "unqualified" voters, conservative Republicans organized Operation Eagle Eye. One of their tactics involved mailing letters to registered minority voters and demanding an answer by mail. Anyone who did not respond was challenged at polling places as not residing at that address. A more threatening tactic was to have election "observers" demand that a voter read from the U.S. Constitution and to challenge the qualifications of anyone whose performance they considered inadequate. The numerous challenges by a particularly aggressive young attorney created long lines at the polling places and an atmosphere of intimidation. In response, election officials threw him out of polling places at Southminster Presbyterian Church and at the Bethune School. Those officials—Manuel Pena and Rev. Brooks—later identified him as William Rehnquist, future Supreme Court justice. In 1965 the U.S. Congress outlawed literacy tests and other forms of voter intimidation, but Arizona did not formally repeal this provision until 1972.[66]

The lack of progress in employment and housing led Brooks and Ragsdale to meet with leading businesses and demand, successfully, that they integrate their workforces. They also increased public protest activities. In conjunction with a public march on July 26, 1963, the Maricopa NAACP printed *Equality in Employment*, a booklet detailing what problems needed to be addressed. It noted that African Americans held few government positions and that nearly all of those were as laborers, while they filled only six of more than six hundred positions on the police force. Private employers hired few African Americans and virtually none for clerical, sales, or skilled positions. Schools remained functionally segregated, with fewer African Americans holding teaching positions than ten years previously, and all of the elementary teachers taught in schools having mostly or only African American children. Access to public accommodations remained a major problem: many restaurants and half of the motels and hotels refused to accept African Americans. Finally, de facto housing segregation persisted in all public housing units, and African Americans were unable to purchase homes outside of South Phoenix.[67]

The city responded to these conditions by prohibiting discrimination by private parties. It adopted a public accommodations ordinance in July 1964; its leaders pushed for a state civil rights law, passed in January 1965, banning discrimination in employment, voting, and public accommodations; and in 1968 the city banned discrimination in housing. But implementing these measures proved difficult, and economic progress was slow and incomplete. Frustration exploded in riots on July 25 and 26, 1967, near one of the largely African American public housing projects, but these ended relatively quickly due to the persuasive intervention of Rev. Brooks and a curfew lasting until July 31. Called a "major disturbance" by the 1968 Kerner Report on civil disorders, the incident prompted additional efforts to attack the problems of unemployment and poverty.[68]

While city leaders slowly recognized and addressed the problems of discrimination, they also rediscovered the existence of poverty. Even more than most Americans in the 1950s who were enamored of newfound affluence, the postwar vision of Phoenix leaders and their efforts at implementing it had focused entirely on attracting and expanding the middle class. While the seeming obliviousness to race—following an approach developed in the late nineteenth century—was somewhat studied, the inattention to issues of class and how they interacted with race bespoke a larger national belief that "a rising tide lifts all boats," that economic prosperity for some would assist all citizens. This economic notion mirrored Charter Government's political goal of dispassionately creating policies that were expected to benefit the entire public, all of which came into question during the 1960s.[69]

The postwar housing crisis had prompted the city to provide additional public housing, a concern with dilapidated housing drove efforts to formulate a city housing code, and a desire to revitalize several multiblock areas produced a modest urban renewal plan, but a larger intellectual context for these efforts was lacking.[70] That change in perspective among Phoenix leaders began in the early 1960s with the efforts of the Community Council, a coalition of organizations focused on community social problems. A study of census tract data from the 1960 Census led the council to identify a substantial area of South Phoenix with high levels of unemployment, poor housing, low income, and inadequate city services, an area where the population was dominated by African Americans and Mexican Americans. Using ideas and language common in discussions across the nation, the council described this as the "Inner City" and portrayed the conditions as being connected to both race and class (figure 8.3). Through other investigations, programs, and conferences, the council sought to educate the city's leaders and to solve these

Figure 8.3 Phoenix Inner City, 1963. Note: "Inner City" boundaries as defined by the Phoenix Community Council; downtown is the center rectangular area. *Source:* Redrawn from map in *Social Background Paper,* General Plan Update Information Series 1990 (Phoenix: City of Phoenix Planning Department, 1990), figure 3; modified from information in City of Phoenix, "Precinct Map, 1963," in Arizona Vertical Files, Phoenix Public Library; Inner City boundaries from "History of Operation 'LEAP'" [2 November 1964] 8, report in box 3, folder 21, City of Phoenix Government Records Collection, Arizona Historical Society, Tempe.

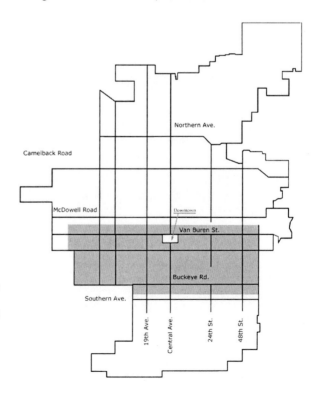

serious problems. The council's activities, along with the organized protests, prompted an accelerating series of events that would refocus city policies.[71]

In the summer of 1963 the city created a Human Relations Commission (HRC) to investigate a wide range of issues, and in October the HRC held hearings on education and housing. The Community Council then held a conference on the Inner City in November, appointed an Inner City Committee in December, and in January 1964 began discussing these issues with the mayor and city council. In February, another volunteer group, the Valley Beautiful Citizens Council, held a conference on housing. In March, responding to this growing interest, understanding the seriousness of these issues, and recognizing that South Phoenix had voted strongly for the ACT slate in the recent election, newly elected Mayor Graham invited inner city pastors and community leaders to meet with the city council on April 15, 1964.

The meeting attracted an overflow crowd and impressed Graham, who appointed a steering committee and a series of task forces. Based on their work, in November the city council created Operation LEAP–Leadership and Education for the Advancement of Phoenix—a private commission, to address numerous community issues, funded with $50,000 from the city and the obligation to obtain $25,000 from private donors. City leaders proudly described this as a new and innovative approach to the problem of poverty: where residents "provide much of the initiative and leadership," while the entire community provided resources, and instead of "existing agencies working in semi-isolation," having those agencies work together within a single organization.

The effect on the perspective of city leaders was striking. The city applied for the All-America City Award in 1965 and 1966, championing LEAP as its central accomplishment. The 1965 application explained that "LEAP has been influential in changing the priority list of Phoenix problems. In years past most leading citizens have considered the major local problems to be a lack of city facilities. . . . After LEAP focused attention on the poverty program, the main problems now receiving major attention include" better housing, a housing code, minority employment, and other ways to fight poverty.[72]

Although LEAP was begun as a modest, public-private effort, the organization immediately confronted new circumstances, requiring city and LEAP leaders to abandon its novel structure. The federal government's creation of numerous War on Poverty programs offered great opportunities, but to obtain federal funds, LEAP had to shed its hybrid character and become either a public agency or a nonprofit corporation. The leadership consensus was to make it a Community Action Agency within the city administration, and in January 1966 it became a city department. Federal funding also influenced LEAP's focus and activities. Within a year it had obtained federal funds of more than $1.5 million and local funds of about $250,000. It administered the Head Start and Youth Corps job programs; it organized neighborhood councils; and it worked on numerous other programs, such as park and street improvement, adult education, clothing distribution, legal aid funding, and a small-business loan program. It also had plans for numerous additional projects and had already applied for some of them. When Phoenix applied for the All-America City Award in 1968, it highlighted its efforts to reduce unemployment in the inner city. This type of increased planning on social and economic problems, along with relatively successful efforts at acquiring federal funds through the next decade, continued and strengthened the city's shifting focus, away from a narrow focus on services and toward programs that touched people's lives.[73]

During the 1970s, conservative fiscal policy reduced the city's social spending (table 8.2). African Americans made important gains on various fronts, but still fell below the norms of the white population. The percentage of high school graduates nearly doubled, reaching 55.7 percent, compared with 77.0 percent for whites. Although median income doubled, it still measured only two-thirds of the city average. African Americans remained more vulnerable to economic downturns, and their unemployment reached 10.6 percent in 1980, double the rate for whites. The distribution of occupations improved, and a number of individuals obtained white-collar positions. Although African Americans still concentrated in South Phoenix, a third had moved north into other areas of the city. The most visible gain, and one that also contributed to future progress, was the growing power of African American politicians, like Calvin Goode in the city council (1972–1994) and Clovis Campbell and Art Hamilton in the state legislature.[74]

MEXICAN AMERICAN POLITICAL ACTIVISM

The experience of Mexican Americans both resembled and differed from that of African Americans. Mexican Americans suffered discrimination and poverty, responded by creating organizations and engaging in protest activities, and produced politicians who became politically important in the larger community. They filed a lawsuit that ended school segregation of Mexican American children in 1955, and they resided in many of the same South Phoenix neighborhoods as African Americans. They were equally interested and involved in LEAP and related programs dealing with poverty, unemployment, neighborhood improvement, and education. But, partly because their population was larger and racially diverse, and partly because Anglo American racial attitudes were more accepting of nonblacks, more Mexican Americans were able to live outside of South Phoenix and to achieve greater economic success. They were able, as Matthew Whitaker phrased it, to "overcome discrimination and segregation in some socioeconomic areas in Phoenix long before black people secured such freedoms."[75]

As a result, these two groups had a somewhat uneasy relationship. Their traditional competition over limited public resources continued regarding LEAP and other programs, and it affected larger sociopolitical strategies. Brad Luckingham concluded that "few Mexican Americans joined blacks in local sit-ins and marches; in fact, Mexican American leaders persuaded their followers not to march with blacks."[76] In some cases, Mexican Americans even supported discrimination. A glaring instance of this occurred in July 1963, when the El Rey Café owners refused service to four African American youths. This incident and the resulting protests led the city council to establish the city's Human Relations Commission and a month later to adopt a policy "to eliminate discrimination against any person on account of his race, color, creed, or national origin." While the Leaders' Conference of the Spanish-Speaking Community of Phoenix passed a resolution favoring a solution to the issue, Commission officials communicated with the Café owners, explaining the city's now-public opposition to such discrimination, and the owners changed their policy.[77]

Various community leaders understood the importance of cooperation. The director of the Community Council wrote to the new LEAP director in October 1965 that "there could be nothing more disastrous for this antipoverty program than the development of ill will between the two major racial and ethnic minority groups, namely the Mexican-American and the Negro. Fortunately, the bulk of the leadership on this commission and the leadership in the community, generally, is aware of this potential difficulty, and they are striving to not only prevent difficulties, but to work toward positive programs of understanding and cooperation."[78] But some conflicts were difficult to avoid.

Mexican American political activity developed in two phases. Beginning in 1941, a chapter of the League of United Latin American Citizens (LULAC) represented their interests. Although initially focused on social activities and promoting education, through the 1950s it helped sponsor the lawsuit against school segregation, encouraged voter registration, and supported political leaders like city council members Adam Diaz (1954–56) and Val Cordova (1956–1960), who later served as a county and then federal district judge. During the 1960s other political leaders emerged, like Manuel Pena, who served in the state legislature (1966–96) and city councilman Frank Benites (1966–70).[79] During this period LULAC's political interests increased, but its focus remained on social events and self-improvement.[80]

Mexican American political activism received a major boost in the late 1960s from the emerging Chicano Movement. In 1968 a new organization of Chicano students at Arizona State University held sit-ins and forced the university not to renew its contract with a linen company that was discriminating against minorities. The following year, Joe Eddie Lopez and other community activists joined student leaders, including Alfredo Gutierrez, to organize Chicanos Por La Causa (CPLC), soon aided by a $22,000 grant from the Southwest Council of La Raza. The organization's first major activity came in the fall of 1970, when it entered a conflict involving Phoenix Union High School. Smoldering complaints about abuse by African American students and about various educational failings related to Mexican American students—the high dropout rate, curricular limitations, and counselors directing students into vocational tracks instead of toward college—burst into flames of interracial violence. CPLC responded by organizing a month long boycott of the school. The boycott concluded with useful educational changes, but also with heightened interracial suspicions. CPLC leaders like Ronnie Lopez continued to speak out, emphasizing Chicano pride, denouncing the nation's hypocrisy, and claiming that "in reality [the United States] has progressed very little in the way it treats its minorities."[81]

Spurred by this new group's activism and rhetoric, LULAC shifted to greater activism. In 1970 it initiated two housing projects, and in 1972 it criticized the discriminatory hiring practices of three large corporations that had recently moved into Phoenix. Most significantly, it regularly organized voter registration drives and campaigns for election turnout. These efforts reflected a broad increase in political interest among Mexican Americans and supported a growing number of Mexican American leaders who were achieving political influence and prominence. The most important Mexican American figure in Phoenix politics was Rosendo Gutierrez, a civil engineer, who was active in numerous community groups, including the Urban League and the Community Council, and had chaired Operation LEAP in the mid-1960s. Supported by Charter Government for city council in 1973, he ran successfully without its endorsement in 1975. Elected as vice mayor in 1976, he conflicted strongly with Mayor Hance and challenged her, unsuccessfully, in the 1977 mayoral election.[82]

CPLC also served as an incubator for politicians. Alfred Gutierrez won election to the state senate in 1972 (beating Clovis Campbell in the primary), where he remained until 1986, eventually moving into the senate leadership. Joe Eddie Lopez served on the county board and later in the state legislature; Ronnie Lopez held various positions, including chief of staff for Governor Bruce Babbitt; and Earl Wilcox served in the state legislature. The movement of these and other men from protest into leadership paralleled CPLC's growth and maturation. An initial grant from the Ford Foundation in 1972, coupled with federal government antipoverty funds, enabled CPLC to become a highly effective community organization. While its early strategy focused on referring people to existing social service agencies, CPLC soon began developing its own services. By 1980 it offered housing, education, job training and help for small businesses, health care, and a credit union, and outside assessors called it "one of the premier Latino community development corporations . . . in the country."[83]

These services were especially important because of the continuing influx of relatively poor, uneducated immigrants, mostly from Mexico. Family income remained roughly in the middle between those of whites and African Americans, while the proportion on public assistance (9.1 percent) was half that of the other minority group. Their unemployment level had been low (3.7 percent in 1970), but in the hard economic times of

Figure 8.4 Joe Eddie Lopez and Daniel Ortega at Chicanos Por La Causa meeting. *Source:* Where Worlds Meet Collection, Chicano Research Collection, Arizona State University Libraries. Courtesy Arizona Humanities Council.

1980 it increased to 8.9 percent, nearly the same level as African Americans'. Finally, the proportion of high school graduates rose from 35 to 45 percent, but that was still the lowest level of the three population groups. Although economic improvement did occur during these decades, the record was not an especially heartening one.[84]

The norms and expectations of Phoenix politics and government in 1980 looked and felt very different than they had only twenty years before. Charter Government's controlling structure, agenda, and leadership were gone, replaced by a council whose members advanced competing agendas and conflicting perspectives. In a 1976 interview Harry Rosenzweig voiced the complaints of old Charter Government leaders who felt appalled by the loss of common purpose in the city's politics: "[in] the last 10 years or so, they gotta have a Mexican, a Negro, gotta have somebody from Maryvale, somebody this and that, and everybody's now getting interested like [Rosendo] Gutierrez, a nice guy, but he's trying to form a power base for himself. He wants to go further in politics."[85]

Coming from a major Republican power broker, the complaint was somewhat ironic, particularly given Charter Government's constant efforts to balance its slates, and since some previous city leaders had gone on to hold other offices. But Rosenzweig correctly observed a fundamental shift in the nature of officeholding from what it had been when he had served in 1950. Some of the beliefs that Charter Government had consistently championed—a general public interest and selfless public service—were being replaced by an interest-group perspective, whose adherents accepted the legitimacy of competing group interests and of council members representing the interests of racial and economic groups. Significantly, this did not reflect a repudiation of growth and the high-tech suburban vision. But when Phoenix leaders expanded the range of city services and obligations, they changed the dynamic of city governance, and listening to citizens who had not benefited from growth altered the nature of city politics. A more fundamental threat to the dominant vision was that some city leaders began addressing the impact of rapid and continuing growth on the Valley's fundamental structure and its touted suburban lifestyle.

9

Changing the Urban Form:
The Politics of Place and Space

The emergence of minority and interest-group politics in Phoenix, and the changing focus of city government from narrowly defined services to a broader perspective that also addressed issues of poverty, coincided with the rise of major problems plaguing the older city. The decay of Phoenix's center-city housing and the virtual collapse of its downtown echoed the experiences of cities across the nation, but their occurrence within a community so committed to suburban sprawl and so oriented to automobile use created public policy discussions with a different dynamic than those that occurred in many other urban areas. Debates over specific policies prompted more general discussion about the nature of growth and, ultimately, about the city's ability to plan adequately for the future. The focus of city politics, newly broadened to connect government with all of the city's population, also expanded to include contested issues of place and space.

The initial postwar vision outlined a system whereby the city council would decide on general goals, city officials would develop specific proposals, and the council would make the final decisions. The system operated largely in this fashion during the 1950s, but a different process began developing after

1960. During its first decade, Charter Government effectively managed public opinion, mobilizing it for specific purposes. After 1960 Charter Government could no longer control public opinion on all issues, and public conflict began to shape city policy independently of the council's efforts. This process affected not only social policies, but also transportation and neighborhood development. An even more striking challenge to the postwar vision and growth politics came from an environmental critique, raising concerns about air pollution, the use of resources, landscape and architectural designs, and, more generally, how to live in a desert. During the 1970s, then, many people began asking serious questions about the form the city was taking, the built environment that was being created, and the area's future. Some skeptics were relative newcomers to the Valley, but many who asked the most probing questions had created the growth vision and the policies that had brought it about.

THE POLITICS OF HOUSING

The emergence of the civil rights movement and the politicization of minority groups in Phoenix transformed city politics. Rather than just reflecting the interests of a single group, it displayed the concerns of many; instead of a narrow, progrowth, service-and-taxes focus, public discussion broadened to include larger social issues like education and jobs. The most troublesome of these issues were housing and where people lived. The city's rapid growth created a housing shortage, which—exacerbated by the poor quality of some existing housing—stimulated demands for government involvement. This in turn prompted opposition from the housing industry and some home owners, and it produced a unique crisis.

Phoenix had begun addressing the serious problems of woefully dilapidated housing and unhealthy conditions in the southern part of the city by constructing three public housing projects just before World War II. When the huge expansion of wartime manufacturing created a housing shortage, the federal government built several neighborhoods of "temporary" housing. The postwar boom worsened the housing shortage, but efforts to resolve this by building additional, permanent public housing were stymied until passage of the 1949 National Housing Act. In 1950 the city council authorized construction of 1,000 units, and in the following two years the city built 484 units adjacent to the original three inner city sites. The 1954 National Housing Act provided additional funding, but construction was delayed because the city had not produced the law's required "workable plan" to eliminate and prevent urban blight and slums.[1]

The city's interest in these larger questions had been stimulated in 1950 by the organization and activities of a citizens' committee, and that concern grew substantially after housing reports in the 1950 census and a 1953 housing survey by the Phoenix Health Department showed areas of significant blight.[2] After passage of the national 1954 housing law and state-enabling legislation, the city created an Urban Renewal Department and began developing plans for slum clearance and renewal projects. To get federal funding for these projects and for public housing, the city needed to adopt a code outlining minimum standards for housing. The city also needed this code to improve housing outside of the specially designated slum-clearance areas.

Starting in 1956, Phoenix moved ahead effectively on these matters. In July the city council passed a code, and in 1957 it restarted the stalled public housing program, authorizing an additional 200 units, and pushed ahead with urban renewal. After a federal housing official required additions to the code, the city created a large revision committee and, following a public hearing, passed a revised measure in April 1959.[3] The city then resumed work on the public housing, and plans for its two urban renewal projects were completed by April 1960. The city also implemented the first stages of its program of housing repairs, picking two target neighborhoods, where it identified needed repairs and required that a number of unfixable structures—mainly alley shacks—be razed.[4] Thus, by 1960 Phoenix had worked with federal administrators and engaged its citizens to create and implement programs in public housing, urban renewal, and repair of deficient housing in the central and southern areas of the city. But this rosy situation quickly wilted.

Theoretical objections to taking federal funds started the collapse. Eugene Pulliam, a frequent critic of the federal government, published editorials in April and May claiming that accepting a federal "handout" for urban renewal would be "morally bankrupt." The *Phoenix Gazette* argued that "civic renewal of the dilapidated areas of Phoenix can and should be done by local enterprise and initiative" and asserted that federal slum-clearance programs just moved slums elsewhere in town.[5] In short order, important members of the city's urban renewal committees echoed these views. At the same time, efforts to place public housing outside of the inner city generated resistance from the new neighbors.[6] Even more troublesome was protest over the housing code itself—a protest that mixed concerns about urban renewal, slum clearance, and mandatory housing improvement and that employed images of lawless invasions and even forced demolitions of homes.[7]

Led by Rev. Aubrey Moore, critics attended city council hearings in

December 1960 and January 1961, demanding the code be repealed, and they presented a petition with more than ten thousand signatures calling for a referendum on the issue. Since this question would have to be included on the May election ballot, when voters would decide about the city's spending and bond proposals, and fearing that this might torpedo those plans, the council repealed the code in February 1961. This left the city temporarily ineligible for federal urban funds, but after the bond measures passed, Charter Government resumed its traditional approach to solving troublesome issues. It adopted a revised code created by a broadly representative committee, and after letting opponents force a referendum on the measure, it organized a well-funded, thoughtful explanation of the new code. But unlike all previous occasions, this time Charter Government failed: at a special election on May 28, 1963, a majority of voters rejected this code.[8]

City leaders were shocked and disappointed but not deterred, and three years later, prompted by concerns about the inner city, they tried again. They used a sixty-person committee to draft a further revised code, and thirty thousand people signed a petition circulated by the Junior Chamber of Commerce calling for a referendum on the issue. But despite new support for this code from the newspaper and some former opponents, voters rejected it as well.[9] Throughout the 1960s, then, the city's failure to obtain federal funds and embrace serious housing reform did not reflect the preferences of city leaders. Nor was the inaction because housing conditions were improving, for the 1960 census had provided a detailed analysis of the woeful condition and significant deterioration of housing in key areas of the center city.[10] Instead, the initial anticode campaign had been forged by a group of citizens with fearful beliefs and a commitment to vote, and the unusual repudiation of the leaders' recommendations stymied timely action. But the repeated campaigns and code revisions ultimately had an effect. In 1970, on its fourth attempt, the city council adopted a code that did not generate a referendum, and only then could the city obtain federal funds from the Model Cities Program.[11]

But the consequences of the city's inaction were serious, as the quality of city housing continued to deteriorate. Between 1960 and 1972 the proportion of substandard housing in the city more than doubled (rising from 7.9 to 18.4 percent), and the city neighborhoods dominated by such housing expanded from the area directly south of downtown to the entire section designated as the "inner city" in 1963 (figure 8.3). From 1972 to 1980 the number of census tracts in which more than half the dwelling units were substandard rose from 26 to 58 (out of 151 tracts), encompassing an area roughly nine by six miles.[12]

THE POLITICS OF PLACE AND SPACE:

Downtown

After 1960 Phoenix politics began focusing on the nature of specific places within the city—a politics of space and place. Much of the city's development had proceeded from private impulses, occasionally and indirectly aided by government. Although the city established basic guidelines through zoning, the growth of Phoenix and its subdivisions essentially followed developers' notions and initiatives. Over time, seeing growth and its resulting problems, many Phoenicians began to demand a larger public role in shaping the city's growth, but restrictions on suburban expansion were always contested. By contrast, in the beginning of the postwar era Phoenicians generally acknowledged some public responsibility for the older, central part of the city, but city leaders had difficulty determining exactly how to shape and improve the changing character of the downtown and older neighborhoods.

Like most cities during the postwar era, Phoenix struggled with its declining downtown area. While problems of the inner city raised complex issues and hard choices, the downtown crisis reflected a less comprehensible combination of changes—a fundamental structural shift in the nature of American cities, as well as historic changes in affluence, consumption, and transportation. In part, of course, it was the flip side of suburbanization. But if Americans had some understanding of that phenomenon, they found downtown transformations much more perplexing. In this regard, Phoenix leaders were not unique, but like many other Sunbelt leaders they were more sanguine about the process, or perhaps more distracted, since they focused primarily on understanding and dealing with the sprawl of subdivisions and suburbs. Phoenix had designed two urban renewal projects in the 1950s, but these were modest in size and on the edges of the downtown, and when they fell afoul of debates over a housing code, leaders simply moved onto other issues.[13]

Phoenix's downtown problems appeared in slight form even before the war, with increasing traffic congestion, but downtown's role as the political, economic, and social center of the community continued into the postwar era. The most evident problem after the war was parking. Already in 1946 the Adams Hotel announced plans to build a five-story parking garage, its representatives explaining that "the great changes in our downtown business situation in the last three years have made automobile parking and storage next to impossible." The other, large hotels eventually followed this example, as did the Luhrs Hotel in 1957.[14] Owners of retail businesses also considered parking a serious problem, prompting Mayor Ray Busey to establish a committee in 1946, which soon led to the creation of the Phoenix Downtown Parking Association. A decade later the head of this organization complained to City Manager Ray Wilson:

> There have been ever so many meetings and discussions regarding our parking and traffic problems. There have been at least a dozen surveys, a number of expensive engineering reports and hundreds of experts telling us over and over again what our problems are. We are all aware of our problems, but apparently no one is doing anything about them.[15]

Downtown merchants tried various remedies. Only a few stores could afford their own parking lots, but the parking association purchased three lots and leased others. Stores began to validate parking, but this, too, proved expensive, with annual costs up to $40,000 for large stores. Merchants argued repeatedly that parking was the city's responsibility and urged it to pursue federal funding for this and related projects. The issue was complicated by increased traffic. Most proposals dealing with that problem involved eliminating curb parking, as well as changing the traffic flow and improving streets, all of which required city approval and action. These deliberations also touched on other urban issues, with proposals for shuttle buses, a highway system to bring in suburban shoppers, landscaping, public events, and slum clearance to eliminate the increasing problems of urban decay.[16]

Parking and traffic problems not only touched other issues, they were part of the larger shift that involved suburbanization and the development of other shopping areas, especially malls. Downtown merchants complained about this, claiming that their taxes were disproportionately high, while noting "how easy it is to operate in a shopping center."[17] They reported the out-migration of Phoenix retailers and cited national figures to put this in context. Many of their proposals sought to imitate mall attractions, such as landscaping and free parking, and by the late 1950s they increasingly mentioned the notion of creating a "downtown mall," with numerous references to Victor Gruen's master plan for Fort Worth.[18]

City officials and managers listened to these concerns but offered only limited support. In a memo entitled "The City Is Doing Its Part," the transportation department supervisor characterized merchant complaints as "rather thoughtless in many respects" and recommended that employees and shoppers use the bus.[19] City Manager Ray Wilson saw the problem as simple competition between downtown and suburban shopping centers: the latter had gained an advantage by providing free parking for customers, but downtown merchants wanted the city to cover this added expense for their stores. Mayor Jack Williams claimed that Phoenix government did many things to help downtown, but he also argued that downtown's needs must be weighed against those of other city areas. He advised the merchants to seek more support from other downtown businesses, such as banks and insurance companies.[20] Attempting to reinforce his notions of a reasonable strategy for downtown merchants, Williams questioned their basic premise and asked, "Is the problem the growth of regional and suburban shopping centers, or the deterioration of downtown Phoenix?"[21]

Williams posed these as alternative explanations for the immediate changes affecting downtown; in reality they were interrelated elements in a larger transformation of downtown's role within the metropolitan region. In 1956 the head of the parking association characterized downtown as "the heart of the city" and "the pulse of all our growth," and he confidently described it as the political, economic, communications, and transportation center.[22] Several years later the Downtown Merchants Association president reiterated the importance of its remaining "the hub." While accepting the city's need to annex shopping centers and suburban areas, he argued, somewhat plaintively, "They have to be suburban to something, don't they? And, if the major stores downtown can't make a go of it, and if something isn't done, there's nothing at the hub to be suburban to but a ghost city or something approaching it."[23]

Although not quite a ghost city, the Phoenix downtown was declining rapidly, especially the retail sector. In 1948 downtown accounted for 52 percent of the city's considerable retail sales; that proportion fell to 38 percent in 1954 and to 28 percent in 1958. During the next five years the actual value of retail sales in downtown declined by half; a decade later their dollar amount remained the same, but inflation had eroded their value by one-quarter.[24] In the immediate postwar years overall retail capacity in Phoenix increased enormously, with shopping centers developing by the late 1940s and malls after 1957 (see chapter 7). While that initial growth added to the city's retail capacity, new retail venues soon began drawing businesses out of downtown, as the number of stores there dropped from 518 in 1948 to 410 in 1958.

The shift was most apparent in malls, and particularly for department stores. Park Central Shopping Center drew the first department store in 1957, and within a few years both local and national department stores began leaving downtown. Within a decade J. C. Penney's, which had constructed a new building in 1952, was the only department store left in downtown, and it soon left.[25] Other retail businesses followed a similar pattern. Clothing and shoe stores, important adjuncts to department stores, whose downtown numbers briefly increased after the war, soon began leaving for shopping centers and malls. By 1960 those stores still downtown constituted only a quarter of all the city's clothing and shoe stores. Before the war all jewelers had been located in downtown; by 1960 that proportion fell below half. Even movie theaters left the area: by 1966 only five of eighteen were there—and ten of the non-downtown theaters were drive-ins.[26]

Downtown's role as the city's prime office and financial center also diminished, aided by the city's acquiescence in a rezoning request. Starting in 1958, David Murdock and Del Webb erected a cluster of substantial office buildings a few miles north of downtown. This business district—initially labeled Uptown but later renamed Midtown as development proceeded further north—included five buildings with more than sixteen stories and represented a significant alternative to downtown. Since the 1940s, downtown had attracted only one new office building; by 1969 it contained 1.2 million square feet of office space. Midtown had "more prestige value" and was larger (1.9 million square feet), so that "when someone wanted newer, more modern or expanded space, there was little choice but to move north." And in the 1970s a third business district, the Camelback Corridor, began.[27]

While unwilling to challenge the dispersion of either retail businesses or office buildings, city officials were not unconcerned about the rapid collapse of downtown, particularly since it occurred simultaneously with decay of housing in the inner city. But they saw little opportunity for specific action. Downtown had always been the center of city, county, and state government, and the city reinforced this by constructing the Municipal Building (1963) and the Maricopa County Complex (1965). However, it ignored opportunities to use public funds to enhance downtown by locating two public recreational structures—the Municipal Stadium (1963) and the Veterans Memorial Coliseum (1965)—outside of the downtown area.

In 1965 Mayor Milton Graham announced a new policy of promoting downtown redevelopment, and the centerpiece of his effort was a civic center. First suggested in the late 1950s and modeled after a project in Dallas, the final plans for the civic center included both a concert hall, a longstanding need, and a convention facility, which was expected to yield greater economic benefits. Despite some opposition, voters approved a special sales tax to help fund it, and the center was completed in 1972. This development strategy of promoting urban tourism tapped into the growing market for conventions, but the city also faced serious competition, as more than a hundred centers opened across the nation in little over a decade after 1970.[28] The civic center also attracted support because constructing these facilities enabled the city to practice some urban renewal and eliminate an area known as the Deuce, several blocks of dilapidated buildings dominated by pawnshops and bars and populated by the poor and homeless. A second project, Patriots' Park (1974), was at the center of downtown. Besides creating open space, supporters touted it as a way to "get rid of the pawnshop atmosphere" for "a whole city block of blight."[29]

The Phoenix Civic Center did have some immediate impact: its development encouraged the construction of two major hotels, the Adams Hotel (1974) and the Hyatt Regency (1975). Separately, but no less vitally for downtown, each of the three major banks constructed a significant office building downtown—the First Interstate Bank (1972), Valley National Bank (1973), and Arizona Bank (1976). These structures increased the available office space in downtown by more than 2 million square feet, they reestablished downtown as the city's financial center, and they changed the city's skyline.[30] This construction, reflecting a belated recognition that downtown retained some importance, would eventually fuel additional downtown projects. Other business areas continued to grow, however, sometimes with city encouragement, and city leaders had not developed a clear and viable alternative to the traditional form of downtown. But while Phoenix had not created a plan of action, one advantage of this failure was that it had not demolished massive sections of its built past.[31]

THE POLITICS OF PLACE AND SPACE:

Older Neighborhoods

The postwar urban transformation affected not only downtown and the inner city, but also the traditionally prestigious older neighborhoods (figure 9.1). Located north of downtown in a 1.5 mile square, they had been built in the early part of the century, generally as the city's better residential neighbor- hoods and housing the city's elite. In the postwar sprawl, however, many of these residents joined the outward migration to larger and newer suburban homes, and the status of the Roosevelt, Kenilworth, Encanto, and similar neighborhoods declined. Initially, they suffered only a market disadvantage: most buyers preferred newer homes and newer styles, and builders could offer optimal financing. Over time, however, as these areas continued to decline in status, they continued to lose population and housing. They suffered further because the city's planned highway was expected to cut through these areas, which resulted in less upkeep, increasing deterioration, and declining home values. By the 1960s they resembled other areas of the city in the proportion of home ownership, but the quality of some housing declined significantly: roughly one-third was deemed "substandard," prompting city leaders to call for "action to *eliminate* slums and blight." By 1970 family income for these once-prestigious neighborhoods had fallen below the median city value.[32]

By the early 1970s it seemed quite likely that these neighborhoods would decline further and merge into the blighted inner city area. Instead, adversity and new attitudes about the city arrested that decline. The city's freeway plans, which had first contributed to the decline, now served as a catalyst for

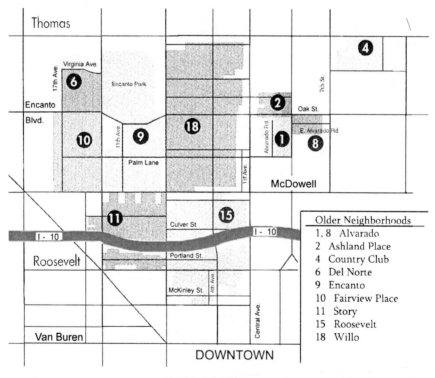

Figure 9.1 Older neighborhoods immediately north of downtown. *Source:* Based on the map in *Historic Neighborhoods of Phoenix* (Phoenix: Phoenix Historic District Coalition, 1999). Courtesy Helen Prier.

neighborhood organization and preservation. In 1969 the city announced that the route would go through the Story and Roosevelt neighborhoods, but to reduce the impact on them, it proposed to elevate the roadway and landscape the section below it (figure 8.2) But even if the park feature of that design might offer some community benefits, the construction would still demolish some six hundred buildings. Many residents in these and surrounding neighborhoods rejected the notion and organized to fight the plan.[33]

They were joined by other Phoenicians who opposed freeways on various grounds, including an aesthetic critique of the proposed new "skyline." Part of what fueled this revolt was changing ideas about the purpose and consequences of urban highways—both nationally and in Phoenix. Initially, the plan had attracted support because it would provide suburbanites with easier access to downtown, but by 1970 the outward march of suburbs and the decline of downtown raised questions about the proposed location and the purpose of the highway itself. The delay in implementation also proved important because this struggle occurred after many other cities had battled over building freeways, enabling Phoenicians to see the negative consequences of freeways and some methods of opposing them.[34] Some critics, including newspaper publisher Eugene Pulliam, opposed any highway construction as encouraging additional sprawl, traffic, and air pollution. Others advocated some system of public transportation, while still others opposed the construction on fiscal grounds.[35]

Freeway opponents were victorious in May 1973, when Phoenix voters rejected the proposal. But the victory was only temporary: proponents revived the project in 1975, and voters endorsed that below-ground-level proposal. The victory was also hollow, for the highway department had already removed the vast majority of buildings in the projected route—80 percent, by one estimate.[36] As a result, the final stage of the antifreeway struggle focused, not on the entire neighborhood, but on the remaining historic and prehistoric sites. While opponents could not prevent construction, they did manage to alter the route to protect certain key historic buildings and to salvage more archeological material.[37]

Although freeway opponents failed to defeat the project or prevent the building destruction, the struggle prompted the growth of neighborhood identity and organizations, like the Greater Alvardo–Los Olivas Neighborhood Association, and it influenced subsequent city policy. In 1977 the mayor appointed a committee to consider central city redevelopment. In 1978 the city council authorized tax incentives for in-fill housing projects and created a "special conservation district" program "to address the special conditions and unique needs of Phoenix' older neighborhoods." This program aided organized neighborhoods by enabling them to obtain enhanced zoning and planning powers, recognizing their historic character, but not requiring the special qualities and detailed documentation to be named as a historic district. Within five years a number of neighborhoods had achieved this status. Many of them also organized preservation groups, such as the Roosevelt Action Association and the Encanto Citizens Association, which surveyed areas and obtained a listing on the National Register of Historic Places for numerous structures.[38]

These historic preservation efforts connected with a broadening appreciation of local history, which was reflected in the organization and growth of local historical societies in Phoenix and throughout the Valley. The city's centennial in 1970 prompted only a low-key celebration, but it also led to the Phoenix History Project, which collected and preserved many historical materials. Mayor John Driggs played a key role in arranging public and private support for this and other projects. He obtained federal funds to purchase a Victorian-era residence, the Rosson House, and raised private funds to restore and move the structure to a nascent Heritage Square, east of the new Phoenix Civic Center, which would eventually showcase other restored structures.[39]

By the 1970s, then, a new dynamic was emerging that combined opposition to urban sprawl and consciousness of the Valley's past. An interest in preserving the older, prewar city meant appreciating the visible structures that remained, a sentiment shared by some native Phoenicians and by some immigrants. It was far more difficult to generate interest in preserving the part of the Valley's past that was really starting to disappear—its agricultural heritage. The Valley's rapid sprawl had overwhelmed the meager efforts at planning and by the 1970s began significantly affecting overall patterns of land use.

PLANNING, LAND USE, AND SPRAWL

Phoenix's rapid postwar growth surprised even its initiators. Their vision had focused on stimulating and accommodating growth, but they had not expected it to be so continuous, fast, and unruly. Nor had they anticipated the persistent and increasingly disturbing feature of leapfrog growth, which made regional planning seem increasingly necessary. To be sure, population dispersion in the form of agricultural villages and towns had characterized the Valley since the nineteenth century, but these communities had been relatively distant from one another. Noncontiguous growth around Phoenix had begun largely in the 1930s, encouraged by the availability of cars, but this pattern exploded after the war. Land-use studies in the 1950s and 1960s highlighted this "uneven patchwork pattern of urban development," and the public grew increasingly concerned about this pattern and "the phenomenon of 'gobbling up land.'"[40]

The emerging ambivalence of some Phoenicians towards growth mirrored the feelings of other Americans, who were finding that the benefits of growth came with the problems of "sprawl." The obviously unplanned nature of this growth roused concern on several counts, and a 1965 report on future economic growth in Maricopa County warned that this "plays havoc with the orderly planning and management of public revenues and expenditures" and that it could even "stop growth in its tracks."[41] Six years later, Phoenix Forward, a citizens' advisory group on expenditures, counseled the city to "discourage urban sprawl and guide and control the orderly growth and expansion of the City to insure a centrally-oriented community and an optimum usage of land."[42]

Besides fearing for the health of the city center, Phoenicians began worrying about the proliferation of auto-dependent suburbs, with single-family homes of ever-increasing size. Many local critics, echoing the views of those elsewhere, objected to the patterns of land use, sometimes for consuming agricultural land, but otherwise for developing former wilderness areas. Of course, the Valley posed different choices than many other places, because the area's natural state was desert, and both agriculture and urban expansion were possible only through the creation of water systems. Urban growth did consume substantial agricultural land in the Valley, especially in the Salt River Valley Project lands, but by extending irrigation systems, farmers were able to bring new land into cultivation. Consequently, the total agricultural acreage in Maricopa County actually increased from 1955 to 1975, but by the mid-1970s the loss "of valuable agricultural land" generated increasing concern.[43]

Growth more directly affected the county's desert land during these decades, with roughly 3 percent of it being converted to agriculture, mainly on the Valley's western and eastern peripheries.[44] Another 3 percent of desert land was transformed into urban space, especially to the north and east of Phoenix, and in leapfrog developments (particularly in larger planned communities) scattered to the east and west of the Valley.[45] In terms of direct conversion, 60 percent of the new urban territory added from 1955 to 1975 came from desert, particularly after the mid-1960s, while 40 percent (declining over time) came from farmland.[46]

"Disorderly," or leapfrog, development fit the short-term interests of developers and home owners. Lower land costs meant cheaper houses and greater profits; larger land parcels meant builders could more easily benefit from economies of scale and could design entire communities, with amenities that made their houses more attractive to buyers. These advantages to builders and buyers were countered by the greater cost of providing infrastructure and services, generally borne by the city and its current residents. And, of course, there were the indirect costs from extending highways to enable longer commutes. What made this possible was not the absence of planning efforts by the county, but its inability to enforce planning and zoning requirements and the ability of developers to play cities off against each other.[47]

By the U.S. census standards (persons per square mile of city territory), Phoenix in 1970 and 1980 had the lowest population densities of any large American city, which fits the common image of the city as a sprawling suburb. Yet this measure was misleading, for it reflected the combined effect of leapfrog development and the city's aggressive annexation policy. The low-density figure did not reflect new spatial configurations of subdivisions, for lot sizes remained roughly the same over this period and were comparable to those in other large cities. Instead, Phoenix responded to leapfrog development and annexation threats from other cities with a policy of continuing annexation (figure 9.2).

In the early 1960s and in 1972–73, it annexed northern areas in Deer, Moon, and Paradise valleys. Only the 1961 annexation in Deer Valley generated any controversy, and the city overcame this by showing residents how annexation would reduce the annual cost of their services by $149, while their new property tax would be roughly a third of that amount.[48] By 1974, however, the city's growth and plans again conflicted with expanding goals of surrounding cities (whose plans also conflicted with those of the other cities). From 1976 to 1978 Phoenix aggressively used strip annexation in the west and southeast to stake out areas it intended to annex in the future, and it countered the ambitious plans of Avondale, Tolleson, Chandler, and Tempe.[49]

This protected the city from becoming landlocked, from losing developed territory immediately contiguous to the city, and from losing valuable sales tax revenues. It also meant, however, that a substantial portion of the land within city boundaries was vacant: 63 percent of the city's Planning Area in 1972. Thus, leapfrog settlement and rapid annexation reinforced a perception that Phoenix was sprawling, but the city's continued growth, plus some deliberate policies, brought relatively rapid changes: measures of vacant land in the city declined to 50 percent in 1974 and 40 percent in 1980.[50]

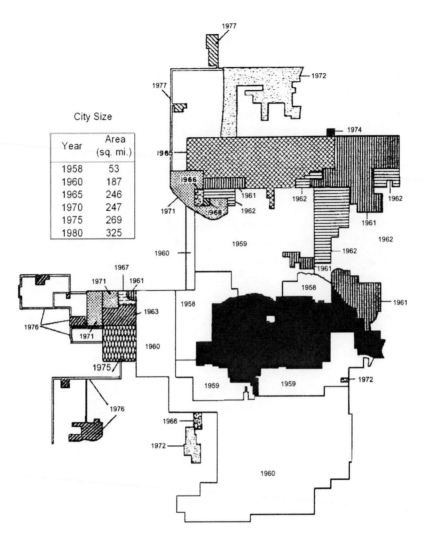

City Size	
Year	Area (sq. mi.)
1958	53
1960	187
1965	246
1970	247
1975	269
1980	325

Figure 9.2 Annexation and city size, 1958–78. *Source:* Modified from *Annual Financial Report, 1979* (Phoenix: City of Phoenix, 1979); "Statistical Profile," *Annual Financial Report* (Phoenix: City of Phoenix), 1960–80 editions.

PLANNING TO LIVE IN THE DESERT

The nature and increased extent of sprawl during the 1960s and 1970s prompted many Phoenicians to look more critically at the benefits and consequences of growth. This shift in attitude was occurring throughout the nation, but the Phoenix experience differed because the city grew so rapidly and because of its location and environment. This new perspective was partly evident in the report of the Phoenix Forward planning group. Unlike earlier committees, it focused on broader planning issues, and by questioning the nature of growth in the Valley, it set the tone for subsequent local and external planning groups. The group's report, *Phoenix Forward*, called on the city to discourage urban sprawl and to promote "high density development"; it recommended the establishment of open space, a series of greenbelts, and development of the Salt River bed; and it promoted metropolitan planning.[51] In January 1974 a report on Phoenix by a study group from the American Institute of Architects warned about the dangers of sprawl and recommended creating a greenbelt around the metropolitan area. A few months later the report of the Regional-Urban Design Assistance Team to the city council outlined all of the harmful economic and social consequences of "continuing limitless expansion."[52] The mayor and planning director reacted coolly to the group's proposals for urbangrowth boundaries and a greenbelt, but in November the city council agreed to study methods to encourage in-fill construction. In 1975 the Land-Use Committee of the Urban Form Directions Study—a citizen committee appointed by the city—recommended what they called "a familiar refrain in Phoenix: Stop the sprawl."[53]

What encouraged this refrain, besides an interest in the social and political consequences, was a growing public awareness of sprawl's damaging impact on the environment. The emerging national environmental movement provided a broad ideological framework that encouraged Phoenicians to question growth, and they resembled other Americans in such views as opposing the loss of farmland, the waste of resources, and the negative effects on the health.[54] But this movement also coincided with and reinforced a growing local appreciation of the Sonoran Desert's unique environment. Breaking from traditional preferences and the effort to create a green, or mesic, environment like those in the eastern United States, some Phoenicians championed a desert vision that had previously attracted only a minority of residents, like the early Arizona Cactus and Native Flora Society. A mix of natives and newcomers increasingly promoted a desert landscape, or an oasis style that included some greenery.[55]

The environmental issue generating the broadest interest was air pollution. Public warnings and opinion polls in early 1961 indicated substantial concern, leading to a university study of conditions in the state. A national study in 1962 found that Phoenix ranked "among the top five cities for dirty air," but local officials dismissed these findings, claiming that the only problem was dust and harmless particulates. This attitude dispersed quickly, however, in the face of more studies and worsening conditions. Groups like the Valley Beautiful Citizens Council raised air pollution as a serious concern. As one of its members, Leonard Huck, explained, "Phoenix averages more hours of sunlight than any other city in the Western hemisphere, but this God-given treasure will be rendered useless if a smog cover precludes the inhabitants from enjoying it."[56]

By 1966 it was widely understood that air pollution threatened public health and that auto emissions were a primary cause, and in 1969 the *Phoenix Forward* report described pollution as "the greatest immediate threat to the community." The state legislature responded by creating pollution control agencies and standards, but no serious regulations were adopted until mandatory vehicle emissions testing began in 1973. Foul air alerts in 1975 and 1979 increased public recognition of the problem, and in 1980 Mayor Margaret Hance announced solemnly that "either we comply with the Clean Air Act or we lose our ability to grow and prosper."[57] Despite public awareness and growing concern, little substantive change occurred because Valley residents also retained a fundamental commitment to the primary cause of the problem—the single-occupant automobile transportation system.

Water posed a second environmental concern. In the early years, availability and flood control had been important issues, but the construction of numerous dams throughout the Valley during the 1920s and 1930s had helped guarantee a stable supply and furthered the vision of a tamed and predictable environment. After 1960, however, the validity of that vision was thrown into doubt. In 1954 a heavy storm in Queen Creek flooded that mostly agricultural southeastern area of the Valley. Failure of the marginal water-control structures there crystalized efforts to create a responsive agency. The Maricopa Flood Control District was organized in 1959, modeled directly after the system in Los Angeles; and its managers immediately began proposing various flood control projects.[58] And none too soon. In 1963, a second and more serious postwar flood caused considerable damage in the west Valley, covering some sixty-five hundred acres.[59] Two years later, in December 1965 and January 1966, flood waters swept down the Salt River for the first time in decades, wrecking utility towers, damaging airport runways, damaging or destroying sixteen of seventeen river crossings, and causing an estimated $6 million in destruction.[60]

These events shocked Valley residents, but their significance was completely overshadowed by the incidents that followed. From 1967 to 1980 ten floods struck the Valley, disrupting normal patterns of life, causing serious property damage, and taking lives. Waters from some of the "smaller" floods came mainly from the north, like the flood in June 1972, which broke through canals and destroyed homes, with a final cost of more than $10 million.[61] Much more severe flooding affected the Salt River and occurred in five episodes from March 1978 to February 1980. This repeatedly blocked all but two bridges and destroyed six of them, producing massive traffic jams, wrecking utility towers, cutting telephone connections, demolishing homes, and forcing the evacuation of numerous residents. In the flood of December 1978, Sky Harbor Airport lost its radar system and half of a runway, twelve persons died, and the final damage assessment topped $52 million (exceeding the $44 million total for the March 1978 flood) (figure 9.3). The worst flood, in February 1980, not only mimicked these damages but also threatened Stewart Mountain Dam, whose failure would have been catastrophic.[62]

The flood damage was worse than it might have been because, over the decades, the riverbed had become clogged with salt cedar, an invasive small tree. Furthermore, the construction of gravel businesses, homes, and other structures in or very near the riverbed was imprudent, and some of the bridges were clearly underbuilt. The sprawl of buildings and pavement in the northern area also influenced the nature and severity of flooding by directing the increased runoff from periodic high rainfall into narrowed and channeled washes, creeks, and rivers, instead of allowing it to disperse over a wider area.[63] Of course, the main floods were

Figure 9.3 Floodwaters hit Sky Harbor Airport, 1979. *Source:* Mesa Tribune Collection, Arizona State University Libraries. Courtesy East Valley Tribune.

produced by unusually severe storms and were not fully preventable, but for Phoenicians to grasp that reality—discarding the sense of a predictable and controllable environment and recognizing that water in the desert was not always invisible and benign—represented a crucial change in perspective.

Besides their use for flood control, dams functioned as part of a highly successful system that provided water to the Valley, meeting the two-thirds increase in demand during these decades. Water usage by agriculture in Maricopa County rose substantially by 1970 and dropped slightly thereafter, but the water needs of the burgeoning urban population reduced the share of water devoted to farming from 90 to 80 percent by 1980. The continued supply and low price sustained a relatively high level of use in Phoenix, compared to other southwestern cities (table 9.1), one that had begun a century before. What especially elevated this level was that residential use made up a very high 70 percent of the total, with more than 40 percent of all city water going to "outdoor residential uses." This included not only the traditional mesic landscaping of lawns, gardens, and trees, but also the proliferation of swimming pools and the hundreds of acres of manmade lakes.[64]

The traditional contrast in appearance with Tucson, always a desert or oasis type of city, became more striking during this era. Although this older southern city grew substantially—its population rose from 34,954 in 1950 to 330,537 in 1980—it lagged well behind Phoenix, having shown less interest and less success in pursuing economic growth. Equally important, it had far fewer water resources, which led to a fundamental divergence in policy and practice. In Phoenix, per capita water usage rose between 1950 and 1981 from 195 to 271 gallons daily. Water usage also rose in Tucson, from 160 gallons in 1959 to 205 in 1975, but serious supply problems led the city to change direction. Its leaders mounted a significant conservation campaign, which dropped its water usage by 25 percent and confirmed in appearance and culture its identity as a desert city.[65]

Through this era Valley cities met the rising demands for water, but they faced problems fundamentally as serious as those of their southern rival. While it had far more surface water than Tucson did, a third of the Valley's supply came from groundwater. Many of the area's original wells had been drilled to drain waterlogged farm land, but wells drilled to supply postwar urban needs rapidly depleted the groundwater basin. A 1955 report explained that the water table in the Salt River Project (SRP) area had dropped 57 feet in five years, but that non-SRP areas in the Valley (to the southeast and especially

Table 9.1 Per capita water use in southwestern cities, 1981.

City	Gallons per capita daily
Phoenix	271
Albuquerque	242
Denver	213
Los Angeles	172
Tucson	150

Source: William Chase, "Phoenix: How a City Plans Future Water Use," in *Arizona Waterline,* ed. Athia L. Hardt ([Phoenix:] Salt River Project, 1989), 25.

the west) relied much more on groundwater. In 1963 a U.S. Geological Survey study pointed to a massive overdraft of groundwater and announced that "Arizona's water problem is grave." In subsequent years the problem grew even more serious, as agricultural pushed further into areas with only groundwater sources and as suburban areas and uses burgeoned.[66]

Two possible remedies to this problem—conservation and use of reclaimed wastewater, or effluent—would not provide a sufficient solution and, in the view of some leaders, would jeopardize the area's image. Instead, planners adopted the same solution that had made the initial growth possible: a major federally funded water project. Starting at the turn of the century, Arizona and the states abutting the Colorado River began struggling over its waters. Arizona had pursued its own course, competing especially with California. After a complex trail of debates, federal legislation, and court decisions, Arizona achieved its goal in 1968, when Congress authorized construction of the Central Arizona Project (CAP), which would pump water through canals to Phoenix and Tucson to be stored in four reservoirs. Construction began in 1973, but within a few years the entire project was threatened.[67]

The precipitating factor was the growing federal budget deficit, but President Jimmy Carter's decision to exclude this project (and other western water projects) from proposed federal funding in 1977 indicated a basic shift in public policy. In part, this reflected greater skepticism of traditional large public works projects, particularly the claims that they would be self-funding. It also reflected an environmental critique of water and dam projects. The administration's plan produced a tremendous negative reaction, and it was forced to backtrack. The modified plan funded the CAP canal and pumping system, but not the dams, and despite subsequent efforts to revive or modify, no additional dam was built.

This policy pleased the growing environmental movement in the Valley, while the Fort McDowell Yavapai nation, which had refused to cede any of its reservation lands, created an annual celebration of the decision and called it "Orme Dam Victory Days." Equally important, as a condition for restoring the funding, Arizona had to address its groundwater problem. In 1980 Governor Bruce Babbitt forged a compromise Groundwater Management Act, which created regional management districts that were to force a reduction in the use of groundwater. Rather than simply providing more water, the first priority for CAP water usage was to replace the use of groundwater, and only secondarily was it to provide an additional source. This did not end the overuse of water, nor did it indicate as marked a cultural shift as occurred in Tucson, but it did represent the emergence of forces opposing the traditional view of the Valley's environment.[68]

Part of this shift included changing ideas about the nature of landscapes. While the initial settlement and development vision aimed to transform the desert into a garden city of residential areas with lawns, shrubs, and trees, the dramatic postwar growth, involving commercial expansion and sprawling residential areas, raised other issues. In 1956 Mayor Jack Williams concluded that "it is becoming more and more obvious that the City must pass some ordinance relating to shrubs and trees and plantings in front of buildings, on parking lots, etc. If we don't we will wind up as Walter Lucking of Public Service says, with acres and acres of hot macadam." Williams suggested that local garden clubs might create "a Master Plan for Beautification of Phoenix," but he was most concerned about commercial areas. He included ideas for "green spots" in the downtown, but he also proposed requiring shopping centers to landscape their environs. The city's efforts at downtown landscaping won praise a few years later, but complaints continued about problems caused by construction and urban expansion. Norman Dibble wrote to Mayor Samuel Mardian that "the valley is fast becoming a vast wasteland of dust, gravel, bricks, concrete, and black topped parking lots. . . . I can drive from here [Tempe] to Phoenix or particularly Scottsdale and along the sidewalks rarely ever a tree, just mile upon mile of filth and dust surfaces between curbs and property lines."[69]

The change involved more than the planting of additional trees; urban expansion literally undercut the forested landscape that Phoenix had grown since the nineteenth century. Part of this occurred because the numerous street-broadening projects required tree removals, but even more consequential was SRP's involvement in the federal Rehabilitation and Betterment Program. The primary motive for this program of infrastructure improvement was to reduce water loss from seepage and vegetation along the banks. Starting in 1950, SRP began lining canals, laterals, and drainage ditches with concrete, plus putting some laterals in pipes (table 9.2). This process included eliminating bank vegetation in Phoenix and throughout the project area, and during the 1950s an estimated twenty thousand cottonwoods were cut down. Additional cause for transforming canals and laterals was increased public agitation over drownings. This prompted not only the enclosure of many urban laterals in underground pipes, but also a new urban canal landscape: raised, vegetation free, and completely fenced off. Instead of being an integral part of the city's landscape and recreation, the canal system was now hidden or a scar.[70]

A changed landscape also followed suburban sprawl. The use of closed pipes instead of open canals and laterals produced streets with less shade. The availability of air-conditioning (and to a lesser degree, evaporative coolers) encouraged developers to design homes without traditional shading features like broad eaves and porches. Their limited landscaping offered few trees or bushes, and even those were not for shade. While the yards of older homes had tall trees like ash or cottonwood, developers in the 1960s and 1970s favored modest numbers of smaller varieties, such as olive, mulberry, and African sumac.[71]

A second impulse began to produce different landscaping for yards. During the 1950s some landscape architects championed the use of desert plants in place of traditional shrubs, and a more minimalist approach to yard design appealed to developers who advertised a care-free lifestyle. In some hands this amounted to replacing lawns and bushes with bare lava or river rock, but to others it meant using drought-tolerant plants. Promoting this ecologically sensitive form of xeriscaping (not the empty rock yard of "zero-

Table 9.2 Condition of Salt River Project canals and laterals, 1956–73.

Year	Canals			Laterals		
	Total miles	Lined miles	%	Total miles	Lined or piped miles	%
1973	131	54	41.2	876	653	74.5
1965	138	47	34.1	868	413	47.6
1957	138	38	27.5	858	223	26.0

Source: *Salt River Project Annual Report* (Phoenix: Salt River Project), 1956–73 editions.

scaping") involved not only basic aesthetics, but also major efforts at public education. While Phoenix and other Valley cities cautiously advocated this approach, private groups were more active. Community college and adult education classes provided some initial training, but the Desert Botanical Garden was the most influential proponent of desert landscaping. By the mid-1970s, with a membership of nearly fourteen hundred and a paid staff of fourteen, the garden emerged as a major Valley organization and a destination for visitors. It offered classes and produced pamphlets explaining desert gardening; in conjunction with the SRP it sponsored an annual contest to reward landscaping that employed drought-resistant plants; and it brought in docents to provide an interpretive program for visitors.[72]

An expanding appreciation of the natural environment stemmed partly from the city's consumption of agricultural and desert lands, and from increasing concerns about preserving accessible public space in the Valley. The 1960s campaign to save Camelback Mountain from private development fostered a broader appreciation of area mountains as a "crucial element of the Valley's scenic environment," and this came to fruition in the effort to preserve the Phoenix Mountains as public parks. The success in persuading citizens to use public funds to acquire this land depended on a perceived connection between open space and this particular environment—not a recontoured garden space, but a natural area. Acknowledging this as a crucial development, the city based its 1973 application for an All-America City Award on this accomplishment.[73]

PLANNING AND THE URBAN VILLAGE

Phoenix came slowly to serious urban planning, planning that constrained as well as enabled. In size and function the city's Planning Department (created in 1951) resembled those in cities of comparable size, but its efforts focused on services or dealt with limited areas, primarily for annexation purposes. An interest in planning for the city's general future appeared in the 1960s. The first institutional form of this came in 1963 with the formation of the Valley Beautiful Citizens Council, which included some of the Valley's most influential leaders and was charged with examining widely varying issues from urban rehabilitation and transportation to trees, signboards, and training young leaders. By 1965 some residents criticized this group for inactivity, and a survey of major leaders demonstrated a strong belief, in the words of Arizona Bank President Lloyd Bimson, that "we need a well-publicized long-range growth plan, including urban renewal."[74]

Evidence of different planning activities and support cropped up increasingly in subsequent years. The Valley Forward Association (1967) was formed to coordinate the efforts of various groups like Valley Beautiful. Working under ASU Dean of Architecture James Elmore, several ASU architecture classes created a Rio Salado proposal to transform the largely dry and unused Salt River bed into a recreation area. The 1970 report of the Phoenix Forward task force addressed many crucial planning issues, including slum clearance, high-density developments, green belts, and transportation, but they also called for "a creative general Phoenix City Plan" and proposed some key provisions to be included.[75] During this period the Planning Department and city council began to grapple with the larger issues of growth.

In 1971 the city adopted its first land-use plan, the *Central Phoenix Plan*, which dealt with downtown, and the following year it incorporated this into *The Comprehensive Plan—1990*. Both plans endorsed the existing patterns of downtown and uptown development, proposing to link them in a corridor of high-rise office buildings, as well as endorsing the existing pattern of suburban expansion.[76] However, emerging concerns about sprawl coincided with the city's growing planning impulse. This prompted its first suburban planning exercise, in Deer Valley, but more importantly it led the city to appoint an Urban Form Directions Committee. As noted earlier, its report in November 1975 denounced sprawl as wasteful and expensive and complained that it produced an increasingly impersonal society. The report also recommended a new approach to planning that would support a diversity of places within the city, including center city redevelopment and a low-density periphery; that would protect open space and the natural environment; that would preserve historical areas and reflect the southwestern heritage; and that would encourage community identity. Its central recommendation was that the city adopt an "urban village" planning strategy.[77]

Working from that approach, the council created a planning committee, and in 1978 it adopted the committee's plan for redeveloping downtown. This included improved transportation, city partnership with private entities to design and fund development projects, and encouragement of private development efforts. The city also worked to "convince some business leaders of the *real* need to revitalize the central city." Despite this increased commitment, the city's larger planning perspective emphasized a new, multinodal urban model, in which downtown had prominence but an unclear priority.

In 1979 the city accepted the urban village model by adopting the *Phoenix Concept Plan 2000*. This would divide the city into nine "villages," each having planning authority, and, at least eventually, they were expected to contain the full range of urban features such as employment centers, high-density commercial development, recreation areas, and various types of housing (figure 9.4). Each of the main business districts—downtown, uptown, and Camelback—constituted the economic core of a village, while major malls served that role for several other villages. The plan's motivating concern was that "Phoenix was spreading into an urban morass"; it was essential to create a form that would nurture "a sense of community."[78]

The emphasis on community was both a real and a perceived strength of this plan. The city clearly needed to avoid a formless sprawl and to link discrete neighborhoods and subdivisions. In essence, the urban village model built on the language, concepts, and interests evident in numerous projects throughout the Valley, from retirement communities to master planned communities to new towns. It offered a clear approach to planning future expansion, although it would not, of course, eliminate conflicts with developers or others whose personal goals might conflict with the larger plan.

The larger issue was the existing city. Nearly every village included some vacant land, offering some development options, but the built structures and forms necessarily constrained any reshaping of these areas to advance the interests of community. A strength of this model, however, was its endorsement of the multinodal reality that was already forming. The presence of multiple business centers within the city was the most obvious manifestation of this, but the model also spoke to emerging theories about urban development. The city's plan addressed important problems, and urban analysts would tout this as a farsighted effort to create a "multinucleated metropolitan region," or an "Edge City," but naming a pattern was not the same as solving a problem, and public debate over the city's form would continue in the coming years.[79]

THE GROWTH CRISIS

Discussions about the future of Phoenix in the 1970s were louder and included more diverse voices than before, reflecting both the growing complexity of Phoenix and larger, national currents of change. Questions about suburbia, downtowns, inner cities, environmental change, and political leadership resonated in new ways between this burgeoning southwestern metropolis and America's varied cities. Previously, Phoenix's development and locals' reactions to it had been somewhat out of step with national trends, but by the 1970s Phoenix was confronting the same types of challenges as other cities, and public debates reflected and invoked national perspectives and ideas

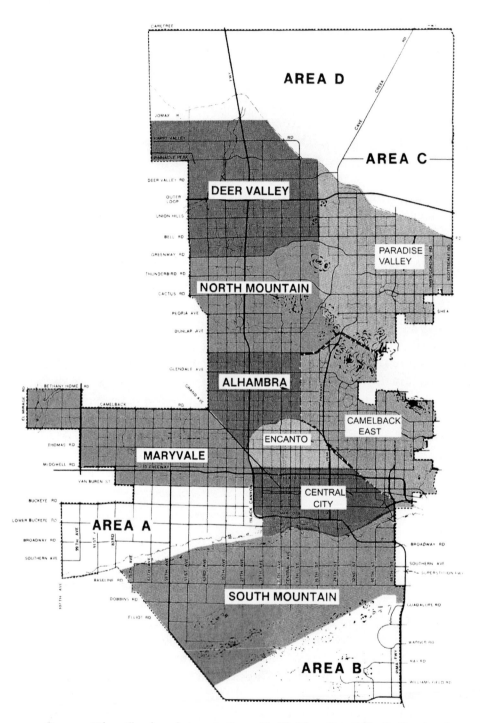

Figure 9.4 Urban village boundaries, 1985. *Source:* Modified from *General Plan for Phoenix, 1985–2000* (Phoenix: City of Phoenix Planning Department, 1985), attached map.

about growth. But the balance of views and the expectations of Phoenicians were somewhat different because of who they were and why they were there.

The criticisms by Phoenicians about the declining downtown, the troubled inner city, and suburban sprawl, with its attendant auto dependence, congestion, and environmental damage, sounded much like what people were saying in many other American cities. But public discussions were made more complex because of the considerable mobility of the city's population. Some migrants criticized growth for threatening the traits that had drawn them to the Valley, but more new residents, often arriving from areas with declining industries and rising unemployment, relished the opportunities created by a growing Phoenix. Their views of the city were shaped, not by Phoenix's past, but by their own. Thus, migrants from California, for example, found the Valley cheaper and less crowded than places they had left. Midwesterners could view the desert environment, not as diminishing, but as vast and exotic.

Among older residents, some continued to accept the basic patterns of growth as good—or perhaps inevitable. Their eyes were focused on the prosperous periphery, not on the decaying center, and they took continuing pride in the city's rising size and status. But others saw things differently, and this most strikingly included leaders who had helped initiate the changes. Many of them were surprised by the extent of the city's increased size and scope, and they were disturbed by the unintended consequences of the growth. Margeret Kober wished that Phoenix had remained the "lovely little place" it had been when she had arrived, because now, she complained, "I get off the beaten path and I'm completely lost in our big city." Patrick Downey explained that "I, like most old-timers, am a little disappointed in the crowded condition and the sprawl and all that, but we only have ourselves to blame for it." Bud Jacobson clarified this view, noting the problems with air pollution, transportation, and building, and explaining that "very little thought then was given to the future or that what you were doing today would have an impact on tomorrow. The only thought was, let's go and let's grow."[80]

Perhaps the most troubling aspects of growth were the city's increased physical size and the resulting loss of community. John Driggs described the shift from the world of the 1950s, where "you'd meet people in the stores and talk to them on the corners and the sidewalks downtown," to a society filled with new residents whose social groups were "pushed out further and further, and therefore, [had] less continuity with any traditional early Phoenix group." A desire for community permeated many of the comments by these leaders. John Long explained his interest in building the community of Maryvale by saying that "a person seems to lose his identity in a city." Newton Rosenzweig observed that growth had brought economic leaders who were "temporarily residing in Phoenix on almost like a transient basis" and that it was harder to get people involved in civic projects. He concluded that he had become "a 'no-growth' person, or at least indifferent to growth."[81]

The deaths of Eugene Pulliam and Walter Bimson in the mid-1970s symbolized another crucial aspect of change, not only the passing of a generation, but a basic shift in the nature of Phoenix politics, leadership, and decision making. The postwar system had involved deference and consultation, inclusion and hierarchy, a balance of elements that could work in a modest-sized city. With a relatively limited number of institutions and a physically compact city, a small group of (mostly) men with personal connections and frequent contact had made decisions and then worked to obtain public endorsement. But the tremendous postwar growth and changes in American political culture had eliminated that system.

Shortly before his death, Pulliam attempted to create more formal replacement for the informal leadership, helping to organize the Phoenix 40, a group of business and community leaders. Although slightly more inclusive than the informal group it sought to replace, and valued for touting civic participation and some worthy projects, it generated as much criticism as success, and by the mid-1980s it had changed into the broadly inclusive business-community group Greater Phoenix Leadership. In reality, the city had grown too large for a single group, for leadership came from multiple centers reflecting various institutions, different areas of the city, and competing values.[82] Instead of private decisions and a consensus vision on developing the entire city, policy decisions were public and reflected conflicts in values and objectives. Just as minority groups had legitimized debates over social policy, so area-based groups forced public discussion of their concerns. Residents of older neighborhoods objected to the destruction caused by urban highways that benefited distant subdivisions. Inner city residents complained about the poor quality of their services, while the city subsidized services for new city areas.

By the late 1970s there was an undercurrent of dissatisfaction with the shape the city was taking and interest in creating alternative policies. The valid concerns of those who were unhappy with the city's changed scale and its consequences for personal interaction and community were often difficult to translate into specific policy alternatives. Some critics argued for a denser, more centralized, more focused city, stressing the need to rebuild downtown and to revitalize older neighborhoods. Others wanted to stop suburban sprawl, particularly because of the environmental consequences of continued growth. While many Phoenicians continued to give general support to the postwar suburban ideal, this emerging intersection of criticisms initiated thoughts of replacing the high-tech suburban vision. But it would be changing economic conditions and social realities that would force more explicit deliberations about a different direction for the city's future.

10

An Uncertain Future:
Looking for a New Vision

Phoenicians continued to demonstrate enthusiasm for growth during the last decades of the twentieth century and into the next millennium. In 2004, under a puckish headline of "Git Along, Little Philly," the *Arizona Republic* trumpeted the claim that Phoenix had passed the City of Brotherly Love to become the nation's fifth largest city.[1] Such praise for the city's continued population growth was characteristic, as many Phoenicians treated new population statistics like a sports box score—the report of the local team's success and an occasion to cheer. Celebrations of growth and a respect for quantitative measurements are traditionally American, but they had been an even more intrinsic part of the Valley's culture since the 1950s. Phoenix residents' desire for prestige and status strongly encouraged this emphasis, but it was also encouraged by a more tangible goal—federal monies and state sales-tax revenues that were allocated according to population.

At the same time, more Phoenicians were becoming increasingly skeptical or even hostile to expanding a metropolis in the desert, prompting serious debates over the city's development. Many residents continued to champion the area's growth, its attractions, and its potential, often repeating arguments used since the 1940s. Some critics focused on specific concerns that needed attention, but others argued that the size of the metropolis was seriously straining the Valley's resources and destroying its appeal. Proponents of no growth, smart growth, and no controls on growth battled for public support. A mixture of optimism and concern, of pride and regret, ran through these years like water in the Salt River bed, offering benefits but threatening to flood.

Discussions of growth had rested on the postwar high-tech suburban vision for growth. This comprehensive perspective had presented an inter-related set of economic, social, cultural, and political goals. The breadth of that vision and the common commitment of the civic leaders to implement it had yielded impressive change and growth. But by the 1980s the limitations inherent in the vision, changes in the position of Phoenix and in the national context, and a failure to adjust the vision to changing circumstances had taken the city farther from what city leaders had expected and produced a building crisis.

The most significant flaw in the original vision of politics was the exclusion of minorities. By the 1970s national and local pressures had largely remedied the legal and political inequities they had faced, but Phoenicians did not address the exclusion of the poor and poorly educated, both whites and minorities, from the primary economic opportunities. Despite the area's continued economic growth, the economy was also flawed by the failures, first, to sustain the original economic vision, and then to update it to address changing realities. Major elements of the original plan included creating a diverse economy, recruiting high-tech firms—aerospace and electronic— and bolstering them with an excellent educational system. By the late 1960s, however, the commitment to those goals began to erode: the larger planning effort died, the focus on education shifted from an emphasis on excellence to a celebration of enrollment and size, and the vision of high tech had become a fixed stare. By the 1990s some Phoenicians began seeking ways to stimulate the economy.

Phoenix also grappled with changes in the national economy and with the nation's largest urban centers. Competing with second- or third-level regional centers, as it had through the 1950s, was much less difficult than vying with the nation's largest and most dynamic urban centers for businesses and growth. Older cities had established networks of large businesses and accumulated wealth, which aided and directed economic development through investment and philanthropy. Some newer, dynamic cities had a few residents who invested substantial personal wealth in enterprises that greatly benefited those communities. Phoenix was home to fewer wealthy individuals and hosted fewer large businesses or business headquarters, reinforcing its second-tier image and hampering its ability to create the most desirable types of economic growth.

The transformation of the city's politics that began in the 1970s continued during the following decades. The political system was reshaped to address more adequately the diverse interests within the city, but the basic questions remained the same. What levels and types of city services should the city support? What should the city do to shape or slow suburban expansion? How important was it to revitalize downtown, and how could the city best accomplish that? The city's efforts to address these questions were increasingly limited by the expansion of its surrounding communities. The location of growth, the city's share of the area's population, and the greater number of separate communities within the Valley meant that most problems involving either the built or natural environment were metropolitan in nature. While Phoenix exercised the greatest influence on Valley decisions and policies, increasingly it had to seek partners, foster cooperation, and offer leadership, rather than simply acting on its own.

During the 1950s Phoenix had vied for territory with several of its surrounding suburbs, but after 1980 annexation struggles proliferated among numerous Valley communities. While public discussions might focus on pride of size, the role of sales taxes in municipal finances was a more compelling motive behind efforts at expansion and annexation. Issues of resource management, environmental protection, transportation, and community planning also depended increasingly on complex agreements between multiple public and private parties.

Within this growing metropolis, Phoenicians and the residents of other Valley communities increasingly struggled with questions of identity. In a new and rapidly growing area with many fresh arrivals, where human history had a limited known imprint on the land and where the landscapes had been significantly recontoured, what tied people together? Developers and city planners sought to create community through built environments. Neighborhood residents tried to foster social networks and community identification, while other citizens found connections through voluntary associations, often drawing members from across the Valley. As memories of Arizona's recent western past receded and as the culture of the area became more diverse—in areas ranging from dining to the arts—residents struggled to define a specific and unique character of Phoenix. While some promoted the value of imported, human-made features like professional sports teams, others championed the area's desert environs, part of the Valley's continuing conflict between the natural and constructed environments.

CREATING A NEW ECONOMIC VISION

Prelude: A Maturing Economy, 1960–1980

Through the 1960s and 1970s the Phoenix economy grew as city leaders had directed, with agriculture's role diminishing while the importance of manufacturing and tourism blossomed. The Chamber of Commerce and other groups touted the Valley's economic attractions, but by the late 1960s the area's booming economy made most business recruitment seem unnecessary. The efforts, mainly involving larger companies, included some successes. By 1973 Phoenix was home to national headquarters for the Best Western Motel chain, Ramada Inn, Greyhound, and Armour-Dial. Major business expansion included Western Electric's building the nation's largest telephone-cable plant in 1968, while American Express completed a regional center for its credit card division in 1970.[2]

The most important economic development during these years was the continued expansion of the high-tech sector, as Digital, Honeywell, GTE, and Litton joined earlier arrivals like General Electric and Sperry Rand. Motorola was by far the most important firm, however, and its expansion completely overshadowed the activities of other companies. In its various plants throughout Phoenix and the East Valley suburbs, it built integrated circuits and semiconductors for its consumer and government electronics divisions, with the latter producing important products in navigation and missile guidance. In all, Motorola employed twenty-two thousand people, fully one-fourth of the Valley's manufacturing workforce. Together with the continuing expansion of other firms in aerospace and electronics such as AiResearch, Kaiser, and Goodyear Aerospace, this meant that manufacturing continued to employ roughly 20 percent of the Valley's workforce.[3]

Other sectors generally kept pace with economic expansion. Phoenix held its prominence as a regional wholesaling center and a government hub, with federal, state, and local governments employing roughly one in six workers. Retail sales grew nearly sevenfold from 1960 to 1980, rising from 57 to 61 percent of all sales in Arizona.[4] Phoenix also hosted most of the state's financial institutions. In 1960 this included the three largest banks—Valley National, First National, and Arizona—which held the vast majority of Arizona's bank deposits. Decisions by federal regulators and the economy's growth encouraged the creation of additional banks during the 1960s.

Through personal services and judicious mergers the newer banks prospered, but in 1968 the big three banks still controlled more than 80 percent of Arizona's bank deposits. Savings and loan associations also were concentrated in Phoenix and were dominated by a few institutions, but their numbers grew as well during these decades. Although smaller than the banks (having one-quarter the resources), they grew very rapidly in this era and provided important financing for home mortgages.[5]

Construction benefited from the population influx and the growing economy, employing 6 to 8 percent of the workforce, with another 2 or 3 percent in related areas of real estate or banking. Home building provided two-thirds of this employment, as the value of construction rose in Phoenix and the major suburbs. Building patterns reflected national economic factors and the typical volatility of this industry, but they also followed a speculative optimism characteristic of Valley builders. After a long downturn in construction activity from 1963 to 1968, Phoenix experienced significant growth interrupted by sharp declines from 1974 to 1976 and 1980 to 1982.[6]

Tourism continued its rapid postwar expansion, aided by the promotional efforts of the Chamber of Commerce and the visitors bureau and by inclusion in county and city planning efforts such as the Phoenix Forward report. By 1967 visitors spent almost $250 million a year, which made tourism the area's third largest income producer; by 1979 tourism generated $1.6 billion, supplanting agriculture as the Valley's second leading economic sector.[7] New resorts were built, especially in northeastern Phoenix and Scottsdale, while older resorts were remodeled, air-conditioned for summer use, and expanded. One such change involved the Arizona Biltmore Resort, a Valley landmark, which the Wrigley family sold in 1973. When a fire caused extensive damage, the architects at Frank Lloyd Wright's Taliesin West redesigned the facilities, and over the next five years the resort doubled its accommodations.[8]

Air travel proved crucial to the growth of Arizona tourism, and passenger traffic at Sky Harbor Airport escalated at a stunning annual rate of 11 percent. Airport funding and expansion kept pace: Terminal 2 opened in 1962, and a much larger Terminal 3 followed in 1979. Phoenix benefited from airline deregulation in 1978, attracting three more airlines and so much more business that the planned destruction of Terminal 1 was postponed.[9] Much of this traffic involved tourists, often winter visitors. The city also began attracting some convention business, but this was largely state or regional rather than national, and in 1981 Phoenix ranked only twenty-eighth nationally in convention business.[10]

Continuing Economic Strengths after 1980

This portrait of health and vibrancy for the Phoenix economy in 1980 seems, at a glance, equally true of the economy in 2005, judging by that era's vitality in general conditions and strength in particular sectors. Increases in the size of the economy (gross domestic product) and employment had outpaced national growth, while unemployment levels had remained below the national average and lower than those of most other western metropolitan areas. The health sector grew, especially with Banner Health's expanding number of hospitals and the arrival of a Mayo Clinic facility in 1987. Retail sales reached nearly 70 percent of the state's total sales by 2006, while employment in both retail and wholesale areas was high relative to many cities.[11] The city remained the region's dominant financial center, as its range of services expanded. After a state law in 1989 removed fees from credit cards, various national banks moved their credit card operations to the Valley. By 1999 this involved a dozen firms employing some ten thousand persons, and their numbers continued to rise. Investment firms prospered, partly by catering to the pockets of wealthier or older Valley residents. The city's role as a regional center for insurance businesses significantly expanded after 2001 with the arrival of USAA, a firm that specialized in serving military personnel. By early 2007 it had twenty-eight hundred employees, and it projected that it would increase that number to fifteen thousand in less than a decade.[12]

Tourism continued to outpace most other sectors and became an evermore important element in the Phoenix economy. Between 1979 and 1988 the income from tourism nearly doubled, to $2.9 billion; by 2005 it had nearly quadrupled again, to $11 billion, funding ninety-one thousand jobs and producing $679 million in government revenues. Tourist spending affected many aspects of the Valley's economy, from food and lodging to transportation, from the proliferating golf courses to arts and entertainment venues. Visitors filled lodgings across the Valley, some in the expensive, highly rated resorts, many more in the range of motels, and some in private homes. Those who resided longer but still part-time in the Valley (one to four months) came during the winter. By 2000 these "snowbirds" included one hundred ninety thousand persons living in parks for mobile homes, RVs, or travel trailers, and they added roughly $500 million to the area economy. From 2001 until the market decline in 2008 an increasing number of part-time residents were buying second homes in the area. Tourism also stimulated migration to Arizona: visits had encouraged two-thirds of all migrants to move and had significantly influenced one in five visitors.[13]

The growth of tourism paralleled the increase in air travel. By the mid-1980s all of the major national airlines, plus numerous others, flew into Phoenix, and international carriers began operating there in the 1990s. Passenger traffic at Sky Harbor Airport increased at a frenetic pace, rising more than 500 percent between 1980 and 2006. This influx quickly overwhelmed existing plans, making the addition of Terminal 3 (1979) insufficient and requiring the hurried addition of a fourth terminal in 1990. Increased traffic also necessitated the building of a third runway in 2000 and a new air traffic control tower in 2007.[14]

Not everyone appreciated this activity. Tempe residents and city officials regularly complained about noise.[15] Beginning in the 1980s, such complaints encouraged the suggestion, previously just a fanciful notion, of building an alternative, regional airport between Phoenix and Tucson. Another airport controversy arose after 2000 over limiting high-rise buildings near the flight path. But most Phoenicians and other Valley residents liked Sky Harbor's accessibility, as well as its ability to finance its operations and expansion through its own revenue sources.[16] Moreover, Sky Harbor had a directing role in the Valley's larger aviation system.

All but one of the Valley's World War II airports continued to operate in the postwar era, and by the 1970s they, plus several additional fields, offered significant opportunities for smaller passenger and cargo planes. Phoenix acquired and expanded general aviation airports at Goodyear (1968) and at Deer Valley (1971), which by the 1990s claimed to be the nation's busiest general aviation airport (one that handles nonscheduled civilian flights). Other general aviation airports operated by Mesa, Scottsdale, Chandler, and Glendale also grew much busier after 1980.[17] Potentially the most important facility was Williams Air Force Base, which was decommissioned in 1993, with Mesa obtaining its main aviation facilities. For a decade Mesa labored to develop a reasonable plan to build this into an economic development site and a passenger airport. Finally, in 2006, as population expansion and freeway construction provided a suitable context, and with traffic increasing at Sky Harbor, Mesa established a partnership with Phoenix to operate the Phoenix-Mesa Gateway Airport, which was intended to operate as a reliever airport for Sky Harbor.[18]

While very different from Sky Harbor, each of these airports was threatened by the spread of housing developments, and each confronted criticism from new neighbors regarding noise and traffic. Home owners and developers were powerful political forces, but airports generally won these conflicts.[19] They did so because airports were, in reality or in future plans, generators of significant economic development. Of course, Sky Harbor had the greatest importance, with a direct economic impact of $6.5 billion in 2003. Its on-airport employment exceeded thirty-one thousand, with another thirteen thousand jobs directly related to airport operations, and another ninety-two thousand jobs related to aviation. The combination of Sky Harbor's passenger and air cargo opportunities made it one of the Valley's major economic centers.[20]

Scottsdale followed this model and, growing very rapidly after 1989, created the Valley's third largest economic center. By 2006 the Scottsdale airport facility employed some two thousand persons, but the surrounding Airpark contained more than twenty-two hundred firms and more than forty-five thousand employees. Mesa's Falcon Field concentrated more on aviation and on aerospace businesses, with more than sixteen thousand employees in the area and an economic impact of $866 million. Encouraged by this pattern of success, the Chandler, Glendale, Goodyear, and especially the Phoenix-Mesa Gateway airports created plans in the 1990s and expanded them after 2000 to pursue similar types of economic development.[21]

Aviation also provided another form of employment. Taking advantage of airline deregulation and the continuing demand for travel to Arizona, in 1983 a group of Valley investors organized America West Airlines. Expanding at a breakneck pace, by 1989 the new firm had nearly fifty planes, employed fifty-seven hundred people, and continued to add routes. Overextended by such rapid expansion and facing stiff competition from Southwest Airlines, which made Phoenix one of its major hubs, America West operated from 1991 to 1994 under Chapter 11 bankruptcy protection. It emerged in a surprisingly vibrant state. By 2000 it employed ninety-seven hundred workers and ranked as the nation's eighth largest airline, and after merging in 2005 with U.S. Airways it became the fifth largest airline, with ten thousand employees in Arizona.[22]

Rising Economic Problems

Phoenicians could delight in the expansion of these sectors and the general rise in employment, but other aspects of the local economy during these years caused them increasing alarm. One problem concerned the relative prosperity of the city's residents, as measured by per capita income. The Phoenix area had slightly exceeded the national figure from 1970 to 1988, but thereafter per capita income dropped to roughly 96 percent of national levels. Comparisons with other urban areas were more alarming: by 2006 Phoenix ranked 131st

Figure 10.1 Aviation in Phoenix. The continuing growth of aviation in Phoenix led to the rise of America West Airlines and the expansion of Sky Harbor Airport. *Source:* City of Phoenix. Photo by Bob Rink.

among the nation's metropolitan areas, trailing all of the nation's 25 largest cities. The weakness of this, the state's strongest economic area, affected the decline of Arizona's per capita income to 86 percent of the national figure and ranking 38th in the nation. Wages in Phoenix (as elsewhere in the country) had jumped substantially from 1996 to 2000, but they subsequently leveled off, and in 2002 roughly two-thirds of those working in the Phoenix area earned less than $27,000. While boosters could be pleased that the economy continued to generate additional jobs, far too many of them were low paying.[23]

Poor wages partly influenced the city's high poverty level: in 2000 Phoenix ranked 7th worst among the nation's top 25 metropolitan areas, and increasing areas of the city were dominated by poverty. Other economic problems touched even more people. Traditionally, one of the city's greatest appeals had been its claim to affordability, and throughout these years its cost-of-living index continued to compare relatively favorably to those of most large U.S. cities and only slightly above the average for all U.S. cities. While the city's rating on the different components of the COL index shifted over time, its primary strength rested in its relatively inexpensive housing. But even that was jeopardized, as an increase in housing values of more than 50 percent during 2005 reduced that advantage, particularly when combined with the city's lower income. Among the top 20 metropolitan areas in 2006, Phoenix ranked 12th in the share of affordable housing (at 28.2 percent), measured in terms of cost and median income. (Within a few years, however, as the real estate bubble burst, unemployment and massive numbers of foreclosures created yet another problem.)[24]

A second cluster of structural problems followed national trends, to an extent, but they also revealed serious dilemmas facing the city. One such problem involved the patterns of business ownership and the decreasing role of local native business leaders. During the 1960s the three locally owned department stores—Korrick's, Goldwater's, and Diamond's—were bought by outside chains. Though obviously part of a national pattern, these sales had major consequences, for they removed local control of important economic institutions and ended the local public role of men who had championed a commercially vibrant central city. During the 1970s most important local builders either sold their companies to national firms or simply retired. This change also mirrored a nationalizing trend, but it, too, eliminated important local leaders, and it brought in economic players whose commitment to the long-term prosperity of the Valley was far more tenuous.[25]

During the 1980s and early 1990s another national trend transformed Valley financial institutions. In 1985, cued by forthcoming federal legislation, Arizona legalized the out-of-state purchase of Arizona banks. The result was instantaneous and crucial, as major national banks in New York (Citibank and Chase) and California (Security Pacific and Bank of America) bought many Arizona banks, large and small. Waves of successive consolidations followed Arizona's legalization of full interstate banking in 1992, prompting one person to suggest that banks affix their new names with Velcro, to await the next change. The size of these new institutions, together with their new banking practices, affected lending patterns throughout the Valley, reducing the role of personal contacts and risk taking based on familiarity with individuals. New ownership patterns also ensured that no one could—or might care to—aspire to the kind of supportive and promotional role that Walter Bimson had played.[26] The arrival of more national grocery store chains—such as Albertson's and Fred Meyer's—caused further reshuffling, with the disappearance or weakening of some local stores (ABCO, Smitty's, and Basha's) and the takeover of others, like Fry's. Wal-Mart entered the Valley like a tornado, setting up megastores that eliminated competition and reshaped areas, and provoking major public protest. By 2001 Wal-Mart had become Arizona's fourth largest employer. More generally, the number of mergers and acquisitions in Arizona continued to increase, rising from 158 in 2002 to 261 in 2006.[27]

Each of these industry transformations raised serious questions. Thoughtful civic leaders wondered if transplanted managers of national businesses would commit time and money to the community, crucial factors in the city's previous development. A second issue was that entrepreneurial opportunities were limited and declining, and wealth was departing from the state. While the city had successfully persuaded national businesses to establish branch offices, plants, or divisions in Phoenix, it attracted virtually no additional corporate headquarters since the few it had gained in the 1960s. After 1992, the only locally based firms among the city's major employers were Arizona Public Service, Banner Health System, Basha's Supermarkets, and America West Airlines—all of which were local service and goods providers.[28]

Nor had the Valley done well after the 1970s in stimulating or supporting the creation of local businesses—a third basic economic problem. In 1987 a successful entrepreneur, Wally Rainesen, succinctly stated a common view that "the Phoenix area has been a disaster for venture capital and start-ups." In 1992, responding to "persistent complaints there was a dire shortage of venture capital," the Arizona Venture Capital Conference began to bring representatives of venture capital firms to hear presentations by certain Arizona start-up firms. This did increase the funds available for Valley businesses, but only two of the investment firms were from the Valley (and even they had non-Arizona investors), and out-of-state firms often required those start-up companies to move. In 1999 a group of Phoenix investors formed the Arizona Angels to invest in Arizona firms and enable them to remain in the state, and in 2004 they took over Arizona's effort to encourage investment. But despite the developing activities, the dimensions of this problem remained very serious: businesses in the state received 1 percent of the national investment, and a study in 2007 reported that Phoenix businesses received only a fraction of the investments obtained by businesses in competing western cities like Austin, Denver, San Diego, and Seattle.[29]

The Collapse of High Tech

The changing role of high-tech manufacturing was a fourth problem, and in many respects the most disturbing. Phoenix had successfully recruited high-tech firms during the 1950s, when various companies (commonly termed the "Seven Dwarfs") aspired to compete in the mainframe computer business with IBM. Despite the often high quality of their machines, by 1970 this window of hope was closing, affecting both the industry and Phoenix. General Electric sold its Phoenix computer operations to Honeywell in 1970; Sperry Rand fared somewhat better economically, but during the 1970s its management felt compelled to reduce significantly its operations in the Phoenix area. By that time, of course, the industry had begun shifting from mainframes to microcomputers, which involved the design and production of various types of semiconductors. Phoenix had considerable success in this area, particularly with Motorola and with Intel, which arrived in 1979, yet it was unable to parlay this into a larger enterprise. In 1983 Phoenix was not even a finalist in the effort to attract the Microelectronics and Computer Technology Corporation, a consortium of high-tech firms that eventually located in Austin. Nor was it a serious contender a few years later for Sematech, a consortium of semiconductor manufacturers.[30]

These failures presaged a much larger problem. After four decades in which manufacturing—particularly electronics and aerospace—had led the economy's advance, the number of manufacturing employees plateaued in the late 1980s, electronics employment then declined, and by 2005 manufacturing accounted for only 6 percent of the nonagricultural workforce.[31] While aerospace firms like Honeywell and Boeing held their own, electronics companies generally did not. Some success stories included small specialty semiconductor design firms that subcontracted production, while Microchip Technology specialized in microcontrollers and managed to maintain a workforce of 2,000.[32] However, most of the Valley's high-tech firms began experiencing serious difficulties by 2000, and in the next seven years employment in semiconductor companies dropped by a third, from 33,565 to 23,179.[33]

Intel did better than most firms. Through substantial investment in facilities, it grew its workforce to roughly 10,000 workers by the late 1990s, but it faced increasing problems in a highly competitive industry. After investing $3 billion in upgraded facilities in 2005, in 2007 the company laid off 1,000 employees. Then, after careful evaluation, in February 2009 Intel management decided to invest the same amount in another upgrade, attracted by Arizona's research and development tax credit. Other semiconductor or circuit manufacturers with substantial numbers of employees were even less successful in avoiding layoffs and declining business during this period. STMicroelectronics had opened a fabrication plant in Phoenix in 1995, but in July 2007 it began laying off employees, and the firm announced it would close this 900-person factory in 2010. Sanmina, which in 2000 had purchased a plant that previously employed some 2,000 workers, announced in July 2007 that it was closing the plant and laying off the remaining 600 workers.[34]

These stories of decline paled in comparison with the disaster experienced by the Valley's leading high-tech firm, Motorola (figure 10.2). From a workforce of more than 20,000 in the 1990s, the company shrank to 1,000 employees by 2007. This deterioration started in 1997, when the company moved the headquarters of its semiconductor activities to Austin, and continued with the bankruptcy of its ill-fated Iridium cell phone network in 1999. As the market for its cell phone microchips declined, the company first laid off thousands of employees and then successively sold off whole divisions. In 1999 it spun off ON Semiconductor, which eventually found a niche market for chips for cell phones and other devices and employed 1,200. In 2004 it spun off its Semiconductor Products Division into a new firm, Freescale Semiconductor, which by 2007 had 3,500 Valley employees at chip plants in Chandler and Tempe. But these surviving pieces were a fraction of the original firm.[35]

The decline of the semiconductor business was disheartening, since its employees received relatively high salaries, but even more because it

Figure 10.2 The collapse of Motorola, the area's preeminent high-tech firm, meant the loss of many jobs and significant manufacturing capability. This facility in Mesa was torn down in 2005. *Source:* Photo by the author.

represented a failure of economic development. In reality, Phoenix had never become a really important high-tech center. This was becoming apparent to some observers by the early 1980s; rankings in the 1990s showed the Valley only near the middle of western cities and below the nation's top ten high-tech cities. Its employment was heavily concentrated in one area (semiconductor manufacturing), with some additional employment from firms like Avnet and Insight, which successfully marketed high-tech equipment. But the Valley failed to attract or develop a cluster of firms doing significant work in research and development.[36]

A Building and Financial Crisis

Always an important element of the Valley's economic expansion, construction (especially residential) grew even more significant as a basis for economic development and an influence on the area's prosperity. Seven percent of the workforce labored in this sector, and a roughly equivalent share owed their jobs to related economic activities like finance and realty. In addition, by linking construction activities to a larger assessment of in-migration and growth, some analysts argued that roughly a third of the area's economy depended in some fashion on new residential or commercial construction. The connection of construction with real estate development and finance also led to several economic disasters during this era, with far-reaching effects on Arizona's economy and institutions.[37]

The traditional volatility of the construction sector held true in Phoenix during this period, but unlike previous economic slowdowns, when real estate trailed a declining economy, in the 1980s real estate caused the decline. Recovery from the economic and construction slump of 1980–82 led to unprecedented amounts of construction. While Phoenix builders had always been optimistic, during this time their motto seemed to be "If we build it, it will sell." Although true initially, building activity soon raced well past demand. By 1986 commercial space in the Valley was vastly overbuilt, with vacancy rates for offices (30 percent) and apartments (13 to 17 percent) well into the danger zone. The glut of residential properties was even more severe. The result was devastating, as commercial foreclosures ran to $1 billion in 1986 and $2.5 billion in 1988, while nearly half of all residential closings were foreclosures. Home building, and especially apartment building, collapsed (figure 10.3).[38]

Several factors fueled this situation and reflected forces outside the Valley. Between 1977 and 1986 the number of builders in Arizona increased sevenfold. Some were local start-ups, but many came from outside the state, including nationally prominent firms, and many of those came from Texas, fleeing the serious downturn of that state's economy and building industry. The strategy frequently employed by national builders was "build to maintain a market share," an approach that increased land and housing prices, as well as flooding the housing market. It also drove out numerous local builders, bankrupting some, like Quail Home and Bowen Homes, and forcing others from the Valley, like Cardon Homes and Haman Homes. In 1990, veteran Phoenix builder Dave Brown observed that "all the local guys are gone. I'm the last privately owned builder in town. What you're seeing is the extinction of the small- and middle-sized builder."[39]

Construction had also been unduly encouraged by the federal tax system, but the 1986 Tax Reform Act ended those advantages and the strategy. The final and most important factor were laws in the early 1980s that deregulated savings and loan institutions, allowing them considerable liberty to make and sell loans, while still insuring their deposits. Savings and loans, which traditionally loaned money for single-family homes, now began handing out money for many types of real estate development, and this shift greatly affected the Valley's economy. Without adequate government regulation and restrictions, savings and loans paid grossly inflated land prices or funded

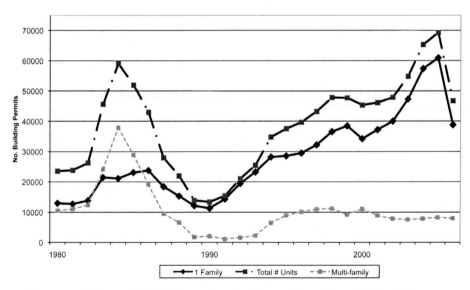

Figure 10.3 Building activity in Maricopa County, 1980–2006. *Source:* Texas Real Estate Center, Texas A&M University, "Metropolitan Residential Building Permit Activity," http://recenter. tamu.edu/data/bpm/.

proposals with virtually no investment by the developer and split the expected profits. Brought in to clean up Security Savings in 1989, Bill Crocker observed that "this institution, like many savings and loans in Arizona, was run like a venture capital company."[40]

Some developers simply used poor judgment, but others, especially under worsening economic conditions, acted fraudulently. The most egregious instance involved Charles Keating, who used a Phoenix financial services company, American Continental Corporation, to buy Lincoln Savings and Loan in Irvine, California, which he utilized to defraud investors in a desperate effort to keep his Arizona developments afloat. American Continental filed for bankruptcy in 1989, but federal authorities charged Keating with bilking Lincoln Savings. Repaying the Lincoln creditors cost taxpayers $3.2 billion, the most expensive such disaster in the country. Keating himself was convicted in 1993 on seventy-three criminal charges. A less costly but equally significant case involved Fife Symington, who received sweetheart deals from Southwest Savings, on whose board of directors he served. He then parlayed his reputed business acumen into election as governor of Arizona, but the economic downturn forced him to seek refinancing of his projects, which he obtained by providing fraudulent information. Ultimately, his activities led to criminal charges, his conviction, and his resignation from office.[41]

These and similar cases seriously affected both the short- and long-term economic development of the Valley. In the two years after February 17, 1989, nine of Arizona's ten savings and loans failed, costing taxpayers more than $5 billion. Federal regulators filed civil charges against directors and officers of six thrifts and criminal charges against three. Yet the crisis could have destroyed even more institutions. Arizona banks had also made ill-advised loans, and as the economy declined, their losses mounted. Their fortunes differed from those of the savings and loans, however, first, because they did not act fraudulently, but also because the two largest Arizona-owned banks— Valley National and First Interstate—plus the out-of-state banks had sufficient resources to withstand the serious losses (Security Pacific lost $1.1 billion in 1989). The 1985 law allowing out-of-state banks to buy Arizona banks saved a number of those institutions.[42]

As Arizona's savings and loans and a number of its small banks began folding in 1989, larger banks, especially the Bank of America, scooped them up. This led to a series of buyouts and mergers, especially from 1992 to 1994, and the pattern was repeated after June 1997, when federal legislation permitted full interstate branch banking. As a result, the four largest banks in Arizona, all based in other states, controlled 90 percent of Arizona's bank assets. Many people criticized this concentration of economic power, one further evidenced by the declining number of banks in the state from fifty-three in 1985 to twenty-nine in 1996. Surprisingly, just as the concentration reached its greatest extent, a countertrend emerged: a dozen banks organized from 1996 to 2000. Often calling themselves "community banks," these institutions aimed to offer the style of personal banking that large banks were abandoning. By 2007 a very different system had emerged. Three major banks—Wells Fargo, Bank of America, and J. P. Morgan Chase & Company—still dominated the state, but their share of all Arizona deposits had fallen to 62 percent, as the number of banks, most of them community banks and many based out of state, rose to sixty-eight.[43]

Construction activity eventually resumed and then boomed by the late 1990s. The profits and competition for markets led to another wave of buyouts, as major national construction companies purchased other Arizona builders. The sales included most of the remaining Arizona-based builders of appreciable size: Pulte purchased Del Webb Homes, D. R. Horton bought Continental Homes, and K. B. Homes took over the Estes Company. Together with other companies involved in land sales, these firms were vocal in local debates over possible controls on growth, and they took strength from the argument that a third of the area's growth was connected to construction.[44]

But, just as in the 1980s and in eerily similar fashion, larger market conditions with an admixture of greed pushed construction and financial miscalculations past reason and into disaster. With the downturn of the stock market after 2000, investors began seeking other opportunities, and real estate seemed profitable. Housing construction then boomed tremendously, and housing sales jumped, as some speculators bought and resold new homes while others bought, refurbished, and sold older homes. This created a substantial increase in construction-related employment and a huge escalation in price, with related demand for easier financing. The result was a variety of unsafe mortgage financing schemes. By 2007 Phoenix, like the rest of the country, began witnessing waves of foreclosures and another looming financial disaster, and in 2008 and 2009 the Valley was near the top of the housing disaster charts.[45]

Planning and Responses to Economic Challenge

The economic plan that Phoenix pursued after World War II was developed by private leaders, particularly in the Phoenix Chamber of Commerce, and implemented with the occasional assistance of city leaders, and it included efforts to develop institutions of culture and higher education. Planning efforts dwindled during the 1960s, and the Chamber of Commerce struggled to deal with the public's changing expectations and with the emerging metropolitan context. In 1977 it transferred the promotion of tourism and conventions to a Valley-wide agency. In 1983 it renamed itself the Phoenix Metro Chamber, but it abandoned the title after a few years, reflecting the growth and independence of suburban chambers. And over the next several years its membership declined by roughly half.[46]

As the chamber's role dwindled, new public-private groups emerged to address the topic of economic planning for Phoenix and the Valley. Phoenix Mayor Terry Goddard pushed the organization of the Phoenix Economic Growth Corporation (1985), a mixed public-private group, to plan the city's economic future. This was soon subsumed into the Greater Phoenix Economic Council, which grew out of Mayor Goddard's 1988 call for a summit of business, civic, and political leaders from the Valley to deal with the immediate economic crisis and to create a Valley-wide strategy for economic development. In their 1989 All-America City Award proposal, city leaders identified "inter-community cooperation" as Phoenix's primary weakness and specifically noted "the failure to construct a single, unified economic development program." The increased population and economic interests in the surrounding suburbs fostered the organization and operation of separate groups—the East Valley Partnership (1982) and Westmarc (1990) for the West Valley—yet they worked to overcome competition and to cooperate. Together with the Greater Phoenix Convention and Visitors Bureau, Greater Phoenix Leadership, and other groups, they formed the Greater Phoenix Business Leadership Coalition to consider a range of economic development policies.[47]

Planning efforts also involved statewide interests and efforts. A public-private group (Arizona Strategic Planning for Economic Development) started in 1990 and led to a state-sponsored group in 1992 and another group in 1999 to plan for the New Economy. Multiple private studies encouraged significant rethinking about the future. The Arizona Town Hall organization sponsored forums and reports concerning different economic issues; Arizona State University's Morrison Institute of Public Policy generated a flurry of insightful studies; ASU's Greater Phoenix 2100 project presented scientific and technical data to facilitate long-range planning; and the *Arizona Republic* published numerous series of articles assessing the region's condition and future prospects.[48]

These studies came to many common conclusions. Like the original economic vision, they argued for attracting high-wage jobs, noting that most of the city's new jobs were relatively low paying. They also revived the earlier emphasis on the crucial role of education, especially higher education. While ASU's business and engineering schools had continued to develop useful programs and the university had created a research park, which had generated some activity, it had not been asked for nor had it provided the kind of significant economic drive that successfully developing communities had received from their universities.[49] What differed most from the prior plan, besides a broader emphasis on education, was the shift in focus from computers and semiconductors to biomedical research. In this, the city and state were not alone: by 2006 most states were targeting biosciences, and two-thirds provided funding for research and development facilities. But despite this competition, Phoenix and Arizona moved ahead fairly quickly after 1999, aided by state and private funding, especially from Arizona's emerging philanthropic foundations, and by determined action by ASU and the city of Phoenix.[50]

The initial step was the most crucial: a concerted effort begun in 1999 by state, city, and industry leaders succeeded in attracting the Translational Genomics Research Institute and the International Genomics Consortium to Phoenix in 2002. The expectation was these organizations would win substantial grant funding and attract related businesses. The following year ASU began collaborative programs with the Mayo Clinic in medical research and development, as well as in clinical work; and in 2004 ASU opened the door for a new University of Arizona Medical School to be part of a Phoenix Biomedical Campus. ASU also expanded its territorial and intellectual scope in 2004 through a joint venture with Scottsdale to create an ASU Scottsdale Center for New Technology and Innovation, which would "include traditional and non-traditional business incubators, as well as programs focusing on technologies at the intersection of engineering, art, and bioscience."[51] These developments depended on significant changes in the university: creating a School of Life Sciences and a School of Sustainability; establishing the Arizona Biodesign Institute; luring the Center for Science, Policy, and Outcomes from Columbia University, and achieving from these and other parts of the university a significant increase in research funding.[52] Given the significant competition for developing a biotech industry, it would take years to see if this new venture succeeded, but the initial results in terms of institutions and funded projects, plus the attraction of both public and private investment, were promising.[53]

CREATING A NEW POLITICAL VISION

In the years after 1980 the city's political culture and vision were transformed in ways no less profound than the redirection of economic goals and policies. This post–Charter Government era highlighted significantly new patterns of leadership, political organization, and responsibilities for council members. Yet these changes did not affect city administration, which remained highly effective despite the continuing challenges of growth.

The city's increased population, the rise of minority politics, and the emergence of new political issues stimulated the citizen demands that brought these changes, and popular concerns for government openness and public decision making continued throughout this era. However, low levels of voter turnout and limited turnover among officeholders indicated limits to popular engagement and participation in Phoenix politics. One explanation for this general condition was the absence of formal political organization or partisan activity in city politics.[54] The mobility of the population—the high amount of turnover and the high proportion of new, young residents—also produced lower levels of political involvement for the population as a whole.[55] Whatever the cause, this muted political participation had various implications for the nature of politics and the role of government. Most importantly, mayors faced a much greater responsibility than before to articulate a vision for the city and provide the leadership to achieve specific policies.

Leadership and a New Politics

Margaret Hance initiated the transformation of the political system when she broke the hold of the Charter Government on Phoenix government in 1975. While her decision to run and her subsequent actions were personal, they were not idiosyncratic, for the profusion of twenty-six city council candidates in that year demonstrated a rejection of elite control over political nominations, a desire for greater popular access to office, and changing public attitudes about political power. But public desires soon fell victim to the limitations of political structure: the number of council candidates fell, competition diminished, and in 1981 voter turnout dropped below 20 percent—lower than in the Charter Government era. A key reason for this was the problem of running a citywide campaign in a city of more than three hundred square miles and with three-quarters of a million people. The city's mobile population and the passing of the "founding fathers" was reflected in low name recognition, with no one candidate topping 15 percent recognition. And few persons had sufficient money to run or could raise adequate campaign funds. Thus, even though the CGC nomination system was discredited, CGC endorsement at least offered some recognition and electoral advantage.[56]

These frustrations bolstered the longstanding proposal to elect council members from districts. Encouraged by polls showing support from two-thirds of the public, a Committee for District Representation organized a successful petition drive that forced the city council to allow a popular vote on the plan, but it auspiciously scheduled this for 1 December 1982—a Wednesday—to discourage voter turnout. The proposal to elect council members from eight districts (up from the current six at-large members) roused many important opponents: Mayor Hance, her Charter Review Committee, the Charter Government Committee, the Phoenix 40 group of notables, the Chamber of Commerce, and major business interests. They recycled the arguments dating back to the 1940s about the dangers of "old-fashioned, ward politics," while the *Arizona Republic* hysterically denounced it as the "balkanization" of the city and a plot to allow "union bosses to seize control of city hall." More thoughtful critics worried about excessive localism and competition among districts, but offered no solutions to the problems with at-large election.

The Committee for District Representation's leading spokesman, Terry Goddard, relished the elite's united opposition as showing their desire to maintain a system in which "a small group of self-appointed manipulators control who is elected to the City council." Goddard and the committee touted a district system as bringing government closer to the public and as enabling representation for diverse communities and interests. Facing a well-financed campaign of opposition, the district forces waited until the end of the campaign to use television ads. Despite the unusual election day, voter turnout exceeded that of the previous city election, and the district plan won a narrow victory.[57]

This nascent system created a new political dynamic for the 1983 election. Mayor Hance's decision to retire leveled the field considerably. In her stead was Pete Dunn, a conservative Republican and former state legislator who championed her conservative fiscal policies and emphasis on crime, limited support for social programs, and support for annexation with minimal restraints on urban expansion. His opponent was Terry Goddard. A young lawyer who had not held political office, Goddard had gained recognition as an effective spokesman for the district committee, and he had previously been active in opposing the Papago Freeway. Also important was his political experience working with the Democratic Party's county organization and the fact that his father, Sam Goddard, was a former governor and state party chairman. But Goddard's greatest assets were his ability as an articulate, ebullient, and effective campaigner and his focused campaign message calling for open, responsive, and active government. Labeling Dunn "the henchman of the status quo" and denouncing CGC and the Phoenix 40, he called for balancing development with quality-of-life concerns. Voter turnout doubled over the 1981 election, and Goddard won a solid 53.8 percent of the vote, a clear defeat for the Hance-CGC forces.[58]

Goddard's tenure as mayor (1984–1990) marked a distinct shift in city governance, policies, and politics, but in various ways he confounded conservative expectations (figure 10.4). He revived efforts to promote economic development, but he did so through his newly created Phoenix Economic Growth Corporation, a public-private partnership. This measured approach surprised some opponents from 1983 and helped win support from the city's newspapers and some key economic leaders. The *Arizona Republic* observed:

> Some feared that a Goddard administration would cripple devel-
> opment. They were wrong. Under Goddard, commercial and
> home development have thrived like bougainvillea, even though
> they've been forced to accept a few more stipulations, acquiesce in
> more neighborhood concerns and . . . finance more infrastructure
> improvements.

When Valley's economy weakened in 1989, he used the occasion to push for regional economic development through the development of the Greater Phoenix Economic Council.[59]

Goddard invigorated city government. He inherited an able city administration, which he later likened to "a race car usually kept in the garage with the motor idling." He decided to take it out on the track and see what it could do. He spent considerable effort on evaluating zoning and planning cases, seeking to direct growth into patterns that reflected thoughtful public choices rather than developer initiatives. He sought to encourage in-fill growth and discourage expansion and annexation. His efforts had some success, but the actions of developers and urban competition, especially in terms of sales tax revenues, prevented him from making the degree of change he had hoped for.[60]

Goddard also viewed the nature of the city very differently than had previous mayors, focusing not on making Phoenix like other cities, but on developing and encouraging its own qualities and unique identity as a desert city. A native Arizonan, he appreciated the city's historical and archeological

Figure 10.4 Mayor Hance's reaction to Goddard's 1983 victory. *Source:* Steve Benson, *Arizona Republic,* 3 November 1983.

heritage, values that were strengthened by his involvement in the highway fight. As mayor he established historic preservation as an important policy, creating the historic preservation ordinance and program in 1985 and including substantial funding of $15 million in a 1989 bond issue. With this support, the program developed quickly and within twenty years had surveyed and registered nearly fifty districts and 181 properties.[61] For Goddard, historic preservation was about "pride of place," and it connected to the larger goal of valuing and stabilizing older neighborhoods. "We had to start by telling them they would be heard, that they had a reason for existence, and that these neighborhoods would survive." Goddard's perspective on transforming the city included supporting cultural institutions, backing public art, and encouraging desert-appropriate architecture, but his growing passion for revitalizing downtown left his most tangible legacy. Besides the buildings and projects begun during his term in office, the passage of a billion dollar bond issue in 1988 funded projects that appeared during the next decade and that created the first possibility for a successful downtown since the 1950s.[62]

While Goddard had considerable success as mayor, he did not win endorsement for all of the major projects that he recommended. Although

America West Arena was built with city assistance, which he recommended, voters refused to fund a downtown baseball-football stadium; voters supported a massive highway project, but they rejected a mass transit system and the Rio Salado project to develop the Salt River bed as a recreation area. Moreover, despite working to build in-fill and opposing annexation, he wound up supporting annexation as a lesser evil. His willingness to consider large projects, to envision a different polity and different policies, and to risk his political capital marked him as a visionary leader who changed the direction of the city's development.[63]

Goddard's tenure as mayor ended in 1990, when he resigned to run (unsuccessfully) for governor. His chosen replacement was Paul Johnson, another young Democrat, who had won election to city council three times, initially with Goddard's help and the next times without opposition. Acknowledged as very hardworking, Johnson skillfully outmaneuvered more senior and better-known colleagues to win the council's election as interim mayor, holding the office until the next general election. During that period he reportedly compiled what was, for the time, a very sizable campaign fund of $200,000. This, combined with his effective actions as mayor, discouraged all opposition in 1991—only the third uncontested mayoral election in the postwar era.[64]

While Goddard governed as a visionary leader, developing new priorities and programs, Johnson's mayoralty focused more on management, as he sought to implement the ideas of his predecessor. In part, this was unavoidable, given the number of projects that Goddard had started. In addition, Johnson faced different circumstances, for during his first years in office Phoenix confronted a worsening economic climate and growing problems. As city revenues shrank, Johnson met the crisis by cutting the budget and postponing the expenditures approved in the 1988 bond election. Although emphasizing economic development and community-based crime programs, Johnson also promoted environmental programs, including protection of the mountain preserve and expansion of the city's recycling program. Johnson's resemblance to Goddard also extended to his interest in becoming governor, and in March 1994 he resigned as mayor to compete with Goddard for the Democratic nomination for governor. (Neither man won the nomination.)[65]

Johnson's successor was a friend, Councilman Skip Rimsza (Johnson was best man at Rimsza's wedding), a Republican and the owner of a realty company. First elected to the council in 1989, Rimsza won a special mayoral election to replace Johnson and then regular elections in 1995 and 1999 with a relatively unassuming and balanced agenda. He supported in-fill development and maintained existing efforts to create a more vibrant downtown; he continued to support impact fees for new developments, pushed a modest program to expand the city's desert preserve, and built more parks. Rimsza particularly emphasized reducing crime by hiring more police officers, particularly community-based forces, by forming special police units, and by encouraging neighborhood action.[66]

Rimsza's approach to city government as reflected in his first full term was utilitarian and uninspired. "There's nothing magical about municipal government," he claimed in his 1999 campaign. "No lofty philosophical debates. We simply provide the basic services." Nor, in contrast to Goddard and Johnson, did he see the job as requiring long hours. The *Arizona Republic* concluded that "Rimsza sees himself as CEO of a vast corporation, successfully delivering services." His reelection reflected some voter satisfaction, but serious criticism of his leadership was growing steadily.[67] Rimsza responded by expanding his vision and his programs during his second term, campaigning for a light rail system, obtaining voter approval of a major bond initiative for infrastructure and cultural services, winning support for a major expansion of the convention center, and beginning the city's connection with biotechnology initiatives. As he left office in 2003, the result of term limits, some critics still argued that he had not offered "any inspired vision" or plans of his own, and others complained about his political style and limited involvement, but most conceded that he had grown in the job and that his final years had produced some significant accomplishments.[68]

Rimza's successor was Phil Gordon, who had been Rimsza's chief-of-staff in 1997, a councilman since 1998, and a visible candidate-in-waiting soon afterward. Like Rimsza and Johnson, Gordon maneuvered carefully to reduce opposition in 2003. The *Arizona Republic* observed that "through a combination of money, powerful friends, obsessive work habits, and some bluffing, he has outmaneuvered or intimidated away nearly every challenger."[69] His only opponent attempted to win by injecting party politics and running as a Republican, but this gained him little support, while Gordon's $1 million campaign fund, his political skills, and his broad set of policy goals earned him an easy victory.[70]

Gordon's early political reputation came through his work as an advocate of neighborhood concerns, and he achieved wider support by his willingness to seek many opinions and to negotiate effectively to reach solutions. But though he was praised for his political skills and commitment, some questioned whether he had an adequate vision for the city. By 2007, when he ran for reelection, he could claim success in answering those concerns. While maintaining an emphasis on neighborhood services, Gordon made significant progress on projects to foster economic development and to create the vibrant downtown that citizens had desired for decades. Besides advancing the light rail system and the convention center, which he began previously, he spearheaded even more significant efforts for planning and funding an ASU campus downtown, as well as creating a Biomedical Campus that included a campus for the University of Arizona Medical School.[71] In so doing, Gordon continued to expand the role of mayors in Phoenix politics and governance.

Representing Citizens and Governing the City

The job of a council member changed after 1980 because the council's structure had altered and the city had grown, but the challenges for city government remained largely the same. The political environment for council members shifted with the new district election system in 1983 and the new direction offered by Mayor Goddard. The most obvious difference was heightened political competition: the first election drew fifty-one candidates for the eight council seats. Name recognition and experience continued to shape the outcome, as three of the four incumbent council members running for reelection were successful. But two were forced into a runoff election, another incumbent lost, while two councilmen from the 1970s who changed residence to run in District 4—Rosendo Gutierrez and Gary Peter Klahr—lost to John Nelson, a Maryvale activist and political newcomer. The new system's impact was most evident in the election of persons whose political and social backgrounds were different from those of past council members: a former fireman, Duane Pell, and a Mexican American neighborhood organizer, Mary Rose Wilcox.[72]

Subsequent elections attracted fewer candidates; usually a couple of districts saw minimal or no opposition, but most had at least two candidates. Nevertheless, incumbents enjoyed a major advantage: three elections were held before any incumbent lost (in 1989), and in the next decade only three more suffered defeat. District races, like citywide contests, were influenced by visibility and money.[73] A clear difference from officeholding in the CGC era was that council members after 1980 remained in office longer, some for many terms: Howard Adams, a conservative progrowth Republican, sat on the council from 1978 to 1990; John Nelson represented West Phoenix from 1984 until retiring in 2000; and Calvin Goode from South Phoenix had the longest tenure, retiring in 1994 after twenty-two years in office.[74] Thus, political careers differed from those of the Charter Government era, when elected city officials held office briefly and without moving subsequently to other political posts. These council members intended to remain in that office, except for the one or two who, when the opportunity arose, sought to become mayor. For most, the office was an end in itself; a few saw this as a potential springboard for higher political rewards.

City council service changed appreciably after 1983 because of the nature of district politics and because of Goddard's efforts. Previously, the council's only help came from two aides, the members shared a secretary, and they worked in an open office with four phones and three or four desks. When Councilman Ed Korrick had complained, the deputy city manager told him in effect, "That's the best we can do; you're only temporary help."[75] And, with meetings only two days a week and some evenings, it was "a very part-time job," as Mayor Goddard observed. Goddard changed this by pushing a more demanding agenda, increasing council meetings, setting meetings for places and times accessible to the public, and providing each council member with an office and an aide. Equally important, the district system fostered a new culture of constituency service and empowered neighborhoods and their leaders to connect with and even fight against city hall. The district system encouraged citizens to contact their representatives, made this easier through regular district forums and public communication, and thus "increased the volume of traffic dramatically." As a consequence, council members spent between thirty and seventy hours per week on their duties, and a majority of this time involved working on district issues and providing constituency services.[76]

Such time demands necessarily limited who could or was willing to hold the office. John Nelson was the only person during this period who worked a full-time job; many held no outside job. The higher workload made salary an increasingly important issue. After raising council salaries from $12,000 to $18,000 in 1983, voters rejected further hikes in 1987 and 1991. But continuing arguments about equitable compensation, comparisons with salaries in other cities, and the quality of public service changed public opinion. Between 1995 and 2005 voters supported four salary increases, boosting the yearly take to a respectable $61,000. While the decision to hold office would still involve economic choices, doing so would not be prohibitively burdensome for most people.[77]

Opponents of the district system had predicted that it would diminish citywide planning and policy making and that it would reduce citizen interest in government. Unlike council members elected from the entire city, district representatives did spend considerable time on narrower, more specific services or problems facing their constituencies, yet their increased time spent on council work still left them adequate opportunities to deal with citywide concerns. In addition, council members who stayed longer in office developed considerable expertise and were able to work more effectively on various city issues.[78]

After an initial upsurge, voter turnout in the post-Charter Government era dropped below previous levels, running about 10 percent of the age-eligible population (and roughly 16 percent of the registered voters), which was low compared to other Sunbelt cities and very low compared with large cities in other regions.[79] While these overall turnout figures suggest that popular interest in city politics was very limited, other indicators suggest a somewhat different perspective. First, contests in individual districts periodically offered voters substantial differences and generated much greater interest. Voters were also involved in policy making through referenda and initiatives, which averaged seven per election. The city continued the tradition of organizing large committees with hundreds of members to prepare plans for spending programs, and voters regularly endorsed these large spending programs. Finally, with the shift to the district system the city revived its efforts to involve citizens in various community organizations. Phoenix called for "thousands of citizens . . . to serve on more than 120 new and expanded citizen committees" dealing with zoning, the arts, historic properties, economic development, and various other activities. Among the most interesting endeavors was the Phoenix Forums project, which met from 1988 to 1990 and brought citizens together to address a wide range of community planning issues.[80]

All council members looked closely at city finances, and the starting point was revenue. Although the city's continued expansion brought increased revenues, Phoenix also faced important choices. The most significant change in city revenues involved funds from the federal government. During the 1980s the Reagan administration reduced federal spending on cities, and during the mid-1980s it eliminated revenue sharing. While Phoenix was hurt less than some other cities, the loss of these funds posed a serious problem, which the city confronted by increasing its sale tax from 1 to 1.2 percent.[81] In response, the council appointed a task force in 1986 to evaluate the city's tax structure, and the administration announced "a clear need to switch to a much broader tax base," but by 1987 the city had abandoned that effort and announced the creation of a task force working on "an aggressive effort to strengthen the City's sales tax revenue base." Because of these continuing attempts to foster retail development and the subsequent increase of the city's sales tax to 1.8 percent, those revenues rose from 24.9 to 39 percent of the city's total revenues from 1980 to 2005.[82]

City spending during these years rose also substantially, from $221 million to $1,032 million, but this inflation-adjusted rate of 70.1 percent lagged behind the city's population increase. Real spending on police grew more rapidly (137 percent), boosted by federal grants for community policing starting in the mid-1990s, and the number of officers doubled during these twenty-five years. In Phoenix, as in other cities, crime was always an important political issue. During the 1980s and early 1990s, the city's crime rate increased, especially for violent crimes, but these rates were lower and increased less than in other southwestern cities. However, when these rates began falling in the mid-1990s, those other cities experienced more rapid declines. This contrast, and the continued fluctuation in Phoenix's crime rates after 2000, became issues in council and mayoral election campaigns.[83]

The city's physical expansion also shaped the budget. Spending rose even more rapidly on the fire department (157 percent): the number of firemen nearly doubled, and seventeen fire stations were built in new neighborhoods (for a total of fifty-two), which kept the department's good national rating. New neighborhoods also benefited from the planned development of other facilities, such as six branch libraries. In addition, the expansion of city parks and the acquisition of desert and mountain preserves also affected the same, mostly northern areas of the city. Such geographically based spending differences roused relatively few splits within the council, partly because other programs benefited other districts, but most differences among council members ran along ideological rather than geographical lines.[84]

The effectiveness and efficiency of Phoenix government during these years was evidenced by numerous awards and outside evaluations. For example, the city won its third and fourth awards as an All-America City in 1979 and 1989. Then, in 2009, after not competing for two decades, the city entered the competition again and won its fifth All-America City Award. *Financial World* magazine rated Phoenix the "Best Managed" of the nation's thirty largest cities, while a German organization in 1993 declared it to be one of the two best-run cities in the world. In 2000 several studies named it the best-run American city, while another ranked it top in efficiency nationally from 1995 to 2000. One reason for the city's success was its able administrators. Longtime city manager Marvin Andrews won many honors, including City

Manager of the Year in 1986, while his successor, Frank Fairbanks, was equally honored.[85] Although the Charter Government vision about politics had been repudiated, its notions about government and administration continued to bear fruit.

A NEW URBAN VISION

Concerns about the basic shape and direction of Phoenix that had been voiced during the 1970s in various reports and public discussions were translated during the next several decades into various plans, actions, groups, and other concrete forms. While proponents of some of these efforts differed and even conflicted in certain ways, they shared a rejection of the postwar vision's exclusive focus on peripheral suburban development—a centrifugal model—and instead favored a centripetal urban model, fostering the development of the core area. The renovation of downtown was the central issue, but creating a workable plan and achieving it were very difficult. The tremendous amount of new construction represented a major advance in creating a viable downtown, but also vital was the expansion and enlivening of the city's cultural opportunities and facilities, to create a cosmopolitan atmosphere that would both please locals and attract visitors. But the encouragement of culture was not simply in aid of an abstract ideal, for supporters of the arts increasingly noted their important economic impact. Even more significant in economic terms and in generating community identity during these years was the presence of professional sports teams. At the same time, however, they fostered political conflict, for each of the four major sports teams were involved with controversial decisions about their facilities. Finally, urban identity in Phoenix was increasingly tied to matters of neighborhood connections and organization. These issues were key elements in what would emerge as a new vision for Phoenix's future.

Building the City: The Downtown Era

The focus of postwar city leaders on the city's rapidly expanding suburban neighborhoods began changing during the 1970s, when rising concerns about that sprawl fueled desires to control or channel it. The alternative to expansion was in-fill growth and redevelopment of older neighborhoods, but the success of these efforts depended on the existence of a vibrant and self-sustaining downtown. Phoenix leaders had avoided downtown partly because of their fascination with suburban growth, but also because, like most urban leaders across the nation, they had no clear and viable ideas for downtown development to replace the traditional retail model that cars, malls, and sub-urbia had destroyed.[86] The combination of inattention and uncertainty meant that by the early 1980s—apart from some municipal and office buildings, plus the convention center and several hotels—the Phoenix downtown was largely a wasteland of weedy parking lots and boarded-up stores. Looking back on it later, Mayor Johnson called it "a rat hole."[87] The election of Terry Goddard put into power an able politician who cared about downtown and who had ideas about development, initiating a fundamental shift in the city's focus and two decades of major activity.

Living in an older, near-downtown neighborhood and familiar with neighborhood preservation efforts, Goddard entered office wanting to improve downtown, but during his terms as mayor he "got more and more passionate about it." While the urban village plan included downtown as one of nine villages, Goddard argued that "downtown is everybody's neighborhood—an asset for all Phoenix."[88] His plans for downtown fit a broad vision for economic and cultural development, one that resembled the efforts occurring in other cities, but Goddard also pursued ideas that would highlight the city's unique character. As with his economic development efforts, Goddard sought public-private cooperation, and he worked closely with the Phoenix Community Alliance and the Downtown Phoenix Partnership. To get private investment he had to convince developers that the city was serious about downtown development and that, while fostering village "cores," it would not permit zoning variations to create alternate downtowns.[89]

Within a few years major developers had finished several projects, the first private construction in a decade and the first construction besides hotels or offices in nearly twenty-five years. Completion of condominium units at Renaissance Park in 1986 was followed a few years later by the Renaissance Square office buildings. Shortly thereafter several mixed development projects were completed. The Phoenix Community Alliance worked with the city, Gruen Associates, and the Rouse Corporation to develop the Arizona Center, which opened in 1990 with retail shops, restaurants, office space, and entertainment venues. The Mercado, designed as a Mexican-style marketplace, opened in 1989 to provide shopping, restaurants, and office space.

Even more significant to the attractiveness of downtown, both symbolically and in drawing people to the area, was the development of cultural and entertainment facilities. The city partially underwrote construction of America West Arena, home to the Phoenix Suns basketball team and venue for various concerts and other sporting events. Matching the privately funded construction of the Herberger Theater was the city's purchase and subsequent refurbishing of the Orpheum Theater, an elegant movie palace, into a facility for live performances.[90] The development of cultural facilities received a substantial boost from the passage of a major capital-spending bond initiative in 1988. The Museum of Science and Technology and the Phoenix Museum of History moved from essentially storefront operations into impressive new facilities, which prompted museum management to make major improvements to their exhibits. The city's outdated cultural complex was redone, as both the Phoenix Little Theater and the Phoenix Art Museum were significantly expanded, and a new, architecturally striking library was built.[91]

The pace of renewal accelerated during the next decade, with the completion of new and expanded facilities of various types. A series of public buildings—a new city hall (1993), a county courthouse (1999) and a federal courthouse (2001)—added to the existing complex of government offices. A county-financed baseball stadium (1998) for the city's new expansion team attracted millions of fans and generated significant investment in the surrounding area, particularly for restaurants. Two major office buildings, the Phelps Dodge Center and the Collier Center, housing the Bank of America, expanded the area's available office space, while additional hotel space was also constructed. The Heard Museum of Native Cultures and Art undertook a major expansion and then a renovation of its facility, while private investors built the Dodge Theater. Passage of a bond election in 2001 provided support for still more facilities, including a Children's Museum of Phoenix and a Valley Youth Theatre; for repairing Symphony Hall; and for expanding eight museums and theaters.[92]

All of these facilities significantly increased the cultural activities and opportunities in the downtown, but the transformation remained incomplete. Although many more people were drawn to the area, they commonly made hit-and-run appearances, sporadic visits that did not create the kind of critical mass of people necessary for a successful downtown. The lack of attractive, even decent, housing in the area clearly presented a major obstacle, and one that planners struggled to solve. By the later 1980s, following the development of Renaissance Park, developers began constructing apartment buildings. Seeing the expanding construction market and the completion of additional buildings downtown, the Downtown Phoenix Partnership in 1997 established a goal of building five thousand units over the next five years. By 2000 various homes and apartments were being built, with an increasing number of lofts, and prospects and prices rose in the following years.[93]

Downtown development continued to flourish after 2000, but it soon took a somewhat different direction. In 2000 the primary debate over the city's future direction focused on the convention center. It had been expanded in 1982, and the city's ranking among convention cities rose from twenty-eighth in 1981 to tenth in 1992, with estimated revenues of more than $40 million. Attendance began to sag soon afterward, however, dropping by half between 1997 and 2003. This had serious financial consequences, since city officials estimated that each conventioneer generated $1,500 in spending. The decline, according to city officials, occurred because other cities now had bigger centers. In response, Mayor Rimsza pushed a plan to triple the size of the convention center. Voter approval of bond funding in 2001 plus state funding awarded in 2003 enabled the project to begin, and the second of two stages was opened in 2008 to hoopla and hopes. But some questioned the wisdom of this development strategy, since hundreds of communities across the country were continuing to do the same thing. The number of convention centers had been growing dramatically since 1975, while the amount of exhibit space grew even faster, jumping by a third from 2000 to 2006; not coincidentally, at the same time convention attendance was falling in many cities.[94]

Did the convention center expansion represent the pursuit of a continually moving goal? Was it a necessary effort to maintain and perhaps strengthen the city's larger tourist economy? Or was its main value as a symbol of the city's status? While differences over the wisdom of this project persisted, by the time funding was approved, its role in the plans for downtown economic development had been at least reduced. The attraction of the Translational Genomics Research Institute and the International Genomics Consortium in 2002 (as noted above) and the completion of the institute's facility in 2004 initiated a new developmental emphasis on biotechnology and biomedicine, and it soon began drawing complementary businesses to the area. The most significant addition to this project came after 2004 with the creation, on a neighboring site, of the Phoenix Biomedical Campus, to include medical, pharmacy, and nursing schools of the University of Arizona and Arizona State University, both of which had ties to the institute.[95]

A second significant change was ASU's decision in 2003 to create a major downtown campus immediately north of the center of the downtown area. This reuse of existing facilities and major construction of new ones was funded substantially by city monies authorized in a bond election. The campus opened in 2006, serving three thousand students, with plans to expand quickly to fifteen thousand.[96] The addition of so many people in the downtown area offered a realistic hope of providing the long-sought critical mass for a successful downtown, bolstering markets for restaurants and retail services. It also provided passengers for the light rail system that began operating in December 2008, and reinforced the escalating construction of housing: between 1996 and 2008 a total of 6,350 residential units were built in the downtown area, with 10 major high-rise housing projects in various stages of development.[97]

These elements comprised key parts of the city's new downtown plan in 2004, but that redesign also addressed the look and feel of the area and its relationship to the environment. During the 1980s a few people, including Terry Goddard, had talked about Phoenix as a desert city and about using architecture to provide shade from the summer sun. After twenty years, that recommendation finally began getting serious attention. The *Arizona Republic* reported on the limited adoption of this design strategy and urged more action. ASU's College of Architecture and Environmental Design produced various innovative plans. The city's 2004 plan admonished developers to "use shade everywhere," as well as including various small parks and plazas to create a walkable downtown. In 2006 the city began carrying out these goals by initiating its Urban Form Project, which aimed to create a "Connected Oasis" with walkable, shady spaces, "a new 'circulation' plan for traffic, as well as a master plan for public space and public art."[98]

The Reemerging Role for Culture and the Arts

The broadening view of downtown development that Phoenicians were seeking to implement was evident not only in buildings and structural factors but also their changing attitude toward the arts. Early signs of a new perspective appeared in 1985–86 with the creation of the Phoenix Arts Commission and the requirement that 1 percent of the budgets of city construction projects be spent on public art. While some projects generated controversy, during the next two decades the proliferation of interesting fountains, statues, freeway murals, and bus shelters won wide support for this manner of enriching public spaces. Art became even more visible in Phoenix starting in 1989, after artists initiated an annual open house of their galleries and studios. In the late 1990s they added First Friday, a monthly open house offered by up to ninety studios, galleries, and art spaces; First Fridays drew thousands of visitors. The success of these ventures highlighted the complex and expanding role of the arts in city development. Artists were located in the poorer parts of downtown, precisely the areas most vulnerable to redevelopment. Construction of

America West Arena and the baseball stadium in the 1990s replaced artist-occupied areas of the warehouse district, to the south of downtown. A decade later the cluster of artists north and west of downtown faced a similar threat of removal, yet some of them owned their properties and might, thus, be able to avoid being displaced. In addition, the city leaders' attitude toward cultural tourism and its larger economic benefits was much different than it had been at the start of downtown redevelopment.[99]

The changed views toward local artists were part of a much larger transformation in the role of culture and the arts in the city. In the 1950s support for the arts reflected a belief that satisfying the new, educated, high-tech workforce required improving the Valley's culture, but the drive and support for this effort relied especially on a few key individuals like Walter Bimson. That, plus the periodic financial assistance from the city for expansion, enabled the Phoenix Art Museum and the nationally renowned Heard museum to grow apace with the city. The various performing arts organizations faced greater and roughly parallel difficulties. City growth and increasing expectations in the 1970s coincided with the deaths of the first generation of supporters, making the next several decades troubled times.[100]

The Arizona Theatre Company brought a full season of serious professional theater to Phoenix in 1983; while the Actors Theatre of Phoenix began in 1986. Both found homes on stages at the Herberger Theater, both benefited from major grants from the National Arts Stabilization Program in the 1990s, and both entered the next decade in relatively secure positions. During the 1990s live theater in the Valley was expanded by creation of the Southwest Shakespeare Company (in Mesa), several alternative theater troupes, two ethnic companies, and various suburban community theaters, as well as productions by ASU.[101] In 1986 three struggling dance groups united to form Ballet Arizona, which emerged from a financial crisis in the late 1990s in a relatively secure position.[102]

The Phoenix Symphony also faced money problems, partly because it became a full-time, professional orchestra during the 1980s. Aided by a National Arts Stabilization grant in 1997, it slowly achieved greater financial security over the next decade through a combination of fund raising and greater concert attendance.[103] The Arizona Opera company began performing in Phoenix in 1975, but by 1983 it was nearly bankrupt. A new general director saved the organization, and when he retired in 1997, it was solvent, active, and critically acclaimed.[104] The experience of Valley choral music groups was quite different, primarily since few were professional. By the 1990s two of the

Valley's older choral groups—the amateur Phoenix Boys Choir (1947) and the Phoenix Bach Choir (1958), a professional group—had achieved national recognition (including Grammy awards) and significant audiences, while highly skilled groups such as the ASU Choral Union, the Phoenix Symphony Chorus, the Orpheus Male Chorus of Phoenix, Arizona Masterworks Chorale, and Cantemus offered numerous additional concert opportunities. The *Arizona Republic*'s music critic concluded enthusiastically, "Choral music flourishes here."[105]

The venues for live performances increased dramatically after 1980, reflecting the broadening support for the arts throughout the metropolitan area. The Herberger Theater, ASU's Galvin Playhouse, and the Chandler Center for the Arts opened in the 1980s. During the following decade Phoenix's Symphony Hall, ASU's Gammage Auditorium, the Phoenix Little Theater, and the Orpheum were remodeled. In 2005 the $98 million Mesa Arts Center opened, followed in 2007 by Tempe's $66.5 million cultural center.[106] Together with the dozens of museums, many with new or expanded facilities after the mid-1990s, Phoenix and the Valley could reasonably boast of having major cultural resources for residents and destinations for visitors.[107] The prevalence of facilities and the growing success of widely diverse cultural and arts groups prompted three reports on the arts in the Valley in 2002 and 2003, all of which described a cultural scene that was substantial, growing, and seeking more resources. The reports argued that culture and the arts offered economic benefits through employment and by creating a cultural scene that attracted and retained a skilled, educated workforce.[108] In the city's 2004 plan Phoenix leaders accepted this basic idea, suggesting an entertainment district and support for existing private and public activities and facilities.[109]

While attendance at arts facilities and events continued to increase, financial support remained a serious issue.[110] The problem, as observers began noting by the mid-1990s, was related to age and mortality. Jim Ballinger, director of the Phoenix Art Museum, explained that "a city doesn't take off with serious philanthropy until it has a core of third-generation families that support the arts."[111] A decade later, however, when the art museum raised more than twice its initial fund-raising goal, conditions looked very different. The Arizona Grantmakers Forum, a small group of Arizona foundations begun in 1985, were joined after 1995 by many additional foundations, most notably three very wealthy foundations: the Pulliam ($411 million), Piper ($589 million), and Helios (more than $600 million). While not eliminating financial constraints, their largesse, and that of other donors, offered a very different future. Besides foundations, an increasing number of wealthy individuals began to support these institutions (as well as contributing to other causes, notably substantial gifts from home builder Ira Fulton and Intel CEO Craig Barrett to ASU).[112]

Sports, Politics, and Identity

Professional sports, like culture and the arts, acquired an importance in Phoenix beyond that normally given to leisure-time activities. The director of the Downtown Phoenix Partnership observed in 1995 that "sports is far more visible than the arts, but I think both have changed the public perception of Arizona and the Valley."[113] After the Diamondbacks won a heart-stopping World Series victory in 2001, an *Arizona Republic* editorial saw a broader meaning:

> This desert place no longer is an isolated outpost; it no longer is just another adolescent Sun Belt metropolis exhilarated at the sight of its own growth. It is a city of champions, and true champions carry themselves with purpose.[114]

Beyond providing inspiration and identity, sports teams were also valuable as major economic enterprises and were pursued for their potential effect on economic development.[115] In 1989, supporting efforts to acquire a major league baseball team, Terry Goddard explained that "baseball is big business. It gives us a shot in the arm that we can't get any other way. It brings in the new taxes that we need to pay for other things that this city needs: police, fire, whatever."[116] An economic impact analysis done in 1993 projected that a baseball team would benefit the economy by $230 million of income, 340 jobs, and $9 million in direct tax revenues.[117] Teams also generated revenue by enabling Phoenix to host special events—the NBA All-Star game in 1995 and the Super Bowls in 1996 and 2008 had economic impacts of, respectively, $25 million, $187 million, and more than $500 million.[118]

Professional sports also paralleled culture and the arts in that its managers sought public support for facilities. But whereas cultural facilities were typically considered a public responsibility—if perhaps a low priority—many citizens viewed public funding of stadiums and arenas as unnecessary and perhaps improper. The recognition that teams were privately owned businesses seeking profits, that sports figures made huge salaries, and that there were competing needs for public funds conflicted with Phoenicians' desire for entertainment and the notion of sports activities as a means of economic development. This clash, plus debates over the precise method of public financing and questions about locations, made sports facilities and professional sports a serious and continuing matter of political debate during these years.

As of the late 1980s Phoenix hosted only two professional sports teams. A minor league baseball team played in the small Phoenix Municipal Stadium, while the Arizona Veterans Memorial Coliseum, a general-purpose indoor facility, served as home to the Phoenix Suns NBA basketball team. Although the Suns had arrived in 1968 as an unheralded expansion team in a second-tier sport, by the 1980s their success in this increasingly popular game had generated strong support and community pride. More striking changes occurred in only a few years as Phoenix acquired teams in the other three major sports: the transfer to Phoenix of the St. Louis Cardinals football team (1988) and the Winnipeg Jets (renamed Coyotes) hockey team (1996) and the winning of the expansion baseball team, the Arizona Diamondbacks (1995).[119]

Debates over the funding and location of facilities for these teams began even before they arrived, starting with unsuccessful efforts in 1989 to fund a baseball stadium with a property tax.[120] At the same time, however, the city concluded an arrangement with the Suns to finance a new arena, located downtown because of the preference of general manager and part owner Jerry Colangelo. The city's share of the costs were to be paid through a new method, a tourism tax on motels, hotels, and car rentals, which would be partially repaid by the Suns.[121] Council member Mary Rose Wilcox strongly supported the agreement, arguing that sports is "one of the biggest economic development tools a city can use."[122]

A third development in 1989 that further altered the position of sports in the Valley concerned baseball's spring training in Arizona. After rising complaints about Cactus League facilities, plus Florida's attempts to lure Cactus League teams, Governor Rose Mofford appointed a task force to study the issue. Noting that spring training provided national recognition and $150 million from tourists, the task force recommended funding new and improved facilities. In 1990 the Arizona legislature enabled Maricopa and Pima counties to fund stadium improvements—also by using a tourism tax on motels, hotels, and rental cars. Valley municipalities responded enthusiastically, and within three years four stadiums were improved and two were being built. By 1998 Valley cities had used the promise of new stadiums to attract three more teams.[123]

Efforts to acquire a major league baseball franchise for Phoenix created far more controversy. While baseball was quite popular in the Valley, major league teams were highly sought, very expensive ($130 million for the franchise), and required a suitable stadium. After a failed attempt by one

Phoenix group in 1990, Suns owner Jerry Colangelo was asked to manage the next effort. Colangelo was the ideal and significant choice for the position. A former college baseball player, he had adroitly managed the Suns franchise over the years, his flexibility and popularity helped obtain city funding for America West Arena, and he had played a major role in getting it placed it downtown. That talent, reputation, and commitment were crucial to the success of this effort.

He put together an attractive proposal in 1993 and began negotiating with the county supervisors to finance a domed stadium in downtown Phoenix. After lengthy discussions, on February 17, 1994, the county supervisors voted for a stadium to be financed by a quarter-cent county sales tax. This action produced a firestorm of criticism, but the resulting protests, lawsuits, and an attempted referendum failed to reverse the decision.[124] There were important consequences, however: two supervisors lost subsequent elections, while Supervisor Mary Rose Wilcox was shot and seriously wounded.[125] In the end, Colangelo's group won the franchise, the tax ended after two and a half years, the stadium opened in 1998 to public acclaim, and the team drew impressive crowds.[126] But the controversy seriously complicated the efforts of the other two teams still seeking a home.

When the Coyotes hockey team came to Phoenix, they played in America West Arena, but they were soon dissatisfied with the venue and financing, and they sought their own facility. After failing to conclude a deal with Mesa, in 1999 they won approval from Scottsdale voters for a hockey arena financed by sales taxes revenues as part of a redevelopment project.[127] But after this arrangement languished for several years, owner Steve Ellman made a surprise shift and concluded a deal whereby Glendale would provide land and build an arena, while Ellman would develop retail projects for the surrounding area. While attracting hockey legend Wayne Gretzky as part owner and, starting in 2005, as head coach brought some luster, the team's weak performance drew too few fans, sparking financial difficulties and a changes in ownership. In May 2009, after the Coyotes' owner Jerry Moyes abruptly filed for bankruptcy, he announced the team had been sold and was being moved to Ontario. While the National Hockey League stalled this with legal action, and alternate buyers were being pursued, the team's future was uncertain, as were the financial implications for the city of Glendale.[128]

The most contested path to a new stadium involved the Cardinals football team. Within its first two years in Arizona, the team's owner, Bill Bidwell, ruined negotiations with Phoenix by offering too little investment in a stadium and seriously alienated many residents with high ticket prices, miserly treatment of players, and losing teams. As negotiations floundered and Phoenix focused on baseball, the Cardinals began negotiating in January 1996 with the East Valley Partnership for a stadium in the East Valley. After several revisions, and with both Tempe and Scottsdale dropping out of participation, Mesa finalized a proposal tying a sizable multipurpose stadium to a convention center, large hotels, restaurants and shops, plus residential and recreation areas. But with concerns about the magnitude of the project and objections to the financing source—a twenty-year sales tax on Mesa—in May 1999 that city's voters soundly rejected the proposal.[129]

With no clear stadium prospect and fearing the Cardinals might move elsewhere, Governor Jane Hull created a task force to craft a workable and winnable solution.[130] The proposal ultimately adopted by the legislature and sent to voters involved a now-familiar tourism tax on hotels and car rentals, plus charges on stadium-related activities. To increase support the task force packaged the proposal for a multipurpose stadium with funding for Cactus League facilities, tourism, and amateur sports facilities. Voters approved the package in November 2000.[131]

Bids for the newly funded stadium soon arrived from Mesa, Tempe, downtown Phoenix, and the West Valley. The site committee awarded the stadium to Tempe, but intercity conflict confounded these plans. Phoenix objected to a stadium in the Sky Harbor flight path, and when opposition from antitax conservatives killed a bid from Mesa, Glendale snatched the prize by concluding a deal with the Cardinals. This victory came on top of the city's previous success in luring the Coyotes away from an increasingly testy relationship with Scottsdale. Although the team remained inconsistent on the field, their games in the new stadium in 2006 drew public attention and sold-out crowds. Even more importantly, the team's surprising charge to the Super Bowl in 2009, despite falling short of victory, gained it substantial public support and enthusiasm for the first time.[132]

The battle over these facilities and the reaction to the teams' successes and failures highlighted deeper currents of change within the Valley. The initial decisions to locate America West Arena and the baseball stadium in downtown Phoenix demonstrated the city's political dominance and reflected its ideas for downtown redevelopment. After 2000, the city's primary goals for downtown and economic development had shifted away from sports facilities. At the same time, changing patterns of population growth reduced Phoenix's proportion of the Valley's population and its political clout, while giving each of the major suburbs a legitimate chance at winning the stadium. But this opportunity produced different reactions, accentuating divisions within East Valley communities while encouraging cooperation in the West Valley. A new team's success could stimulate great public enthusiasm, but because they had only a relatively short history, they lacked the reservoir of goodwill that older teams could rely on to draw crowds during weaker seasons. Thus, while success could encourage identification with the "community's" team, failure could bring serious economic hardship or worse.

Envisioning "Neighborhoods That Work"

While the city's policy for transforming downtown represented a fundamental shift, its approach to neighborhood development substantially reinforced a change in direction begun in the 1970s. By 1989 nine neighborhoods had developed as Special Planning Districts, with enhanced zoning and planning powers over land use, traffic patterns, public art, streetscapes, and landscapes. Planning committees in three of these neighborhoods wrote plans that also included historic preservation, empowering them to require that the exterior of neighborhood structures fit the area's historic character. This designation was separate from but reinforced the status of historic district that the city's Historic Preservation Program had begun in 1985. The Roosevelt Special Planning District, for example, included five such historic districts. By 2007 the city had thirty-five residential historic districts, which provided some authority to regulate structural changes, and some of these were included in other Special Planning Districts.[133]

A second approach to improving neighborhoods involved "redevelopment programs." Building on the earlier federal Community Development Program, Phoenix reorganized its efforts "to stabilize and regenerate blighted areas." Located in the city's older and typically poorer sections, including areas of South Phoenix, these programs involved improvements in public infrastructure and services, rehabilitation of individual homes, and efforts to obtain private investment. From seven areas in 1985, the program grew to sixteen two decades later.[134] In 1993 the city created the Neighborhood Initiative Program, which also sought to deal with blighted areas needing less structural assistance and more economic development. Associated with these programs but also operating independently were city efforts at encouraging in-fill construction through tax incentives, fee waivers, and modified development procedures.[135]

These programs focused on stimulating redevelopment in targeted areas, but by the mid-1980s deteriorating housing conditions had been spreading rapidly and causing public alarm. U.S. Census data showed that 36,640 of the city's housing units (18.4 percent) were substandard in 1972; by 1980 the figure had risen to 82,920 units, or a third of all city housing. A collection of some forty associations formed the Neighborhood Coalition of Greater Phoenix. Working with the newly districted city council, this organization crafted an effective property maintenance code, which voters adopted in 1987. More than 45,000 complaints were filed in the first year, but in the third year that number had dropped to 8,580, suggesting a considerable improvement on at least some level. These efforts also prompted a reorganization of some of the city's administrative structure dealing with neighborhoods in 1987, with a more substantive restructuring of all neighborhood services into the Neighborhood Services Department in 1993.[136]

By the 1980s, then, city leaders had begun to define their efforts to improve city life and to serve their constituents as involving neighborhood development. Councilwoman Peggy Bilsten explained that "stronger neighborhoods make for a stronger city." Increasingly concerned about sprawl, these leaders sought to foster a greater sense of community connection within neighborhoods, and neighborhood organizations provided a primary method for doing so. The numbers of these groups grew dramatically, reaching 465 in 1996, 806 in 2000, and 1,030 in 2008. They were of different types, however, reflecting neighborhood conditions as well as the nature of the area's development, but following no simple pattern. By 2008 block watches and other groups focused on crime comprised roughly a third of the groups (a larger share than in 1996); neighborhood associations, which had broader purposes, comprised roughly a fourth of the groups; while home owners' associations and organizations addressing an array of specific purposes (such as businesses, parks, or PTAs) made up the remainder.[137] Some organizations were only marginally active, but some of them, notably the Roosevelt and Garfield associations in two older neighborhoods, demonstrated the power of activity to bring about positive changes.[138]

Neighborhood associations also connected to the urban village aspect of the city's General Plan. This had been intended to create smaller, semiautonomous communities within the city, each having the full range of urban functions, such as employment centers, high-density commercial development, recreation areas, and various types of housing. While the plan encouraged some diversity of functions, it was soon apparent that these villages were unable to develop villages cores as planners had hoped, that residents generally worked and shopped outside of their villages, and that few people seemed to know what village they lived in. But even though the larger criticisms of urban villages were accurate, neighborhood organizations had begun providing some connection between residents and their villages. They also made an understandable link with the larger planning issues that village planning groups considered.[139] Along with efforts to build a more dynamic city core, they constituted a serious effort to reenvision the city.

POPULATION AND COMMUNITIES: GROWTH IN THE DESERT

A Hispanic City?

"Hispanic Majority in Phoenix by 2007" ran the front-page headline in the *Arizona Republic* on January 22, 2003. Although based on faulty assumptions for projecting population growth, it highlighted a dramatic increase in the proportion of Hispanics in Phoenix, from 17 percent in 1990 to 34 percent in 2000.[140] What made this change—and the headline—even more significant was that a central feature of Phoenix throughout the twentieth century had been the dominance of the Anglo population and relatively small proportion of Mexican Americans (consistently around 15 percent). In the early twentieth century, boosters had explicitly touted this aspect of Phoenix, describing the city as "American," and that sense of distinction among southwestern cities had persisted, albeit less vocally, in subsequent decades. In the postwar era, as noted above, the CGC slated Mexican Americans for city council, and some individuals achieved high economic mobility, but in general the group's political influence was limited, and the problems of poverty, discrimination and segregation, and inadequate services remained serious.

Mexican Americans had traditionally concentrated in South Phoenix, but by the 1960s they had begun spreading into neighborhoods west of downtown. After 1980 the population moved further to the north, and by 2005 it comprised an important part of neighborhoods throughout the city.[141] Although this dispersion was an important factor in the city's transformation, the continuing concentration was also significant. By 2000 Mexican Americans comprised more than half the population in the area extending two miles north of downtown. A census bureau study concluded that in 2000 Phoenix ranked as one of "the five most segregated metropolitan areas for Hispanics."[142] The core of this area was also the most impoverished in the city, with more than half the residents living below the poverty level. Adding to this was a significant gap in educational levels and achievement compared to the rest of the population.[143]

City services were largely inadequate to assist this population, although they improved over time, and voluntary organizations offered key assistance, especially Chicanos Por la Causa (CPLC). Adding to the efforts of Friendly House, a social service organization founded in 1920, and aided by the subsequent formation of groups like Centro de Amistad and Valle del Sol, CPLC grew rapidly during the 1970s and established a range of valuable programs. Severe reductions in federal support in the early 1980s shrank the program by half, but during the 1990s money from various public and private sources revitalized the organization. It was, by this point, one of the largest community development corporations in the nation, with more than eight hundred employees and having a budget that exceeded $10 million.[144]

The growing size of this population also had an economic impact. By 2000 Hispanic businesses had taken over twenty-five neighborhood shopping centers and innumerable small strip malls, where "the marketing and advertising and sales force, signage, frontage, and approaches are Hispanic." Marketing firms specifically targeting Hispanic consumers increased from several in the early 1990s to thirty by 2005.[145] This marketing involved using Spanish, which became an increasingly audible presence in the Valley—on the streets, on ten radio stations, and on two television stations by 2000—and employers sought workers fluent in both English and Spanish.

Language also became an increasingly divisive political issue. In 1988 Arizona voters passed an initiative declaring English the state's "official language." Although defeated in the courts, its passage reflected growing concern about whether Hispanics were assimilating into mainstream American society or remaining separate. The issue reemerged in 2000, when state voters approved another language law, this one prohibiting bilingual education in favor of English-immersion instruction.[146] Public concern over assimilation, combined with growing fear and anger over illegal immigration, led to the passage of state laws in 2006 that heightened the political division within the state and the city. The issues also began to affect city politics, as Mayor Gordon decided in December 2007 to revise the rules restricting the police from asking about a person's immigration status.[147] Immigration "sweeps" in Valley cities instituted by Maricopa County Sheriff Joe Arpaio, allegedly to catch illegal immigrants, and state legislation in 2010 requiring police to seek and arrest illegals caused increasing political turmoil throughout the Valley and the state. Given the complexity of the immigration issue, the nature of the Valley's economy, and the growing presence of legal Hispanic residents and citizens, only a comprehensive immigration reform package will diminish this conflict. It is also apparent that the police and legislative "crackdown" have had a polarizing effect, with unknown political consequences.

A Growing City

The increased Hispanic population in 2000 comprised only one part of a larger demographic pattern. In the years after 1980 the Phoenix metropolitan area continued to grow at a tremendous rate, making it a continuing national story. This growth enhanced the status and ranking of Phoenix, but it also produced a metamorphosis in the structure of the larger metropolitan region. The area's growth occurred in roughly three stages. By 1960 Phoenix had emerged as a leading western city, using annexation to acquire the vast majority of the area's population. In the next two decades it grew by nearly 80 percent (table 10.1), and its national ranking rose from twenty-ninth to ninth. Like many Sunbelt cities, Phoenix overshadowed its suburbs, but although the metropolitan area ranked only twenty-fourth in the nation, important changes had been occurring in the Valley's population distribution. By 1980 the first-tier suburbs (Mesa, Tempe, Scottsdale, and Glendale) had grown significantly, each ranking among the nation's fastest growing cities. As a result, Phoenix's proportion of the Valley's population had fallen to 57 percent.

Between 1980 and 2008 the distribution of the Valley's population entered a new phase. While Phoenix continued to grow very rapidly (98.5 percent), faster than all other major U.S. cities except Las Vegas, suburban expansion was even more striking. The first-tier suburbs ranked among the nation's fastest growing cities of more than 100,000, and each attained enough population, resources, and maturity to pursue distinct paths of development and separate identities. The second ring of suburbs also began to emerge, led by the East Valley community of Gilbert, the nation's fastest growing community after 1990. By the late 1990s development began to reshape the more distant agricultural communities of the West Valley, as the cities of Avondale, Surprise, and Goodyear burgeoned at a prodigious, Gilbert-like pace. As a result, by 2008 Phoenix's share of the Valley's population had fallen to 41.5 percent, while the national ranking of the metropolitan population jumped from twenty-fourth in 1980 to thirteenth in 2008.[148]

Population projections may vary greatly, depending on the assumptions behind them, and the economic slowdown starting in 2007 highlighted some important limits to predictions. Still, a twenty-five-year forecast done in 2005 offered a rough sense of the future areas of growth, even though its projected pace would need revision. Phoenix was projected to grow impressively, though at a rate slower than in prior decades; more significantly, suburbs were expected to grow at a faster pace, which would diminish Phoenix's share of the Valley's population to 37 percent by 2030. Much of that development was

Table 10.1 Population of metropolitan Phoenix, 1980–2008.

	1980	1990	2000	2008	1980–2008
Phoenix	789,704	983,403	1,321,045	1,567,924	99%
Suburbs	597,207	1,027,088	1,612,174	2,210,949	270%
All urban places	1,386,911	2,010,491	2,933,219	3,778,873	172%
Maricopa	1,509,175	2,122,101	3,072,149	3,954,598	162%
Phoenix: % of urban	56.9%	48.9%	45.0%	41.5%	
East Valley					
Mesa	152,453	288,091	396,375	463,552	204%
Chandler	29,673	90,533	176,581	247,140	733%
Tempe	106,919	141,865	158,625	216,449	102%
Gilbert	5,717	29,188	109,697	175,523	2970%
Sun Lakes	1,944	6,578	11,936	NA	
Guadalupe	4,506	5,458	5,228	5,948	32%
North East Valley					
Scottsdale	88,364	130,069	202,705	235,371	166%
Fountain Hills	2,771	10,030	20,235	25,227	810%
Paradise Valley	10,832	11,671	13,664	14,990	38%
Cave Creek	1,589	2,925	3,728	5,428	242%
Carefree	986	1,666	2,927	3,862	292%
West Valley					
Glendale	96,988	148,134	218,812	251,522	159%
Peoria	12,251	50,618	108,364	157,960	1189%
Sun City	40,664	38,126	38,309	NA	
Sun City West	3,741	15,997	26,344	NA	
Youngtown	2,254	2,542	3,010	4,896	117%
Surprise	3,723	7,122	30,848	92,897	2395%
El Mirage	4,307	5,011	7,609	24,751	475%
Tolleson	4,433	4,434	4,974	7,199	62%
Litchfield Park	3,657	3,303	3,810	5,126	40%
Goodyear	2,747	6,258	18,911	59,508	2066%
Buckeye	3,434	5,038	6,537	47,261	1276%
Avondale	8,134	16,169	35,883	81,299	899%
Gila Bend	1,585	1,747	1,980	1,831	16%
Wickenburg	3,535	4,515	5,082	6,620	87%

predicted for the West Valley, whose population was expected to rise from 20.6 to 32.7 percent of the metropolitan population, led by the two cities of Buckeye and Surprise, each of which was anticipated to top a surprising 400,000 population level.[149] Both grew prodigiously after 2000, and although Surprise was larger, in 2007 alone Buckeye approved plans for twenty-three housing communities totaling 275,000 homes.[150]

What most distinguished the projections for these communities was their incorporated size. While Phoenix expanded significantly after 1980 (from 321 to 514 square miles), the first-tier suburbs more than doubled in size, to 474 square miles. Far more striking was the expansion by the second-tier suburbs. Between 1980 and 2004 they increased their incorporated areas tenfold, to 760 square miles, and this included only half of the land in their planning areas.[151]

Although Phoenix continued to annex more territory after 1980, those actions occurred within a very altered context and represented a new rationale. Starting in the 1950s, the city had pursued annexations as an ambitious, prosperous, and protective approach to growth. The rising criticism of growth during the 1970s included concerns about the costs, environmental consequences, and inequities caused by sprawl, as well as a growing interest in developing downtown and in improving existing neighborhoods. The combined impact of these criticisms created doubt about and sometimes opposition to further annexations. By the early 1980s city policy began changing to reflect this shift in public opinion. Having preemptively used strip annexation to isolate its southwestern area of Laveen from annexation by other Valley cities, the Phoenix city council determined to let it remain undeveloped and unincorporated. This left the territory to the north for future expansion, and city leaders intended to spread there only slowly, after planning.[152] However, as growth in the Valley continued, developers and other cities raised economic and political pressures that Phoenix could not ignore.

During 1984 Charles Keating secretly bought more than a thousand acres of land just north of the city boundary and of the Central Arizona Project (CAP) canal, and by December he was aggressively pursuing annexation. The

Opposite: Source: U.S. Bureau of the Census, "Population Estimates, 2008," http://www.census.gov/popest/cities/files/SUB-EST2008-ALMO.csv (accessed 20 June 2009); Arizona Department of Economic Security, "Decennial Census Population of Arizona, Counties, Cities, Places: 1860 to 1990," http://www.workforce.az.gov/?PAGEID=67&SUBID=129 (accessed 7 January 2008).

city had established a rule to wait before extending water service to that area, but, as Terry Goddard later recounted, "when Keating played Phoenix off against Scottsdale, we really felt in a bind . . . and essentially we made a deal with the devil and incorporated his land" on December 20 (figure 10.5). If this situation was unsavory, the consequences of not dealing with a developer could be worse. A month later, Harrison Merrill, an Atlanta-based developer, sought to manipulate the annexation of his property adjacent to Keating's and set off a major fight. On January 17, 1985, Peoria leaders acted on Merrill's invitation and annexed his land north of Phoenix and west of I-17, while the Scottsdale City Council announced plans to annex an odd-shaped section running north, west to I-17, and south to the Phoenix border, effectively landlocking the city—exactly what it had fought against since the 1950s (figure 10.6). Goddard returned early from a trip to Washington, DC, and with Councilman Korrick and the city manager he pleaded with the Scottsdale City Council not to reopen the border wars settled two decades before.[153]

Scottsdale ultimately agreed not to annex Merrill's property. Peoria eventually rescinded its annexation after the powerful House majority leader, Burton Barr, "sat down in the basement of the legislature with the mayor of Peoria and their city attorney" and threatened them "with the wrath of Burton Barr."[154] Phoenix subsequently annexed this territory, but over the next twenty years the two cities continued to struggle over annexation of the area to the north of this.[155] The conflict also prompted overdue legislation on annexation that instituted a thirty-day waiting period before signatures could be collected and required signatures from half of the property owners (rather than just owners of half of the property).[156]

By the late 1980s and even more strongly during the next decade, members of city council debated annexation. Mary Rose Wilcox and Linda Nadolski argued that annexations were becoming too costly and unnecessary; Thelda Williams, Duane Pell, and Tom Simplot contended that additional acquisitions delayed needed services for areas already in the city. And several members complained that further annexations detracted from efforts to encourage in-fill development. A continuing majority on the council, including Mayors Goddard, Johnson, and Rimsza, argued that growth was inevitable, that expansion need not prevent growth within the city, and that in balance and with proper planning annexation made sense. They also used arguments that originated in the 1950s—fear of the city becoming landlocked and the beneficial impact of the city's stricter planning and zoning regulations. Perhaps their most powerful reason for annexation, however, was the city's tax system, for

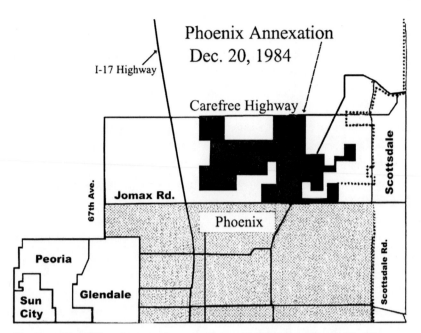

Figure 10.5 City of Phoenix annexation, 1984. *Source:* Modified from *Phoenix New Times,* 30 January–5 February 1985, 6.

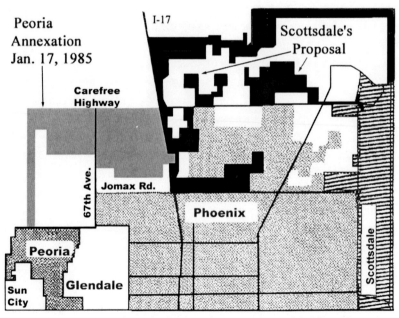

Figure 10.6 Annexation conflict in north Phoenix, 1985. *Source:* Modified from *Phoenix New Times,* 30 January–5 February 1985, 6.

Phoenix, like other cities, depended excessively on sales tax revenues. This fact drove it to chase after commercial enterprises, as in 1996 when it annexed twelve square miles solely because they included an outlet mall.[157]

Communities and Community

The growth of Phoenix after 1980 occurred amid changes within and outside the city. Public consensus for development and expansion was replaced by open debate; while prodevelopment sentiments were commonly voiced, they were as commonly challenged. A significant instance of this occurred in a 1985 conflict over the upscale Esplanade development at 24th Street and Camelback. Based on the area's village plan and strong neighborhood opposition, the city council rejected the developer's proposal and forced him to lower the height of the proposed buildings.[158] At the same time, the shifting patterns of development within the Valley created different stresses. Thus, Phoenix continued to annex more territory, albeit sometimes reluctantly and under pressure, but its larger development policies followed a different direction. Its emphasis on downtown development was matched with various efforts to encourage in-fill construction. Besides creating neighborhood programs, city leaders also pushed the Rio Salado Project in 1987, a proposal for dense, mixed development along the Salt River bed. Support for a mass transit system—a failed effort in 1989 and a successful one in 2000—represented efforts to promote a larger transformation of the city.[159]

The city's policies toward growth on the periphery demonstrated this new perspective. Through its General Plan and in specific area policies, the city sought to ensure that new construction occurred near existing developments, to prevent leapfrog growth.[160] In 1987 the city began assessing impact fees on developers, to shift the cost of providing services from the city to the developers and new owners. By 2000 these fees ranged from $4,000 to $7,000 in southern parts of the city and more than $12,000 in northern subdivisions; in 2006 the fees for the southernmost subdivisions were raised to $17,500.[161]

The nature of growth also prompted other new policies. By the 1980s the look of the housing built in some Phoenix subdivisions and suburbs began reverting to the sterility of the 1950s suburbs. The style was different—two-story stucco with tile roofs—but the bland, repetitive similarity was familiar. This pattern resulted partly from the competition between builders, especially given the influx from other states, and the tremendous increase in home building during the 1980s (see figure 10.3). Like mass builders in the early wave of subdivision construction, they reduced price by producing similar homes, and they sought to boost sales by increasing the sizes of the houses while reducing the lot sizes. In the two decades after the early 1970s, the average house size in Maricopa County rose from 1,420 to 1,900 square feet (28 percent), while the average lot size dropped from 7,435 to 6,599 square feet (11 percent). Lot size rebounded briefly in the late 1990s, but the housing boom after 2001 resulted in a substantial decline: average lot size for new homes dropped 1,000 square feet, while lots closer to the Phoenix core shrank to between 3,000 and 4,000 square feet.[162]

As disturbing as the similar style was the form of these houses and the consequences for neighborhoods. Sitting on narrow lots with little or no side yards, they had shallow setbacks from the street, largely hidden front entries, and protruding two- or three-stall garages (figure 10.7). This pattern for new construction represented the antithesis of what the city was encouraging in existing neighborhoods, and it prompted the city council to revise building standards in 1998. Reflecting new urbanist influences, the changed standards included narrower streets, varied sidewalk patterns, and more natural systems for storm-water runoff. The minimum lot width was increased, variety for design and setbacks was established, while developers were required to include a visible front entry and reduce the prominence of the garage.[163]

The city's reputation for sprawl persisted after 1980, even though its new policies such as in-fill and impact fees, its increased physical size, plus rising land costs significantly changed the pattern of city expansion.[164] What obscured the public's understanding of the changes resulting from policy and economic forces was its traditional focus on the city's continuing annexation and population growth. A closer examination shows that in basic development patterns, Phoenix was becoming more like the nation's other major cities. Instead of using population within the city limits as a gross measure of density, a more accurate representation excludes public open space and peripheral, vacant land. Applying this approach to the post-1980 population figures shows, not worsening sprawl for Phoenix, but the reverse. Between 1982 and 1997 the population density of Phoenix increased 21.9 percent, ranking third among all metropolitan areas. By that end date density in the Phoenix metropolitan region ranked eleventh in the nation, ahead of Chicago, Washington, DC, and Boston. Finally, the common comparison made between Phoenix and Atlanta shows that "Atlanta urbanized five times as much land to accommodate" population growth as did Phoenix.[165]

While decreasing lot size, center city in-fill, and continued contiguous expansion produced these significant changes, other trends—toward larger

Figure 10.7 Stucco-tacky housing. Some neighborhoods were built as block after block of stucco and tile homes with prominent garages and little social face to the neighborhood. *Source:* Photo by the author.

developments and more master planned communities—and a demand for cheaper, larger homes encouraged sprawl, though less in Phoenix and more in other Valley communities. By the 1990s, the spread of population in the Valley was being shaped not only by topography and distance, but also by the state's ownership of its trust land, lands received from the federal government at the time of statehood that were to be sold or leased for their maximum value to benefit public education. This requirement and the irregular pattern of public and private landholding complicated the process of development. Although various groups within the state sought to create a logical, equitable method for mixed development, the complexity of the task continued to thwart the participants. As a result, large areas to the southeast were unavailable for development, at least temporarily, which increased the pressures on development to the west and south. And planners increasingly considered a future in which developments in Phoenix and Tucson connected.[166]

Three of the first master planned communities in the 1970s were large developments, with architectural and landscaping controls, social and recreational amenities, mixed housing, and some commercial development. Several comparable communities were begun in Scottsdale during the 1980s, but the most of the increased numbers of master planned communities in that decade were smaller—under 1,000 acres—and offered fewer amenities. By the 1990s developers began shifting to larger projects, and, in a replay of earlier trends, this meant moving further to the periphery of the Valley. While some of these projects, such as Desert Ridge (with 5,700 acres), were built within Phoenix, most were located elsewhere. North Scottsdale included six communities of between 1,100 and 3,200 acres, and far eastern Maricopa County (extending into Pinal County) included several developments of about 2,000 acres, but building in the far western Valley was simply in another dimension. Five communities developing in Buckeye by 2000 held between 8,800 and 14,000 acres, while Douglas Ranch included 35, 000 acres.[167]

By 2000 Maricopa County included roughly 400 such communities in various stages of development (with another 131 in the neighboring Pinal County). Their size and growing numbers over these decades meant that they increasingly came to define new home ownership and neighborhood residence in the Valley. Of all homes built and sold in the Valley, roughly half in the 1990s and three-fourths a decade later were in master planned communities.[168] But while this implied some larger architectural and landscape design, it did not necessarily indicate the same levels of social and recreational amenities or convenient access to commercial and employment opportunities.

Golf courses were featured in many planned communities, serving as the center green space for one or several of the community's neighborhoods. In addition, some smaller (500 to 850 acres) expensive developments were designed as golf communities; two-thirds of such neighborhoods in north Scottsdale were gated, and half of those had guards. Other specialty communities included one airpark and four water ski communities.[169] Retirement communities, another specialty type, continued to flourish in the Valley. As Sun City West and Sun Lakes grew to their planned maximums, seven communities were added to the existing cluster of communities in east Mesa. The Del Webb company altered its model after 1998, building two versions of Sun City within incorporated cities as well as smaller retirement neighborhoods within larger planned communities.[170]

The Webb company also built Anthem, a popular community with numerous amenities, but a poster child for sprawl and manipulative development. In 1998 the firm began constructing a large community north of Phoenix city boundaries and beyond any other development. Before the first resident moved in, the company spent more than $180 million on housing infrastructure, a wide range of recreation amenities (a lake, a golf course, and a community center), community facilities (a school, fire station, health center, water treatment facility), and basic stores. The response was striking: almost a thousand houses sold in the first week after the models opened in March

1999; by July 2001 the population reached fifty-one hundred, and by 2008 it was estimated at thirty-five to forty thousand.

The largest problem with developing this area was the scarcity of water, since it was far from any municipal or private water source. The Webb company solved this by a 100-year arrangement with the Ak-Chin Indian Community to purchase part of their allocation of CAP water. The second problem was the lack of adequate employment. Though not unusual, this was particularly troublesome because the area's terrain funneled all traffic to Phoenix down the already-crowded I-17 highway. By 2007 the state highway department was forced to start widening the road, but the process would be lengthy and, functionally, a tax on Arizonans levied by the Webb company and the residents of Anthem.[171]

While Anthem and similar developments used sprawl to obtain lower land costs and larger lots, other developers pursued other objectives. The clearest alternatives were variants on new urbanist styles. Opened in 2004 to considerable publicity, the community of Verrado, 8,800 acres within Buckeye, features narrow streets and prominent front entryways, alleys and rear garages, numerous small parks, and a central, pedestrian-accessible Main Street (figure 10.8). With retail and office space, and with neighboring access to future industrial sites, it aims to provide substantial employment to residents.[172] In nearby Surprise the same developer created the similarly designed residential community of Marley Park, advertised as "A Celebration of Home," which emphasized a traditional lifestyle and bungalow architecture.[173]

Several developments in the East Valley resemble these but with an agricultural theme. Agritopia, a relatively small residential community (220 acres), offers a similar emphasis on the street and front porch, but its featured housing styles are bungalow and Arizona Ranch, with picket fences. It has a garden and orchard at the center and remodeled farm buildings for a farm stand, grill, and coffee shop. A second Gilbert community, Morrison Ranch, also reflects the farming roots of the community and the owners. This mixed development combines an area of employment, substantial open space, and a residential component reminiscent of the shade and grass of the area's agricultural past.[174]

A desire for community encouraged the rise of home owner associations (HOA), but other factors reinforced their growth. Becoming visible in the 1970s, largely through their role in the larger master planned communities, these associations proliferated rapidly and became a standard part of urban life in the Valley. Although initiated by developers, the creation of an HOA was required by most cities for any community development having over a certain number of homes; Phoenix required an HOA for any development with a common area. By 2007 Arizona had more than 8,900 HOAs, which included 1.2 million homes, with the bulk of them in the Valley. These organizations played a key role in shaping community life, serving as quasi governments with explicit authority to create and enforce significant restrictions about the appearance and use of private property. Complaints about the extent and misuse of those powers increased, however, and between 2000 and 2006 the state legislature passed six laws restricting HOAs, in particular, limiting their ability to place liens on homes for unpaid fines and protecting displays of political signs or flags. Complaints relating to HOAs were sometimes directed against the community management companies, used by two-thirds of the associations. As a result, the associations formed a state Association of Community Managers in 2003, to provide significant training and information for these firms.[175]

Figure 10.8 Housing in Verado. Designers of houses in this new urbanist community place garages and cars in the rear, with a prominent front door and often a porch. There are also numerous neighborhood parks. *Source:* Photo by the author.

Besides questions related to property rights, HOAs also prompted questions about privatizing government. In cities with at-large council representation, an HOA could easily take on the political task of negotiating for the area's residents. For example, the Dobson Ranch HOA negotiated with Mesa to secure a recycling program for the area. HOA boards could also operate like a municipal government, supervising public areas and recreation facilities and even making financial contributions, as Dobson's HOA did when it contributed to the Mesa Symphony. HOA boards, with their committees, meetings, and annual elections, had significant representative features, and they could serve important social and public roles within communities. Yet despite their value, these were not inclusive, democratic institutions, for HOA membership was restricted to home owners. Moreover, despite additional safeguards provided in state legislation, procedures and structures were less transparent and less geared toward ensuring public participation. Reliance on HOAs as local self-government, then, effectively disfranchised not only the less affluent but also the more geographically mobile citizens.[176]

Living Together in a Desert: Metropolitan Issues

Phoenicians had always lived as part of a region and a metropolitan area, but the nature and importance of that relationship changed substantially as the Valley grew—especially the suburbs—and as people looked beyond political boundaries to socioeconomic and ecological relationships. Economic and residential development created clear needs for cooperation, but transportation and environmental issues prompted the first and most deliberate efforts at regional action. The Maricopa Association of Governments (MAG), formed in 1967, began driving the transportation issues with the adoption of a plan in 1980. Worsening traffic conditions and inadequate funding for highway construction prompted a concerted regional effort in 1985, which won overwhelming voter support for MAG's comprehensive regional plan involving 271 miles of freeways. Financed by a twenty-year half-cent county sales tax, the plan also provided nominal funding for a Regional Public Transit Authority.

The initial efforts to implement this plan bogged down by inadequate management, declining revenues, and debates about where and when to build particular sections of highway. In 1994, voters rejected the proposed solution of an additional road tax, but with the improved economy and rising revenues enough mileage was completed by the end of the 1990s to reduce traffic congestion—temporarily. Faced with the public's revived interest and the increasing need, in 1999 the state legislature provided an additional $1.6 billion for highways. In 2004, with the same two elements of construction progress and increasing traffic, voters extended the sales tax highway funding for another twenty years.[177]

While highway construction proved a remarkably ephemeral, even illusory, solution to the problem of traffic congestion, it had other, more permanent consequences. In the Valley's development up to the 1980s, in the absence of highways, the locations of housing and shopping facilities had been determined according to factors other than transportation. The construction of significant highway mileage changed this pattern. Increasingly, highway location shaped the sequence of residential construction, but it had even more power to determine the life and death of malls. Of the thirteen malls constructed through 1973, seven closed during the 1990s, and none had close highway access. Three of the survivors were high-end malls, and two of other three had close highway access. All of the malls built after 1974, except the high-end mall in Paradise Valley, had close highway access, as did nearly all of the malls constructed after 2000. Factors besides transportation also influenced this pattern, such as the outward migration of population, but two of the newest malls were built in Tempe and Mesa, and a number of older malls with highway access were remodeled, rather than being torn down.[178]

Demands for an effective mass transit system grew steadily during this period, for despite the continuing construction of an extensive freeway system, traffic and travel times continued to increase, as did the concerns about rising levels of air pollution and the costs of auto commuting. Virtually every plan put before voters during this era involved increased funding for local or regional bus service. These expansion measures included extended hours, Sunday service, more frequent service, bus pullouts and shelters, and better schedules. In Phoenix bus ridership increased after each improvement and infusion of funds. After the 1985 plan was adopted, ridership rose 60 percent in the next four years, but it leveled off during the 1990s; additional funding in 2000 boosted ridership by a third. But despite the improvements, few Phoenician believed that a stand-alone bus system could substantially address the Valley's transportation needs. While some persons remained wedded to cars and freeways, and others doubted that Arizonans would adequately use mass transit, Valley opinion shifted during this era to support a transit system in which buses played a supporting role to some type of rail system.[179]

The first effort to create a mass transit system with a rail component occurred in 1989 with ValTrans, a complex transportation plan including a 103-mile rail system costing $8 to $10 billion, to be funded by a half-cent sales tax. Concerned about the cost, the specific plan, and the practicality of a rail system that included areas with low population densities, voters refused. Given the immediate need to create a broad freeway system and its funding problems, efforts to create a rail system went into limbo—but the notion did not die. In 1996 Phoenix and Tempe began initial planning efforts. When new proposals for a light rail system emerged in 1997, both Phoenix and Scottsdale voters initially rejected them, as did Chandler in 1999. But public sentiment was changing. In 2000 Phoenix voters overwhelmingly endorsed a revised proposal, setting off a cascade of transit plans and actions by cities across the Valley. Tempe and Mesa voted to link with the Phoenix system, and as construction got underway in 2006, the other major suburbs shifted their planning to a more serious level. The initial phase opened in December 2008, and the level of use exceeded all projections.[180]

Transportation and growth affected air quality in the entire Valley and required both county and state action. Valley residents had protested air pollution beginning in the early 1960s; by the 1980s it had become a crisis. Particulates, ozone, and especially carbon monoxide levels plagued Valley residents. Besides the smells and the visible brown cloud, a 1996 study determined that the annual cost of pollution per year in economic and health consequences was $432 million. The worst problem was carbon monoxide, caused almost entirely by cars: in 1981 Valley air violated the maximum standards of the Environmental Protection Agency on thirty-seven days, and in 1984 the total was ninety-nine days, the worst record in the nation. In 1985 the Arizona Center for Law in the Public Interest filed suit to force the state to comply with EPA standards. Ensuing negotiations led to a 1988 state law mandating the use of fuel additives during the winter, higher emission-testing standards, and efforts to reduce automobile driving. Considering the plan inadequate, the center appealed to federal court, which ordered the EPA to demand stricter standards. It eventually did so, threatening to withhold federal highway funds from Arizona to force compliance.[181]

The state legislature responded by raising the standards for gasoline and auto emissions testing, mandating no-burn days to prohibit fires on high pollution days, and providing a token $10 million for mass transit. Initially, these measures brought little improvement, and in 1995 the Valley suffered repeated no-burn days and air quality alerts. The following year the EPA noted that despite some improvement over the decade, the Valley ranked worse than any western city except Los Angeles and classified conditions as "serious." In subsequent years, however, the various restrictions had an effect, and the number of air quality violations fell.[182] Particulate pollution, linked in part to growth, remained very high, averaging eighty-three violations annually from 1997 to 2003. Carbon monoxide levels remained below EPA maximums, but ozone levels worsened, and in 2004 the EPA labeled the county a "nonattainment area." An even more serious issue for the Valley was the long-delayed tightening of EPA's ozone standards, announced in March 2008. The head of the county's air quality department confessed that "we will have a problem with meeting the (new) federal standard." Public concern over these conditions, plus the likely threats of federal highway money being withheld, may well prompt significant action in the future.[183]

Water provoked even greater interest during this era. This was, of course, the oldest and most basic issue for living in central Arizona. An interest in water had concentrated tremendous energies within the area—to create canals, to produce the Roosevelt Dam and related dams, to plant farms and vegetation, to construct water systems for the expanding settlements in the Valley, and to build the CAP and distribute water from the Colorado River. The mounting concern during the 1970s that had led to the passage of the Groundwater Management Act (GMA) represented the first recognition that "more" might no longer be an adequate response to the issues of water supply and quality. The importance of the former issue came home with greater weight as a drought began during the 1990s, which challenged assumptions about how much water would actually be available to the Valley.[184]

Passed in 1980, the GMA defined four areas for managing water and required all Valley municipalities (the Phoenix Active Management Area) to draw less groundwater. One response was "water farming," in which Valley cities purchased water rights from rural areas of Arizona. First Scottsdale and then Phoenix purchased rights in the McMullen Valley in La Paz County, but the uproar from rural counties ultimately led to legislation prohibiting such actions in the future.[185] Without that option, cities had to reduce their use of groundwater through a combination of conservation and purchasing CAP water. This did occur, as groundwater usage by cities in the Phoenix Active Management Area declined by a third between 1985 and 1998. What prompted this shift, besides concerns over the declining water table, were the discoveries that many groundwater sources were contaminated by agricultural and industrial pollutants.

City officials were pleased by a one-quarter decline in per capita water usage in the twenty-five years after 1980, but the city's tremendous growth in that era continued to drive up total water consumption. More troubling was a change in how development affected water use. Postwar urbanization had generally meant shifting from agricultural to residential or industrial water use patterns, with a net gain in available water. But this had begun to alter, as agricultural usage became more efficient, development increasingly occurred on nonagricultural land, and residential areas were more densely populated. By 2000 urbanization began to produce higher water use.[186]

While the city certainly had sufficient water in the short term, a growing number of Valley residents recognized the long-term problem was becoming more serious and had to be addressed by individuals and by cities. Conservation was encouraged—but rarely mandated—in many forms, from efficient appliances to xeriscaping. Starting in the 1980s, John Long had campaigned for more effective use of treated water. Appalled by the use of "regular" water for the proliferating numbers of decorative lakes in the Valley, he led a campaign to require the use of effluent. Seemingly the most wasteful water usage was in maintaining the Valley's vast number of golf courses, but by 2004 most of that water was effluent, and many courses used sophisticated irrigation systems to regulate and monitor water use. Overall, reclaimed water comprised 7 percent of the city's water. The state also pioneered alternative methods for the use and storage of water through its recharge and recovery programs and the Central Arizona Groundwater Replenishment District, as well as the Arizona Water Banking Authority. But despite these advances, more difficult choices clearly loomed ahead.[187]

A shortage of water remained the greatest threat in this desert, but there could still be too much of a good thing. The years after 1980 did not repeat the numbers or severity of floods in the previous two decades, but unpredictable rain patterns, combined with the recontouring of land by urban development, continued to cause problems. A flood in 1993 destroyed a million-dollar bridge being constructed over the usually dry riverbank; in 2000 another storm caused more than $1 million in damage to bridges and roads. Increasing the height of the Roosevelt Dam reduced the danger of floods from the east, but north-central and northwestern areas of the Valley remained vulnerable to periodic heavy rains, particularly because development affected drainage patterns. Of further concern was the mutation of the Salt River bed into Tempe Town Lake. Created after the defeat of the Rio Salado project in 1987, it opened in

1999 as a very different type of feature: a two-mile lake filled with CAP water and contained at both ends by inflatable dams. The anomalous project had served as a magnet for multistory developments along its banks—and as a hostage to the vagaries of desert weather.[188]

An increasing public awareness of metropolitan and ecological issues in the years after 1980 appeared in various forms. Several Valley institutions became major proponents of desert living, heightening public interest in these larger questions. The Desert Botanical Garden developed programs in ecological and environmental education, opening a demonstration desert garden in 1984 and creating an interpretive master plan, with the Plants and People of the Sonoran Desert Trail in 1988 as a model ethnobotanical exhibit. In 1993, working in conjunction with five other agencies, the garden management built the Desert House, to study conservation. In similar fashion the Phoenix Zoo evolved into an institution of ecosystem exhibition, education, and conservation. Created in the early 1960s, partly for status, it adopted the then-standard zoo practices of presenting animals from all parts of the world. This categorical approach, with some shift in design, lasted into the 1980s, when the zoo board redefined its goals to reflect national trends and to offer an interpretation of its animals within their worlds, rather than being separate from plants, landscapes, and human influences. Zoo operators cooperated with the Heard museum and the Desert Botanical Garden in a Desert Connections program, it partnered with the Salt River Project to sponsor Clean Air Day, and in 1999 it began an Arizona Wildlands project to increase desert awareness. What began as an effort to bring the world to Phoenix in ordered cages became an attempt to explain to Phoenicians how people and animals lived together in a desert.[189]

Phoenicians had always embraced outdoor living, and the creation of the Phoenix Mountain Preserve starting in 1971 reflected their desire to protect this landmark area for recreation and as visible reminders of the natural environment. But the desert floor was considered developable space, to be cleared, leveled, and built upon. In opposing a Phoenix annexation proposal in 1989, Cave Creek Mayor Jack Davis complained that Phoenix "doesn't understand the desert," using bulldozers "to redefine the landscape" when it should "build with the vegetation." While this description certainly represented the city's basic approach for many years, over time a different sensibility had crept into the minds of planners and the public. From 1970s land use reports touting open space and 1980s public discussions about a desert city came an altered perspective on building and living in the desert. The city's General Plan increasingly reflected these goals for land use, by limiting the recontouring of washes and other features and encouraging desert landscaping. In 1995 the city began planning for a desert preserve of twelve to sixteen thousand acres, which voters supported in 1999. The Sonoran Desert Preserve is also part of a larger system, connected to other public lands, to flood control basins or parks, and through paths and trails along canals.[190]

The desert also became more visible within Phoenix and the Valley during these years. Concerns about water usage led to increased planting of drought-tolerant plants, such as native mesquite and palo verde trees and sage or creosote bushes. Such landscaping was most characteristic in the more recently developed areas, especially high desert areas in the north, areas that had never been farmed. But throughout the Valley, in public and private spaces, a shift occurred in the use of vegetation and space.

The effect of urban development on the Valley became inescapably apparent to residents with the growth of an "urban heat island." The Valley's early development, particularly its agriculture, had spread water and shade, which may have provided some general cooling, and certainly cooled particular places. But postwar urbanization, with its proliferation of housing and pavement (one-third of the urban surfaces), the destruction of Valley vegetation, and the covering of canals reversed that condition. Because of the increase in heat-absorbing surfaces, which released the heat more slowly during the night, in the years after 1948 the average minimum temperature in the Valley rose 10.9 degrees (to 64.9 degrees). The worst aspect of this was that it could extend summer's day temperatures of more than 100 degrees well into the nighttime. This rise turned the 1980s interest in shaded buildings into a clear directive after 2000 and an aesthetic appreciation of tree planting into a survival technique. The striking difference in heat from roofs of dark or white surfaces prompted repeated discussion by the *Arizona Republic*.

The area most adversely affected by increasing heat was the Phoenix downtown, and the Downtown Urban Form Project, initiated by the city council in 2004, began to address this issue. Its 2008 report included a detailed and thoughtful analysis, with numerous recommendations. But despite the increasing level of concern during these years, zoning requirements did not change, developers continued to produce heat-absorbing buildings, and the temperature kept rising.[191]

Fighting over Growth

By the late 1980s increasing numbers of Phoenicians worried about growth, about the danger of "becoming another L.A."[192] Novelist Glendon Swarthout gave voice to some of these sentiments in 1991:

> When we came, the Valley was an Eden. There was ample room, a population which fit, air as clean as a mirror, and a lovely lifestyle. Then for thirty years we let the businessmen and politicians who ran the Valley lead us down the garden path of unplanned growth. Crime, traffic, heat, air pollution, bankruptcies, unemployment, corruption—the quality of our lives is pathetically diminished and what have we been given as compensation? Professional sports.[193]

The late 1990s saw the beginning of a broad discussion of growth in the Valley. Periodic reports in the *Arizona Republic* raised significant issues. In 1995 the Greater Phoenix Economic Council began holding public summits and polling Valley leaders, and in 1996 it combined with various Valley groups to create the Greater Phoenix Quality of Life Stewardship Council.[196] While business leaders and groups focused generally on growth, citizens in the Valley and state who were associated with numerous conservation, environmental, and public interest groups began raising issues of public control. The major obstacle to managing growth was what it had been since the 1940s—weak county controls and low standards—although the proliferation of communities accentuated the problem. Faced with an increasingly conservative state legislature opposed to using government to remedy the situation, this group decided to work around the legislators and go directly to the voters. After considering various methods for controlling growth, they drafted the Citizens Growth Management Initiative (CGMI) in 1997 and began circulating this proposal with the aim of placing it on the fall 1998 ballot.[197]

Governor Jane Hull had also been developing a growth-control proposal, but she had been opposed by the conservative Republican legislative leaders from the Valley, who resisted any interference with growth or private property. However, as Rob Melnick observed, "the fear that the citizens' initiative could pass into law . . . helped many business and political leaders in the state recognize that the debate over growth had changed significantly," and lawmakers enacted a version of the governor's Growing Smarter plan in May 1998.[198]

This measure boosted the powers and obligations of municipal governments. It required local governments to develop ten-year plans dealing with the environment, open space, and transportation; mandated public participation to approve or amend the plan; required developers to pay their "fair share" of costs for public services; and encouraged building in vacant inner land, rather than in fringe areas. It also sought voter approval to spend $20 million annually for eleven years to purchase state trust lands for conservation purposes. However, it banned any mandatory state plans or growth boundaries—an attraction for developers and conservatives—and it included the promise that money would not be spent on open space if the CGMI passed–a threat to the supporters of control.[199]

Ironically, CGMI was not on this ballot, because organizers, running short of time and money, opted to wait for the 2000 election.[200] Seeking to avoid having voters decide this issue, or at least hoping to defeat it, Governor Hull appointed a commission to draft additional growth-management tools. The resulting proposal won over some, but not most, CGMI supporters.[201] The legislature then enacted this measure, Growing Smarter Plus, which restricted cities' annexation powers; allowed them to designate nongrowth areas where they could deny services; let counties charge impact fees; and expanded voters' control of plan changes. The legislature also proposed constitutional amendments allowing the sale for preservation of 3 percent of the state trust land and the exchange of state trust lands for other public lands.[202]

The 2000 election involved two separate but related issues: controlling sprawl and maintaining open space.[203] The citizens' initiative proposed that local governments be able to establish firm urban-growth boundaries and that developers pay the full costs of expansion. The open space issue was more complicated because much of the land in question (particularly in the northern and western parts of the Valley) was state trust land, which was legally required to be sold or leased for maximum profit to fund public schools. Some open space advocates questioned whether maximum value was an appropriate standard in relation to another public use, rather than development. CGMI supporters also argued that 3 percent was too little land.

At first, the public strongly favored both the CGMI and the state lands proposals. However, the 70 percent support for CGMI in late summer began to drop as opponents launched a furious and expensive attack, with glossy mailings and television ads calling CGMI unfair and warning that it would bring economic disaster. The significantly outgunned CGMI supporters defended their proposal and denounced the lands proposal as a fraud, claiming that 3 percent would actually be the limit of public land for open space. The lands measure narrowly lost, but the CGMI was soundly defeated by a two-to-one margin, in the state and throughout the Valley.[204] As the reverberations of electioneering died down, it was clear that while Valley residents rejected these growth limits at this time, the center of the debate and the nature of government involvement in growth-related issues had shifted significantly. Concern about the city's future was spreading as fast as the city itself. The following years would be rife with planning reports and studies, all noting the significant issues and suggesting useful ways to proceed.[205] But there would still be no clear link between these plans and clear, realizable, and enforceable methods for action. Ultimately, thinking about the city's future requires understanding its past.

Conclusion:
Desert Vision, Desert City

Growth has been central to Phoenix's history, but its importance, meaning, and value have changed considerably over the years. From its beginning, Phoenix sought to grow. As in virtually all new communities, its citizens saw growth as the normal condition and goal. Phoenicians knew that not all communities thrived, of course, and some even busted, but these seemed exceptions that proved the rule. A town's exact future was unclear, but in the hopeful nineteenth century of an expanding nation, when town founding was a common experience and the country's urban hierarchy was constantly changing, the inhabitants of any new town had dreams. And in the century's last decades, with increasing scientific knowledge and technological capacity, and with a firm belief in people's ability to master their world, Phoenicians envisioned turning their desert into a "land of milk and honey." While such biblical phrases and imagery provided the impetus for their Edenic vision, they put it in a specific territorial and regional context with booster language to describe their bountiful land of alfalfa, cattle, citrus, and cotton. Their ambitious but realizable goal was to develop Phoenix's agricultural economy and marketing position within Arizona and to some extent within the Southwest.

Size and distance shaped the community's mental map. Though growing steadily, especially after construction of the Roosevelt Dam, Phoenix lagged behind the West's urban centers of the late nineteenth and early twentieth century. And while resolutely and successfully pursuing improvements in transportation and communications, Phoenix remained an essentially remote location, with only indirect ties to the nation's larger cities. As the frontier closed and the urban hierarchy became more settled, Phoenicians, like residents of many urban areas, reconciled themselves to their city's relatively low prominence, but they still sought self-improvement and recognition. While not oblivious to their location, they created a built environment with national standards in mind. They built in brick forms, not just from memory or tradition, but to assert a national connection. They organized cultural and intellectual groups, not only for self-improvement or intellectual curiosity, but as statements to an American audience. And their political forms and debates resonated with an expression of common ideas and familiar patterns of action. Thus, the city's seven decades of modest growth shaped its self-image and limited expectations and also created patterns of behavior.

The city's next seventy years followed quite a different course. The two periods differ significantly, but some threads of change connected them. The shift was enabled by two new technologies. Aviation diminished space and connected Phoenix directly to places that had been multiples stops and great distances away. Evaporative coolers and air conditioners overcame the onerous burden of summer heat. These developments were not unique to Phoenix, of course, so they alone did not create or impel its growth, but beginning in the 1930s they made it possible.

Other influences on growth involved the extension of existing conditions. Already in the late nineteenth century, the Valley's warmth and low humidity had begun drawing people with respiratory or arthritic conditions. Because these ailments hit all classes, they brought to the Valley persons with standing and wealth who would not otherwise have moved to such a remote and underdeveloped area, and this migration increased in the 1920s and 1930s. Tourism, present from the early days, also grew, despite the limitations imposed by the Depression and war years. And postwar affluence significantly enhanced each of these prewar patterns.

The war also created new opportunities. The construction of airfields and factories provided wartime construction work and employment, but no guarantees of postwar benefits, even for the two air bases. The factory buildings had potential uses, but many places across the country had excess capacity, and those facilities were larger than the ones in Phoenix. So, while the physical structures would prove useful, the war and its related activities were far more important for demonstrating other possible futures, for connecting the city to other places, and for providing experience in how to get things done. It made some Phoenicians think about the future in an international context. It taught city leaders not just to draw on their own experiences but to look elsewhere, especially at California—for ways to plan development, for ideas about neighborhoods and subdivisions, and for financial support. Most importantly, it provided Phoenicians with experience in creating public-private partnerships to pursue development. This involved using political power, thinking about the larger issues, and negotiating satisfactory arrangements.

Postwar Phoenicians deliberately and intentionally pursued growth, and in ways quite beyond their prior behavior. In part this was born of a general postwar optimism in which the inhabitants of Phoenix, like those of many cities, saw a better future in an economy relying on aerospace, electronics, and the military. The Phoenix effort differed, partly because its high-tech suburban vision was more comprehensive. The reform of urban politics and the creation of a highly efficient administration was the essential basis for this effort. A public-private partnership attracted suitable businesses and created the range of necessary improvements and support, from utilities to education. Although the cultural institutions paled by comparison with those of older and larger cities, the creation of new groups and facilities offered excitement, opportunities, and hope for the future.

Success also required effective leadership. In this regard the city was helped by its relatively modest prewar growth. Its size and expansion had encouraged the maintenance of a single leadership group, open to talented newcomers and personally connected. It was certainly hierarchical, but it also fostered cooperation and consultation, and this characterized the operation of politics, government, economic expansion, and cultural development.

A comprehensive plan, effective leadership, and the right opportunities were essential, but Phoenix also benefited greatly from timing. The 1950s were uniquely suited to the development of this approach, and it was vital for Phoenicians to have had a decade to root this firmly in Valley soil. The 1960s saw rising challenges on nearly every front, changing economic circumstances in the 1970s undermined various aspects of the older visions, and new ideas about the environment and cities made urban planning vastly more complicated. The postwar vision continued to serve as an effective blueprint for community development through the 1970s, but by the 1980s problems and criticisms began to overshadow it.

The initial and most apparent problem was politics. The Charter Government group generally succeeded in controlling politics through slate making and by claiming the political center. Its first serious challenge came in the 1960s, when racial minorities and the poor, who had been ignored as political actors in the original vision, challenged their exclusion from political office and the narrow focus of city government. CG responded by slating minority candidates and by starting to address larger social problems. But after Charter Government turned conservative in the 1970s, and with the city's increasing diversity, the original system broke down in the mid-1970s.

The city's urban form also developed significant problems. The spread of affordable suburban homes generated traffic snarls and air pollution. Growth fostered the creation of identical rather than distinctive neighborhoods, and it threatened to destroy the unique environment that many people had found so appealing. As sprawling suburbs overtook the desert, they left behind declining neighborhoods and a near-vacant downtown and in the process created distances and divisions that demolished the earlier social networks and personal connections. While the design of individual neighborhoods and communities could resolve some of the concerns about living patterns, the most serious problems involved larger questions of urban design and required thoughtful decisions about the city and the metropolitan region, and these were beyond the ability of the aging postwar leadership to resolve.

The economic model experienced difficulties by the 1980s and began to falter visibly in the 1990s. One problem was that the city's rapid growth had suddenly brought it into competition with America's large and dynamic cities before it had created the kind of economic and financial infrastructure vital for competing in such an environment. Organized efforts at business recruitment had dwindled in the 1960s, key economic institutions and businesses had been purchased by outside companies starting in the 1970s, and the Valley lacked individuals with significant wealth whose investments or philanthropy could significantly direct and assist its future.

Changes in the nation's economy starting in the 1970s also forced Phoenicians to make important and difficult decisions. In the 1950s the city had successfully targeted certain types of businesses, notably computer companies, but that model began to fade in the 1970s, partly because the computer business entered a new phase of development. Phoenicians' amazement at the city's growth fostered complacency, and without the leadership to develop a new, broad development strategy, a "growth machine" emerged. Construction and development, which had previously been facilitating the expansion of manufacturing, now emerged as a major end in itself, a larger part of the economy, and an active force in trying to define the area's long-term goals.

The pursuit of sprawl as a deliberate economic objective reflected a substantial shift from the initial postwar vision. This strategy roused a growing popular opposition to the social and environmental consequences of such growth. It also faced severe criticism on economic grounds. Resting a plan on the assumption that in-migration would continue indefinitely, regardless of other factors, was delusional at best and a Ponzi scheme at worst—something that the housing collapse of 2007 began to show. This strategy also failed to provide the kinds of higher paying jobs necessary for a twenty-first century economy. By the late 1990s a coalescence of different political and economic forces had begun to forge a new economic vision, one that included a significant biomedical element and offered an alternative future. This vision depended on considerable economic strengths in the area and had some notable successes, but the supporters of this new perspective also faced significant competition from places across the nation and a difficult struggle with opponents of any planning and with supporters of the growth machine.

The broadening of city politics that had begun in the 1960s continued in the 1970s and early 1980s. Prompted by the city's increasing size and diversity, demands for participation and leadership led to a new political system: one in which mayors were expected to provide vision and active leadership and in which council members connected different parts of the city to its center. This new structure and leadership produced a fresh strategy for the city's shape, one that reversed the previous focus on the periphery in favor of the core. Although it took two decades to develop, by 2005 city leaders had created a relatively clear notion of what downtown should be and how to produce it.

The pride of early residents in Phoenix as a modern American city changed to a postwar desire that it become a major American city. Size was the initial standard for claiming this status, but Phoenicians recognized that other measures were also vital. While pursuing affordable housing and strong neighborhoods for their own sake, Phoenicians also realized that people would consider these attributes in evaluating their community. Sports and the arts offered additional ways to enhance the city's image. The postwar leaders had included the arts as an important component in the city's development, but increasingly over time Phoenicians saw beyond their value for education, status, and entertainment, and began to see their economic benefits. Professional sports provided many of the same advantages, reached a different and larger segment of the population, and introduced the potential for emotional identification with the area. Sports and the arts also became crucial additions to the increasingly successful efforts to build a viable and vital central urban core. Public facilities, the expanded convention center, retail businesses, a university campus, government and office buildings, and residential development offered the first realistic chance at a creating a successful downtown area since the 1940s.

While Phoenicians struggled with developing a viable economic strategy and meeting the expectations of a major city, they also confronted anew the challenge and meaning of their environment. The nineteenth-century belief that human habitation could permanently transform a desert into a garden and the 1920s theme of "Let's do away with the desert" gave way to more somber realities. Belief in the essential manageability of the environment has been confounded by the heat island, pollution, and drought. Rather than ignoring or conquering its environment to make Phoenix fit a single model of a modern or a major American city, some city leaders began seriously considering the meaning and importance of its location. Doing so does not mean simply abandoning all the elements of past visions or rejecting any future growth. But it does require effective leadership and different thinking about growth, incorporating the new ideas about city politics and form, and having the next vision be focused on what it means to be a desert city.

Notes

PART I

1. See, for example, *Arizona Business Directory and Gazetteer, 1881* (San Francisco: W. C. Disturnell, 1881), 83; *Phoenix Arizona: City of Progress* (Phoenix: Board of Trade, 1914), 1; Jas. H. McClintock, *Phoenix Arizona in the Great Salt River Valley*, Bulletin No. 4 (Phoenix: Board of Trade, 1908), 5–6; *Salt River Valley: Its Attractions for the Immigrant, the Capitalist, the Invalid* (Phoenix: Maricopa County Immigration Union, 1894), 5–8, 10.

2. Besides comments in the sources noted above, see *Phoenix, Arizona: In the Great Salt River Valley* (Phoenix: H. I. Latham, 1908), 4–5; *Phoenix Directory for the Year 1892* (Phoenix: Bensell Directory Company, 1892), 17, 19; and *Phoenix Directory, 1899–1900* (Phoenix: Phoenix Directory Company, 1899–1900), 16. On western urban planning see John Reps, *Cities of the American West: A History of Frontier Urban Planning* (Princeton: Princeton University Press, 1979).

3. For example, see *Phoenix Directory, 1899–1900*, 15; *Salt River Valley: Attractions*, 11, 15; and McClintock, *Phoenix Arizona*, 3.

CHAPTER 1

1. Various authors define this area differently. Some focus on historical patterns of cultivation and settlement, which relied on the flowing Salt River, while contemporary analysts looking at urban growth see the "transportability" of water and the spread of population not limited by soil and the agricultural potential. Obviously, different boundaries will yield different notions about the size of this area. My description here uses the basic geological features as the outer limits of the Valley, which I see as balancing the historical and contemporary realities. See, for example, the descriptions in *Bird's Eye View of Phoenix, Maricopa Co., Arizona*, Sketched by

C. J. Dyer W. Byrnes Litho. (Phoenix: Schmidt, Label & Litho. Co., 1885); Stephen C. Shadegg, *Century One: One Hundred Years of Water Development in the Salt River Valley* (Phoenix: Lithographed by W. A. Krueger, 1969), 5; Greater Phoenix 2100 Project, *Greater Phoenix Regional eAtlas*, http://www.gp2100.org/eatlas/map.jsp?map=5 (accessed 14 July 2005). Cf. Leon Kolankiewicz and Roy Beck, *Sprawl City: Weighing Sprawl Factors in Large U.S. Cities*, U.S. Bureau of the Census (March 2001), 40, http://www.sprawlcity.org/studyUSA/ (accessed 14 July 2005).

2. W. Eugene Hollon, *The Great American Desert: Then and Now* (New York: Oxford University Press, 1966), 5, 9–11, 142–48; Wallace Stegner, *Beyond the Hundredth Meridian: John Wesley Powell and the Second Opening of the West* (1954; repr., New York: Penguin Books, 1992), 1–7, 215–7; and Martyn J. Bowden, "The Great American Desert in the American Frontier, 1800–1882: Popular Images of the Plains," in *Anonymous Americans: Explorations in Nineteenth-Century Social History*, ed. Tamara Hareven (Englewood Cliffs, NJ: Prentice-Hall, 1971), 48–79. Stephen M. Sloan discusses many aspects of perception in "Negotiating a Sense of Place in the Salt River Valley: Urbanites and the Desert" (PhD diss., Arizona State University, 2003).

3. The others are the Great Basin, centered in Utah and north central Nevada; the Chihuahuan Desert, stretching from New Mexico into central Mexico; and the Mojave Desert, in southern California and southern Nevada. For a convenient map of the desert see Henry P. Walker and Don Bufkin, *Historical Atlas of Arizona*, 2nd ed. (Norman: University of Oklahoma Press, 1986), 7–8.

4. Quotation from John P. Andrews and Todd W. Bostwick, *Desert Farmers at the River's Edge: The Hohokam and Pueblo Grande*, 2nd ed. (Phoenix: Pueblo Grande Museum and Archaeological Park, 2000), 7. More generally see ibid., 7–8; Edwin Corle, *The Gila: River of the Southwest* (1951; repr., Lincoln: University of Nebraska Press, 1964), 342–56; Shadegg, *Century One*, 8–9; and Arizona-Sonoran Desert Museum, "Desert Natural History," http://desertmuseum.org/desert/sonora.html (accessed 14 July 2005).

5. Every tour book describes the Phoenix climate, but the descriptions vary widely, and, as I will discuss later, the weather patterns have changed somewhat over time. David M. Hendricks, *Arizona Soils* (Tucson: College of Agriculture, University of Arizona, 1985), also available online at http://southwest.library.arizona.edu/azso/ (accessed July 17, 2005), provides a useful, brief discussion of the Valley's climate (33–40) and soil (75). The best source for weather data is Robert J. Schmidli, "Climate of Phoenix, Arizona: An Abridged On-Line Version of NOAA Technical Memorandum NWS WR-177," rev. ed. (Phoenix: Weather Service Forecast Office, 1996), online version by R. S. Cerveny (Phoenix: Office of Climatology, Arizona State University, December 1996), http://geography.asu.edu/cerveny/phxwx.htm (accessed 17 July 2005). Also useful is Western Regional Climate Center, "Historical Climate Information: Arizona Climate Summaries," http://www.wrcc.dri.edu/summary/climsmaz.html (accessed 17 July 2005). See also the discussion of weather from 1896 to 1907 in L. N. Jesunofsky, *Climate of the Salt River Valley*, pamphlet reprint from the *Arizona Republican*, 1910 (Hayden Library, Arizona State University). As one example of booster reasoning see McClintock, *Phoenix Arizona*, 4–6. The *Arizona Republican* changed its name in 1930 to the *Arizona Republic* (hereinafter *AR* will be used to refer to either version of the paper).

6. See, for example, Jay J. Wagoner, *Early Arizona: Prehistory to Civil War* (Tucson: University of Arizona Press, 1975); and Walker and Bufkin, *Historical Atlas*, 13–20.

7. The watershed is explained in Arizona Department of Water Resources, *Arizona Statewide*

Watershed Framework (Phoenix: Arizona Department of Water Resources, 2000), chap. 5, 2, and chap. 5, 9. Cf. Karen L. Smith, *The Magnificent Experiment: Building the Salt River Reclamation Project, 1890–1917* (Tucson: University of Arizona Press, 1986), 73. On soils, see Hendricks, *Arizona Soils*, passim.

8. As quoted in Andrew M. Honker, "A River Sometimes Runs Through It: A History of Salt River Flooding and Phoenix" (PhD diss., Arizona State University, 2002), 18. See D. Jacobs and S. E. Ingram, "Vegetation Map of Phoenix, Arizona, 1867–1868," Central Arizona–Phoenix Long-Term Ecological Research Contribution 3 (Tempe, AZ: International Institute for Sustainability, Arizona State University, 2003), http://caplter.asu.edu/docs/contributions/Vegetation_of_Phx_bw.pdf (accessed 29 June 2005).

9. Thomas E. Sheridan discusses the broader Anglo-Indian conflict in Arizona in *Arizona: A History* (Tucson: University of Arizona Press, 1995), 73–99; Walker and Bufkin, *Historical Atlas*, 24, 26, 37–38.

10. Todd W. Bostwick, *Beneath the Runways: Archaeology of Sky Harbor International Airport* (Phoenix: Pueblo Grande Museums, 2008); Thomas Edwin Farish, *History of Arizona*, 8 vols. (San Francisco: Filmer Brothers Electrotype Co., 1918), 2:251–57; and Shadegg, *Century One*, 10–13, which nicely encapsulates Swilling's troublesome character: "He was inspired by adversity and failure. Success made him quarrelsome."

11. For information on the Hohokam see Andrews and Bostwick, *Desert Farmers at the River's Edge*; and Michael H. Bartlett, Thomas M. Kolaz, and David A. Gregory, *Archaeology in the City: A Hohokam Village in Phoenix, Arizona* (Tucson: University of Arizona Press, 1986). Justin Juozapavicius reports on recent excavation of large canals in Mesa in "Past, Future Meet at Riverview," *AR*, 11 July 2005, B1, B9. Estimates of total canal mileage vary, with more recent statements usually being higher.

12. The Pueblo Grande Museum in Phoenix and the Park of the Canals in Mesa have preserved some prehistoric canals, so that contemporary visitors can experience the same intuitive leap that Swilling experienced.

13. Farish, *History of Arizona*, 6:70–90, 99–102, 158–67; Geoffrey P. Mawn, "Promoters, Speculators, and the Selection of the Phoenix Townsite," *Arizona and the West* 19 (Fall 1977): 207–24; G. Wesley Johnson, *Phoenix, Valley of the Sun* (Tulsa, OK: Continental Heritage Press, 1982), 25–29; and Bradford Luckingham, *Phoenix: The History of a Southwestern Metropolis* (Tucson: University of Arizona Press, 1989), 13–17. Reps, *Cities of the American West*, 631, describes the dimensions and plan of the town site; Richard V. Francaviglia, *Main Street Revisited: Time, Space, and Image-Building in Small-Town America* (Iowa City: University of Iowa Press, 1996), 87–108, discusses the different types of downtown platting.

14. In this regard the classic study is Robert Dykstra, *The Cattle Towns* (New York: Knopf, 1968). On mining towns in Arizona see Eric L. Clements, *After the Boom in Tombstone and Jerome, Arizona: Decline in Western Resource Towns* (Reno: University of Nevada Press, 2003); and Thomas J. Dorich, "A Socioeconomic Portrait of Jerome, Arizona, 1877–1935" (PhD diss., Arizona State University, 1996).

15. Shaddeg, *Century One*, 13–14; Salt River Project, *A Valley Reborn* (Tempe, AZ: Salt River Project, 2002), 32–34; Johnson, *Phoenix*, 32–34, 38–40; Shara Forrister, "Understanding Gilbert and Queen Creek, Arizona, 1880–1941," unpublished paper in the author's possession.

16. The communities of Higley and Rittenhouse (now Queen Creek) started in the same period, but they were not part of the Salt River Project area, and lacking access to that water, they developed much more slowly. Forrister, "Understanding Gilbert and Queen Creek"; and

Sue Sossaman, *Higley, Arizona: A Rural Community* (Queen Creek, AZ: San Tan Historical Society, 1999). Two other communities were established in the West Valley: Avondale (1892), on the Agua Fria River, and Buckeye (1880), which was on a stage line and drew water from wells and from the Gila River. Charles Sargent, ed., *Metro Arizona* (Scottsdale, AZ: Biffington Books, 1988), 99, 103.

17. See, for example, Michael Dear and Steven Flusty, "Postmodern Urbanism," *Annals of the Association of American Geographers* 88 (March 1998): 50–72; Rob Kling, Spencer Olin, and Mark Poster, eds., *Postsuburban California: The Transformation of Orange County Since World War II*, rev. ed. (Berkeley: University of California Press, 1995); and Joel Garreau, *Edge City: Life on the New Frontier* (New York: Doubleday, 1991).

18. The reality of this created system—which persisted until after World War II, when the canals were effectively fenced, lined, and then covered—runs contrary to Donald Worster's claim that "the modern canal, unlike a river, is not an ecosystem." *Rivers of Empire: Water, Aridity, and the Growth of the American West* (New York: Pantheon Books, 1985), 5. Quotations from Patrick Hamilton, *The Resources of Arizona: Its Mineral, Farming, and Grazing Lands, Towns, and Mining Camps; Its Rivers, Mountains, Plains, and Mesas; With a Brief Summary of Its Indian Tribes, Early History, Ancient Ruins, Climate, etc. etc. A Manual of Reliable Information Concerning the Territory* (Prescott, AZ: Arizona Territorial Legislature, 1881), 23; the panoramic map, Dyer, *Bird's Eye View of Phoenix*; and *Salt River Valley: Its Attractions*, 8. See also *Arizona Directory, 1881*, 83–84; Farish, *History of Arizona*, 6:143; Alfred Simon, "Mixing Water and Culture: Making the Canal Landscape in Phoenix" (PhD diss., Arizona State University, 2002), esp. 30–49; Honker, "A River," 25; and Sloan, "Negotiating a Sense of Place," 104, 198. Cf. Richard E. Sloan, *Memories of an Arizona Judge* (Palo Alto, CA: Stanford University Press, 1932), 6.

19. J. W. Crenshaw, *Phoenix and the Salt River Valley, Arizona* (Phoenix: Board of Trade, 1911), 4; and *Salt River Valley: Attractions*, 2–3, 8.

20. *Arizona Directory, 1881*, 83–84; *Phoenix Directory, 1892*, 15–17; and *Phoenix Directory, 1899–1900*, 6–11; Hamilton, *Resources of Arizona*, 82–83; Sheridan, *Arizona*, 199–203; Richard E. Lynch, *Winfield Scott: A Biography of Scottsdale's Founder* (Scottsdale: City of Scottsdale, 1978), 106–16.

21. David F. Myrick, *Railroads of Arizona* (San Diego: Howell-North Books, 1980), 2, esp. 484–502; and *Salt River Valley: Attractions*, 13. D. W. Meinig, *Southwest: Three Peoples in Geographical Change, 1600–1970* (New York: Oxford University Press, 1971), 35–52, esp. 43, 51, provides an broader analysis of the changing transportation system; Sheridan, *Arizona*, 115–23, conveniently summarizes railroad building in Arizona; and Walker and Bufkin, *Historical Atlas*, 41, 46–47, has maps of the wagon roads and railroads. On competition with California see *Salt River Valley: Attractions*, 5.

22. *Arizona Directory, 1881*, passim.; Hamilton, *Resources of Arizona*, 29; Mark E. Pry, "The Growth of an Early Sunbelt City: Urban Structure in Phoenix, Arizona, 1880–1910" (master's thesis, Arizona State University, 1988), 56, 58; Larry Schweikart, *A History of Banking in Arizona* (Tucson: University of Arizona Press, 1982), 9–33; Johnson, *Phoenix*, 36; and Mark E. Pry, *Immigrant Banker: The Life of Emil Ganz* (Tempe, AZ: Southwest Historical Services, 2001).

23. Hamilton, *Resources of Arizona*, 29; *Arizona Directory, 1881*, 150–51, 153; Carol Osman Brown, "Phoenix—100 Years Young," essay, n.d., Arizona Historical Foundation, 10; and Janet Suzanne McFarland, "A Power for Good in the Community: The Phoenix Woman's Club, 1900–1930" (master's thesis, Arizona State University, 1994), 74, 32. See Don Doyle on "The

Social Functions of Voluntary Associations in a Nineteenth-Century American Town," *Social Science History* 1 (Spring 1977): 333–55.

24. Jerry Reynolds, *The Golden Days of Theaters in Phoenix: A Dramatic Tableau of the Theaters and Amusements in Greater Phoenix from 1877 to 1982* (Glendale, CA: Associated Media Services, 1982), 12–17. On the structure and role of early Arizona saloons see Harry David Ware, "Alcohol, Temperance, and Prohibition in Arizona" (PhD diss., Arizona State University, 1995), 65–74, 80; and on the concept of "semi-public space," see Perry R. Duis, *The Saloon: Public Drinking in Chicago and Boston, 1880–1920* (Urbana: University of Illinois Press, 1983). The *Arizona Gazette* (hereinafter *AG*), 31 December 1881, 3, reports fifteen saloons, but Pry, "Early Sunbelt City," 58, relying on the *Arizona Directory, 1881*, reports nine. The directory's lower number probably reflects the fact that it took little money to start a "saloon" and little skill to operate one, for a time. However, their numbers fluctuated, because competition was steep—the first wood frame and brick buildings were saloons (Ware, "Alcohol," 72, 73).

25. See, for example, the standard described in Francaviglia, *Main Street Revisited*, xix–xx.

26. *Phoenix Directory, 1892*, 17–19, 117–24; *Phoenix Directory, 1899–1900*, 179–207; *The Taming of the Salt* (Phoenix: Salt River Project, 1979), 41–44; Johnson, *Phoenix*, 40–43, 190, 196–97, 228; Pry, "Early Sunbelt City," 18–21.

27. *Phoenix Directory, 1892*, 118, 123–24; *Phoenix Directory, 1899–1900*, 32–38. On the Ladies Benevolent Society see Aimee de Potter Lykes, "Phoenix Women in the Development of Public Policy: Territorial Beginnings," in G. Wesley Johnson, ed., *Phoenix in the Twentieth Century: Essays in Community History* (Norman: University of Oklahoma Press, 1993), 39–40. On classifying churches see Philip R. VanderMeer, "Religion, Society, and Politics: A Classification of American Religious Groups," *Social Science History* 5 (Winter 1981): 3–24; for the general contours of this group and era see Marin E. Marty, *Righteous Empire: The Protestant Experience in America* (New York: Dial Press, 1970), 166–87.

28. Quotation from "Salt River Valley, Attractions," 15. *Phoenix Directory, 1892*, 17, 116–22; *Phoenix Directory, 1899–1900*, 16, 31–32, 38; Reynolds, *Golden Days of Theaters*, 25. The importance of education is commonly stressed in promotional literature, as noted also by Marienka J. Sokol, "From Wasteland to Oasis: Promotional Images of Arizona, 1870–1912," *Journal of Arizona History* 34 (Winter 1993): 374–5.

29. My analysis of culture is influenced by Lawrence W. Levine, *Highbrow/Lowbrow: The Emergence of Cultural Hierarchy in America* (Cambridge: Harvard University Press, 1988); Michael Kammen, *American Culture, American Tastes: Social Change and the 20th Century* (New York: Knopf, 1999), esp. 3–14; and David D. Hall, "A World Turned Upside Down?," *Reviews in American History* 18 (March 1990): 10–14.

30. Reynolds, *Golden Days of Theaters*, 25–26, 33–41, 49–53; on the context see David Nasaw, *Going Out: The Rise and Fall of Public Amusements* (Cambridge: Harvard University Press, 1993). Built as the Patton Grand Opera House in 1898, it was sold in 1899 and renamed.

31. Ware, "Alcohol, Temperance, and Prohibition in Arizona," 78–135; Pry, "Early Sunbelt City," 108; *Phoenix Directory, 1899–1900*, 204; *Sanborn Fire Insurance Map of Phoenix, June 1893*, Digital Sanborn Maps, 1867–1970, http://sanborn.umi.com.ezproxy1.lib.asu.edu/az/0169/dateid-000003.htm (accessed 12 August 2005); and Reynolds, *Golden Days of Theaters*, 18–24. The 1894 city ordinance restricted prostitution to Block 41, which was between current streets of Madison, 6th, Jackson, and 5th. *A Teacher's Guide to the Phoenix Museum of History*, 2nd ed. (Phoenix: Phoenix Museum of History, n.d.), 19. On cultural conflict over liquor see Norman H. Clark, *Deliver Us from Evil: An Interpretation of American Prohibition* (New York:

Norton, 1976); on morality see Peggy Pascoe, *Relations of Rescue: The Search for Female Moral Authority in the American West, 1874–1939* (New York: Oxford University Press, 1990); and on the WCTU see Ruth Bordin, *Women and Temperance: The Quest for Power and Liberty, 1873–1900* (Philadelphia: Temple University Press, 1981).

32. Luckingham, *Phoenix*, 33; Peter Iverson, *Carlos Montezuma and the Changing World of American Indians* (Albuquerque: University of New Mexico Press, 1982); Peter MacMillan Booth, "Akimel O'odham (Pima)," *Encyclopedia of North American Indians*, Frederick E. Hoxie, ed. (New York: Houghton Mifflin, 1996), http://college.hmco.com/history/readerscomp/naind/html/na_000600_akimeloodham.htm (accessed 5 September 2005); *Phoenix Directory, 1892*, 118, 123; and *Phoenix Directory, 1899–1900*, 33; Matthew C. Whitaker, "The Rise of Black Phoenix: African-American Migration, Settlement, and Community Development in Maricopa County, Arizona, 1868–1930," *The Journal of Negro History* 85 (Summer 2000): 197–209; Bradford Luckingham, *Minorities in Phoenix: A Profile of Mexican American, Chinese American, and African American Communities, 1860–1992* (Tucson: University of Arizona Press, 1994), 79–97, 129–31.

33. Their proportion varied by time and by place. Opportunities for agricultural work were greater in or near smaller Valley settlements, and by one estimate they comprised about half of the Tempe population before 1900. "A Brief History of Hispanic Tempe" (Tempe, AZ: Tempe Historical Museum, 2000), http://www.tempe.gov/tardeada/t_hist.htm (accessed 18 August 2005).

34. Luckingham, *Minorities*, 16–25; *Phoenix Directory, 1899–1900*, 32–33, 36; quotation from *Phoenix Directory, 1892*, 19.

35. *Arizona Directory, 1881*, 149; Francaviglia, *Main Street Revisited*, 21; *Historic Homes of Phoenix: An Architectural & Preservation Guide*, Cooper/Robert Architects (Phoenix: City of Phoenix, 1992), 28, quotation from 30. Significantly, the first wood frame structure in town was the Magnolia Saloon in 1878, *Salt River Herald*, 27 April 1878, 4.

36. *Historic Homes*, 35–43; Johnson, *Phoenix*, 44; *Salt River Valley: Attractions*, 8; quotation from *Phoenix Directory, 1899–1900*, 16. Certainly the most visible example of this style is the Rosson House, placed at Heritage Square in 1976; Johnson, *Phoenix*, 178–79.

37. Charles S. Sargent, Jr., "Evolution of Metro Phoenix," in James W. Elmore, ed., *A Guide to the Architecture of Metro Phoenix* (Phoenix: Phoenix Publishing, 1983), 9; and Pry, "Early Sunbelt City," 27, and Janus Associates, "Commerce in Phoenix, 1870 to 1942: A Context for Preserving Historic Properties" (Phoenix: State Historic Preservation Office, 1989), 17–18.

38. These features are clear in photographs from the era, most conveniently seen in Herb McLaughlin and Dorothy McLaughlin, *Phoenix, 1870–1970, in Photographs* (Phoenix: privately printed, 1970). On the architectural features see Francaviglia, *Main Street Revisited*, 30, 40–42, 117, 125.

39. *AR*, 5 March 1891 and 24 February 1891, 2; *Arizona Daily Gazette*, 24 February 1891, 2; as quoted in Honker, "A River," 43–45. James H. McClintock, *Arizona: Prehistoric-Aboriginal, Pioneer-Modern* (Chicago: S. J. Clarke, 1916), 2:570.

40. *Phoenix and the Salt River Valley, Arizona, 1893–1894* (Phoenix: Phoenix National Bank), 3, quoted in *Historic Homes*, 34–35.

41. *Historic Homes*, 28; Gregory Mawn, "Phoenix, Arizona: Central City of the Southwest, 1870–1920" (PhD diss., Arizona State University, 1979), 74–80; Luckingham, *Phoenix*, 23–26.

42. *AG*, 1 January 1883, 4 May 1883, and 16 August 1883; Luckingham, *Phoenix*, 26; and Pry, "Early Sunbelt City," 18–21.

43. Sargent, "Evolution of Metro Phoenix," 10–11; Johnson, *Phoenix*, 189, 210; Pry, "Early Sunbelt City," 19–26.

44. *Appleton's Annual Cyclopedia and Register of Important Events of Year 1889*, new series (New York: D. Appleton & Co., 1889), 29:156.

45. Pry, "Early Sunbelt City," 21.

46. Luckingham, *Phoenix*, 27; Mawn, "Phoenix," 74–80; and Bradford Luckingham, *The Urban Southwest: A Profile History of Albuquerque—El Paso—Phoenix—Tucson* (El Paso: Texas Western Press, University of Texas, 1982), 24.

47. Robert A. Trennert, Jr., *The Phoenix Indian School: Forced Assimilation in Arizona, 1891–1935* (Norman: University of Oklahoma Press, 1988).

48. Sheridan, *Arizona*, 200.

49. Honker, "A River," 30–49, provides a detailed and insightful discussion of this flood; see also Myrick, *Railroads of Arizona*, 2:508–9.

50. Authors differ on periodizing the drought and its severity. Earl Zarbin, "In Pursuit of a Reservoir," in Johnson, ed., *Phoenix in the Twentieth Century*, 146; Jack L. August, *Vision in the Desert: Carl Hayden and Hydropolitics in the American Southwest* (Fort Worth: Texas Christian University Press, 1999), 18; and Honker, "A River," 53. But using the U.S. Weather Bureau's measured rainfall, as reported by Jesunofsky, in *Climate of the Salt River Valley*, 5, shows the first shortfall in 1898 (1 inch), roughly 2-inch shortfalls in 1899–1901, near average rainfall in 1902–3, and 1.5 inches below average in 1904. The problems may have been seriously accentuated by lower rain in the watershed or by concentrated rainfall in a few storms—and they may have been emphasized when Valley residents lobbied for the Roosevelt Dam. On Phoenix businesses see Janus Associates, "Commerce in Phoenix," 6.

51. Smith provides detailed coverage of the entire period in *Magnificent Experiment*; for another treatment focusing on the politics, see Zarbin, "Pursuit of a Reservoir," 139–53. Reid W. Teeples and Richard E. Lynch briefly discuss the construction era in "Salt River Project Born in Effort to Fight Drought," in Athia L. Hardt, ed. *Arizona Waterline* (Phoenix: Salt River Project, 1988), 60–62; the construction of canals is noted in *A Valley Reborn*, 32–34; canal purchase and consolidation is described in *AR*, 19 February 1907, 10.

52. Rainfall data from the Phoenix Weather Bureau of the U.S. Department of Commerce was reported in *AR*, 22 November 1942, 2:6.

53. Arizona Academy, *Do Agricultural Problems Threaten Arizona's Total Economy?*, Tenth Arizona Town Hall (Phoenix: Arizona Town Hall, 1967), 74, 84, provides the acreage data. In 1890, compared with other western states and territories using irrigation, Valley farms were relatively small: U.S. Department of Interior, Census Office, *Eleventh Census, 1890*, vol. 5, *Report on Agriculture by Irrigation in the Western Part of the United States* (Washington, DC; Government Printing Office, 1894), 6. *Phoenix Arizona: Where Winter Never Comes* (Phoenix: Phoenix Arizona Club, 1927), 21, described the Valley in 1927 as "a land of small farms." The number of farmers is taken from the pamphlet "Phoenix" (Phoenix: Chamber of Commerce, 1923).

54. On Goodyear towns see P. W. Litchfield, *Industrial Voyage: My Life as an Industrial Lieutenant* (Garden City, NY: Doubleday & Company, 1954), 159–62; Scott Solliday, *Chandler: Pioneer City of the New West* (Chandler: Chandler Historical Society, 1996), 32–34; City of Goodyear, Arizona, "History," http://www.ci.goodyear.az.us/index.asp?NID=384 (accessed 12 December 2005); and "Litchfield Park, Arizona," http://www.arizonan.com/litchfieldpark/ (accessed 12 December 2005). Tolleson (1912), Guadalupe (1910), and the Goodyear towns

were essentially housing for agricultural laborers, while a few people lived in the former mining area of Cave Creek. Until the 1980s, these towns were small, with a very limited connection with Phoenix.

55. Quotation from *Phoenix, Arizona* (Phoenix: Chamber of Commerce, 1922), 3. Arizona Academy, *Agricultural Problems*, discusses Arizona's agricultural history in detail and with substantial data; also *Phoenix, Arizona: The New Winter Playground* (Phoenix: Chamber of Commerce, 1929), 21; and "Commerce in Phoenix," 7. The number of farmers is taken from the pamphlet "Phoenix" (Phoenix: Chamber of Commerce, 1923). See also discussions in Sheridan, *Arizona*, 212–16; and Michael Kotlanger, "An Overview of Economic Development in Phoenix in the 1920s," in Johnson, *Phoenix in the Twentieth Century*, 93–96; plus comments in Smith, *Magnificent Experiment*, 111, 143, 158.

56. For discussion of the dams see Teeples and Lynch, "Salt River Project," 64–65; *A Valley Reborn*, 17–19; and Honker, "A River," 62–64 (and 76–84 on the 1938 flood). The Flood Control District of Maricopa County Web site has a partial list of floods and some history, http://www.fcd.maricopa.gov/Flooding/History.asp (accessed 10 August 2005). Vince Murray provides a more detailed discussion in "Origins of the Maricopa Flood Control District," unpublished seminar paper, 2002.

57. Hodge, *Arizona*, 29–29; Hamilton, *Resources of Arizona*, 91–92.

58. John Louis Waslif, "Health Seekers in the Salt River Valley, Arizona: A Burden on the Southwest?" (master's thesis, Arizona State University, 1996), 24–34.

59. *Phoenix Directory, 1899–1900*, 13–15; McClintock, *Phoenix Arizona in the Great Salt River Valley*, 5–6; Jesunofsky, *Climate of the Salt River Valley*, 8; *Salt River Valley: Its Attractions*, 10; and Waslif, "Health Seekers," 17.

60. J. W. Crenshaw, *Salt River Valley, Arizona* (Phoenix: Maricopa County Board of Trade, 1907); *Phoenix—The Salt River Valley* (Phoenix: Santa Fe Railroad, 1916), 13; *Phoenix City and Salt River Valley Directory, 1925* (Phoenix: Arizona Directory Company, 1925), 673; Phoenix Arizona Club, *Arizona: Information Data of Principal Cities and Towns, Industries, Hotels and Auto Courts, Guest and Dude Ranches, Summer and Winter Resorts, Sanatoriums . . .* (Phoenix: Phoenix Arizona Club, 1931), 14, lists twenty facilities in the Phoenix area; and Waslif, "Health Seekers," esp. 17–18, 41–53.

CHAPTER 2

1. E.g., Raymond E. Murphy, *The American City: An Urban Geography* (New York: McGraw-Hill, 1974), 35–81; William Cronon, *Nature's Metropolis: Chicago and the Great West* (New York: W. W. Norton, 1991), 46–54, 263–309; James E. Vance, Jr., *The Continuing City: Urban Morphology in Western Civilization* (Baltimore: Johns Hopkins University Press, 1990), 12–14; D. W. Meinig, *Southwest: Three Peoples in Geographical Change, 1600–1970* (New York: Oxford University Press, 1971), 50–51.

2. Salt River Herald, 2 March 1878. See also Patrick Hamilton, *The Resources of Arizona: Its Mineral, Farming, and Grazing Lands, Towns, and Mining Camps; Its Rivers, Mountains, Plains, and Mesas; With a Brief Summary of Its Indian Tribes, Early History, Ancient Ruins, Climate, etc. etc.; A Manual of Reliable Information Concerning the Territory* (Prescott, AZ: Arizona Territorial Legislature, 1881), 81, 405–8.

3. Quotation from *AR*, 3 April 1911, 1. On the Valley cities see Charles Sargent, "Towns of the Salt River Valley, 1870–1930," *Historical Geography Newsletter* 5 (Fall 1975): 1–9; on Tucson and southwestern competition see Meinig, *Southwest*, passim, and Bradford Luckingham,

The Urban Southwest: A Profile History of Albuquerque—El Paso—Phoenix—Tucson (El Paso: Texas Western Press, University of Texas, 1982), 1–53. John Reps, *Cities of the American West: A History of Frontier Urban Planning* (Princeton, NJ: Princeton University Press, 1979), 631, 678, stresses the importance of getting the railroad connection for the city's success.

4. Quotation from *AR*, 6 April 1911, 8. Sargent, op cit., 5, minimizes the domination, claiming that because travel limited the connections, the other towns duplicated low-order functions of Phoenix. But these functions were the first basis for any town; only the duplication of more specialized functions would invalidate the argument. The city directories show that this did not occur. For example, in the *Phoenix Directory, 1925*, Phoenix had 26 of the Valley's 29 dentists, 143 of 149 lawyers, all 11 architects, 4 accountants, and 7 brokers. By contrast, 7 of the 23 blacksmiths, 4 of the 9 ice houses, and 4 of the 16 photographers were in the other Valley towns. Moreover, the retail structures of both Tempe and Glendale in 1929 (as shown in per capita numbers of stores, employees, and sales) reflect a clear dependence on Phoenix. U.S. Department of Commerce, Bureau of the Census, *Fifteenth Census of the United States, 1930: Distribution*, vol. I, *Retail Distribution*, part 1 (Washington, DC: Government Printing Office, 1933), 96.

5. Johnson's "Directing Elites: Catalysts for Social Change," in G. Wesley Johnson, ed., *Phoenix in the Twentieth Century: Essays in Community History* (Norman: University of Oklahoma Press, 1993), 13–32, offers a particularly insightful analysis for this period.

6. Quotation from Orme Lewis, interview by Phoenix History Project, 13 December 1977, transcript, 53, in Phoenix History Project Collection, 1974–85, Arizona Historical Society, Tempe (hereinafter PHPC). Johnson notes that it was a commercial elite in ibid., 22, and Karen Smith discusses aspects of cooperation and land development in *The Magnificent Experiment: Building the Salt River Reclamation Project, 1890–1917* (Tucson: University of Arizona Press, 1986), 157–58; also Johnson, *Phoenix*, 59–63; and *The Taming of the Salt* (Phoenix: Salt River Project, 1979), 80–83.

7. Richard V. Francaviglia, *Main Street Revisited: Time, Space, and Image-Building in Small-Town America* (Iowa City: University of Iowa Press, 1996), xix, 1–8. This and the subsequent discussions of business clustering rely on Mark E. Pry, "The Growth of an Early Sunbelt City: Urban Structure in Phoenix, Arizona, 1880–1910" (master's thesis, Arizona State University, 1988), 50–105, plus my analysis of his data and information in the related city directories.

8. On CBD see Robert M. Fogelson, *Downtown: Its Rise and Fall, 1880–1950* (New Haven: Yale University Press, 2001), passim; David Ward, *Cities and Immigrants: A Geography of Change in Nineteenth-Century America* (New York: Oxford University Press, 1971), 85–102, 118–20; and Vance, *The Continuing City*, 384–441.

9. Their locations changed slightly over time and were also influenced by expansion and fire, as discussed in Jerry Brisco, "The Department Store Industry in Phoenix, 1895-1940" (master's thesis, Arizona State University, 2000), 23–26, 36–38, 77–78. Quotation from Patrick Downey, interview by Phoenix History Project, 8 July 1978, transcript, 3, PHPC.

10. This discussion of the distribution of businesses and offices is based on my analysis of data in various city directories, most systematically the *Phoenix Directory, 1925*, and *Phoenix Directory, 1935* (Phoenix: Arizona Directory Company, 1935). Cf. Kotlanger, "An Overview of Economic Development," 93–103; and Peter Lee Russell, "Downtown's Downturn: A Historical Geography of the Phoenix, Arizona, Central Business District, 1890–1986" (master's thesis, Arizona State University, 1986) 45–75.

11. In addition, another quarter had offices still further north, out of downtown and closer

to hospitals. The pattern for dentists was similar: from nearly all in the 1920s to a third in downtown, while the others had offices slightly to the north of downtown. *Phoenix City Directory, 1940* (Phoenix: Arizona Directory Company, 1940), 555–56.

12. David F. Myrick, *Railroads of Arizona* (San Diego: Howell-North Books, 1980), 2:781–802; Rob Bohannan, "Phoenix Union Station: History," www.azrail.org/station/az/phoneix/history.htm (accessed 3 July 2005).

13. Janus Associates, "Commerce in Phoenix, 1870 to 1942: A Context for Preserving Historic Properties" (Phoenix: State Historic Preservation Office, 1989), 10.

14. *Phoenix Directory, 1925*, 625–27, 699–701, 691, 32–33, 120–21; *Phoenix Directory, 1940*, 551; Michael Kotlanger, "An Overview of Economic Development in Phoenix in the 1920s," in Johnson, *Phoenix in the Twentieth Century*, 97–99, and Pry, "Early Sunbelt City," 134. Pry argues convincingly from his data that a warehouse district did not develop before 1920.

15. Ruth M. Reinhold, *Sky Pioneering: Arizona in Aviation History* (Tucson: University of Arizona Press, 1982), 86–91, 109–12, 184–90; and Arthur Horton, *An Economic, Political, and Social Survey of Phoenix and the Valley of the Sun* (Tempe, AZ: Southside Progress, 1941), 270–71.

16. The various hotels are noted in *Buck's Directory of Phoenix and the Salt River Valley for 1909* (Phoenix: Buck Directory Co., 1909), 434, 453–54; *What to See in Phoenix* (Phoenix: Chamber of Commerce, 1917), 15; and *Phoenix Directory, 1925*, 673–74; but there were many other boardinghouses: the 1909 directory (p. 6) reports a total of thirty-eight. Robert A. Melikian, *Hotel San Carlos* (Charleston, SC: Arcadia Publishing, 2009).

17. *Phoenix Directory, 1899–1900*, 17; Pry, "Early Sunbelt City," 27; Brisco, "Department Store in Phoenix," 32; *Historic Homes of Phoenix: An Architectural & Preservation Guide*, Cooper/Robert Architects (Phoenix: City of Phoenix, 1992), 45. Bicycles also had some impact, providing another form of transportation, inspiring regulatory city ordinances, and demonstrating the problems of unpaved streets. Mark E. Pry, "Everybody Talks Wheels: The 1890s Bicycle Craze in Phoenix," *Journal of Arizona History* 31 (January 1990): 1–18.

18. Auto registration figures are from *Arizona Blue Book for 1929–30* (Phoenix: Secretary of State, 1930), 155; *Arizona Blue Book, 1930–31*, 237; and Horton, *Economic, Political, and Social Survey*, 273. One-third of the county's population lived in Phoenix, but the city included two-thirds of the essential auto services (gas stations and garages). The city held an estimated fifteen thousand dwellings, and thus roughly that many households. My estimate is based on the assumptions that some households did not own a car and that some of those who did own had two vehicles, balanced with the importance of auto services. *Phoenix Directory, 1925*, 664–65; "Phoenix Growth in Relation to Maricopa County, Arizona, and the U.S." (Phoenix: City of Phoenix, Planning Department), undated data sheet.

19. *Phoenix Directory, 1909*, 432; *Phoenix Directory, 1925*, 628–33; Bureau of the Census, *Fifteenth Census, 1930: Distribution*, vol. I, *Retail Distribution*, part 1, 238–39. The 1925 listings had forty-eight garages, thirty-five gas stations, and six insurance agents working solely on automobiles.

20. Kotlanger describes highway construction and paving in "An Overview of Economic Development," 100–101; see a more detailed analysis in Melissa Keane and J. Simon Bruder, *Good Roads Everywhere: A History of Road Building in Arizona* (Phoenix: Environmental Planning Section, Arizona Department of Transportation, 2003), 41–61, http://www.azdot.gov/Highways/EEG/documents/files/cultural/good_roads/gdrds_chapter_4.pdf (accessed 17 June 2005). Road construction and paving were important, but in 1931 less than one-third of the Arizona State Highway system miles in Maricopa County were all or partly concrete; the rest was equally split between oil surfaced and gravel (or gravel and dirt).

Arizona Blue Book for 1930–31 (Phoenix: Secretary of State, 1931), 239. Among county roads, only 264 of roughly 3,800 miles were paved by 1940. Horton, *Economic, Political, and Social Survey*, 272. On taxes see Keane and Bruder, *Good Roads*, 48–50; and *Arizona Blue Book, 1930–31*, 238. Hal Barron provides a good analysis of the larger context of the roads movement in *Mixed Harvest: The Second Great Transformation in the Rural North, 1870–1930* (Chapel Hill: University of North Carolina Press, 1997), 19–41.

21. Bureau of the Census, *Fifteenth Census, 1930: Distribution*, vol. I, *Retail Distribution*, part 1, 96, 242, as discussed in Brisco, "Department Store in Phoenix," 75. The strength may have even exceeded this reported analysis: checking a random selection of eight pages of listings for all cities with populations over ten thousand shows only one city (Asbury Park, NJ) that exceeded Phoenix's per capita sales figures. U.S. Department of Commerce, Bureau of the Census, *Abstract of the Fifteenth Census of the United States* (Washington, DC: Government Printing Office, 1933), 818–93.

22. Brisco, "Department Store in Phoenix," 84–85.

23. James W. Elmore, ed., *A Guide to the Architecture of Metro Phoenix* (Phoenix: Phoenix Publishing, 1983), passim; Leslie Mahoney, interview by Phoenix History Project, 6 November 1975, transcript, 2, 15, PHPC.

24. Fogelson, *Downtown*, 5.

25. On the key role of downtown see Fogelson, *Downtown*; Alison Isenberg, *Downtown America: A History of the Place and the People Who Made It* (Chicago: University of Chicago Press, 2004); and Jon Teaford, *The Twentieth-Century American City*, 2nd ed. (Baltimore: Johns Hopkins University Press, 1993). On public space see Peter C. Baldwin, *Domesticating the Street: The Reform of Public Space in Hartford, 1850–1930* (Columbus: Ohio State University Press, 1999); and David Waldstreicher, "Two Cheers for the 'Public Sphere' . . . and One for Historians' Skepticism," *William and Mary Quarterly* 62 (January 2005): 107–12.

26. On the development of suburbs during this era see Sam Bass Warner, *Streetcar Suburbs: The Process of Growth in Boston, 1870–1900* (Cambridge: Harvard University Books, 1962); Dolores Hayden, *Building Suburbia: Green Fields and Urban Growth, 1820–2000* (New York: Pantheon, 2003), 71–127; Ward, *Cities and Immigrants*, 105–43; and Kenneth T. Jackson, *Crabgrass Frontier: The Suburbanization of the United States* (New York: Oxford University Press, 1985), esp. 118–89.

27. See "Pre-1950 Historic Residential Resources Reconnaissance Survey Report" (Phoenix: City of Phoenix, Planning Department, 1990), 38–44, quotation from 44; Charles S. Sargent, Jr., "Evolution of Metro Phoenix," in Elmore, *Guide to the Architecture of Metro Phoenix*, 10–11; and Daniel C. Davis, "Phoenix, Arizona, 1907–1913," 54, essay, 1976, Arizona Historical Foundation. The lines took more complex paths than a verbal description can easily convey, largely because "every mile of track" served Sherman's properties or was subsidized by another developer; "Pre-1950 Residential Report," 38. The area to the south of the railroad tracks grew somewhat during this period. It included but was not exclusively populated by minorities. In this period only a small area was within the city boundaries.

28. "Pre-1950 Residential Report," 33, 37, 66; Sargent, "Evolution of Metro Phoenix," 18; *Historic Homes*, 49–59; quotations from *AR*, 21 April 1909, 9; "Roosevelt Neighborhood: Special District Plan" (Phoenix: City of Phoenix, Planning Department, 1989), 5–7; "Phoenix—The Salt River Valley"; cf. *AR*, 23 October 1905, 17. The current Roosevelt Historic District, which includes the Kenilworth subdivision and others, displays this housing and landscaping style. Popularity of bungalows connected the city with Los Angeles, which also began supplying architects to the desert city.

29. "Pre-1950 Residential Report," 47.

30. Horton, *Economic, Political, and Social Survey*, 273.

31. Ibid., 45, 46, 68; "Out of the Ashes: The History of the City of Phoenix," City of Phoenix, http://phoenix.gov/CITYGOV/history.html#ESTABLISH (accessed 15 August 2005); e.g., ad in *AR*, 5 February 1927, sec. 2, 8.

32. "Pre-1950 Residential Report,," 34, 36, 41, 45–47, 51, 67–68; *Historic Homes*, 60–67; *AR*, 3 October 1926, sec. 3, 1, 6; *AR*, 6 February 1927, sec. 2, 8; "Cheery Lynn Historic District" at http://www.historicphoenix.com/historic_districts/Cheery_Lynn_main.html.

33. This figure represents the 1940 census report of Phoenix homes built between 1920 and 1929. Despite possible minor discrepancies, this is preferable to using the number of building permits (4,003), since those were only for construction within the then-current city boundaries, and it is uncertain whether all of those projects were completed. U.S. Department of Commerce, Bureau of the Census, *Sixteenth Census of the United States, 1940: Housing*, vol. 2 (Washington: Government Printing Office, 1943), 99; and *Historic Homes*, 215.

34. *Historic Homes*, 66; "Phoenix—The Salt River Valley" (1916).

35. *AR*, 25 February 1927, 9; *AR*, 11 November 1929, 3. Hayden, *Building Suburbia*, 88–93 critiques this rationale; see also the ad on 106.

36. Carl Bimson, "Thirty Years of Progress in Arizona Home Financing," *Arizona Review of Business and Public Administration* 12 (February 1963): 2; *Sixteenth Census, 1940: Housing*, 99. This falls below the state level of 38.8 percent in William S. Collins, *The New Deal in Arizona* (Phoenix: Arizona State Parks Board, 1999), 326. Bimson reports on a 1934 study, showing home ownership at roughly a fourth, and while the Depression might have reduced that level slightly, this fits with earlier data. The 1940 census analysis of home ownership by age of home shows ownership in 1940 of pre-1930 homes at 17 percent. Of these explanations, the investment strategy issue is the most difficult to evaluate, and the costs of ownership are easiest, although not simple. As a starting point, one can note that according to various ads in the *AR* and those printed in *Historic Homes*, inexpensive houses in the 1920s cost upwards of $1,500, upper middle class homes were $4,000 to $7,000, while wealthier homes were offered at $9,000.

37. The City Beautiful movement encompasses different elements: architecture, city beautification, and, as discussed in chapter 3, municipal housekeeping. William H. Wilson, *The City Beautiful Movement* (Baltimore: Johns Hopkins University Press, 1989), and Jon A. Peterson, "The City Beautiful Movement: Forgotten Origins and Lost Meanings," *Journal of Urban History* 2 (August 1976): 415–34.

38. Janet Suzanne McFarland, "A Power for Good in the Community: The Phoenix Woman's Club, 1900–1930" (master's thesis, Arizona State University, 1994), 85–86; *AR*, 21 April 1909, 9; *Phoenix Arizona: City of Progress* (Phoenix: Board of Trade, 1914), 1; and Bradford Luckingham, *Phoenix: The History of a Southwestern Metropolis* (Tucson: University of Arizona Press, 1989), 80.

39. *New York World*, 15 May 1921, as reprinted in Horton, *Economic, Political, and Social Survey*, 35; *Phoenix Arizona: Where Winter Never Comes* (Phoenix: Phoenix Arizona Club, 1927), 3.

40. *Phoenix: Winter Never Comes*,12; *Phoenix Arizona: City of Progress*, 1. The discussion of canals in these paragraphs draws primarily on the excellent discussion in Alfred Simon, "Mixing Water and Culture: Making the Canal Landscape in Phoenix" (PhD diss., Arizona State University, 2002), 50–75, which reports on numerous interviews.

41. Quotations from ibid., 69.

42. Robert C. Balling, Jr., and Sandra W. Brazel, "The Myth of Increasing Moisture Levels in Phoenix," in Robert J. Schmidli, "Climate of Phoenix, Arizona: An Abridged On-Line Version of NOAA Technical Memorandum NWS WR-177," rev. ed. (Phoenix: Weather Service Forecast Office, online version by R. S. Cerveny, Office of Climatology, Arizona State University, December 1996), http://geography.asu.edu/cerveny/phxwx.htm (accessed 17 July 2005).

43. Kevin Norton, "'The Swimming Pool Capital of the World': The Development of Private Swimming Pools in Phoenix, Arizona" (master's thesis, Arizona State University, 2005), 71–81; he also notes that several public pools were built in minority neighborhoods after 1927.

44. *Phoenix, Arizona: The New Winter Playground* (Phoenix: Chamber of Commerce, 1929), 5; in *Phoenix: Winter Never Comes*, 20, the section is titled "Nature's Fantastic Flower Garden"; and James P. Burke and Joseph M. Ewan, "Sonoran Desert Preservation: An Open Space Plan for the City of Phoenix, Arizona," National Planning Conference, 1999, http://www.asu.edu/caed/proceedings99/NSC/EWAN.HTM (accessed 14 September 2005).

45. Dixie Legler, *Frank Lloyd Wright: The Western Work* (San Francisco: Chronicle Books, 1999), 8–13, 19–31, quotation from 8.

46. Tara A. Blanc, *Oasis in the City: The History of the Desert Botanical Garden* (Phoenix: Heritage Publishers, Inc., 2000), 9–13. Compare with the related developments in Tucson, discussed in Janice Bowers, *A Sense of Place: The Life and Work of Forrest Shreve* (Tucson: University of Arizona Press, 1988).

CHAPTER 3

1. Jas. H. McClintock, *Phoenix Arizona in the Great Salt River Valley*, Bulletin no. 4 (Phoenix: Board of Trade, 1908), 3.

2. Advertisement in *Mesa Free Press*, March 1905, as quoted in Andrew M. Honker, "A River Sometimes Runs Through It: A History of Salt River Flooding and Phoenix" (PhD diss., Arizona State University, 2002), 55; John Louis Waslif, "Health Seekers in the Salt River Valley, Arizona: A Burden on the Southwest?" (master's thesis, Arizona State University, 1996), 35. Paul Thomas Hietter shows that Arizona was neither especially violent not plagued by crime in "Lawyers, Guns, and Money: The Evolution of Crime and Criminal Justice in Arizona Territory" (PhD diss., Arizona State University, 1999).

3. On the importance of statehood see, for example, Barton Wood Currie, "The Transformation of the Southwest through the Legal Abolition of Gambling," *Century Illustrated Monthly Magazine* 75 (1908): 905–10.

4. On the nature of moral reform generally during this era see, for example, Morton Keller, *Regulating a New Society: Public Policy and Social Change in America, 1900–1933* (Cambridge: Harvard University Press, 1994); Clark, *Deliver Us from Evil*; John Burnham, *Bad Habits: Drinking, Smoking, Taking Drugs, Gambling, Sexual Misbehavior, and Swearing in American History* (New York: New York University Press, 1993); and Peggy Pascoe, *Relations of Rescue: The Search for Female Moral Authority in the American West, 1874–1939* (New York: Oxford University Press, 1990). On liquor see James H. Timberlake, *Prohibition and the Progressive Movement, 1900–1920,* (Cambridge: Harvard University Press, 1963); Thomas Pegram, *Battling Demon Rum: The Struggle for a Dry America, 1800–1933* (Chicago: Ivan R. Dee, 1998); Thomas J. Noel, *The City and the Saloon: Denver, 1858–1916* (Lincoln: University of Nebraska Press, 1982); and K. Austin Kerr, *Organized for Prohibition: A New History of the Anti-Saloon League* (New Haven: Yale University Press, 1985). On moral reform see Alison M. Parker,

Purifying America: Women, Cultural Reform, and Pro-Censorship Activism, 1873–1933 (Urbana: University of Illinois Press, 1997); David J. Pivar, *Purity Crusade: Sexual Morality and Social Control, 1868–1900* (Westport, CN.: Greenwood Press, 1973); and Mark Thomas Connelly, *The Response to Prostitution in the Progressive Era* (Chapel Hill: University of North Carolina Press, 1980).

5. Janet Suzanne McFarland, "A Power for Good in the Community: The Phoenix Woman's Club, 1900–1930" (master's thesis, Arizona State University, 1994), 36–43, 85; Harry David Ware, "Alcohol, Temperance, and Prohibition in Arizona" (PhD diss., Arizona State University, 1995), 150–54; Aimee de Potter Lykes, "Phoenix Women in the Development of Public Policy: Territorial Beginnings," in G. Wesley Johnson, ed., *Phoenix in the Twentieth Century: Essays in Community History* (Norman: University of Oklahoma Press, 1993), 34–39; Richard E. Lynch, *Winfield Scott: A Biography of Scottsdale's Founder* (Scottsdale, AZ: City of Scottsdale, 1978), 131.

6. Ware, "Alcohol, Temperance, and Prohibition in Arizona," 155–61, 234; on gambling also see Jerry Reynolds, *The Golden Days of Theaters in Phoenix: A Dramatic Tableau of the Theaters and Amusements in Greater Phoenix from 1877 to 1982* (Glendale, CA: Associated Media Services, 1982), 54.

7. Ware, "Alcohol, Temperance, and Prohibition in Arizona," 166–275; Lykes, "Phoenix Women," 38. James McClintock claimed in 1908 that gambling had been banned by state law and the city's "rigid anti-gambling ordinance" and that "there are few saloons." *Phoenix Arizona in the Great Salt River Valley*, Bulletin No. 4 (Phoenix: Board of Trade, 1908), 3.

8. Ware, "Alcohol, Temperance, and Prohibition in Arizona," 150–51; Heidi J. Osselaer, *Winning Their Place: Arizona Women in Politics, 1883–1950* (Tucson: University of Arizona Press, 2009), 65; McFarland, "A Power for Good," 36–46, 52–58, 85–88. On clubwomen and on municipal housekeeping see Anne Firor Scott, *Natural Allies: Women's Associations in American History* (Urbana: University of Illinois Press, 1991), and Karen Blair, *The Club Woman as Feminist* (New York: Holmes and Meir, 1980). McFarland, 73, also notes that not all Phoenix clubs (namely, the Harmony and Friday clubs) engaged in reform activities.

9. As quoted in Reynolds, *Golden Days of Theaters*, 83.

10. Reynolds, *Golden Days of Theaters*, 38–53, 99, 116; "Society in Phoenix," 5, ms., box 10, folder 207, PHPC; Margaret Helen Tuveson, interview by Phoenix History Project, 29 February 1976, transcript, PHPC; Newton Rosenzweig, interview by Phoenix History Project, 5 October 1978, transcript, 5–6, PHPC. The Community Concert Association also began a series in 1931. Arthur G. Horton, *An Economic, Political, and Social Survey of Phoenix and the Valley of the Sun* (Tempe, AZ: Southside Progress, 1941), 257.

11. *Buck's Directory of Phoenix and the Salt River Valley for 1909* (Phoenix: Buck Directory Co., 1909), 81, 432, 460; Rosenzweig interview transcript, 4; Horton, *Economic, Political, and Social Survey*, 257; *AR*, 3 November 1959, 20, and 8 November 1959, 1; and Ed Korrick, interview by Arizona Jewish Historical Society, transcript, http://info.lib.asu.edu/NetAns2/gate.exe?f=doc&p_d=ajhs&state=3k6kf6.1.27 (accessed 27 August 2005).

12. "Historical Note to Manuscript Guide," Phoenix Little Theatre Records, 1922–1994, Arizona Historical Society, Tempe (hereinafter AHS); and "Society in Phoenix," 3. Dorothy Chansky, *Composing Ourselves: The Little Theatre Movement and the American Audience* (Carbondale: Southern Illinois University Press, 2004).

13. It is very difficult to assess the quality of locally produced art or to determine whether any of the local "artists" were "professionals," i.e., at least partly self-supporting, but descriptions of

the more celebrated artists help clarify these questions. Ann E. Marshall, Mary H. Brennan, Juliet Martin, *The Heard Museum: History & Collections*, rev. ed. (Phoenix: Heard Museum, 2002); Michelle M. Bayes, "Collecting Culture: A History of the Heard Museum, 1929–1999" (master's thesis, Arizona State University, 2000); McFarland, "A Power for Good," 93–95; Horton, *Economic, Political, and Social Survey*, 258–60; John P. Andrews and Todd W. Bostwick, *Desert Farmers at the River's Edge: The Hohokam and Pueblo Grande*, 2nd ed. (Phoenix: Pueblo Grande Museum and Archaeological Park, 2000), 73; *Teacher's Guide to the Phoenix Museum*, 26; Whitney Chadwick, et al., *American Dreamer: The Art of Philip C. Curtis* (New York: Hudson Hills Press, 1999), 26. One example of local work was the Arts and Crafts Studio advertised in *Phoenix Directory, 1909*, 432.

14. Quotation from Lykes, "Phoenix Women," 240, note 3. McFarland, "A Power for Good," 36, 61–62, 58–61, 74–80; Lykes, "Phoenix Women," 42–44; and "A Short History of Carnegie Corporation's Library Program," http://www.carnegie.org/reporter/07/library/shorthistory_low.html (accessed 28 August 2005).

15. *Phoenix Directory, 1909*, 25–26; *What to See in Phoenix* (Phoenix: Chamber of Commerce, 1917), 13; *Phoenix Directory, 1925* (Phoenix: Arizona Directory Company, 1925), 117–18; *Phoenix, Arizona: The New Winter Playground* (Phoenix: Chamber of Commerce, 1929), 7; Orme Lewis, interview by Phoenix History Project, 13 December 1977, transcript, 2–3, PHPC; *AR*, 6 April 1991, B1; Bradford Luckingham, *Minorities in Phoenix: A Profile of Mexican American, Chinese American, and African American Communities, 1860–1992* (Tucson: University of Arizona Press, 1994), 133–37, 143–44. Segregation also existed in other Valley schools, *AR*, 14 April 1991, E2.

16. Michael Kammen, *American Culture, American Tastes: Social Change and the 20th Century* (New York: Knopf, 1999), 3–46, esp. 22.

17. *Phoenix, New Winter Playground*, 5, 24, 30; Reynolds, *Golden Days of Theaters*, 59–61, 84; and Newton Rosenzweig, interview, 5–6. The Phoenix amusement park differed from those in east in that it had no streetcar connection and no rides.

18. *Phoenix, New Winter Playground*, 3; the Thunderbirds were young men, generally less interested in formal activities of the Chamber of Commerce, who organized the Open and other sporting events to advertise the city. Orme Lewis, interview by Phoenix History Project, 13 December 1977, transcript, 28, PHPC; Harry Rosenzweig, interview by Phoenix History Project, tape recording, 29 July 1976, PHPC; Robert Nelson, "Par Tee On!" *Phoenix New Times*, 18 January 2001, http://www.phoenixnewtimes.com/Issues/2001-01-18/news/feature_print.html (accessed 7 Feb. 2005).

19. Quotations from *AR*, 2 May 1915, 2. Further indicating baseball's importance is the fact that the club president was E. L. O'Malley, one of the city's elite; Jeb Stuart Rosebrook, "Diamonds in the Desert: Professional Baseball in Arizona and the Desert Southwest, 1915–1958" (PhD diss., Arizona State University, 1999), 122.

20. Rosebrook, "Diamonds," 53, 64, 85, 135.

21. Ibid., 44 fn. 33, 123; Bob Jacobsen, "A Man for All Seasons," http://www.asu.edu/alumni/vision/01V05N01/cover16.htm (accessed 22 September 2005); Robert A. Trennert, Jr., *The Phoenix Indian School: Forced Assimilation in Arizona, 1891–1935* (Norman: University of Oklahoma Press, 1988), 128–31.

22. *Phoenix Directory, 1909*, 27; *What to See in Phoenix*, 9; Reynolds, *Golden Days of Theater*, 58–74, 88–93; "The Phoenix Fox Theater, with Photos and History," http://www.acmeron.com/puhs/puhs_page_5.htm (accessed 29 June 2005); and Luckingham, *Minorities*, 161.

23. Horton, *Economic, Political, and Social Survey*, 262–64; Johnson, *Phoenix*, 113, 203.

24. *Phoenix Directory, 1925*, 120–23; *Phoenix Directory, 1935* (Phoenix: Arizona Directory Company, 1935), 31–36; *Arizona Blue Book, 1929–30*, (Phoenix: Secretary of State, 1930) 146–47. The Luis H. Cordova Papers, 1936-1990, at Arizona State University, contain materials relating to organizations and protests against unequal treatment.

25. See previously cited directories; Jeffrey Charles, *Service Clubs in American Society: Rotary, Kiwanis, and Lions* (Urbana: University of Illinois Press, 1993); "Organization of the Rotary Club of Phoenix Arizona," http://www.rotaryhistoryfellowship.org/clubs/cities/clubs/100phoenix.htm (accessed 27 August 2005); "Kiwanis History, 1914–1917," http://www.scottsbluffkiwanisclub.org/history.html (accessed 27 August 2005); and *AR*, 22 November 1942, 2–5; Osselaer, *Winning Their Place*, 73–79.

26. Religious organizations are listed in *Phoenix Directory, 1909*, 23–25; *What to See in Phoenix*, 12; *Phoenix Directory, 1925*, 119–20; *Phoenix Directory, 1935*, 30–31; and *Phoenix Directory, 1940* (Phoenix; Arizona Directory Company, 1940), 29–30.

27. County-level religious membership data comes from the religious censuses taken by the U.S. Census Bureau in 1906, 1916, 1926, and 1936. The data and citation information are online in the American Religion Data Archive, http://www.thearda.com/Archive/Files/Descriptions/BAINCITY.asp (accessed 29 August 2005). The figures for church membership as a percentage of the population are a linear interpolation of census figures for the county population thirteen years and over for the years 1900–40. Mormons averaged 11 percent of the county data, but they concentrated heavily in the East Valley, esp. Mesa, and a 1940 religious survey of Phoenix suggests that they constituted probably about 2 percent of the Phoenix population. Data reported in Horton, *Economic, Political, and Social Survey*, 253–54. African American churches are discussed in David R. Dean and Jean A. Reynolds, *African American Historic Property Survey* (Phoenix: City of Phoenix, Historic Preservation Office, 2004), 21–24.

28. McClintock, *Phoenix in the Great Salt River Valley*, 3.

29. Quotations from Luckingham, *Minorities*, 136, and Horton, *Economic, Political, and Social Survey*, 105. On issues of identity and perception see, for example, George J. Sanchez, *Becoming Mexican American: Ethnicity, Culture, and Identity in Chicano Los Angeles, 1900–1945* (New York: Oxford University Press, 1993); Ronald Takaki, *Strangers from a Different Shore: A History of Asian Americans* (New York: Penguin Books, 1989); and Keith Jerome Crudup, "African Americans in Arizona: A Twentieth-Century History" (PhD diss., Arizona State University, 1998).

30. The benign view of Indians is typified by picture captions in *Phoenix and the Interesting Salt River Valley* (Phoenix: Chamber of Commerce, 1927), 18, and comments in McClintock, *Phoenix in the Great Salt River Valley*, 3. Other Phoenix ethnic groups are discussed in Luckingham, *Minorities*, 25–47, 97–111, 139–56; Dean and Reynolds, *African American Survey*, passim; and Eric Walz, "The Issei Community in Maricopa County: Development and Persistence in the Valley of the Sun, 1900–1940," *The Journal of Arizona History*, 38 (Spring 1997): 1–22.

31. Keith Blakeman, "Divided Opportunity in a Migrant City: Phoenix, Arizona, 1910–1916," unpublished seminar paper, Arizona State University, 1999. This study rests on a 50 percent sample of the 1910 population census, tracked to city blocks and traced through the 1911, 1913, and 1916 city directories.

32. See Emmett McLoughlin, *People's Padre: An Autobiography* (Boston: Beacon Press, 1954), 36;

Adam Diaz, interview by Phoenix History Project, 14 April 1976, transcript, 2, PHPC; and Jacqueline Shoyeb, "Immaculate Change: Phoenix's Oldest Hispanic Church Comes Full Circle," *Devil's Tale*, http://cronkitezine.asu.edu/spring2005/immaculate.html (accessed 9 May 2006).

33. The two classic works, still useful, which deal with change and the governmental and political responses to change in this period are Samuel P. Hays, *Response to Industrialism, 1885–1914* (Chicago: University of Chicago Press, 1995), and Robert H. Wiebe, *The Search for Order, 1877–1920* (New York: Hill and Wang, 1967). Ballard C. Campbell, *The Growth of American Government: Governance from the Cleveland Era to the Present* (Bloomington: Indiana University Press, 1995), 8–82, provides a good context for understanding the operations of governments; Jon C. Teaford, *The Unheralded Triumph: City Government in America, 1870–1900* (Baltimore: Johns Hopkins University Press, 1984), includes an excellent analysis of the connection between socioeconomic groups and governmental positions; Martin L. Schiesel, *The Politics of Efficiency: Municipal Administration and Reform in America, 1800–1920* (Berkeley: University of California Press, 1977), and Bradley Robert Rice, *Progressive Cities: The Commission Government Movement in America, 1901–1920* (Austin: University of Texas Press, 1977), analyze commission and manager forms of government; in *Reform in Detroit: Hazen S. Pingree and Urban Politics* (New York: Oxford University Press, 1969) Melvin G. Holli made an important distinction between structural and social reformers; while Samuel P. Hays, "The Politics of Reform in Municipal Government in the Progressive Era," *Pacific Northwest Quarterly*, 55 (Oct. 1964): 157–169, remains essential reading for understanding this reform movement.

34. Janus Associates, "Commerce in Phoenix, 1870 to 1942: A Context for Preserving Historic Properties" (Phoenix: State Historic Preservation Office, 1989)," 6; *AR*, 5 March 1907, 1; *AR*, 16 June 1910, 2; *AR*, 16 December 1910, 4; and Daniel C. Davis, "Phoenix, Arizona, 1907–1913," essay, 1976, Arizona Historical Foundation 12, 72–73. Geoffrey Mawn provides a detailed narrative of city services in "Phoenix, Arizona: Central City of the Southwest, 1870–1920" (Ph.D. diss., Arizona State University, 1979), 360–87, 401–4.

35. See the earlier discussion of liquor control in the section on "Making a Moral City."

36. Quoted in Ware, "Alcohol, Temperance, and Prohibition in Arizona," 215. For the city officials and their occupations see *Phoenix Directory for 1899–1900* (Phoenix: Phoenix Directory Company, 1899–1900) and *Phoenix Directory, 1909*.

37. See Rice, *Progressive Cities*, passim.

38. *AR*, 3 April 1915, 4; although he also notes that Farish caused some of the problems, Luckingham, *Phoenix*, 69–73, accepts this perspective; Amy Bridges, *Morning Glories: Municipal Reform in the Southwest* (Princeton: Princeton University Press, 1997), 81–82; Richard S. Childs, *The First 50 Years of the Council-Manager Plan of Municipal Government* (New York: National Municipal League, 1965), 91, describes Phoenix as the "black sheep" of the flock; Leonard D. White, *The City Manager* (Chicago: University of Chicago Press, 1927), 219–20; Leonard E. Goodall, "Phoenix: Reformers at Work," in Leonard E. Goodall, ed., *Urban Politics in the Southwest* (Tempe, AZ: Arizona State University, 1967), 110–27; and Mawn, "Phoenix, Arizona," 419–48.

39. Horton *Economic, Political, and Social Survey*, 198, 193; *AR*, 22 November 1942, 2–7. Criticism of the Phoenix government often included the term *corruption*, but in many instances without a clear meaning or directly addressing the various possible meanings.

40. Horton, *Economic, Political, and Social Survey*, 194–95, 198; "The History of the Phoenix

Fire Department," http://phoenix.gov/FIRE/history.html (accessed 2 September 2005); "Pre-1950 Historic Residential Resources Reconnaissance Survey Report" (Phoenix: City of Phoenix Planning Department, 1990), 58; Douglas E. Kupel, *Fuel for Growth: Water and Arizona's Urban Environment* (Tucson: University of Arizona Press, 2003), 95–100, 109–17; Karen L. Smith, "Community Growth and Water Policy," in Johnson, *Phoenix in the Twentieth Century*, 157–59.

41. *Historic Homes of Phoenix: An Architectural & Preservation Guide*, Cooper/Robert Architects (Phoenix: City of Phoenix, 1992), 60; "Commerce in Phoenix," 9, 12; Julie Miller, "The Phoenix Planning Department," unpublished seminar paper, 1995, and Elizabeth Burns, "Urban Planning Within the Salt River Valley," in Charles Sargent, ed., *Metro Arizona* (Scottsdale, AZ: Biffington Books, 1988), 166; and Larissa Larsen and David Alameddin, "The Evolution of Early Phoenix: Valley Business Elite, Land Speculation, and the Emergence of Planning," *Journal of Planning History* 6 (May 2007): 102–9.

42. On liquor, see Ware, "Alcohol, Temperance, and Prohibition in Arizona," 286–87, 318–28; Burnham, *Bad Habits*, 154–61, discusses the context for gambling; and Horton, *Economic, Political, and Social Survey*, 241, notes the debate over legalization in Arizona.

43. Horton, *Economic, Political, and Social Survey*, 242–43, provides a detailed description of conditions and the system, including long excerpts from newspaper articles; Charles Winick and Paul M. Kinsie, *The Lively Commerce: Prostitution in the United States* (Chicago: Quadrangle Books, 1971), 155–62, 254–53, discuss prostitution in the interwar years and the role of the military; Joel Best, *Controlling Vice: Regulating Brothel Prostitution in St. Paul, 1865–1883* (Columbus: Ohio State University Press, 1998), esp. 4–5, discusses a system whose operation and rationale are reflected in Phoenix; while David J. Pivar, *Purity and Hygiene: Women, Prostitution, and the "American Plan," 1900–1930* (Westport, CN: Greenwood Press, 2002), provides an excellent context for understanding the larger issues.

44. *Arizona Business Directory and Gazetteer, 1881* (San Francisco: W. C. Disturnell, 1881), 83; Johnson, *Phoenix*, 44; *Salt River Valley: Its Attractions for the Immigrant, the Capitalist, the Invalid* (Phoenix: Maricopa County Immigration Union, 1894), 8. Cf. Bradford Luckingham, "The Promotion of Phoenix," in Johnson, *Phoenix*, 83–88.

45. Johnson, *Phoenix*, 76; Davis, "Phoenix, Arizona, 1907–1913," 44–45; and for tourist estimates see *Phoenix Arizona: City of Progress* (Phoenix: Board of Trade, 1914), 1; *Phoenix, Great Salt River Valley*, 4; *Phoenix—The Salt River Valley* (Phoenix: Santa Fe Railroad, 1916).

46. The first prominent winter visitor was *New York Tribune* editor Whitelaw Reid, in 1895–96, who rented the house of Roland Rossen. Johnson, *Phoenix*, 52. On early resorts see Charles S. Sargent, Jr., "Evolution of Metro Phoenix," in James W. Elmore, ed., *A Guide to the Architecture of Metro Phoenix* (Phoenix: Phoenix Publishing, 1983), 17; the changing approach is evident in *Phoenix—The Salt River Valley* and in *What to See in Phoenix*; and on the 1920s see Waslif, "Health Seekers," 86–87, 81.

47. *Phoenix, Winter Never Comes* (Phoenix: Phoenix Arizona Club, 1927), 31, 5; *Phoenix, Summer Day All Winter* (Phoenix: Arizona Club, 1927), 1; *Phoenix, New Winter Playground*, 5; *AR*, 19 February 2004, E1, E3; *AR*, 13 September 2004, E1; Charles S. Stevenson, "*We Met at Camelback!*" (Scottsdale, AZ: Arizona Desert Publishing Company, 1968); Peter Aleshire, "The Old Kid on the Block," *Phoenix*, February 2004, 101–5; Sylvia Evans Byrnes, *Jokake Inn: One of the Earliest Desert Resorts* (Arizona?: n.d.); Dixie Legler, *Frank Lloyd Wright; The Western Work* (San Francisco: Chronicle Books, 1999), 19–23. Dude ranches were not located immediately near Phoenix; the closest were in Wickenberg, with others in Prescott

and Tucson: *Arizona: Information Data of Principal Cities and Towns, Industries, Hotels and Auto Courts, Guest and Dude Ranches, Summer and Winter Resorts, Sanatoriums...* (Phoenix: Phoenix Arizona Club, 1931), 7. On accommodations see Sargent, "Evolution of Metro Phoenix," 17; Horton, *Economic, Political, and Social Survey,* 134–35.

48. "Royal Palms Resort and Spa: A Distinguished History," http://www.royalpalmshotel.com/ press_release/history.pdf (accessed 3 January 2006); Johnson, *Phoenix,* 99–100; *AR,* 13 September 2004, E1–2; Stevenson, *"We Met at Camelback!,"* 205–12.

49. Horton presents economic and travel data, the comprehensive promotional materials, and the chamber's strategy in *Economic, Political, and Social Survey,* 121–38, 145; Thomas Charles Cooper, "*Arizona Highways:* From Engineering Pamphlet to Prestige Magazine" (master's thesis, University of Arizona, 1973), 21–31; *Phoenix, New Winter Playground,* 31, discusses transportation; and chair of the chamber's advertising committee, Al M. Zellmer, presents data on visitors, economic impact, and travel through 1941 in "Welcome Stranger!," *Arizona Highways,* August 1943, 20, 21, 59.

50. For discussions of the impact see Jay Edward Niebur, "The Social and Economic Effect of the Great Depression on Phoenix, Arizona, 1929–1934" (master's thesis, Arizona State University, 1967), and the bibliography in William S. Collins, *New Deal in Arizona* (Phoenix: Arizona State Parks Board, 1999), 422–28. Collins reports basic economic data in *New Deal in Arizona,* 22, 25; Thomas E. Sheridan notes New Deal expenditures in *Arizona: A History* (Tucson: University of Arizona Press, 1995), 255.

51. Carl Abbott provides a useful overview of "The Federal Presence" in *The Oxford History of the American West,* Clyde A. Milner, II, Carol A. O'Connor, and Martha A. Sandweiss, eds. (New York: Oxford University Press, 1994), 469–99.

52. Quotations in Horton, *Economic, Political, and Social Survey,* 223, 145. Nor were these just temporary agencies: see the two-page list of agencies in *Phoenix Directory, 1940,* 25–26. Luckingham, *Phoenix,* 104, claims that all spending totaled $10 million in 1937, but Horton, 221, 223, claims that in 1940 spending on equipment alone was $10 million.

53. Horton, *Economic, Political, and Social Survey,* 182; figures calculated from Horton, 181, 186–88; Ruth M. Reinhold, *Sky Pioneering: Arizona in Aviation History* (Tucson: University of Arizona Press, 1982), 191–93. The federal government spent $20 million just on highway construction in Arizona, 1933–39, Melissa Keane and J. Simon Bruder, *Good Roads Everywhere: A History of Road Building in Arizona* (Phoenix: Environmental Planning Section, Arizona Department of Transportation, 2003), 50, http://www.azdot.gov/Highways/EEG/ documents/files/cultural/good_roads/gdrds_chapter_4.pdf (accessed 17 June 2005).

54. *Annual Report, Housing Authority of the City of Phoenix, AZ, 1961* (Phoenix: Phoenix Housing Authority, 1961), 1–2; McLoughlin, *People's Padre,* 53–57. See Bruce I. Zachary, "The Effects of the Federal Public Housing Movement upon Phoenix, Arizona, 1937–1949" (master's thesis, Arizona State University, 1997). Collins describes homestead projects in *New Deal in Arizona,* 339–41.

55. Quotation from Horton, *Economic, Political, and Social Survey,* 181, which lists the number of building permits in table 27, 180. Kenneth T. Jackson, *Crabgrass Frontier: The Suburbanization of the United States* (New York: Oxford University Press, 1985), 195–97, explains the basic impact of HOLC, and Collins, *New Deal in Arizona,* 326–37, discusses its impact in the state.

56. Carl Bimson, "Thirty Years of Progress in Arizona Home Financing," *Arizona Review of Business and Public Administration,* (February 1963), 12: 1–4; Larry Schweikart, *A History of Banking in Arizona* (Tucson: University of Arizona Press, 1982), 104; Jackson, *Crabgrass*

Frontier, 204–5; permits are listed in Horner, *Economic, Political, and Social Survey*, 181; data on home construction and ownership is from the U.S. Department of Commerce, Bureau of the Census, *Sixteenth Census of the United States: 1940, Housing*, vol. 2 (Washington: Government Printing Office, 1943), 99; and Kristen C. Pumo reports the FHA mortgage levels in "The Home Builders Association of Central Arizona and the FHA: Phoenix Residential Housing, 1920–1970" (master's thesis, Arizona State University, 2002), 32. Bimson, "Arizona Home Financing," 2, reported that the 1934 survey showed ownership at 28 percent, which may mean that ownership declined after 1930 and that HOLC improved the levels.

57. Jackson, *Crabgrass Frontier*, 205; Dolores Hayden, *Building Suburbia: Green Fields and Urban Growth, 1820–2000* (New York: Pantheon, 2003), 123; Marc A. Weiss, *The Rise of the Community Builders: The American Real Estate Industry and Urban Land Planning* (New York: Columbia University Press, 1987); Greg Hise, *Magnetic Los Angeles: Planning the Twentieth-Century Metropolis* (Baltimore: Johns Hopkins University Press, 1997), 65–85; and cf. Collins, *New Deal in Arizona*, 362.

58. Horton, *Economic, Political, and Social Survey*, 181; Pumo, "Home Builders Association," 36–40; Collins, *New Deal in Arizona*, 355.

59. *Fairview Place Historic District, 1928–48* (Phoenix: City of Phoenix Historic Preservation Office, n.d.), 3–4; *Cheery Lynn Historic District, 1928–45* (Phoenix: City of Phoenix Historic Preservation Office, n.d.), 5; Collins, *New Deal in Arizona*, 364; Pumo, "Home Builders Association," 35. On postwar changes see chapter 7, below.

60. William H. Jervey, "When the Banks Closed: Arizona's Bank Holiday of 1933," *Arizona and the West*, 10 (Summer 1968): 127–52; Schweikert, *Banking in Arizona*, 83–108; "Commerce in Phoenix," 11; Carl A. Bimson, *Transformation in the Desert: The Story of Arizona's Valley National Bank* (New York: Newcomen Society, 1962); and Horton, *Economic, Political, and Social Survey*, 171, 174.

61. Arizona Academy, *Do Agricultural Problems Threaten Arizona's Total Economy?* Tenth Arizona Town Hall (Phoenix: Arizona Town Hall, 1967), 82–85; Collins, *New Deal in Arizona*, 189–91, 193–97; Sheridan, *Arizona*, 257–58, explains the profitable and increasingly important role of cotton; Robert C. Balling, Jr., and Sandra W. Brazel, "The Myth of Increasing Moisture Levels in Phoenix," in Robert J. Schmidli, "Climate of Phoenix, Arizona: An Abridged On-Line Version of NOAA Technical Memorandum NWS WR-177," rev. ed. (Phoenix: Weather Service Forecast Office, online version by R.S. Cerveny, Office of Climatology, Arizona State University, December, 1996), http://geography.asu.edu/cerveny/phxwx.htm (accessed 17 July 2005); and data from the Phoenix Weather Bureau in *AR*, 22 November 1942, 2–6. Annual Phoenix temperatures were two degrees warmer after 1924 than before, but temperatures were fairly consistent from 1925 to 1940. The sole exception was 1934, but the warmer temperatures came January to June, not during the summer.

62. These conclusions reflect data and my analysis of the data reported in Horton, *Economic, Political, and Social Survey*, 143–47.

63. Ibid., 149–50; and "Commerce in Phoenix," 12.

64. Horton, *Economic, Political, and Social Survey*, 153–55.

65. "15th November Anniversary Symposium," *Phoenix Magazine*, November 1980, 98.

66. On air-conditioning see Gail Cooper, *Air Conditioning America: Air Conditioning and the Controlled Environment, 1900–1960* (Baltimore: Johns Hopkins University Press, 1998); and Ray Arsenault, "The End of the Long Hot Summer: The Air Conditioner and Southern

Culture," in Raymond A. Mohl, *Searching for the Sunbelt: Historical Perspectives on a Region* (Knoxville: University of Tennessee Press, 1990), 176–211. On air-conditioning in Phoenix during this period see Sargent, "Evolution of Metro Phoenix," 17; Jerry Brisco, "The Department Store Industry in Phoenix, 1895–1940" (master's thesis, Arizona State University, 2000), 129–30; George H. N. Luhrs, Jr., *The Geo. H. N. Luhrs Family in Phoenix and Arizona, 1847–1984* (Phoenix: Jean Stroud Crane, 1988), 177; and *AR*, 19 August 1943, 1. According to Martin L. Thornburg and Paul M. Thornburg, a three- to five-ton refrigeration unit cost $2,000 to $3,000, *Cooling for the Arizona Home*, Extension Circular no. 105, University of Arizona, Agricultural Extension Service (Tucson: University of Arizona, 1939), 16.

67. Milton G. Sanders, "Not So Crazy with the Heat," *Arizona Highways*, August 1943, 34–37, 54; Bob Cunningham, "The Box That Broke the Barrier: The Swamp Cooler Comes to Southern Arizona," *Journal of Arizona History*, 26 (Summer 1985): 145–62; Bimson, "Arizona Home Financing," 4; and the pamphlet by Thornburg and Thornburg, *Cooling for the Arizona Home*, 13, describes how to make a simple unit and the prices. Prominent early experimenters with coolers in Phoenix were Frank Harmonson of Southwest Manufacturing and Supply Company and Oscar Palmer. Paul W. Pollock, *Arizona's Men of Achievement*, 6 vols. (Phoenix: Paul W. Pollock, 1958), 1:246, 280. Milton Sanders explained that around 1936 or 1937 the utility company he worked for sent out descriptions of how to make a cooler, and he claimed that Palmer opposed using coolers because of the humidity, in "15th Anniversary Symposium," 98.

68. Quotations from *AR*, 22 November 1942, 2:5; Horton, *Economic, Political and Social Survey*, 154, 181. Thornburg and Thornburg, *Cooling for the Arizona Home*, 13; Horton, *Economic, Political and Social Survey*, 154, 184; Sanders, "Not So Crazy," 54, estimates that between twenty and twenty-eight thousand of the thirty thousand power company customers had units; Cunningham, "The Box," 162; Oscar Palmer, interview by Phoenix History Project, tape recording, 17 January 1975, PHPC; Chuck Rayburn, "He Tamed the Searing Summer Sun," *PG*, 14 August 1973; and "Adam Duane Goettl," in Pollock, *Arizona's Men of Achievement*, 1:45; and Bill Goettl, interview by Phoenix History Project, tape recording, 7 April 1977, PHPC.

69. Frank L. Snell, interview by Phoenix History Project, transcript, 13–27, 25 May 1977, 28 September 1978, and 7 December 1978, PHPC; G. Wesley Johnson, "Directing Elites: Catalysts for Social Change," *Phoenix in the Twentieth Century*, 23–24; Johnson, *Phoenix*, 99–109; and Luhrs, *Luhrs Family in Phoenix*, 156–59, 165–77.

70. On Heard see Earl Zarbin, *All the Time a Newspaper: The First 100 Years of the Arizona Republic* (Phoenix: Arizona Republic, 1990); "Charles Albert Stauffer," in *Arizona's Men of Achievement*, 1:24; "W. W. Knorpp," in Pollock, *Arizona's Men of Achievement*, 1:26; Dean Smith, *The Goldwaters of Arizona* (Flagstaff, AZ: Northland Press, 1986), esp. 164–75; and Peter Iverson, *Barry Goldwater: Native Arizonan* (Norman: University of Oklahoma Press, 1997) 14–15, 28.

71. Walter Bimson, interview by Phoenix History Project, tape recording, 27 December 1975, PHPC; Carl Bimson, interview by Phoenix History Project, tape recording, 23 July 1976, PHPC; a series of articles in *AR*, 22–25 October 1961; "Walter Reed Bimson," in Pollock, *Arizona's Men of Achievement*, 1:14; "Carl A. Bimson," in Pollock, *Arizona's Men of Achievement*, 1:16; Keith Monroe, "Bank Knight in Arizona," *The American Magazine*, November 1945, 24–30; and Schweikert, *Banking in Arizona*, 84–90, 102–6.

72. For Snell's basic biography see *AR*, 7 September 1994, 1; *Phoenix Gazette*, 7 September 1994, 1; Paul W. Pollock, *American Biographical Encyclopedia: Profiles of Prominent Personalities, Arizona Edition*, 6 vols. (Phoenix: P. W. Pollock, 1967–81, 1:32. More details are in Snell interview transcript, with details about with business contacts on 20, 46, 50, 74, and 138.

73. Quotations from Snell interview transcript, 41, 42. *AR*, 22 November 1942, 2–5.

74. Quotations from Snell interview transcript, 45, 46, and Newton Rosenzweig interview transcript, 19–20. See also Snell interview transcript, 14–16, 32–37, 75, 80–82; Judith Anne Jacobson, "The Phoenix Chamber of Commerce: A Case Study of Economic Development in Central Arizona" (master's thesis, Arizona State University, 1992), 1–19; George Luhrs on the Arizona Club in *Luhrs Family in Phoenix*, 143, 177; and biographical sketches, e.g., Charlie Korrick, in *AR*, 3 November 1959, 20.

75. Quotations from Zellmer, "Welcome Stranger!," 23; and "City of Homes," *Arizona Highways*, August 1943, 26. And in the same issue of this magazine, Harry L. Crockett, "Of Schools and Learning," 12–15, and "Parks and Playgrounds," 38–41.

76. Quotations from Horton, *Economic, Political, and Social Survey*, 158.

77. "Phoenix 1993," *Arizona Highways*, August 1943, 43.

78. This reflects my analysis of wage, payroll, and employee data for various groups as reported in Horton, *Economic, Political, and Social Survey*, 143–55; compared with information in U.S. Bureau of the Census, *Historical Statistics of the United States, Colonial Times to 1957* (Washington, DC: Government Printing Office, 1961), 168.

79. Bimson, "Arizona Home Financing," 2; Horton, *Economic, Political, and Social Survey*, 183, 184; and McLoughlin, *People's Padre*, 41–42, 53.

PART II

1. *AR*, 22 November 1942, 1–11.

CHAPTER 4

1. Quotation from Gerald D. Nash, *World War II and the West: Reshaping the Economy* (Lincoln: University of Nebraska Press, 1990), 1. See Roger W. Lotchin, *Fortress California, 1910–1961: From Warfare to Welfare* (New York: Oxford University Press, 1992); a series of articles on the war's impact by Arthur C. Verge, Marilynn S. Johnson, Paul Rhode, and Roger Lotchin in *Pacific Historical Review*, 63 (August 1994); Carl Abbott, *The Metropolitan Frontier: Cities in the Modern American West* (Tucson: University of Arizona Press, 1994), 3–29; and Gerald D. Nash, *The Federal Landscape: An Economic History of the Twentieth-Century West* (Tucson: University of Arizona Press, 1999), 41–54.

2. Nash, *World War II and the West*, 7–17, 165–75.

3. A chemical engineer trained at MIT, Litchfield started with Goodyear in 1900, two years after it began, and his work on tread designs, multiple-ply cord for tires, and a pneumatic truck tire were important for the company's success. P. W. Litchfield, *Industrial Voyage: My Life as an Industrial Lieutenant* (Garden City, NY: Doubleday, 1954), 159–62; Scott Solliday, *Chandler: Pioneer City of the New West* (Chandler, AZ: Chandler Historical Society, 1996), 32–34.

4. Quotations from Litchfield, *Industrial Voyage*, 164, 324; discussion, 141–44. *AR*, 15 March 1970, K1; *The Wingfoot Clan*, 20 March 1959, Goodyear newspaper at Arizona State University, Architecture Library, Litchfield Park Collection (hereinafter LPC); Litchfield, *Industrial Voyage*, 227; "About Goodyear," http://www.ci.goodyear.az.us/index.asp?NID=384 (accessed 12 December 2005); "Litchfield Park, Arizona," http://www.arizonan.com/litchfieldpark/ (accessed 12 December 2005); "The Wigwam Resort," http://www.asu.edu/caed/HCDE/herberger/publications/designlink/Vo13n03.html (accessed 12 December 2005).

5. Litchfield, *Industrial Voyage*, 137–39, 177–78, 245–46; "Litchfield, Paul W.," *Encyclopædia Britannica*, 2005, http://search.eb.com/eb/article-9048505 (accessed 13 December 2005);

"Modern Airships," http://www.centennialofflight.gov/essay/Lighter_than_air/modern_airships/LTA18.htm (accessed 18 December 2005); "Airships and Balloons in the WWII Period," http://www.centennialofflight.gov/essay/Lighter_than_air/Airships_in_WWII/LTA10.htm (accessed 18 December 2005); "Our History," http://www.goodyear.com/corporate/history/history_overview.html (accessed 13 December 2005). President (1926–40) and chairman of the board (1930–58), Litchfield also instituted "welfare capitalism" as Goodyear policy, with employee health and education benefits, stock sharing, recreation, and bicameral employee representation; see Litchfield, *Industrial Voyage*, passim.

6. Lichtfield, *Industrial Voyage*, 286.

7. Brad Melton and Dean Smith, eds., *Arizona Goes to War: The Home Front and the Front Lines during World War II* (Tucson: University of Arizona Press, 2003), 11, 105, 111, 161; *AR*, 22 November 1942, 1–2; "About Goodyear." These workers were housed in the new town of Goodyear, as Southwest Cotton Company sold its land—and the original town of Goodyear—in the southeast valley; Solliday, *Chandler*, 34.

8. *AR*, 22 November 1942, 1–5, 2–2; on temporary housing see William S. Collins, *The Emerging Metropolis: Phoenix, 1944–1973* (Phoenix: Arizona State Parks Board, 2004), 3, 265, and *Annual Report, Housing Authority of the City of Phoenix, AZ, 1961* (Phoenix: City of Phoenix, 1961), box 4, folder 46, in Samuel Mardian, Jr., Papers, Arizona State University (hereinafter SMJP); Melton and Smith, *Arizona Goes to War*, xxi, 11, and many stories of increased wages, e.g., 111; and Larry Schweikart, *A History of Banking in Arizona* (Tucson: University of Arizona Press, 1982), 108. The Allison Steel Company was the only prewar firm that engaged in any substantial war-related manufacturing; *AR*, 22 November 1942, 1–7; Arthur Horton, *An Economic, Political, and Social Survey of Phoenix and the Valley of the Sun* (Tempe, AZ: Southside Progress, 1941), 153.

9. *AR*, 22 November 1942, 2–2.

10. Ruth Reinhold, *Sky Pioneering: Arizona in Aviation History* (Tucson: University of Arizona Press, 1982), 191–94; Reinhold, interview with Phoenix History Project, 25 August 1976, transcript, 12–13, PHPC; "Civilian Pilot Training Program," http://www.centennialofflight.gov/essay/GENERAL_AVIATION/civilian_pilot_training/GA20.htm (accessed 19 December 2005); Melton and Smith, *Arizona Goes to War*, 62–64, 98–101; *AR*, 22 November 1942, 1:10, 2:4; Paul W. Pollock, *Arizona's Men of Achievement*, 6 vols. (Phoenix: Paul W. Pollock, 1958), 1:114, 194; and David A. Walker, "Where a Hollywood Contact Helped Win a War," *AOPA*, April 1984, http://www.ci.mesa.az.us/airport/falconhollywood.asp (accessed 19 December 2005). Southwest directors had wanted to label all of their airfields Thunderbird, but the British insisted that the Mesa facility be named Falcon, to reflect British tradition.

11. *AR*, 15 January 1941; Melton and Smith, *Arizona Goes to War*, 11, 98–99, 190–93; Bradford Luckingham, *Phoenix: The History of a Southwestern Metropolis* (Tucson: University of Arizona Press, 1989), 136–38; and Matthew McCoy, "The Desert Metropolis: Image Building and the Growth of Phoenix, 1940–1965" (PhD diss., Arizona State University, 2000), 51–55. During the war the army also established many auxiliary airfields near Luke. Paul Freeman, "Abandoned & Little-Known Airfields: Arizona—Southwest Phoenix area," http://www.airfields-freeman.com/AZ/Airfields_AZ_Phoenix_SW.htm (accessed 10 January 2006).

12. McCoy, "Desert Metropolis," 51–55; Melton and Smith, *Arizona Goes to War*, 89–91, 98–101; "Williams Campus: History," http://www.cgc.maricopa.edu/wc/williamshist.shtml (accessed 20 December 2005).

13. Frank L. Snell, interview by Phoenix History Project, 28 September 1978, transcript, 49,

quotation from 62, PHPC; Ross R. Rice, *Carl Hayden: Builder of the American West* (Lanham, MD: University Press of America, 1994), esp. 49–53, 173; Jack L. August, *Vision in the Desert: Carl Hayden and Hydropolitics in the American Southwest* (Fort Worth: Texas Christian University Press, 1999), does an excellent job discussing Hayden's involvement in water issues, and Bruce Babbitt's introduction to that volume offers useful insights into the nature of Hayden's political service. Hayden also helped get three bases placed in the Tucson area, plus others elsewhere in the state. Although only in his first term, Arizona's other senator, Ernest McFarland, also aided the state's pursuit of federal largess. James Elton McMillan, Jr., *Ernest W. McFarland: Majority Leader of the United States Senate, Governor, and Chief Justice of the State of Arizona: A Biography* (Prescott, AZ: Sharlot Hall Museum Press, 2004), 96–97.

14. Information on Webb is drawn from various sources, including Arelo Sederberg and John F. Lawrence, "Del Webb, the Bashful Barnum," *Los Angeles Times WEST Magazine* (14 September 1969), 16–20; Steve Bergsman, "Del Webb," *Phoenix* (August 1991), 81–89; Tom Chauncey, *Tom Chauncey: A Memoir* (Tempe, AZ: Arizona State University Libraries, 1989), 130; Harry Rosenzweig, interview by Phoenix History Project, 29 July 1976, tape recording, PHPC; *AR*, 5 July 1974; Del Webb Biography file, Hayden Collection, Arizona State University; and Margaret Finnerty, *Del Webb: A Man, A Company* (Flagstaff, AZ: Heritage Publishers, 1991).

15. Quotation from Horton, *Economic, Political, and Social Survey*, 181. Finnerty, *Del Webb*, 25–34, notes the various projects.

16. E. V. O'Malley, interview by Phoenix History Project, 12 July 1976, transcript, 21, PHPC.

17. George W. Howard, "The Desert Training Center/ California-Arizona Maneuver Area," *Journal of Arizona History*, 26 (Autumn 1985): 273–94; Melton and Smith, *Arizona Goes to War*, 95–97, 193–95.

18. *AR*, 1 December 1942, 1, 4. Earl Zarbin, *All the Time a Newspaper: The First 100 Years of the Arizona Republic* (Phoenix: Arizona Republic, 1990), 170–73, notes that the military had put part of the city out of bounds in June, a common tactic during World War I. Charles Winick and Paul M. Kinsie, *The Lively Commerce: Prostitution in the United States* (Chicago: Quadrangle Books, 1971), 247–51.

19. *AR*, 1 December 1942, 4.

20. *AR*, 1 December 1942, 1, 4; *AR*, 2 December 1942, quotation on 1. In a 1989 Goldwater Lecture Series roundtable, Barry Goldwater agreed with the "nonprofessional" claim and quipped that more venereal disease came from Glendale High School than from prostitutes. 1989 Goldwater Lecture Series, roundtable, video (in possession of Peter Iverson). On the renewed political interest of businessmen see Snell interview transcript, 80–82.

21. *AR*, 11 December 1942, 1, 2.

22. *AR*, 15–19 December 1942; quotation from *AR*, 15 December 1942, 2; Earl Zarbin, *All the Time a Newspaper: The First 100 Years of the Arizona Republic* (Phoenix: Arizona Republic, 1990), 172; Snell interview transcript, 80–86.

23. Zarbin, *All the Time*, 173; *AR*, 1 May 1943, 1; and Dennis Preisler, "Phoenix, Arizona, During the 1940s: A Decade of Change" (master's thesis, Arizona State University, 1992), 23–39, also summarized in Collins, *Emerging Metropolis*, 46–47.

24. Charles Hyer, "Falcon Field Beginnings," *American Aviation Historical Society Journal* 30 (Fall 1985): 175, http://www.cityofmesa.org/airport/falconfieldbeginnings.asp (accessed 10 January 2006); "Scottsdale Airport History," http://www.ci.scottsdale.az.us/Airport/ History.asp (accessed 10 January 2006); "Historic California Posts; California/Arizona

Maneuver Area (Desert Training Center)," http://www.militarymuseum.org/CAMA. html (accessed 10 January 2006); U.S. Environmental Protection Agency, "Phoenix-Goodyear Airport Area," http://yosemite.epa.gov/r9/sfund/overview.nsf/0/0511a5f2a604 caaa88256ca600721061?OpenDocument#descr (accessed 10 January 2006); *AR*, 2 October 1946, 4; *AR*, 3 October 1946, 1, 3.

25. *AR*, 3 April 1947, 1–2; and Matthew G. McCoy, "Base Instinct: Phoenix and the Fight Over Luke Field, 1946–1948," *Military History of the West*, 35 (2005): 57–76.

26. Al Moriarty reported the hopes for Alcoa in *AR*, 5 September 1945, 1; Collins, *Emerging Metropolis*, 24–25; Nash, *World War II and the West*, 109–121. Even the Communist Party Club of Phoenix supported the continued operation of these plants: *AR*, 5 September 1945, 7.

27. John Shirer, "Shifting Trends in Employment, 1939–1953: Arizona and the United States," *Arizona Business and Economic Review*, 3 (September 1954): 1, 5; quotation from Joseph Stocker, "Phoenix: City Growing in the Sun," *Arizona Highways*, April 1957, 36.

28. On the nature of growth in southwestern cities see Amy Bridges, *Morning Glories: Municipal Reform in the Southwest* (Princeton: Princeton University Press, 1997), 26–29, 158.

29. Melissa Keane and J. Simon Bruder, *Good Roads Everywhere: A History of Road Building in Arizona* (Phoenix: Environmental Planning Section, Arizona Department of Transportation, 2003), 53, 60, http://azdot.gov/Highways/EEG/documents/files/cultural/ good_roads/gdrds_cover_preface_abstract.pdf (accessed 17 June 2005); U.S. Department of Transportation, *America's Highways, 1776–1976: A History of the Federal-Aid Program* (Washington, DC: U.S. Department of Transportation, 1976); and Mark H. Rose, *Interstate: Express Highway Politics, 1941–1956,* (Lawrence, KS: Regents Press of Kansas, 1979); William Graebner, *A History of Retirement: The Meaning and Function of an American Institution, 1885–1978* (New Haven: Yale University Press, 1980); Cindy S. Aron, *Working at Play: A History of Vacations in the United States* (New York: Oxford University Press, 1999); Hal K. Rothman, *Devil's Bargains: Tourism in the Twentieth-Century American West* (Lawrence, KS: University Press of Kansas, 1998); and Edward L. Ullman, "Amenities as a Factor in Regional Growth," *Arizona Business and Economic Review*, 3 (April 1954): 1–6.

30. Judith Anne Jacobson, "The Phoenix Chamber of Commerce: A Case Study of Economic Development in Central Arizona" (master's thesis, Arizona State University, 1992), 44–46; Thomas Charles Cooper, "Arizona Highways: From Engineering Pamphlet to Prestige Magazine" (master's thesis, University of Arizona, 1973), 93, 104. Regular city contributions began in 1950–51 at $20,000, *Annual Report of the Finance Director, 1951* (Phoenix: City of Phoenix, 1951), vi.

31. Up to the 1920s boardinghouses had rooms for working class and temporary residents, but downtown expansion largely eliminated that by the 1950s. The roster of hotels changed over time by additions and subtractions; it also depended on the definition of the term. In 1955 the Phoenix directory listed sixty-four hotels. The 1961 directory included sixty-seven hotels: fifty-six in downtown, four north, one west, five on Van Buren, and one at Sky Harbor Airport. *Mullin-Kille of Phoenix, Arizona, ConSurvey City Directory, 1955* (Phoenix: Mullin-Kille, 1955), 68–69; *Mullin-Kille of Phoenix, Arizona, ConSurvey City Directory, 1961* (Phoenix: Mullin-Kille, 1961), 114 (hereinafter *Phoenix Directory, 1961*); *Analysis of Transient Housing* (Los Angeles: Western Real Estate Research Corp., 1960), 6–13, in box 8, folder 4, SMJP.

32. Al M. Zellmer, "Welcome Stranger!," *Arizona Highways*, August 1943, 22; *AR*, 31 July 1999, SD3; *AR*, 19 February 2004, E1, E3; *AR*, 13 September 2004, E1; Peter Aleshire, "The Old Kid

on the Block," *Phoenix*, February 2004, 101–5; *Phoenix Directory, 1955*, 13, 95; *Phoenix Directory, 1961*, 111, 159; *Analysis of Transient Housing*, 6–8. Older resorts, the Wigwam in Litchfield Park and San Marcos in Chandler, continued to prosper. Wickenburg, some forty miles west of Phoenix, hosted another seven ranches.

33. Robert E. Waugh, "Winter Tourist Markets of Central and Southern Arizona," *Arizona Business and Economic Review* 12 (December 1955): 1–9; *The Economy of Maricopa County, 1965 to 1980: A Study for the Guidance of Public and Private Planning* (Phoenix: Western Management Consultants, 1965), 199–215.

34. John A. Jakle, Keith A. Sculle, and Jefferson S. Rogers, *The Motel in America* (Baltimore: Johns Hopkins University Press, 1996); Waugh, "Winter Tourist Markets"; Zellmer, "Welcome Stranger!," 23; *Phoenix Directory, 1955*, 193–94; *Phoenix Directory, 1961*, 4, 6, 8, 139–40, 174; *Mobile Homes in Phoenix, Arizona* (Phoenix: Phoenix City Planning Department, 1971) 3–6, 19, 20. Half the motels were on east Van Buren; another third were on the rest of U.S. Highway 80; a number were on Grand, while the remaining ones were scattered on twenty-one different streets. A quarter of the 189 trailer courts were on U.S. Highway 80, while the rest were in a west-north-east arc on the outskirts of town, scattered on sixty-five different streets. Some were relatively large, like two on the Black Canyon Highway with 36 and 43 spaces; most others seem to have had only 3 to 8 spots. *Phoenix Directory 1961*, 174. *Analysis of Transient Housing*, 5, which reported many fewer trailer parks (117) than the directory, reports a total of 6,277 available spaces.

35. Quotation from Stocker, "Phoenix," 39; John Shirer, "The Arizona Winter Visitor, 1951–1952 Season," *Arizona Business and Economic Review*, 1 (October 1952): 1–6; *Arizona Statistical Review, 1951*, 6 (hereinafter *ASR*); "Phoenix," *Reynolds Review*, December 1958, 11; *Phoenix Directory, 1961*, 6; City of Phoenix and Maricopa County Advance Planning Task Force, May 1959, *Land Use of the Phoenix Urban Area: A Study Basic to Long Range Planning* (Phoenix: City of Phoenix, 1959), 12, 14; *Analysis of Transient Housing*, 7–8, chart 10a, 12–13; and "Estimated Tourist Expenditures in Arizona" from *ASR*, 1950–1961.

36. Quotations from Zellmer, "Welcome Stranger!," 23, and Sylvia Byrnes, *Jokake Inn: One of the Earliest Desert Resorts* (Arizona?: n.d.), 17; Ullman, "Amenities as a Factor in Regional Growth," 2–3; Melton and Smith, *Arizona Goes to War*, 100, 93.

37. Quotation from Stocker, "Phoenix," 38; examples of letters to mayors are in box 4, folder 23, City of Phoenix Government Records Collection, 1955–1966, Arizona Historical Society, Tempe, Arizona (hereinafter PCGR).

38. "Arizona: Industry and People Find Living Good in the Desert," *U.S. News and World Report*, 43 (11 October 1957): 77; *AR*, 25 March 1956.

39. Ullman, "Amenities as a Factor in Regional Growth," 4; "Royal Palms Resort and Spa: A Distinguished History," http://www.royalpalmshotel.com/press_release/history.pdf (accessed 3 January 2006); *AR*, 8 November 1959, 1; Carl Bimson, interview by Phoenix History Project, 23 July 1976, tape recording, PHPC; "Carl Bimson," in Paul W. Pollock, *American Biographical Encyclopedia: Profiles of Prominent Personalities, Arizona Edition (ABE Arizona)*, 6 vols. (Phoenix: P. W. Pollock, 1967–70), 1:16.

40. See, for example, the letter from Mrs. R. Bouldin to Mayor Mardian, 2 October 1961, in box 4, folder 23, PCGR. A fascinating character, Lincoln (1866–1959) founded a company in 1895 that became hugely successful, based on his innovative work on arc welding. A devotee of land and tax reformer Henry George, he ran for vice president in 1924 on the Commonwealth Land Party ticket, served as president of the Henry George School of

Social Science in New York City, and established the Lincoln Foundation (1947), which funded research on land policy issues. He also gave substantial sums to establish the John C. Lincoln Hospital. Charles S. Stevenson, "*We Met at Camelback!*" (Scottsdale, AZ: Arizona Desert Publishing Company, 1968), 206–12; "John C. Lincoln—He Was Our President!," http://www.cooperativeindividualism.org/lincoln-john_remembrance-hgeorge-news. html (accessed 11 January 2006); "Lincoln Electric: 110 Years of Excellence," http://www. lincolnelectric.com/corporate/about/history.asp (accessed 11 January 2006); Collins, *Emerging Metropolis*, 341–42.

41. *AR*, 9 November 1952, 7:2; "Arizona: Industry and People," *U.S. News and World Report*, 78; Ralph C. Hook, Jr., and Paul D. Simkins, *Recent Migration to Arizona: A Study Prepared for the Arizona Development Board* (Phoenix: Arizona Development Board, 1959), 5.

42. "William. H. Goettl," Pollock, *ABE Arizona*, 3:230; Bill Goettl, interview by Phoenix History Project, 7 April 1977, tape recording, PHPC; *AR*, 28 May 2000, F5; Michael F. Konig, "Toward Metropolis Status: Charter Government and the Rise of Phoenix, Arizona, 1945–1960" (PhD diss., Arizona State University, 1983), 23; *AR*, 25 April 1973, A7.

43. *Arizona Days and Ways Magazine*, 11 February 1962, 103; Arizona Public Service Company, *Annual Report, 1951–1964*, esp. *1953*, 9, and *1955*, 9; *Annual Report, 1958* (Phoenix: Salt River Project), 7, and Annual Report, *1959* (Phoenix: Salt River Project), 8; Gail Cooper, *Air Conditioning America: Air Conditioning and the Controlled Environment, 1900–1960* (Baltimore: Johns Hopkins University Press, 1998), 124–27, 136–67, 216 notes 2 and 3; Ralph E. Staggs, interview by Phoenix History Project, 18 May 1977, transcript, 18–22, PHPC.

44. *Arizona Days and Ways Magazine*, 11 February 1962, 103.

45. *AR*, 21 February 1945, 1; *Historical Statistics of the United States, Colonial Times to 1970*, 2 pts. (Washington, DC: U.S. Bureau of the Census, 1975), 2:727–30; the map of Arizona railroads in *Arizona Industrial Facts* (Phoenix: Arizona Development Board, 1964), 8.

46. Keane and Bruder, *Good Roads Everywhere*, 41–56; auto expenses accounted for between 20 and 25 percent of tourism expenses during the 1950s, *ASR*, 1950–1961; Shirer, "Arizona Winter Visitor," 3, 5.

47. Grady Gammage, Jr., *Phoenix in Perspective: Reflections on Developing the Desert* (Tempe, AZ: Herberger Center for Design Excellence, College of Architecture and Environmental Design, Arizona State University, 1999), 33.

48. Quotations from *AR*, 22 November 1942, 4:6; *AR*, 18 October 1944, 4.

49. "Phoenix: City on Wings," *Arizona Highways*, April 1957, 26; *ASR*, 1950, 4; *Arizona Industrial Facts*, 1964, 10; *Historical Statistics of the United States*, 769; annual passenger traffic listed in *ASR*, 1952–1961; Michael D. Jones, *Desert Wings: A History of Phoenix Sky Harbor International Airport* (Tempe, AZ: Jetblast Publications, 1997), 18–25; and Nicholas Udall describes the expansion of the airport into residential areas in John Nicholas Udall, interview by Phoenix History Project, 21 December 1977, transcript, 14, PHPC.

50. *AR*, 23 February 1945, 7; Nash, *World War II and the West*, 206–7. A respected industrial leader, Hoffman was an internationalist who later headed the U.S. Marshall Plan to aid European economic recovery after World War II. Alan R. Raucher, *Paul G. Hoffman, Architect of Foreign Aid* (Lexington: University Press of Kentucky, 1985).

51. Roger W. Lotchin, *Fortress California, 1910–1961: From Warfare to Welfare* (New York: Oxford University Press, 1992), 156–61.

52. *AR*, 7 October 1944, 2; quotations from 19 October 1944, 5. An *AR* editorial explicitly recommended following the San Diego model in 1 September 1945, 1.

53. Nash, *World War II and the West*, 169–73, 190–202.

54. *AR*, 13 October 1944, 13; *AR*, 8 December 1944, 1. The day after the Osborn-Hayden announcement, GOP congressional nominees lambasted Democrats as being antibusiness and demanded to be included in meetings to encourage industry to stay. *AR*, 14 October 1944, 2. Collins, *Emerging Metropolis*, 11–13, discusses Osborn's legislative suggestions, primarily proposals for highway development and some social welfare initiatives.

55. *AR*, 17 December 1945, 2.

56. Jacobson, "Phoenix Chamber of Commerce," 19, 23–29, 56–58; *AR*, 5 September 1945, 2; Snell interview transcript, 77–82, 106–108, 112–18.

57. G. Wesley Johnson, Jr., discusses the nature of Phoenix leadership in "Directing Elites: Catalysts for Social Change," in G. Wesley Johnson, ed., *Phoenix in the Twentieth Century: Essays in Community History* (Norman: University of Oklahoma Press, 1993), 17–27. The 1989 Goldwater Lecture Series roundtable (with Frank Snell, Barry Goldwater, Jack Pfister, and Budge Rufner) contains comments on the close connection of this leadership group. 1989 Goldwater Lecture Series, roundtable, video (in possession of Peter Iverson). Collins, *Emerging Metropolis*, 204–51, includes good discussions of many of these leaders.

58. Udall interview transcript, 11; Ed Korrick, interview by Arizona Jewish Historical Society, 31 January 2000, http://info.lib.asu.edu/NetAns2/gate.exe?f=doc&p_d=ajhs&state=i557f2.1.27 (accessed 25 February 2003).

59. "Edward V. (Ted) O'Malley," in Pollock, *ABE Arizona*, 2:188; Harry Rosenzweig interview tape recording.

60. Russell Pulliam, *Publisher: Gene Pulliam, Last of the Newspaper Titans* (Ottawa, IL: Jameson Books, 1984); Zarbin, *All the Time*, esp. 180–87.

61. *ASR*, 1961, 17; Carl A. Bimson, *Transformation in the Desert: The Story of Arizona's Valley National Bank* (New York: Newcomen Society, 1962), 22–25; Pam Haitt, *The Arizona Bank: Arizona's Story* (Phoenix: Arizona Bank, 1987), 133–67; Schweikart, *Banking in Arizona*, 107–31.

62. Walter Bimson, interview by Phoenix History Project, 27 December 1975, tape recording, PHPC; Carl Bimson, interview by Phoenix History Project, 23 July 1976, tape recording, PHPC; *AR*, 22–25 October 1961; "Walter Reed Bimson," in Pollock, *ABE Arizona*, 1:14; "Carl A. Bimson," in Pollock, *ABE Arizona*, 1:16; and Keith Monroe, "Bank Knight in Arizona," *The American Magazine*, November 1945, 24–30.

63. *AR*, 7 September 1994, A8.

64. *AR*, 7 September 1994, 1; *Phoenix Gazette*, 7 September 1994, 1; "Frank Snell," in Pollock, *ABE Arizona*, 1:32; Sam Mardian, interview by Phoenix History Project, 20 July 1978, transcript, 2, PHPC.

65. *Thunderbird, Special Issue* 50 (1996): 2–7, 42–43.

66. Newton Rosenzweig interview transcript, 20.

67. Edward Jacobson, interview by Arizona Historical Society, 17 December 1992, transcript, 1–2, quotations 15, 16, at Arizona Historical Society.

CHAPTER 5

1. Amy Bridges discusses approaches to growth in *Morning Glories: Municipal Reform in the Southwest* (Princeton: Princeton University Press, 1997), 26–29, 218–20.

2. Bridges' *Morning Glories* is an outstanding analysis of the larger questions of urban development in the Southwest. While I interpret some parts of Phoenix history differently,

I profited greatly from her sophisticated study. On the league see Frank Mann Stewart, *A Half-Century of Municipal Reform: The History of the National Municipal League* (Berkeley: University of California Press, 1950), while Richard S. Childs discusses *The First 50 Years of the Council-Manager Plan of Municipal Government* (New York: National Municipal League, 1965). The useful guide to NML's papers included the "Historical Chronology," http://carbon. cudenver.edu/public/library/archives/nml/nml_main.html#HISTORICAL (accessed 3 February 2006). The relationship of the two organizations is discussed in Alfred Willoughby, dittoed form letter, 12 August 1959, 3 in series 5, container 69, folder 18, National Municipal League Papers, Auraria Library, University of Colorado, Denver (hereinafter NMLP-AA).

3. One example of their efforts against vice was their unsuccessful attempt to have "bookmaking establishments" automatically declared to be public nuisances. *AR*, 4 October 1944, 1. On reform see Arthur G. Horton, *An Economic, Political, and Social Survey of Phoenix and the Valley of the Sun* (Tempe, AZ: Southside Progress, 1941), 195, 197; *AR*, 5 September 1945, 1; *AR*, 9 November 1945, 1.

4. *AR*, 22 December 1945, 2; *AR*, 5 September 1945, 1.

5. Stories on these reports appeared on page 1 of *AR* on 16, 17, 19, 20, 22, 23, 26, 27, and 28 December 1945.

6. Many historians offer detailed narratives of the political events from 1946 through 1949, and my description benefits from their accounts. As the subsequent pages show, however, my understanding of those events differs from theirs (as do theirs from each other on some points) regarding the nature of political factionalism, the escalation of the conflict, the changing roles of James Deppe and Ward Scheumack, and the validity of the bossism and corruption charges. See Michael F. Konig, "Toward Metropolis Status: Charter Government and the Rise of Phoenix, Arizona, 1945–1960" (PhD diss., Arizona State University, 1983), 24–73; Michael F. Konig, "The Election of 1949: Transformation of Municipal Government in Phoenix," in G. Wesley Johnson, ed., *Phoenix in the Twentieth Century: Essays in Community History* (Norman, OK: University of Oklahoma Press, 1993), 167–82; Brent Whiting Brown, "An Analysis of the Phoenix Charter Government Committee as a Political Entity" (master's thesis, Arizona State University, 1968), 22–33; and William S. Collins *The Emerging Metropolis: Phoenix 1944–1973* (Phoenix: Arizona State Parks Board, 2004), 46–60.

7. [John] Nicholas Udall, interview by Phoenix History Project, 21 December 1977, transcript 1-6, PHPC; *AR*, 19 June 2005, B9. The family included State Supreme Court judges and Congressmen Stewart Udall and Morris Udall from Tucson.

8. *AR*, 3 March 1946, 2. The *Arizona Republic* had also alleged the dangers of gambling and prostitution in the 1946 election: Earl Zarbin, *All the Time a Newspaper: The First 100 Years of the Arizona Republic* (Phoenix: Arizona Republic, 1990), 175.

9. *AR*, 21 February 1948, as reprinted in Collins, *Emerging Metropolis*, 53. In the next city campaign the *AR* noted this simple slogan in amazement, *AR*, 6 November 1949, 1.

10. *AR*, 3 August 1948, 1; Udall interview transcript, 18. Udall later admitted that he had exaggerated and that Scheumack "liked to call himself the 'City Boss.'" Lacking criminal charges, it is impossible to be sure what sort of "corruption" he was associated with, since the term is typically used loosely and often refers to moral rather than legal judgments. But, most likely, he was at least receiving and influencing favorable paint contracts. Ironically, Busey had been Scheumack's first employer in the Valley, but had fired him for alleged misdealings with city employees. Cf. Collins, *Emerging Metropolis*, 51–52, with Konig, "Toward Metropolis Status," 27.

11. The criticism of transient managers is virtually universal among historians of Phoenix government, but no one presents substantial evidence that changes before the 1940s materially affected the quality of city services. It is the city's growth, combined with political factionalism, that made this a problem.

12. Ray Busey, untitled memorandum on Charter Revision Committee, 1961, in box 2, folder 7, City of Phoenix Government Records Collection, Arizona Historical Society, Tempe (hereinafter PGRC); "Charter Revision Committee," in PCGR; Rhes Henry Cornelius, interview by Phoenix History Project, 22 June 1976, transcript, 23, PHPC.

13. Williams, quotation from Jack Williams, "Talk to the National Municipal League Convention," Colorado Springs, 16 September 1958, 1, in box 2, folder 7, PCGR; also a dittoed letter from NML Executive Director Alfred Willoughby, 12 August 1959, in series 5, container 69, folder 18, in NMLP-AA; Bridges, *Morning Glories*, 101–18.

14. *AR*, 17 November 1948, 1; *AR*, 30 November 1948, 1; *AR*, 10 January 1949, 1; *AR*, 30 January 1949, 1; *AR*, 6 April 1949, 1; *AR*, 7 March 1949, 1; *AR*, 15 June 1949, 1; and quotation from *AR*, 14 July 1949, 1.

15. The analysis of the origins and initial character of this group differ in Brown, "Phoenix Charter Government," 31–32; Collins, *Emerging Metropolis*, 58; Konig, "Toward Metropolis Status," 53–54; and Bridges, *Morning Glories*, 119–20. Quotation from *AR*, 6 July 1949, 1.

16. *AR*, 6 July 1949, 1; Bridges, *Morning Glories*, 119–22, quotation from 119; Cornelius interview transcript, 25; Harry Rosenzweig, interview by Phoenix History Project, 29 July 1976, tape recording, PHPC; Louis Fraga, "Domination through Democratic Means," *Urban Affairs Quarterly*, 23 (June 1988): 531–33.

17. Harry Rosenzweig interview tape recording; Margaret Kober biography sheet, accompanying Margaret Kober interview by Phoenix History Project, 18 June 1976, transcript, PHPC; *AR*, November 12, 1951.

18. Harry Rosenzweig interview tape recording; Frank G. Murphy, interview by Phoenix History Project, 10 February 1976, transcript, 13, PHPC; Kober interview transcript, 15; Dean Smith, *The Goldwaters of Arizona* (Flagstaff, AZ: Northland Press, 1986), 186–90; Barry M. Goldwater, with Jack Casserly, *Goldwater* (New York: Doubleday, 1988), 86–90, quotation 89; Peter Iverson, *Barry Goldwater, Native Arizonan* (Norman, OK: University of Oklahoma Press, 1997), 66–72.

19. *AR*, 6 November 1949, 1–2; 10 November 1949, 2; quotations from *AR*, 6 November 1949, 6; Konig, "Election of 1949," 174–79.

20. Total votes and total registered voters from *Registered Voters and Votes Cast for Mayor and Council, Primary and General Election, Phoenix, 1949–1979* (Phoenix: City of Phoenix, 1980); votes for individual candidates from *AR*, 9 November 1949, 1, and *AR*, 10 November 1949, 1–2, while votes by precinct are listed in *AR*, 10 November 1949, 23. Split support for the entire CGC council slate is measured by the coefficient of variation, which was 0.102 (or 10 percent). Turnout increased because of interest but also because voters no longer had to register separately for municipal elections: Brown, "Phoenix Charter Government," 47.

21. Quotations from "Official Entry of the City of Phoenix, Arizona, for the 1958 All-America Cities Awards," series 5, carton 10, folder 64, 1958, All-America Cities Award, NMLP-AA; and "The Phoenix Story of Municipal Government Since 1950," 9 October 1961, typescript in box 2, folder 11, PCGR (emphasis in the original). For examples of personal reminiscences offering such exaggerations see Cornelius interview transcript, 22–26, and comments in *AR*, 5 November 1961, 1; and Harry Rosenzweig interview tape recording. Cf. the milder

comments in Udall interview transcript, 16, and "15th November Anniversary Symposium," *Phoenix Magazine*, November 1980, 101. The most notable awards were as an All-America City in 1950 and 1958, but Paul Kelso lists the sixty-nine others in *A Decade of Council-Manager Government in Phoenix, Arizona* (Phoenix?: 1960), 52–58.

22. *AR*, 10 November 1949, 2; *AR*, 15 July 1949, 1.

23. Hereinafter, discussions regarding the actions of the Charter Government Committee will continue to use the abbreviation *CGC*, while the term *Charter Government* will be used to refer to the larger group, officeholders and supporters acting separately from the CGC.

24. Bridges, *Morning Glories*, 120–23, explains the Cincinnati approach; quotation from Jack Williams letter to R. L. Thomas, 25 May 1959, in box 3, folder 18, PCGR; while the importance and use of citizen committees is discussed in "Phoenix Story," 2–3. Cf. Chandler Davidson and Luis Ricardo Fraga, "Slating Groups as Parties in a 'Nonpartisan' Setting," *Western Political Quarterly*, 41 (June 1988): 373–90.

25. Cornelius interview transcript, 31; Williams letter to Thomas, 1; Adam Diaz, interview by Phoenix History Project, 14 April 1976, transcript, 14, PHPC.

26. Bridges, *Morning Glories*, 122–24; Fraga, "Domination through Democratic Means"; also see Jack Williams's 1959 letter to Thomas. Goldwater to John B. Bebout, 27 November 1950; Goldwater to Alfred Willoughby, 10 December 1951; Goldwater to George Gallup, 9 January 1952; all in Goldwater correspondence, series 3, container 21, folder 57, NMLP-AA; "Finalist and Winners List" for 1949–1994, in series 1, carton 35, folder 7, NMLP-AA.

27. Biographical information on CGC and other candidates for city office obtained from newspaper stories and ads that appeared during the campaign.

28. On these economic conflicts see Bradford Luckingham, *Phoenix: The History of a Southwestern Metropolis* (Tucson: University of Arizona Press, 1989), 157–59, and the discussion below in chapter 6, "Planning for Manufacturing."

29. Total votes for each election come from *Registered Voters and Votes, Phoenix, 1949–1979*; votes by precinct are listed in *AR*, 10 November 1949, 23; *AR*, 13 November 1957, 2; and a map titled "Phoenix Municipal Primary Election, November 19, 1959," in box 1, folder 8, PCGR. The significant changes in precinct boundaries from election to election prevent a more precise statistical analysis. Diminished turnout is, of course, the finding of virtually every study of nonpartisan municipal voting systems.

30. The coefficient of variation (which norms the standard deviation to different means) averaged only 0.046.

31. During each campaign the newspaper published brief biographies of each candidate, and campaign ads often included biographical information. Early, influential discussions of the socioeconomic differences of leaders, especially as related to citywide campaigns, include Robert A. Dahl, *Who Governs? Democracy and Power in an American City* (New Haven: Yale University Press, 1961), 63–84, and Samuel P. Hays, "The Politics of Reform in Municipal Government in the Progressive Era," *Pacific Northwest Quarterly*, 55 (October 1964): 157–69. Cf. Carol A. Cassel, "Social Background Characteristics of Nonpartisan City Council Members: A Research Note," *Western Political Quarterly*, 38 (September 1985): 495–501.

32. Leonard E. Goodall, "Phoenix: Reformers at Work," in Leonard E. Goodall, ed., *Urban Politics in the Southwest* (Tempe, AZ: Arizona State University, 1967), 118–20; Brown, "Phoenix Charter Government," 48–55, and Collins, *Emerging Metropolis*, 62–64, provide brief accounts of individual elections.

33. E.g., *AR*, 5 November 1953, 1; *AR*, 4 November 1959, 1; *AR*, 6 November 1950, 6; *AR*, 9 November 1950, 12.

34. *AR*, 5 November 1953, 1; quotation from *AR*, 8 November 1953.

35. *AR*, 2 November 1951, 1; *AR*, 3 November 1957, 1; *AR*, 13 November 1957, 2; *AR*, 8 November 1959, 8, 19. Collins, *Emerging Metropolis*, discusses aspects of party ties related to city elections (62–64) and analyzes the conflict over county government, focusing on the role of party (69–82).

36. As just one example of political migration, noted Valley banker Frank Brophy supported FDR in the 1930s, backed Republicans Wendell Wilkie and then Robert Taft in the 1940s, shifted to the States Rights Party in 1956, and in the 1960s belonged to the John Birch Society. Paul W. Pollock, *Arizona's Men of Achievement*, 6 vols. (Phoenix: Paul W. Pollock, 1958), 1:12; Pam Haitt, *The Arizona Bank: Arizona's Story* (Phoenix: The Arizona Bank, 1987), 104.

37. *AR*, 13 November1951, 1; *AR*, 7 November 1955, 1; *AR*, 2 November 1951, 10; *AR*, 11 July 1957, 1; *AR*, 7 November 1957, 1; quotation from *AR*, 7 November 1955, 1.

38. *AR*, 13 November 1951, 1; *AR*, 8 November 1953, 1; *AR*, 7 November 1957, 1; *AR*, 6 November 1959, 18; *AR*, 8 November 59, 12; *AR*, 6 November 1955, 1; *AR*, 1 November 1955, 2; *AR*, 22 November 1957, 1; quotation from Phoenix Ticket news release, 4 November 1959, in box 1, folder 7, PCGR.

39. *AR*, 8 November 1959, 12; *AR*, 8 Nov. 1953, 1; *AR*, 9 Nov. 1953, 1.

40. *AR*, 2 November 1955, 4; *AR*, 6 November 1957, 1; *AR*, 9 November 1959, 19.

41. *AR*, 4 November 1955; *AR*, 6 November 1955; also *AR*, 9 November 1957, 1.

42. *AR*, 9 November 1957, 1; property and sales tax data, per capita, adjusted for inflation for 1937–67, are reported in *Annual Financial Report, 1966–67* (Phoenix: City of Phoenix, 1967), 12; Kelso, *Decade of Council-Manager Government*, 43.

43. Philip G. Hudson, "Arizona's Tax Structure: A Comparative Study," Arizona Business *Review*, 2 (April 1953): 3, reports tax data, which is given here in simplified form:

Type of Tax	Arizona	Rocky Mountain	United States
Property tax	9.0%	9.0%	2.0%
Sales tax	31.2	23.4	17.6
Income tax	10.7	13.5	16.0
Other taxes	49.1	54.1	64.4

44. Calculated from budget data, excluding utilities, reported in *Financial Report, 1966–67*, 9; *Annual Financial Report, 1960–61* (Phoenix: City of Phoenix, 1961), xii, iv–v (hereinafter *AFR*); and *Annual Budget, 1956–57* (Phoenix: City of Phoenix, 1957), xxxiv–xl.

45. See Hudson, "Arizona's Tax Structure," 2; Phoenix, *City Code*, Ordinance No. 5121, sec. 2-9(f)2; Kelso, *Decade of Council-Manager Government*, 43. The effort to tax tourists also included "rooming houses" and "apartment buildings," thus raising rents for some longer term residents.

46. *Annual Budget, 1950–51* (Phoenix: City of Phoenix, 1951), vi.

47. *AFR, 1965–66*, 12; and *Annual Report of the Finance Director, 1951* (Phoenix: City of Phoenix, 1951), iv.

48. *Phoenix Reports: 2 ½ Years of Progress: January 1, 1950, to June 30, 1952* (Phoenix: City of

Phoenix, 1952), 6–7. The pay schedule was based on a Public Administration Service study; Kelso, *Decade of Council-Manager Government*, 58.

49. "Phoenix Story," 12; Kelso, *Decade of Council-Manager Government*, 35, 38–40.

50. *Budget, 1950–51*, v.

51. *Budget, 1950–51*, vii.

52. *Report of Finance Director, 1951*, vi.

53. *Phoenix Reports: 2½ Years*, 9; reports are listed in Kelso, *Decade of Council-Manager Government*, 58–65. In per capita measures for twenty-six cities of 250,000 to 500,000 population, it ranked fifth in number of employees and eighth in expenditures. *The Municipal Year Book, 1961* (Washington, DC: International City Management Association, 1961), 274.

54. Jack Williams, "Talk to National Municipal League Convention," 16 September 1958, 1–4, in box 2, folder 7, PCGR; "Official Entry 1958 All-America Cities Awards," 2–4; and "Phoenix Story," 2, 4–6. Membership lists in box 6, folder 28, and in box 2, folder 14, SMJP.

55. *Budget, 1950–51*, vi; *Report of Finance Director, 1951*, ii, iv. The average annual capital expenditures from 1943 to 1950 were $296,631 and from 1950 to 1957 they were $1,794,455. *Budget, 1956–57*, xi.

56. *Budget, 1956–57*, x; *Financial Report, 1965–66*, 6; Bridges, *Morning Glories*, 160–62.

57. *Official Statement, Relating to the Issuance of $9,000,000 Water System Revenue Bonds, Series 1960 (Payable Solely from Water System Revenues): Interest Exempt from All Present Federal Income Taxes* (Phoenix: City of Phoenix, [1960]), 13, 15, 17; University of Arizona, *Arizona's Water Supply*, Report for the Fourth Arizona Town Hall (Phoenix: Arizona Academy, Hall, 1964), 33–34; and Williams, "Talk to National Municipal League," 3. Karen L. Smith, "Community Growth and Water Policy," in Johnson, *Phoenix in the Twentieth Century*, 155–63; Douglas E. Kupel, *Fuel for Growth: Water and Arizona's Urban Environment* (Tucson: University of Arizona Press, 2003), 157–61. The city bought water previously allotted to agricultural land; with bond money it bought thirty-six small water companies in 1948–49, five in 1957, and three in 1960.

58. *Official Statement, Water Bonds, 1960*, 11–12, 15–17; "Phoenix Story," 6.

59. City of Phoenix, Arizona Water & Sewers Department, four-page memo, with "Water Rate History" and "Water Rate Comparison," 11 September 1963, in box 2, folder 12, PCGR; *Official Statement, Water Bonds, 1960*, 16.

60. *AR*, 21 February 1945, 1, 4. The state's 1948 Groundwater Code attempted to deal with some of these issues. University of Arizona, *Arizona's Water Supply*, 57.

61. Kelso, *Decade of Council-Manager Government*, 22–23.

62. Ibid., 25–27; Williams, "Talk to National Municipal League," 3; on disease see Collins, *Emerging Metropolis*, 26–27; in 1953 there were forty-seven thousand cesspools, privies, and septic tanks "in the fringe areas" of Phoenix, *Phoenix Reports 2½ Years*, 29.

63. Arizona Highway Department, in cooperation with the City of Phoenix and Maricopa County and the U.S. Department of Commerce, Bureau of Public Roads, *A Street Arterial Plan for Phoenix, Arizona* (Phoenix: [s.n.], 1950), 8–10, 14–15; and *Better Roads for Tomorrow: Phoenix-Maricopa County Traffic Study* (Phoenix: Arizona Highway Department, 1957), 14–15; national figures calculated from *Historical Statistics of the United States, Colonial Times to 1970*, 2 pts. (Washington, DC: U.S. Bureau of the Census, 1975), 1:8, 716.

64. *Personalized Transit Study: History of Mass Transit and Travel Time Studies for Automobile and Transit* (Phoenix: City of Phoenix, 1969), 3–4. Cf. Owen D. Gutfreund, *Twentieth-Century Sprawl: Highways and the Reshaping of the American Landscape* (New York: Oxford University

Press, 2004), 73–74, and Kenneth T. Jackson, *Crabgrass Frontier: The Suburbanization of the United States* (New York: Oxford University Press, 1985), 168–71.

65. *Phoenix Reports: 2½ Years*, 24; *Personalized Transit Study*, 4–5. Jerry W. Abbitt presents a detailed history in "A History of Public Transportation in Phoenix, Arizona, 1887–1989" (master's thesis, Arizona State University, 1989).

66. Sources for street mileage are noted on table 5.2 (slightly different figures are offered in "Phoenix Story," 7, and Kelso, *Decade of Council-Manager Government*, 27); Mardian, Statement at Swearing in Ceremonies, 4 January 1960, 4–5, in box 1, folder 7, PCGR; and on the influence of the FHA on the county, see Collins, *Emerging Metropolis*, 111.

67. *Phoenix Reports: 2½ Years*, 18; *Financial Report, 1960–61*, xiv, 42. A change occurred in the procedure, as the 1952 description mentions a majority of the "front footage," while the 1960 source (vii) refers to a majority of "the people."

68. *Street Deficiency Study, 1961: A Report to the City Council* (Phoenix: City of Phoenix, 1961), 31–32.

69. Quotation from Advance Transportation Planning Team, *Epilogue '83: An Update of Transportation—1980, Then and Now* (Phoenix: City of Phoenix, 1983), 22. The 1960 common plan is touted in "Phoenix Story," 6, and Kelso, *Decade of Council-Manager Government*, 27–28. Konig presents a detailed and useful discussion in "Toward Metropolis Status," 252–83. The planning studies were *Master Street Plan* (Phoenix: City of Phoenix, 1949); *Street Arterial Plan; Better Roads for Tomorrow; A Major Street and Highway Plan for the Phoenix Urban Area* (San Francisco: Wilbur Smith and Associates, 1960); and *Street Deficiency Study, 1961*.

70. Bruce B. Mason and Leonard E. Goodall, "Arizona," in Eleanore Bushnell, ed., *Impact of Reapportionment on the Thirteen Western States* (Salt Lake City: University of Utah Press, 1970), 49–69; Advance Transportation Planning Team, *Epilogue '83*, 24; Konig, "Toward Metropolis Status," 252–83; *AR*, 28 February 1957, 1.

71. This takes issue with a major point in Gutfreund, *Twentieth-Century Sprawl.*

72. Kelso, *Decade of Council-Manager Government*, 35; *Report of Finance Director, 1951*, iv; *A History of the Phoenix Police Department* (Phoenix: Phoenix Police Department, 1975), 22; *Budget, 1950–51*, x; *Annual Report, 1972* (Phoenix: Phoenix Police Department, 1972), 4; *Municipal Year Book, 1961*, 402.

73. *Financial Report, 1965–66*, 6; "Phoenix Story," 10; *Report of Finance Director, 1951*, iv; *Fire Station Plan for the City of Phoenix: A Long Range Planning Study* (Phoenix: City Planning Department, [1961?]), i, 6, 8; *Municipal Year Book, 1961*, 362. See also the Stay America Committee press release, [6?] November 1961, in box 2, folder 10, PCGR; and [City of Phoenix?], "What About the City of Phoenix Fire Rating?," 25 October 1963, box 2, folder 12, in PCGR.

74. Quotation from Maricopa County Planning Department, *A Comprehensive Plan for Land-Use in Paradise Valley* (Phoenix: Maricopa County, 1957), 39; *Phoenix Reports: 2½ Years*, 19, 25–27; Kelso, *Decade of Council-Manager Government*, 28–30; "Phoenix Story," 9–11.

CHAPTER 6

1. On postwar western economic growth see Michael P. Malone and Richard W. Etulain, *The American West: A Twentieth-Century History* (Lincoln: University of Nebraska Press, 1989), 219–63; Carl Abbott, *The Metropolitan Frontier: Cities in the Modern American West* (Tucson: University of Arizona Press, 1994), 3–78; Gerald D. Nash, *World War II and the West: Reshaping the Economy* (Lincoln: University of Nebraska Press, 1990); Roger W. Lotchin, *Fortress California, 1910–1961: From Warfare to Welfare* (New York: Oxford University Press,

1992); and Gerald D. Nash, *The Federal Landscape: An Economic History of the Twentieth-Century West* (Tucson: University of Arizona Press, 1999), 41–54. Jason Howard Gart analyzes aspects of Arizona's experience with the military and technology aspects of this in "Electronics and Aerospace Industry in Cold War Arizona, 1945–1968: Motorola, Hughes Aircraft, Goodyear Aircraft" (Ph.D. diss., Arizona State University, 2006).

2. *ASR, 1960*, 10; John Shirer, "Shifting Trends in Employment, 1939–1953: Arizona and the United States," *Arizona Business and Economic Review* 3 (September 1954): 1–6.

3. *ASR, 1956*, 22; *ASR, 1960*, 10, 37; *Official Statement, Relating to the Issuance of $9,000,000 Water System Revenue Bonds, Series 1960: (Payable Solely from Water System Revenues): Interest Exempt from All Present Federal Income Taxes* (Phoenix: City of Phoenix, [1960]), 35; *Phoenix City Directory, 1961*, (Dallas: R. L. Polk & Company, 1961), 12–13.

4. John Shirer, "Business in Arizona, 1929–1951, as Reflected in Phoenix Department Store Sales," *Arizona Business and Economic Review*, 1 (March 1952): 1–6; annual data taken from *ASR*, 1948–1961; John D. Wenum, *Annexation as a Technique for Metropolitan Growth: The Case of Phoenix, Arizona*, Research Study no. 11 (Tempe, AZ: Institute of Public Administration, Arizona State University, 1970), 37; *Phoenix Directory, 1961*, 5.

5. Annual data taken from *ASR*, 1948–1961.

6. *ASR, 1961*, 13.

7. Ibid.

8. The Goettl brothers were especially important, starting International Metal Products (cooler manufacturing), and William shifted the focus of Goettl Brothers Metal Products to air conditioners and heating pumps. Oscar Palmer sold his firm in 1952. Oscar Palmer, interview by Phoenix History Project, 17 January 1975, tape recording, PHPC; William Goettl, interview by Phoenix History Project, 7 April 1977, tape recording, PHPC; *AR*, 12 April 1959, 2:13; *AR*, 28 May 2000, F5; biographical sketches of Adam, William, Henry, and Gust Goettl in Paul W. Pollock, *American Biographical Encyclopedia: Profiles of Prominent Personalities, Arizona Edition*, 6 vols. (Phoenix: P. W. Pollock, 1967–81), 1:224–25, 2:161, 3:230, 5:46; Phoenix, *Official Statement, Water Bonds, 1960*, 33. Heat pumps slowly gained popularity: 1,238 were operating in Phoenix in 1959; *Annual Report* (Phoenix: Salt River Project, 1959), 8.

9. "Phoenix," *Reynolds Review*, December 1958, 10–14; Michael F. Konig, "Toward Metropolis Status: Charter Government and the Rise of Phoenix, Arizona, 1945–1960" (PhD diss., Arizona State University, 1983), 210–11; William S. Collins, *The Emerging Metropolis: Phoenix 1944–1973* (Phoenix: Arizona State Parks Board, 2004), 24–25.

10. Judith Anne Jacobson, "The Phoenix Chamber of Commerce: A Case Study of Economic Development in Central Arizona" (master's thesis, Arizona State University, 1992), 24, 27, 36, 48.

11. [John] Nicholas Udall, interview by Phoenix History Project, 21 December 1977, transcript, 22, PHPC; *AR*, 10 November 1949, 1; Michael F. Konig, "The Election of 1949: Transformation of Municipal Government in Phoenix," in G. Wesley Johnson, ed., *Phoenix in the Twentieth Century: Essays in Community History* (Norman: University of Oklahoma Press, 1993), 177–78; Konig, "Toward Metropolitan Status," 94–95, 215. Most voters accepted the notion that these were indirect taxes that penalized business activity.

12. Mal Hernandez, "Electronics: A Dynamic New Force on the Horizon," *Arizona Days and Ways Magazine*, 11 February 1962, 445; Daniel E. Noble, "Motorola Expands in Phoenix," *Arizona Business and Economic Review*, 3 (June 1954): 1–2; Joseph Stocker, "Phoenix: City Growing in the Sun," *Arizona Highways*, April 1957, 36–39; Collins, *Emerging Metropolis*,

38–43; and Margaret Finnerty, "The Bug in the Desert: The Labor Movement in Phoenix, 1940–1950," in Johnson, *Phoenix in the Twentieth Century*, 183–95.

13. *290 New Manufacturers in the Phoenix Area Since March 1, 1948* (Phoenix: Phoenix Chamber of Commerce, 1960), 1; *AR*, 9 November 1952, 7:4, 3; "Phoenix," *Reynolds Review*, December 1958, 10–14; on Goodyear see Gart, "Electronics and Aerospace Industry," 244–71.

14. Roger W. Lotchin, "The Origins of the Sunbelt-Frostbelt Struggle: Defense Spending and City Building," in Raymond A. Mohl, *Searching for the Sunbelt: Historical Perspectives on a Region* (Knoxville: University of Tennessee Press, 1990), 47–68; *AR*, 9 November 1952, 7:4, 2; *AR*, 8 September 1957; *AR*, 2 June 1959; *290 New Manufacturers*, 3; Hernandez, "Electronics," 442; *Arizona Days and Ways Magazine*, 11 February 1962, 321; Stocker, "Phoenix: City Growing in the Sun," 38; and "Arizona: Industry and People Find Living Good in the Desert," *U.S. News and World Report*, 43 11 October 1957, 80. On Fort Huachuca, see Collins, *Emerging Metropolis*, 161, 165–69.

15. Patrick Downey, interview by Phoenix History Project, 8 July 1978, transcript, 8, PHPC; Frank Snell, interview by Phoenix History Project, 25 May 1977, 28 September 1978, and 7 December 1978, transcript, 116, PHPC; "15th November Anniversary Symposium," *Phoenix Magazine*, November 1980, 103; Larry Schweikart, *A History of Banking in Arizona* (Tucson: University of Arizona Press, 1982), 183; and Matthew McCoy, "Desert Metropolis: Image Building and the Growth of Phoenix, 1940–1965" (PhD diss., Arizona State University, 2000), 228–42. Examples of the public-private partnership are Ray Wilson's letter thanking the chamber in Wilson to Lewis Hass, 26 December 1958, box 1, folder 1, PCGR, and the letter from Charles E. Hoover of the Municipal Industrial Development Corporation thanking Mayor Jack Williams, 13 June 1956, box 4, folder 22, PCGR.

16. Quotations from Downey interview transcript, 8–9; Carl Bimson, interview by Phoenix History Project, 23 July 1976, tape recording, PHPC.

17. *AR*, 9 November 1952, 7:1; *290 New Manufacturers*, passim. Other summaries of manufacturing firms and employment are *Phoenix City Directory, 1955* (Dallas: R. L. Polk & Company, 1955), 7; *Official Statement, Water Bonds, 1960*, 33; cf. Hiram S. Davis, "New Manufacturing Plants Strengthen the Phoenix Economy," *Arizona Business and Economic Review* 6 (February 1957): 1–3.

18. Newton Rosenzweig , interview by Phoenix History Project, transcript, 33, PHPC; Snell interview transcript, 108; Charles E. Hoover to Jack Williams, 13 June 1956, in box 4, folder 22, PCGR; Collins, *Emerging Metropolis*, 179–80.

19. Hernandez, "Electronics," 441, 442; *Arizona and Electronics* (Phoenix: Arizona Development Board, [1957]; H. R. Oldfield, "General Electric Enters the Computer Business-Revisited," *IEEE—Annals of the History of Computing*, 17 (Winter 1995): 53, 55; Jane King and W. A. Shelly, "A Family History of Honeywell's Large-Scale Computer Systems," *IEEE—Annals of the History of Computing*, 19 (October–December 1997): 42.

20. William L. Everitt, "A Man for His Season: A Tribute to Dan Noble," *Motorola Monitor*, vol. 12, no. 1 (1973), 1–3; *AR*, 15 October 1973, "Sun Living," 1; *AR*, 5 February 1962; and Gart's chapter on Motorola in "Electronics and Aerospace Industry," 117–60. I sketched Noble's life in Philip R. VanderMeer, *Phoenix Rising: The Making of a Desert Metropolis* (Carlsbad, CA: Heritage Media, 2002), 35.

21. Noble may also have been predisposed to Arizona, having spent 1919–20 in Prescott, in an effort to rest his ailing eyes. *AR*, 4 February 1962, 1. "January 1974 Marks Motorola's 25th Year in Phoenix!," unsigned article in Motorola Collection, Arizona Historical Society, Tempe;

AR, 15 October 1973, "Sun Living," 1; Daniel Noble, interview by Phoenix History Project, 26 September 1976, transcript, passim, PHPC; Gart, "Electronics and Aerospace Industry," 137–42; Edwin Darby, "Motorola Ties Illinois to Arizona," *Chicago Sun Times*, 22 September 1962; John Shirer, "The Motorola Research Laboratory in Phoenix," *Arizona Business and Economic Review*, 2 (February 1953): 1–4.

22. Quotation from Noble interview transcript, 18; *AR*, 11 December 1960; Noble interview transcript, passim; Edwin Darby, "Motorola Making Hay in Arizona," *Chicago Sun Times*, 23 September 1962; Edwin Darby, "Motorola Racking up Advances, *Chicago Sun Times*, 24 September 1962.

23. Quotations from *AR*, 18 March 1956, 1; and *AR*, 7 November 1959, 1. Cf. Charles Warner, "Noble Face of Arizona: Dr. Daniel E. Noble, Electronic Pioneer," *Point West*, June 1963, 36–38. *AR*, 25 March 1956; Ernest J. Hopkins and Alfred Thomas, Jr., *The Arizona State University Story* (Tempe, AZ: Arizona State University, 1960), 287–95.

24. *AR*, 1 June 1957; Oldfield, "General Electric," 53; cf. Margaret Pugh O'Mara, *Cities of Knowledge: Cold War Science and the Search for the Next Silicon Valley* (Princeton: Princeton University Press, 2005).

25. Hopkins and Thomas, *Arizona State University*, 295–302; Earl Zarbin, *All the Time a Newspaper: The First 100 Years of the Arizona Republic* (Phoenix: Arizona Republic, 1990), 218–19; Peter Alshire, "It's All about U," *ASU Magazine* 11 (March 2008): 6–19.

26. On program development see *AR*, 12 December 1962, A14; *AR*, 9 December 1963, 12A; *AR*, 6 February 1962, A1.

27. Quotation from *AR*, 6 February 1962, A1. Cf. Charles Warner, "Noble Face of Arizona: Dr. Daniel E. Noble, Electronic Pioneer," *Point West*, June 1963, 36–38. *AR*, 6 February 1962, A1; Ernest J. Hopkins and Alfred Thomas, Jr., *The Arizona State University Story* (Tempe, AZ: Arizona State University, 1960), 287–95. On university-business linkage see *AR*, 8 December 1963, 17A; *AR*, 9 December 1963, 1A; *AR*, 9 December 1962, A1, A9; *AR*, 9 December 1962, 1A, 17A. G. Homer Durham describes the state of the university as of 1962 in "'Ditat Deus' Is a Working Goal," *Arizona Days and Ways Magazine*, 11 February 1962, 154–55.

28. Quotation from *AR*, 8 December 1963, 1A.

29. See, for example, *Arizona Life in the Valley of the Sun* ([n.p]: Hillman-Wood, Inc., [1937]).

30. Quotation from "Phoenix," *Reynolds Review*, December 1958, 10–11, cf. *City Directory, 1961*, 6. On movies see, for example, Jerry Reynolds, *The Golden Days of Theaters in Phoenix: A Dramatic Tableau of the Theaters and Amusements in Greater Phoenix from 1877 to 1982* (Glendale, CA: Associated Media Services, 1982), 97, 101, and Anne M. Butler, "Selling the Popular Myth," in Clyde A. Milner II, Carol A. O'Connor, and Martha A. Sandweiss, eds., *The Oxford History of the American West* (New York: Oxford University Press, 1994), 771–801.

31. See "Scottsdale's Development as an Arts Colony and Tourism Destination Context," www.scottsdaleaz.gov/historiczoning/arts.asp (accessed 15 August 2006). In 1962 Scottsdale was noted as a "play-haven for millionaires" and a "home for the arts," in *Arizona Days and Ways Magazine*, 11 February 1962, 460. Russanne Erickson, "Legend City Amusement Park: A Case Study of a Twentieth Century Amusement Park" (master's thesis, Arizona State University, 2006); VanderMeer, *Phoenix Rising*, 110–11.

32. Quotations from *City Directory, 1961*, 6; and Oren Arnold, "Counter Points," *Point West*, April 1963, 53. Maggie Savoy, "Arizona Originals Go Anywhere," *Arizona Days and Ways Magazine*, 11 February 1962, 119–27.

33. Analysis of restaurants listed in *City Directory, 1961*, 159–62, and *Point West*, 1963 issues.

34. Edward H. Peplow, Jr., "You'll Like Living in Phoenix," *Arizona Highways*, April 1957, 14–35; *Arizona Days and Ways Magazine*, 11 February 1962, 497–517; Dave Hicks, "Sports," *Phoenix Metro*, November 1986, 170–75; Harry Rosenzweig, interview by Phoenix History Project, 29 July 1976, tape recording, PHPC; "Arizona State University Football," Tempe Historical Museum, http://www.tempe.gov/museum/FOOTBALL/fbasu.htm (accessed 28 April 2006).

35. *Arizona Days and Ways Magazine*, 11 February 1962, 497–99, 503–9; Hicks, "Sports," *Phoenix Metro*, 170–75; *City Directory, 1961*, 8.

36. Jeb Stuart Rosebrook, "Diamonds in the Desert: Professional Baseball in Arizona and the Desert Southwest, 1915–1958" (PhD diss., Arizona State University, 1999).

37. Vic Wilmot, "There's Gold in Them Thar Diamonds," *Point West*, April 1963, 24–29; Brian L. Laughlin, "A History of Baseball Spring Training in Arizona" (master's thesis, Arizona State University, 1991); "History of the Cactus League," http://www.cactusleague.com/c_history. php (accessed 25 January 2006).

38. Quotations from Samuel Mardian, Jr., interview by Phoenix History Project, 20 July 1978, transcript, 18, PHPC; Daniel Noble expressed similar views.

39. Quotation from Sam P. Applewhite, Jr., interview by Phoenix History Project, 2 February 1977, transcript, 19, PHPC; Walter Bimson, interview 1 and interview 2 by Phoenix History Project, 6 May 1976, PHPC; Carl Bimson interview, tape recording; Rhes Henry Cornelius, interview by Phoenix History Project, 22 June 1976, transcript, 42, PHPC.

40. Applewhite interview transcript, 19–20; Walter Bimson, "The Story of the Phoenix Art Museum," *Point West*, November 1963, 21; Tim Kelly, "The Phoenix Art Museum," *Arizona Highways*, March 1966, 4–27; Ann Elizabeth Marshall, "Arts and Cultural District Formation in Phoenix, Arizona" (DPA thesis, Arizona State University, 1993), 88–89; Mardian interview transcript, 18.

41. Applewhite interview transcript, 19–25; Bimson, "Phoenix Art Museum," 21, 49–51; *AR*, 8 November 1959, 1.

42. Bimson interview tape recording; *AR*, 25 October 1961, 1; Joseph Stocker, "Curtis," *Point West*, February 1963, 36–41.

43. Peplow, "You'll Like Living in Phoenix," 29; Bobby Johnston, " Mrs. Linde: The Desert Impresario," *Point West*, November 1963, 22–25; Joseph Stocker, "Mrs. Archer Linde, Beloved Impresario," *Phoenix*, January 1985, 94–96; Margaret Helen Tuveson, interview by Phoenix History Project, 29 February 1976, transcript, PHPC.

44. Reynolds, "Golden Days," 109–11; *AR*, 12 February 2006, E6; Collins, *Emerging Metropolis*, 361–63.

45. "Historical Note to Manuscript Guide," Phoenix Little Theatre Records, 1922–1994, AHS; Reynolds, "Golden Days," 122. Interestingly, after 1968, the Phoenix Children's Theater occasionally used the Sombrero Playhouse for their productions. Collins, *Emerging Metropolis*, 361, n. 62.

46. Collins, *Emerging Metropolis*, 357–58, discusses the prewar symphonies. Other major groups included the Phoenix Boys Choir (1947), the Phoenix Bach Choir (1958), and the Phoenix Chamber Music Society (1961), as well as various groups associated with ASU. Richard Edward Shaffer, "History of the Phoenix Boys Choir: From 1947 through 1989" (master's thesis, Arizona State University, 1992); "Phoenix Bach Choir," http://www.bachchoir.org/ about.html (accessed 30 April 2006); *Arizona Days and Ways Magazine*, 11 February 1962, 467.

47. Blanche Korrick, interview by Phoenix History Project, 18 July 1977, transcript, PHPC; *AR*, 11 January 1998, PS3.

48. *AR*, 11 January 1998, PS3; *AR*, 1 May 1958, 1; *AR*, 24 June 2001, B7; A. Nannette Taylor, "Louise Lincoln Kerr: Grand Lady of Music," www.asukerr.com/more/aboutkerr.shtml (accessed 30 April 2006); *AR*, 11 January 1998, PS8.

49. Bryan C. Stoneburner, "The Phoenix Symphony Orchestra, 1947–1978: Leadership, Criticism, and Selective Commentary" (master's thesis, Arizona State University, 1981); Dixie Legler, *Frank Lloyd Wright: The Western Work* (San Francisco: Chronicle Books, 1999), 111–15; Mardian interview transcript, 15–17; Collins, *Emerging Metropolis*, 364–66.

50. Tim J. Kelly, "The Question of Subsidy in the Arts," *Point West*, November 1963, 35.

51. Communities not listed in table 6.3, which were unincorporated and too small to be registered in the population census, include Guadalupe, Higley, Laveen, Cashion, Queen Creek, Litchfield Park, Ocotillo, Chandler Heights, and Surprise. Wickenburg, which had shifted from mining gold in the nineteenth century to mining "dudes" in the twentieth, was too distant to be considered within the metropolitan area, as was Gila Bend. Mark E. Pry, *The Town on the Hassayampa: A History of Wickenburg, Arizona* (Wickenburg, AZ: Desert Caballeros Western Museum, 1997). Charles Sargent, ed., *Metro Arizona* (Scottsdale, AZ: Buffington Books, 1988), 99, 102.

52. Scott Solliday, *Chandler: Pioneer City of the New West* (Chandler, AZ: Chandler Historical Society, 1996); *Our Town: History of Mesa*, centennial ed. (Mesa, AZ: Mesa Public Schools, 1978); and John Harrison Akers, "From Dale to Hollow?: The Urban Transformation of Glendale, Arizona, 1940–1990" (master's thesis, Arizona State University, 1997).

53. John D. Wenum provides a thoughtful and detailed analysis of annexation in *Annexation*, but see also Collins, *Emerging Metropolis*, 83–104, and Konig, "Toward Metropolitan Status," 86–112.

54. See the census reports, U.S. Department of Commerce, Bureau of the Census, *1950 Census of Population, Advance Reports, Population of Arizona*, (Washington, DC: Government Printing Office, 1951), 1–3; U.S. Department of Commerce, Bureau of the Census, *1950 Census of Population*, vol. II, part 3, *Characteristics of the Population: Arizona* (Washington, DC: Government Printing Office, 1952), 3, 6–10; U.S. Department of Commerce, Bureau of the Census, *Census of Population, 1960*, vol. I, part 4, *Characteristics of the Population: Arizona*, (Washington, DC: Government Printing Office, 1961), 9–11.

55. Quotation from Wenum, *Annexation*, n. 2, 51.

56. Udall interview transcript, 13; Edward Jacobson, interview by Phoenix History Project, 9 May 1980, transcript, 1–12, PHPC.

57. Jacobson interview transcript, 2.

58. Wenum, *Annexation*, 52; *Phoenix Reports: 2½ Years of Progress: January 1, 1950, to June 30, 1952* (Phoenix: City of Phoenix, 1952), quotations on 24; Advance Planning Task Force, Phoenix and Maricopa County, *Land Use of the Phoenix Urban Area*, ([Phoenix]: [City of Phoenix], 1959), 11–12, 15–17, quotation on 4.

59. Information and quotation from *Phoenix Reports: Years*, 24; *Look*, 3 February 1959, 83.

60. Aaron Marsh, "Municipal Public Relations Plays Lead Role in Phoenix Annexation Program," *The American City*, November 1952, 122–23; Paul Kelso, *A Decade of Council-Manager Government in Phoenix, Arizona* (Phoenix: 1960), 25–27; Jack Williams, "Talk to the National Municipal League Convention," Colorado Springs, 16 September 1958, 3, in box 2, folder 7, in PCGR; Wenum, *Annexation*, 69.

61. Quotation from *City Manager's News Bulletin*, vol. 9, no. 52 (24 December 1958), 1, in box 1, folder 1, PCGR.

62. *AR*, 22 November 1942, 11, and *City Directory, Phoenix and Vicinity, 1948–1949* (Phoenix: Arizona Directory Company, 1949), 167. Edna McEwen Ellis offers a community history in *Sunny Slope: A History of the North Desert Area of Phoenix* (Phoenix: Art Press, 1990). The lack of poverty and illness is disputed by local historian Don Taylor, *AR*, 2 March 1994, 1.

63. Ellis, *Sunny Slope*, 96–111; *AR*, 1 April 1958, 1; *AR*, 2 May 1958, 2; *AR*, 30 November 1948, 17; quotation from *City Manager's News Bulletin*, vol. 9, no. 52, 1. Cf. Collins, *Emerging Metropolis*, 90–94.

64. *ASR, 1951*, 31; U.S. Department of Commerce, Bureau of the Census, *Census of Population and Housing, 1960*, Final Report PHC(1)-117 (Washington, DC: Government Printing Office, 1961), table P, 19; *AR*, 28 October 1952, 1; *AR*, 18 February 1953, 1; *AR*, 10 December 1959, 1; William Kantz, "An Account of the Participation of W. E. Kantz in the Controversy over the Incorporation of South Phoenix," in box 1, folder 4, plus miscellaneous materials in box 1, folder 9, in William Kantz Collection, 1952–54, Arizona Historical Foundation; Travis Williams, interview by Fred Amis, tape recording, 4 April 2001, in the author's possession; George E. Wickman to Ray W. Wilson, 29 March 1960, in box 2, folder 11, PCGR.

65. Collins, *Emerging Metropolis*, 99–104; Downey interview transcript, 13–20; Wenum, *Annexation*, 78, 84.

66. Wenum, *Annexation*, 82–89.

67. Wenum, *Annexation*, 76, 81. The high proportion living in annexed areas compares with the marginally higher 78.5 percent in Tucson and with otherwise lower figures, like 29.1 percent in Mesa, and an average of 25 percent for the major Texas cities of San Antonio, Dallas, and Houston. The process was more contentious in other places, such as Tucson and Albuquerque, as noted by Michael F. Logan in *Fighting Sprawl and City Hall: Resistance to Urban Growth in the Southwest* (Tucson: University of Arizona Press, 1995), e.g., 33–39, 109.

68. E.g., *U.S. News & World Report*, 11 October 1957, 77–82, 96–97.

69. Oklahoma City was larger, but its merger of city and county—like other cases later on—put it in a different category.

CHAPTER 7

1. *Historical Statistics of the United States: Colonial Times to 1970*, part II, Bicentennial ed. (Washington, DC: Government Printing Office, 1975), 639–40, 646; U.S. Census Bureau, *Census of Housing*, "Historical Census of Housing Tables," http://www.census.gov/hhes/www/housing/census/ historic/owner.html (accessed 12 September 2006). Arizona home ownership rose from 47.9 percent to 68.3 percent.

2. "Urban and Rural Populations," from U.S. Bureau of the Census, *1990 Census of Population and Housing*, "1990 Population and Housing Unit Counts: United States" (CPH-2), 5, http://www.census.gov/population/censusdata/table-4.pdf (accessed 12 September 2006); Frank Hobbs and Nicole Stoops, *Demographic Trends in the Twentieth Century*, Census 2000 Special Reports, Series CENSR-4 (Washington, DC: Government Printing Office, 2002), 33.

3. For good overviews of suburbanization see Kenneth T. Jackson, *Crabgrass Frontier: The Suburbanization of the United States* (New York: Oxford University Press, 1985), 231–71; Dolores Hayden, *Building Suburbia: Green Fields and Urban Growth, 1820–2000* (New York: Pantheon Books, 2003), 128–53; David L. Ames and Linda Flint McClelland, "Historic Residential Suburbs: Guidelines for Evaluation and Documentation for the National Register

of Historic Places," *National Register Bulletin* (Washington, DC: U.S. Department of the Interior, National Park Service, 2002), http://www.cr.nps.gov/nr/publications/bulletins/suburbs/index (accessed 12 September 2006); Carl Abbott, *The Metropolitan Frontier: Cities in the Modern American West* (Tucson: University of Arizona Press, 1993), 3–29, 149–72; Barbara M. Kelley, *Expanding the American Dream: Building and Rebuilding Levittown* (Albany: State University of New York Press, 1993); and Barbara M. Kelly, ed., *Suburbia Re-examined* (Westport, CT: Greenwood, 1989).

4. Besides the works in note 3 above, see Tom Martinson, *American Dreamscape: The Pursuit of Happiness in Postwar Suburbia* (New York: Carroll & Graf, 2000); Maurice R. Stein, *The Eclipse of Community: An Interpretation of American Studies* (1960; repr., New York: Harper & Row, 1964), 199–226; and Jon C. Teaford, *The Metropolitan Revolution: The Rise of Post-Urban America* (New York: Columbia University Press, 2006), 62–107.

5. See, for example, Ann Forsyth, *Reforming Suburbia: The Planned Communities of Irvine, Columbia, and Woodlands* (Berkeley: University of California Press, 2005), 24–25; Andrew Duany, Elizabeth Plater-Zyberk, and Jeff Speck, *Suburban Sprawl: The Rise and Decline of the American Dream* (New York: Farrar, Straus, and Giroux, 2000); Dolores Hayden, *A Field Guide to Sprawl* (New York: W. W. Norton, 2004), 7–8; Philip Langdon, "Sprawl," in Morrison Institute for Public Policy, *Growth in Arizona: The Machine in the Garden* (Tempe, AZ.: Morrison Institute for Public Policy, 1998), 107–8; and the more positive view in Robert Bruegmann, *Sprawl: A Compact History* (Chicago: University of Chicago Press, 2005).

6. Forsyth, *Reforming Suburbia*, 27–28, citing a 1971 Urban Land Institute report.

7. On the New Town movement see Forsyth, *Reforming Suburbia*, 2–3, 27–35; Carol A. Christensen, *The American Garden City and the New Towns Movement* (Ann Arbor: UMI Research Press, 1986); J. A. Prestridge, *Case Studies of Six Planned New Towns in the United States* (Lexington: Institute for Environmental Studies, University of Kentucky Research Foundation, 1973), 1–2, 21; Gideon Golany and Daniel Walden, eds., *The Contemporary New Communities Movement in the United States* (Urbana: University of Illinois Press, 1974); Irving Lewis Allen, *New Towns and the Suburban Dream: Ideology and Utopia in Planning and Development* (Port Washington, NY: Kennikat Press, 1977); and James Bailey, ed., *New Towns in America: The Design and Development Process* (New York: Wiley, 1973), 41–43, 56, 103.

8. E.g., Greg Hise, *Magnetic Los Angeles: Planning the Twentieth-Century Metropolis* (Baltimore: Johns Hopkins University Press, 1997).

9. See, for example, Michael Dear and Steven Flusty, "Postmodern Urbanism," *Annals of the Association of American Geographers*, 88 (March 1998): 50–72. This discussion also relates to David Rusk's concept of "elastic cities" in *Cities without Suburbs*, 2nd ed. (Washington, DC: Woodrow Wilson Center, 1995).

10. The census lists Anchorage, Jacksonville, Oklahoma City, Nashville, and Indianapolis as being larger, but these represented city-country mergers, rather than the areas within a city's boundaries or the urbanized areas. See Campbell Gibson, "Population of the 100 Largest Cities and Other Urban Places in the United States: 1790 to 1990," Population Division Working Paper No. 27, Population Division, U.S. Bureau of the Census (Washington, DC: U.S. Bureau of the Census, 1998), www.census.gov/population/www/documentation/twps0027. html (accessed 5 November 2003).

11. For Webb's observation see Arthur Horton, *An Economic, Political, and Social Survey of Phoenix and the Valley of the Sun* (Tempe, AZ: Southside Progress, 1941), 181. See Marc A. Weiss, *The Rise of the Community Builders: The American Real Estate Industry and Urban Land*

Planning (New York: Columbia University Press, 1987); Hise, *Magnetic Los Angeles*, passim; Hayden, *Building Suburbia*, 123–25, 131–33; Jackson, *Crabgrass Frontier*, 190–218.

12. As quoted in the National Association of Home Builders Convention Report, in *America Builder*, March 1958, 20–21.

13. E.g., Edward H. Peplow, Jr., "You'll Like Phoenix," *Arizona Highways*, April 1957, 15.

14. "Subdivisions Require Lot of Planning," *AR*, 7 November 1954; Ralph Staggs, interview by Phoenix History Project, 18 May 1977, transcript, 12–13, PHPC. In Mesa, at least (and perhaps in others suburbs), the shift to larger-scale development came later: Liz Wilson and Debbie Abele, *Mesa Postwar Modern Single Family Subdivision Development, 1946–1973*, Report for the Mesa Housing Division (Mesa, AZ: City of Mesa, 2004), 8, 30, 42–43, 51.

15. Staggs interview transcript, 3; clippings from 1954 *AR* dated 6 June, 11 July, 23 May, 10 June, and 2 May in box 1, folder 5, Homebuilders of Central Arizona Collection, Arizona Historical Society, Tempe, Arizona (hereinafter HCAC); *AR*, 14 October 1979. See also William S. Collins, *The Emerging Metropolis: Phoenix, 1944–1973* (Phoenix: Arizona State Parks Board, 2005), 325–29; and Erika Finbraaten, "Post World War II Homebuilding: An Industrial Revolution" (master's thesis, Arizona State University, 2003).

16. Sam Mardian, interview by Phoenix History Project, 20 July 1978, transcript, 1–5, PHPC; Harold H. Martin, "The New Millionaires of Phoenix," *Saturday Evening Post*, 30 September 1961, 25–33.

17. Based on annual employment data in *ASR*, 1950–1980 editions, and data in *ASR*, *1957*, 31. The value of building permits in major suburbs compared with value in Phoenix rose from 50 percent in the 1950s, to 60 percent in the 1960s, and up to 80 percent in the 1970s.

18. *Arizona Business Gazette* (hereinafter *ABG*), 13 August 1998, 1; [Associated General Contractors], "Special Report: Arizona: Air-Conditioned Boomland," *This Earth*, August/ September 1963, 7. Perhaps the most prominent victim of the collapse was commercial builder David Murdock, whose assets dwindled from more than $100 million to less than $1 million. Collins, *Emerging Metropolis*, 246.

19. *AR*, 27 February 1998, A2; Staggs interview transcript, 31; *AR*, 7 January 1968. Wilson and Abele, *Mesa Postwar Development*, mention "thirty-four well-known subdivision builders," and the Arizona Home Builders Association (started in 1951) claimed forty-three members: attachment to confidential letter from President Ralph Burgbacher to Arizona Home Builders Association members, 22 November 22, 1954, in box 1, folder 7, HCAC.

20. See also the case of the only African American construction firm in town, the Williams and Jones Construction Company, in Philip R. VanderMeer, *Phoenix Rising: The Making of a Desert Metropolis* (Carlsbad, CA: Heritage Media, 2002), 72.

21. *AR*, 30 July 1964; *AR*, 3 February 1967; *AR*, 18 October 1967; *AR*, 7 January 1968; *AR*, 28 February 1969; and *AR*, 21 December 1970. Cf. City Planning Department, *Mobile Homes in Phoenix, Arizona* ([Phoenix]: City Planning Department, 1971).

22. *ASR*, 1969–1981; *ABG*, 13 August 1998, 1; *Phoenix Magazine*, November 1986, 85; Staggs interview transcript, 32; and John F. Long, interview by Phoenix History Project, 21 December 1977, transcript, 16–17, PHPC.

23. For national discussions of this see Kelley, *Expanding the American Dream*, and Hise, *Magnetic Los Angeles*, 153–85.

24. *AR*, 27 June 1954, and *AR*, 9 May 1954, in box 1, folder 5, HCAC.

25. Arthur David Pieper, "John Long: Planning Total Industrialization by 1961," *House & Home*, March 1960, 158–69; *AR*, 4 March 1962, E20; Martin, "New Millionaires of Phoenix," 30; Long interview transcript, 2–3; *American Builder*, June 1958, 74–75.

26. Staggs interview transcript, 5, 32–34; *AR*, 4 July 1954; *AR*, 4 March 1962; *AR*, 14 October 1979; Dan Lee, "Dwelling on the Middle Class," *Arizona*, in *AR*, 30 July 1978, 6–8; Finbraaten, "Post World War II Homebuilding," 101, 120, 130; "How to Start a One-man Boom: The John Long Story," *House & Home*, February 1957, 124–25.

27. Staggs interview transcript, 8–13, 25–28; *AR*, 27 June 1954, in box 1, folder 5, HCAC; labor materials in box 1, folder 5, and in box 8, folders 67 and 69, HCAC; Frank Snell, interview by Phoenix History Project, 7 December 1978, transcript, 117, PHPC; *AR*, 12 April 1959, 5:22; Lee, "Dwelling on the Middle Class," 4. Mardian interview transcript, 22, also noted labor-management cooperation.

28. Wilson and Abele, *Mesa Postwar Development*, 13; Hise, *Magnetic Los Angeles*, 78–84, 100–106, 173–74; Alfred Bruce and Harold Sandbank, *A History of Prefabrication* (1943; repr., New York: Arno Press, 1972); Pieper, "John Long," 161; Lee, "Dwelling on the Middle Class," 8–9.

29. Staggs interview transcript, 15–16; *This Is Arizona: Fiftieth Anniversary* (special edition of *Arizona Days and Ways Magazine*, 11 February 1962), 412; "Special Report: Arizona: Air-Conditioned Boomland," 9–10; Wilson and Abele, *Mesa Postwar Development*, 13, 61.

30. Martinson, *American Dreamscape*, 157–67; David Bricker, "Cliff May," in Robert Winter, ed., *Toward a Simpler Way of Life: The Arts and Crafts Architects of California* (Berkeley: Norfleet Press/University of California Press, 1997), 283–90; David Bricker, "Ranch Houses Are Not All the Same," in Deborah Slaton and William G. Foulks, eds., *Preserving the Recent Past 2* (Washington, DC: Historic Preservation Education Foundation, National Park Service, and Association for Preservation Technology International, 2000), 115–23.

31. *Pre-1950 Historic Residential Resources Reconnaissance Survey Report* (Phoenix: City of Phoenix Planning Department, 1990), 68–69; *Historic Homes of Phoenix: An Architectural and Preservation Guide*, Cooper/Robert Architects (Phoenix: City of Phoenix, 1992), 100–114; Wilson and Abele, *Mesa Postwar Development*, 13–29, 66: Pieper, "John Long," 168; *This Is Arizona*, 75, 81–83. The "Neighborhood Inventory Forms" from the "Pre-1950 Historic Residential Survey," detail the overwhelming shift to ranch homes and the strong shift to block construction in Phoenix neighborhoods built from 1945 to 1950; "Craftsmen Constructed Homes of Roaring '20s" in *AR*, 13 November 1966, E5, discusses a progression from simple houses built before 1950 to homogeneous neighborhoods built into the later 1950s, followed by more variety and quality in housing built into the 1960s.

32. Staggs interview transcript, 15; *AR*, 21 December 1970; Wilson and Abele, *Mesa Postwar Development*, 29; *Phoenix Magazine*, October 1979, demonstrates both housing diversity and the emphasis on insulation; Hogan Smith, "The House That Phoenix Builds," *Phoenix Magazine*, February 1967, 17, quotation on 47; *AR*, 12 August 2006, SR1; Grady Gammage, Jr., *Phoenix in Perspective: Reflections on Developing the Desert* (Tempe, AZ: Herberger Center for Design Excellence, College of Architecture and Environmental Design, Arizona State University, 1999),104; and Elizabeth S. Wilson, "Postwar Modern Housing and a Geographic Information System Study of Scottsdale Subdivisions" (master's thesis, Arizona State University, 2002), 87.

33. *AR*, 15 September 1957, 5:11; Wilson and Abele, *Mesa Postwwar Development*, 13; U.S. Census Bureau, *Statistical Abstract of the United States* (Washington, DC: Government Printing Office, 1997), 718; Avi Friedman and David Krawitz, *Peeking through the Keyhole: The Evolution of North American Homes* (Montreal: McGill-Queen's University Press, 2005); Christopher Solomon, "The Swelling McMansion Backlash," http://realestate.msn.com/buying/Articlenewhome.aspx?cp-documentid=418653 (accessed 17 August 2006).

34. Wilson and Abele, *Mesa Postwar Development*, 57; Tom Rex, *Housing in Metropolitan Phoenix* (Tempe, AZ: Morrison Institute for Public Policy, Arizona State University, 2000), 12; Barbara M. Kelly, "The Houses of Levittown in the Context of Postwar American Culture," *Preserving the Recent Past*, Deborah Slaton and Rebecca A. Schiffer, eds. (Washington, DC: Historic Preservation Education Foundation, 1995), 5, http://www.cr.nps.gov/nr/publications/bulletins/suburbs/Kelly.pdf (accessed 12 September 2006). Phoenix housing size information from box 1, folder 1, HCAC; *PG*, 13 September 1954; ads from *AR*, 1 February 1953, 25 April 1954, 1 November 1959, 11 November 1959, 1–7 November 1961, 11 February 1962, 11 February 1966, 10–16 November 1966; *This Is Arizona*, passim. Scottsdale housing analysis based on data in Wilson, "Postwar Modern Housing," 145.

35. *Arizona Homes and Gardens*, September-October 1953, as noted in Kristen C. Pumo, "The Homes Builders Association of Central Arizona and the FHA: Phoenix Residential Housing, 1920–1970" (master's thesis, Arizona State University, 2002), 66; *AR*, 12 April 1959, 5:2; *AR*, 12 September 1958, 16; *AR*, 8 July 1962, E14; *AR*, 15 September 1959, 5:11; quotation from *AR*, 20 September 1953, clipping in box 1, folder 2, HCAC; Peplow, "You'll Like Phoenix," 16; quotation from *This Is Arizona*, 75; Smith, "House That Phoenix Builds," 17.

36. Quotation from *Sunset*, April 1950, 50. See similar comments in *Sunset*, May 1950, 44, and *Sunset*, August, 1950, 38.

37. Kevin Norton, "The Swimming Pools Capital," 87–89, 119; *This Is Arizona*, 59, 494. But builders differed on pools: Long began offering pools in 1956; in 1962 Staggs still did not offer them, citing safety concerns. Manya Winsted, "Pioneer Builder John F. Long Celebrates an Anniversary," *Phoenix Magazine*, February 1977, 48; *AR*, 8 July 1962, E14.

38. *This Is Arizona*, 81.

39. Quotation from Peplow, "You'll Like Phoenix," 25.

40. *AR*, 11 February 1962, 16E; *This Is Arizona*, 81. Melvin E. Hecht offers a more cautious view—mainly reflecting personal observation—in "Climate and Culture, Landscape and Lifestyle in the Sun Belt of Southern Arizona," *Journal of Popular Culture*, 11 (Spring 1978): 941–44.

41. Price and size data in box 1, folder 1, HCAC; *PG*, 13 September 1954; ads from *AR*, 1 February 1953, 25 April 1954, 12 April 1957, 1 November 1959, 11 November 1959; Wilson and Abele, *Mesa Postwar Development*, 7, 40, 51; analysis of data reported in Finbraaten, "Post World War II Homebuilding," passim; Winsted, "Pioneer Builder John F. Long," 47–49; Alan C. Reed, "Dream Homes by the Dozens," *Arizona Highways*, September 1954, 25; Peplow, "You'll Like Phoenix," 15. Levittown price data from Greg Knight, "The Suburbanization of America: The Rise of the Patio Culture," http://www.patioculture.net/paper.html (accessed 5 September 2006).

42. *This Is Arizona*, 81, 77, and passim; *AR*, 8 July 1962, E9; Wilson and Abele, *Mesa Postwar Development*, 40; price information from *AR*, 1–7 November 1961, 11 February 1962, 11 February 1966, 10–16 November 1966, 21 December 1970, 30 April 1978; price information from *Phoenix Magazine*, October 1979, 107–33; Anne Mello, "Home Buying . . . Can You Afford to Wait?," *Phoenix Magazine*, October 1979, 111. Median home values during the 1960s rose 15 percent, or an inflation-adjusted rate of only 1 percent; the inflation-adjusted rate for the 1970s was 77 percent. Data from *Inside Phoenix, 1968* (Phoenix: Arizona Republic and Phoenix Gazette, 1968), 34; *Inside Phoenix, 1978*, 62; Rex, "Housing in Metropolitan Phoenix," 15.

43. Staggs interview transcript, 22.

44. *AR*, 26 September 1954.

45. *This Is Arizona*, 263; Staggs interview transcript, 7. (Cf. Wilson and Abele, *Mesa Postwar Development*, 7, which offers similar figures but no source information.) Porter Womack also paid $2,500 for land in 1954. Bert Fireman, "Under the Sun," *PG*, 27 December 1954. By 1969 the value of land on Camelback Road had increased fifty times from its 1945 value; Stephen C. Shadegg, *Century One: One Hundred Years of Water Development in the Salt River Valley* (Phoenix: W. A Krueger, 1969), 5. Of course land in some developments was more expensive, such as the $8,950 per acre parcels in a Scottsdale development in 1963. *Point West*, April 1963, 22.

46. This is based on an analysis of data from Staggs interview transcript, passim; Finbraaten, "Post World War II Homebuilding," passim; and *Phoenix Magazine*, October 1979, 114. Cf. Pumo, "Home Builder Association," 93.

47. Based on an analysis of the data and discussion in *Land Use of the Phoenix Urban Area: A Study Basic to Long Range Planning* (Phoenix: City of Phoenix and Maricopa County Advance Planning Task Force, 1959); *AR*, 12 April 1959, 5:22; Wilson and Abele, *Mesa Postwar Development*, 44–46.

48. Lynne Pierson Doti and Larry Schweikart, "Financing the Postwar Housing Boom in Phoenix and Los Angeles, 1945–1960," *Pacific Historical Review*, 58 (May 1989): 173–94; "How to Start a One-Man Boom," 118; Gammage, *Phoenix*, 46; Pumo, "Home Builders Association," 84–86.

49. *ASR*, 1961, 27; *Inside Phoenix*, 1968, 9; *Inside Phoenix*, 1978, 18; *ASR*, 1984.

50. *Inside Phoenix*, 1968, 9–11, 30; *Inside Phoenix*, 1978, 61.

51. Quotations from Shadegg, *Century One*, 43.

52. Hugh Knoell, press release, 17 September 1953, in box 1, folder 1, HCAC.

53. E.g., plat maps in Scott Solliday, "Post World War II Subdivisions: Property Register Second-Tier Resources, Neighborhood and House Type Context Development, Property Survey Update," Tempe Historic Commission, 2001, http://www.tempe.gov/historicpres/PostWWII (accessed 14 September 2006); *Land Use of the Phoenix Urban Area*, 16; see my discussion of city services in chapter 4, above.

54. On national trends see sources in notes 3 and 4, esp. Kelly, *Suburbia Re-examined*.

55. *AR*, 28 March 1954, Special Section, and *AR*, 19 May 1954, clippings in box 1, folder 5, HCAC; and Collins, *Emerging Metropolis*, 233–36. The property ran from Thomas to Osborn streets and extended from Central as far west as 7th Avenue.

56. Long interview transcript, 1–16; *AR*, 7 January 1968 and 14 November 1971; Winsted, "Pioneer Builder John F. Long," 47–49; Dan Lee, "Dwelling on the Middle Class," *Arizona Magazine*, in *AR*, 30 July 1978, 6; Jeffrey Hardwick, *Mall Maker: Victor Gruen, Architect of an American Dream* (Philadelphia: University of Pennsylvania Press, 2004), 104–59; and Alex Wall, *Victor Gruen: From Urban Shop to New City* (Barcelona: Actar, 2005), 65–158. For a more extended discussion of Maryvale see Finbraaten, "Post World War II Homebuilding," 79–90; also Collins, *Emerging Metropolis*, 313–4.

57. *This Is Arizona*, 87, 92–93; "What Is Dreamland Villa and the Dreamland Villa Community Club?," members.cox.net/bobbiesum/dvcc/directory_2005.html (accessed 17 September 2006); "Dreamland Villa Golf Club," http://www.golflink.com/golf-courses/golf-course.asp?course=356 (accessed 19 September 2006). Dreamland became chartered in 1961 and took over the community assets in 1972. The seminal work classifying different types of retirement housing is Michael Hunt et al., *Retirement Communities: An American Original* (New York: Haworth Press, 1984), esp. 252–73.

58. *This Is Arizona*, 74, 87–93.

59. VanderMeer, *Phoenix Rising*, 66; Steve Bergsman, "Del Webb," *Phoenix Magazine*, August 1991, 81–89; Arelo Sederberg and John F. Lawrence, "Del Webb, the Bashful Barnum," *Los Angeles Times WEST Magazine*, 14 September 1969, 16–20; *Time*, 3 August 1962, 47–48; *AR*, 13 February 2000; *AR*, 14 January 1973, 1; *AR*, 5 July 1974, clipping from Del Webb Biography Collection, Arizona Collection, Arizona State University Library; *AR*, 11 November 1961; Tom Chauncey, as told to and edited by Gordon A. Sabine, *Tom Chauncey: A Memoir* (Tempe, AZ: Arizona State University Libraries, 1989), 131; and Margaret Finnerty, *Del Webb: A Man, A Company* (Flagstaff, AZ: Heritage Publishers, 1991).

60. Besides sources in the previous note, see also Joyce Rockwood Muench, "Sun City Arizona, USA," *Arizona Highways*, November 1967, 4–5, 32; *Time*, 3 August 1962, 46–49; Charles S. Sargent, Jr., *Planned Communities in Greater Phoenix: Origins, Functions, and Control*, Papers in Public Administration no. 25 (Tempe, AZ: Institute of Public Administration, Arizona State University, 1973), 82–85; Patricia Gober, "The Retirement Community as a Geographical Phenomenon: The Case of Sun City, Arizona," *Journal of Geography*, 84 (September/October 1985): 189–98; John M. Findlay, *Magic Lands: Western Cityscapes and American Culture after 1940* (Berkeley: University of California Press, 1992), 160–213.

61. *AR*, 13 February 2000; Gober, "The Retirement Community," 191, 193–94; Sargent, *Planned Communities*, 84–85; Findlay, *Magic Lands*, 206–8.

62. *AR*, 13 February 2000, 14 Jan. 1973, 1; *AR*, 5 July 1974, clipping from Del Webb Biography; *Time*, 3 Aug. 1962, 48.

63. Sargent, *Planned Communities*, 70–73, 85–86. In subsequent years more retirement housing communities were built, for both year-round and seasonal use. These were smaller than Sun City, because few companies could match Webb's resources, but also because land ownership in Mesa was more fragmented. Wilson and Abele, *Mesa Postwar Development*, 8.

64. On Arizona towns see Charles Sargent, ed., *Metro Arizona* (Scottsdale, AZ: Buffington Books, 1988), 60–61, 102; and "History of Goodyear," http://www.ci.goodyear.az.us/index.asp?NID=384 (accessed 15 December 2005).

65. See discussions of New Towns in Forsyth, *Reforming Suburbia*, 2–3, 27–35; Wall, *Gruen*, 201–4; Christensen, *The American Garden City and the New Towns Movement*; Prestridge, *Case Studies*, 1–2, 21; Golany and Walden, *Contemporary New Communities Movement*; and Allen, *New Towns and the Suburban Dream*. On Arizona see Wilbur Smith and Associates, *Arizona New Town Development Concepts* (Phoenix: City of Phoenix, Department of Economic Planning and Development, 1971), esp. 1–2 to 1–5; Sargent, *Planned Communities*, passim; and William R. Gable, "Arizona," in JeDon A. Emenhiser, ed., *Rocky Mountain Urban Politics*, Monograph Series, 19 (Logan, UT: Utah State University, 1971): 27–32. Hise in *Magnetic Los Angeles* demonstrates the precedent-setting and pioneering efforts of California builders.

66. Bobbi Holmes, "Lake Havasu City History," *Havasu Magazine*, http://havasumagazine.com/history_of_lake_havasu_city.htm (accessed 20 September 2006); Thomas E. Sheridan, *Arizona: A History* (Tucson: University of Arizona Press, 1995), 334–45; cf. Findlay, *Magic Lands*, 52–116, 216, which shows the influence of Disneyland on urban planning and that the alumni of this project worked on other western cities, such as Seattle.

67. Sargent, *Planned Communities*, 64–70; "Fountain Hills History," *Fountain Hills Times Online*, http://www.fhtimes.com/cominfo/06historyff.htm (accessed 28 September 2006).

68. *AR*, 3 November 1957, 5:16; and Teresa Baker, "The Litchfield Park Collection," seminar paper, Arizona State University, 1995. The company's aviation facility was in the adjacent town of Goodyear.

69. Quotations from Marshall Kaplan, "Report of Interview with Patrick J. Cusick, Jr.," 3 December 1964, in box 136, folder 1, Litchfield Park Collection, ASU (hereinafter LPC); "Litchfield Park," *The Wingfoot Clan, Arizona Edition*, 18 September 1969, 2, in box 159, LPC.

70. Victor Gruen, *The Heart of Our Cities; The Urban Crisis: Diagnosis and Cure* (New York: Simon and Schuster, 1964); Wal, *Gruen*, 209–11; Victor Gruen Associates, *Proposed General Plan for Litchfield Park Area, Maricopa County, Arizona* (Phoenix: Victor Gruen Associates, 1966), 11–19; "Objectives for the Development of Litchfield Park, Arizona, 18 June 1965," and Patrick J. Cusick, "Summary of Significant Matters Discussed and Decisions Made 22, 23, and 24 November 1965," in box 136, folder 1, LPC; and "Declarations of Restrictions, Subdivision 12, April 1966," in box 143, folder 8, LPC; and "'New Town' Begun in Phoenix Area," *National Civic Review*, December 1967, 643.

71. Sargent, *Planned Communities*, 73–77; quotation from memo, Hugh S. Kelly to Patrick J. Cusick, 30 June 1966, in box 136, folder 1, LPC; Mark Scott, "Litchfield Park: The Failure of an Arizona Planned Community," unpublished paper in possession of the author. Lichtfield Park's long-term prospects as a residential center were damaged by proximity to Luke Air Force Base and its noise. Fountain Hills incorporated in 1989; "Fountain Hills History."

72. Sargent, *Planned Communities*, 5–8, lists the characteristics of "planned communities" as of 1972 and uses 640 acres as an "arbitrary" but somewhat useful division between conventional subdivision and planned suburb. I have added to Sargent's information the data from "Large-Scale Developments in Metropolitan Phoenix," *Inside Phoenix*, 1978, 55. My discussion excludes several exurban communities (three subdivisions in far north Carefree, plus Queen Creek in the far southeast) as being too distant from the populated area to be directly relevant to this analysis. I also omit Long's two additions to Maryvale, since their structure essentially reflects the perspective he developed in the 1950s. Thus, my analysis adds twenty communities to the five that Sargent uses.

73. *AR*, 14 November 1971.

74. His analysis is based on information in "Large-Scale Developments," as well as these websites (accessed 28 November 2006): "Find a Neighborhood," http://www.aznb.com/findneighborhood; City of Phoenix, "Neighborhood Associations," http://phoenix.gov/phxb/NSDAssoc/search-alpha-init.do; and Map Quest, http://www.mapquest.com/main.adp. Another option for smaller upper-end developments was building in cooperation with resorts. E.g., "A Way of Life," *Phoenix Magazine*, February 1967, 18–19.

75. One subdivision included two thousand acres in its long-term plan; one of the two Phoenix subdivisions was the posh Biltmore Estates, only seven miles from downtown.

76. William S. Worley, *J. C. Nichols and the Shaping of Kansas City: Innovation in Planned Residential Communities* (Columbia: University of Missouri Press, 1990); Evan McKenzie, *Privatopia: Homeowner Associations and the Rise of Residential Private Government* (New Haven: Yale University Press, 1994); Robert H. Nelson, *Private Neighborhoods and the Transformation of Local Government* (Washington, DC: Urban Institute Press, 2005). Joel Garreau discusses these "shadow governments" in *Edge City: Life on the New Frontier* (New York: Doubleday, 1991), 185–208.

77. Sargent, *Planned Communities*, 58–59; Martin W. Gibson, *Phoenix's Ahwatukee-Foothills* (Charleston, SC: Arcadia, 2006), 67–90; "Ahwatukee History," www.ahwatukeehoa.com/sub_category_list.asp?category=4&title=ABM+History (accessed 1 October 2006); Carol E. Heim, "Border Wars: Tax Revenues, Annexation, and Urban Growth in Phoenix," Working Paper 2006-01, Department of Economics, University of Massachusetts, Amherst, 10–13.

Typically, the developer operated the HOA until most homes were sold; home owners took control in Ahwatukee in 1988, when 90 percent of the lots were sold.

78. *Proposed Comprehensive General Plan, Scottsdale, Arizona* (South Pasadena, CA: Eisner-Stewart & Associates, 1966); Gruen Associates and Environmental Planning Consultants, *Kaiser Aetna–McCormick Ranch, Scottsdale, Arizona: Policy for Creating a Quality Environment* (Scottsdale: Kaiser Aetna, 1971) and *Kaiser Aetna–McCormick Ranch, Scottsdale, Arizona: Master Development Plan, January, 1971* (Los Angeles: The Associates, 1971); "The History of McCormick Ranch," http://www.mccormickranchpoa.com/history. htm (accessed 25 September 2006); City of Scottsdale, "Scottsdale's Past," http://www. scottsdaleaz.gov/generalplan/Introduction.asp (accessed 9 May 2005); and Sargent, *Planned Communities*, 77–79.

79. Dwight L. Busby, *Dobson Ranch: A Planned Community* (Phoenix: Busby Associates, 1972); Sargent, *Planned Communities*, 63–64; Tray C. Mead and Robert C. Price, *Mesa: Beneath the Shadows of the Superstitions* (Northridge, CA: Windsor Publications, 1988), 122–23, 146; Dobson Association, "About Us," www.dobsonranchhoa.com/outside_frame.asp (accessed 18 November 2006).

80. On HOAs see McKenzie, *Privatopia*, and Nelson, *Private Neighborhoods*. HOAs were also used for another nine Planned Area Developments in Phoenix started between 1965 and 1975, but these were generally small in-fill projects. Of the twenty-nine that were for single-family homes, the median size was sixty-four homes and 17.3 acres. The HOAs maintained the private streets, common landscape areas, and some recreation areas, usually just a swimming pool. *A Study of Planned Area Development (PAD)* (Phoenix: City of Phoenix Planning Department, 1975), 2–7; calculations based on data on 26–35.

81. *General Plan, 2030, City of Tempe* (Tempe, AZ: City of Tempe Development Services Department, 2003), 22; Heim, "Border Wars," 10–14.

82. Abbott, *Metropolitan Frontier*, 142; Rusk, *Cities without Suburbs*, 83; Jason Hackworth calls these four communities "satellite municipalities" in "Local Planning and Economic Restructuring: A Synthetic Interpretation of Urban Redevelopment, *Journal of Planning Education and Research* 18 (June 1999): 293–306; while both Arizona and Phoenix city planners used the term *satellite* more restrictively to refer to a separate but dependent community, namely, Fountain Hill; see Smith, *Arizona New Town*, 3–7, and *Self-Contained Community* (Phoenix: City of Phoenix Planning Department, 1982), 4–5. Cf. Leo F. Schnore, "Satellites and Suburbs," *Social Forces*, 36 (December 1957): 121–27; and Sargent, *Planned Communities*, 52–56.

83. Ernest J. Hopkins and Alfred Thomas, Jr., *The Arizona State University Story* (Tempe, AZ: Arizona State University, 1960), 284–304; Michael J. Schmandt, "Local Government Decision and Landscape Change: Downtown Tempe, 1972–1991" (master's thesis, Arizona State University, 1991); Harry Mitchell, interview by Mill-Avenue-Oral-History-Project, 18 May 1988, transcript, Hayden Arizona Collection, Arizona State University Library; *AR*, 15 February 1987, AZ section; *General Plan, 2030, City of Tempe*; Patricia Gober, *Metropolitan Phoenix: Place Making and Community Building in the Desert* (Philadelphia: University of Pennsylvania Press, 2006), 174, 186–96; Robert E. Lang, "The Boomburbs at 'Buildout': Future Development in Large, Fast-Growing Suburbs," 17–18, draft essay, Metropolitan Institute at Virginia Tech, 2005, http://www.mi.vt.edu/uploads/SGOE.pdf (accessed 27 February 2007).

84. Wilson, "Postwar Modern Housing," 60; cf. *Proposed Comprehensive General Plan, Scottsdale, Arizona* (South Pasadena, CA: Eisner-Stewart & Associates, 1966), 9.

85. Data in *General Plan, 2030, Tempe*, 22; Wilson and Abele, *Mesa Postwar Development*, 40, 51; and *The Economy of Maricopa County, 1965 to 1980: A Study for the Guidance of Public and Private Planning* (Phoenix: Western Management Consultants, Inc., 1965), fn. 5, 227. See too the discussions in passing in *A Comprehensive Plan for Scottsdale, Arizona; "The West's Most Western Town"* ([Phoenix]: Maricopa County Planning and Zoning Department, 1960–62) and *Proposed Comprehensive General Plan, Scottsdale.*

86. This shift to more affluent residences also fostered a different type of politics, one based more on wealth than previously City of Scottsdale, "Scottsdale Airport History," www.scottsdaleaz. gov/Airport/History.asp (accessed 25 February 2007); City of Scottsdale, "Scottsdale's Past," www.scottsdaleaz.gov/generalplan/Introduction.asp (accessed 9 May 2005); Lang, "The Boomburbs at 'Buildout.'"

87. Mark C. Simpson, "The Role of Leisure Activities in the Development of a Sunbelt Suburb: Parks and Recreation in Mesa, Arizona, 1980 to 2000" (master's thesis, Arizona State University, 2006), 26–36; Wilson and Abele, *Mesa Postwar Development*, 34, 49; *Our Town, Mesa Arizona, 1878–1978* (Mesa, AZ: Mesa Public Schools, 1978) 150–54, 162–64; Mead and Price, *Mesa*, 93–122.

88. Quotation from Wilson and Abele, *Mesa Postwar Development*, 40; *General Plan, 2030, Tempe*, 22; *AR*, 9 March 2006, Mesa section, 1.

89. *Thunderbird, Special Issue*, 50 (1996); Dean Smith, *Glendale: Century of Diversity, An Illustrated History* (Glendale, AZ: City of Glendale, 1992), 110–34.

90. Elizabeth Burns, "Vance's Commuting Analysis Extended to the Suburban Southwest: Tempe, Arizona," *Yearbook of the Association of Pacific Coast Geographers*, repr. no. 67 (Berkeley: Transportation Center, University of California, 1992), 10, 13–17, www.uctc.net/papers/067.pdf (accessed 15 February 2007).

91. *Edge City*, 4–15; Rob Kling, Spencer Olin, and Mark Poster, *Postsuburban California: The Transformation of Orange County since World War II* (Berkeley: University of California Press, 1991).

92. Janus Associates, Inc., *Commerce in Phoenix, 1870 to 1942: A Context for Preserving Historic Properties* (Phoenix: State Historic Preservation Office, 1989), 27–28.

93. *Land Use of the Phoenix Urban Area*, quotation on 3, 14–15; *A Comprehensive Plan for Land-Use in Paradise Valley* (Phoenix: Maricopa County Planning Department, 1957), 31–33; *AR*, 1 November 1961, B1; Peplow, "You'll Like Living in Phoenix," 24–25; *Inside Phoenix, 1968*, 1978. Three larger centers offered from 245,000 to 350,000 square feet and included dime stores and even a department store.

94. James J. Farrell, *One Nation under Goods: Malls and the Seductions of American Shopping* (Washington, DC: Smithsonian Institution, 2003); and the "AHR Forum" on malls, *American Historical Review* 101 (October 1996), including Lizabeth Cohen, "From Town Center to Shopping Center: The Reconfiguration of Community Marketplaces in Postwar America," 1050–81, Thomas W. Hanchett, "U.S. Tax Policy and the Shopping-Center Boom of the 1950s and 1960s," 1082–110, and Kenneth Jackson, "All the World's a Mall: Reflections on the Social and Economic Consequences of the American Shopping Center," 1111–21.

95. *Inside Phoenix*, 1965, 1968, 1973, and 1978 editions. Chris-Town Mall grew the most: it began in 1963 with roughly 60 tenants and 680,000 square feet and after fifteen years had 160 tenants and took up 1,250,000 square feet.

96. *AR*, 1 November 1994; Farrell, *One Nation under Goods*; Hardwick, *Mall Maker*, 214–24.

CHAPTER 8

1. See, for example, Robert A. Beauregard, *Voices of Decline: The Postwar Fate of U.S. Cities* (Cambridge, MA: Blackwell, 1993); Alison Isenberg, *Downtown America: A History of the Place and the People Who Made It* (Chicago: University of Chicago Press, 2004), 166–202; Kenneth T. Jackson, *Crabgrass Frontier: The Suburbanization of the United States* (New York: Oxford University Press, 1985), 272–305; and Amy Bridges, *Morning Glories: Municipal Reform in the Southwest* (Princeton: Princeton University Press, 1997), 151–91.

2. Bridges, *Morning Glories*, provides an insightful perspective on Phoenix policies in the context of other southwestern cities. For discussions of growth machines see John R. Logan and Harvey L. Molotch, *Urban Fortunes: The Political Economy of Place* (Berkeley: University of California Press, 1987); Andrew E. G. Jonas and David Wilson, eds., *The Urban Growth Machine: Critical Perspectives, Two Decades Later* (Albany: State University of New York Press, 1999); and David R. Johnson, "Growth Machines Revisited," paper presented at Social Science History Association Conference, Portland, OR, 3 November 2005.

3. Mardian quotation from Swearing-in Statement, 4 January 1960, in box 1, folder 7, PCGR. See the discussion in Chapter 5, above; "Phoenix Growth Committee, 1957," in box 6, folder 28, SMJP; "Growth Committee, 1961," in box 2, folder 14, SMJP; Phoenix Forward Task Force, *Phoenix Forward—Citizen Participation in Planning: A Citizen Report on Objectives and Goals for Metropolitan Phoenix* (Phoenix: City Council and The Task Force, 1970); *National Civic Review* 57 (October 1975): 489 (hereinafter *NCR*); *NCR* 69 (April 1980): 83; *AR*, 29 December 1974, A1; *AR*, 23 November 1975, B1; *AR*, 7 December 1975, B2. In the following discussion I use *Charter Government* to refer to the elected city officials nominated as Charter Government candidates; in using *CGC*, or *Charter Government Committee*, I am referring to the larger group of former and current officials and committee members, plus like-minded individuals.

4. *AR*, 5 May 1967, 2–3; *AR*, November 1967; *PG*, 3 November 1975; *AR*, 5 November 1975.

5. Quotations from Jack Williams letter to R. L. Thomas, 25 May 1959, in box 3, folder 18, PCGR; Margaret Kober, interview by Phoenix History Project, 18 June 1976, transcript, 16, PHPC. For descriptions of how the Charter Government Committee was formed and operated in a single year (1967), see *AR*, 29 May 1967, A1; *AR*, July 1967, A1; *PG*, 8 September 1967, A1; *PG*, 20 October 1967, A1.

6. E.g. *AR*, 22 October 1967 and 8 November 1967, clippings in "Phoenix—Elections—1967" folder, Arizona Vertical File, Phoenix Public Library (hereinafter AVF). The mayoral workload is obvious from the records of Phoenix government, in SMJP and PCGR. See also Leonard E. Goodall, "Phoenix: Reformers at Work," in Goodall, ed., *Urban Politics in the Southwest* (Tempe, AZ: Arizona State University, 1967), 123.

7. Leonard E. Goodall analyzed the nature of Charter Government in "Phoenix: Reformers at Work," 124–25. Bridges, *Morning Glories*, passim, offers important insights into nonpartisan politics, but she focuses more on the relative neglect of certain liberal issues than on CGC's efforts to claim the political center. She also sees the main shift in Phoenix politics as occurring in the 1960s, with the political activation of minority groups linked to the rise of antigrowth policies. As I argue later in this chapter, that shift came in the 1970s and resulted more from multiple problems related to growth.

8. The unique nature of this campaign was noted in *AR*, 12 November 1961, A22; I analyze this campaign in detail in "Conservatism and Urban Development in Phoenix," paper presented at Social Science History Association Conference, Portland, OR, 3 November 2005.

9. Aubrey Moore, transcript of radio broadcasts, 24 October 1961 and 30 October 1961, in box 2,

folder 8, PCGR; *AR*, 7 November 1961, A8, A11; *AR*, 11 November 1961, A8; *AR*, 12 November 1961, A12.

10. *AR*, 12 November 1961, A23; quotation from SAC press release, 16 October 1961, in box 2, folder 9, PCGR.

11. *AR*, 4 November 1961, A7; *AR*, 7 November 1961, A8, A11; *AR*, 12 November 1961, A23; "Release from Mayor's Office," 19 October 1961, in box 2, folder 8, PCGR; quotation from SAC press release, 2, in box 2, folder 9, PCGR; SAC "Statement of Issues," 18 October 1961, in box 2, folder 8, PCGR.

12. *AR*, 5 November 1961, A12, B1; *AR*, 4 November 1961, A12; *AR*, 12 November 1961, A22; *AR*, 11 November 1961, A22; *AR*, 15 November 1961, A5; *AR*, 2 November 12A; Samuel Mardian remarks to Northside Republican Club, 30 October 1961, in box 2, folder 9, PCGR.

13. *AR*, 5 November 1961, A5; *AR*, 12 November 1961, A22; *AR*, 13 November 1961, A7–A8; "Television Spots," in box 2, folder 9, PCGR; and Mayor's Office statement, 19 October 1961, in box 2, folder 9, PCGR.

14. *AR*, 11 November 1961, A8; *AR*, 6 November 1961, A21; *AR*, 10 November 1961, A5; *AR*, 12 November 1961, A22.

15. See VanderMeer, "Conservatism and Urban Development in Phoenix"; "Smear Campaign" materials in series 5, subject files, container 69, folders 12–14, 19–23, NMLP-AA; *AR*, 2 November 1961, A1, A12; *AR*, 12 November 1961, A22; *AR*, 4 November 1961, A12; "Editorial," *Arizona Sun*, in box 2, folder 8, PCGR; "Memo: SAC Meeting, November 3, 1961," in box 2, folder 8, PCGR; Mardian, personal correspondence, in box 2, folder 9, PCGR.

16. Summary election data is in *Registered Voters and Votes Cast for Mayor and Council, Primary and General Election, Phoenix, 1949–1979* (Phoenix: City of Phoenix, 1980); for complete 1961 returns see "Certificate of Election," in box 2, folder 8, PCGR. Cf. election analysis in Goodall, "Phoenix," 119.

17. See the responses in *AR*, 22 December 1961, A5, to an article in the *Washington Post* on conservatism in the Valley.

18. The most detailed candidate biographies for ACT nominees are the press release biographies, "ACT Candidate," in "Phoenix—Elections—1963" folder, AVF. Charter Government candidates were profiled in *AR*, 23 October 1963, clipping in AVF; HEAR candidates were best profiled in *Evening American* (hereinafter *EA*), 13 October 1963, A1. On Ragsdale see Matthew C. Whitaker, *Race Work: The Rise of Civil Rights in the Urban West* (Lincoln: University of Nebraska Press, 2005); on Pena see "Biography of Manuel 'Lito' Peña, Jr., 1924–1955," Chicano Research Collection, and Manuel "Lito" Peña Biography File, Arizona Collection, Arizona State University.

19. Quotation from "ACT Platform," in "Phoenix—Elections—1963" folder, AVR; *AR*, 17 October 1963, A20; *AR*, 9 October 1963, A1; *PG*, 17 October 1963, A1; *EA*, 31 October 1963, A1.

20. "ACT Platform"; *AR*, 27 September 1963, A1; *AR*, 29 October 1963, A1; *AR*, 12 November 1963, A17; *EA*, 17 October 1963, A1; and *AR*, 4 December 1963, A1.

21. Some of the position papers are included in box 1, folder 5, PCGR; see the handwritten summary numbers, dated 8 October 1963, in box 2, folder 12, PCGR; quotations from *AR*, 13 November 1963, A4; *AR*, 17 October 1963, 8A; *AR*, 8 November 1963, A1; *AR*, 12 November 1963, A17.

22. *AR*, 29 August 1963, A1; *Arizona Journal* (hereinafter *AJ*), 13 October 1963, A1; *EA* A1, on 13 October 1963, A1; *EA*, 22 October 1963, A1; *EA*, 28 October 1963, A1; *AR*, 18 Oct., A5; *AR*, 28 October, A1.

23. *AJ*, 8 December 1963, A1. Summary election data in *Registered Voters and Votes*; primary election results in *AR*, 13 November 1963, A1, and *AR*, 14 November 1963, A1, with complete returns and maps in box 1, folder 5, PCGR; general election analysis in *AR*, 11 December 1963, A1.

24. *AR*, 7 November 1963, A1, A3, A8; *AR*, 10 November 1963, A1; *Registered Voters and Votes*; and Brent Whiting Brown, "An Analysis of the Phoenix Charter Government Committee as a Political Entity" (master's thesis, Arizona State University, 1968), 90.

25. *AR*, 7 November 1965, A3; Brown, "Phoenix Charter Government," 80–83; and clippings in "Phoenix—City Elections—1967," AVF; *PG*, 21 November 1966; *AR*, 11 [July?] 1967; *AR*, 26 August 1967; *AR*, 24 October 1967; *PG*, 19 October 1967; *AR*, 24 October 1967; *PG*, 31 October 1967; and *AR*, 3 November 1967.

26. *AR*, 4 November 1967, A1; *AR*, 11 November 1967, A1; *PG*, 6 November 1967, A8; *PG*, 8 November 1967, A1; and esp. *AR*, 12 November 1968, A20–A21. Cf. *NCR*, 57 (January 1968): 49.

27. Brown, "Phoenix Charter Government," 69–78, provides a detailed discussion of this process.

28. See the *AR*'s candidates' biographies in "Phoenix—Election—1969" folder, AVF; *PG*, 6 November 1969, A20.

29. *AR*, 5 November 1969, A23; "Phoenix—Election—1969" folder, AVF.

30. John Driggs, interview by Phoenix History Project, 13 July 1978, transcript, 1–5, PHPC; for voting returns see *Registered Voters and Votes*. The normal variation in Charter Government's vote was 3.8 percent; in the 1969 elections it reached 13.6 and 11.2 percent—only slightly below the range for its opponents.

31. *PG*, 14 November 1969, A1, A4.

32. He placed second. His major impact on Arizona politics came from filing a lawsuit that forced reapportionment of the state legislature in 1966. Amy Silverman, "Old Glory: Veteran Phoenix Lawyer Gary Peter Klahr Fought the Bar and the Bar Won," *New Times*, 4 July 2002, www.phoenixnewtimes.com/search/results.php?issue=170995 (accessed 27 June 2007).

33. Quotations from "Charter Government," *Phoenix Magazine*, 8 August 1973, 98; Driggs interview transcript, 18–19.

34. *Registered Voters and Votes*; Lila Cockrell of San Antonio, elected a few months earlier, was the first. Texas Women's Hall of Fame, "Lila Cockrell," www.twu.edu/twhf/tw-cockrell.htm (accessed 28 June 2007); Judith A. Leavitt, ed. *American Women Managers and Administrators: A Selective Biographical Dictionary of Twentieth-Century Leaders in Business, Education, and Government* (Westport, CN: Greenwood Press, 1958), 47–48.

35. *AR*, 5 November 1975, A1; *AR*, 10 December 1975, A1; *Registered Voters and Votes*. On measure of the dramatic shift: Charter Government's voter cohesion was worse than its opponents: 12.7 to 10.9 percent.

36. This discussion rests on my analysis of the city's financial data as presented in two document series produced by the City of Phoenix from 1960 to 1980: *(Comprehensive) Annual Financial Report* (hereinafter *AFR*) and the *Annual Budget of the City of Phoenix* (hereinafter *ABP*). Besides the revenue sources discussed below, the city also drew from less significant and less controversial sources such as construction-related fees, fines, licenses, rents, and special excise taxes.

37. Dennis R. Judd and Todd Swanstrom discuss revenues for all cities in *City Politics: Private Power and Public Policy*, 2nd ed. (New York: Longman, 1998), 333–38. Local property taxes also helped fund public schools, but Phoenix schools, like those in most American cities, were operated by independent school boards.

38. See also the earlier discussion of services in chapter 5. [City of Phoenix], "Fact Sheet," [1959], 12–16, in box 1, folder 7, PCGR; Paul Kelso, *A Decade of Council-Manager Government in Phoenix, Arizona* ([Phoenix?]: 1960), 20–23; *AFR, 1960/61*, vi–vii; City of Phoenix, Arizona Water and Sewers Department, untitled memo, including "Water Rate History" and "Water Rate Comparison," 11 September 1963, in box 2, folder 12, PCGR; "1975–76 Annual Budget Message," *ABP, 1973/74*, 55; "1975–76 Annual Budget Message," *ABP, 1975/76*, 52. The airport was a self-supporting city service.

39. David R. Berman, *Arizona Politics and Government: The Quest for Autonomy, Democracy, and Development* (Lincoln: University of Nebraska Press, 1998), 151; *AFR, 1970/71*, II; *AFR, 1965/66*, 8–13; "Annual Budget Message," *ABP, 1973/74*, 52–53; "Annual Budget Message," *ABP, 1975/76*, 50–51. Gas taxes were further increased in 1974.

40. *NCR*, June 1975, 315–16; Jon C. Teaford, *The Metropolitan Revolution: The Rise of Post-Urban America* (New York: Columbia University Press, 2006), 129–39; Judd and Swanstrom, *City Politics*, 324–37; Helen Ladd, "Big City Finances," in George E. Peterson, *Big-City Politics, Governance, and Fiscal Constraints* (Washington, DC: Urban Institute Press, 1994), 201–60; *Phoenix Magazine*, November 1986, 92; "Annual Budget Message," *ABP, 1975/76*, 2–3, 7, 11–12; *ABP, 1980/81*, 13; Margaret T. Hance, *Mayor's Budget Message, 1980–1981* (Phoenix: City of Phoenix, 1980), 1–2.

41. "Federal Grants-in-Aid to State and Local Governments" [1958], in box 2, folder 11, PCGR; Judd and Swanstrom, *City Politics*, 217–21, 231–35; and Timothy J. Conlan, *From New Federalism to Devolution: Twenty-five Years of Intergovernmental Reform*, rev. ed. (Washington, DC: Brookings Institute Press, 1998), passim.

42. Catherine H. Lovell, "Coordinating Federal Grants from Below," *Public Administration Review*, 39 (September–October 1979): 432–39; Judd and Swanstrom, *City Politics*, 223–24; Conlan, *From New Federalism to Devolution*, 36–92.

43. Jack Williams to Rep. L. H. Fountain, 30 January 1958, in box 2, folder 11, PCGR.

44. On the conservative shift see VanderMeer, "Conservatism and Urban Development in Phoenix." Federal grants and revenue-sharing funds are listed annually in *AFR* and summarized in *AFR, 1975/76*, 156–57; *AFR, 1980/81*, 165–66; on newspaper opinion, see, for example, the editorials in *PG*, 4 August 1967 and 20 November 1967.

45. Driggs interview transcript, 8, 10–11, 15; *AFR, 1975/76*, 156–57; *AFR, 1980/81*, 165–66; "Annual Budget Message," in *ABP, 1975/76*, 13. Spending on police had comprised 38.6 percent of revenue-sharing funds in 1972–76, for a combined figure of 44 percent of the 1972–80 total of $83 million. On Hance's policies see David L. Altheide and John S. Hall, "Phoenix: Crime and Politics in a New Federal City," in Anne Heinz, Herbert Jacob, and Robert L. Lineberry, eds., *Crime in City Politics* (New York: Longman, 1983), 230–34.

46. Josh Protas, "The Straw That Broke the Camel's Back: Preservation of an Urban Mountain Landscape," *Journal of the Southwest* 43 (Autumn 2001): 379–421; Peter Iverson, *Barry Goldwater, Native Arizonan* (Norman, OK: University of Oklahoma Press, 1997), 205–11; cf. *AR*, 3 June 2007, V1; Driggs interview transcript, 11; Dorothy Gilbert, "A History of the Phoenix Mountains Preserve," 1993, unpublished paper, Arizona Collection, Arizona State University; *AFR, 1975/76*, 156–57.

47. Driggs interview transcript, 10–12; Judd and Swanstrom, *City Politics*, 233–34.

48. "Annual Budget Message," in *ABP, 1980/81*, 7, 9.

49. All-America City Award, in series 1, carton 1, folder 55, NMLP-AA. The figures for employees per 10,000 population for "common functions" of government are from *The Municipal Year*

Book (Chicago: International City Managers' Association), 1960–1980 editions. The closest competitors were also southwestern cities—San Diego and San Antonio.

50. *AFR, 1980/81,* 174; "Annual Budget Message," *ABP, 1975/76,* 52; City of Phoenix, Arizona Water and Sewers Department, four-page untitled memo, including "Water Rate History" and "Water Rate Comparison," 11 September 1963, in box 2, folder 12, PCGR; *ABP, 1980/81,* 13.

51. See the discussion in chapter 5; "Statistical Profile," *AFR,* 1960–1980; "Capital Improvement Plans, 1963–1965," in box 2, folder 12, PCGR; *1970 Mayor's Annual Report, Mayor Milt Graham* (Phoenix: City of Phoenix, 1970), 12; "Annual Budget Message," in *ABP, 1975/76,* 11–12.

52. Michael D. Jones, *Desert Wings: A History of Phoenix Sky Harbor International Airport* (Tempe, AZ: Jetblast Publications, 1997); passenger data from *ASR,* 1960–1980; "History and Statistics" on Deer Valley and Goodyear airports, http://phoenix.gov/deervalleyairport/about/history.html and http://phoenix.gov/goodyearairport/about/index.html (accessed 5 July 2007); Pete R. Dimas, *Progress and a Mexican American Community's Struggle for Existence: Phoenix's Golden Gate Barrio* (New York: Peter Lang, 1999).

53. Quotation from Mardian, Swearing-in Statement, in box 1, folder 7, PCGR; *Street Deficiency Study, 1961: A Report to the City Council* (Phoenix: City of Phoenix, 1961), 31–32; "Streets for the People of Phoenix," in box 2, folder 12, PCGR; *1969 Street Needs Study: A Report to the City Council and the Citizens of Phoenix* (Phoenix: City of Phoenix, 1969), 15–16; Advance Transportation Planning Team, *Epilogue '83: An Update of Transportation—1980, Then and Now* (Phoenix: City of Phoenix, 1983), 28, 14–16, 29; *AFR, 1975/76,* 156–57; *AFR, 1980/81,* 165–66. On street widening see William S. Collins, *The Emerging Metropolis: Phoenix, 1944–1973* (Phoenix: Arizona State Parks Board, 2004) 109–17.

54. Quotation from "Official Entry of Phoenix, Arizona, 1973 All-America City Award," in series 5, carton 10, folder 65, NMLP-AA; *Epilogue '83,* 30–31. See the contemporary critique of urban transportation in University of Arizona, *Preserving and Enhancing Arizona's Total Environment: Research Report* (Phoenix: Arizona Academy, 1970), 152–57, compared with *History of Mass Transit and Travel Time Studies for Automobile and Transit,* vol. 1 of *Personalized Transit Study* (Phoenix: City of Phoenix, 1969). Jerry W. Abbitt presents a detailed history in "A History of Public Transportation in Phoenix, Arizona, 1887–1989" (master's thesis, Arizona State University, 1989).

55. See the discussion in chapter 5.

56. *Epilogue '83,* 12–14; Earl Zarbin, *All the Time a Newspaper: The First 100 Years of the Arizona Republic* (Phoenix: Arizona Republic, 1990), 304–9; Kevin R. McCauley, "Public Transportation and Streets in Phoenix, 1950–1980," in G. Wesley Johnson, ed., *Phoenix in the Twentieth Century: Essays in Community History* (Norman, OK: University of Oklahoma Press, 1993), 197–213; and Ian P. Johnson, "Mountain Tops and Valley Houses: Preserving the Western Cityscape in Phoenix, 1954–1985," seminar paper, Arizona State University, 2005. See also the discussion in Chapter 9.

57. Altheide and Hall, "Phoenix: Crime and Politics," provides an excellent analysis of this entire issue. See also campaign materials relating to crime and police in box 2, folder 6, PCGR; *PG,* 29 October 1963, A1; *AR,* 27 September 1963, A1; *AR,* 3 January 1964, A1.

58. Crime statistics from *Annual Police Report, 1980* (Phoenix: City of Phoenix Police Department, 1980), 36, and *Phoenix Magazine,* November 1986, 86–88; annual budget figures from *AFR,* 1960–1980, which also include an annual "Statistical Profile" with numbers of police; comparative force data from the *National Municipal Yearbook* (Chicago: International City Managers' Association); on modernization see *A History of the Phoenix Police*

Department (Phoenix: City of Phoenix Police Department, [1978?]).

59. Herbert Jacob and Robert L. Lineberry, "Crime, Politics, and Cities," in Heinz, Jacob, and Lineberry, *Crime in City Politics*, 1–22.

60. Altheide and Hall, "Phoenix: Crime and Politics," 214–15, quotation from 227 (citing *PG*, 2 October 1974); *National Municipal Yearbook, 1971*, 64.

61. *Phoenix Magazine*, November 1986, 86–99; Pat Murphy, "Riding a Racehorse Named Growth," *Phoenix Magazine*, November 1991, 87; Michael F. Wendland, *The Arizona Project*, rev. ed. (Mesa, AZ: Blue Sky Press, 1988); *AR*, 3 June 2001, A18; Altheide and Hall, "Phoenix: Crime and Politics," 216-17, 228.

62. *Fire Station Plan for the City of Phoenix: A Long Range Planning Study* (Phoenix: City of Phoenix Planning Department, 1961); *Fire Station Plan, 1980* (Phoenix: City of Phoenix, 1974), 8; annual data from the *National Municipal Yearbook*, 1960–1980. See also the Stay America Committee press release, [6?] November 1961, in box 2, folder 10, PCGR; and [City of Phoenix], "What About the City of Phoenix Fire Rating?," 25 October 1963, in box 2, folder 12, PCGR.

63. Quotation from U.S. Commission on Civil Rights, *Hearings before the United States Commission on Civil Rights, Phoenix, Arizona* (Washington, DC: Government Printing Office, 3 February 1962), 55. Minorities and civil rights in Phoenix are well discussed in Whitaker, *Race Work*, 133–212; David R. Dean and Jean A. Reynolds, *African American Historic Property Survey* (Phoenix: City of Phoenix Historic Preservation Office, 2004), 60–90; Bradford Luckingham, *Minorities in Phoenix: A Profile of Mexican American, Chinese American, and African American Communities, 1860–1992* (Tucson, AZ: University of Arizona Press, 1994); and Mary Melcher, "Blacks and Whites Together: Interracial Leadership in the Phoenix Civil Rights Movement," *Journal of Arizona History*, 32 (Summer 1991): 195–216.

64. U.S. Commission on Civil Rights, *Hearings, Phoenix*, 135–57, 127–29, and 125–27.

65. Mardian's material in U.S. Commission on Civil Rights, *Hearings, Phoenix*, 7–12 and 12–16, quotation from 10; quotation from Ragsdale on 58; Brooks's comments, 55.

66. *AR*, 12 January 1991, A2; *Pittsburgh Post-Gazette*, 2 December 2000; Melcher, "Blacks and Whites," 208–9; David R. Berman, *Arizona Politics and Government: The Quest for Autonomy, Democracy, and Development* (Lincoln: University of Nebraska Press, 1998), 31, 76.

67. *Equality in Employment: A Community Responsibility* (Phoenix: Maricopa County NAACP, 1963), in box 2, folder 13, PCGR.

68. Whitaker, *Race Work*, 190–98; City of Phoenix, "Official Entry for All-American City Award, 1968," 4, in series 5, carton 10, folder 67, NMLP-AA; Luckingham, *Minorities in Phoenix*, 173–82.

69. William Julius Wilson, *The Truly Disadvantaged: The Inner City, the Underclass, and Public Policy* (Chicago: University of Chicago Press, 1987); W. J. Wilson and R. Aponte, "Urban Poverty," *Annual Review of Sociology* 11 (August 1985): 231–58.

70. See the discussion below on the "Politics of Housing."

71. "History of Operation 'LEAP,'" [2 November 1964], 1–3, ms. in box 3, folder 21, PCGR.

72. City of Phoenix, "Official Entry of Phoenix for a 1965 All-American City Award," in series 5, carton 10, folder 65, NMLP-AA; "History of Operation 'LEAP,'" 4–17; Mardian charge to HR Commission, 16 July 1963, in box 2, folder 12, PCGR; Selden G. Kent to Gustav M. Ulrich, 21 November 1963, in box 3, folder 19, PCGR; and "Operation LEAP," July 1964, in box 3, folder 21, PCGR; quotations from "Official Entry of Phoenix for a 1965 All-American City Award," 3, 6.

73. City of Phoenix, "Official Entry" for All-American City Award, 1966, and City of Phoenix, "Official Entry" for All-American City Award, 1968, in series 5, carton 10, folders 66 and 67, NMLP-AA; Rosendo Gutierrez, "Special Report to the Phoenix City Council on Operation 'LEAP,' July 13, 1965," in box 3, folder 20, PCGR; "Status of Program Approval for LEAP Projects, July 30, 1965," in box 3, folder 20, PCGR; Milton Gan to Robert Coop, 11 October 1965, in box 3, folder 20, PCGR; Marvin Andrews to Randy H. Hamilton, 17 March 1966, in box 3, folder 21, PCGR; and *Annual Report, 1970* (Phoenix: State of Arizona Economic Opportunity Office, 1970), 30–32.

74. U.S. Bureau of the Census, *1970 Census of Population*, vol. I, *Characteristics of Population*, Part 4, *Arizona* (Washington, DC: Government Printing Office, 1973), 135–56, 168–74; U.S. Bureau of the Census, *1970 Census of Population and Housing: Series PHC(1) Census Tracts* (Washington, DC: Government Printing Office,1972), P3–P12, P85–P97; U.S. Bureau of the Census, *1980 Census of Population and Housing: Census Tracts* (Washington, DC: Government Printing Office, 1983), P75–P76, P114–P126; Luckingham, *Minorities in Phoenix*, 177–85. See the discussion of Arizona's minority leadership in Philip R. VanderMeer, "The Historical Patterns of Arizona Leadership," *Building Leadership in Arizona*, Arizona Town Hall, 80 (Spring 2002): 22–23; also Whitaker, *Race Work*, 192–93.

75. Quotation from Whitaker, *Race Work*, 205; see also the larger discussion on 199–221. For general coverage of Mexican Americans see Luckingham, *Minorities in Phoenix*, 39–75; and David R. Dean and Jean A. Reynolds, *Hispanic Historic Property Survey* (Phoenix: City of Phoenix Historic Preservation Office, 2006), 68–116.

76. Luckingham, *Minorities in Phoenix*, 177.

77. *AR*, 22 July 1963, A1; and materials in box 3, folder 15, PCGR: William P. Reilly, Phoenix Commission on Human Relations, to Mr. and Mrs. Gabriel Peralta, 5 September 1963; Phoenix Human Relations Commission, "Meeting Report," 3 September and 10 September 1963; and Selden G. Kent to Michael Case, 29 November 1963.

78. "Statement by Milton Gan to 'LEAP' Commission," 20 October 1965, 6, in box 3, folder 21, PCGR.

79. Dean and Reynolds, *Hispanic Historic Property Survey*, 89, 109–10; Adam Diaz, interview by Phoenix History Project, 14 April 1976, PHPC; *AR*, 20 June 1988; and VanderMeer, "Historical Patterns of Arizona Leadership," 23–25.

80. See, for example, stories in *AR* on 3 July 1966, A14; 25 June 1967, B1; 28 December 1967, A17; and 25 May 1969, A25.

81. Arturo Rosales, *Chicano: The History of the Mexican American Civil Rights Movement* (Houston: Arte Publico Press, 1996); Whitaker, *Race Work*, 210–11; Luckingham, *Minorities in Phoenix*, 61–62; Patricia Adank, "Chicano Activism in Maricopa County: Two Incidents in Retrospect," in Manuel P. Servin, ed., *An Awakened Minority: The Mexican-Americans*, (Beverly Hills: Glencoe Press, 1974), 246–66; quotation from *PG*, 26 May 1972, 22.

82. On housing see *AR*, 8 July 1970, A8; *AR*, 13 November 1970, A10; *AR*, 2 May 1971, K1; *AR*, 25 May 1972, A24. The corporate criticism is in *PG*, 16 August 1972, A18. Registration and election drives noted in *PG*, 22 June 1972, 18; *AR*, 21 May 1973, A3; *AR*, 27 June 1975, A3.

83. Quotation and organizational information from Pratt Center for Community Development, "Chicanos Por La Causa (CPLC), Phoenix, AZ," CDC Oral History Project, http://www.prattcenter.net/cdc-cplc.php (accessed 12 January 2005); Luckingham, *Minorities in Phoenix*, 62–63; Dean and Reynolds, *Hispanic Historic Property Survey*, 111–13; documents on "The

Chicana/Chicano Experience in Arizona," web exhibit, www.asu.edu/lib/archives/website//
organiza.htm (accessed 15 July 2007); "Personal Data Sheet: Alfredo Gutierrez," CB Bio
Gutierrez, Chicano Research Collection, Arizona State University; VanderMeer, "Historical
Patterns of Arizona Leadership."

84. *1970 Census of Population,* vol. I, *Characteristics of Population,* part 4, *Arizona,* 135–56, 168–74;
1970 Census of Population and Housing: Series PHC(1) Census Tracts, P3–P12, P85–P97; *1980
Census of Population and Housing: Census Tracts,* P75–P76, P114–P126; Luckingham, *Minorities
in Phoenix,* 177–85.

85. Harry Rosenzweig, interview by Phoenix History Project, 29 July 1976, tape recording, PHPC.

CHAPTER 9

1. *Annual Report, Housing Authority of the City of Phoenix, AZ, 1961* (Phoenix: City of Phoenix,
1961), 2, in box 4, folder 46, SMJP. William Collins, *The Emerging Metropolis: Phoenix, 1944–
1973* (Phoenix: Arizona State Parks Board, 2004), 261–73, provides a detailed discussion of
temporary and permanent public housing.

2. See, for example, U.S. Bureau of the Census, *1950 Census of Housing Advance Reports,* series
HC-8, no. 3 (3 October 1952); "Urban Renewal in Phoenix, Arizona" (Phoenix: City of
Phoenix Urban Renewal Department, 1 December 1960), in box 4, folder 48, SMJP.

3. S. E. Vickers, "Background and History of 1958 Housing Code Committee," memo to mayor
and council, 7 July 1961, in box 5, folder 12, SMJP; *Housing Authority of Phoenix, 1961,* 3, 6–7;
"Chronology of the Housing Code," 1, typescript, in box 5, folder 7, SMJP; "Urban Renewal in
Phoenix," 3, in box 4, folder 48, SMJP.

4. *Redevelopment Plan for Southwest Urban Renewal Area* (Phoenix: Urban Renewal
Commission, 1960); *Redevelopment Plan for East Jefferson Urban Renewal Area* (Phoenix:
Urban Renewal Commission, 1960), in box 8, folder 4, SMJP; City of Phoenix Urban Renewal
Department, Neighborhood Improvement and Housing Code Enforcement, "Progress
Report, September 1959–March, 1961," in box 5, folder 12, SMJP.

5. *PG,* 4 May 1960; also *AR,* 12 April 1960; clippings in box 4, folder 48, SMJP.

6. Edward Jacobson, chair of the Citizens Urban Renewal Finance Study Committee, to
Mayor Mardian and the council, 16 November 1960, in box 8, folder 3, SMJP. See the
public housing protest documents in box 6, folder 31, SMJP: Roy B. Yanez to Samuel
E. Vicker, 8 August 1961; G. E. Cornforth to Sam Mardian, 9 January 1961; "300 Plan to
Fight Housing Project," *AR,* 11 November 1960; "Creighton District Resident Will Battle
Housing Project," *PG,* 11 November 1960.

7. "A Formal Protest to the City Council of the City of Phoenix: In Regards to Ordinance No.
G-293, et al.," 20 December 1960, 1–3, in box 4, folder 48, SMJP; and mimeographed petition
and protest document addressed to the mayor and council from Citizens for the Preservation
of Property Rights [n.d.], in box 4, folder 47, SMJP.

8. "Chronology of the Housing Code," 3; Philip R. VanderMeer, "Conservatism and Urban
Development in Phoenix," paper presented to Social Science History Association Conference,
Portland, OR, 3 November 2005, 17, 24–25.

9. *AR,* 1 November 1966, A1, A8; *AR,* 2 November 1966, A4, A19; *AR,* 3 November 1966, A4; *AR,*
9 November 1966, A1.

10. The basic areas and related data are reported in Neighborhood Improvement and
Housing Code Enforcement, "Progress Report, September 1959—March 1961." Tables
of census data are included in "Summary of Selected Data Re Housing Characteristics,

Phoenix, Arizona," typescript attached to Phoenix Community Council minutes, 18 April 1963, in box 5, folder 7, SMJP.

11. John Driggs, interview by Phoenix History Project, 13 July 1978, transcript, 9–10, PHPC.

12. *Housing Authority of Phoenix, 1961*, 3–4; Housing and Community Development Department, *Housing Assistance Plan* (Phoenix: City of Phoenix, 1979), 7-1; *Social Background Paper* (Phoenix: City of Phoenix Planning Department, 1990), 15–17.

13. Alison Isenberg, *Downtown America: A History of the Place and the People Who Made It* (Chicago: University of Chicago Press, 2004), 166–311; Robert M. Fogelson, *Downtown: Its Rise and Fall, 1880–1950* (New Haven: Yale University Press, 2001), 366–98; Bernard J. Frieden and Lynne B. Sagalyn, *Downtown, Inc.: How America Rebuilds Cities* (Cambridge: MIT Press, 1989), 1–106; and Carl Abbott, "Five Strategies for Downtown: Policy Discourse and Planning Since 1943," *Journal of Policy History*, vol. 5, no. 1 (1993): 5–27.

14. *AR*, 3 March 1946, A1. George H. N. Luhrs, Jr., *The Geo. H. N. Luhrs Family in Phoenix and Arizona, 1847–1984* (Phoenix: Jean Stroud Crane, 1988), 272.

15. Leonard Goldman to Ray Wilson, 30 April 1956, in box 4, folder 22, PCGR.

16. See the following correspondence in PCGR: Ed Korrick to Jack Williams, 19 April 1958, in box 3, folder 17; Fred Porter to Jack Williams, 30 August 1958, 2, in box 3, folder 17; Leonard Goldman to Jack Williams, 10 September 1956, in box 4, folder 22; Fred Porter to Jack Williams, 21 January 1958, in box 4, folder 22; Ed Korrick to Jack Williams, 8 January 1959, in box 3, folder 17; Leonard Goldman to Jack Williams, 21 December 1957, in box 4, folder 22; Wilbur S. Smith to John Beatty, 25 August 1958, in box 3, folder 17. See also, Luhrs, *Luhrs Family*, 268–69.

17. Quotation in Porter to Williams, 30 August 1958; *Luhrs Family*, 269.

18. Goldman to Wilson, 30 April 1956; Porter to Williams, 30 August 1958; Phoenix Progress Committee materials, in box 4, folder 22, PCGR. On Gruen's Fort Worth plan, see Jeffrey Hardwick, *Mall Maker: Victor Gruen, Architect of an American Dream* (Philadelphia: University of Pennsylvania Press, 2004), 166–98; and Alex Wall, *Victor Gruen: From Urban Shop to New City* (Barcelona: Actar, 2005), 126–38.

19. Carl Rawlings to Ray Wilson, 10 May 1956, in box 4, folder 22, PCGR.

20. Porter to Williams, 30 August 1958; Jack Williams to Fred Porter et al., 13 February 1959, in box 3, folder 17, PCGR.

21. Quotation in Jack Williams to Fred S. Porter, 9 March 1959, in box 3, folder 17, PCGR.

22. Goldman to Wilson, 30 April 1956.

23. Porter to Williams, 30 August 1958.

24. Peter Lee Russell, "Downtown's Downturn: A Historical Geography of the Phoenix, Arizona, Central Business District, 1890–1986" (master's thesis, Arizona State University, 1986), 101–2.

25. *Phoenix City Directory* (Dallas: R. L. Polk & Company), 1958–1968 editions; Jerry Brisco, "Korrick's: From Big Fish to Minnows in the Ocean," unpublished ms. in author's possession; Russell, "Downtown's Downturn," 102–5; Luhrs, *Luhrs Family*, 268–71.

26. Based on an analysis of data in the *Phoenix City Directory* for 1940, 1955, 1960, and 1966. See also the analysis of 1955 in Russell, "Downtown's Downturn," 78–94.

27. Michael F. Konig, "Toward Metropolis Status: Charter Government and the Rise of Phoenix, Arizona, 1945–1960 (PhD diss., Arizona State University, 1983), 141–46; Central Phoenix Committee, *Downtown Phoenix: A 25 Year Vision* (Phoenix: City of Phoenix, 1991), 57; Russell, "Downtown's Downturn," 105–7; Marvin A. Andrews to Mayor Mardian, 21 July

1961, "Value of Buildings in Downtown Core Area," in box 8, folder 2, SMJP; quotations from Edward H. Peplow, Jr., "The Downtown Decision," *Phoenix Magazine*, August 1973, 134, 137; Charles Sargent, ed., *Metro Arizona* (Scottsdale, AZ: Biffington Books, 1988), 149.

28. *AR*, 9 January 1965, A1; Rhes Cornelius, interview by Phoenix History Project, June 22, 1976, transcript, 19–21, PHPC; Eric E. Duckstad, *The Need for Convention-Cultural Facilities in Phoenix: A Reassessment* (Menlo Park, CA: Stanford Research Institute, 1966); Julie Spiller, "History of Convention Tourism," in Karin Weber and Kaye Chon, eds., *Convention Tourism: International Research and Industry Perspectives*, (New York: Haworth Hospitality Press, 2002), 3–20; Kent A. Robertson, "Downtown Redevelopment Strategies in the United States: An End-of-the-Century Assessment," *Journal of the American Planning Association*, 61 (Autumn 1995): 429–37; Frieden and Sagalyn, *Downtown, Inc.*, 270.

29. Luhrs, *Luhrs Family*, 297–301, 414; Richard T. Lai, comp., "The Deuce: Its Past, Present, and Potential; A Developmental Study of the Phoenix, Arizona 'Skid Row,'" Barton Barr Central Library, Phoenix; Driggs interview transcript, 11–12; *AR*, 9 December 1974, A1, as quoted in Russell, "Downtown's Downturn," 121.

30. Peplow, "Downtown Decision," 76, and Edward H. Peplow, Jr., "Downtown Vision," *Phoenix Magazine*, August 1973, 78, 139. This Adams Hotel (later renamed) replaced an older structure.

31. Abbott, "Five Strategies"; and Isenberg, *Downtown America*, 255–311.

32. These neighborhoods were identified through the City of Phoenix Historic Preservation Office's "Historic District" pamphlets and the online "Map of All Residential Historic Districts," http://phoenix.gov/ftpalias/HISTORIC/allresdists.pdf (accessed 12 August 2007); they were linked to appropriate census tract maps and data in Research Section, City of Phoenix Planning Department, *Community Profile and Needs Assessment, City of Phoenix, Arizona, 1977–1980* (Phoenix: City of Phoenix Planning Department [1977 or 1978]), 36–37, 47, 55, quotation 44. Information on the decline also in Terry Goddard, interview by Philip VanderMeer, 27 September 2001, tape recording, in the author's possession.

33. See the discussion of highway plans in chapter 5. The number of buildings demolished is noted in Cooper/Roberts Architects, *Historic Homes of Phoenix: An Architectural and Preservation Guide*, (Phoenix: City of Phoenix, 1992), 10.

34. See Raymond Mohl, "Stop the Road: Freeway Revolts in American Cities," *Journal of Urban History* 30 (July 2004): 674–706.

35. These perspectives and the larger history of this topic are covered in Earl Zarbin, *All the Time a Newspaper: The First 100 Years of the Arizona Republic* (Phoenix: Arizona Republic, 1990), 304–7; Kevin R. McCauley, "Public Transportation and Streets in Phoenix, 1950–1980," in G. Wesley Johnson, ed., *Phoenix in the Twentieth Century: Essays in Community History* (Norman, OK: University of Oklahoma Press, 1993), 201–14; and Ian P. Johnson, "Mountain Tops and Valley Houses: Preserving the Western Cityscape in Phoenix, 1954–1985," seminar paper, Arizona State University, 2005.

36. Johnson, "Mountain Tops," 24, citing an interview with James Garrison, the state historic preservation officer (2007). Figures from the regular 1970 and special 1975 censuses show that 678 "dwelling units" were removed from the primary area, tract 1130. Phoenix Planning Department, *Community Profile, 1977–1980*, 9. Driggs interview transcript, 30–31.

37. Goddard interview tape recording; Johnson, "Mountain Tops," 20–24.

38. *Profile of the Special Conservation District, December 1982* (Phoenix: City of Phoenix Planning Department, 1982), 3; Phoenix, *Community Profile*, 53; *Historic Homes of Phoenix*, 10–13.

39. Johnson, "Mountain Tops," 18–19; G. Wesley Johnson, *Phoenix, Valley of the Sun* (Tulsa: Continental Heritage Press, 1982), 178–79. Johnson's Phoenix book is a product of the project, and the project files are stored at the Arizona Historical Society, Tempe.

40. *The Economy of Maricopa County, 1965 to 1980: A Study for the Guidance of Public and Private Planning* (Phoenix: Western Management Consultants, Inc., 1965), 139, 236.

41. Ibid., 238.

42. Phoenix Forward Task Force, *Phoenix Forward: Citizen Participation in Planning, a Citizen Report on Objectives and Goals for Metropolitan Phoenix* (Phoenix: City Council and The Task Force, 1970), 135.

43. Eva Eagle, *Land Use Planning and Regulation in Arizona's Counties* (Tempe, AZ: Center for Public Affairs, Arizona State University, 1976), 21. My land-use analysis is based on *Economy of Maricopa County*, 139–48, and on data and maps in Kim Knowles-Yanez, Cherie Mortiz, Jana Fry, Charles L. Redman, and Matt Bucchin, *Historic Land Use: Phase I Report on Generalized Land Use*, Central Arizona–Phoenix Long-Term Ecological Research Contribution no. 1 (Tempe, AZ: Center for Environmental Studies, Arizona State University, August 1999), 9–11, 16, http://caplter.asu.edu/docs/contributions/HistoricLandUse_Color.pdf (accessed 22 April 2004).

44. The county is large (9,224 square miles), so the low percentage still yields substantial acreage.

45. Additional desert lands were set aside for recreation, so that a tenth of all Valley desert land was transferred in some fashion during these two decades.

46. *Economy of Maricopa County*, 139–48, 226–38; and Knowles-Yanez et al., *Historic Land Use*, 9–11, 16.

47. Eagle, *Land Use Planning*, 21; *AR*, 7 July 1974, B1; Pam Hait, "A Long-Range Look at the Valley," *Phoenix Magazine*, August 1973, 44–48.

48. Phoenix City Manager, "What Annexation Can Do for You," 24 May 1961, dittoed sheet in box 4, folder 14, SMJP.

49. *AR*, 7 October 1961; *AR*, 10 November 1962, 1; *AR*, 30 March 1974; *AR*, 25 June 1976; *AR*, 23 July 1976; *AR*, 7 July 1977; *AR*, 17 June 1980; James E. Buchanan, comp., *Phoenix: A Chronological and Documentary History, 1865–1976*, American Cities Chronology Series (Dobbs Ferry, NY: Oceana Publications, 1978); and the sense of Valley-wide annexation in Carol E. Heim, "Border Wars: Tax Revenues, Annexation, and Urban Growth in Phoenix," Working Paper 2006–01, Department of Economics, University of Massachusetts, Amherst, 12–14.

50. *The Comprehensive Plan—1990* (Phoenix: City of Phoenix, 1972), 103; *AR*, 21 June 1974, A1; Bradford Luckingham, *Phoenix: The History of a Southwestern Metropolis* (Tucson: University of Arizona Press, 1989), 193. On sales tax revenues see Heim, "Border Wars."

51. *Phoenix Forward*, xiii–xviii.

52. *AR*, 21 January 1974, and *AR*, 7 July 1974, B1–B2.

53. *AR*, 23 November 1975, B1, B18.

54. See, for example, Hal K. Rothman, *Saving the Planet: The American Response to the Environment in the Twentieth Century* (Chicago: Ivan R. Dee, 2000).

55. For the early development of these ideas, see the discussion in chapter 3. For a discussion of landscaping styles, see Chris A. Martin, Kathleen A. Peterson, and Linda B. Stabler, "Residential Landscaping in Phoenix, Arizona, U.S.: Practices and Preferences Relative to Covenants, Codes, and Restrictions," *Journal of Arboriculture*, 29 (January 2003): 9–16.

56. Buchanan, *Phoenix*, passim; *AR*, 24 February 1963; quotations from *AR*, 12 December 1962, A1, and *AR*, 3 October 1965, A16.

57. *AR*, 23–26 October 1966; University of Arizona, *Preserving and Enhancing Arizona's Total Environment: Research Report* (Phoenix: Arizona Academy, 1970), 27–66; *Phoenix Magazine*, August 1973, 58, 124–26; *Phoenix Magazine*, November 1986, 66–97; quotations from *Phoenix Forward*, xv–xvi, and *Phoenix Magazine*, November 1986, 98.

58. U.S. Army Corps of Engineers, *Gila Floodway, Maricopa and Pinal Counties, Arizona: Summary Report for Flood Control* (Los Angeles: U.S. Army Corps of Engineers, 1977), A1–A9; Vincent Smith Murray, "A History of Flooding and Flood Control in Maricopa County" (master's thesis, Arizona State University, 2006), 56–97.

59. U.S. Army Engineer District, Los Angeles, Corps of Engineers, *Flood-Damage Report on Storm and Flood of 16–17 August 1963: Glendale-Maryvale Area near Phoenix, Arizona* (Los Angeles: The District, 1964), 2–4, 12.

60. U.S. Army Engineer District, Los Angeles, Corps of Engineers, *Flood-Damage Report on Flood of December 1965–January 1966: Salt and Gila Rivers, Granite Reef Dam to Gillespie Dam, Arizona* (Los Angeles: The District, 1966). See also the description in Andrew M. Honker, "A River Sometimes Runs Through It: A History of Salt River Flooding and Phoenix" (PhD diss., Arizona State University, 2002), 138–42.

61. U.S. Army Engineer District, Los Angeles, Corps of Engineers, *Report on Flood of 22 June 1972 in Phoenix Metropolitan Area, Arizona* (Los Angeles: The Corps, 1972), 2, 55.

62. U.S. Army Engineer District, Los Angeles, Corps of Engineers, *Flood Damage Report: 28 February–6 March 1978 on the Storm and Floods in Maricopa County, Arizona* (Los Angeles: The Corps, 1979); U.S. Army Engineer District, Los Angeles, Corps of Engineers, *Flood Damage Report, Phoenix Metropolitan Area, December 1978 Flood* (Los Angeles: The Corps, 1979), 24, 36, 41; *AR*, 19–21 December 1978; *AR*, 16–21 February 1980; *Phoenix Magazine*, November 1986, 94–98; and Honker, "A River," 147–68, 191–212, 218–39.

63. Murray, "Flooding and Flood Control," 46–47; and Honker, "A River," 99–125.

64. Based on Bob Moore, "Agriculture Developed, Managed Water Early in State's History," in Athia L. Hardt, ed., *Arizona Waterline* ([Phoenix]: Salt River Project, 1989), 14–16, and William Chase, "Phoenix: How a City Plans Future Water Use," in *Arizona Waterline*, 25–26. In general, the basic quality of municipal water was not an issue: School of Renewable Natural Resources, College of Agriculture, University of Arizona, *Managing Water Quality in a Water Scarce State*, Forty-Seventh Arizona Town Hall (Phoenix: Arizona Academy, 1985), 31–54.

65. University of Arizona, *Arizona's Water Supply*, Report for the Fourth Arizona Town Hall (Phoenix: Arizona Academy, 1964), 18; Hugh A. Holub, "Water Conservation and Wealth (A Tale of Two Cities),"in Hardt, *Arizona Waterline*, 21–22. See also Douglas E. Kupel, *Fuel for Growth: Water and Arizona's Urban Environment* (Tucson: University of Arizona Press, 2003), 177–80; Michael F. Logan, *Desert Cities: The Environmental History of Phoenix and Tucson* (Pittsburgh: University of Pittsburgh Press, 2006), 174–82; and Bradford Luckingham, *The Urban Southwest: A Profile History of Albuquerque—El Paso—Phoenix—Tucson* (El Paso: Texas Western Press, University of Texas, 1982).

66. U.S. Department of the Interior, Bureau of Reclamation, "Report on Proposed Rehabilitation and Betterment of Salt River Project, Arizona," April 1955, 11, 15, 16, record 19550400, group 470.1, Salt River Project (hereinafter *SRP*) Archives, Phoenix; Chase, "Phoenix: How a City Plans," 24; U.S. Geological Survey quotation taken from *Arizona's Water Supply*, 2; SRP, *Annual Report* (Phoenix: SRP), 1955–1980 editions.

67. Among the numerous works on this topic, see Donald Worster, *Rivers of Empire: Water, Aridity, and the Growth of the American West* (New York: Pantheon, 1985), 194–212, 272–76;

Philip L. Fradkin, *A River No More: The Colorado River and the West* (Tucson: University of Arizona Press, 1981), 258–62; Thomas E. Sheridan, *Arizona: A History* (Tucson: University of Arizona Press, 1995), 340–46; U.S. Bureau of Reclamation, "Colorado River Basin Project, Central Arizona Project," http://www.usbr.gov/dataweb/html/crbpcap.html (accessed 22 June 2005); *Arizona's Water Supply*; and essays in Hardt, *Arizona Waterline*.

68. Cecil Andrus, interview with Central Arizona Project, 6 June 2005, http://www.cap-az.com/pdfs/oral/Interview%20with%20Cecil%20Andrus.pdf (accessed 10 August 2007); Morris Udall, "A Toast: To a Water Settlement," *Congressman's Report*, vol. XV, no. 1 (15 May 1977), http://www.library.arizona.edu/exhibits/udall/congrept/95th/770515.html (accessed 10 August 2007); Wendy Nelson Espeland provides a detailed study of the Orme Dam issue in *Struggle for Water: Politics, Rationality, and Identity in the American Southwest* (Chicago: University of Chicago Press, 1998); Honker, "A River," 168–78, 198–203, 241–54; and Hardt, *Arizona Waterline*, passim.

69. Quotations in Jack Williams to Leonard Goldman, 17 September 1956, in box 4, folder 22, PCGR; Norman Dibble to Sam Mardian, 13 November 1961, in box 2, folder 10, PCGR.

70. For data and description see SRP, *Annual Report,* 1956–73; Bureau of Reclamation, "Proposed Rehabilitation and Betterment"; and Jay C. Ziemann, "The Modernization of the Salt River Project: The Impact of the Rehabilitation and Betterment Program" (master's thesis, Arizona State University, 1988). By 1969 the Rehabilitation and Betterment Program had financed roughly half of the improvements, as calculated from data in H. Shipley to Stephen H. Poe, 8 September 1969, record group 470.1, SRP Archives. Alfred Simon discusses canals in "Mixing Water and Culture: Making the Canal Landscape in Phoenix" (PhD diss., Arizona State University, 2002), 91–95; Collins, *Emerging Metropolis,* 31–32, says that street widening was the "main reason" for tree removal in the 1950s.

71. Melvin E. Hecht, "Climate and Culture, Landscape and Lifestyle in the Sun Belt of Southern Arizona," *Journal of Popular Culture,* 11 (Spring 1978): 936–38; Charles Kelly, "Roots of Landscaping," *AR,* 25 March 2001, F1; and Dwight L. Busby, *Dobson Ranch: A Planned Community* (Phoenix: Busby Associates, 1972). However, some pine varieties grew quite tall.

72. *AR,* 12 April 1959, E20; Martin, "Residential Landscaping"; and Tara A. Blanc, *Oasis in the City: The History of the Desert Botanical Garden* (Phoenix: Heritage Publishers, 2000).

73. Paul W. Van Cleve, *An Open Space Plan for the Phoenix Mountains* (Phoenix: City of Phoenix, 1971), quotation from 26; Dorothy Gilbert, "A History of the Phoenix Mountains Preserve," 1993, Arizona Collection, Arizona State University; and "Official Entry of Phoenix, Arizona, 1973 All-America City Award," in series 5, carton 10, folder 69, NMLP-AA.

74. Quotation from *AR,* 3 October 1965, A16. On city planning departments, see data in the *Municipal Yearbook* (Chicago: International City Managers' Association), 1960–75 editions. *AR,* 24 February 1963, A1; *AR,* 3 October 1965, A1.

75. *Phoenix Magazine,* August 1973, 49; "Rio Salado," http://www.asu.edu/lib/archives/asustory/pages/13accp.htm (accessed 20 March 2007); *Phoenix Forward,* 135–36, xiii–xviii, 119–33.

76. *Comprehensive Plan—1990,* 108ff; James M. Barney et al., eds. *History of the City of Phoenix, Arizona* (Phoenix: City of Phoenix Planning Department, 1975), 11.

77. Deer Valley Citizens Planning Committee, *Deer Valley Area Plan* (Phoenix: City of Phoenix Planning Department, 1972); *AR,* 7 December 1975, B2; *Urban Form Directions: Committee Summary Reports* (Phoenix: City of Phoenix Planning Commission, 1975), esp. 3, 8–11; *AR,* 23 November 1975, B1; *AR,* 7 December 1975, B2; *AR,* 20 April 1976, B1.

78. City of Phoenix, "Official Entry for 1979–1980 All-America City Award," and "All-America City Award Presentation," 13 November 1979 (quotation from page 4), in series 5, carton 10, folder 70, NMLP-AA; *Phoenix Concept Plan, 2000: A Program for Planning* (Phoenix: City of Phoenix Planning Department, 1979).

79. On the questions of urban form see, for example, Joel Garreau, *Edge City: Life on the New Frontier* (New York: Doubleday, 1991); M. Gottdiener and George Kephart, "The Multinucleated Metropolitan Region: A Comparative Analysis," in Rob Kling, Spencer Olin, and Mark Poster, *Postsuburban California: The Transformation of Orange County since World War II* (Berkeley: University of California Press, 1991), 31–54; and Michael Dear and Steven Flusty, "Postmodern Urbanism," *Annals of the Association of American Geographers*, 88 (March 1998): 50–72.

80. Margaret Kober, interview by Phoenix History Project, 18 June 1976, transcript, 25, PHPC; Patrick Downey, interview by Phoenix History Project, 8 July 1978, transcript, 38, PHPC; Edward "Bud" Jacobson, interview by Arizona Historical Society, 17 December 1992, transcript, 20, Arizona Historical Society, Tempe.

81. Driggs interview transcript, 38; Manya Winsted, "Pioneer Builder John F. Long Celebrates an Anniversary," *Phoenix Magazine*, February 1977, 49; Newton Rosenzweig, interview by Phoenix History Project, 5 October 1978, transcript, 40, 62, 64, PHPC.

82. See, for example, Peter Wiley and Robert Gottlieb, *Empires in the Sun: The Rise of the New American West* (New York: G. P. Putnam's Sons, 1982), 174–75; Greater Phoenix Leadership, "Our History and Milestones," http://www.gplinc.org/about/our-history.aspx (accessed 20 July 2009); *Phoenix New Times*, 23–29 April 1975, 3, 17; and G. Wesley Johnson, Jr., "Directing Elites: Catalysts for Social Change," in Johnson, *Phoenix in the Twentieth Century*, 27–32.

CHAPTER 10

1. *AR*, 20 June 2004, V1.

2. Judith Anne Jacobson, "The Phoenix Chamber of Commerce: A Case Study of Economic Development in Central Arizona" (master's thesis, Arizona State University, 1992), 36–39, 43, 83–85; Edward Peplow, Jr., "Growth Patterns," *Phoenix Magazine*, August 1973, 74; data from James E. Buchanan, comp., *Phoenix: A Chronological and Documentary History, 1865–1976*, American Cities Chronology Series (Dobbs Ferry, NY: Oceana Publications, 1978), 51–60. See also Bradford Luckingham, *Phoenix: The History of a Southwestern Metropolis* (Tucson: University of Arizona Press, 1989), 185–90; William S. Collins, *The Emerging Metropolis: Phoenix, 1944–1973* (Phoenix: Arizona State Parks Board, 2005).

3. William L. Everitt, "A Man for His Season: A Tribute to Dan Noble," *Motorola Monitor*, vol. 12, no. 1 (1973): 1–3; *AR*, 15 October 1973, "Sun Living," 1; *AR*, 5 February 1962, clipping in Daniel Noble folder, Luhrs Reading Room, Arizona State University; "January 1974 Marks Motorola's 25th Year in Phoenix!," unsigned article in Motorola Collection, Arizona Historical Society, Tempe; Daniel Noble, interview by Phoenix History Project, 26 September 1976, transcript, PHPC; Peplow, "Growth Patterns," 72–74; and employment data from Arizona Regional Economic Analysis Project (hereinafter AREAP), "Full-time and Part-time Employment by Major Industry," www.pnreap.org/PNREAP.Report (accessed 20 December 2007).

4. *ASR*, 1960–1980; AREAP, various data; Peplow, "Growth Patterns."

5. Larry Schweikart, *A History of Banking in Arizona* (Tucson: University of Arizona Press, 1982), 132–74; Pam Haitt, *The Arizona Bank: Arizona's Story* (Phoenix: Arizona Bank, 1987), 159–282; data from *ASR*, 1960–1980.

6. Based on analysis of numbers of units constructed, value of building permits, and employment data from *ASR*, 1960–1980; also *ASR*, 1981, 44. See figure 7.4 and the discussion in chapter 7.

7. Jacobson, "Phoenix Chamber of Commerce," 44, 49; Phoenix Forward Task Force, *Phoenix Forward: Citizen Participation in Planning, a Citizen Report on Objectives and Goals for Metropolitan Phoenix* (Phoenix: City of Phoenix, 1970), 168–74; *Inside Phoenix, 1968* (Phoenix: Arizona Republic and Gazette, 1968), 42; *Arizona Index: Arizona's Travel Resort Convention Index* (Phoenix: Holland/Qualman Publishing, 1968; *Inside Phoenix, 1980*, 38.

8. *AR*, 19 February 2004, E1; *The Economy of Maricopa County, 1965 to 1980: A Study for the Guidance of Public and Private Planning* (Phoenix: Western Management Consultants, 1965), 199–215; Peter Aleshire, "The Old Kid on the Block," *Phoenix Magazine,* February 2004, 101; Candice St. Jacques Miles, *Arizona Biltmore: Jewel of the Desert* (Phoenix: Arizona Biltmore, 1985).

9. Michael D. Jones, *Desert Wings: A History of Phoenix Sky Harbor International Airport* (Tempe, AZ: Jetblast Publications, 1997); passenger data from *ASR*, 1960–1980. Still, a majority of winter visitors came by car; Hiram S. Davis and Mary Jane Digges, "Tourism in Maricopa County," *Arizona Review* 15 (March 1966): 9–11.

10. Jacobson, "Phoenix Chamber of Commerce," 44–49; *Inside Phoenix, 1968*, 42; Dennis R. Judd and Todd Swanstrom, *City Politics: Private Power and Public Policy,* 2nd ed. (New York: Longman, 1998), 372.

11. *Arizona Indicators*, "Taxable Retail Sales," https://webapp4.asu.edu/corda/dashboards/EconomicIndicators_public/main.dashxml (accessed 11 January 2008); Tom R. Rex, "Development of Metropolitan Phoenix: Historical, Current, and Future Trends," report for the Morrison Institute for Public Policy (Tempe, AZ: Morrison Institute for Public Policy, 2000), 13, http://wpcarey.asu.edu/ seid/reports.cfm (accessed 22 March 2006). Employment and unemployment data from AREAP and compiled by the U.S. Bureau of Labor Statistics at http://recenter.tamu.edu/data/empm/ MT043806.html (accessed 12 December 2007); *What Matters in Greater Phoenix: Indicators of Our Quality of Life, 1998 Edition* (Tempe, AZ: Morrison Institute for Public Policy, 1998), 36; *What Matters—The Maturing of Greater Phoenix, 2004 Edition* (Tempe, AZ: Morrison Institute for Public Policy, 2004), 27. Basic economic analysis using data and analysis from Arizona State University Center for Business Research, "Economy of Phoenix," Arizona Community Economic Base Studies, (Phoenix: Arizona Department of Commerce, 2004), http://www.azcommerce.com/Research/BaseStudies/Economic+Base+Studies.htm (accessed 13 October 2007).

12. *AR*, 26 December 1999, D1; *AR*, 24 September 2001, D1; *AR*, 24 March 2004, D5; *AR*, 20 November 2004, D5; *AR*, 19 March 2007, A14.

13. *Inside Metro Phoenix, 1990* (Phoenix: the Arizona Republic/Phoenix Gazette, 1989), 20; Dean Runyan Associates, *Arizona Travel Impacts, 1998–2006P* (Phoenix: Arizona Department of Tourism, 2007), http://www.azot.gov/section.aspx?sid=74 (accessed 12 December 2007); Timothy Hogan and Stephen K. Happel, "Mobile/RV Parks Statewide Report Fewer Winter Residents," *Arizona Business*, 47 (July 2000): 1–3; Timothy Hogan, Stephen K. Happel, and Katrina S. Walls, "State's 'Snowbird' Count Estimated at 300,000 or More," *Arizona Business*, 50 (June 2003): 1–3; *AR*, 29 March 2001, D1. See also Patricia Gober, *Metropolitan Phoenix: Place Making and Community Building in the Desert* (Philadelphia: University of Pennsylvania Press, 2006), 122–23.

14. Sky Harbor Airport, "Historical Traffic Statistics" and "Airport History," http://phoenix.gov/skyharborairport/about (accessed 14 January 2008).

15. *AR,* 9 September 1989, B1; Sky Harbor's Web site contains numerous documents relating to this controversy, as well as to the airport's actions, at http://phoenix.gov/skyharborairport/about/comm-noiseinfo.html (accessed 17 January 2008). See esp. Coffman Associates, *F.A.R. Part 150 Study, Noise Compatibility Program for Sky Harbor International Airport, Phoenix, Arizona* (Phoenix: City Aviation Department, 1989).

16. "Phoenix Sky Harbor International Airport 2005 Poll" results at http://www.supportskyharbor.com/linkonea.asp (accessed 17 January 2008).

17. "About Goodyear" and "About Deer Valley," http://phoenix.gov/goodyearairport/about/index.html and http://phoenix.gov/deervalleyairport/about/index.html (accessed 17 January 2008); *AR,* 16 June 1999, Sun City section, 1; *Chandler Republic* (hereinafter *CR*), 25 May 2006, 4.

18. Urban Land Institute, *Williams Gateway Area, Mesa, Arizona,* Advisory Services Panel Report, 2006, http://www.uli.org (accessed 2 January 2008); Coffman Associates, *Williams Gateway Master Plan,* 2008 draft, http://www.coffmanassociates.com/public/Williams/ (accessed 14 February 2008); Phoenix-Mesa Gateway Airport, "History," http://www.phxmesagateway.org/history.asp (accessed 15 January 2008); *AR,* 16 October 2007, D1; *Business Journal of Phoenix,* 17 August 2007; *AR,* 18 February 2008, A1.

19. *CR,* 25 May 2006, 4; *Scottsdale Republic* (hereinafter *SR*), 7 November 2003, 16; *AR,* 10 July 2001, B1. See also the sources relating to protection of Luke Air Force Base: City of Glendale, "Our Partnership with Luke Air Force Base," http://www.glendaleaz.com/lukeafb/ (accessed 20 January 2008).

20. Sky Harbor Airport, "Economic Impact," http://phoenix.gov/skyharborairport/about/airfig-economic.html (accessed 13 January 2008); *Phoenix Business Journal,* 15 June 2004.

21. *AR,* 1 December 2006, D1; *AR,* 31 October 2005, D1; *SR,* 7 November 2003, 16; *CR,* 19 August 2006, 3; *CR,* 30 April 2005, 1; Arizona Department of Transportation, "Mesa Falcon Field Airport: Economic Impact and Aviation Services," http://azdot.gov/aviation/library/pdf/ECON_IMPACT_FFZ.pdf (accessed 21 January 2008); *Glendale Republic,* 9 May 2007, 26; *AR,* 12 June 2007, A9.

22. Helen Feger, "America West Sets a Risky New Course," *Arizona Trend,* January 1987, 55–62; *AR,* 30 December 1989, F1; *AR,* 26 December 1999, D1; William Lehman, "US Airways: A Heritage Story, Part VIII—America West," http://www.usairways.com/awa/content/aboutus/pressroom/history/americawest.aspx (accessed 13 January 2008); *AR*'s annual ranking of largest Arizona employers, various dates, 1995–2007.

23. "Per Capita Personal Income, Per Cent of U.S.," table CA1–3, and "Personal Income for Metropolitan Areas, 2006," http://www.bea.gov (accessed 21 January 2008); *AR,* 28 October 2007, A26; *What Matters—The Maturing of Greater Phoenix,* 27; calculations based on data in Phoenix Planning Department, "Phoenix Statistical Summary," 16, phoenix.gov/PLANNING/resdat35.pdf (accessed 23 December 2007).

24. Census and wage data, http://www.metrocouncil.org/Census/MetroComparisons/MetroComparisons_poverty.pdf (accessed 21 January 2008); *Inside Phoenix, 1978,* 32; *Inside Metro Phoenix, 1990,* 8, 16, 18; *What Matters in Greater Phoenix: Indicators of Our Quality of Life, 1999 Edition* (Tempe, AZ: Morrison Institute for Public Policy, 1999), 46; Phoenix Planning Department, "Phoenix Statistical Summary," 21; *What Matters—The Maturing of Greater Phoenix,* 34–35; *AR,* 13 May 2000, 1; *AR,* 2 August 2006, B8; *AR,* 28 October 2007, A24; W. P. Carey School of Business, Arizona State University, "Housing Affordability Indices," http://www.poly.asu.edu/realty/market_update.html#affordability (accessed

12 December 2007); "NAHB Housing Opportunity Index," National Association of Home Builders, 4th quarter 2006, http://www.stlrcga.org/x436xml (accessed 10 January 2008).

25. Jerry Brisco, "Korrick's: From Big Fish to Minnows in the Ocean," unpublished essay in the author's possession; Collins, *Emerging Metropolis*, 201–30; on builders see discussion in chapter 7.

26. *AR*, 2 January 1986, C3; *ABG*, 19 October 1987, 6; *PG*, 20 March 1992, D1; *PG*, 28 October 2995, D1; *AR*, 7 May 1995, D1; *AR*, 29 June 1992, D1; and *PG*, 2 September 1993, C1.

27. *PG*, 14 September 1989, A1; *AR*, 28 May 1999, E1; *AR*, 3 June 1999, D1; *AR*, 20 June 1999, D1; *AR*, 16 May 2007, D5.

28. *Inside Metro Phoenix, 1990*, 13; discussions of businesses in *AR*, 15 February 1987, passim; *AR*, 29 December 2000, D3 ; *AR*, 20 May 2007, D6; *AR*, 5 October 2003, D1; *AR*, 31 December 1999, D1; Phoenix Planning Department, "Phoenix Statistical Summary," 17.

29. *AR*, 15 February 1987, AZ11; *AR*, 21 July 1999, E1; *AR*, 12 December 1999, D1; *AR*, 2 December 2004, D1; *AR*, 11 April 2005, D1; *AR*, 28 October 2007, A24, A25.

30. *AR*, 24 October 2000, A1; John Couleuer, "The Core of the Black Canyon Computer Corporation," *IEEE—Annals of the History of Computing*, 17 (Winter 1995): 56–60; H. R. Barney Oldfield, "General Electric Enters the Computer Business—Revisited," *IEEE—Annals of the History of Computing*, 17 (Winter 1995): 46–55; G. T. Gray, and R. Q. Smith, "Sperry Rand's Third-Generation Computers, 1964–1980," *IEEE—Annals of the History of Computing*, 23 (January–March 2001): 3–16; Collins, *Emerging Metropolis*, 185–87; *AR*, 4 November 2007, A21; *The Handbook of Texas Online*, http://www.tshaonline.org/handbook/online/articles/MM/dnm1.html (accessed 8 January 2008).

31. AREAP data; *ASR*, 1980–1996; and U.S. Bureau of the Census, *1980 Census of Population: General Social and Economic Characteristics: Arizona* (Washington, DC: Government Printing Office, 1982); U.S. Bureau of the Census, *1990 Census of Population: Social and Economic Characteristics: Arizona* (Washington, DC: Government Printing Office, 1993); U.S. Census Bureau, *Census 2000 Supplementary Survey Profile: Phoenix*, http://www.census.gov/acs/www/Products/Profiles/Single/2000/C2SS/Tabular/160/16000US0455003.htm (accessed 23 August 2007).

32. *AR*, 22 April 2007, D1; *CR*, 17 November 2004, 3; *AR*, 20 December 2006, D1.

33. *AR*, 23 November 2003, D1; *AR*, 13 January 2008, D1.

34. *CR*, 6 September 2006, 6; *AR*, 25 October 25, 2007, CH2; *Phoenix Business Journal*, 10 February 2009, http://assets.bizjournals.com/phoenix/stories/2009/02/09/daily22.html (accessed 12 June 2009); *AR*, 11 July 2007, A10; *Phoenix Business Journal*, 21 November 2008, http://phoenix.bizjournals.com/phoenix/stories/2008/11/24/story9.html (accessed 12 June 2009); *AR*, 1 June 2007, D1.

35. *AR*, 14 May 2000, S8; *AR*, 10 March 2001, A1; *AR*, 27 January 2002, D1; *AR*, 22 May 2006, D1; *AR*, 12 October 2007, D3; *AR*, 14 October 2007, D3; *AR*, 22 August 2007, D1.

36. *What Matters: Indicators of Our Quality of Life, 1999*, 51; *Five Shoes Waiting to Drop on Arizona's Future: Arizona Policy Choices, 2001* (Tempe, AZ: Morrison Institute for Public Policy, 2001), 26; *Phoenix Business Journal*, 5 March 1997, http://www.bizjournals.com/phoenix/stories/1997/03/03/daily5.html (accessed 16 January 2008); but other retailers were less successful: Microwave went bankrupt in 2000, *AR*, 14 April 2000, A1.

37. AREAP employment data; *AR*, 28 November 2004, A1; *AR*, 12 December 2004, A1, A26.

38. *PG*, 14 September 1989, A1; *AR*, 6 June 1990, A1; Kirsten Mouton, "Welcome to Hard Times," *Arizona Trend*, January 1987, 40–47; *AR*, 2 January 1986, C1.

39. Mouton, "Welcome to Hard Times," 42; Kirsten Mouton, "A Steep Climb for Homebuilders," *Arizona Trend*, June 1987, 60–65; *PG*, 14 September 1989, A1; quotation from *AR*, 6 June 1990, A1.

40. Quotation from *PG*, 14 September 1989, A1; *PG*, 2 June 1990, A1; Kitty Calamita, Henry N. Pantile, and Robert Tollman, *Big Money Crime: Fraud and Politics in the Savings and Loan Crisis* (Berkeley: University of California Press, 1997); and David L. Mason, *From Buildings and Loans to Bail-Outs: A History of the American Savings and Loan Industry, 1831–1995* (New York: Cambridge University Press, 2004), 213–65.

41. E.g., Michael Binstein and Charles Bowden, *Trust Me: Charles Keating and the Missing Billions* (New York: Random House, 1993); James W. Johnson, *Arizona Politicians: The Noble and the Notorious* (Tucson: University of Arizona Press, 2002), 167–76; *New York Times*, 5 September 1997, 1.

42. *AR*, 20 February 1994, H1; *PG*, 20 January 1990, D1; *AR*, 11 February 1990, F1; *AR*, 22 February 1990; *AR*, 2 June 1990, C1. Seven of the nine savings and loans were based in Phoenix.

43. On mergers see *AR*, 3 August 1994, C1; *AR*, 30 September 1995, E1; *AR*, 28 January 1996, D1; *AR*, 14 April 1996, D1; *PG*, 28 October 1995, D1; on community banking see *AR*, 22 March 1997, E1; *AR*, 18 April 2004, D1; on banking trends see *Phoenix Business Journal*, 24 December 2004, 8 June 2007, 26 October 2007; and analysis of deposit data from FDIC, http://www2.fdic.gov/sod/index.asp (accessed 23 December 2007).

44. *AR*, 9 January 1999, E1; *AR*, 8 May 2001, D1; *AR*, 12 December 2004, A26.

45. *AR*, 7 March 2004, HV1; *AR*, 1 August 2004, D1; *AR*, 6 February 2005, A1; *AR*, 2 October 2005, A1; *AR*, 28 December 2005, D1; *AR*, 2 August 2006, B8; *AR*, 27 December 2007, A1; *AR*, 2 February 2008, A1; *AR*, 15 February 2009, A1.

46. Jacobson, "Phoenix Chamber of Commerce," 49, 57, 66, 79–83.

47. *AR*, 26 December 1999, D1; *AR*, 26 April 1998, D1; *AR*, 7 November 1999, D1; Phoenix, "Official Entry, 1989," All-America City Award, in series 15, carton 16, folder 69, NMLP-AA, 9; *AR*, 7 May 1995, A13; *AR*, 1 May 1999, B1; *AR*, 23 June 2000, Glendale/Peoria Community section, 2; *AR*, 28 October 2007, A25; *AR*, 11 May 2003, D1.

48. *Arizona Daily Star* (hereinafter *ADS*), 8 November 1993, 10D; *ADS*, 20 June 1992; for information on the Arizona Town Hall and its reports see http://www.aztownhall.org; among the Morrison Institute for Public Policy reports are *Organizing Economic Development in the 1990s: The Price of Prosperity* (1990); *What Matters: Indicators of Our Quality of Life* (1998); *Hits and Misses* (2000); *The New Economy: Policy Choices for Arizona* (2000); *Five Shoes* (2001); *What Matters—The Maturing of Greater Phoenix* (2004); and *Making Arizona Competitive in Science, Engineering, and Medical Research and Innovation: Understanding the Pathway to Success* (2006), which are noted and generally available at http://www.asu.edu/copp/morrison/; the Greater Phoenix 2100 site (http://www.gp2100.org/) contains descriptions, data, and reports; and examples of reports published in *AR*, 3 March 2003, V1–V3; *AR*, 23 February 2003, V1–V3; *AR*, 10 April 2005, V1–V3; *AR*, 28 October 2007, A24.

49. R. Towse, "The ASU Research Park," in Charles Sargent, ed., *Metro Arizona* (Scottsdale, AZ: Biffington Books, 1988), 134–35; Philip R. VanderMeer, *Phoenix Rising: The Making of a Desert Metropolis* (Carlsbad, CA: Heritage Media, 2002), 81–82; Margaret Pugh O'Mara, *Cities of Knowledge: Cold War Science and the Search for the Next Silicon Valley* (Princeton: Princeton University Press, 2005).

50. E.g., *Making Arizona Competitive*, 4–5, 20; *AR*, 17 February 2002, V1.

51. *AR*, 22 May 2002, D1; *AR*, 13 June 2003, D1; "Translational Genomics Research Institute

Formally Launches in Arizona: Dr. Jeffrey Trent to Be Named President and Chief Scientific Officer," City of Phoenix news release, 26 June 2003, http://www.phxskyharbor.com/ NEWSREL/tgri.html (accessed 22 June 2004); *AR*, 2 June 2004, A1; *Northeast Phoenix Republic*, 19 December 2007, 27; *AR*, 17 August 2005, B1; *AR*, 27 May 2006, B4.

52. "About the School of Life Sciences," http://sols.asu.edu/text/aboutsols.php (accessed 24 June 2004); Kerry Fehr-Snyder, "ASU Chief Lures Science Think Tank; Group Seeks to Develop Policy," *AR*, 23 January 2004, http://www.azcentral.com/arizonarepublic/local/ articles/0123asuscience23.html (accessed 15 June 2004).

53. E.g., *Making Arizona Competitive*; *AR*, 11 April 2005, D1; *AR*, 15 January 2006, V2; *AR*, 6 February 2008, D1.

54. On the connections between voting systems, turnout, and officeholding, see Dennis R. Judd and Todd Swanstrom, *City Politics: Private Power and Public Policy*, 2nd ed. (New York: Longman, 1998), 84–106; Amy Bridges, *Morning Glories: Municipal Reform in the Southwest* (Princeton: Princeton University Press, 1997), 141–50, 200–203; Samuel P. Hays, "The Politics of Reform in Municipal Government in the Progressive Era," *Pacific Northwest Quarterly*, 55 (1964): 157–169; Zoltan L. Hajnal and Paul G. Lewis, "Municipal Institutions and Voter Turnout in Local Elections," *Urban Affairs Review* 38 (2003): 645–68; Jerry L. Polinard, Robert D. Wrinkle, and Thomas Longoria, Jr., "The Impact of District Elections on the Mexican American Community: The Electoral Perspective," *Social Science Quarterly* 71 (1991): 608–14.

55. Terry Goddard made this argument specifically for Phoenix in Terry Goddard, interview by author, 27 September 2001 and 2 October 2001, tape recording, in the possession of the author. Another structural factor was the shift to four-year terms and staggered elections for council.

56. *Registered Voters and Votes Cast for Mayor and Council, Primary and General Election, Phoenix, 1949–1979* (Phoenix: City of Phoenix, 1980); *PG*, 4 November 1981, A1; Goddard interview tape recording.

57. Earl Zarbin, *All the Time a Newspaper: The First 100 Years of the Arizona Republic* (Phoenix: Arizona Republic, 1990), 349–51; Bridges, *Morning Glories*, 193–97; Goddard interview tape recording; *AR*, 28 November 1982, A1.

58. Goddard interview tape recording; *AR*, 2 November 1983, A1.

59. *AR*, 26 December 1999, D1; quotation from *AR*, 29 August 1987.

60. Goddard interview tape recording.

61. Goddard interview tape recording; Ian P. Johnson, "Mountain Tops and Valley Houses: Preserving the Western Cityscape in Phoenix, 1954–1985," seminar paper, 2007, 30–35, Arizona State University; materials at Phoenix Historic Preservation Office, http://phoenix. gov/HISTORIC/index.html (accessed 25 October 2007).

62. Goddard interview tape recording; *AR*, 4 October 1989, A1; *PG*, 12 September 1990, B1; *PG*, 31 October 1990, B1; *AR*, 7 May 1995, A13.

63. *AR*, 21 December 1989, B1; *AR*, 22 April 1990, AA1; *AR*, 4 October 1989, A1; *AR*, 9 October 1985, A1; Howard Fischer, "ValTrans Derailed," *Phoenix New Times*, 5 April 1989, http:// phoenixnewtimes.com/1989-04-05/news/valtrans-derailed/ (accessed 18 December 2007); Goddard interview tape recording; *PG*, 6 July 1989, G1; and *PG*, 21 September 1989, A10.

64. *AR*, 18 September 1989, A2; *AR*, 29 September 1991, VG3; *AR*, 12 March 1994, A1.

65. *PG*, 31 October 1990, B1; *AR*, 7 December 1991, C1; *AR*, 29 September 1991, B6; *AR*, 12 March 1994, A1.

66. *AR*, 15 October 1994, A1; *AR*, 5 October 1995, A7; *AR*, 4 October 1995, A1; *AR*, 24 September 1995, F4.

67. Quotations from *AR*, 3 September 1999, B9, and *AR*, 8 September 1999, A1; *AR*, 18 February 1999, B6; Goddard interview tape recording.

68. *AR*, 28 December 2003, A17; *AR*, 4 January 2004, V1.

69. *AR*, 3 December 2002, B1; *AR*, 1 March 2003, B6; quotation from *AR*, 27 April 2003, A1.

70. *AR*, 20 July 2003, B1; *AR*, 29 August 2003, B1.

71. *AR*, 27 April 2003, A1; *AR*, 20 September 2003, B10; *AR*, 29 August 2007, Phoenix Republic section, 17.

72. *AR*, 2 November 1983, A1; 14 December 1983, A1; *AR*, 26 January 2003, V1.

73. On incumbency see election reports and *AR*, 15 October 1994, A1; on the incumbents' edge in funding, see, e.g., the six-to-one report in *PG*, 27 September 1995, 1.

74. This reflects my analysis of election returns and candidate materials presented in the *AR*, e.g., 30 September 1987, B2; 2 October 1987, [Elect. Supp.], 1–11; 4 October 1989, A; 29 September 1991, VG1–12; 6 October 1993, A1; 5 October 1995, A1; 8 September 1999, A1; and 10 September 2003, A1, B10.

75. As reported by Terry Goddard in Goddard interview tape recording.

76. *AR*, 24 August 1987, A6; Goddard interview tape recording; "Official Entry, 1989," All-America City Award, 9, NMLP-AA; *AR*, 26 January 2003, V1; *AR*, 7 October 1987, B1; *AR*, 4 October 1991, B1.

77. Comments on occupations reflect officeholder statements in *AR*, such as the editions cited in note 74 above. Information on council salaries can be found in *AR*, 7 October 1987, B1; *AR*, 4 October 1991, B1; *AR*, 5 September 1999, B6; *AR*, 28 August 2003, B8; *AR*, 14 September 2005, B6.

78. Goddard interview tape recording; *AR*, 26 January 2003, V1; Kathleen Stanton, "The Balance of Power," *Phoenix New Times*, 25 September 1991.

79. Turnout calculated from vote totals and a linear interpolation of census population figures. See also Bridges, *Morning Glories*, 180–81.

80. For referenda see the election reports cited above in note 74; on bonds see *PG*, 12 September 1990, B1; City of Phoenix, "2006 Bond Program," http://www.phoenix.gove/2006bond (accessed 20 February 2008); "Official Entry, 1989," All-America City Award, 4–9, quotation from 3, NMLP-AA; Dennis M. Burke, "Remembering the Future: The Phoenix Futures Forum," http://goodgovernment.org/phoenixfutureshistory.htm (accessed 9 April 2007).

81. *AFR*, *1985–86*, 9, and *AFR*, *1986–87*, 9–10; Judd and Swanstrom, *City Politics*, 236–37, 336.

82. Quotations from *AFR*, *1985–86*, 10; *AFR*, *1986–87*, 12; *AFR*, *1987–88*, 6. Data on revenue and spending in this and subsequent discussions are from *AFR*, 1980–2007 editions.

83. Crime data from *The Municipal Year Book*, 1980–1991; *What Matters: Indicators of Our Quality of Life, 1999 Edition*, 28, 29; City of Phoenix Police Department, "Uniform Crime Reporting (UCR), Part I," http://phoenix.gov/POLICE/crista1.html (accessed 25 February 2008); as election issue see, e.g., *PG*, 20 September 1995, 3; *AR*, 8 September 1999, A1; *Ahwatukee Republic*, 16 May 2007, 6. For program innovations see *Phoenix General Plan* (Phoenix: City of Phoenix, 2002), 432–33.

84. *Phoenix Budget, 2007–08* (Phoenix: City of Phoenix, 2007), 19; *Phoenix General Plan*, 334–40, 424–28.

85. *AR*, 20 June 2009, A1; *AR*, 25 June 2009, B1; City of Phoenix, "Phoenix is Named All-America City," http://www.phoenix.gov/news/061909phxaac.html (accessed 22 June

2009); Janet Vinzant and Robert B. Denhardt, *Creating a Culture of Innovation: 10 Lessons from America's Best Run City,* Transforming Organization Series, January 2001 (Arlington, VA: PricewaterhouseCoopers Endowment for the Business of Government, 2001), www.businessofgovernment.org/pdfs/denhardtreport.pdf (accessed 4 March 2004); *AFR, 1990–91,* VI; Adrian T. Moore, James Nolan, and Geoffrey F. Segal, with Matthew Taylor, *Competitive Cities: A Report Card on Efficiency in Service Delivery in America's Largest Cities* (Los Angeles: Reason Public Policy Institute, 2001), http://www.reason.org/ps282.pdf (accessed 3 March 2004); and *AR,* 12 July 2004, B6.

86. For useful summaries of various downtown strategies see Carl Abbott, "Five Strategies for Downtown: Policy Discourse and Planning Since 1943," *Journal of Policy History,* vol. 5, no. 1 (1993): 5–27; and Kent A. Robertson, "Downtown Redevelopment Strategies in the United States: An End-of-the-Century Assessment," *Journal of the American Planning Association* 4 (Autumn 1995): 429–37. On post-1980 development see Larry R. Ford, *America's New Downtowns: Revitalization or Reinvention?* (Baltimore: Johns Hopkins University Press, 2003).

87. *AR,* 24 June 1990, C1.

88. Quotations from Goddard interview tape recording and in Luckingham, *Phoenix: The History of a Southwestern Metropolis* (Tucson: University of Arizona Press, 1989), 237.

89. *AR,* 22 October 1995, D1, and *AR,* 20 September 1997, E1; Goddard interview tape recording. On downtown development see Ford, *America's New Downtowns,* as well as a previous study: Bernard J. Frieden and Lynne B. Sagalyn, *Downtown, Inc.: How America Rebuilds Cities* (Cambridge, MA: MIT Press, 1989).

90. *AR,* 4 February 1990, C1; *AR,* 24 June 1990, C1; *PG,* 2 August 1990, A1; *AR,* 9 July 1995, B1; City of Phoenix, *Downtown Phoenix: A 25 Year Vision* (Phoenix: Central Phoenix Committee, 1991), 61–65. On the Arizona Center and Mercado see Jason R. Hackworth, "Local Politics and Structural Change: Commercial Landscape Production in the Phoenix Metropolitan Area" (master's thesis, Arizona State University, 1996), 35–47, 96–104; on downtown Phoenix see Gober, *Metropolitan Phoenix,* 177–86.

91. *ABG,* 9 October 1997, 8; *AR,* 20 April 1997, C1; *AR,* 7 July 1995, B4.

92. *AR,* 22 December 1996, A1; *AR,* 22 September 2000, B1; *AR,* 26 January 2001, A1; *AR,* February 10, 2001, B1; *AR,* 7 April 2002, A10; *AR,* 23 October 2007, B1.

93. E.g., *AR,* 17 December 1989, S1; *AR,* 5 July 1992, F1; *AR,* 10 September 1997, E1; *ABG,* 30 October 1997, 6; *AR,* 15 December 2000, D1; *AR,* 25 February 2003, A4; *AR,* 15 May 2005, B1; *AR,* 12 January 2008, A18.

94. Judd and Swanstrom, *City Politics,* 370–73; *Inside Metro Phoenix, 1990,* 20; *AR,* 21 May 2000, B10; *AR,* 5 July 2001, A1; "Fact Sheet: Expansion Project," http://phoenix.gov/CIVPLAZA/overview.pdf (accessed 12 December 2007); *AR,* 27 June 2004, D1; Heywood Sanders, *Space Available: The Realities of Convention Centers as Economic Development Strategy,* Research Brief (Washington, DC: Brookings Institution, 2005), 2, 15; Dave Kovaleski, "Aiming High," MeetingsNet, 1 January 2007, http://meetingsnet.com/strategy/costcontrol/meetings_aiming_high_19_19_010107/ (accessed 14 January 2007); *AR,* 26 December 2008, B1.

95. E.g. *AR,* 10 August 2004, A1; see information on the Arizona Bioindustry Organization at http://www.azbio.org/ (accessed 13 February 2008). On the evolving planning discussions see *AR,* 9 June 2002, A4; *AR,* 27 November 2003, A1; *AR,* 17 October 2004, V1; *AR,* 6 October 2005, A1; and *AR,* 13 February 2006, D1.

96. *AR,* 2 October 2005, A1, A26; *AR,* 15 March 2006, A1.

97. *AR,* 12 January 2008, A18; *AR,* 18 May 2006, D1; Gober, *Metropolitan Phoenix,* 164–66.

98. *AR,* 28 November–1 December 2004; "For Phoenix to Flourish," *Shade,* October–November 2004, 50–96; *Downtown Phoenix: A Strategic Vision and Blueprint for the Future* (Phoenix: City of Phoenix, 2004), 37, 28; *AR,* 18 January 2008, B1.

99. *AR,* 15 July 2001, A1; *AR,* 23 December 2001, E5; *AR,* 29 August 2004, E5: *AR,* 3 March 2008, E1.

100. Ann E. Marshall, Mary H. Brennan, and Juliet Martin, *The Heard Museum: History and Collections,* rev. ed. (Phoenix: Heard Museum, 2002); Michelle M. Bayes, "Collecting Culture: A History of the Heard Museum, 1929–1999" (master's thesis, Arizona State University, 2000); *AR,* 19 November 1989, VA17; *AR,* 22 March 1998, G15.

101. Arizona Theater Company, "Decade by Decade: An Overview of ATC's 35 years," http://www.aztheatreco.org (accessed 15 July 2001); Actors Theatre, "Our History" http://www.atphx.org (accessed 3 May 2002); *AR,* 1 July 2001, E8; *AR,* 12 February 2006, E6.

102. "History of Ballet Arizona," http://www.balletaz.org (accessed 2 March 2008); *AR,* 10 September 2000, E8.

103. *AR,* 11 November 1998, A1; *AR,* 11 January 1998, PS1–PS9; *AR,* 9 December 2007, D1.

104. *AR,* 16 January 2000, E3; *AR,* 21 July 2002, E7; *AR,* 29 July 2005, B9.

105. *AR,* 7 May 1999, D10; *AR,* 28 August 2005, E6; *AR,* 9 November 1999, D1; *Scottsdale Republic North,* 30 November 2007, 24; *AR,* 10 September 2000, E8.

106. *Mesa Republic,* 8 September 2007, 4.

107. Central Arizona Museum Association, http://www.azcama.com (accessed 5 November 2006).

108. *The Arts in Arizona: A Discussion Document* (Phoenix: Flinn Foundation, 2002); Batelle Memorial Institute, *Learning from Others: Benchmarking the Maricopa Region against Other Regions' Efforts to Build a Vibrant Arts and Cultural Sector* (Phoenix: Maricopa Regional Arts and Culture Task Force, 2003); Morrison Institute for Public Policy, "A Place for Arts and Culture: A Maricopa County Overview," September 2003 draft, online at http://morrisoninstitute.asu.edu/publications-reports (accessed 5 October 2009). Terry Nichols Clark provides a valuable perspective in *The City as an Entertainment Machine* (Oxford, UK: Elsevier, 2003).

109. *Downtown Phoenix: A Strategic Vision,* 19–24.

110. *What Matters—The Maturing of Greater Phoenix,* 43–45; *What Matters: Indicators of Our Quality of Life, 1998 Edition,* 74–75.

111. *AR,* 22 December 1996, A1. Cf. *AR,* 7 May 1005, A13, and *AR,* 20 April 1997, C1.

112. *AR,* 6 November 2006, A1; *AR,* 18 March 2005, B8; *Business Journal,* 22 April 2005, 9; Arizona Grantmakers Forum, http://www.arizonagrantmakersforum.org/ (accessed 22 June 2005).

113. *AR,* 7 May 1995, A13.

114. *AR,* 7 November 2001, B10.

115. Len Sherman, *Big League, Big Time: The Birth of the Arizona Diamondbacks, the Billion-Dollar Business of Sports, and the Power of the Media in America* (New York: Pocket Books, 1998), 66, 69, 110; Lee Shappell, *Phoenix Suns: Rising to the Top with the "Team of Oddities"* (Champaign, IL: Sagamore Publishing, 1993), 13–15; *AR,* 13 December 2000, C1, C7.

116. *PG,* 25 August 1989, B1.

117. *PG,* 21 December 1993, A1.

118. *ABG,* 1 February 1996, 22; *AR,* 12 May 2008, B1. Other sports also provided important economic benefits. Besides the regular racing contests, major one-time events like the FBR/Phoenix Open for golf and the Fiesta Bowl and Insight Bowl games brought in substantial revenue.

119. Tony Salem, "A History of Professional Sports in Arizona: 1968–Present," (honor's thesis, Arizona State University, 1999); *AR,* 27 January 2008, C12; VanderMeer, *Phoenix Rising,*

124–25, 129. Jerry Colangelo also brought teams in the Womens National Basketball League and the Arena Football League.

120. *PG*, 1 September 1989, B1; *AR*, 7 September 1989, A1; *PG*, 25 September 1989, B1; *PG*, 29 September 1989, B7; *AR*, 4 October 1989, A1.

121. *AR*, 24 October 1989, A1; *AR*, 21 December 1989, B1; *AR*, 22 April 1990, AA1; *PG*, 2 August 1990, A1.

122. *PG*, 2 August 1990, A1.

123. *The Governor's Special Task Force on Cactus League Baseball, Final Report, June 1989* (Phoenix: Arizona Department of Commerce, Arizona Office of Tourism, 1989); *AR*, 19 September 1993, C13; Sherman, *Big League*, 72–74.

124. *AR*, 12 February 1994, A1; *AR*, 15 January 1994, A1; *PG*, 18 February 1994, A1; *AR*, 21 May 1994, A1; *AR*, 8 August 1996, B1.

125. *AR*, 23 November 1997, A1; *AR*, 14 August 1997, A1.

126. *AR*, 5 March 1995, A1; *PG*, 9 March 1995, A1; *AR*, 26 November 1997, A1; *AR*, 1 April 1998, A1.

127. *AR*, 19 May 1999, B1; *AR*, 4 November 1999, A1.

128. *AR*, 11 April 2001, A1; *AR*, 18 July 2001, A1; *AR*, 7 May 2009, A1; *AR*, 17 May 2009, B1.

129. *AR*, 9 October 1997, A2; *AR*, 10 October 1997, A1; *AR*, 30 January 1998, B1; *AR*, 13 May 1999, A10; *AR*, 18 May 1999, B1; *AR*, 19 May 1999, A1.

130. *AR*, 6 November 1999, A1.

131. *AR*, 19 April 2000, A12; *AR*, 28 April 2000, A1; *AR*, 27 September 2000, Sun Cities/Surprise Community section, 1; *AR*, 14 November 2000, B1.

132. *AR*, 2 February 2001, A1; *AR*, 14 February 2001, A1; *AR*, 18 November 2001, A13; *AR*, 1 March 2002, A1; *AR*, 30 April 2002, B1; *AR*, 29 August 2002, A1; *AR*, 30 August 2002, A2; *AR*, 11 September 2002, B5; *AR*, 2 August 2006, A1.

133. On SPDs see *General Plan for Phoenix, 1985–2000* (Phoenix: City of Phoenix, 1985), 38–39; *Phoenix General Plan*, 2002, 231–32, 244–48; *Special District Plan for the Roosevelt Neighborhood* (Phoenix: City of Phoenix Planning Department, 1989); and the list and map of historic districts, http://phoenix.gov/HISTORIC/residents.html (accessed 22 March 2006).

134. *General Plan, 1985–2000*, 38–43; *Phoenix General Plan*, 2002, 254–56.

135. *Phoenix General Plan*, 2002, 75–77, 161, 249–52; *General Plan, 1985–2000*, 40–43; *AR*, 5 October 2005, B1.

136. "Official Entry, 1989," All-America City Award, 4–6, NMLP-AA; *Social Background Paper*, General Plan Update Information Series (Phoenix: City of Phoenix Planning Department, 1990), 15–21; *Annual Report, 1986–1987; City of Phoenix Neighborhood Improvement and Housing Department* (Phoenix: The Dept., [1987]), 2–4, 6; *Phoenix General Plan*, 2002, 247–48.

137. *AR*, 16 November 1994, B3; *Phoenix General Plan*, 2002, 233. Analysis based on association lists in *Neighborhoods That Work: A Directory of Neighborhood Successes* (Phoenix: City of Phoenix Neighborhood Services Department, 1996), and "Neighborhood Associations by Council District," http://phoenix.gov/APPINTRO/nbhdassoc.html (accessed 5 February 2008).

138. *AR*, 5 October 2005, B1; *AR*, 4 March 2008, B1; *AR*, 2 June 2000, A1.

139. For criticism of urban villages see Gober, *Metropolitan Phoenix*, 155–58, and Grady Gammage, Jr., *Phoenix in Perspective: Reflections on Developing the Desert* (Tempe, AZ: Herberger Center for Design Excellence, College of Architecture and Environmental Design, Arizona State University, 1999), 54–58.

140. *AR,* 22 January 2003, A1, and *AR,* 3 March 2003, A1; *AR,* 28 March 2001, A10–A11; U.S. Bureau of the Census, USA Counties, "Table 22: 50 Largest Metropolitan Statistical Areas— Population by Race and Hispanic Origin, 2006," http://censtats.census.gov/usa/usa.shtml (accessed 22 August 2007).

141. See the analysis by Alex P. Oberle and Daniel D. Arreola, "Resurgent Mexican Phoenix," *Geographical Review,* 98 (April 2008): 171–96.

142. Housing and Community Development Department, *Housing Assistance Plan* (Phoenix: City of Phoenix, 1979), 57–59; U.S. Bureau of the Census, *Residential Segregation of Hispanics or Latinos: 1980–2000,* quotation 85, http://www.census.gov/hhes/www/housing/housing_ patterns/pdf/ch6.pdf (accessed 7 March 2008).

143. U.S. Bureau of the Census, "TM-P004H: Percent of Persons Who Are Hispanic or Latino (of Any Race), 2000," http://www.census.gov/, Factfinder (accessed 6 January 2008); *Five Shoes,* 16–23, especially map 3, showing population concentration and educational achievement; Bradford Luckingham, *Minorities in Phoenix: A Profile of Mexican American, Chinese American, and African American Communities, 1860–1992* (Tucson: University of Arizona Press, 1994), 65–72; *Hits and Misses,* 22–23.

144. *AR,* 21 February 2006, A21; Pratt Center for Community Development, "Chicanos Por La Causa (CPLC), Phoenix, AZ," CDC Oral History Project, http://www.prattcenter.net/ cdc-cplc.php (accessed 12 January 2005); pages at Chicanos Por La Causa, Inc., http://www. cplc.org/default.aspx (accessed 15 July 2007).

145. Quotation from *AR,* 25 June 2000, D1; *AR,* 13 April 2005, D1. See also Oberle and Arreola, "Resurgent Mexican Phoenix," 179–82.

146. *AR,* 12 January 1999, A1; *AR,* 28 February 2006, A12; *AR,* 23 February 2008, B1.

147. *AR,* 4 December 2007, A1.

148. U.S. Bureau of the Census, USA Counties, "Table 22: 50 Largest Metropolitan Statistical Areas—Population by Race and Hispanic Origin, 2006," http://censtats.census.gov/usa/ usa.shtml (accessed 22 August 2007). See *AR,* 24 June 2001, V1.

149. "Total Resident Population by Municipal Planning Area, Maricopa County, July 1, 2005, and Projections July 1, 2010, to July 1, 2030," in *Socioeconomic Projections of Population, Housing, and Employment by Municipal Planning Area and Regional Analysis Zone* (Phoenix: Maricopa Association of Governments, 2007), 4, www.workforce.az.gov/admin/UploadedPublica tions/2538_2006MAGprojectionsJURI.pdf (accessed 7 January 2008). See also "Arizona, Nevada, and California Cities Show Fastest Growth, Census Bureau Says," U.S. Bureau of the Census News, 24 June 2004, http://www.census.gov/Press-Release/www/releases/ archives/population/001856.html (accessed 7 January 2008).

150. *AR,* 12 May 2003, A1; *AR,* 14 May 2003, A1; *AR,* 4 November 2007, V1.

151. "Table 0–2: Jurisdictional Summary of MAG Municipalities," *Regional Report: A Resource for Policy Makers in the Maricopa Region* (Phoenix: Maricopa Association of Governments, 2005), 3, http://www.mag.maricopa.gov/publications.cms (accessed 15 March 2006). Buckeye and Goodyear annexed another 175 square miles in 2006–7, *Southwest Valley Reporter,* 11 August 2006, 12, and *Southwest Valley Reporter,* 28 March 2007, 1.

152. *Annexation Implications, Western and Southwestern Phoenix, Arizona* (Phoenix: City of Phoenix Planning Department, 1982); and *PG,* 2 November 1994, A1.

153. Quotation from Goddard interview tape recording; Andy Zipser, "Growing by Leaps and Bounds: Behind the Scenes at the Phoenix-Scottsdale Turf Wars," *Phoenix New Times,* 30 January–5 February 1985, 6.

154. Goddard interview tape recording.

155. *AR*, 5 April 1993, 1N1; *Glendale/Peoria Republic*, 1 April 2000, 1; *AR*, 5 December 2002, A1; *AR*, 6 December 2002, B1. Cf. the argument with Cave Creek stemming from 1986 in *AR*, 17 September 2004, B6.

156. In addition to the sources in note 155, see Carol E. Heim, "Border Wars: Tax Revenues, Annexation, and Urban Growth in Phoenix," Working Paper 2006–01, Department of Economics, University of Massachusetts, Amherst, http://scholarworks.umass.edu/cgi/viewcontent.cgi?article=1049&context=econ_workingpaper (accessed 16 October 2009).

157. *AR*, 25 January 1989, A1; *AR*, 28 April 1993, A1; *AR*, 19 August 2003, B1. On the impact of tax policy see Heim, "Border Wars."

158. Dennis Burke, "Remembering the Future"; *Phoenix New Times*, 3 November 1994, http://www.phoenixnewtimes.com/1994-11-03/news/a-new-chapter-in-the-esplanade-saga (accessed 25 June 2008).

159. On Rio Salado see *PG*, 16 January 1987, A1; *PG*, 4 November 1987, A1.

160. *AR*, 25 January 1989, A1.

161. *Phoenix General Plan, 2002*, 161; *Hits and Misses*, 35; *AR*, 23 October 2006, B1; *Ahwatukee Republic*, 16 November 2006, 6. Cf. Jana Bommersbach, "Developers' Blues," *Phoenix New Times*, 15–21 April 1987, 26.

162. Tom R. Rex, "Housing in Metropolitan Phoenix," 12, and "Population Density in Metropolitan Phoenix," 13–15, Reports Prepared for the Morrison Institute for Public Policy, 2000, http://wpcarey.asu.edu/seid/reports.cfm (accessed 22 March 2006); *AR*, 27 September 2006, D1. On house size see Alex Wilson and Jessica Boehland, "Small Is Beautiful: U.S. House Size, Resource Use, and the Environment," *Journal of Industrial Ecology*, 9 (Winter–Spring 2005): 277–87. The pattern repeated itself after 2007.

163. Gammage, *Phoenix in Perspective*, 104–11; Gober, *Metropolitan Phoenix*, 104. Andrew Duany, Elizabeth Plater-Zyberk, and Jeff Speck explain the new urbanist perspective in *Suburban Sprawl: The Rise and Decline of the American Dream* (New York: Farrar, Straus and Giroux, 2000).

164. See, for example, Robert Bruegmann, *Sprawl: A Compact History* (Chicago: University of Chicago Press, 2005); Dolores Hayden, *A Field Guide to Sprawl* (New York: W. W. Norton, 2004), 7–8; and Philip Langdon, "Sprawl," in *Growth in Arizona: The Machine in the Garden* (Tempe, AZ.: Morrison Institute for Public Policy, 1998), 107–8.

165. William Fulton, Rolf Pendall, Mai Nguyen, and Alicia Harrison, "Who Sprawls Most? How Growth Patterns Differ across the U.S.," *Brookings Institution, Survey Series* (July 2001), esp. 6, 8, 15, http://www.brookings.edu/es/urban/publications/fulton.pdf (accessed 14 July 2005). Cf. Leon Kolankiewicz and Roy Beck, "Sprawl City: Weighing Sprawl Factors in Large U.S. Cities: Analysis of U.S. Bureau of the Census data on the 100 Largest Urbanized Areas of the United States," March 2001, http://www.sprawlcity.org/studyUSA/ (accessed 14 July 2005); and Robert E. Lang and Patrick A. Simmons, "'Boomburbs': The Emergence of Large, Fast-Growing Suburban Cities in the United States," *Fannie Mae Foundation Census Note 06* (June 2001), http://www.fanniemaefoundation.org/programs/census_notes_6.html (accessed 12 September 2006); *Hits and Misses*, 10–11, 46.

166. *AR*, 11 May 2003, A1; *AR*, 5 October 2005, A1; *AR*, 13 November 2005, A1; *AR*, 2 April 2006, A1, V1; *AR*, 9 April 2006, A1; Gammage, *Phoenix in Perspective*, 114–20; *Megapolitan: Arizona's Sun Corridor* (Tempe, AZ: Morrison Institute for Public Policy, 2008); and "We Create Our Future: Pinal County Comprehensive Plan," draft plan, http://pinalcountyplan.com/PDF/

022409PinalCompPlanCPCDraftFINAL.pdf (accessed 15 July 2009).

167. *Regional Growing Smarter Implementation Project: Final Report* (Phoenix: Maricopa Association of Governments, 2003), 42; *AR*, 12 May 2003, A2; *Surprise Republic*, 5 October 2007, 12. Terri Lynn Shepherd summarizes the planning features of twenty-three of the post-1980 planned communities in "The Influence of Garden Cities on New Communities in the Phoenix Metropolitan Area" (master's thesis, Arizona State University, 2000).

168. *AR*, 28 February 1999, A1; *Regional Growing Smarter Report*, 42; Tim Rogers, "Master-Planned Communities," http://phoenix.about.com/cs/real/a/masterplanned. htm (accessed 13 March 2008); Alice Held, "The Difference between Masterplanned Communities, Subdivisions, and Horse Properties," http://www.come2az.com/forsale/homelife/Difference.html (accessed 22 February 2008).

169. Many golf communities are in north Scottsdale, "Northeast Valley," http:// www.come2az. com/forsale/homelife/MPC-NEValley.html (accessed 27 February 2008); maps with the nearly 200 golf courses are printed annually in the *AR*, e.g., 18 January 2007, C8–C9; "Stellar Airpark Estates," http://www.stellarairpark.com/AirPark_old/AirPark_NEW/index.asp (accessed 8 October 2007); Gordon Baker Homes, "Water Ski Property and Communities" http://www.myhomeinaz.com/waterfront.htm (accessed 13 March 2008).

170. "Retirement Communities," http://www.azhomefront.com/Category. aspx?CategoryID=1066 (accessed 11 March 2008). See also the map in *Hits and Misses*, 16.

171. *AR*, 28 February 1999, A1; *AR*, 14 January 2000, D1; *AR*, 5 July 2001, A1; *AR*, 29 September 2005, B4; "Anthem," http://www.anthemarizona.com/ (accessed 23 January 2008). On Anthem and other periphery developments see Gober, *Metropolitan Phoenix*, 101–22.

172. *Verrado: A Hometown Takes Shape* (Menlo Park, CA: Sunset Publishing, 2005); *AR*, 22 March 2006, B5; *AR*, 18 January 2004, D1.

173. "Marley Park: A Celebration of Home," http://www.marleypark.com/index.asp (accessed 13 March 2008); *Northwest Valley Republic*, 4 November 2005, 10; *AR*, 19 May 2006, NHA16.

174. *Gilbert Republic*, 14 September 2004, 3; *AR*, 2 October 1999, Gilbert Community section, EV1; *AR*, 20 March 2004, HO12; "Agritopia," http://www.agritopia.com/index.html (accessed 3 March 2007); "The Joe's Farm Grill Story," printed handout, Agritopia; Morrison Ranch, http://www.morrisonranch.com/home.asp (accessed 13 March 2008); *AR*, 9 January 2003, Gilbert and Queen Creek Community section, 1; cf. Gober, *Metropolitan Phoenix*, 117–21.

175. AR, 3 August 2004, A1; *AR*, 11 June 2006, B1; *2007 Arizona Community Management Impact Study* (Phoenix: Arizona Association of Community Managers, 2007), 2, 4, http://www. aacmonline.org/doc/toc.asp?assn_id=10622 (accessed 14 March 2008); *Basics of Association Management* (Phoenix: Arizona Association of Community Managers, 2007); Barbara Coyle McCabe, "Privatizing Urban Services through Homeowners Associations: The Potential and Practice in Phoenix," *International Journal of Public Administration*, vol. 29, nos. 10–11 (2006): 841–42. The HOA Network, a strongly anti-HOA group in Arizona, publishes and links to useful information online at http://www.starman.com/HOA/hoa_info.htm.

176. For conflicting views on HOAs see Evan McKenzie, *Privatopia: Homeowner Associations and the Rise of Residential Private Government* (New Haven, CT: Yale University Press, 1994) and Robert H. Nelson, *Private Neighborhoods and the Transformation of Local Government* (Washington, DC: Urban Institute Press, 2005). Evan McKenzie, "Gated Communities and Homeowner Associations," http://tigger.uic.edu/~mckenzie/hoa.html (accessed 21 December 2007).

177. *FY 2007–2011 Transportation Improvement Program* (Phoenix: Maricopa Association of Governments, 2006), 5–7; *Certification of Revenue and Construction Costs for the Regional Freeway System* (Phoenix: Arizona Department of Transportation, 2007), 1–4; *Hits and Misses*, 14–15; and Arizona Rail Passenger Association, "A Brief History of Public Transportation in Metro Phoenix," http://www.azrail.org/trains/transit/transit-history/ (accessed 13 March 2008).

178. E.g., *AR*, 7 May 2004, D1; *AR*, 25 January 2007, D1; *Mesa Republic*, 20 October 2007, 4; and "Dead Mall," http://mallsofamerica.blogspot.com/2006/11/swanky-sears-inphonenix.html (accessed 3 January 2007).

179. *Phoenix Budget, 2003–2004* (Phoenix: City of Phoenix, 2003), 29; *Phoenix Budget, 2007–2008*, 109; Arizona Rail Passenger Association, "Brief History of Public Transportation," passim. On travel patterns and attitudes see *What Matters—The Maturing of Greater Phoenix*, 37–38.

180. *AR*, 25–29 March 1989; *AR* 13 September 1997, A1; *AR*, 22 March 2000, A1; *AR*, 29 March 2000, B1; *AR*, 25 January 2005, A1; *FY 2007–2011 Transportation Improvement Program*, 5–6; and Arizona Rail Passenger Association, "Brief History of Public Transportation."

181. *AR*, 4 February 1996, A1; *AR*, 22 November 1996, B1; *AR*, 31 March 1990, A1; *AR*, 26 July 1990, A1.

182. *AR*, 27 June 1991, A1; *AR*, 13 November 1993, B10; *AR*, 3 February 1996, A1; *AR*, 8 May 1996, A1; *AR*, 22 November 1996, B1; *AR*, 31 December 1998, D3.

183. Quotation from *AR*, 13 March 2008, A1; *Regional Report for Policy Makers*, 40–43; *The Maturing of Greater Phoenix*, 31.

184. E.g., "Statewide Drought Program," http://www.azwater.gov/dwr/drought/ (accessed 15 March 2008). The best general guide to Arizona water issues is Bonnie G. Colby and Katharine L. Jacobs, eds., *Arizona Water Policy: Management Innovations in an Urbanizing, Arid Region* (Washington, DC: Resources for the Future, 2007).

185. *AFR, 1986–87*, 11; "Central Arizona: The Endless Search for New Supplies to Water the Desert," in *Water Transfers in the West: Efficiency, Equity, and the Environment* (Washington, DC: National Academy Press, 1992), 194–212.

186. University of Arizona, *Arizona's Water Future: Challenges and Opportunities*, Background Report Prepared for the Eighty-fifth Arizona Town Hall, 2004, http://oed.arizona.edu/Lib/Media/Docs/watertownhall.pdf (accessed 6 March 2006); data from the Governor's Water Management Commission, part four, chapter I, draft report, 2001; Mark Frank, "Municipal Water Use in the Phoenix Active Management Area," http://cals.arizona.edu/OALS/urbanization/water.html (accessed 21 June 2001); *AR*, 3 January 2005, A4; *Phoenix General Plan*, 2002, 320–32; Phoenix Water Services Department, *Phoenix Water Resources Plan, Update 2005* (Phoenix: City of Phoenix, 2005), 10, 30–36; *AR*, 4 May 2008, B6. West Valley cities, lacking surface water, were less successful in reducing groundwater use.

187. *What Matters: Indicators of Our Quality of Life, 1999 Edition*, 61; Rebecca Mong, "John F. Long: Maryvale Developer Harnesses Sun, Fights for Water and West Side," *Phoenix Magazine*, November 1986, 281–83, 370–75; *AR*, 5 June 2004, A1; *AR*, 5 January 2005, A8; *Phoenix Water Resources*, 21, 29; *Water Conservation Plan, 1998* (Phoenix: Phoenix Water Services Department, 1998); Sharon B. Megdal, "Arizona's Recharge and Recovery Programs," in Colby and Jacobs, *Arizona Water Policy*, 188–203; Douglas E. Kupel, *Fuel for Growth: Water and Arizona's Urban Environment* (Tucson: University of Arizona Press, 2003), 211–17.

188. Flood Control District of Maricopa County, "History of Maricopa County Flooding," http://www.fcd.maricopa.gov/Education/history.aspx (accessed 3 July 2005); and Andrew M. Honker, "A River Sometimes Runs Through It: A History of Salt River Flooding and Phoenix" (PhD diss., Arizona State University, 2002), 261–76.

189. Tara A. Blanc, *Oasis in the City: The History of the Desert Botanical Garden* (Phoenix: Heritage Publishers, 2000); Dick George, *One of a Kind: An Informal History of the Phoenix Zoo, 1961–1982* (Phoenix: Arizona Zoological Society, 1982); *The Phoenix Zoo: Case Statement, 1999–2000* (Phoenix: Phoenix Zoo, 2000).

190. *AR*, 21 Sept. 1989, A10; *Phoenix General Plan, 2002,* 276–92; Adelheid Fischer, "Make No Small Plans," *ASU Research* (Winter 2004), 34–37.

191. *AR*, 20 August 2004, B1; *AR*, 29 November–1 December 2004; *AR*, 14 May 2005, B3; Anthony Brazel, Nancy Selover, Russell Vose, Gordon Heisler, "The Tale of Two Climates—Baltimore and Phoenix Urban LTER Sites," *Climate Research*, 15 (2000): 123–135; *Phoenix General Plan, 2002,* 271–72; *Downtown Phoenix Plan* (Phoenix: City of Phoenix, 2008), chapter 4, http://phoenix.gov/urbanformproject/dtplan04.pdf (accessed 11 August 2009).

192. See the *PG* series on "Survival in the Valley," especially 14 September 1989, A14; 20 September 1989, A1; and 21 September 1989, A10. Another example of the L.A. fear is in *PG*, 20 April 1990, B7.

193. Pat Murphy, "Riding a Racehorse Named Growth," *Phoenix Magazine,* November 1991, 86–89.

194. In Community Roundtable, "Making the Valley More Livable," *PG*, 18 May 1995, B9.

195. *What Matters: Indicators of Our Quality of Life* (1998), 9, 19, 23; *AR*, 14 September 1997, Special Report, 1.

196. Mark DeMichele, "Valley Needs to Chart Future," *AR*, 1 August 1996, E2; and "Growing Better—What's Next? Improving Quality of Life Starts by Assessing Valley's Problems," *AR*, 2 February 1997, H1.

197. David S. Baron, "Initiative Lets Voters Set Course on Growth," *AR*, 19 April 1998, H1; *AR*, 4 June 1998, B4; and *ADS*, 31 May 1998, 1B.

198. Melnick, "Growing Smarter and the Citizens Growth Management Initiative: Early Lessons," *Growth in Arizona,* 200; similarly, *AR*, 10 June 1998, B6, and *AR*, 14 June 1998, A1; *ADS*, 31 May 1998, 1B.

199. Steve Betts, "Growing Smarter in Arizona," in *Growth in Arizona,* 95–98; Paul Babbitt, "Growing Smarter in Arizona: The Northern Arizona Experience," in *Growth in Arizona,* 102–5; *ADS*, 31 May 1998, 1B.

200. *AR*, 10 June 1998, B6; *AR*, 14 June 1998, A1; *ADS*, 31 May 1998, B1; *ADS*, 31 May 1998, 1B; and *ADS*, 14 June 1998, 1F.

201. *Tucson Citizen,* 26 November 1998, 1A; Steve Wilson, "Placing Faith in Honest Dialogue about Growth," *AR*, 18 January 2000, B2; and *AR*, 12 February 2000, B4.

202. *AR*, 11 February 2000, B6; *AR*, 12 February 2000, B4; *AR*, 28 February 2000, B7; and *ABG*, 27 February 2000, 1.

203. The most useful evaluation of the issues and conditions in the Valley is *Hits and Misses; Growth in Arizona* includes essays relating directly or generally to the debate; Gammage, *Phoenix in Perspective,* critiques the CGMI approach.

204. *AR*, 22 August 2000, A2; *AR*, 24 September 2000, A1; and election returns, at http://www.sosaz.com/results/2000/general/CTYSUM.HTM.

205. E.g., Grady Gammage, Jr., *The Treasure of the Superstitions: Scenarios for the Future of Superstition Vistas, Arizona's Premier State Trust Land in the Southeast Valley* (Tempe, AZ: Morrison Institute for Public Policy, 2006); Rick Heffernon, Nancy Welch, and Rob Melnick, *Sustainability for Arizona: The Issue of Our Age* (Tempe, AZ: Morrison Institute for Public Policy, 2007); and sources in note 48 above.

Index

ACT. *See* Action Citizens Ticket

Action Citizens Ticket (ACT): African Americans and, 238, 239; diverse slate of, 237–38; election (1963) and, 239; Mexican Americans and, 237–38, 239; platform of, 238

Actors Theatre of Phoenix, 329

Adams, Howard, 320

Adams, John, 21

adobe, 25, 27

African Americans: ACT campaign and, 238, 239; early town and, 24; Mexican Americans and, 259–60; segregation and, 70; social organizations and, 68; South Phoenix annexation and, 177–78. *See also* civil rights

agriculture, 5; canals supporting, 16–18, 17; centrality of, 16; crops grown, 18–19; drought (1898–1904) and, 30; economic growth, long-term, and, 90; hydraulic system and, 29–33; manufacturing as subordinate to, 89–90; New Deal and, 80, 82; postwar, 155; Roosevelt Dam and, 30–31; soil and, 18; sprawl influencing, 277; transportation and, 19–20; World War I and, 32

Agritopia, 348

Ahwatukee subdivision, 219

air-conditioning, 5; central/window, 112–13; early efforts at, 84; industry development, 84–85; manufacturing and, 112; postwar economy and, 155–56

AiResearch company, 98, 105, 157–58

air pollution, 280–81, 352–53

Albury, F. W., 118

Alcoa, 98; postwar and, 106

"American Eden" vision, 6, 89–91, 93, 361; "High-Tech" vision compared with, 94; overview, 9–10

America West Airlines, 302, 303

America West Arena, 325

Andrews, Marvin, 323–24

Anglo settlers, 14

annexation: adjacent cities and, 178; business resistance to, 174–75; challenges of, 174; Charter Government and, 175; city size and (1958–1978), 278, 279; debates about, 342, 344; Keating/Merrill and, 342; key factor in, 179; Mesa and, 224; 1950–1960, 176; Peoria and, 342, 343; post-1980s, 341–42, 343, 344; pseudo, 176–77; Scottsdale and, 178, 222–23, 342, 343; sprawl and, 278, 345–46; suburban incorporation efforts and, 177–78; success of, 178–79; taxes and, 344; Tempe and, 178, 222; undeveloped land and, 179, 179–80; Wilson and, 175–76

Anthem, 347–48

antipoverty program funds, federal, 246, 246

Anti-Saloon League, 59

architecture: automobile influences on residential, 51–52; California style, 50; downtown, early, 46–48, 47; FHA standards and, 81–82; residential, early, 49–50; town, early, 25, 26, 27; Wright and, 55. See also housing

Arizona: interurban competition, 39–40, 40; statehood, 37. See also specific subject

Arizona Biltmore, 78, 107–8

Arizona Cactus and Native Flora Society, 55–56

Arizona Canal, 17, 30

Arizona Cardinals, 334

Arizona Center, 325

Arizona Club, 22, 87, 88, 130

Arizona Diamondbacks, 331, 333

Arizona Improvement Company, 17; citrus crops and, 19

Arizona School of Music, 62

Arizona State College (ASC): becoming ASU, 162–63; Noble and, 162; normal school, 29, 64

Arizona State University (ASU): biotechnology and, 313; downtown campus, 327–28; establishment of, 162–63; football, 166; Motorola and, 162–64; Tempe and, 221–22

Arizona Theatre Company, 329

Arizona Wildlands project, 355

Army Desert Training Center, 103

Arpaio, Joe, 338

arts. See fine arts

ASC. See Arizona State College

Askins, Herbert R., 118

ASU. See Arizona State University

automobiles: air pollution and, 281; distance overcome by, 113–15; postwar and, 146; public revenue from, 46; rapid increase of, 45; related businesses, 45–46; streetcar system influenced by, 50; suburbs transformed by, 50–52; tourism and, 77, 113–14; traffic control and, 147–48, 148; urban form influenced by, 45–46

aviation, 5, 6; America West Airlines and, 302, 303; building industry in, 97–99; city services and, 249; CPTP and, 100; distance overcome by, 114–15; expansion of military, 99–103; general purpose airports and, 301; Hayden and, 102; Korean War and, 158; maturing economy (1960–1980) and, 299; military pilot training and, 100–101; post-1980 economy and, 301–2; Salt River Valley as ideal for, 99–100; tourism and, 78; urban form influenced by, 44–45

awards, 323–24

Babbitt, Bruce, 285

Ballinger, Jim, 330

banking, 21; Bimson, Walter, and, 120; crisis in, 309–11; New Deal and, 82; out-of-state purchasing of, 304; post-1980 economy and, 300

Barnett, John, 170

Barr, Burton, 342

Barrow, Timothy, 241, 247

Barton, Robert, 110

baseball, 66; Arizona Diamondbacks and, 331, 333; leagues, 166–67; major league spring training and, 167, 332–33

Benites, Frank, 239, 240

Bennett, Edward, 75

Bernstein, Charles, 129

Bidwell, Bill, 333–34

Bilsten, Peggy, 336

Bimson, Carl, 81, 86

Bimson, Lloyd, 287

Bimson, Walter, 82, 86, 120, 162, 167–69, 292

biotechnology, 327; ASU and, 313; planning for, 313–14

Bisbee, 39, 40

Biz Vets, 128

Blaine, Jack, 131

block grants, federal, 245–46, 246, 248

Bolles, Don, 253

boosterism, 12; agriculture and, 18; healthy
 climate and, 33–34; minority groups and,
 24–25; societal divide and, 22–23

Breen, Thomas, 212

Bridges, Amy, 130, 143, 395

Brooks, George, 254, 255, 256

Brown, Dave, 309

Buckeye, 340, 341

building industry: aviation and, 97–99. See also
 construction; home building

Burgbacher, A. J., 208

Burgbacher, Ralph, 208–9

Burke, John, 176

buses, 146, 250; tourism and, 77, 77; traffic
 congestion and, 351–52

Busey, Ray, 105, 127, 129, 131, 174, 270

business service clubs, 68

cactus, 13

California style architecture, 50

Camelback Inn, 107–8

Camelback Mountain preservation, 247, 287

Camp McDowell, 14

canals: condition of (1956–1973), 286; desert
 transformation and, 53–55, 54; drownings
 and, 286; flooding of, 30; Hohokam, 15, 15;
 modern, 16–18, 17; social environment and,
 54–55

CAP. See Central Arizona Project

carbon monoxide, 352–53

"card room putsch" deal, 104, 126

Carter, Jimmy, 284

Casa de Sol, 211, 212

CBD. See central business district

CCC. See Charter Commission Committee

Central Arizona Project (CAP): cutbacks
 on, 284–85; establishment of, 284;
 Groundwater Management Act and, 285

central business district (CBD): architecture,
 early, 46–48, 47; businesses initially
 attracted to, 43–44; consumer culture, 48;
 1920s, 43, 43, 46–47; retail business in, early,
 46; street paving in, 45; transportation
 influencing, 44–46

Central Phoenix Plan (City of Phoenix), 288

central place theory, 38

CGC. See Charter Government Committee

CGMI. See Citizens Growth Management
 Initiative

Chamber of Commerce: decline of, 312;
 economic elite and, 87; opposition
 to district plan by, 315; planning for
 manufacturing and, 156–60; postwar
 planning and, 117–18; postwar tourism
 promoted by, 107

Chandler: canals and, 18; growth of, 224;
 population and, 172, 173–74, 191

Chandler, Alexander J., 55

Chanen, Herman, 194

Charlton, Richard, 169

Charter Commission Committee (CCC),
 73

Charter Government: administrative reforms
 by, 141–42; annexation and, 175; charter
 reform producing, 129–33; conservative
 turn of, 240–41; core value of, 233;
 demise of, 241–42, 242; efficiency issues
 surrounding, 139–40; election campaign
 (1961), 235–37; election campaign (1963),
 237–39; election campaign (1967), 239–40;
 elections (1949–1959) and, 136, 137;
 employees per capita in, 143; as liberal
 movement, 235–40; nature of, 134–36; as
 nonpartisan, 234; party affiliations and,
 139; planning department in, 142; planning
 for manufacturing and, 156–60; political
 debates and, 138–40; politics of center
 and, 232–35; public safety services, 149–51;
 SAC frustrating, 237; success of, 136, 137,
 138; taxes and, 140; transportation reforms
 of, 146–49; water issues and, 143–45;
 weaknesses/challenges faced by, 184–85

Charter Government Committee (CGC), 126;
 campaign (1949) by, 131–33, 132; campaign
 (1949) victory of, 133; candidate selection
 process of, 134–35; formation of, 130;
 Goldwater, Barry, and, 131; initial candidate
 selection by, 130–31; operational strategy
 of, 134; opposition to, 138; opposition
 to district plan by, 315; organized labor
 and, 135–36; party affiliations and, 139;
 Southwest influence of, 135

charter reform: Charter Government resulting from, 129–33; stages of, 126

Charter Revision Committee, 129; NML and, 130

Cheney, Merle, 111

Chicano Movement, 261

Chicanos Por La Causa (CPLC), 261, 262, 262, 338

Chinese: early town and, 24; segregation and, 70; social organizations and, 68

Christy, Lloyd, 73

Christy, William: banking and, 21; leadership and, 41

churches, 68–69

The Cincinnati Plan of Citizen Organization for Political Activity (NML), 130

Citizens Growth Management Initiative (CGMI), 357–59

citrus crops, 19

city council: competition and, 320; duty increases for, 321; salaries, 321–22; term limits and, 320–21

Civilian Pilot Training Program (CPTP), 100

civil rights, 6–7; background regarding, 253–54; employment/housing and, 256; hearings, 254–55; 1950s and, 254; Operation Eagle Eye and, 255

Civil Rights Commission, U.S., 254–55

climate: air-conditioning overcoming, 112–13; consumptives and, 34; control, 83–85; health and, 33–34; landscaping changing, 54; migration and, 110–11; Sonoran Desert, 13–14

clothing, 203

Colangelo, Jerry, 332, 333

Cold War, 6, 154

Collins, M. E., 28

Colorado River, 145

Committee for District Representation, 315

community building: city policies toward, 344–45; during 1950s, 208; "High-Tech Suburbia" vision and, 184; legislation influencing, 215; Litchfield Park and, 216–17; Long on, 292; new towns and, 215–17; Park Central and, 208–9; planned communities and, 217–21; retirement communities and, 210–15; shift to, 207–10

Community Council, 257–58

Community Development Block Grant Program, 245

The Comprehensive Plan (City of Phoenix), 288

computer industry, collapse of, 306

construction, 5; boom in (late 1990s), 311; crisis in, 308–10, 309, 311; fluctuation in housing, 194, 195; maturing economy (1960–1980) and, 299; postwar leadership in, 119; prewar vs. postwar, 192–93. *See also* community building; home building

consumptives, 34

convention center, 272–73, 327

Cooke, Delos Willard, 78

Cornelius, Rhes, 168

cotton crop, 32

Coyotes hockey, 332, 333–34

CPLC. *See* Chicanos Por La Causa

CPTP. *See* Civilian Pilot Training Program

credit card operations, 300

crime, 251–53, 323

crops, 18–19

cuisine, 165–66

culture, 3; art museum and, 167–68; cuisine and, 165–66; development of, 61–64; downtown consumer, 48; downtown renewal and, 326; early popular, 23; early town, 20–27; fine arts, 63; high, 167–71; libraries and, 64, 151; local artists, 62–63; music, 62, 170–71; Musicians Club and, 61; outdoor activities and, 65–66, 166; overview regarding, 5; Phoenix Women's Club and, 63–64; popular vs. mass, 65; public education and, 64; radio and, 67–68; reemerging role for, 328–31; rodeos and, 164; societal divide in, 22–23; sports and, 66, 166–67; theater, 62–63, 169–70; western/outdoor, 164–67

Curtis, Philip, 63, 168–69

dams, 30–33, 40, 41, 77, 79–80, 216, 282–85, 355

Daniels, Hayzel, 254

Davidson, Lyman, 241

decentralization, 1

defense spending, western metropolitan (1940–1945), 95–96, 96

Deppe, James, 128, 129–30

Depression, 79; manufacturing and, 83; New Deal programs during, 79–82 desert: canals and, 53–55, 54; climate/natural environment of, 13–14; definitions of, 13; landscaping, 286–87; planning to live in, 279–87; recontouring of, limiting, 355–56; remaking, 52–55; saving, 55–56; Sonoran, 4, 11, 13–14; sprawl influencing, 277; Tucson and, 283

Desert Botanical Garden, 287, 355

Desert Crest, 212

Diamond, Harold, 118

Diaz, Adam, 135, 138

discrimination, 69–71. *See also* civil rights

district plan victory, 315

Dobson Ranch subdivision, 219–20

doctors, CBD and, 44

Dolan, John, 197

Dorne, Maxwell, 193

Dorris Opera House, 23, 61

Douglas, 39, 40

Downey, Patrick, 44, 291

downtown, 3; architecture, early, 46–48, 47; businesses initially attracted to, 43–44; CBD (1920s), 43, 43, 46–47; changing urban form of, 42–48; consumer culture of, early, 48; convention center and, 272–73, 327; culture/entertainment and, 326; decline of, postwar, 269, 271–72; environment and, 328; as heat island, 356–57; housing, 325, 326–27, 328; malls regarding, 270–71, 271–72; parking and, 269–70; politics regarding, 269–73; redevelopment of, 272–73; renewal, 324–28; renewal (1980s), 325–26; renewal (1990s), 326–27; renewal (2000s), 327–28; retail business in, early, 46; street paving in, 45; Tempe, 222; traffic and, 270; transportation influencing, 44–46

Dreamland Villa, 211, 211, 214

Driggs, John, 240, 241, 247, 276, 291

drought: 1895–1904, 30–31; tolerant plants, 356

Dunn, Pete, 315

Dwight B. Heard Building, 46

East Valley Partnership, 312

East Valley retirement community, 214

economy: agriculture and, 90; biotechnology and, 313–14; building crisis and, 308–10, 309, 311; challenges in, planning/response to, 311–14; competition with national urban centers and, 296–97; cost of living and, (post-2000), 303–4; creating new vision of, 298–314; early town, 20, 21–22; education and, 161–64; elite of, 85–88; financial crisis and, 309–11; growth of postwar, 154–56; high-tech firms and, 160–64; home building mass production and, 198, 199; local business creation and, (post-1970), 305; maturing (1960–1980), 298–99; Mexican Americans and, 338; New Deal and, 80; new postwar vision and, 118–21; out-of-state business purchases and, 304–5; overview regarding, 5; per capita income (post-1988) and, 302–3; Phoenix Economic Growth Corporation, 312; planning for manufacturing and, 156–60; post-1980 strengths of, 300–303; postwar, 105–6; postwar planning and, 115–18; poverty and, 303; problems in (post-1980), 302–5; Scottsdale and, 223; sports and, 331; tourism and, 109, 299, 300; World War II soldiers and, 103–4

Eden, William, 117

education: ASC and, 162; early institutions of, 20, 22; economy and, 161–64; establishing public, 64; Noble/Motorola and, 161–64; Operation LEAP and, 258–59, 260; playgrounds and, 151

election: 1949, 131–33; 1961, 235–37; 1963, 237–39; 1967, 239–40; 1983, 315–16; results 1949–1959, 137

electronics, 5; decline of, 306–7; Korean War and, 158; Tempe and, 222

Ellin, Nan, 3

Elliott, Frank, 86

Ellman, Steve, 333

Elmore, James, 288

El Rey Café, 260

environment, natural: defining features of, 11; isolation of, 12; overview regarding, 3; Salt River, 14; Sonoran Desert and, 13–14; urban planning and, 280; visions prompted by, 6–7

Esplanade development, 344

Falcon Field, 100, 105, 173, 223, 302

Farish, William, 73–74

Farnsworth, Ross, 211
Federal Arts Center, 63
federal government: antipoverty program
 funds, 246, *246*; block grants, 245–46, *246*,
 248; housing, funds for, 267–68; influence,
 79–80; revenue from, 245–48, *246*
Federal Housing Authority (FHA), 84;
 affordable housing and, 192, 205–6; air-
 conditioning and, 112–13; standards, 81–82
FHA. *See* Federal Housing Authority
fine arts, 5; critics regarding, 171; culture, 63;
 financial support for, 330–31; First Fridays
 and, 328; live performance venues, 330;
 local, 168–69; museum, 167–68; music and,
 170–71, 329–30; reemerging role for, 328–31;
 Scottsdale and, 223; Tempe and, 222;
 theater and, 169–70, 329
fire department, 28, 73, 74, 127, 150–51, 253, 323
First Fridays, 328
Fleming, J. R., 116
flooding, 30, 31, 33, 281–83, *282*, 354–55
football, 66; ASU, 166; Cardinals, 334
Foss, John W., 49
Foster, Hohen, 131
Fountain Hills, 216
Fountain of the Sun, 214
Fox Theater, 67, *67*
Friday Club, 64

gambling, 130; Charter Government and,
 138–39; saloons and, 59; during World
 War II, 103
Gammage, Grady, 162
Ganz, Emil, 20; bankers and, 21; leadership
 and, 41
garbage disposal, 151
Garden City, 215
Garvey, Dan, 116
GE. *See* General Electric
General Electric (GE), 160, 162
Gilbert: canals and, 18; population growth
 (1980–2008), 339, *340*
Glendale: annexation and, 178; canals and, 17,
 17; Cardinals football and, 334; as edge city,
 224–25; population growth (1960–1980),
 191; population growth (1980–2008), 339,
 340; population projections (done in 2005),
 341; population regarding, *172*, 173–74, *191*,

339, *340*, 341; as supersuburb, 224
GMA. *See* Groundwater Management Act
Goddard, Terry, 312, 344, 357; annexation and,
 342; background on, 315–16; council agenda
 and, 321; district plan and, 315; downtown
 vision of, 325; tenure as mayor, 316–18, *317*
Goettl brothers, manufacturing and, 85, 111,
 112, 156
Goldwater, Baron, 41, 86
Goldwater, Barry, 80, 118; CGC and, 131;
 election (1949) victory of, 133; mountain
 preservation and, 247; NML and, 135; SAC
 and, 236
Goldwater, Bob, 118
golf, 166, 220; planned communities and, 347;
 water conservation and, 354
Goode, Calvin, 241, 242, 320–21
Goodyear, 32, 215; aviation industry and,
 97–98; Litchfield Park and, 216–17; postwar
 withdrawal of, 106
Goodyear Aircraft Corporation, 98, *99*, 157
Gordon, Phil, 319–20, 338
government: awards and, 323–24; change
 reluctance of, 116–17; from charter reform
 to charter, 129–33; charter revisions and,
 72–74; city planning and, 75; crime and,
 251–53; debates, 71; early, 28–29; early
 county, 28; election (1949) and, 131–33; as
 liberal movement, 235–40; mayors, role
 of, 28, 73–74, 129, 234, 314, 317–20, 365;
 morality regulation and, 72, 75–76; New
 Deal and, 79–82; politics of center and,
 232–35; postwar planning and, 115–18; postwar tourism promoted by, 107; prostitution
 and, 75–76; Public Administration Service
 study (1945) and, 126–27; public services
 and, 71–72, 74–75; territorial, 29; Webb
 and, 102–3. *See also* Charter Government;
 Charter Government Committee; federal
 government; politics
Graham, Milton, 234, 239, 240, 246, 252,
 258, 272
Great American Desert, 13
Greater Phoenix Business Leadership
 Coalition, 312
Greater Phoenix Leadership, 292
Gretzky, Wayne, 333
groundwater, 283–84, 285, 353

Groundwater Management Act (GMA), 285; requirements of, 353

Growing Smarter plan, 357–59

growth: attitudes, 185–86; as central, 361; CGMI and, 358–59; Chandler, 224; crisis, 289, 291–93; of economy, 90, 154–56, 312; fighting over, 357–59; future, 7; Gilbert, 339, *340*; Glendale, *191*, 339, *340*; Mesa, *191*, 221, 339, *340*; Mexican Americans and, 337; Phoenix Economic Growth Corporation and, 312; Phoenix Growth Committee and, 142; population, 7, 38, *39*, 171, *172*, 295, 339, *340*, 341; Scottsdale, *191*, 222–23, 339, *340*; seven decades of modest, 361–62; seven decades of robust, 362–66; suburbs, 187–90, 339, *340*; supersuburbs, 221, 339, *340*; Tempe, 221, 339, *340*; tourism, 76–79, 106–9

Gruen, Victor, 209, 210; Litchfield Park and, 216; malls and, 226, 227; McCormick Ranch subdivision and, 219

Gutierrez, Alfredo, 261, 262

Gutierrez, Rosendo, 242, 261–62, 320

Haas, Lewis E., 118

Hall, John C., 111, 194, 196; affordable homes and, 204; economies of scale and, 198; mass production used by, 197–98

Hance, Margaret, 241, 262; air pollution and, 281; federal funds and, 247; Goddard and, 317; opposition to district plan by, 315

Hancock, Glen, 195, 196

Hanner, Buck, 237

Harless, Richard, 237

Harris, Ann Lee, 169

Hart, James G., 193

Hayden, Carl, 101–2

health, 5; climate promoting, 33–34; consumptives and, 34; migration and, 111–12; post-1980 economy and, 300; tourism and, 76, 78

Heard, Dwight, 63, 86; leadership and, 41; subdivisions developed by, 49

Heard, Maie Bartlett, 62, 63

Heard Museum, 63, 329

heat island, urban, 356–57

Heyman Furniture Building, 26

Highland Canal, 30

high-tech industries: collapse of, 305–8;

economy and, 160–64. *See also specific industry*

"High-Tech Suburbia" vision, 6; community building and, 184; "Eden" vision compared with, 94; elaborating/modifying, 183–86; growth attitudes altering, 185–86, 295–96; housing and, 183–84; minorities and, 296; overview, 93–94; results of, 180–81

highway system, 3; improvement efforts, 250–51, *251*, 350–51; malls and, 351. *See also* Papago Freeway

Hinkhouse, Forest M., 168

historic districts, 335

historic preservation, 276

HOAs. *See* home owner associations

hockey, 332, 333–34

Hodge, Leslie, 170

Hoffman, Paul, 116

Hohokam settlements, 14–15, *15*

home building: affordable, 203–6; backyard and, 201–2; boom in (late 1990s), 311; casual living and, 203; collapses of, 195–96; crisis in, 308–9, *309*; design diversity in, 200–201; economies of scale in, 198, *199*; FHA impacting, 192; for growing population, 190, *191*, 192; home ownership (1940–1980) and, 187; inflation and, 204; initial postwar, 193–94; labor relations in, 198; land cost and, 205; loans and, 205–6; in Maricopa County (1961–1981), *194*, *195*; mass production and, 197–98; materials used in, 198–99; outdoor living and, *202*, 202–3; in Phoenix, 196–201; pools and, 202–3; ranch style of, 199–200; room arrangement and, 201; shift from individual to corporate, 196; size and, 201, 345; stucco-tacky, 345, *346*; vertical integration of, 193

home owner associations (HOAs), 218, 221, 348–50

hotels: downtown, early, 45, 46; postwar and, 107–8; tourism and, 77–78

housing: affordable, declining, 304; civil rights and, 256; federal funding for, 267–68; "High-Tech Suburbia" vision and, 183–84; National Housing Act and, 266; politics of, 266–68; public, 267. *See also* Federal Housing Authority; home building

Hoyt, Ross, 103–4

HRC. *See* Human Relations Commission

Huck, Leonard, 281

Hull, Jane, 334, 357

Human Relations Commission (HRC), 258

hydraulic system: dams and, 31–33; drought (1895–1904) and, 30–31; Roosevelt Dam and, 31–32; Salt River flooding and, 30; Salt River irregular flow and, 29–30

immigration status, 338–39

incorporation efforts, 177–78

Indians: early town and, 24; segregation and, 70; water and, 145

Industrial Development Committee, 157

inflation, 204

Inner City, 257, 257–58

insurance industry, 300

Intel, 306

International Genomics Consortium, 313

internment camps, 103

irrigation: canals supporting, 16–18, 17; Hohokam, 15, 15

Jacobsen, Bud, 291

Japanese: internment camps and, 103; segregation and, 70; social organizations and, 68

J. C. Penney, 46, 271–72

Johnson, Paul, 318–19, 344

Kapp, Russell, 139–40

Keating, Charles, 341

Kerr, Louise Lincoln, 171

Kersting, Bob, 100

Klahr, Gary Peter, 241, 320

Knier, Carl, 100

Knight, Alfred, 130

Knoell, Frank, 196

Knoell, Hugh, 197, 207–8

Knorpp, Wes, 86, 104

Kober, Les, 119

Kober, Margaret, 131, 234, 291

Korean War, 157–58

Korrick, Abe, 41, 118

Korrick, Blanche, 62, 170

Korrick, Charles, 41, 119

Korrick, Ed, 237, 239, 241, 321

Kraft, Howard, 241

labor: home building and, 198; organized, 135–36

Lake Havasu City, 216

landscaping, 2, 5; canals and, 53–55, 54; desert, 285–87; drought tolerant plants and, 356; tree planting and, 53

laterals: condition of (1956–1973), 286; drownings and, 286

Lawrence, Robert, 170

leadership, 5; Greater Phoenix Business Leadership Coalition and, 312; Hayden and, 101–2; from informal to more formal, 292; military facilities and, 101; new politics and, 314–20; new postwar vision and, 118–21; Operation LEAP and, 258–59, 260; postwar planning and, 115–18; urban form influenced by, 41–42. *See also* Charter Government; government

Leadership and Education for the Advancement of Phoenix. *See* Operation LEAP

League of United Latin American Citizens (LULAC), 260–61

leapfrog development, 51, 146, 150, 179, 185, 188, 276–79, 344

Leisure World retirement community, 214

"Letter to Patriotic Leaders" (SAC), 236

Levitin, Sam, 140

Lewis, Orme, 64

libraries, 61, 64, 151, 323, 326; association, 20, 64; importance, 22; mentioned, 127, 131, 208, 210, 220, 226

light rail system, 3, 327–28, 352

Lincoln, John C., 78

Linde, Jessie E., 61–62

Litchfield, Paul, 32, 97–98, 116

Litchfield Park, 32, 216–17

Long, John F., 193, 194, 240; affordable homes and, 204, 205; block use by, 199; on community, 291; economies of scale and, 198, 199; mass production used by, 197–98; no down payment and, 205; philanthropic character of, 210; planned community and, 209–10; response to housing collapse by, 195–96; union labor and, 198; water conservation and, 354

Lopez, Joe Eddie, 261, 262

Lopez, Ronnie, 261, 262

Luce, Clair Booth and Henry, 111, 168
Luckingham, Bradford, 3
Luhrs, George, 85
Luhrs Building, 46
Luhrs Tower, 46
Luke Field, 100–101; closing of, 105
LULAC. *See* League of United Latin American Citizens

Mahoney, Les, 41
malls, shopping, 226, 226–27; downtown and, 270–71, 271–72; highways and, 351
manufacturing: agriculture, as subordinate to, 89–90; air-conditioning and, 112; decline of, 305–8; Depression and, 83; Goettl brothers and, 85, 111, 112, 156; high-tech firms and, 160–64; Industrial Development Committee and, 157; Korean War and, 157–58; Mesa and, 223; migration and, 110; new (1948–1960), 158–60, 159; planning for, 156–60; postwar, 105–6, 155–56, 156; smokeless industry and, 158; Tempe and, 222
Mardian, Sam, 119, 147, 194, 234; civil rights and, 254–55; on culture, 167; election results summary and, 137; federal funds and, 246; SAC and, 236, 237; on selfless civic participation, 233; street improvement and, 249
Maricopa County: auto registrations in, 45; establishment of, 28; home building in (1961–1981), 194, 195; population (1940–1960), 171, 172; population (1960–1980), 191; population (1980–2008), 339, 340, 341; postwar tourism promoted by, 107
Maricopa Flood Control District, 281
Maryvale, 178; home building and, 198, 199; as planned community, 209–10
mass production, home building, 197–98, 199
mass transit, 351–52. *See also specific form of*
May, Cliff, 199, 202
mayors, role of, 28, 73–74, 129, 234, 314, 317–20, 365
McArthur, Albert, 55
McClintock, C. E., 20
McCormick Ranch subdivision, 219
McCulloch, Robert, 216
McLoughlin, Emmett, 80

Melnick, Rob, 357
Mercado, 325
Meredith, Herman, 193
Merrill, Harrison, 342
Mesa: canals and, 17, 17; decentralization and, 223–24; Dobson Ranch subdivision and, 219–20; Dreamland Villa and, 211, 211; as edge city, 224–25; Falcon Field and, 100, 173, 302; growth of, 221; house size in, 201; malls, 226; manufacturing and, 223; Phoenix-Mesa Gateway Airport and, 301; population growth (1960–1980), 191; population growth (1980–2008), 339, 340; population projections (done in 2005), 341; population regarding, 172, 173–74, 191, 339, 340, 341; Southwest Shakespeare Company in, 329; taxes and, 224
Mesa Canal, 30
Mexican Americans: ACT campaign and, 237–38, 239; adobe regarding, 27; African Americans and, 259–60; Chicano Movement and, 261; city services and, 338; CPLC and, 261, 262, 262, 338; discrimination by, 260; economy and, 338; immigration status and, 338–39; language and, 338; LULAC and, 260–61; neighborhoods occupied by, 337–38; political activism of, 259–63; population growth of, 337; religion and, 24; segregation and, 70–71; social organizations and, 68; South Phoenix annexation and, 177. *See also* civil rights
Mickle, George, 41, 85
Midwest, perspectives, 1–2
migration: climate influencing, 110–11; companies regarding, 111; health and, 111–12; moves per area household (1960–1967), 206, 207; openness to, 206–7; postwar, 109–12, 206
military: aviation expansion, 99–103; CPTP and, 100; facility location decisions, 96–97; Hayden and, 102; migration and, 110; pilot training, 100–101; politics and, 103–5; postwar trials regarding, 105–6; Webb and, 102–3; western metropolitan defense spending (1940–1945), 95–96, 96
mining, 14, 16; CBD and, 44; Depression and, 79

minority groups, 7; decline in, 24–25; early, 24; "High-Tech Suburbia" vision and, 296. *See also* African Americans; Chinese; Japanese; Mexican Americans

modern city, or modern American city: described, 4–6, 35; early status as, 35; goal, as a, 9, 29, 365; minorities and, 23–25, 69; requirements for 10, 57, 61, 69

Mofford, Rose, 332

Moore, Aubrey, 235, 246, 267–68

morality: government regulation regarding, 72, 75–76; reform efforts, 57–61

Morrison Ranch, 348–49

motels, postwar and, 108–9

Motorola: ASU and, 162–64; collapse of, 307, 307; founding of, 160; higher education and, 161–64; moves to Arizona, 160–61; Scottsdale and, 222; Semiconductor Products Division of, 161

mountain land preservation, 247–48

movie theaters, 65–67, 272; mentioned, 173, 226, 254

Moyes, Jerry, 333

Murdock, David, 119, 194, 272

Murphy, Frank, 119, 131, 137

Murphy, William: banking and, 21; leadership and, 41

Museum of Science and Technology, 326

music, 61, 62, 170–71, 329–30

Musicians Club, 61, 62

Nadolski, Linda, 342

National Housing Act, 266

National Municipal League (NML), 125–26; *Cincinnati Plan of Citizen Organization* and, 130; Goldwater, Barry, and, 135; operational strategy of, 134; SAC and, 235–36

Neighborhood Coalition of Greater Phoenix, 336

Neighborhood Initiative Program, 335–36

neighborhoods: decline of, 273–74; freeway proposal and, 274–75; historic districts and, 335; historic preservation and, 276; locations of older, 274; Mexican American, 337–38; organizations, 337; politics and, 273–76, 274; redevelopment and, 275–76, 335–36; urban village and, 336–37

Nelson, John, 320, 321

New Deal programs, 6; agriculture and, 80, 82; banking and, 82; construction and, 80; federal government and, 79–80; FHA, 81–82; for private home ownership, 80–81

Nichols, J. C., 218

Nixon, Richard, 245

NML. *See* National Municipal League

Noble, Daniel, 110–11; Arizona promotion by, 160–61; background of, 160; higher education and, 161–64; transistor and, 161

O'Malley, Ted, 119

O'Malley brothers, 41

open space, 358–59

Operation Eagle Eye, 255

Operation LEAP (Leadership and Education for the Advancement of Phoenix), 258–59, 260

Orpheum Theater, 67, 326

Osborn, Sidney, 104, 117

ozone, 353

Palace Saloon, 59

Papago Freeway, 250–51, 251, 274–75

Paradise Valley, 178

Paradise Valley Mall, 227

Park Central, 208–9

Park Central Mall, 226

parking, downtown, 269–70

park system, 151

Patriots' Park, 273

PCGGC. *See* Phoenix Citizens Good Government Council

Pell, Duane, 320

Pena, Manuel, 237–38, 255

Peoria: annexation and, 342, 343; canals and, 17, 17; school district, 214

Phoenix: criticisms of, 1; defining boundaries of, 4; establishment of, 15–16; future growth of, 7; identity issues surrounding, 295–98; Midwest compared with, 2; in 1940, 88–91; 1930s and, 79–83; perspectives on, 1–4; as territorial capital, 29; tipping point in, 3; topics covered on, 4–5; visions influencing, 6–7; western towns compared with, 16. *See also specific subject*

Phoenix Art Museum, 167–68, 326, 329

Phoenix Arts Commission, 328

Phoenix Children's Theater, 169–70
Phoenix Citizens Good Government Council (PCGGC), 126, 127
Phoenix Civic Center, 272–73
Phoenix Concept Plan 2000 (City of Phoenix), 288–89, *290*
Phoenix Economic Growth Corporation, 312
Phoenix Fine Arts Association, 63
Phoenix 40, 292; opposition to district plan by, 315
Phoenix Forums project, 322
Phoenix Forward: high density development and, 280; pollution and, 281; report by, 280, 281
Phoenix Growth Committee, 142
Phoenix History Project, 276
Phoenix Indian School, 24, 29, 66, 70
Phoenix Little Theater, 63, 169–70, 326
Phoenix-Mesa Gateway Airport and, 301–2
Phoenix Mountain Preserve, 248, 355
Phoenix Museum of History, 326
Phoenix Opera House, 23, 61
Phoenix Suns, 332
Phoenix Symphony Association, 170
Phoenix Theatre Center, 169–70
Phoenix Union High School, 62, 64, 66, 169; civil rights conflict and, 261
Phoenix Union Station, 44
Phoenix Women's Club: activities of, 61, 63–64; antivice campaigns and, 59, 61; culture and, 63–64; "Do Away with the Desert" campaign of, 52
Phoenix Zoo, 355
pilot training, 100–101
planned communities: Anthem, 348; consequences of large, 220–21; HOAs and, 218, 221, 349–50; largest subdivisions, 219–20; Maryvale, 209–10; 1990s, 347; rationale behind, 217–18; smallest/medium sized "large" subdivisions, 218; trust lands and, 346; types of, 347; Verrado, 348, *349*
police department, 127, 149–50, 252–53
politics: of center, 232–35; from charter reform to charter government, 129–33; citizen participation in, 322; city counsel competition and, 320; of city services, 248–53; civil rights and, 253–56; creating new vision of, 314–24; crime and, 251–53;

district plan victory and, 315; diversity and, 263; downtown and, 269–73; election (1949), 131–33; election (1983), 315–16; Goddard's tenure in, 316–18, *317*; Gordon's tenure in, 319–20; housing, 266–68; Johnson's tenure in, 318–19; liberal movement in, Charter Government, 235–40; Mexican American activism and, 259–63; military and, 103–5; neighborhoods, older, and, 273–76, *274*; new (post-1975), 314–20; overview regarding, 4, 5, 231–32; place/space, 269–79; postwar conflicts in, 126–33; poverty and, 256–59, *257*; Rimsza's tenure in, 319; sports and, 331–35. *See also* Charter Commission Committee; Charter Government; city council; government; revenue; taxes
pollution, air, 280–81, 352–53
pools, 202–3
population, 3; adjacent towns and, *172*, 173–74; Arizona early interurban, *40*; densities (1970–1980), 278; growth, 7, 38, *39*, 171, *172*, 295, 339, *340*, 341; home building for growing, 190, *191*, 192; inland West cities growth in, 38, *39*; metropolitan (1960–1980), *191*; Mexican Americans and, 337; 1980–2008, 339, *340*, 341; 1960–1980, 339; projections (done in 2005), 341; sprawl and, 345–46; subdivisions and, 174; town, early, 20, 21; of western cities in 1940, 88, *89*
poverty: background regarding, 256–57; employment/housing and, 256; HRC and, 258; Inner City and, *257*, 257–58; Operation LEAP and, 258–59; program funds, federal, 246, *246*; rising (2000), 303
Price, Dix, 130
prostitution: Charter Government and, 139; government control of, 75–76; World War II soldiers and, 103–4
Public Administration Service study (1945), 126–27
public housing, 256–58, *257*, 267
public safety: fire department and, 150–51; police department and, 149–50
Pulliam, Eugene, 119–20, 267, 292

Quebedeaux, W. C., 116

radio, 67–68

Ragsdale, Lincoln, 238, 254, 255, 256

railroad: distance overcome by, 113; importance, 12, 25, 41–42; lines established, 19–20; promotion of growth and, 31, 33, 76–77; station, 52, 75; urban form influenced by, 44. *See also* light rail system

Rainesen, Wally, 305

ranch style homes, 199–200

recreation, 5, 355; community and, 212, 215, 220–21, 348; outdoor activities as, 65–66, 166; playgrounds/parks and, 151; Rio Salado and, 288, 318; sports and, 66

Rehabilitation and Betterment Program, 285

Rehnquist, William, 255

Reilly, William, 254

religion: churches and, 68–69; early organized, 20, 22; Mexican Americans and, 24

Renaissance Park, 325

resorts: postwar and, 107–8; tourism and, 77–78

resources, 3

retirement communities: conclusions regarding, 214–15; Dreamland Villa, 211, *211*, 214; impetus for, 210; other, 212, 214; in Phoenix area (1980), *211*; Sun City, 212–14, *213*; Youngtown, 210–11, *211*

revenue: antipoverty program funds, 246, *246*; from automobiles, 46; block grants, 245–46, *246*, 248; challenges of (1980–2000), 322–23; from federal government, 245–48, *246*; major sources of, *244*; mountain land preservation, 247–48; sharing, 245, 247; water system, 243–44. *See also* taxes

Reynolds Metals Company, 157

Rialto Theater, 67

Rimsza, Skip, 318–19, 327, 344

Rio Salado, 288, 318

Rio Verde retirement community, 214

Rockwell, John, 100

rodeos, 66, 164

Roosevelt Dam, 30–32

Rosenzweig, Harry, 119, 131, 166, 263

Rosenzweig, Newton, 87–88, 119, 292

Rosing, Kenneth, 193

Ross, John, 111

Rosson House, 276

Ruskin, Lewis J., 111, 168–69

SAC. *See* Stay American Committee

salaries, city council, 321–22

saloons, 23; banning women/gambling from, 59; campaigns against, *59*, 59–60; decline/elimination of, 60; revival of, 75

Salt River, 4, 11; flooding, 30, 31, 33, 282; nature of, 14. *See also* hydraulic system

Salt River Project, 143, 286

Salt River Valley: Anglo settlers of, 14; aviation, as ideal for, 99–100; canal system, 16–18, *17*; dams, 31–33; defining features of, 11; isolation of, 12; trees and, 18

San Carlos Hotel, 45, 107

San Diego, 116

Sanmina, 307

Scheumack, Ward "Doc," 128

Schleifer, Ben, 210

school(s), 22, 61, 62, 170, 208; activities, 23, 62, 66, 166, 170; buildings, 25, 46, 62, 64, 80, 169; importance of, 10, 20, 22, 27, 64, 89; mentioned, 158, 208, 210, 224, 227; playgrounds and, 151; segregation, 64, 70, 238, 254, 256, 259; Sun City conflict over, 214. *See also* Arizona School of Music; Arizona State College; Arizona State University; Phoenix Indian School; Phoenix Union High School

Scott, Winfield, citrus crops and, 19

Scottsdale: annexation and, 178, 222–23, 342, 343; aviation and, 302; canals and, 17, *17*; as edge city, 224–25; growth of, 222–23; house size in, 201; malls, 226; McCormick Ranch subdivision and, 219; Motorola and, 222; population growth (1960–1980), *191*; population growth (1980–2008), 339, *340*; population projections (done in 2005), 341; population regarding, *172*, 173–74, *191*, 339, *340*, 341; resorts and, 108; western theme marketing of, 165

segregation/desegregation, 24, 64, 69–71, 238, 254–56, 259–61

semiconductor industry, decline of, 306–8

Semiconductor Products Division, of Motorola, 161

service clubs, 68

sewage treatment, 145, 248–49

Shadegg, Stephen, 206, 207

Shangri-La Apartments, 212

Sherman, Moses, 21; leadership and, 41; streetcar system established by, 28

shopping: centers, expansion of, 225–26; malls, expansion of, 226, 226–27; postwar, 225

Sims, Carl, 254

Sky Harbor Airport: city services and, 249; CPTP and, 100; early years of, 44–45; expanded service at, 115, 249; flooding and, 282, 282; maturing economy (1960–1980) and, 299; post-1980 economy and, 301–2, 303; postwar expansion of, 114–15

Smith, John Y. T., 14

Smith, Richard, 104

Snell, Frank, 86–87, 104, 116; as great leader, 120–21; on labor relations, 198

social construction: climate control and, 83–85; culture and, 61–64; government and, 71–76; morality influencing, 57–61; 1930s, 79–83; Wild West image and, 57–58

social structures: business service clubs and, 68; canals influencing, 54–55; churches and, 68–69; discrimination and, 69–71; diversity regarding, 68–71; divide in, 22–23; early organizations, 22; early town, 20–21, 22; saloons and, 23; segregation and, 70–71

soil, 18

Sombrero Playhouse, 169, 170

Sonoran Desert, 4, 11; in 1860s, 14; abundant life in, 13; climate of, 13–14

Sonoran Desert Preserve, 356

South Phoenix, 177–78, 237, 253, 257–60, 335

Southwest Airlines, 100

Southwest Cotton Company, 32

Southwest Shakespeare Company, 329

Sperry Phoenix, 160

sports, 3; culture and, 66, 166–67; economy and, 331; funding of, 331–32; politics/ identity and, 331–35; taxes and, 332, 333, 334. See also specific sport

sprawl: agriculture influenced by, 277; annexation and, 278, 345–46; population and, 345–46; of suburbs, 188, 189; urban planning and, 276–79, 279

Staggs, Ralph, 193, 194; affordable homes and, 204; Casa de Sol and, 211–12; economies of scale and, 198; housing business sold by, 196; housing collapse and, 195; land cost and, 205; mass production used by, 197–98

Starck, Gustaf, 55–56

Stauffer, Charles, 41, 86

Stay American Committee (SAC): ideology of, 235; NML and, 235–36; as semisecret national movement, 237; stealth campaign of, 236

STMicroelectronics, 306–7

streetcar system, 28; decline of, 50; demise of, 146; residential development influenced by, 48–49

subdivisions: Heard, Dwight, and, 49; largest, 219–20; population and, 174; smallest/ medium-sized "large," 218

suburbs: architecture of, 49–50; automobile transforming, 50–52; before 1960, 173–74; conclusions regarding, 227–29; growth of (1945–1980), 187–90, 221–25; incorporation efforts and, 177–78; population growth (1980–2008), 339, 340; population projections (done in 2005), 341; sprawl of, 188, 189; streetcar system influencing, 48–49, 50. See also home building; supersuburbs

Suggs, Clarence, 193, 196, 210

Suggs, Ellis, 200

Sun City: criticism of, 213–14; opening of, 212–13, 213; Peoria school district and, 214; success of, 212–13; Webb and, 212

Sun Lakes retirement community, 214

Sunland Village retirement community, 214

Sunnyslope: annexation vs. incorporation in, 177; pseudo annexation and, 176–77

Superlite Builder's Supply Company, 199

supersuburbs: Glendale, 224; Mesa, 223–24; overall growth of, 221; population growth (1980–2008), 339, 340; population projections (done in 2005), 341; Scottsdale, 222–23; Tempe, 221–22

Surprise, 340, 341

Swarthout, Glendon, 357

Swilling, Jack, 14–15

Swilling Canal, 16

swimming pools, 202–3

Symington, Fife, 310

Talton, Jon, 3

Tang, Thomas, 254

taxes: annexation and, 344; Charter

Government and, 140; highway improvement and, 351; Mesa and, 224; 1960s, 244; property, 243, 244, *244, 245*; sales, 244, 245, 322–23; sources of revenue from, (1960–1980), 244; sports and, 332, *333, 334*

Tempe: annexation and, 178, 222; ASU and, 221–22; canals and, 17, *17*, 30; as edge city, 224–25; growth of, 221; population and, *172, 173–74, 191,* 339, *340,* 341; population growth (1980–2008), 339, *340*; population projections (done in 2005), 341

Tempe Canal, 17, 30

term limits, city council, 320–21

theater, 326, 329; culture, 62–63, 169–70; houses, 66–67, *67*

Theilkas, Dorothy, 240

Thomas, Bill, 199

Thomas, Paul, 199

tourism, 5, 6; as automobile based, 77, 113–14; aviation and, 78; buses and, 77, *77*; economic benefits of, 109; growth of, early, 76–79; health and, 76, 78; hotels/resorts and, 77–78; maturing economy (1960–1980) and, 299; post-1980 economy and, 300; postwar growth of, 106–9; postwar hotels/resorts and, 107–8; postwar motels and, 108–9; public/private cooperation and, 107; railroad and, 77; Scottsdale and, 223; trailer courts and, *108,* 108–9; wealthy visitors and, 77–78; Wild West image and, 58

traffic: buses and, 351–52; control, 147–48, *148*; downtown, 270

trailer courts, *108,* 108–9

transistor, 161

Translational Genomics Research Institute, 313

transportation: agriculture and, 19–20; air quality and, 352–53; automobiles, postwar, and, 146; buses and, 146, 250, 351–52; CBD (1920s) influenced by, 44–46; Charter Government reforms in, 146–49; city services and, 249–51, *251*; distance overcome by, 113–15; early urban development and, 40–41; highway improvement and, 250–51, *251,* 350–51; light rail system and, 3, 327–28, 352; malls influenced by, 351; mass transit and, 351–52; post-1980 issues in, 350–53; railroad

establishment and, 19–20; streetcar system and, 28, 146; street conditions and, 146–48, *148*; street improvement and, 249–50; traffic control and, 147–48, *148*

trucking, 114

trust lands, 346

tuberculosis, 34

Tucson: CAP and, 284; as desert city, 283; interurban competition and, 39, *40*; per capita water use in, 283, *284*; Phoenix compared with, 39; railroad and, 19; state university established in, 29

Tuthill, A. M., 104

Udall, Nicholas, 127, 128, 131; election results summary and, *137*; election (1949) victory of, *133*

urban form: architecture influencing, early, 46–48, *47*; Arizona interurban competition and, 39–40, *40*; automobiles influencing, 45–46; aviation influencing, 44–45; central place theory of, 38; changing, 42–52; city planning and, 75; downtown and, 42–48, 324–28; inland West cities growth and, 38, *39*; leadership influencing, 41–42; neighborhoods that work, envisioning, and, 335–37; new vision of, 324–37; overview regarding, 4; railroad influencing, 44; transportation influencing, 44–46

urban heat island, 356–57

urban planning: air pollution and, 280–81; CAP and, 284–85; environmental movement and, 280; flooding and, 281–83, *282*; groundwater and, 283–84, 285; growth crisis and, 289, 291–93; landscaping and, 285–87; to live in desert, 279–87; shift in (mid-70s), 279–80; sprawl/land use and, 276–79, *279*; urban village and, 287–89, *290*

Urban Renewal Department, 267

urban village, 287–89, *290*; neighborhoods and, 336–37

VA. *See* Veterans Administration

Valley Beautiful Citizens Council: activities of, 287; air pollution and, 281; housing conference of, 258

Valley Forward Association, 288

Verrado, 348, *349*

Veterans Administration (VA), 192, 205–6
Vickers, Jim, 131
Victorian homes, 49

Walters, Charles, 131
Warren, Morrison, 239, 240
Warren, Ned, 253
water: Charter Government's management
   of, 143–45; conservation of, 354; consumer
   usage of (1950–1960), 144–45; drought
   (1895–1904) and, 30–31; drought tolerant
   plants and, 356; flooding and, 30, 33, 281–83,
   282, 354–55; GMA and, 353; groundwater
   and, 283–84, 285, 353; Hayden and, 101;
   irregular flow of, 29–30; per capita use of,
   283, 284; public services and, 71–72, 74–75,
   248–49; revenues from, 243–44; Roosevelt
   Dam and, 31–32; Salt River Valley dams
   and, 31–33; sewage treatment and, 145, 248–
   49; supply/quality/delivery (1950–1960),
   143, 144; Tucson and, 283, 284. See also
   irrigation
"water farming," 353–54
Wayland, Roy, 85
WCTU. See Women's Christian Temperance
   Union
Webb, Del, 80, 85, 102–3, 111, 119, 192, 194, 212,
   272
Webster, Gertrude Divine, 56
Webster, Ronald, 130

Westmarc, 312
Westward Ho Hotel, 45, 46, 107
Wetzel, Lawrence, 252
Wilcox, Earl, 262
Wilcox, Mary Rose, 320, 332, 333, 342
Wild West image, 57–58
Williams, Jack, 134, 135, 145, 247, 285; on
   districts, 139; election results summary
   and, 137; federal funds and, 246; Phoenix
   Growth Committee and, 142
Williams Field, 101
Wilson, Ray, 133, 139; annexation and, 175–76;
   downtown vs. malls and, 270–71
women: antivice campaigns and, 60–61;
   banned from saloons, 59; Hance and, 241;
   WCTU and, 58–59, 60. See also Phoenix
   Women's Club
Women's Christian Temperance Union
   (WCTU), 58–59, 60
Women's Enforcement League, 60
Wood, Charles, 216
World War I, agriculture and, 32
World War II, 6; economy and, 103–4; future
   planning following, 115–18; impact of,
   95–97; politics surrounding, 103–5; postwar
   trials following, 105–6
Wright, Frank Lloyd, 55, 78, 171
Wrigley, William, 78

Youngtown, 210–11, 211